Time Out
Madrid

Penguin Books

PENGUIN BOOKS

Published by the Penguin Group
Penguin Books Ltd, 27 Wrights Lane, London W8 5TZ, England
Penguin Putnam Inc., 375 Hudson Street, New York, New York 10014, USA
Penguin Books Australia Ltd, Ringwood, Victoria, Australia
Penguin Books Canada Ltd, 10 Alcorn Avenue, Toronto, Ontario, Canada M4V 3B2
Penguin Books (NZ) Ltd, 182–190 Wairau Road, Auckland 10, New Zealand

Penguin Books Ltd, Registered Offices: Harmondsworth, Middlesex, England

First published 1995
Second edition 1997
Third edition 1999
10 9 8 7 6 5 4 3 2 1

Colour reprographics by Precise Litho, 34–35 Great Sutton Street, London EC1
Printed and bound by William Clowes Ltd, Beccles, Suffolk NR34 9QE

Edited and designed by

Time Out Guides Limited
Universal House
251 Tottenham Court Road
London W1P 0AB
Tel +44 (0) 171 813 3000
Fax +44 (0) 171 813 6001
E-mail guides@timeout.com
www.timeout.com

Editorial

Editorial Director Peter Fiennes
Editor Nick Rider
Contributing Editors Harvey Holtom, Nick Lyne
Copy Editor Lesley McCave
Listings Researcher Lola Delgado
Proofreader Tamsin Shelton
Indexer Julie Hurrell

Design

Art Director John Oakey
Art Editor Mandy Martin
Designers Benjamin de Lotz, Lucy Grant,
Scott Moore, Thomas Ludewig
Scanner Operator Chris Quinn
Picture Editor Kerri Miles
Picture Researcher Kit Burnet

Advertising

Group Advertisement Director Lesley Gill
Sales Director Mark Phillips
Advertisement Sales (Madrid) The Broadsheet
Advertising Assistant Ingrid Sigerson

Administration

Publisher Tony Elliott
Managing Director Mike Hardwick
Financial Director Kevin Ellis
Marketing Director Gillian Auld
General Manager Nichola Coulthard
Production Manager Mark Lamond
Production Controller Matthew Forrester
Accountant Catherine Bowen

Features in this guide were written and researched by:

Introduction Harvey Holtom. **Madrid by Season** Harvey Holtom. **History** Nick Rider. **Architecture** Harvey Holtom. **Madrid Today** Nick Lyne. **Stormy weather** Nuria Barrios. **Sightseeing** Nick Lyne, Robert Latona, Anne Salmerón. **Museums** Harvey Holtom, Nick Rider, Anne Marie de la Fuente. **Art Galleries** Harvey Holtom. **Accommodation** Mary de Sousa. **Restaurants** Nick Lyne, Harvey Holtom, Vicky Hayward. **Tapas** Harvey Holtom, Vicky Hayward. **Cafés & Bars** Nick Lyne, Harvey Holtom. **Nightlife** Tom de Castella. **Shopping** Harvey Holtom. **Services** Harvey Holtom. **Children** Harvey Holtom. **Bullfighting** Nick Lyne, Nick Rider. **Dance** Harvey Holtom. **Film** Nick Lyne. **Gay & Lesbian Madrid** Juan Ignacio Durán. **Media** Nick Lyne. **Music: Classical & Opera** Harvey Holtom, Stephen Mackey. **Music: Rock, Roots & Jazz** Harvey Holtom. **Flamenco** Larry Lilue, Nick Lyne, Nuria Barrios. **Sport & Fitness** Harvey Holtom. **Theatre** Harvey Holtom, Stuart Green. **Trips Out of Town** Nick Lyne, Robert Latona, Grant Bracey, Nicholas Law, María Victoria Bocos, Vicky Hayward, Nick Rider. **Directory** Harvey Holtom, Nick Rider.

The editors, writers and publisher would like to thank the following:

Javier Aldecoa and Miguel Angel Delgado of the Consorcio de Transportes de Madrid, Outline S.L., Museo del Prado commercial office, Museo Nacional Reina Sofía press office, Teatro Real press office, the staff of the Museo Municipal de Madrid, the Ayuntamiento de Buitrago de Lozoya, Galería Helga de Alvear, Melanie Pindado and Sala Triángulo, Daniel Charquero, Lyn Corewyn, Sarah Dague and Javier Olaciregui, Mary de Sousa and all at The Broadsheet, Magín Fernández Perandones, Rafael Fernández, Irene Franco, Stuart Green, Andrew Hall, Laura Kumin, Lesley McCave, Harvey for 'exemplary dedication', Maggi Riach and Ethel Rimmer.

Maps on pages 277-89 supplied by the Consorcio de Transportes de Madrid.
Map on page 290 by Mapworld, 71 Blandy Road, Henley-on-Thames, Oxon RG9 1QB.

Photography by Andrew Hall except: page 3 **Sofia Moro/Cover**; page 8 **Quim Llenas/Cover**; page 17, 21, 23, 26, **Museo Municipal de Madrid**; page 15, 25, 28 **Efe Agency**; page 27 **Tony Stone Images**; page 29 **Jordi Socias/Cover**; page 30, 44 **Matias Nieto/Cover**; page 66 **Jon Santa Cruz**; page 72 **Museo del Prado**; page 74, 81 **Museo Thyssen-Bornemisza**; page 79 **Ministerio de Cultura Museo de America**; page 184 **Image Bank**; page 189 **Warner Bros. Inc.**; page 88, 216 **Platou/Cover**; page 212 **Flamenco 2000**; page 220 **F. J. Rodriguez/Cover**; page 223 **Pepe Franco/Cover**; page 225 **Chris Parker/Axiom**; page 227 **Carma Casulá**; page 229 **Stuart Black/The Travel Library**; page 231,246 **José Manuel Navia/Cover**; page 236 **Jose R. Flaton/Cover**; page 241 **J. Costa/Cover**; page 244 **Erika Barahona Ede/FMGB Guggenheim**.
The following photographs were supplied by the featured establishments: 77, 86, 90, 99, 101, 103, 105, 185, 233.

Contents

About the Guide

This is the third edition of the *Time Out Madrid Guide*, one in an expanding series of city guides that includes over 20 cities worldwide. For this new edition our resident writers have revisited restaurants and tapas bars, galleries and festivals, to give as complete a picture as possible of the city today – not only Madrid's superb art museums and world-famous attractions like Toledo, but cafés and flamenco cellars, fringe theatres and backstreet shops, architectural eccentricities and the latest currents in the ever-changing nightlife scene.

The *Madrid Guide* covers every aspect of the city. It's also more than a book solely for tourists and casual visitors. We look at gourmet cuisine and food delivery, explain how to see a football match and, if you're staying for a while, how to handle residency and other aspects of living.

In response to reader demand, in this new edition of the guide several chapters – Sightseeing, Restaurants and others – are organised on a uniform area basis. Boundaries between districts in Madrid are sometimes open to argument, but the division we have followed in the centre of the city is shown *right*. Map references with guide entries refer to the four double-page maps on pages 278 to 285.

CHECKED & CORRECT

We've tried to make this book as useful as possible. All information was checked and correct at the time of going to press, but please bear in mind that, as in most cities, places can close and owners and managers can change their arrangements at any time. In addition, in Madrid small shops and bars often do not keep precise opening hours, and may close earlier or later according to the level of trade. Similarly, arts programmes are often finalised very late, and dates can fluctuate from year to year. Before going anywhere out of your way it's as well to phone to check times, dates and other details.

RIGHT TO REPLY

The information we give is impartial. No organisation or enterprise has been included in this guide because its owner or manager has advertised in our publications. Their impartiality is one reason why our guides are successful and well respected. We hope you will enjoy the *Time Out Madrid Guide*, but if you disagree with any of our judgements, let us know; comments on places you have visited, and tips for inclusion in future editions, are always welcome. You'll find a reader's reply card at the back of this book.

Prices

The prices listed in this guide should be treated as guidelines. Fluctuating exchange rates and inflation can cause prices, especially in shops and restaurants, to change rapidly. But, if prices and services ever vary wildly from those quoted, ask if there's a good reason. If there's not, go elsewhere and, then, please let us know. We try to give the best and most up-to-date advice, so we always want to hear if you've been overcharged or badly treated.

Telephone numbers

Since 1998 it has been necessary to dial provincial area codes with all numbers in Spain, even for local calls. Hence all Madrid numbers have to begin 91, whether or not you're calling from outside the city. From abroad, you must dial 34 (Spain) + 91. The 91 is still not shown on the signs or stationery of many hotels, restaurants and so on.

Credit cards

The following abbreviations are used for credit cards throughout this guide: **AmEx** – American Express; **DC** – Diners Club; **EC** – Eurocheque; **JCB** – Japanese credit bank card; **MC** – Mastercard; **TC** – travellers' cheques in any currency; **$TC**, **£TC** – travellers' cheques in US dollars or pounds sterling; **V** – Visa.

> There is an online version of this guide, as well as weekly events listings for several international cities, at **www.timeout.com**

Introduction

Over the last 400 years Madrid has been capital of many things. Initially of an immense overseas empire – the role for which it was dragged out of obscurity – and then, after this empire was lost, capital of a nation. Twice capital of a Republic, the second time besieged and bombed, the city was then for 40 years the grey capital of Franco's grey regime. With the political transition of the 1970s, Madrid suddenly became the fresh, sparkling capital of the *Movida* and all things wild and modern (and in an exercise of self-delusion even believed itself capital of the world for a while). In 1992 it was European Capital of Culture, but not many people seemed to notice. These days, Madrid is above all *capital del ambiente*.

Ambiente means atmosphere, ambience, or maybe 'the scene' (the word can also refer, much more specifically, to the gay scene alone). Madrid can still rightly claim to be the capital of many scenes – the flamenco scene, Spain's dance scene, the theatre scene, the nightlife scene.

Which might seem a touch paradoxical in the light of events of the last few years. After the *Movida* died a natural death (probably not a bad thing, as the frantic pace of those times threatened a collective coronary), the economy also took a nose dive. That, combined with ten years of attacks on the city's partying tendencies orchestrated from the *Partido Popular* city hall and fought for by its grey-suited infantrymen, might well have turned Madrid into the Mediterranean Oslo its one-time court jester, Pedro Almodóvar, once feared it would. Nothing of the sort.

Paradoxes. Readers' letters in the local press frequently abuse Mayor Alvarez del Manzano and his control-freak henchmen. If these letters really reflected the opinions of most Madrileños, then surely the PP's days must be numbered, but the party is still there, and has been re-elected several times. Conversely, the *capital del ambiente* tag also still stands firm, in the face of all the official obsession with surface respectability. Anyone who has seen Madrid's buzzing night world will confirm it. If enforced, current restrictions on closing times and noise levels would shut Madrid down before 3am every night, but the revelling still goes on regardless way beyond that point, into the following day. In apparently very conservative times, Madrid's gay scene, one particular *ambiente*, has become one of the most dynamic sectors of the local economy, and is thriving more than ever. Looked at in the cold light of logic, none of this

adds up. An explanation is probably to be found, though, in the Madrileño approach to life.

Several years ago, a leading Dutch newspaper and a Spanish one invited their respective correspondents in Madrid and Amsterdam to write their impressions of their adopted cities. What most struck the Dutch journalist was the refreshing attitude Madrileños showed to life. Instead of worrying about how they *ought* to be living, he noted, they just got on with it.

It's a *carpe diem* mentality, an attitude that means going out and having fun is a priority not to be interfered with, and not necessarily to be squared entirely rationally with other things you might have on your mind. It can be seen in the way that, despite the fact that the onset of more international working patterns has been threatened and talked about for years, nobody has yet been able to mess with the sacred Spanish lunch, long drawn-out and leisurely. It also means blowing a raspberry at perceived impositions from above.

A recently revised set of city by-laws for drivers and pedestrians includes fines of up to 5,000ptas for jaywalking, running and jumping in the street (yes, just that), as well as for waiting for buses outside of a bus shelter. These wonderful regulations were greeted, not unsurprisingly, with hoots of derision. They will also, of course, be completely ineffectual. If people didn't run and jump in the streets previously, now they probably will, because it's another rule to buck, and because they have been told that they can't.

Anyone who knew Madrid back in the wild mid-'80s might think that the city has grown up a little, even become a touch more staid, but they will also recognise, just below the surface, that naughty child who likes to stay up all night. So it's best to go with the flow. Stay out extra late, take three hours over lunch, and, if you've got 5,000ptas to spare, try sprinting up the Gran Vía and blowing a raspberry of your own. *Harvey Holtom*

In Context

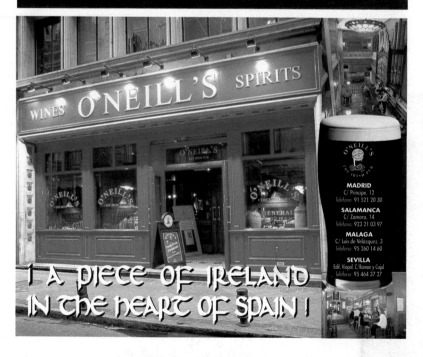

Madrid by Season

As one season runs into the next, Madrid's modern festivals, traditional fiestas and sessions of just plain revelling follow hard on each other's heels.

You like raucous street parties full of local colour? Madrid is your kind of town. Cutting-edge art fairs? It can sort you out there, too. Or if your thing is ceramics, dance, or fashion, or ethnic music, photography, opera, antiques or bullfighting, Madrid has something going on. Paradoxes abound: there is much that is highbrow, and lots that is quite a bit lower; independent initiatives are as popular as officially backed events; and recently coined festivals share the calendar with *fiestas* with medieval origins. Some events are international in flavour, others smack of the parochial. Whatever you want, this city has it.

In Madrid there is much doom-laden criticism of the cultural philistinism of recent governments. The various official arts festivals during the year present a patchy balance of successes and medio-crity. Both the **Veranos de la Villa** (Summers in the City) and **Festival de Otoño** (Autumn Festival) have suffered cuts in recent years, but their programming still throws up

some top-calibre artists, alongside others that are, well, less so. The international art fest **ARCO** seems now to be recovering after some years in the doldrums, as does the dance festival **Madrid en Danza**.

Into the institutional vacuum have stepped private promotors: one of the most successful initiatives in recent years has been **Festimad**, an alternative arts jamboree and music festival. And, fingers crossed, the brand new **PHotoEspaña** will become a permanent fixture.

Anyone wishing to witness a proper knees-up in the most traditional Madrid style, on the other hand, should try to be in town for a *verbena* (street *fiesta*), for this is the time when Madrid and the Madrileños really come into their own. **La Paloma** and the other *verbenas* in August are

Not-quite traditional zarzuela *at* La Corrala, *part of the* **Veranos de la Villa** *season. See page 9.*

1664 de KronENbourg

SeGún Pep CarRió

NunCa cuAtro cifRAs DiJeroN tANto

manifestations of a popular culture still in touch with its roots (for which, *see page 8* **Like a *castizo* should**). **Dos de Mayo** and **San Isidro** are two other popular events that are celebrated with great gusto. And don't forget **Carnival** and **Holy Week**, lower-key than in some parts of Spain but a great excuse for a party nonetheless.

Advance information about arts festivals is notoriously hard to come by, as programming details are often not finalised until close to the date, but local listings magazines such as the *Guía del Ocio* and *Metrópoli* usually produce special pull-out supplements in the preceding weeks (for both, *see chapter* **Media**); you can also call the city council's **010** info line (*see chapter* **Directory**) and the regional government's **012** number. They will also have details of admission prices. Events listed that are public holidays are marked *; for a full list of them, *see chapter* **Directory**. For more music festivals, *see chapters* **Music: Classical & Opera**, **Music: Rock, Roots & Jazz** *and* **Flamenco**.

Spring

EXPO-OCIO

Feria de Madrid/IFEMA, Parque Ferial Juan Carlos I. Metro Campo de las Naciones/Arturo Soria, then bus 122. **Information** 91 549 48 00/91 722 50 00/91 722 51 80. **Date** Mar.
At this huge leisure fair, held at the Feria de Madrid complex (*see chapter* **Directory**), you can buy sports gear, adventure holidays, beds, cars, boats and even houses. If you don't have that kind of money, try the virtual reality machines, go indoor rock-climbing or ride on a life-size Scalextrix.

Día de la Mujer/Semana de la Mujer

Various venues. **Route** *normally starts at Plaza Jacinto Benavente. Metro Sol, Tirso de Molina.*
Information Dirección General de la Mujer (91 580 47 00) & Centro de la Mujer, C/Barquillo 44, 1° izq (91 319 36 89). **Date** 8 Mar and surrounding week.
International Women's Day, 8 March, is marked with a march (usually starting at 8pm, and nearly always from Plaza Jacinto Benavente and down Calle Atocha), followed by *fiestas* in bars and clubs at night, organised by women's groups. The official *Dirección General de la Mujer* organises a week of events by female artists and performers.

Semana Santa (Holy Week)

All over Madrid. **Information** City information line (010) and tourist offices. **Date** Easter Week, Mar/Apr.
Holy Week is a less impressive event in Madrid than in southern Spain, but nevertheless there are a number of religious processions in the city during the week, with the traditional hooded figures of the *Penitentes* (Penitents) and huge images of Christ and the Virgin carried on the shoulders of troops of sturdy bearers. The most striking procession in Madrid is that of the brotherhood of *Jesús Nazareno el Pobre*, which winds its way round La Latina. There are also organ concerts in many churches and chapels. Easter is more important in towns around Madrid. The procession in **Toledo**, held in silence, is particularly solemn and ceremonious, and **La Granja** offers the eerie spectacle of the hooded penitents bearing huge crucifixes on their backs. In **Chinchón**, on Good Friday, there is a performance of a medieval Passion Play in the Plaza Mayor. For all these towns, *see pp225-34*.

Fiesta del Trabajo* (May Day)

City centre & Casa de Campo. Metro Lago, Batán/bus 33, 41, 75. **Date** 1 May.
May Day has lost much of its original political and emotional significance since the 1970s, but it still witnesses a sizeable march in central Madrid, organised by a joint committee of the Communist-led CCOO (known as '*Cocos*'), the Socialist UGT and the anarcho-syndicalist CGT. All three organisations are usually at loggerheads, but are sufficiently 'anti' the economic policy of whichever government is in office to put aside their differences for a day. Another march, by the anarchist CNT, runs through the district of Tetuán, along Calle Bravo Murillo and finishes in Cuatro Caminos. After the speeches, a festive spirit takes over and many demonstrators make for the Casa de Campo, where the UGT usually organises a big party with the different *Casas Regionales*, social clubs representing all the different regions of Spain, with *chiringuitos* (makeshift bars and stalls) offering beer, *bocadillos* (rolls) and all kinds of traditional food and drink.

Dos de Mayo*

District of Malasaña. Metro Tribunal, Bilbao, Noviciado/bus 3, 40, 147, 149. **Map E4**
Parque de las Vistillas. Metro Opera/bus 3, 25, 33, 39, 148. **Information** 012. **Date** 2 May. **Map B8**
The 2 May 1808, when the people of Madrid rose up in an attempt to expel Napoleon's invading army (*see chapter* **History**), is a hallowed day in local legend. Today it is the official holiday of the Madrid region, the *Comunidad de Madrid*. Resistance was strongest in the Malasaña area around the Monteleón artillery barracks, which stood where the Plaza Dos de Mayo is today, and the district takes its modern name from the teenage heroine of the struggle, Manuela Malasaña. The modern *fiesta*, the beginning of the summer *verbena* season, is also centred in Malasaña, with bands playing traditional and other dance music in the Plaza Dos de Mayo, and a more mixed crowd in the streets than the young bunch who regularly frequent the *barrio*'s bars. The *Comunidad de Madrid* also organises concerts and dance stages in venues around the city, particularly the Parque de las Vistillas next to the Palacio Real.

Festimad

Parque el Soto, Móstoles. Train Cercanías C-5 Círculo de Bellas Artes, C/Marqués de Casa Riera 2. Metro Banco de España/bus all routes to Cibeles. **Map G7**
Information 91 547 23 85/91 360 54 00. **Date** early May.
This 'Alternative Festival' began in 1994 in the now-defunct Revolver nightclub, with the idea of providing a shop window for Madrid's alternative youth culture. By 1996 it had grown to such an extent that the Bellas Artes building (*see chapters* **Sightseeing**, **Cafés & Bars**, **Art Galleries** *and* **Music: Classical & Opera**) became the venue for a week-long jamboree of sculpture and photography, seminars, a flea market, record launches, dance performances, film screenings, poetry readings and concerts by musicians of all kinds from Spain's young/indie music scene. Meanwhile, the parallel pop-rock festival moved out to a park in the suburban town of Móstoles, where it has continued to grow. In future the organisers, who do not want the event to become unwieldy but at the same time plan to keep the Móstoles dates, may choose alternative venues for some parts of the festival such as the market, **Festimad Mercado**, and parallel activities like **Etnimad** (a mini world music festival, held in several venues around Madrid) and **Festimad Cine**.

Madrid en Danza

Various venues. **Information** 012.
Date early May-mid-June.
Having had a chequered history in its 13 years of existence, this international dance festival seems finally to have got back on the rails. Political differences between City Hall and Regional Government (CAM) resulted in the non-participation of the former for several years, leaving the

Like a castizo should...

London has cockneys, and Madrid has *castizos*. The word *castizo* itself, roughly meaning pure or authentic, was once used to describe things considered distinctly Spanish, but around the end of the last century Madrid appropriated it to refer only to anything of *its* own. It can be applied to anything, from architecture to food. More specifically, though, it became attached to a particular working-class street type that appeared during the rapid growth of Madrid from the 1880s onwards, and which is now enshrined as the classic Madrileño character.

Castizos, descendants of the *Majos* and *Majas* painted by Goya (*see chapter* **History**), had a cocky, street-smart style of their own, always putting on a show of flash even if they had no idea of how they were going to pay the rent. Their slang and humour were celebrated in *zarzuelas*, the archetypal *castizo* art form. Known for their sharp, sarcastic wit, they were full of an attitude known as *chulería*, a combination of aggression, humour and self-sufficiency. Try flicking your head back and clicking your tongue at somebody and you'll get the idea.

Much of this may all be in the past but, in a city where most people are from somewhere else, those who can trace their origins here back more than a generation or so are proud to celebrate the fact. Different districts dispute the status of being the heart of *castizo*-dom, the main contenders being Chamberí and, above all, La Latina and Lavapiés. People turn out in full *castizo* regalia for the most traditional Madrid *fiestas*, **San Isidro** and, particularly, the August *verbenas* leading up to **La Paloma** – men as *chulos* in dog-tooth-check jackets and flat caps, women as *chulapas* in long skirts, lots of petticoats, flowered shawls and headscarfs, with an obligatory carnation in the hair.

It's then you have a chance to gather round the barrel-organ and dance the *chotis*, a bouncy, short stepped dance in which you cling very tightly to your partner in a kind of wobble, and hear 50 times a day the local anthem *Madrid, Madrid, Madrid* (written by a Mexican, Agustín Lara). The open-air *zarzuela* season at **La Corrala** is another major *castizo* event (*see chapter* **Music: Classical & Opera**). It's not necessary to show that your grandma was born in Madrid to go along, and even people who've not been here five years dress their kids in *castizo* rig-out and join in.

festival a little lame. The 1998 festival saw the *Ayuntamiento* coming back into the fold, the inclusion of other cultural institutions, the extension of activities to more fringe venues and towns in the province of Madrid, and, overall, the strongest programme in years. Nederlands Dans Theater and the Limón Dance Company were the major protagonists among the 30-odd who participated, from Spain and abroad, and the festival will hopefully continue along this path in future years.

San Isidro*

Plaza Mayor and all over Madrid. **Information** City information line (010) and tourist offices. **Date** 8-15 May. San Isidro, the humble twelfth-century labourer famed for his many miracles in aid of the needy (*see chapter* **History**), is Madrid's patron saint, and the week leading up to his day, 15 May, is the whole city's *fiesta mayor*, its biggest wing-ding. In the Plaza Mayor there is dance music each night and performances by local bands playing traditional music, modern folk, pop/rock or flamenco, and a giant *cocido* (*see chapter* **Restaurants**), available to anyone who wants some, is cooked up on the Sunday preceding 15 May. This is the most traditional part of the *fiesta*, with the old and the very young dressing up

in *castizo* attire. Many other events are included under the San Isidro umbrella, some of which go on beyond the week itself. In **Las Vistillas**, the park next to the Palacio Real with a view out over the sierra, there is a dance stage with salsa groups, and Spanish bands playing the traditional Madrileño *chotis*. Concerts are also on the bill at many theatres, and in recent years the **Centro Cultural de la Villa** (*see chapter* **Theatre**) has presented a series of shows called *Raíces Españolas*, with classic belters of traditional Spanish popular music (*canción española*), such as Rocío Jurado or Isabel Pantoja (this may not feature every year). The largest music venue, though, is in the **Casa de Campo**, where there are rock/pop gigs from international and Spanish acts. At the **Colegio San Juan Evangelista** (*see chapter* **Music: Rock, Roots & Jazz**) there is a small jazz festival and one-day flamenco festival. San Isidro is also Madrid's (and so the world's) most important bullfighting *feria*, with *corridas* every day for a whole month at Las Ventas (*see chapter* **Bullfighting**). In addition, San Isidro includes a separate children's programme, and many more exhibitions, demonstrations of local cuisine, local events and craft and book fairs, some of which are listed below.

Feria de la Cerámica *Avda de Felipe II. Metro Goya/bus 15, 21, 29, 30, 43, 63, C.* **Map L4/5**

A high-quality ceramics fair which now includes work in a range of other crafts, and continues throughout the week of San Isidro.

Feria de la Cerámica y Cacharrería
Plaza de las Comendadoras. Metro Noviciado, San Bernardo/bus 21, 147. **Map D3**
More of a 'household crockery' fair, and so cheaper, but still featuring a variety of traditional Spanish ceramics.

Feria del Libro Antiguo y de Ocasión
Paseo de Recoletos. Metro Colón, Banco de España/bus all routes to Plaza de Colón. **Map G/H7**
An old and second-hand book fair held usually on weekends only during the San Isidro period, and where you might find rare treasures or recent remaindered editions.

La Feria del Libro (Madrid Book Fair)

Parque del Retiro. Metro Retiro, Ibiza or Atocha/bus all routes to Atocha or Plaza de la Independencia.
Information Asociación de Libreros (91 534 61 24).
Date two weeks end May-June. **Map I/J7-9**
The Book Fair began as a local show 55 years ago, but is now an important international event, with personal appearances by major writers from throughout the Hispanic world and further afield. It gets bigger every year, and the sections of the book trade – distributors, publishers, bookshops – are all represented in the hundreds of stands in the Retiro. Public attendance is massive throughout the two weeks. It is one of the few events to take place in the Retiro, and there has been opposition to it on environmental grounds. However, for the moment, it looks set to continue among the trees, lakes and statues of Madrid's best green lung.

Summer

San Antonio de la Florida

Ermita de San Antonio de la Florida, Paseo de la Florida 5. Metro Príncipe Pío/bus 41, 46, 75.
Information 91 547 07 22. **Date** 12 June. **Map A4**
The hermitage of San Antonio de la Florida, with its Goya frescoes (*see p46*), is also the place where single women looking to find a suitable chap have traditionally gone on the saint's day, 12 June, to leave a needle in the hope that this might get him to intervene and send one along. In former times it was a big day out for Madrid's traditional seamstresses. Today, there's a big street party outside.

PHotoEspaña

Varios venues. **Information** 91 402 93 88/website www.photoes.com. **Date** mid-June-mid-July.
Launched with great success in 1998, PHotoEspaña is the biggest treat photography lovers in Madrid have ever been given, an event that promises much for future years. Using the Castellana as an 'axis', some 72 photo exhibitions take place over a month, including 17 major shows and a further 42 in the 'off' section. All the great art spaces have taken part, together with a host of other museums and private galleries, *Cercanías* stations, colleges and bookshops. Photographers from the world over were featured in the first edition, among them Duane Michals, Wolfgang Tillmans, Irving Penn, Arnold Newman and Spaniards such as Alberto García Alix and Ouka Lele. Theme shows included '100 years of Photography in Cuba', 'Magnum 1968', 'Spanish Photography in the Twentieth Century' and 'A Weekend in Europe', and workshops, seminars, conferences, prizes and a photographic marathon competition also featured on the agenda.

Fiesta Africana/World Music Getafe

C/Hospital de San José and C/General Palacios, Getafe. Bus 441, 442 from Atocha/train Cercanías line C-4 to Getafe Centro. **Information** Cultura Africana, C/San Eugenio 8, Madrid (91 539 32 67) or Getafe town council (91 681 82 12/91 681 60 62). **Date** July.
Really two separate festivals, the Fiesta Africana and

World Music Getafe have been held five minutes' walk from each other in the centre of the industrial suburb of Getafe since 1994. The Fiesta Africana includes batik workshops, storytelling, African cuisine and, of course, music. The 1998 festival was based around the theme of African women. World Music Getafe is now a fixture on the musical calendar, with acts from Spain and across Europe, Africa, Asia and Latin America. The main venue is the old Hospital de San José, on the street of the same name off Getafe's main street, Calle de Madrid, a short walk from the train station.

Veranos de la Villa

Various venues. **Information** City information line (010) and tourist offices. **Date** July-mid-Sept.
Funding cuts may mean fewer big names, but Madrid still offers a summer cultural programme unequalled in many other cities. In former years the 'Summers in the City' formed a strongly themed programme of opera, flamenco, pop, modern dance, jazz, cinema, theatre and much more; since the cuts, it has become more like an umbrella provided by the *Ayuntamiento* under which private venues and promoters can also shelter, including events with no official participation. That said, there are still a few things that tend not to change: principal venue is the patio of the **Centro Cultural Conde-Duque** (*see chapter* **Art Galleries**), the setting for *Música en Verano*, a season of jazz, blues, flamenco and other music. The last three years have seen artists of the calibre of Paco de Lucia, with Al di Meola and John McLaughlin, Elvis Costello, BB King jamming with flamenco guitarist Raimundo Amador, Robert Cray, Ray Charles, Cheb Khaled, Gilberto Gil, Joe Zawinul and Earth Wind & Fire. Concerts, from salsa to rock and pop, also take place in the Las Ventas bullring, a fabulous music venue.

Also presented at the Conde-Duque is a programme of opera, lately dominated by weary ex-Soviet companies. Dance takes place in the Conde-Duque or the **Teatro de Madrid**, and generally means an appearance by a prestigious dance company, such as that of Victor Ullate (*see chapter* **Dance**); 1998 saw performances by the Compañía Clásica de Cali, from Colombia, and Cuba's Conjunto Folklórico Cubano. A programme of *zarzuela* is presented in the **Centro Cultural de la Villa**, while in **La Corrala** one or two works are chosen for a summer-long outdoor run (*see chapter* **Music: Classical & Opera**). Al fresco cinema (*see chapter* **Film**), a wide range of theatre productions in mainstream and alternative theatres and the international puppet festival in the Retiro complete the main programme (*see chapter* **Children**).

Verbenas de San Cayetano, San Lorenzo & La Paloma

La Latina & Lavapiés. Metro La Latina, Lavapiés or Puerta de Toledo/bus all routes to Puerta de Toledo. **Information** City information line (010) and tourist offices. **Date** 6-15 Aug. **Map D/E9**
In August, those who haven't managed to quit Madrid for beach or mountains gather in what seems to be their entirety at these street *fiestas*, the most traditional and *castizo* in Madrid. San Cayetano (7 August), San Lorenzo (10 August) and La Paloma (15 August) follow each other in quick succession, all blending into the one event. The action takes place all around the archetypically Madrileño districts of La Latina and Lavapiés, where just about every street and square is decked out in flowers and bunting, and many people appear in all their *castizo* finery. During the day, there are parades and lots of events for kids. The main *fiesta* really gets going after the sun goes down, and from then until the early hours the drink flows freely, stalls sell nuts, coconut, rolls, sangria and lemonade, and live bands and competing sound systems provide music from pop and salsa to Madrid's very own *chotis*. To take it all in, it's best just to walk around the district from about 9pm onwards, going down as many side streets as you can.

Autumn

Fiestas del Partido Comunista

Casa de Campo. Metro Lago or Batán/bus 33, 41, 75.
Information Partido Comunista de España
(91 300 49 69). **Date** mid-Sept.
The Spanish Communist Party organises this three-day jamboree on a weekend in September in the **Casa de Campo**. As on May Day (*see above*), the *Casas Regionales* provide local delicacies, and there are live bands, theatre performances and stalls set up by campaigning and community groups. Tickets are available from Madrid Rock (*see chapter* **Shopping: Records & Music**).

International Fashion Week

Feria de Madrid/IFEMA, Parque Ferial Juan Carlos I.
Metro Campo de las Naciones, then bus 122. **Information**
91 722 50 00/91 722 51 80. **Date** mid-Sept & mid-Feb.
Fashion aficionados can delight at the sight of the world's top models showing off new creations by every name in Spanish fashion and many designers from abroad. Various sub-sections feature lingerie, sportswear or furs. The similar February event includes summer clothes and swimwear.

Festival de Otoño (Autumn Festival)

Various venues. **Information** Comunidad de Madrid (91 580 25 75) or 012. **Date** late Oct-early Dec.
Initiated in the early '80s as the Madrid International Theatre Festival, this event evolved into something much wider, embracing a complete range of the performing arts. Each year, one or two countries are chosen as a focus – Italy and Argentina have featured recently – and a figure from literature may be taken as a theme, such as Salomé in 1995. During the last few years of Socialist rule in the *Comunidad de Madrid*, it mushroomed into a large-scale international event. Over the years every kind of music imaginable has featured, and top names from the world of dance have graced the city's stages. At the other end of the spectrum, a near-infinite number of little-known theatre groups, from excellent to wacky to the frankly terrible, have appeared in the Sala Triángulo's *Muestra Internacional de Teatro Alternativo*, an avant-garde theatre meet formerly held in parallel to the main festival, although in future it will be presented earlier in the year (*see chapter* **Theatre**). The **Teatro Albéniz** (*see chapter* **Theatre**) hosts most events in the mainstream festival, but many other venues are used. Unfortunately, this is another case in which overspending in previous years has been followed by savage cuts, the result of which is a smaller festival, more limited in scope. Official long-term policy for the festival appeared to be orienting it towards music and away from theatre, but the last two years' events seemed to contradict this with more theatre than any other art form.

Winter

See also above **International Fashion Week**.

Feria de Artesanía

Paseo de Recoletos. Metro Colón, Banco de España/bus all routes to Plaza de Colón. **Date** Dec-6 Jan. **Map G/H7**
Madrid's biggest craft fair takes over Paseo de Recoletos in the weeks before Christmas and continues to the end of the festive season, 6 January. The official covered stalls run from Plaza de Cibeles to Colón, but unlicensed traders, *piratas*, stretch away as far again on each side. There is plenty worth buying, but it's best to go early as the final days are frantic.

Navidad* (Christmas)

All over Madrid. **Date** 25 Dec.
Unlike in other countries nowadays, the Christmas period still only starts in December in Madrid (for the moment, at least). Festivities centre around 24 and 31 December and 6 January,

the Feast of the Three Kings, or Epiphany. Traditionally, the main Spanish Christmas decoration is a crib, not a tree, and children receive their presents from the Three Kings on 6 January, not on Christmas, though in the last few decades Father Christmas and other international trappings of the season have become increasingly visible, while kids sometimes expect to get presents on *both* days. In the weeks preceding Christmas the Plaza Mayor is filled with stalls selling Christmas trees, traditional cribs and other festive trinkets, department stores put on lavish seasonal displays, and Recoletos is packed for the annual crafts fair, great for buying presents. The main Christmas celebrations take place on the night of Christmas Eve, which is when Spanish families have their traditional Christmas meal at home. The streets are consequently empty, although things liven up a little after midnight, and many clubs are open all night. Christmas Day itself is more a day for recovering.

Noche Vieja (New Year's Eve)

Puerta del Sol. Metro Sol/bus all routes to Puerta del Sol.
Date 31 Dec. **Map E7**
As on Christmas Eve, many people start the evening with a traditional meal with family or friends. The place to head for those who don't stay in is the Puerta del Sol, where thousands gather beneath the clock for a communal countdown, fireworks and the grape-stuffing session that is the centre of a Spanish New Year's Eve – you're supposed to eat one grape for each chime of midnight to get good luck for the rest of the year. Then, it's off to the bars for the rest of the night (but be warned that drinks are a lot more expensive than normal).

Reyes* (Three Kings)

All over Madrid. **Date** 6 Jan.
On 5 January, the eve of the arrival of the Three Kings, there is an evening *Cabalgata* (parade) around the city, with hundreds of elaborate floats, from where the costumed riders throw sweets to the children in the crowd. Thousands of people gather to watch the parade, which is televised. Afterwards, adults, as on the main 'eves', enjoy yet another big dinner, while kids are tucked up in bed preparing for their big day on the 6th, when they finally get their presents.

ARCO

Feria de Madrid/IFEMA, Parque Ferial Juan Carlos I.
Metro Arturo Soria, then bus 122. **Information** 91 722
50 00/91 722 51 80. **Date** early/mid-Feb.
After a couple of lean years, this international art fair recovered somewhat in 1995-6 and has made steady progress, even if the word 'crisis' is often heard from Spanish gallery owners. ARCO attracts a bewildering range of galleries from all over the world, providing a unique opportunity to see a huge selection of work under one roof. Recent years have seen more emphasis on multimedia art, as well as gatherings of major collectors to promote their role as patrons of contemporary art (*see also chapter* **Art Galleries**).

Carnaval

Date the week before Lent (usually late Feb/early Mar).
The Carnival celebrations are opened with a speech by a famous artist or writer, followed by a parade, the route of which varies from year to year. In clubs and other venues there are music gigs, ribaldry, drinking, and a fair amount of dressing up, especially in gay clubs in Chueca (*see chapter* **Gay & Lesbian Madrid**). There is also a famous masked ball in the **Círculo de Bellas Artes** (*see chapters* **Sightseeing**), although tickets are pricey and hard to come by. The end of the Carnival on Ash Wednesday is marked by the hilarious procession of the *Entierro de la Sardina* (Burial of the Sardine), a bizarre and ancient ritual in which the said fish is escorted around town in its tiny coffin, nowadays accompanied by a jazz band, before its interment on Paseo de la Florida. This *fiesta* is the subject of a painting by Goya, on show in the **Museo de la Real Academia de Bellas Artes de San Fernando** (*see chapter* **Museums**).

History

The adventures of a city transformed from country town to imperial capital by one man's decision, and which ever since has been pondering its place in the world.

Once the souk of Arab Mayrit, the Plaza de la Villa.

Frontier outpost

In the seventeenth century, after Madrid had become the capital of the Spanish Empire, an attempt was made to give it an ancient past. Several writers developed the story of its descent from a Roman city called *Mantua Carpetana*.

These accounts, however, were almost entirely the product of wishful thinking. The area around Madrid has one of the longest histories of continuous settlement of anywhere in Europe, and is extraordinarily rich in prehistoric relics, many of them now in the **Museo Arqueológico Nacional**. Later, there were Roman towns nearby at Alcalá de Henares (*Complutum*) and Toledo (*Toletum*), and several Roman villas along the valley of the Manzanares. There is, though, no real evidence that there was ever a local Mantua, or that any of these settlements was the origin of modern Madrid.

The story of *Mantua Carpetana*, however, served to obscure the sheer insignificance of Madrid before Philip II moved his Court here in 1561, and particularly the embarrassing fact that it had been founded by Muslims. Specifically, in the reign of Mohammed I, fifth Emir of Córdoba, in about 860.

Following their eruption into the Iberian peninsula in 711 the Arab armies did not occupy the inhospitable lands north of the Sierra de Guadarrama, but established a frontier more or less along the old Roman road linking Mérida, Toledo and Saragossa. The original *Al-Kasr* (a word absorbed into Spanish as *Alcázar*) or fortress of Madrid was one of a string of watchtowers built north of this line in the ninth century, as Christian raids into *Al-Andalus* became more frequent. The rocky crag on which it stood, where the Palacio Real is today, was particularly suited to the purpose, since it had a view of most of the main tracks south from the Guadarrama. It also had

Key Events

Frontier outpost

c860 Madrid founded during the reign of Emir Mohammed I of Córdoba.
1085-6 Alfonso VI of Castile conquers Toledo and Madrid
1109 Madrid besieged by Moorish army
1202 Madrid given *Fuero* (Statutes); population c3,000
1212 Battle of Navas de Tolosa: decisive defeat of Muslims in Spain
1309 First *Cortes* held in Madrid
c1360 King Pedro the Cruel rebuilds Alcázar of Madrid
1476 Isabella becomes unchallenged Queen of Castile
1492 Conquest of Granada. Expulsion of Jews from Spain. Discovery of America
1520-1 Madrid joins *Comuneros* revolt
1547 Birth of Cervantes in Alcalá de Henares

Capital for a Golden Age

1561 Philip II moves Court to Madrid from Toledo; population then c20,000
1562 Lope de Vega born in Madrid
1563-84 Building of El Escorial
1566 Beginning of Dutch Revolt
1574 First theatre in Madrid, the *Corral de la Pacheca*
1588 Defeat of the Armada against England
1599-1600 Plague and famine throughout Castile
1601-6 Court moved to Valladolid
1605, 1615 Don Quijote published, in two parts
1609 Expulsion of the *Moriscos*, the former Moslems
1617-9 Completion of Plaza Mayor
1630-3 Buen Retiro palace built; population of Madrid c150-170,000
1640 Revolts begin in Portugal and Catalonia
1643 Battle of Rocroi: Spanish army in Flanders defeated
1660 Death of Velázquez
1665 Philip IV succeeded by Charles II, then aged four
1700 Charles II dies without an heir

Bourbon Madrid

1702-14 War of the Spanish Succession: Philip V, first Bourbon King of Spain. Population of Madrid c100,000
1715 Decree of *Nova Planta*; Spain created as one state
1734 Alcázar of Madrid destroyed by fire
1761 Charles III bans waste dumping in Madrid streets
1775-82 Paseo del Prado created
1778 Goya moves to Madrid from Aragon
1795 In wars following French Revolution Spain changes sides to form alliance with France
1800 Population of Madrid c180,000

Revolutions & railways

1808-12 Madrid under French occupation
1812 *Cortes* in Cádiz agrees first Spanish constitution
1814 Fernando VII abrogates constitution
1810-24 Latin American Wars of Independence
1820 Military coup begins three years of liberal rule

1823 French army restores Fernando VII to full power
1833 Carlist Wars begin on death of Fernando VII
1836 Main decree on Disentailment of Monasteries
1851 Railway line to Aranjuez inaugurated
1854-62 Puerta del Sol rebuilt
1858 Canal de Isabel II water system inaugurated
1860 Plan for *Ensanche* of Madrid approved
1868 Revolution overthrows Isabel II
1871 Amadeo of Savoy becomes King of Spain. First trams in Madrid, drawn by mules
1872 Population of Madrid 334,000
1873 February: Amadeo abdicates; Republic declared

The Restoration

1874 January: Republic becomes military dictatorship after coup. December: Alfonso XII declared King
1879 Spanish Socialist Party (PSOE) founded
1898 Spanish-American War: disaster for Spain
1900 Population of Madrid 539,835
1907 First registration of motor vehicles in Madrid
1910 Building of Gran Via initiated
1917 General Strike in the whole of Spain
1919 First Madrid Metro line opened
1923 General Primo de Rivera establishes dictatorship
1929-31 Barajas airport opened
1930 Fall of Primo; Madrid's population officially 952,832

Republic & Civil War

1931 14 April: Proclamation of Second Republic
1934 October: General Strike against entry of right-wing ministers into government; in Asturias, bloodily suppressed by General Franco
1936 February: elections won by Popular Front; 18 July: military uprising against left-wing government; 9 November: Francoist forces launch assault on Madrid
1939 1 April: Franco declares war over

The long dictatorship

1946-50 UN imposes sanctions on Spain
1953 Cooperation treaty with USA
1950-60 Population of Madrid passes two million
1959 Stabilisation Plan opens up Spanish economy
1961 First violent attack by Basque nationalists of ETA
1970 Juan Carlos declared Franco's successor; population of Madrid 3,146,000
1975 20 November: Death of Franco

Rebirth

1977 15 June: First democratic general election
1979 April: Enrique Tierno Galván, Mayor of Madrid
1982 Socialists win national elections
1986 1 January: Spain joins European Community
1991 Popular Party wins power in Madrid city council
1992 Madrid, European City of Culture; Barcelona Olympics; Expo '92 in Seville
1996 *Partido Popular* wins power in general election

excellent water, from underground streams within the rock. Madrid's original Arabic name, *Mayrit*, means 'place of many springs'.

The most important of the outposts protecting Toledo, *Mayrit* was more than just a fortress, with an outer citadel or *Al-Mudaina* (later hispanicised as Almudena), the eastern wall of which ran along the modern Calle Factor, and a wider town or *Medina* bounded by the modern Plaza de la Villa and Calle Segovia. A section of wall, the **Muralla Arabe** on Cuesta de la Vega, is the only remnant of Muslim Madrid still visible in the modern city. Citadel and *Medina* consisted mainly of a mass of narrow alleys, like the old quarters of North African cities today. They did, though, have a sophisticated system for channelling the underground springs, which, much extended, would continue to serve Christian Madrid for centuries.

Mayrit was attacked by Christian armies in 932 and 1047, and in the 970s was used by the great minister of Córdoba, Al-Mansur, as a launching point in his celebrated hundred campaigns against the north. By the eleventh century it had a population of about 7,000, among them Abul-Qasim Maslama, mathematician, astronomer, translator of Greek literature and experimenter in magic.

CHRISTIAN CONQUEST

In the early eleventh century the Caliphate of Córdoba disintegrated into a mass of petty princedoms called *Taifas*, and *Mayrit* became part of the Emirate of Toledo. In 1086 Alfonso VI of Castile was able to take advantage of this situation to conquer Toledo, and with it Madrid. The main mosque became the church of Santa María de la Almudena, which would survive until the middle of the nineteenth century.

For many years, though, Madrid continued to be in the front line. In 1109 it was again besieged, by a Moorish army camped below the Alcázar in the place ever since known as *Campo del Moro* ('Field of the Moor'). A new wall was built, enclosing an area between the Alcázar and Plaza Isabel II, Plaza San Miguel and the Plaza Humilladero.

Nevertheless, by 1270 the Castilians had taken Córdoba and Seville. Christian Madrid, however, was a humble place that grew only very slowly. Its population was probably less than 3,000. Only in 1202 was Madrid given its *Fuero*, or Royal Statutes. It was a decidedly rural town, and most of the population who worked did so on the land. Madrid did acquire some large religious houses, notably the Friary of San Francisco, where San Francisco el Grande stands today, supposedly founded by Saint Francis of Assisi himself in 1217.

Madrid was still not entirely Christian. Many Muslims, known as *Mudéjares*, had stayed in the conquered areas, retaining their own laws and religion. They were particularly prized by the Castilian monarchs for their skills as builders and masons. In Madrid they moved into the area known as the *Morería* (*see page 43*). Medieval Madrid also had a smaller Jewish population, believed to have been concentrated outside the walls in Lavapiés.

Very little of medieval Madrid is visible today precisely because it was so undistinguished, and was largely discarded in later centuries. The most important remaining buildings are the towers of **San Nicolás de los Servitas** and **San Pedro el Viejo**, built by *Mudéjar* craftsmen in their distinctive style. Most local notables had their residences around the **Plaza de la Villa**, where the **Torre de los Lujanes** still stands today.

During the Middle Ages Madrid did acquire its future patron saint, San Isidro. He was a local farm labourer, believed to have died in 1172, who with his wife Santa María de la Cabeza was known for great piety and a series of miraculous and saintly acts, among them that of never failing to give food to another member of the poor. The cult of Isidro, remarkable for the very lowly status of its central figure, became extremely popular locally. Once Madrid had become the Spanish capital the couple would both be canonised, the only husband-and-wife saints in history.

ROYAL FAVOUR

Madrid did finally begin to play a slightly larger role in the affairs of Castile in the fourteenth century. In 1309 the *Cortes* or Parliament met here for the first time. Medieval Castile did not have a fixed capital, but instead the Court followed the king around the country, and similarly the *Cortes* met in many different towns at different times.

Fourteenth- and fifteenth-century Castile was dogged by a series of social revolts and civil wars, between the monarchs, the nobility, and rival claimants within the royal family itself. Against this backdrop Madrid began to gain popularity as a royal residence, as a retreat more than as a centre of power. King Pedro 'the Cruel' (1350-69) first began to turn the old Alcázar into something more habitable. That it was not a very prized royal possession, however, was shown when it briefly became Armenian territory. In 1383 Leo V of Armenia lost his kingdom to the Turks, and as consolation Juan I of Castile gave this Christian hero three of his own estates, among them Madrid. Later it reverted to Castilian sovereignty. Madrid was most favoured by Juan II (1407-54) and above all Enrique IV (1454-74), who gave it the title of *muy noble y muy leal* ('very noble and very loyal').

In addition, political instability did not prevent there being substantial economic progress in fifteenth-century Castile, which enabled Madrid to become for the first time a reasonably prosperous trading centre. The old market in Plaza de la Villa became inadequate, and in the 1460s an area east of the twelfth-century wall was built up as a ramshackle market square, the origin of the **Plaza Mayor**. Around 1450 a new town wall was also built, not for defence but so that taxes could be levied in the new parts of the city. Its eastern entrance was a new gate, the **Puerta del Sol**.

At the end of the fifteenth century a new era was opening up in Castilian and Spanish history. In 1476 Enrique IV's sister Isabel and her husband Fernando of Aragon – Ferdinand and Isabella – succeeded in bringing the civil wars to an end. Through their marriage they united the different Spanish kingdoms, although each retained its own institutions for another two centuries. Within Castile they imposed their authority on the aristocracy, establishing an absolute monarchy and a professional army that enabled them to intervene in the wars of Renaissance Italy. The earnestly devout Isabella was also one of the initiators of the militant sense of religious mission that would be a mark of Imperial Spain. Detesting the religious coexistence that had characterised medieval Spain, she ordered the expulsion of all Jews in 1492 and the forcible conversion of the remaining *Mudéjar* Muslims in 1502, with a reinforced Inquisition to police these measures. Also in 1492 came the conquest of Muslim Granada, which won Ferdinand and Isabella the title 'Most Catholic Kings' from the Pope. It was also, of course, in this same year that they sponsored Columbus' first voyage to America.

Madrid retained a degree of royal favour, partly because of its connections with some key figures at Isabella's Court. Most important was Cardinal Cisneros, the austere Franciscan, born just north of Madrid at Torrelaguna, whom she made Archbishop of Toledo and head of the Church in Spain in 1495. It continued its modest growth, and at the end of the Middle Ages had a population of around 10-15,000.

Capital for a Golden Age

On 11 May 1561 the small-time aristocrats who ran the town of Madrid received a letter from their king, Philip II, informing them that he, the entire royal household and all their hundreds of hangers-on would shortly be coming to stay. They immediately set about panic buying of food stocks from surrounding towns, using the money set aside for the *fiesta* of Corpus Christi, much to the irritation of the local population. No one quite realised, though, that this transformation was intended to be permanent.

In the previous 50 years the Spanish monarchy had itself been transformed. Ferdinand and Isabella were succeeded by their grandson Charles of Habsburg (1516-56), who through his father Philip, Duke of Burgundy, also inherited Burgundy (the Netherlands and large parts of eastern France) and the Habsburg lands in central Europe, and would in 1519 receive the title of Holy Roman Emperor, as Charles V. He would also, of course, acquire ever-larger territories in America. Spain thus became part, and increasingly the centre, of a European and world wide empire.

When he first visited Spain in 1517 Charles appointed French speakers to many state offices. This led in 1520 to the revolt of the *Comuneros*, in which the historic towns of Castile, Madrid among them, rose up in opposition to foreign influence and the encroachment of royal power on their traditional freedoms. However, after this uprising had been suppressed in 1521, Charles came to value Spain – above all Castile – more and more, as the most loyal part of his empire.

Charles and his successors had an immense sense of the dignity of their dynasty and their imperial mission, believing that their vast territories had come to them through Providence and that it was their right and duty to defend both them and the Catholic faith. This would involve continual and ever more costly wars, against the French, the Muslim Turks and the northern Protestants. This idea of mission combined perfectly with the crusading spirit already imbued in the Castilian Church and aristocracy. Castile also had a regular army that was establishing a reputation for invincibility, and was a ready source of money, thanks to American metals and to the fact that after the crushing of the *Comuneros* it was incapable of refusing any royal request for funds.

Charles V made no attempt to give Castile a capital. However, on his visits to Spain he did spend considerable time in Madrid, hunting at El Pardo and giving the town another title, *Imperial y Coronada* ('Imperial and Crowned'). In 1525, after his victory at Pavia, he had his great enemy Francis I of France brought to Madrid and imprisoned in the Torre de los Lujanes.

In 1555 Charles abdicated and retired to the monastery of Yuste, in the Sierra de Gredos (*see page 242*). Austria and the title of Holy Roman Emperor went to his brother Ferdinand, but Spain and Burgundy passed to Charles' son, Philip II (1556-98).

The fundamental figure in Madrid's history, Philip was a deeply pious, shy, austere man. Factors personal and political led him to feel a need for a permanent capital. His father had travelled incessantly about his many dominions, and led his armies into battle. Philip, in contrast, ruled his inheritance from behind a desk, as a kind of 'King-Bureaucrat', sometimes dealing with over 400 documents a day. This extraordinary exercise in paperwork naturally required a permanent base.

Moreover, in the 1540s Charles V had introduced Burgundian state ritual into the relatively informal Court of Castile. Every appearance of the monarch – such as meals, in which food could only be served to the royal family by gentlemen-in-waiting, exalted Dukes and Marquises, on their knees – followed a set ceremonial order, in an etiquette that became ever more elaborate as the Habsburgs amplified their idea of their own grandeur. The number of court attendants mushroomed, making an itinerant court all the more impractical.

Precisely why Philip chose Madrid as his capital, a town without a cathedral, a college or a printing press, remains unclear. In the 1540s, as Crown Prince, he had already ordered the extension of Madrid's Alcázar into a large, rambling palace. The fact that Madrid was almost at the dead centre of the Iberian peninsula may have appealed to Philip, who was fascinated by geometry, but his choice made no economic sense at all, since it would give Spain the only major European capital not on a navigable river.

Valladolid and Toledo were both more obvious candidates, but their historic importance seems itself to have been held against them. In contrast Madrid – which for centuries would normally be referred to in Spain as *la Corte*, the Court, never as

a city in its own right, which indeed it wasn't – would be a capital of the monarchy's own creation, a pure expression of royal power.

BOOM TOWN

Having established his ideal capital, Philip strangely did little to build or plan it. After the completion of the Alcázar his attention shifted to **El Escorial**, where he would increasingly spend his time. Royal piety was demonstrated by the endowment of lavish new houses for religious orders, such as the **Descalzas Reales**. Philip II founded 17 convents and monasteries in Madrid, Philip III 14 and Philip IV another 17, and they would cover a third of the city until the nineteenth century. A wider city wall was put up in 1566, and the **Puente de Segovia** in the 1580s. Philip's favourite architect, Juan de Herrera, planned the rebuilding of the **Plaza Mayor**, but the only part built during his reign was the Casa de la Panadería in 1590. Philip's idea of a capital seemed to be

A palace fit for a king

In 1632 the Count-Duke of Olivares presented his sovereign King Philip IV with the keys of a new residence in the royal park to the east of Madrid, the *Buen Retiro* or 'Good Retreat'. More than a palace it was a complex of palatial buildings, centred on a great courtyard presided over by the statue of the king on horseback, designed by Velázquez, which is now in the **Plaza de Oriente**. Olivares' aim in commissioning the palace was to make an emphatic statement of the greatness of the monarchy he served, creating a self-contained compound, with huge formal gardens, in which the Court could be displayed at its maximum splendour. Louis XIV took the idea as his model for Versailles.

The part of the Retiro that was of most interest to Philip IV was the Court theatre. The King had a special fascination for elaborate set designs and visual tricks, and an Italian designer, Cosimo Lotti, was brought in to create extravagant productions that dwarfed the human actors. Writers such as Calderón created dramas, mostly on mythological themes, to fit. Mechanical devices were used, and productions spread out to feature the park lake, with battles between life-size ships, sea-monsters appearing from the depths, and angels flying through the air. Most performances were only for the Court, but several times a year a wider audience was allowed in to be amazed.

The full splendour of the Retiro lasted less than a century, for the Bourbon kings had no great liking for it. Most of the palace was destroyed in

1812-13, during the Napoleonic Wars. Only two sections of it survive, the **Casón del Buen Retiro** and the **Museo del Ejército**, soon to be absorbed by the Prado (*see chapter* **Museums**).

Centrepiece of the Retiro, Philip IV.

more like a functional collection of royal establishments than a living city.

Reality, however, was more powerful than this rudimentary concept. The establishment of the Court and aristocracy in Madrid, the great centres of consumption and patronage, made it a magnet for people from all over Spain and abroad. The population went from around 16,000-20,000 in 1561 to 55,000 in 1584 and close to 85,000 by 1600. Building did not keep up with the influx, and a law decreed that in any house of more than one storey the upper floor could be requisitioned to house members of the Court. In response people simply put up houses with only one floor, and much of the new Madrid grew as a mass of shabby, low buildings slapped together out of mud.

This improvised capital did not impress foreign visitors. Lambert Wyts, a Flemish aristocrat who arrived in 1571, said that it was 'the foulest and filthiest town in Spain'. Thick mud made it impossible to ride a horse down the main streets in winter until a few cobbles were put down in the 1580s, and even then they were grossly inadequate. There were no drains of any kind, and the streets were full of waste thrown out of the houses every night, producing an 'unbearable stench'.

From the start Madrid took on a characteristic that would stay with it to this day – that it was a city of outsiders, in which at least 50 per cent of the population, and often much more than that, were from somewhere else, with a steady flow of new arrivals. Another trait for which Madrid would be repeatedly condemned was that it was a city that consumed but did not produce anything. The trades that did develop in Madrid – carpenters, shoemakers, jewellers, fanmakers, laceworkers – were overwhelmingly oriented to servicing the Court and aristocracy.

The economic frailty of Madrid reflected that of Castile as a whole. The gold and silver of Mexico and Peru seemed to give the Habsburg kings limitless potential wealth. The demands of their wars, however, were immediate, and could only be met by loans from German and Italian bankers. The result was spiralling, uncontrollable debts, which not even American gold could match. Also, the country's political hierarchy had been built on the basis of giving the aristocracy, the *hidalgos* or lesser gentry and the Church immense privileges, very important among them exemption from taxation. This meant that the always-increasing war taxes hit precisely and only the few productive sectors of the population. Young men of working age were also continually being drawn off for the army. For a country with the social system of Castile, constant imperialism was near suicidal; in time, it would lead to the eradication of the growth visible under Ferdinand and Isabella, and a catastrophic decline in the rural population.

One aspect of Spain during its 'Golden Century'

was its intense Christian faith. This was also, though, the golden age of the *picaro*, the chancer, the figure living on his wits portrayed in the *picaresque* novels of the period. In a society that valued aristocracy, status and military or State service over productive activity, and in which the real economy was rapidly dwindling, their numbers naturally multiplied.

The mecca for all *picaros* was Madrid, the one place where ex-soldiers, landless peasants and other drifters would be most likely to find a niche, as servants or bodyguards, or by gambling, prostitution, thieving or many other means. The great poet and satirist Quevedo wrote a whole book cataloguing the varieties of Madrid's low life and how they acquired cash. It also contained a great many of the very poor, for whom the huge number of religious houses in the city, all sources of charity, was a major attraction.

Picaros were not only found among the poor. Madrid also drew in thousands at the other end of society, often *hidalgos* with estates run to ruin, who came hoping to attach themselves to some lordly patron and so break into the circles of the Court. For them, appearance, maintaining the image of aristocracy, was everything. In 1620 Madrid acquired its first guidebook, the 'Guide and advice to strangers who come to the Court, in which they are taught to flee the dangers that there are in Court life', by Antonio Liñán y Verdugo, a lawyer from Cuenca. He warned provincials who might come to do business in Madrid that in 'this Babylon', 'of every four things one sees, one cannot believe even two', for everything was just 'fabulous appearances, dreamed-up marvels, fairytale treasures, and figures like actors on a stage'.

This volatile mass naturally needed entertainment. One source was the theatre, in the *corral* theatres that began to be built in Madrid in the 1570s (*see chapter* **Theatre**), the focus of the extraordinary literary vitality of the city at this time. There were also the major *fiestas* and royal ceremonies, many of them also occasions for mass revelry. And, even foreigners who complained about the mud and the stink were impressed by the variety of luxuries that could be had in Madrid, from Italian lace to 'fresh' fish, brought caked in ice on a five-day journey from the Basque coast.

MADRID ABANDONED

In 1571 came the greatest success of Philip II's reign with the defeat of the Turkish fleet off Lepanto in Greece. In 1580, after the Portuguese throne had fallen vacant, Philip also became King of Portugal. He appeared to be at the height of his strength. However, suspensions of payments on his debts were becoming frequent occurrences, and in the 1560s a rebellion had broken out in the Netherlands that would develop into a morass into which Spanish armies and wealth would disappear

A state reception for the Prince of Wales at the Alcázar of Madrid in 1623.

without trace. His dispute with England, also, not only led to the catastrophe of the Armada but gave the Dutch a vital ally. Interventions in the religious wars in France proved equally costly.

As problems mounted without any ever being resolved, a gnawing frustration spread through Castilian society. The response of Court and Church was to turn in on themselves. The former Muslims (*Moriscos*), nominally converted to Catholicism in 1502, were subjected to increasing pressure that culminated in their expulsion from Spain in 1609, and the Inquisition – if never the all-pervading force of Protestant caricatures – was given great powers to investigate deviations from Catholic orthodoxy.

Philip II died in 1598 at El Escorial, aged 71. His son Philip III (1598-1621) and grandson Philip IV (1621-65) had neither the intelligence, confidence or normally the motivation to carry on with the awesome burden of work he had set as an example. Philip III began the practice of ruling through a favourite or *valido*, for most of his reign the Duke of Lerma. The country's impoverished state, aggravated by a devastating plague in 1599, was impossible to ignore, and Lerma responded by making peace with England and the Dutch.

He also committed the ultimate injury to Madrid by moving the Court to Valladolid, in 1601. The main stated reason was that this would help revive the prostrate economy of northern Castile, although Lerma also stood to benefit personally. He also argued that Madrid, in any case, was so overrun with undesirables that it had become intolerable. The monarchy's purpose-built capital was out of control, and it would be best to write it off and start again.

Within a few months Madrid was so deserted that 'it appeared as if the Moors or the English had sacked and burnt it'. By 1605 the population had fallen back to just 26,000, little more than it had been before Philip II's arrival in 1561. However, the Valladolid experiment did not work, and it became evident that Madrid had acquired a momentum that was difficult to disregard. In 1606 the Court returned, amid huge rejoicing, and only a year later the population was already back to 70,000.

BAROQUE THEATRE

It was after the definitive establishment of Madrid as capital, with Philip III's brief declaration '*Sólo Madrid es Corte*' ('Only Madrid is the Court'), that more was at last done to give it the look of a grand city. The Plaza Mayor was finally completed in 1619, followed by the **Ayuntamiento** or City Hall and, grandest of all, the Buen Retiro palace (*see page 15*). The aristocracy also built palaces around the city once they were assured they would not have to move on again. Madrid still did not have a cathedral, but it did acquire more elaborate church buildings, such as the Jesuit church of **San Isidro**, completed in 1633.

The Plaza Mayor was the great arena of Habsburg Madrid. Able to hold a third of the city's population at that time, it was the venue for state ceremonies, bullfights, public executions, *autos-da-fé* (the ritual condemnation of heretics), mock battles, circus acts and carnival *fiestas*, as well as still being a market. Particularly lavish entertainments were staged in 1623 for the Prince of Wales, the future King Charles I, who arrived under the bizarre alias of 'Tom Smith' in an attempt to negotiate a marriage with the sister of Philip IV.

Habsburg Madrid functioned rather like a giant theatre, a great backdrop against which the monarchy could display itself to its subjects and to the world. On either side were royal estates, which determined the shape of the city left in the middle and its peculiar north-south pattern of growth. Several times a year royal processions were held, nearly always along a similar route: from the Retiro along Calle Alcalá to the Puerta del Sol, Calle Mayor and the Alcázar, then back again via Calle Arenal and Carrera de San Jerónimo, with stops for ceremonies in the Plaza Mayor and High Masses in various churches. For the occasion, buildings were covered in garlands, and temporary arches erected all along the route with extravagant decoration covered in texts and images extolling the virtues of the dynasty. As the Spanish monarchy slid towards economic collapse the lavishness of these ceremonies only increased, maintaining an illusion of power and opulence.

Away from this ceremonial route, the Habsburgs built few squares and no grand avenues, and old Madrid continued to develop along the disorderly, tangled street plan it retains today, as a shabby amalgam of little houses packed in between the looming walls of aristocratic palaces and religious houses. Even so, the opulence of the Court – and the poverty outside the capital – still attracted more and more people into the city's floating population, and in about 1630 Madrid reached its maximum size under the Habsburgs, with possibly as many as 170,000 inhabitants. In 1656 it was given its fifth and final wall, roughly surrounding the area now considered 'old Madrid', and which would set the limits of the city for the next 200 years.

The centre of all the Court pomp was for many years King Philip IV, whose gloom-laden face is familiar from many a Velázquez portrait. His *valido* was the Count of Olivares, who he gave the unique title of Count-Duke, *el Conde Duque*. Philip IV was a great lover of theatre and painting, and in 1623 appointed Velázquez, then only 23 himself, as Court Painter. Like his father Philip III, though, he would feel overwhelmed and exhausted by the responsibilities of his office.

Philip IV combined devout Catholicism with an active if guilt-ridden sex life, and is believed to have fathered 30 illegitimate children. The Habsburg Court was not, though, one like that of Louis XIV of France, where royal mistresses enjoyed semi-queenly status; it was far too formal and decorous for that, and the King's affairs had to be carried on very much below stairs. More prominent were the royal dwarfs and clowns, of whom Philip IV was particularly fond. As their difficulties mounted, the Habsburgs and their Court retreated more and more into rigid ritual. 'The King of Spain', a Dutch visitor wrote in 1655, 'adopts such a degree of gravity that he walks and behaves like a statue'.

Olivares, meanwhile, was struggling to maintain the Spanish empire, embroiled in the Thirty Years' War. In the 1620s Spain won a series of victories, and for a time it seemed as if the rot had been stopped. In 1639, though, a Spanish fleet was destroyed by the Dutch, and in 1643 the French crushed the Spanish army at Rocroi in Flanders, ending the legend of Spanish invincibility. Naval defeats made it ever more difficult for Spain to control the imports of gold and silver from America. Olivares sought to extend taxation in the non-Castilian dominions of the crown, which led in 1640 to revolts in Portugal and Catalonia. Portugal regained its independence, and the Catalan revolt was only suppressed after a 12-year war.

By mid-century the effects of endless wars on Castile were visible to all, in the shape of abandoned villages and social decay throughout the country. Even Madrid went into decline, so that by 1700 the city's population had fallen back to about 100,000. In the 1660s, the total collapse of the Spanish empire seemed an immediate possibility. Characteristic of seventeenth-century Spain was the mood of *desengaño*, disillusion. The heroic efforts, all the posturing at greatness had come to nothing, and left Castile, the first world power, poorer than most of the countries it had tried to dominate.

HABSBURG TWILIGHT

In the Court, meanwhile, life became ever more of a baroque melodrama. Of Philip IV's 12 legitimate children by his two wives, only two girls survived to adulthood – the youngest the Infanta Margarita, the little princess of Velázquez' *Las Meninas*. In 1661, however, when Philip was already prematurely aged, the Queen, Mariana of Austria, gave birth to a son, conceived, the King confided, 'in the last copulation achieved with Doña Mariana'.

The new heir, the future King Charles II, chronically infirm from birth, provided the dynasty with scant consolation. The Habsburgs' marked tendency to ill-health had been accentuated by their habit of marrying cousins or nieces. The formidable Habsburg jaw, the growth of which can be followed through the family portraits, had in Charles become a serious disability. He was unable to eat solid food. Because of this – or more likely, due to the endless cures he was subjected to for his innumerable ailments – he suffered from uncontrollable diarrhoea, which detracted from the stately dignity of Court ceremonies.

In 1665 Philip IV died, leaving as regent his widow Mariana. Born in Vienna, she chose as her adviser her confessor, a Tyrolean Jesuit called Father Nithard, who was the first of many foreigners to attempt to ban bullfighting. She was forced to dismiss him by Juan José de Austria, one of Philip IV's healthier, illegitimate children, who himself had ambitions on the throne. Mariana then took a less pious tack by promoting a good-looking and totally corrupt groom, Fernando Valenzuela, before being obliged to get rid of him too.

In the meantime, the economy and administration of the country continued to slide. Concern centred again on the need for an heir, and Charles was married off twice, despite a general belief that he was both impotent and sterile. As it became evident that the throne of the Spanish empire would soon become vacant, the Court was overrun with bizarre intrigues, with different factions and the agents of European powers jockeying to capture the prize, all waiting on Charles' final demise. In 1695 the French Ambassador reported that the King 'appeared to be decomposing', and could not walk more than 15 paces without assistance. Even so, Charles resisted everything his 'healers' threw at him until the age of 38. In 1700, though, with the pathetic last words *'Me duele todo'* ('It hurts everywhere'), he finally died, and the Spanish Habsburg dynasty came to an end.

Bourbon Madrid

Philip V (1700-46), first Bourbon King of Spain, secured his throne in 1714, after the 12-year War of the Spanish Succession. He was the grandson of Louis XIV of France and María Teresa, daughter of Philip IV of Spain. Castile, abandoning its more usual francophobia, gave him complete support. The alternative, Archduke Charles of Austria, was supported by Catalonia and the other Aragonese territories, to whom he had promised a restoration of their traditional rights. Twice, in 1706 and 1710, Charles' British, Dutch, Portuguese and Catalan army took Madrid, but was unable to hold it.

Once victorious, Philip reformed his new kingdom along lines laid down by his illustrious grandfather in France. In 1715 the remaining rights of the former Aragonese territories were abolished, so that it is from this date that 'Spain' can formally be said to exist.

A French king brought with him other foreign innovations. Philip V, raised at Versailles, and his Italian second wife Isabella Farnese were not taken with Madrid or its gloomy Habsburg palaces, and as consolation built their own Franco-Italian villa at **La Granja**. They were not overly upset when the entire Alcázar burnt down in 1734, and a new **Palacio Real** was commissioned from Italian architects. Philip V and his administrator in Madrid the Marqués de Vadillo also sponsored

Street fashion, 1790

In the eighteenth century, the appearance of ordinary people in European cities became increasingly similar, with three-cornered hats, breeches and mop-caps appearing everywhere. Not so in Madrid, where this era saw the emergence of the *Majos* and *Majas* – the word itself means 'fine' or 'pretty' – also known as *Manolos* and *Manolas*. A *Majo* wore embroidered shirts and a short jacket with a swathe of buttons, his hair was held in a net, and he always carried a knife. *Majas* wore short, mid-calf skirts with a mass of petticoats, pearl-white stockings, embroidered bodices, an intricately braided hairstyle and, on top, a dramatic lace mantilla. Drawn from humble trades such as porters, coachmen, seamstresses, cigarette makers or market traders, they most often hailed from Lavapiés, and were notorious for not being deferential to anybody. *Majas* especially were known for their wit, grace and verbal ferocity.

Majos and *Majas* were seen in all their finery at *fiestas* such as the Romería de San Isidro. Goya depicted them often. Their cocky elegance intrigued the upper classes, so that even *grandes dames* like the Duchess of Alba would dress up as *Majas*, which is what probably gave rise to the story that Goya's nude and clothed *Majas* are portraits of the Duchess herself. It also became quite fashionable for ladies to have a *Majo* somewhere in attendance. *Majos* and *Majas* survived the Napoleonic Wars but had disappeared by the 1850s, although many of their characteristics would reappear in the later *Castizo* (*see page 8*).

other new buildings, such as the Hospice – now the **Museo Municipal** – the **Cuartel Conde Duque** and the **Puente de Toledo**, all by their favoured local architect Pedro de Ribera.

Reform led to economic recuperation and a recovery in Spain's population. Madrid once again had 150,000 inhabitants by 1760, and 180,000 by 1800. People still came and went continually, but it had also acquired a more stable resident population, with a merchant community and a testy artisan and working class (*see above*).

Even so, in many ways Madrid had changed little. Its main function was still to serve the Court, whose ceremonies set the calendar. They were as lavish as ever, particularly the night processions with candles along every balcony on the ceremonial route, creating an effect of 'indescribable grandeur'. Until the 1770s the amount spent annually by the Crown in Madrid was always greater than the entire budget of the Spanish navy.

Within the Court itself the Bourbons introduced a much lighter style. Isabella Farnese was highly educated, and particularly interested in the arts and music. One Italian musician at the Court was Domenico Scarlatti, who arrived in 1729 as music teacher to Bárbara de Braganza, the Portuguese princess who married the future King Fernando VI. Scarlatti spent the last 28 years of his life here, and wrote most of his 555 harpsichord sonatas for her and her Court – and only for them, since they were never performed in public in his lifetime.

THE KING-MAYOR

Fernando VI (1746-59) was a shy but popular King who gave Spain its longest period of peace for over 200 years. Childless, he was succeeded by his half-brother Charles III (1759-88). Previously King of Naples for 20 years, he too was unimpressed by Madrid. However, more than any of his predecessors he set out to improve it, becoming known as Madrid's *Rey-Alcalde* or 'King-Mayor'.

Charles was fascinated by Enlightenment ideas of progress, science and the applied use of reason. No democrat, he sought to bring about rational improvement from the top. Centralising reforms were undertaken in the bureaucracy and armed forces, and to improve trade with Spanish America. He challenged the privileges of the religious orders, and expelled the Jesuits from Spain in 1767 for their refusal to co-operate.

In Madrid, Charles first undertook to do something about the mud in winter, suffocating dust in summer and foul smells at all times noted by every visitor to the city. A 1761 decree banned the dumping of waste in the streets, and the Italian engineer Francesco Sabatini began the building of sewers and street lighting. A string of major buildings was erected, of which the **Casa de Correos** in Puerta del Sol and the **Puerta de Alcalá** are the best-known. A later queen of Spain remarked that it sometimes seemed as if *all* the monuments of Madrid had been built by Charles III.

Charles III's grandest project was the **Paseo del Prado**. He sent scientific expeditions to every corner of his empire, and planned to exhibit the fruits of their varied researches in a Museum of Natural Sciences – now the **Museo del Prado** – and the adjacent **Jardín Botánico**.

Popular reaction to the King's improvements was mixed, some being resented as foreign impositions. A decree of Charles III's Italian minister Squillace provoked one of history's first fashion revolts. In 1766 he banned the traditional long cape and wide-brimmed hat and ordered the use of the international three-cornered hat, with the justification that the capes were used by criminals to conceal weapons. In what became known as the *Motín de Esquilache* (Squillace Riot), a mob marched on the Palacio Real and forced the repeal of the decree.

Reform and improved trade did create a feeling of well-being in late eighteenth-century Madrid. The aristocracy engaged in a new round of palace-building and hedonistic entertaining. Balls went on throughout the night, most famously in the Duchess of Alba's Palacio de Buenavista in Cibeles. This is the world seen in the early Madrid paintings of Goya, who lived in the city from 1778.

Nevertheless, Spain was still a very feudal society, and the real economy remained backward and frail. And, in an absolute monarchy, a great deal depended on the character of the monarch. Charles IV (1788-1808), whose rather dozy face was immortalised by Goya, had none of his father's energy or intelligence. Also, he chose as his minister the corrupt Manuel Godoy. After the French Revolution, Spain joined other monarchies of Europe in attacking the new regime; in 1795, however, Godoy made peace and then an alliance with France, leading to war with Britain. This was highly unpopular, and in 1808, when Godoy was vacillating over changing sides once again, he was forestalled by an anti-French riot in Madrid that proclaimed Charles IV's son Fernando as King in his place. Napoleon sent troops to Madrid, assuming this decrepit state would be as easy to conquer as any other.

Revolutions & railways

The second of May 1808, when the people of Madrid rose up against the French army in hand-to-hand fighting through the streets, has traditionally been seen as the beginning of modern Spanish history. Left to themselves the authorities in the city would certainly have capitulated. The ferocity of popular resistance astonished the French, who could not understand why a people never included in the deliberations of government should care so much about who ruled them.

Napoleon made his brother, Joseph Bonaparte, King of Spain. In Madrid he tried in a well-meaning way to make improvements, among them some squares for which the city has since been very grateful, notably the Plaza de Oriente and the Plaza Santa Ana. However, this did nothing to overcome the animosity around him. In 1812 the Duke of Wellington and his army arrived to take the city, in a battle that destroyed much of the Retiro palace. The French were finally driven out of Spain in 1813.

The suffering and devastation this war caused in Spain is seen with matchless vividness in Goya's *The Disasters of War*. As well as the fighting itself, the year 1812 brought a catastrophic famine, which in Madrid killed over 30,000 people.

The shock of this upheaval initiated a period of instability that continued until 1874, although it could be said that it only really ended with the death of Franco. Taking little part in international affairs, Spain withdrew into its own problems, with one conflict following another between conservatives, reformists, revolutionaries and other factions. Each attempted, unsuccessfully, to impose their model on the State and create a political system that could accommodate, or hold back, the pressures for modernisation and some form of democracy.

During the war a *Cortes* had met in Cádiz in 1812, and given Spain its first-ever Constitution. This assembly also first gave the world the word 'liberal'. However, when Fernando VII (1808-33) returned from French captivity in 1814, his only thought was to cancel the Constitution and attempt to return to the methods of his ancestors. His absolute rule, though, was incapable of responding to the bankruptcy of the country. The regime was also trapped in the futile but immensely costly struggle to hold on to its American colonies, by then in complete rebellion.

In 1820 a liberal revolt among the army forced Fernando to reinstate the Constitution. He was saved three years later, ironically by a French army, sent to restore monarchical rule. Meanwhile, defeat at Ayacucho in Peru (1824) left Spain with only Cuba, Santo Domingo and Puerto Rico of its former American empire.

In 1830, however, Fernando VII's wife Maria Cristina gave birth to a daughter, soon to be Queen Isabel II (1833-68). Previously, the most reactionary sectors of the aristocracy, the Church and other groups deeply suspicious of economic liberalism had aligned themselves behind the king's brother Don Carlos. When Fernando died in 1833, Carlos demanded the throne, launching what became known as the Carlist Wars. To defend her daughter's rights the Regent, Maria Cristina, had no choice but to look for support from liberals, and so was obliged to promise some form of constitutional rule.

For the next 40 years Spanish politics was a see-saw, as conservative and liberal factions vied for power, while the Carlists, off the spectrum for most people in Madrid, occasionally threatened at the gates. Madrid was the great centre for aspiring politicians, and the problems of Spain were discussed endlessly in its salons and new cafés, which multiplied rapidly at this time. This was the era of Romanticism, and writers such as the journalist Larra and poet José Espronceda were heavily involved in politics. Similarly, many of the politicians of the day were also writers.

Much of the time, however, these reformers were shepherds in search of a flock, for there were no real political parties. The only way a faction could really hope to gain power was with the support of a General with troops at his back.

The army had become inextricably involved in politics. The *pronunciamiento*, or coup, was the main means of changing governments, and the soldiers identified with particular sides – Espartero, Serrano and Prim for the progressives,

Madrileños and Napoleon's army battle it out in Sol, 2 May 1808.

There are ways of doing things

In 1833 Mariano José de Larra, the great satirist considered the founder of Spanish journalism, wrote a piece called *Vuelva Usted Mañana* ('Come Back Tomorrow'). He describes how he has met a foreigner, *M. Sans-Delai*, who has arrived in Madrid to sort out a family inheritance and to propose a project of great mutual benefit to the Spanish government. He expects to do all this in 15 days. Larra promises to buy him lunch in 15 months, as he'll assuredly still be here. The man finally gives up and leaves six months later, having achieved nothing he wanted to do. Wherever he goes, he's told it's not quite the right time to see the right person, and that he should come back tomorrow; his grand scheme is passed around between various ministries, and disappears without trace when one ministry declares it has sent it on while another denies ever having received it.

Spain's bureaucracy was first established by the Habsburgs, but became much larger and more professional under the Bourbons, who, inspired by Louis XIV, created Spain as a centralised state. The governments of the nineteenth century gave the administration its system of hierarchies and the examinations for entry to public service that, once passed, guaranteed a job for life. Irrespective of the superficial instability of governments, the bureaucracy's procedures, routines and rituals remained in place. In Madrid, the city whose whole purpose was government, they long set the tone of middle-class life, and even today a read of Larra's articles from the 1830s can still give any resident a shock of recognition.

Narváez and O'Donnell (a descendant of Irish soldiers in the Spanish army – were the heroes of their followers. Later, most of either faction had monuments or streets named after them in Madrid, together with civilian politicians such as Bravo Murillo, Argüelles, Cea Bermúdez and Martínez de la Rosa.

The people of Madrid – an indeterminate group that ran from lawyers to labourers – played an important part in these ebbs and flows. In crisis after crisis they would form a *Milicia Nacional* and march on Charles III's Post Office in the Puerta del Sol, by then the Interior Ministry. For a long time they were not anti-monarchist, but demanded changes in the Constitution, or the replacement of particular ministers. These clashes were never decisive, and it was later said that Spain had gone through 70 years of agitation without ever experiencing a revolution.

CHANGE COMES SLOWLY

This political instability did not mean that life in Madrid was chaotic. Visitors to Madrid in the early 1830s found a small, sleepy, shabby city, seemingly sunk in the past. Convents and palaces still occupied nearly half its area.

It was around this time that Spain acquired its romantic aura. A growing number of foreigners visited the country, drawn above all by its timeless, exotic qualities. The English traveller George Borrow, who arrived in 1836, described Madrid's population as 'the most extraordinary vital mass in the entire world'. Another visitor was the French writer Prosper Merimée, who in 1845 would write his novel *Carmen*. This would fix the image of Spain forever, above all when given music by Bizet, who himself never visited Spain at all.

The 1830s, however, also saw the single most important change in old Madrid during the nineteenth century. In 1836 the liberal minister Juan Alvarez Mendizábal took advantage of the Church's sympathy for Carlism to introduce his law of *Desamortización* or Disentailment, which dissolved most of the country's monasteries. In Madrid, the Church lost over 1,000 properties. Most were demolished remarkably quickly, to the horror of later art historians. An enormous area thus became available for sale and new building.

Some urban reformers saw this as an opportunity to give Madrid broad, airy avenues, following the always-cited example of Paris. Some major projects were undertaken, the most important the rebuilding of the Puerta del Sol, in 1854-62. However, most of the local traders who benefited from *Desamortización* lacked the capital to contemplate any grand projects, and built individual blocks on small plots, without challenging the established, disorderly street plan.

As a result the districts of old Madrid took on the appearance they have largely kept until today, with great numbers of *corrala*-type tenement blocks (*see page 59*). They allowed Madrid to grow considerably in population, without actually going outside its still-standing wall of 1656.

A few factories had appeared in the city, but for the most part the industrial revolution was passing Madrid by. Its overriding business was still government, and it had many more lawyers than industrialists. Constitutional governments expanded the administration, and the ambitions of the middle class were focused on obtaining official posts rather than on business ventures.

Cibeles in the 1830s.

They employed a great many servants, for labour was very cheap. Most other manual work still went on in small workshops, producing goods too expensive ever to sell outside Madrid.

BEYOND THE WALLS

Two major changes arrived in the 1850s. In 1851 Madrid got its first railway, to Aranjuez, followed by a line to the Mediterranean. Railways would transform Madrid's relationship with the rest of the country, opening up a realistic possibility of its fulfilling an economic function. Equally important was the completion of the *Canal de Isabel II*, bringing water from the Guadarrama, in 1858. Madrid's water supply, still partly based on Moorish water courses, had been inadequate for years. The canal, inaugurated with a giant spurt of water in Calle San Bernardo, removed a crippling obstruction to the city's growth.

Madrid's population was by this time over 300,000. Steps were finally taken for it to break out of its old walls, and in 1860 a plan by Carlos María de Castro was approved for the *Ensanche* ('Extension') of Madrid. It proposed the building of an arc of grid-pattern streets within the line of the street called at different points Joaquín Costa, Francisco Silvela and Doctor Esquerdo. However, as with earlier rebuilding, the plan came up against the chronic lack of large-scale investors. Some areas remained empty for decades: the only major development undertaken immediately was the section of Calle Serrano bought up by the flamboyant speculator the Marqués de Salamanca, whose name was later given to the whole district (*see page 65*). Moreover, even he was unable to sell many properties to Madrid's conservative-minded upper classes at a viable price.

Meanwhile, the political situation was deteriorating once again, after a long period of conservative rule that had begun in 1856. Isabel II had become deeply unpopular, discredited by the aura of sleaze and scandal surrounding her Court. In September 1868, yet another military revolt overthrew the government and, this time, dethroned the Queen as well.

There followed six years of turmoil. The provisional government invited an Italian prince, Amadeo of Savoy, to be King of a truly constitutional monarchy. However, in December 1870 General Prim, strongman of the new regime, was assassinated. Carlist revolts broke out in some areas, while on the left new, more radical groups appeared. At the end of 1868 a meeting in Madrid addressed by Giuseppe Fanelli, an Italian associate of Bakunin, led to the founding of the first anarchist group in Spain. The Cortes itself was riven by factions, and Amadeo decided to give up the struggle and go back to Italy.

On 12 February 1873 Spain became a Republic. Rightist resistance became stronger than ever, while many towns were taken over by left-wing *juntas*, who declared them autonomous 'cantons', horrifying conservative opinion. To keep control, Republican governments relied increasingly on the army. This proved fatal, and, on 3 January 1874 the army commander in Madrid, General Pavía, marched into the Cortes, sent its members home, and installed a military dictatorship.

The Restoration

At the end of 1874 the army decided to restore the Bourbon dynasty, in the shape of Alfonso XII (1874-85), son of Isabel II. The architect of the Restoration regime, however, was a civilian politician, Antonio Cánovas del Castillo. He established the system of *turno pacífico* or peaceful alternation in power between a Conservative Party, led by himself, and a Liberal Party made up of former progressives. Their readiness to co-operate with each other was based in a shared fear of the social tensions visible during the previous six years.

The dominance of these 'dynastic parties' over the political system was ensured by election-rigging and occasional repression. Backing up the new regime was the army, in which conservative and progressive wings had similarly buried their differences.

The years after 1874 saw the culmination of a process begun in the 1840s, in which old aristocratic families fused with those who had profited from the acquisition of Church lands to form a new dominant class in the country. Again, they were united by a common desire to protect what they had – and to display it, as seen in the glittering life of Madrid 'society' during the 1880s.

In the late 1870s the wealthy of Madrid set out on a ten-year building boom. They finally overcame their reluctance to leave the old city, and the Salamanca area became the new centre of fashionable life. Most of the district's new apartment blocks had lifts, first seen in Madrid in 1874. In earlier blocks upper floors had been let cheaply, so that rich and poor had often continued to live side by side. With lifts, however, a top floor could be as desirable as a first, and this kind of class mixing soon faded.

The government and official bodies, too, undertook a huge round of new building. The **Banco de España**, the **Bolsa** (Stock Exchange), the main railway stations and even the municipal markets are all creations of the 1880s. It was also proposed that Madrid should at last be given a cathedral, on the site of the former mosque Santa María de la Almudena, demolished as derelict by the progressives in 1870. The building of the **Catedral de la Almudena**, however, would be a saga that has only recently been concluded.

As well as an opulent élite, Madrid also acquired a larger professional middle class, with many more doctors, engineers, journalists and architects. It attracted intellectuals from throughout the country, from the threadbare bohemians seen in the works of the playwright Valle-Inclán, always on the lookout for something to pawn, to professors at the university, transferred to Madrid from Alcalá de Henares in 1836.

At the same time, Madrid was also receiving an influx of poor migrants from rural Spain, with over 200,000 new arrivals between 1874 and 1900. The main work available for them was in building, for men, and domestic service for women. Economic growth was reflected in the appearance of yet more small workshops rather than factories. There were also many in Madrid with next to no work. The presence of beggars in the streets had long been cited as a symbol of the problems of Spain, but the 1880s also saw the beginning of a worsening housing crisis, with the appearance around Madrid of shanty towns, regarded with fear by respectable opinion.

One of the many remedies put forward made Madrid the site of a curiously modern experiment in planning, the *Ciudad Lineal* or 'Linear City', proposed in the 1890s by the engineer Arturo Soria. His idea was that new housing should be organised around a means of transport, the railway line along Calle Alcalá. Each area would consist of small houses with gardens, of different sizes for residents of different incomes, thus ensuring social homogeneity. However, few affluent residents were drawn to the *Ciudad Lineal*, which became a predominantly working-class area.

Despite this poverty, the established order seemed in little danger in the first decades of the Restoration. The events of 1868-74 had discredited the old Romantic idea of the unity of the people in pursuit of democracy. In 1879 the Spanish Socialist Party, the PSOE, was founded in the Casa Labra *taberna* (*see page 127*). Nevertheless, for a long time the level of agitation in the capital was very limited.

BIG CITY: THE SILVER AGE

Just before the end of the century, however, the preconceptions on which Spanish political life had been based received a shattering blow. The Restoration regime presented itself as having returned the country to stability and some prestige in the world. In the 1890s, however, Spain was involved in colonial wars against nationalists in Cuba and the Philippines. In 1898, the government allowed itself to be manoeuvred into war with the United States. In a few short weeks, almost the entire Spanish navy was sunk, and Spain lost virtually all its remaining overseas territories.

Known simply as 'The Disaster', this was a devastating blow to Spain's self-confidence. The pretensions of the regime were seen to be a sham, and it was revealed as a decrepit, incompetent state based on a feeble economy. Among intellectuals, this sparked off an intense round of self-examination and discussion of Spain's relationship with the very concept of modernity. Politically, it signalled the beginning of the disintegration of the cosy political settlement of 1874.

A significant part in all this was played by the King himself, Alfonso XIII (1885-1931). Arrogant and erratic, Alfonso alienated even his right-wing allies. He was a target for several assassination attempts, the most dramatic when a Catalan anarchist, Mateo Morral, threw a bomb at his wedding procession in the Calle Mayor in 1906.

Though the intellectual debates of this time were centred on Spain's apparent inability to deal with the modern world, the problems of the regime were not due to the country being backward. Rather, they spiralled out of control because after 1900 the country began to undergo an unprecedented period of change.

This sudden economic expansion was set off by three main factors. One, ironically, was the loss of the colonies, which led to large amounts of capital being brought back to the country. Most important was World War I, which provided unheard-of opportunities for neutral Spain in the supply of goods to the Allied powers. Then, during the worldwide boom of the 1920s, Spain benefited hugely from foreign investment.

Within a few years Spain had one of the fastest rates of urbanisation in the world. The economic upheaval caused by the global war led to runaway inflation, spurring a massive movement into the cities. Madrid did not grow as rapidly as industrial Barcelona, which had become the largest city in the country. Nevertheless, after taking four centuries to reach half a million, it doubled its population again in only 30 years, to just under a million by 1930. Only 37 per cent of its people had been born in the city.

The most visible manifestation of this growth was a still-larger building boom. Bombastic creations such as the **Palacio de Comunicaciones** were symptomatic of the expansive mood. Most important was the opening of the **Gran Vía** in 1910, a project first discussed 25 years previously, and not completed for another 20, that would transform the interior of the old city with a new grand thoroughfare for entertainment, business and banking.

Another fundamental innovation would be electricity. The city's trams were electrified in 1898, and the first Metro line, between Sol and Cuatro Caminos, was opened in 1919. Electricity allowed Madrid, far from any other source of power, finally to experience an industrial take-off in the years after 1910. It was still a long way behind Barcelona as an industrial city, but was much more important as a base for major banks. The pace and tone of life in Madrid had changed greatly. Larger companies and new industries brought with them more aggressive styles of working, and a much more industrial working class. Many lived in shabby slum districts in the outskirts, or in the 'misery-villes' of shanties that mushroomed around the city. At the same time, expansion in banking and office work was reflected in the large number of white-collar workers.

Madrid was also, more than ever, the mecca for intellectuals and professionals from around the country. This was the background to the enormous vigour of the city's intellectual life at this time, the 'Silver Age' of Spanish literature. From writers of 1898 such as Antonio Machado and Baroja to the poets of the 1927 generation, Rafael Alberti and Garcia Lorca, the city welcomed an extraordinary succession of literary talent, as well as painters, scientists and historians.

The first 35 years of this century were the golden age of the *tertulia*. The word itself means an informal gathering of friends to talk, keeping roughly to a topic, which can be held anywhere, from a shop to a park bench. More formal, intellectual and literary *tertulias* appeared in Madrid with the first modern cafés during the 1830s, and became ever more central to the cultural life of the city as the century went on, their popularity based in a very Spanish love of talk for its own sake. Most of the writers of the Silver Age had their regular *tertulia*, and equally any new arrival in the city could soon find out exactly where they had to go to hear the main figures of the day hold forth on matters sacred and profane. Some figures were better known for their part in *tertulias* than anything else. A legendary character of pre-1936 Madrid was Ramón Gómez de la Serna, who presided over the gathering at the Café Pombo in Calle Carretas, attended by Buñuel and Garcia Lorca and credited with introducing surrealism into Spain. He was the author of over 100 books, but it was always known that his best ideas had gone up in the smoke and coffee fumes.

From the 1910s onward –and despite the condtions of a fairly lenient dictatorship during the '20s – Madrid's cafés were full of talk, forums for discussion and new projects multiplied, and any number of newspapers and magazines were published. The sheer range of activity was remarkable, above all by comparison with the near silence that fell upon the city in the 1940s.

Awaiting the Republic in Sol, 1931.

THE MONARCHY CRUMBLES

In politics, this urban expansion made it impossible for the 'dynastic parties' to control elections in the way they were able to do in small towns and rural areas. In 1910, a Republican-Socialist coalition won the elections in Madrid for the first time. Tensions came to a head in 1917, when a general strike throughout the country demanded sweeping constitutional reform. In the following years the main focus of conflict was in Barcelona, where virtual urban guerrilla warfare broke out between the anarchist workers' union the CNT and employers and the State. In 1923, the Captain-General of Barcelona, General Primo de Rivera, suspended the constitution and declared himself Dictator under the King.

In Madrid, this event was first greeted with relative indifference. However, by his action Primo de Rivera had discredited the old dynastic parties, without putting anything in their place. A widespread movement against the monarchy developed in the '20s, based in a sentiment that a society that felt itself to be increasingly mature should not have a ramshackle, discredited government imposed upon it.

In 1930 Primo de Rivera resigned, exhausted. The King appointed another soldier, General Berenguer, as new Prime Minister. In an attempt to move back towards some form of constitutional rule, the government decided to hold local elections on 12 April 1931. They were not expected to be a referendum on the monarchy. However, when the results came in it was seen that republican candidates had won sweeping majorities in all of Spain's cities.

Republic & Civil War

On 14 April 1931, as the results of the local elections became clear, the streets of Spain's cities filled with people. In Madrid, a vast, jubilant mass converged on the Puerta del Sol. It was the presence of the exultant crowds in the streets that drove the King to abdicate and spurred republican politicians into action, for they had never expected their opportunity to arrive so soon.

The second Spanish Republic arrived amid huge optimism, as the repository of the frustrated hopes of decades. Among the many schemes of its first government, a Republican-Socialist coalition, was a particular project for Madrid, the *Gran Madrid* or 'Greater Madrid' plan, which it was hoped would permit the integration of the sprawling slum and shanty areas around the city's edge.

A key part of the plan was the extension of the Castellana, then blocked by a racecourse above Calle Joaquín Costa. It was demolished, and the Castellana was allowed to snake endlessly northward, becoming one of the modern city's most distinctive features. Another project completed under the Republic was the last section of the Gran Vía, between Callao and Plaza de España, site of Madrid's finest art deco architecture.

Possibilities of further change and renovation, however, were bound up in the accelerating social crisis that overtook the Republic. The new regime aroused expectations that would have been difficult to live up to at the best of times. Instead, its arrival coincided with the onset of the world wide depression. Moreover, Spain's own partly unreal 1920s boom had exceeded the real capacity of the country's economy. Activity slowed down, and unemployment spread.

At the same time, labour agitation and republican legislation brought wage increases for those in work. This caused panic among employers, particularly in small businesses, and they became easy fodder for a belligerent, resurgent right. The optimistic harmony of April 1931 broke down. Tension was even more intense in the countryside, where agrarian reform was bogged down by conservative opposition.

As frustration grew among workers, tendencies grew apace that called for the end of republican compromise in a second, social, revolution, especially the anarchist CNT and the Communist Party. Even the Socialist Party was radicalised. On the right, similarly, the loudest voices were those demanding authoritarian rule as the only means of preserving social order, such as the fascist Falange, founded in 1933 by José Antonio Primo de Rivera, son of the former dictator. The vogue for extremism was intensified by the mood of the times, in which Nazism, Italian Fascism and Soviet Communism appeared as the most dynamic international models.

In 1933 the coalition between Socialists and liberal republicans broke up. With the left vote split, elections were won by conservative republicans backed by the CEDA, a parliamentary but authoritarian right-wing party. For those who had assumed a Republic would be inseparable from sweeping reform, this was a profound shock. In October 1934 the CEDA demanded to have ministers in the government. A general strike was called in response. It was strongest in the mining region of Asturias, where it was savagely suppressed by army units commanded by a rising general called Francisco Franco.

Left-wing parties were subjected to a wave of repression that radicalised their supporters still further. In new elections in February 1936, however, the left, united once again in the *Frente Popular* or Popular Front, were victorious. In Madrid, the Front won 54 per cent of the vote.

A liberal-republican government returned to power, with Manuel Azaña as President. By this time, however, the level of polarisation and sheer hatred in the country was moving out of control. Right-wing politicians called virtually openly for the army to save the country. Among the military, plans had already been laid for a coup.

REVOLUTION AND SIEGE

On 18 July the Generals made their move, with risings all over Spain, while German and Italian aircraft ferried Franco's colonial army from Spanish Morocco to Andalusia. In Madrid, troops barricaded themselves inside the Montaña barracks, the site of which is now in the Parque del Oeste.

The coup was the spark for an explosion of tension. The workers' parties demanded arms. On 20 July, as news came that the army had been defeated in Barcelona and many other cities, the Montaña was stormed and its defenders massacred, despite political leaders' efforts to prevent it.

With the right apparently defeated, Madrid underwent a revolution. Among left-wing militants the mood was ecstatic: factories, schools and public services were taken over, and although the government remained in place it had little effective power.

Among right-wingers trapped in the city feelings were naturally very different. The aristocrat Agustín de Foxá wrote that 'it wasn't Spain any more. In the Gran Vía, in Alcalá, the mob had camped out.' Ad-hoc militias and patrols had become the only power on the streets. Amid the paranoia and hatred that were the other side of revolutionary excitement, summary executions of suspected rightists were common.

In the meantime, the war still had to be fought. During the summer fighting mostly consisted of skirmishes in the Guadarrama. A far more serious threat was approaching, however, in the shape of Franco's regular troops, advancing from Seville preceded by stories of reprisals more terrible than anything done by the 'red terror' in Madrid. The militias seemed powerless to stop them.

Defeat for the Republic seemed inevitable. German planes bombed the city. On 6 November, Franco's advance guard were already in the outskirts, and the government left for Valencia, a move widely seen as desertion.

Without a government, however, a new resolve was seen in the city. In the southern industrial suburbs the troops were resisted street by street. Women, children, the old and the unmilitary joined in building trenches and barricades, and comparisons were immediately drawn with 2 May 1808.

The bitterness of defeat was felt long and deeply after 1939.

On 9 November the first foreign volunteers, the International Brigades, arrived, doing wonders for morale. Madrid, the Imperial Court, had suddenly become the front line of international democracy. After savage fighting, above all in the Ciudad Universitaria, Franco ordered a halt to the frontal assault on Madrid at the end of November 1936.

Madrid saw little more direct fighting. From the Casa de Campo, where the remains of trenches and bunkers can still be uncovered today, the army settled in to a siege. Attempts to push them back north and south of Madrid were unsuccessful. The city was regularly bombed, and bombarded by Nationalist artillery, who took their sights from the Gran Vía, 'Howitzer Avenue'.

People adapted to the situation. One could go to war by tram, and combatants were taken their lunch on the line along the Gran Vía. Right-wingers were scarcely harassed after the first few months. The siege, however, ground down the spirit of November 1936. Shortages were acute, and lentils often the only food available. Particularly terrible was the severe winter of 1937-8, when doors and furniture were burnt for fuel. The powerful role of the Communists, won through the Republic's dependence on the Soviet Union as its only source of arms, alienated many who were not Party supporters.

Franco, meanwhile, was advancing on other fronts. During 1937 his forces overran the Basque Country and Asturias, and in March 1938 they reached the Mediterranean near Castellón. In January 1939 they conquered Catalonia. In Madrid, fighting broke out behind Republican lines between the Communists, committed to resistance to the end, and other groups who wanted to negotiate a settlement with Franco. Those in favour of negotiation won, but found Franco with no intention to compromise. On 28 March the Nationalist army entered Madrid.

The long dictatorship

Madrid emerged from the Civil War physically and psychologically battered. Hundreds of buildings stood in ruins. Buildings, however, could soon be rebuilt; healing the damage done to the city's spirit, on the other hand, would take decades.

The Madrid of the 1940s was the sombre antithesis of the expansive city of ten years previously, or its current vivacious, outgoing self. Most Madrileños had lost someone close to them, either to bombs and bullets or to firing squads and prison camps. The black market rather than art and literature dominated café conversation, and the figures of earlier years were mostly in exile, or keeping indoors.

The existence of 'two Spains' (right-left, traditional-liberal, rich-poor) was all too apparent. When the victors marched into the city they wasted no time in rounding up members (or merely suspected sympathisers) of 'enemy' groups, anarchists, Communists, union members and liberals. Some were turned in by neighbours, which created a sordid atmosphere of bitterness and distrust. During the early '40s, while the rest of the world was wrapped up in World War II, thousands were executed in Spain. Others paid the price of defeat by serving as forced labour on fascist landmarks such as the Valle de los Caídos, Franco's vast victory monument and tomb (*see page 226*).

Madrid's loyalty to the Republic almost led to it losing its capital status. Voices were raised accusing it of having betrayed 'eternal Spanish values' and calling for a more 'loyal' city to represent the country. Franco actually went to Seville to look into the feasibility of moving the capital there.

Tradition and financial interests bore more weight, however, and the capital stayed put. The Falange, official party of the regime, produced

The Franco regime sometimes gave out bread, but didn't organise many circuses.

extravagant plans to turn Madrid into a Spanish version of Imperial Rome, along the lines of the schemes drawn up by Albert Speer for Hitler. However, a dire lack of funding and galloping inflation scotched these nouveau-Imperialist intentions. The Spanish economy was in a desperate state, and the country went through a period of extreme hardship, the *años del hambre* or 'hunger years'. Many people remember not having eaten properly for ten years after 1936. This poverty also led to the phenomenon that would most shape the face of Madrid in the post-war decades: massive immigration from Spain's rural provinces.

THE GREAT CHANGE

Madrid has grown faster than any other European capital this century. A 'big village' of just over half a million at the turn of the century, and 950,000 in 1930, it passed the three million mark by 1970. Rural flight during the '40s and '50s, rapid industrialisation in the 1960s and the no-holds-barred 'modernisation' of the '80s have been most responsible for this metamorphosis.

Until the 1950s, migrants arriving in Madrid found few real opportunities for work, in an economy that was internationally isolated and excluded from Marshall Aid and the other reconstruction packages of post-war Europe. After 1945 many in Spain and abroad assumed that the Franco regime would shortly go the way of its former friends in Germany and Italy.

Most European countries continued to shun the regime, at least in public, but in 1953, as the Cold War intensified, Franco was saved by the US government's 'our son-of-a-bitch' policy in choosing allies. A co-operation treaty provided the regime with renewed credibility and cash in exchange for air and naval bases on Spanish soil, and later President Eisenhower flew in to shake the dictator's hand.

For those not devoted to the regime, life under Franco was often a matter of keeping one's head down, and getting on with things. Football and other means of escapism played an enormous part in people's lives. The late 1950s were the golden years of Real Madrid, whose successes were trumpeted to boost the prestige of the regime.

The national Stabilisation Plan of 1959 gave the fundamental push to Madrid's development, and brought Spain definitively back into the Western fold. Drawn up by technocrats often associated with the Catholic lay organisation the *Opus Dei*, the plan revolutionised the economy of Spain, and particularly that of the Madrid region. During the 1960s, tourism began to pump money into the Spanish economy. Madrid trebled in size and became an industrial powerhouse.

The city was transformed. Quiet tree-lined boulevards were widened to make way for cars, and elegant turn-of-the-century palaces on the Castellana were replaced by glass-sheathed monoliths. Madrid took on much more of the look, and feel, of a big city.

Rebirth

In the '60s, too, opposition to the regime revived in the shape of labour unrest, while in the north the Basque organisation ETA was becoming active. The oil crisis of 1973 coincided with the assassination by ETA of Franco's Prime Minister, Admiral Carrero Blanco, when a bomb planted beneath a Madrid street launched his car right over a five-storey building. The regime, weakened by student protests, now had to deal with rising unemployment, inflation and a moribund Franco. The transition to democracy had begun.

Franco died in November 1975, closing a parenthesis of nearly 40 years in Spanish history. A new age, uncertain but exciting, had dawned. In July 1976 King Juan Carlos, chosen by Franco to succeed him, named a former Falange bureaucrat, Adolfo Suárez, as Prime Minister. Nobody, however, knew quite what was going to happen.

To widespread surprise, Suárez initiated a comprehensive programme of political reform. Clandestine opposition leaders surfaced, parties were legalised and famous exiles began coming home. The first democratic elections since 1936 were held in June 1977, and a constitution was approved in late 1978. Suárez' centrist UCD (Centre-Democratic Union) had won the national elections, but local elections in Madrid in 1979 were won by the Socialists, with Enrique Tierno Galván as Mayor. Democracy was being consolidated rapidly.

The 'other' Spain, though, had not disappeared, and was getting nervous. Hard-core Francoists were horrified at the thought of Socialists and/or Communists coming to power. Many still held influential positions in the privileged armed forces.

On the morning of 23 February 1981 democrats' worst nightmares appeared to come true when a Civil Guard colonel called Tejero burst into the Cortes with a squad of men, firing his pistol into the air and shouting 'Everybody on the floor'. Tanks were in the streets in Valencia, and there was uncertainty everywhere. In Madrid, however, troops stayed in their barracks. At a little after midnight, Juan Carlos appeared on TV and assured the country that the army had sworn him its allegiance and the coup attempt would soon fail. The next day, people poured on to the streets to demonstrate support for freedom and democracy.

The wolf had shown his teeth, but they were not as sharp as had been feared. Moreover, the coup attempt probably helped significantly to win Felipe González and the socialist PSOE their landslide victory in the elections of November 1982.

THE *MOVIDA* AND SOCIALIST SPAIN

The late '70s and early '80s saw the arrival of democracy and free speech, the decriminalisation of drug use and the breakdown of old sexual conventions. Long-repressed creative impulses were

First democratic Mayor, Dr Tierno Galván.

released. The suit and tie-clad, compulsorily staid and gloomy Madrid of earlier years gave way to an anything-goes, vivacious city: an explosion of art, counter-culture and nightlife, creativity and frivolity known as the *Movida* – very roughly translatable as the 'Shift' or 'Movement'.

Madrid's *Movida* propelled some to international fame, such as fashion designer Sybilla, artists like Ouka Lele and, above all, Pedro Almodóvar, who began making films in clubs. For many, though, the *Movida* was simply the discovery by young Spaniards that, after decades in which their country had seemed a hostile place it was best to get out of, they could have the party right now, and on their doorstep.

The Socialists used control of Madrid's *Ayuntamiento* – led by the very fondly remembered Tierno Galván – to renovate the city's infrastructure, with long-overdue facelifts in squares and parks. Mayor Tierno also provided unprecedented support for progressive causes and the arts, and launched a whole string of new festivals.

If Tierno Galván's local administration was happy to be regarded as godfathers to the newly stylish city of the *Movida*, the national government of Felipe González was still more eager to be seen as the leaders of a reborn country. Decades of international isolation definitively ended with Spain's entry into the European Community in 1986. This had a near-immediate effect on the economy, and in the late '80s the country was the fastest-growing member of the EU. The González

Pedro Almodóvar and the crew have one more party before heading off for Oslo.

governments failed to satisfy the expectations of many of their own supporters, but often gave the impression they believed modernisation would solve all Spain's problems more or less by itself.

The apotheosis of the country's transition was the 'Year of Spain' in 1992 – trumpeted as marking the new Spain's definite establishment on the international stage – with the Barcelona Olympics, Expo '92 in Seville and, least successful of the three, Madrid's year as Cultural Capital of Europe. Since then, however, a different mood has been apparent. Spain's boom pre-'92 had only postponed the effects of the international downturn at the end of the '80s, which hit Madrid with a vengeance in 1993. Breakneck growth had created its own problems: prices soared, and land speculation sent property prices and rents through the roof. At the same time, the Socialists, inseparable from the boom, began to be dragged down by a staggering stream of revelations of corruption.

Even before Spain's great year, in 1991, the PSOE had lost control of the Madrid city administration to the re-formed right of the *Partido Popular* (PP). Disenchantment with the Socialists and a newly cautious mood that followed the brash over confidence of the boom years are major factors behind the rise of the PP, led by the deliberately bland José María Aznar. Felipe González, long the great survivor of Spanish politics, lost his overall majority in elections in 1993, but staggered on for another three years by means of a pact with Catalan nationalists. With the elections of 1996, however, the PP won control of all three levels of government in Madrid, city, region and State.

THE NOT-VERY-NAUGHTY-NINETIES

The general election of 3 March 1996 was the tightest and most acrimonious since Spain's transition. In the event, though, the PP ended 14 years of Socialist rule by only the slimmest of margins, and was only able to take power after prolonged haggling with minority parties, particularly the Catalan nationalists led by Jordi Pujol.

In the end, although sleaze and corruption played a part in the Socialists' downfall, their move to the right and Aznar's self-conscious centrism meant that electors were actually given little concrete to choose from. Some of the media trumpeted the PP victory as a symbol of Spain's political maturity: two centrist parties fighting over the middle ground. Others said it showed that the transition was over, and that politics were dead.

In the capital, however, the PP adopted a style in marked contrast to that of Tierno's PSOE. In building up its support the party had discovered there were people in the city who had never been taken with the idea of it as a glossy, new, cosmopolitan 24-hour party town. Licences for new bars and clubs became harder to get, and failure to keep to newly-restrictive licensing hours began to be punished. The heady days of the *Movida* were over, and Pedro Almodóvar was quoted as saying Madrid would soon be as exciting as Oslo. The city's current mayor, José María Alvarez de Manzano, lays great stress on his love of traditional Spanish culture, and on having a crucifix in his office. The stylish, permissive, forget-the-past Madrid of the '80s, like the Francoist gloom before it, had been only part of the story.

Architecture

Grand boulevards and great monuments: Madrid doesn't really have them, but its architectural mix is, like the city itself, unlike any other.

Visitors familiar with the architectural splendours of other European cities are often disappointed by Madrid. Eleven centuries of history, and the city's one-time status as hub of an immense empire are only palely reflected in the modern metropolis. Constrained by its walls until the 1860s, Madrid rebuilt itself so many times over the top of existing constructions that by the late nineteenth century it was pretty much a modern city.

Madrid has a special history, and its architecture is a very special, eclectic, almost eccentric mixture of styles. Despite later rebuilding, traces survive of most of its past epochs – periods of Moorish, Flemish, Italian, French or American influence are all reflected to a greater or lesser degree. As well as a unique stylistic combination, Madrid has many totally unique monuments: a 'typically' Madrileño architectural identity is hard to find, but the city can claim one, typically unusual style as its own, neo-*mudéjar* (*see page 32*).

Buildings highlighted in **bold** in this chapter without a specific page reference are dealt with at greater length in *chapter* **Sightseeing**.

The old city

For those who insist on starting at the beginning, a segment of the **Muralla Arabe**, the first town wall built by the Moors, can be found on Cuesta de la Vega, near the Almudena cathedral. For centuries after they were conquered from their Moorish rulers, Madrid and many parts of Castile continued to have substantial populations of Muslims living under Christian rule, the *mudéjares*. The Castilian monarchs were greatly in thrall to their superior building skills, especially in bricklaying and tiling, and throughout the Middle Ages many of the country's most important buildings were built using techniques and styles that had originated in Muslim Andalusia. Hallmarks of the *mudéjar* style are Moorish arches and intricate geometric patterns in brickwork, which can be seen on the twelfth-century tower of Madrid's oldest surviving church, **San Nicolás de las Servitas**, built by Arab craftsmen (the body of the church was later rebuilt). Madrid's other *mudéjar* tower, on **San Pedro el Viejo**, was built 200 years later in the fourteenth century.

Other medieval buildings in Madrid, such as the fifteenth-century Torre de los Lujanes in the **Plaza de la Villa**, were erected in a much plainer style.

Capital status & the Hapsburgs

The establishment of Madrid as capital, first in 1561 and definitively in 1606 (*see pages 14-18*), utterly transformed the city and its architecture. Since it was above all a royal capital, 'the Court', the tastes of successive rulers would be of special importance. Philip II's favourite architect, Juan de Herrera, was the first to leave a stamp on the city. Although he and his royal master had little idea of urban plan-

*The most elegant product of the Castilian baroque style, the **Plaza Mayor**.*

ning, their major constructions – the **Puente de Segovia** (1584), the initial stages of the **Plaza Mayor**, the widening of Calles Atocha, Segovia and Mayor – gave the city a shape that lasts to the present day. The 'Herreran' style is present all over Habsburg Madrid (although his greatest achievement was **El Escorial**, *see page 225*); austere, sober, rigid and typically employing grey slate for roof tops and the ubiquitous pointed turrets. Now a symbol of the 'Madrid of the Austrias', it is also known as Castilian baroque, but few of its features were especially 'Castilian': the slate pinnacles were taken from Flanders, which appealed to the Flemish-born Charles V and his son Philip.

Herrera's chief disciple, Juan Gómez de Mora, was almost as influential. While owing much to his teacher, Gómez departed from the Herreran tradition. He was responsible for the completion of the **Plaza Mayor** in 1619, and his original plan is still recognisable in the slate spires, high-pitched roofs and dormer windows. The **Palacio de Santa Cruz** of 1629-34, now the Foreign Ministry (*see page 43*), of which he was the chief architect, shows clear Italian baroque influences, with a façade much more

richly shaped than anything Herrera would have attempted; similarly, Gómez de Mora's 1630 **Casa de la Villa**, the City Hall, is a more ornate variation on the basic Castilian baroque style (*see page 50*).

Nevertheless, the overall impression that Madrid, capital of the first worldwide empire, left on the seventeenth-century visitor was one of chaos, dirt and haphazard growth. While the Habsburgs commissioned much that was noble and even palatial, they did not really configure a city in the global sense of the word. Another reason why building was relatively restrained was the rickety state of the economy, which led to bricks and mortar being favoured over expensive stone.

Bourbon Enlightenment

The expiry of the Spanish Habsburgs with King Charles II in 1700 was followed by war, and the arrival of the Bourbons, under Philip V. If anything sums up their architectural achievements, it was their efforts to embellish and dignify Madrid.

The Bourbons were French, and Philip V's highly respected second wife, Isabella Farnese, was Italian, and these two influences would long predominate

Neo-*mudéjar*

The neo-*mudéjar* style of building is one of very few that Madrid can claim as its own. It emerged around 1870, when Madrid's original 1754 bullring near Puerta de Alcalá had to be replaced. Amid the revivalist atmosphere of the Victorian era, the architects Rodríguez Ayuso and Álvarez Capra tired of neo-Gothic and neo-Egyptian styles, and decided to consult their history books for something more home-grown. They opted for the style of the *mudéjar* master bricklayers who served the kings of medieval Castile, with an elegant structure of horseshoe arches and walls of cleverly interlaced brickwork in abstract geometric shapes, on the spot where the Palacio de Deportes now stands. Uniquely Spanish, the style became widely accepted, especially for bullrings. Madrid's *plaza de toros* had to be pulled down itself some years later, but the replacement, **Las Ventas** of 1929-32, also features neo-*mudéjar* techniques.

There are plenty of other examples of the neo-*mudéjar* style around Madrid. Perhaps the finest is the **Escuelas Aguirre**, also by Rodríguez Ayuso, across from the northern side of the Retiro at the intersection of Alcalá and O'Donnell. Originally a school, the 1870s building is dominated by a slim, minaret-style tower, with an iron and glass lookout point on top. It now houses council offices. Other fine neo-*mudéjar* buildings

The tower of the **Escuelas Aguirre**.

around Madrid are the ABC newspaper building, now the **ABC Serrano** mall (*see page 157*), and the 1907-11 water tower on Calle Santa Engracia in Chamberí, which has become the **Canal de Isabel II** exhibition space (*see page xxx*).

in the dynasty's tastes in buildings. Nevertheless, despite these foreign inspirations, Philip V's administrator, the Marqués de Vadillo, saw to it that many projects went to a local architect, Pedro de Ribera. Among them are the 1722 Hospice, now the **Museo Municipal** (*see page 83*), the Cuartel Conde Duque barracks, restored as the **Centro Cultural Conde Duque** (*see page 85*), the **Puente de Toledo** and many churches. Ribera's buildings, though based in the austere Herreran tradition, have exuberant baroque façades and doorways, dripping with heraldic symbols, which lend a touch of fantasy absent in Hapsburg Madrid, while his churches, such as **San José** on Calle Alcalá (*see page 52*), are in a much lighter baroque style.

Elsewhere in eighteenth-century Madrid the influence of the French and Italian architects favoured by Philip V and his sons Fernando VI and Charles III is far more apparent. After the old grey-spired Alcázar burnt down in 1734 Philip V commissioned a new **Palacio Real** mainly from Italian architects, led by Filippo Juvarra and Giambattista Sacchetti. The result, unsurprisingly, is Italianate. Responsible for many projects was Charles III's 'chief engineer', Francesco Sabatini. The greatest practitioners of the sober, 'pure' neo-classicism of the later years of Charles III's reign, however, were Spaniards: Ventura Rodríguez, who had worked on the Palacio Real, and Juan de Villanueva, architect of the **Museo del Prado** and the **Observatorio**. Like the greatest project of the King's reign, the grand boulevard of the Paseo del Prado – of which they were a part – they clearly reflect Enlightenment ideals of architecture and urban planning.

The nineteenth century

Joseph Bonaparte's brief reign (1808-13) saw the first demolition of convents and monasteries, to be replaced by squares such as **Plaza Santa Ana**. On the whole, though, the first half of the nineteenth century was architecturally a period of stagnation. Following the great clearance of monasteries begun in the 1830s many of the buildings that replaced them were simply constructed apartment and tenement blocks, such as the *corralas* (*see page 61*). Public buildings of this time, such as the 1840s **Cortes**, were often in a conservative neo-classical style.

Greater changes came to Madrid after 1860, with the demolition of the walls and Carlos Maria de Castro's plan for the city's extension (*ensanche; see pages 23, 61*). Areas covered by the plan are easy to spot on a map by their grid street pattern. Chief among them is the **Barrio de Salamanca**, named after the 'twice-ruined and three times rich' speculator the Marqués de Salamanca.

Salamanca is still the most self-consciously grand *barrio* of the *ensanche*, with an elegant, slightly Parisian feel. Its wealthiest residents built opulent mansions in a completely eclectic mix of

Madrid's 1927 petrol station. See page 34.

styles – French Second Empire was one of the most popular – several of which still stand on Calles Velázquez and Serrano. Other *ensanche* districts – Chamberi, Argüelles, Delicias – have in common a rational urban layout, wide thoroughfares and regular-sized blocks. Building styles show a certain sameness without being totally uniform.

Public buildings of the first years of the Bourbon Restoration were as eclectic as Salamanca mansions. A style that Madrid created for itself, neo-*mudéjar* (*see left*), was used for official buildings, bullrings, churches, homes and factories. One of the most extraordinary constructions of the time, Ricardo Velázquez' **Ministerio de Agricultura** in Atocha (*see page 65*), is in contrast a remarkable combination of Castilian brickwork and extravagant, French Beaux-Arts style sculpted decoration. This was also the great period of cast-iron architecture in Madrid, with fine structures such as the **Estación de Atocha**, across the *glorieta* from the ministry.

Art nouveau (called *modernismo* in Spain), so characteristic of Barcelona at the turn of the century, aroused little interest in Madrid, but there are a few examples of the style. The iced-cake-like **Sociedad General de Autores** in Calle Fernando VI, by Jose Grasés Riera from 1902, is the best-known, but the **Casa Pérez Villamil** in Plaza Matute, off Calle Huertas, is as distinctive.

Into the twentieth century

As the *ensanche* was built up and Madrid's economy boomed from the 1900s to the 1920s, the city's architects looked for inspiration backwards and forwards in time, as well as abroad and within Spain. The **Gran Vía** was born of this thinking, a slightly weird monument of cosmopolitanism (*see page 55*). Madrid's smart new districts outside the old centre, Salamanca and Argüelles, needed to be joined by a suitably modern thoroughfare.

The Gran Vía project took out 14 streets, and got grander and grander as it progressed. Writer Francisco Umbral has said it recalls New York or Chicago, but its first building of any standing, the 1905 **Edificio Metrópolis**, was very French in inspiration. No.24 shows neo-Renaissance influence, the 1930s **Palacio de la Música** cinema (no.35) has baroque touches, and the 1929 **Telefónica** building is a New York skyscraper in miniature.

The apartment block at Gran Vía 60, built by Carlos Fernández Shaw in 1930, is a classic of the

Madrid-cosmopolitan style. Equally interesting and by the same architect is his futuristic 1927 **petrol station** on C/Alberto Aguilera (two blocks west of San Bernardo Metro). Also working at this time was the highly original Antonio Palacios, chief architect of the **Palacio de Comunicaciones** in Cibeles (1904-18) – an extraordinary hotchpotch of Spanish, American and Viennese art nouveau influences – and the far more subtle **Círculo de Bellas Artes**.

During its brief existence the Spanish Republic further encouraged rationalist, rather self-consciously modern architecture, the progressive style of the time, as seen in the earliest parts of the **Nuevos Ministerios**. Art deco architecture also came into vogue, in office blocks like the **Capitol** building on Gran Vía (corner of Calle Jacometrezo) or the curious model housing district of **El Viso**, near the Nuevos Ministerios, which has some of the most unusual domestic architecture in Madrid.

Grand revamps

One outstanding feature of Madrid since the 1980s has been the approach taken to apparently terminally decrepit historic buildings in the city. Many have been daringly renovated – in some cases through complete internal rebuilding within the old shell – and 'recycled' for new uses. In many cases they are more striking than all-new structures.

The **Estación de Atocha** (*see page 44*) is the most prominent example. Built in 1888-92, Atocha is a classic nineteenth-century iron and glass railway station, which by the 1980s was run down and caked in black grime. In front of its fine façade was a massive flyover across the Glorieta de Carlos V, long a bee in the bonnet of Mayor Tierno Galván. He saw to it that the entire flyover was demolished, the first phase of *Operación Atocha*. This also involved a comprehensive reorganisation of the station's rail services. Much of the building was no longer needed by the railway, and Madrid's specialist in far-reaching renovations, Rafael Moneo, provided an entirely new interior with a tropical garden, complete with micro-climate.

Other impressive 'revamping' projects include the Palacio de Villanueva, which now houses the **Museo Thyssen-Bornemisza**, another shell rebuilt by Moneo in effect to create an entirely new space. Largest of all is the **Museo Reina Sofía**, built by a multinational team of architects inside a 1770s hospital by Francesco Sabatini; the most widely appreciated, perhaps, is the **Centro Conde Duque**, Pedro de Ribera's 1717 barracks.

Francoist fantasies

The 40 years of the Franco regime had a contradictory impact on architecture in Madrid. Falangist thinking on architecture was nostalgic for a glorious past, and architects leant heavily on ill-conceived imperial memories. The early years of the regime brought several monstrous buildings, reaching a peak – literally – in the Otamendi brothers' **Edificio España** of 1948-53, in Plaza de España. It was conceived in line with a fashionable American idea of containing virtually a small city in one huge block, with shops, offices, a hotel and apartments. It was surrounded, though, with neo-Herreran decoration, a multi storey piece of Castilian baroque. The result is megalomaniac in the extreme. Similarly retro is the **Ministerio del Aire** in Moncloa, a pastiche of El Escorial built over 14 years from 1943 to 1957.

Built at around the same time but with no pretence at neo-baroque or anything similar is the tacky 32-floor **Torre de Madrid**, also on Plaza de España, which could have been lifted from any Latin American city in the 1950s. It was also at this time, though, that architects laid down the beginnings of modernity. Francisco Cabrero and Rafael Aburto's plain **Casa Sindical** at Paseo del Prado 18-20, built in 1948-9 for the regime's labour unions and now the Health Ministry, took inspiration from Italian fascist formalist architecture rather than the bogus 'imperial' style. It can be seen as the forerunner of much contemporary rationalist architecture in Madrid.

Until the 1960s the state of the Spanish economy still limited the scope for building. When the economy did open up, Madrid opened up to international influences, but much of its newest buildings were a forest of dreary apartment blocks, for an exploding population in the era of *desarrollismo* (development).

Modern times

One paradoxical effect of the retro-obsessions of the Franco years was that, by the 1980s, Spanish architects felt little need to look back with nostalgia or add neo-classical fronts to new buildings, and took modernity on board with great gusto. The two most influential contemporary architects in Madrid have been Alejandro de la Sota and Francisco Sáenz de Oiza, active from the '50s onwards. Most architects in the city today are directly or indirectly influenced by them, or by Sáenz de Oiza's protégé Rafael Moneo.

The most vigorous contributions to Madrid in the '80s were the aggressively corporate skyscrapers, mostly commissioned by banks, that now line the upper end of the Castellana. Notable among them are the **la Caixa** building (Castellana 51), an inverted chrome pyramid, the **Catalana Occidente** insurance company (no.50), with two superimposed glass prisms, the superb white 1988 **Torre Picasso** by Minoru Yamasaki and the spectacular **Torres KIO** at Plaza de Castilla.

Madrid Today

With a waning interest in politics and a desire for things pleasurable, Madrileños are reassessing their priorities.

Madrid approaches the end of the millennium after a decade run by the *Partido Popular* (PP), which also won national elections in 1996. In some ways the PP's continuing stay at the helm of the *Ayuntamiento* (and the regional government) reflects not so much a right-wing backlash as a broader lack of interest in politics. Indeed, voter levels in local elections barely topped 50 per cent last time. Most Madrileños seem to doubt whether any party can do much about major issues such as unemployment, or the rising cost of housing. And so, in a city which offers much of the familiar (as well as much that is new), they get on with life.

The greatest legacy of the years of rule at city and national level by the Socialist Party, the PSOE, is widely held to be in the support given to arts and culture. The PP came into office on a no-nonsense, balance-the-books ticket, and promptly cut back on all arts festivals. Nobody seems to have complained much, outside the artistic community.

In opposition, the PSOE seems unable to come up with an economic programme to convince the voters, and will have their work cut out to persuade Madrileños that they have more to offer than the PP in the city and regional elections due in 1999. The PP's success is to a great extent due to support from young middle class (or aspiring middle class) voters. They neither remember Franco's Spain nor are particularly interested in it. What they do remember are the boom years of the 1980s, which saw the transformation of Spain, seemingly overnight, from a land of battered Seat 600s into a force in European affairs, symbolised by hordes of Golf GTIs charging down the Castellana.

Ironically enough, the Socialists' core support comes from people over 50, who do remember the bad old days, and who were directly affected by improvements in such things as health care and pensions. In short, many 20-somethings have grown up with high expectations, and are frustrated that the post-boom years have barely yielded them a second-hand Renault, while their 40-something parents, who benefited from the Socialist opening up of the economy in their youth, have become more cautious, and are also seemingly happy with what they see as the common-sense politics of the PP.

PLAYING CATCH-UP

The first years of the PP have been marked by a reaction against the supposed years of moral decline under the PSOE. This has taken the form of chasing after Socialists involved in a whole string of scandals, along with such things as rather futile attempts to restrict bar opening times.

Speeding up traffic flow through the city by the use of tunnels has been a PP obsession, leading to endless road-digging which, with Metro tunnelling, has caused traffic chaos. The party has a special belief in tunnels as a solution to many of Madrid's problems, and projects a massive network of underground routes beneath the city. The logic is simple. More and more cars, and more and more people living outside the city and commuting. And, of course, an economy based on oil and car use. Which isn't to say that public transport has been abandoned. Thankfully, the PP has got on with extending the Metro, which is finally due to reach the airport at Barajas.

Madrid is slowly taking on the shape of a more uniformly modern city, like many in Europe. However, its working practices are still far away from those of most of the continent, with longer lunches, later starts and finishes and a still-ferocious appetite for late-night living which means that restaurants and bars are full at midnight, even during the week.

AND THE GOOD NEWS

The city has changed in other, positive, ways as well. It is now a more cosmopolitan city. In just a few years it has become commonplace to see African, Arab, Chinese and East European faces on the streets. This isn't to say that there is no longer any hostility towards non-white foreigners. It is not so much rooted in unemployment – there are still plenty of low-paid jobs that Madrileños won't do – as in a resistance to change in a society which still lays – or tries to lay – great store on having been somewhere, or done something, *de toda la vida*, 'for the whole of your life'.

The new generation of Madrileños that is growing up are also more tolerant in many ways than their parents, less dependent on tradition and routine. Nowhere is this more evident than in the birth rate, currently at zero or negative population growth. Amid the apparent conservatism, and in the absence of the official funding of a decade ago,

Some are born *guiri...*

Baseball cap, Hard Rock T-shirt, shorts, white socks and trainers. Climbing out of a tour bus looking completely confused, or wandering around with a backpack and a guidebook in hand, squinting up at the street signs. A complete lack of Latin style or basic bodily coordination. Must be American, British, Nordic. These poor souls are *guiris*.

Madrileños will apply this pejorative term to any foreigner who doesn't show the requisite respect or street savvy. While other countries just get on cheerfully with the business of ripping off ignorant tourists, many Spaniards are genuinely hurt and disappointed at what they see as foreigners' lack of real appreciation of the country. Madrileños in particular believe their city is worthy of the utmost respect. Also, perhaps due to a lingering inferiority complex, Spaniards often like to feel superior to klutzy foreigners. *Guiris* are frequently told that they've missed the point. This is part of their role.

Small wonder that so many visitors, expats and short-stay residents take great pride in speaking the most up-to-date slang and knowing the most out of the way places, in a desperate struggle not to be just one more dumb *guiri*. Most *guiris* make the mistake of overdoing culture, thinking this is an appropriate way to understand Madrid. Wrong. Its museums and galleries may be its most famous glories, but the pulse of the Spanish capital is to be taken on the street. Madrid is a night city. Many *guiris* give themselves away totally by going out to lunch at 1pm, and having dinner at 7pm. If you're going to do the culture bit, get it over by midday, have a late lunch and then lie down for a couple of hours.

Dine as late as humanly possible, and don't think of going to a bar until after midnight. Madrileños don't actually stay out any longer than other people. They just start later.

Don't feel self-conscious when trying to speak Spanish. Failure to make an effort will be interpreted as blatant imperialism.

Areas to concentrate on are those highlighted in this book: Malasaña, Chueca, Lavapiés and the oldest part of the city, which we have called Villa y Corte. Huertas and Santa Ana is verging on *guirilandia*, and don't eat out anywhere around Sol, unless in a basic *menú del día* place. Forget all about the Plaza Mayor. If you want to see the city's expats immersing themselves in local culture to escape *guiri* status, check out the **Nuevo Cafe Barbieri**, and finish off the night with the flamencos in **Candela** (*see chapters* **Cafés & Bars** *and* **Flamenco**). This guide offers the places to go to. It's been written by people who've spent years trying to avoid being tagged as *guiris*.

Disguises won't help.

independent alternative events such as Festimad (*see page 7*) have appeared. Madrid's cosmopolitan tendency is also reflected in the club scene.

The last decade has seen Madrid come to terms with reality. The heady days of the '80s *movida*, decadent and self-indulgent, when sex, drugs and rock'n'roll were the order of the day or night, actually affected few people's lives, for better or worse. The *movida* failed to put down real cultural roots, despite massive government arts subsidies.

And the next century? The drift out of the city by those few with children will probably continue, and lower property prices in the centre will no doubt keep the heart Madrid beating with

younger, single people. True, prices have risen, but a walk round the centre late at night is proof that there are just as many bars as there were a decade ago. And, in areas such as Lavapiés and Malasaña, the roads have actually been made more pedestrian-friendly, with limited access and no on-the-street parking. In short, the streets are still full.

As for politics, it seems that for most of Madrid's residents it matters little which lot is in power, and whether it's going to make much difference. For most who live here, it largely comes down to enjoying the place for its human side: the eternal pleasure of staying out late at night, the bar at the end of the street, or that friendly little restaurant where they do a great *menú del día*.

Stormy weather

Writer Nuria Barrios watches the horizon.

The worst storms in Madrid come in summer, when the pavement is steaming, the light blinding, and the air so hot it can burn the lungs as you breathe. They happen at night: sudden outbursts of thunder, lightning, sheets of rain and hail, leaving the city's people relieved, excited, irritated, concerned and finally resigned at so much natural extremism. This excess, this chaos, is an essential part of the city. Nobody should come here looking for balance, moderation and harmony of yin and yang. Madrid is a city of contrasts, which is the source of its strengths and its defects. The beauty of its storms, and its frequent patches of turbulence.

Madrid is not on the sea. This is obvious. However, many try to make up for this lack with other liquids, preferably consumed at night. After dark a tide runs through the city, carrying with it the many in Madrid who avoid daylight to find shelter in the shadows. The people on the streets at night form an ever-growing republic who slip away from the dictates of a Mayor who has tried, unsuccessfully, to control the uncontrollable. God knows, even Velázquez, who loved Madrid's light more than most, would have become one of the nocturnals if he had been faced with the daily roar of road works and building sites that are currently inflicted on the city.

And, since he has come up, we should talk about José María Alvarez del Manzano, the Catholic Mayor of a chaotic city which sells more candles to bars than to chapels. A city where the churches are ever more empty, and where an enclosed order of nuns chooses salsa as the background music for their answerphone message; a city where religious processions are more like carnivals, and in the Puerta del Sol blend in with the prostitutes who work the surrounding streets. Alvarez del Manzano

represents another face of Madrid: a place where the blood of a saint punctiliously liquifies once a year, and where the Cortes, the parliament, is itself built over the site of an old church. Thanks be to God, the Mayor never quite gets a proper grasp on this city, which runs through his hands like water.

In Madrid, which has been 'Cultural Capital of Europe' in 1992 and many grand things besides, there is still a long-standing tradition of letting kids pee in the street, in spite of the installation of modern, enclosed, automatic toilets a few years ago. The technique has been handed down from generation to generation since time immemorial: down come the knickers of the infant, then the child is lifted up by the shoulders and carefully positioned with bended knees over the gutter. There are more contrasts at every turn. Madrid has an old river, the Manzanares, that's crowded in by buildings and supplanted by thousands of underground rivers, where the flow is not of water and boats but speeding cars. There are more international restaurants all the time, but the *pincho* of tortilla and *caña* of beer still reign supreme. And let's not forget that monument to be found in one of the capital's most traditional establishments: an ornate urn which dispenses *salsa brava* on to your chips.

But, above all, Madrid has a sense of humour, to make the squalls more bearable and the storms more enjoyable. There is a very high bridge here, the *Viaducto* on Calle Bailén, which crosses over the Calle Segovia, far below it. Over the years many Madrileños have come here, to linger and gaze across to the Guadarrama, on their way somewhere, or to take their last steps on earth, since this is also the city's favourite place for suicide attempts. To reduce the risk of this happening, and keep the traffic flowing, the good Mayor has proposed to line the viaduct with giant glass screens. It could just be that after so many years here (he was originally from Málaga), the city's black humour has rubbed off on him.

Me? I have my roots here, sometimes slightly strange and ethereal ones, despite the follies of Mayors and the never-ending changes of a city where they haven't cloned sheep, so much as buildings and motorways.

Nuria Barrios was born in Madrid in 1962. She has recently published a novel, *Amores patológicos* (Pathological Loves), and her stories *El Cuerpo* (The Body) and *Alarma Roja* (Red Alert) have been published in two collections, *Páginas Amarillas* (Yellow Pages), and *Relatos de Mujeres* (Women's Stories) respectively. She writes regularly in *El Pais*.

Telefónica:
espacio para
el Arte y la Cultura.

"La Figuración Renovadora.
Pintores de la Escuela de París
y de la Escuela de Madrid"

"Muntadas. Proyectos"
(29/9 al 22/11)

"PHotoEspaña 98.
Exposición Virtual en Internet"

"Historia del Teléfono"

FUNDACIÓN
ARTE Y TECNOLOGÍA

Madrid, C/ Fuencarral, 3. Martes a viernes de 10 a 14 h.
y de 17 a 20 h. Sábados, domingos y festivos de 10 a 14 h.
Lunes cerrado.
Entrada gratuíta, previa exhibición del D.N.I.

Internet: http://www.telefonica.es/fat/
InfoVía: telefonica.inf/fat/

Sightseeing

Sightseeing

Compact and walkable, Madrid is by turns grand avenues, smart shopping districts, a jigsaw of timeworn alleys – but, above all, a city bustling with life.

Even for those on a tight schedule, it's easy to get a feel of Madrid. The city's most famous attraction, the Prado, and its two other major art museums (the Thyssen and the Reina Sofía) are all on the same avenue, forming Madrid's *Paseo del Arte* or 'Art Promenade'. Most historic buildings are not far away either, as they too fall inside the area of 'Old Madrid', which until the nineteenth century made up the entire city. It was built to the scale of humans on foot, and you often find that even when you consider taking public transport to get somewhere, you end up deciding you might as well make a stroll of it instead. A map is handy, but even visitors who prefer to wander without a specific destination in mind needn't lose out, for wherever they are in the city centre some of Madrid's eclectic sights will be within reach.

Despite its compactness, Madrid is a city of *barrios* or neighbourhoods, each with its own distinct identity. The qualities that give each *barrio* its character are elusive. To their inhabitants, however, a myriad of details make up the vital differences, and even new arrivals to the city soon form an attachment to their particular patch.

BUILDING THE CITY

Propelled by royal whim into becoming the seat of Court and empire, this former Moorish town above the Manzanares was never in a hurry to alter its way of life and become like any other European capital. It wasn't until the seventeenth century that Madrid acquired its first monumental flourishes. From the moment it became Spain's capital in 1561 observers and aspiring urban planners have complained endlessly about its lack of grandeur and a suitably orderly structure. Meanwhile, the shabby city walls put up in 1656 to ensure that tolls and taxes were charged on incoming goods continued to mark its limits until well into the 1860s.

Under the eighteenth-century Bourbons new monuments, churches and convents were added. Between the 1760s and 1780s Charles III added promenades, fountains and arches, street lighting and the city's first sewers. A couple of streets away from the King's monuments, though, life went on pretty much as normal. Madrid continued to be slammed for seediness and lack of amenities, even by visitors such as nineteenth-century Romantics who found its people utterly fascinating.

The last half of the nineteenth century saw major infrastructure improvements to the capital. The walls came down, the railway came in and the Canal de Isabel II brought an (almost) unlimited supply of water down from the sierra. The wealthy began to move out to the Salamanca district, the new hub of fashionable society. These transformations paved the way for a demographic upheaval as countryfolk began to migrate from rural Spain into the big cities. In the twentieth century, Madrid has sprawled out into entirely new areas miles beyond the old city, with factories, dormitory suburbs and a manic radial road system.

At the same time, old Madrid, much of it rebuilt in the last century after the clearance of the city's monasteries, remains very much the city's centre, the site of its most important attractions, cinemas, government institutions and nightlife rounds. Only the business world has really managed to move outside it, up the great spine of the Castellana. *Barrios* of the old centre such as Lavapiés, Malasaña and Chueca still draw in a steady flow of new residents – from Spanish families and students to young Northern Europeans or Moroccans, Chinese and West Africans. Many of the old local population have stayed on, too, and far more than in most cities at the end of the twentieth century these city-centre districts still have a very visible life of their own. This is one of Madrid's essential attractions.

Free entry days

On at least one day a week, usually **Wednesday**, admission is free to most of the monuments administered by Spain's *Patrimonio Nacional*, including the Palacio Real, Descalzas Reales and the Encarnación, (officially) for European Union citizens only. There is also free entry for all visitors to the state museums (which does not include the Museo Thyssen) on **Saturday afternoons** and **Sundays**. For full details, *see p69*.

Holes in the ground

Madrid in the 1990s is a city of building schemes and tunnelling projects. They are never so obtrusive as to ruin a visit to the city, but can be frustrating when you come upon them unannounced. The scale of construction, however, makes writing guidebooks a complex business. Projects are delayed, officially announced completion dates are often quietly forgotten, and it's impossible to produce a reliable list of all the *obras* (works) that may make themselves noticed across the cityscape at any one time.

For the duration of this Guide, car users will likely find themselves caught up in jams resulting from the extension of the Metro, especially on the Castellana near Calle José Abascal and towards the airport. Work also goes on on creating a never-sufficient number of underground car parks.

An essential part of old Madrid, the **Arco de Cuchilleros**. *See page 43.*

Three plazas

Every city has its essential reference points. In Madrid, if you're driving, you're likely first to notice the **Paseo de la Castellana**, the great, north-south avenue that cuts through the city almost from top to bottom, connects the old town to the new northern business districts and forms one of Madrid's most unusual features. On foot, on the other hand, you're likely to begin with the **Puerta del Sol**, which is very literally the centre of the city, in that all street numbers in the city count up outwards from Sol, and it contains *kilómetro cero*, the point from which distances from Madrid to other parts of Spain are measured. Equally, Sol is also the main hub of the transport system, an automatic magnet for people coming in from the city suburbs or arriving from out of town.

Puerta del Sol is also a neutral meeting point for many of the districts of the old city – the old town of the early Habsburgs, Huertas, the streets leading up to Malasaña and Chueca to the north. East of Sol, the Calle de Alcalá, built as a grand ceremonial approach to Madrid, runs down to another vital point on the map, **Plaza de Cibeles**, symbol of Madrid for Spaniards and the junction of the old city, the Castellana and the new city built up from the nineteenth century. To the west, Calle Mayor leads from Sol towards the **Plaza Mayor**, core of Madrid throughout its imperial golden age.

Plaza de Cibeles

Metro Banco de España/bus all routes to Cibeles. **Map H7**
Midway between the Puerta del Sol and the Parque del Retiro, this four-way intersection and its statue and fountain signify Madrid to Spaniards as much as Nelson's Column, the Eiffel Tower or the Empire State Building identify their particular cities. It's surrounded by some of the city's most prominent buildings. Clockwise from the most imposing of the four, the **Palacio de Comunicaciones**, they are the **Banco de España** (for more details on both of these, *see pp44-5*), the **Palacio Buenavista** (now the Army headquarters) and the **Palacio de Linares**, which now houses the **Casa de América** (*see chapter* **Art Galleries**). The Ventura Rodríguez statue in the middle is of *Cybele*, a Graeco-Roman goddess of fertility and symbol of natural abundance, on a chariot drawn by lions. The goddess and the fountain around her were for years the gathering point for victorious Real Madrid fans (Atlético supporters soak themselves in the fountain of Neptune, by the Museo Thyssen) and the place where national football wins were celebrated. However, following the theft of Cybele's arm in one bout of revelry during the 1994 World Cup and some disorder that nearly got out of hand after Real's 1998 European Cup win, the statue, since repaired, has in theory been closed off to such activities. North of Cibeles the Paseo changes name to Paseo de Recoletos, shortly to become the Castellana, Madrid's endless north-south artery.

Plaza Mayor

Metro Sol/bus all routes to Sol. **Map D8**
Madrid's grand main plaza was the city's hub for centuries. It was first built in the fifteenth century as a humble market square, then called the *Plaza del Arrabal* (Square outside the Walls). After Madrid was made capital of Spain by Philip II, Juan de Herrera drew up plans for it to be completely rebuilt, but the only part constructed immediately was the **Casa de la Panadería** (the Bakery). Dominating the square, with

The Paseo del Arte

A joint *Paseo del Arte* ticket is available for all of Madrid's 'Big Three', price 1,050ptas. For details, and full information on these and the city's other art museums, *see chapter* **Museums**.

Museo Nacional Centro de Arte Reina Sofía

C/Santa Isabel 52 (91 467 50 62). Metro Atocha/bus all routes to Atocha. **Open** 10am-9pm Mon, Wed-Sat; 10am-2.30pm Sun. Closed Tue. **Admission** *Mon, Wed-Fri, 10am-2.30pm Sat* 500ptas; 250ptas students; free under-18s, over-65s. *2.30-9pm Sat, Sun free. Paseo del Arte ticket* 1,050ptas. **Map G10**

This giant slab-sided building was originally the Hospital de San Carlos, another project commissioned by Charles III, and designed by Francesco Sabatini. Built in 1776-81, it remained a hospital until 1965. It lay idle until 1977, when work began on its conversion into a museum, exhibition and cultural centre. It opened as an exhibition space in 1986, but was not completed until 1990, with the installation of a permanent collection of contemporary art and the glass lifts either side of the entrance. In 1992 it controversially acquired its greatest attraction, Picasso's *Guernica*. It also hosts major temporary exhibitions and a range of other activities, and has a fine bookshop. *See also chapter* **Art Galleries**.

Museo del Prado

Paseo del Prado (91 420 37 68). Metro Atocha, Banco de España/bus 10, 14, 27, 34, 37, 45. **Open** 9am-7pm Tue-Sat; 9am-2pm Sun, public holidays. Closed Mon. **Admission** *Tue-Fri, 9am-2.30pm Sat* 500ptas; 250ptas students; free under-18s, over-65s. *2.30-7pm Sat, Sun free. Paseo del Arte ticket* 1,050ptas. **Map H8**

This neo-classical structure was designed by Juan de Villanueva in 1785 for King Charles III, who died before it was finished. The King had intended it to be a Museum of Natural Sciences (*see chapter* **History**). However, the massive building, of three sections linked by galleries with an elegant Doric façade at the centre, eventually opened in 1819 as an art museum to display the Spanish royal picture collection. Few visitors to Madrid dare miss this, one of the world's greatest galleries, with, many say, more masterpieces than any other. It is so full of treasures that it is only possible to display a small part of its 9,000-piece collection at any one time.

Museo Thyssen-Bornemisza

Palacio de Villahermosa, Paseo del Prado 8 (91 369 01 51). Metro Banco de España/bus 9, 10, 14, 27, 34, 37, 45. **Open** 10am-7pm Tue-Sun. Closed Mon.

Admission *museum* 700ptas; 400ptas students, over-65s; free under-12s; *temporary exhibitions* 500ptas; 300ptas students, over-65s; *joint ticket for both* 900ptas; 500ptas students, over-65s; *Paseo del Arte ticket* 1,050ptas. **Map G7**

Spain's landing of the art hoard of Baron Hans-Heinrich Thyssen-Bornemisza could easily be the country's greatest coup, however much it had to pay out in the process. It really breaks all the norms, with works from just about every major figure in the history of Western art – Ghirlandaio, Goya, Degas, Picasso, Warhol – and it might be easier to list artists not featured than those present. The building, the Palacio de Villahermosa, is an aristocratic residence from 1805 by Silvestre Pérez and Antonio López Aguado, which had stood empty for several years. To house the Thyssen, architect Rafael Moneo gave it an entirely new interior, with salmon-coloured walls, marble floors and superbly elegant lighting, making the museum stunning even without the works of art. Curiously, it is easy to overlook the plain building from the outside, especially since the entrance is through a courtyard that could be mistaken for a private garden.

OTHER ART HIGHLIGHTS

The 'Big Three' tend to dominate everyone's attention, but Madrid also has many other artistic treasures in less world-renowned locations. For museums listed, *see chapter* **Museums**.

Basílica de San Francisco el Grande (*see p46*) Goya's *San Bernardino de Siena.*
Casón del Buen Retiro (*see chapter* **Museums**) Nineteenth-century Spanish painting, and frescoes by Luca Giordano.
Ermita de San Antonio de la Florida (*see p49*) Extraordinary frescoes by Goya, and his tomb.
Museo Cerralbo El Greco, Zurbarán, Alonso Cano.
Museo Lázaro Galdiano An unknown treasure house: major works by Goya, plus Bosch, Rembrandt and many Flemish, Spanish and English painters.
Museo Municipal Minor works by Goya.
Museo de la Real Academia de Bellas Artes de San Fernando Many Goyas, and Arcimboldo.
Museo Romántico Goya's *San Gregorio el Grande.*
Museo Sorolla The artist's home and his personal collection.
Palacio Real (*see p46*) Frescoes by Giaquinto and Tiepolo, and Goya royal portraits.
Real Monasterio de las Descalzas Reales (*see p53 and chapter* **Museums**) Titian, Breughel, Zurbarán, among others.

---

two pinnacle towers, it was completed under the direction of Diego Sillero in 1590. In the early 1990s, in a move that would not even be contemplated in most countries, this historic edifice was decorated with some eye-catching, hippy-ish murals. The rest of the plaza was built by Juan Gómez de Mora for Philip III, and completed in 1619. Large sections had to be rebuilt after a disastrous fire in 1790. Bullfights, carnivals and all the great festivals and ceremonies of imperial Madrid were held here (*see chapter* **History**). At its centre today is a 1616 statue of Philip III on horseback by Giambologna and Pietro Tacca, originally in the Casa de Campo and moved here in the last century. The ample expanse of the plaza can be enjoyed in different ways at different times. Weekday mornings are calm, a perfect time to study the architecture or enjoy breakfast in one of the attractive (but expensive) cafés. Jewellery, hats, fans and other souvenirs can be bought in the plaza's shops, many of which retain their traditional façades. On Sunday mornings the plaza bustles with a stamp and coin market (*see chapter* **Shopping**); other activities include the serving of giant paellas and the **San Isidro** *cocido* to long lines of Madrileños. For Christmas, it houses a traditional fair with stalls offering trees, nativity scenes, decorations and jokes and toys for kids (for both events, *see chapter* **Madrid by Season**). From the south side of the Plaza, Calle Toledo runs down towards the *barrios* of La Latina and Lavapiés, and the Rastro market.

Puerta del Sol

Metro Sol/bus all routes to Sol. **Map E7**

It's nearly impossible to visit Madrid and not pass through this semicircular space, if only because it is very much the hub of the public transport system. From here, too, Calles Arenal and Mayor lead away to the opera house, the Palacio Real and the Plaza Mayor, while to the east Calle Alcalá and Carrera de San Jerónimo run to the Huertas area, the Paseo del Prado and the main museums. It is called a *puerta* (gate) because this was indeed the main, easternmost gate of fifteenth-century Madrid. Under the Habsburg kings it was surrounded by churches and monasteries, and the space between them supplanted the Plaza Mayor as the city's main meeting place. It was rebuilt in its present form in 1854-62. It still is Madrid's most popular meeting point, particularly by the monument with the symbols of Madrid, a bear and a *madroño* or strawberry tree, at the junction with Calle Carmen. Across from there is the square's most important building, the **Casa de Correos**, built in 1766 by Jaime Marquet as a post office for Charles III. Today it houses the Madrid regional government, the *Comunidad de Madrid*. It was altered significantly in 1866 when the large clock tower was added. Some find it architecturally objectionable, but this clock is the best-known feature of the building today, since it's the one the whole country looks to on New Year's Eve, when Madrileños crowd into the square to await the 12 chimes (*see chapter* **Madrid by Season**). In recent years the clock tower developed a rather precarious incline due to rot in its timbers, but in 1996-7 work was undertaken virtually to rebuild it completely, and the lovingly restored building was unveiled once again at the beginning of 1998. In front of it is *kilómetro cero*, the mark from which distances to Madrid are measured.

Villa y Corte

Between Sol, the Palacio Real and San Francisco el Grande, and containing within it the oldest part of the city, this area is often labelled rather floridly the 'Madrid of the Austrias' or 'Habsburg Madrid' although Philip II and his dynasty can scarcely claim responsibility for very much of it. At its core is the greatest monument they did build, the **Plaza Mayor**, archetypal creation of the Castilian-baroque style (*see page 41*). When it was first built up in the 1460s, however, the plaza had actually been outside the twelfth-century walls of little Madrid.

Battered and sometimes burnt over the years, the Plaza Mayor has been expensively restored since 1980. Most of its walls have been recoloured in a gloriously baroque vermilion, but the plaza's 1590 centrepiece, the **Casa de la Panadería**, has been adorned with a set of fey, semi-psychedelic murals. But then, the Plaza Mayor has seen it all: executions, riots, bullfights, wild Carnival revels and the nastier doings of the Inquisition. Nowadays, coin and stamp collectors turn out in force on Sundays for their market, bands play during *fiestas* and at year's end the plaza is given over to a traditional Christmas fair. It's also a magnet for tourists all year long, with caricature artists, souvenir stalls and some genuinely interesting shops. As much of a draw are its pavement cafés and restaurants, some of them very overpriced, but pleasant nonetheless.

In the south-west corner of the plaza, near the tourist office, is an arch, the **Arco de los Cuchilleros** (Knifemakers' Arch), with a spectacular bank of steps leading down through Calle de los Cuchilleros to the Plaza de la Puerta Cerrada, decorated with some engaging '70s murals. South of that is Calle Cava Baja, along the line of the twelfth-century wall. This is home to the most celebrated *mesones*, temples to Madrid's traditional cuisine (*see chapter* **Restaurants**). Directly south of the Plaza Mayor in Calle Toledo stand the twin towers of **San Isidro**, the temple that contains the bones of the city's patron, and which served as Madrid's cathedral up until 1993.

To the south-east, where Calle Atocha runs up to the Plaza Mayor in the Plaza de la Provincia, is another major work of Castilian baroque, the squatly proportioned **Palacio de Santa Cruz** of 1629-34. Its architect is believed to have been either Juan Bautista Crescenci or Juan Gómez de Mora. Despite its grand appearance it was originally the Court Prison, with a dungeon so deep that prisoners had to rub their rags with lard and set them alight to stop themselves going blind, although it now has a more dignified role as the Foreign Ministry. In former times executions often took place in the **Plaza de la Cebada**, just a tumbril ride away. The best attended of them all was that of Madrid's own Robin Hood, the bandit Luis Candelas, in 1837.

The area between Cebada, Mayor and the Palacio Real really is the oldest part of the city, the site of the Muslim town and of most of medieval Madrid. The beautifully restored **Plaza de la Paja** ('Straw Square') on Calle Segovia probably marked the southernmost point of the Muslim wall. The surrounding streets all mainly follow their original medieval lines. The knot of streets just to the west formed the **Morería**, where during the Middle Ages Madrid's community of *Mudéjar* Muslims (*see chapter* **History**) were confined. The little **Plaza de la Morería** (also called Plaza del Alamillo) was the site of the Mosque and the *Aljama*, the Muslim community courts. The former inhabitants are also remembered in **Plaza Puerta de los Moros**, once the site of the 'Moors' Gate'.

Getting a sense of medieval or early Habsburg Madrid requires an exercise of the imagination. Beyond the street plan and the interconnecting squares – Paja, Plaza de la Cruz Verde, Plaza de los Carros – not much solid remains, and even the sixteenth-century exteriors that once fronted the squares were replaced in the last century. Tucked away in sidestreets are **San Pedro el Viejo** and, across Calle Mayor, **San Nicolás de las Servitas**, the only two *Mudéjar* towers in Madrid. If you continue down Calle Segovia beneath the viaduct you will pass Madrid's oldest relic, a forlorn fragment of the **Muralla Árabe** (Arab Wall), embedded in a rocky ridge.

Grand avenue: the Castellana

Look at any map of Madrid and you see it. A long, sometimes curving, sometimes dead-straight road, running north-south for miles through the city, and called at different points along its length the Paseo del Prado, Paseo de Recoletos and Paseo de la Castellana. It is as if, in a city where people had so often complained of the lack of grand avenues, somebody had suddenly decided to silence the critics with one single thoroughfare like they'd never seen before.

In fact, this endless strip developed gradually rather than out of one decision. Its oldest section, the **Paseo del Prado**, once an open space between the city wall and the Retiro, was given its present form as the most important of Charles III's attempts to give his shabby city the kind of urbane dignity he had seen in Paris and Italy.

As well as Charles' creations such as the **Jardín Botánico** and the **Museo del Prado**, it contains the rest of Madrid's 'Golden Triangle' of art museums, **Atocha** station and such important elements in local life as the **Hotel Ritz**, the **Bolsa** (Stock Exchange) and the second-hand bookstalls on **Cuesta de Moyano** (*see chapter* **Shopping**).

The **Paseo de Recoletos**, north of Cibeles, was mostly added in the 1830s and 1840s. It is as green and elegant as its predecessor, but busier, with fashionable cafés such as **El Espejo** and the famous **Café Gijón** (*see chapter* **Cafés & Bars**). The curiously grand white marble palace a little further north on the right, now the **Banco Hipotecario**, is the one that was the residence of the Marqués de Salamanca, Madrid's one-time huckster-in-chief (*see page 65*).

At the end of Recoletos on the right stands the huge building housing the **Biblioteca Nacional** and, behind it, the **Museo Arqueológico Nacional**. The most ambitious project of the reign of Isabel II, it was commissioned in 1865, but only completed in 1892. It overlooks the **Plaza de**

Colón, where, at Columbus' feet, a cascading wall of water, beautifully cool in summer, conceals the entrance to the **Centro Cultural de la Villa** (*see chapters* **Art Galleries**, **Dance** *and* **Theatre**).

In 1860, when he designed Madrid's *Ensanche* ('Extension'; *see chapter* **History**), Carlos Maria de Castro took the significant decision, since the Paseo del Prado and Recoletos were already there, to continue along the same route with the main avenue of the new district. Thus, the Castellana was born. Until the Republic of 1931 demolished Madrid's old racetrack it reached only as far as Calle Joaquin Costa. Today it snakes away freely northwards, through thickets of office blocks. This is also, though, the home of Madrid's 'beach' of night-time terrace bars, especially around Calle Juan Bravo (near which junction is the unique **Museo de Escultura al Aire Libre**), and prestige shopping complexes such as **ABC Serrano** (*see chapter* **Shopping**).

In the '70s and '80s banks and insurance companies vied with each other to commission in-vogue architects to create corporate showcases here. Constructions to see and judge in the initial stretch include **Bankinter** at no.29, and **Bankunión** at no.46. The junction with Joaquin Costa is marked by the Kafkaesque bulk of the **Nuevos Ministerios** government buildings.

Beyond that, a huge branch of the Corte Inglés signals your arrival at the **AZCA** complex, a monument to '80s corporate taste. A little further up again, opposite each other, are Real Madrid's **Estadio Bernabéu** and the **Palacio de Congresos** conference centre. By this time, the view up the Castellana is dominated by the two leaning towers known as the **Puerta de Europa** at Plaza Castilla. These remarkable smoked-glass blocks, 15° off perpendicular, are perhaps the greatest monument to Spain's '80s boom, begun with finance from the Kuwait Investment Office (so the towers are often called the *Torres KIO*) and left unfinished for years after a financial scandal in 1992. With their phallic fountain in the middle, they have now joined the landmarks of modern Madrid.

Sites along the Castellana are listed here from bottom to top, south to north.

Estación de Atocha

Glorieta de Emperador Carlos V. Metro Atocha/bus all routes to Atocha. **Map H10**
Madrid's classic wrought-iron and glass main rail station was built in 1888-92, to a design by Alberto del Palacio. It remained much the same, gathering a coating of soot, until the 1980s, when Rafael Moneo – he of the Museo Thyssen

– gave the station a complete renovation in preparation for 1992, Spain's golden year. Entirely new sections were added for the AVE high-speed train (*see p245*) and Madrid's expanded local rail network. Also, as well as the building being cleaned up, an indoor tropical garden was installed. Even if you're not catching a train, a visit to Atocha is worthwhile to see this imaginative blend of old and new.

Jardín Botánico

Plaza de Murillo (91 420 30 17). Metro Atocha/bus all routes to Atocha. **Open** *Oct-Apr* 10am-dusk, *May-Sept* 10am-9pm, daily. **Admission** 200ptas; 100ptas students; group discounts. **Map H9**
Madrid's luscious botanical gardens were created for Charles III by Juan de Villanueva and the botanist Gómez Ortega in 1781. They are right alongside the Paseo del Prado, just south of the Prado museum, but inside this green oasis, with more than 30,000 plants from around the globe, it's easy to feel that city life has been put on hold. Ideal for a stroll or a moment's peace in spring, early summer or autumn.

Bolsa de Comercio de Madrid

Plaza de la Lealtad 1 (91 589 26 00). Metro Banco de España/bus 10, 14, 27, 34, 37, 45. **Open** *exhibition space* 10am-2pm Mon-Fri. **Admission** free. **Map H7**
In the same plaza as the Hotel Ritz, Madrid's stock market is a landmark as well as a business centre. Enrique María Repullés won the competition to design the building in 1884, with a neo-classical style chosen to reflect that of the nearby Prado. The building now has two distinct areas. One, the trading area; the second, open to the public, houses an exhibition on the market's history. *See also chapter* **Directory**.

Paseo del Prado

Metro Atocha, Banco de España/bus 9, 10, 14, 27, 34, 37, 45. **Map G/H7-9**
Visitors to the major art museums become familiar with this tree-lined boulevard between Atocha and the Plaza de Cibeles, with the **Museo del Prado** and **Museo Thyssen** either side of its central plaza. The Paseo itself, chiefly designed by José de Hermosilla, was laid out in 1775-82 for King Charles III, as part of his plan to give his capital a grand avenue lined by centres of learning and science (*see chapter* **History**). The form of the main section, from Cibeles to Plaza Cánovas del Castillo and originally called the *Salón del Prado*, was modelled on the Piazza Navona in Rome, with three fountains by Ventura Rodríguez: Cibeles at the most northerly point and Neptune to the south, with a smaller figure of Apollo in the middle. The southern stretch of the Paseo, tapering down to Atocha, has another statue, the *Four Seasons*, in front of the Museo del Prado. Traffic is often heavy on the Paseo today, but in the nineteenth century this was the great promenade of Madrid. Virtually the entire population, rich and poor, took a turn along it each evening, to see and be seen, pick up on the latest city gossip, make assignations, and show off their clothes and carriages.

Banco de España

Plaza de Cibeles. Metro Banco de España/bus all routes to Cibeles. **Map G6**
A grandiose pile designed in 1882 by Eduardo Adaro and Severiano Sainz de la Lastra to house the recently created Bank of Spain. The style is eclectic, but most influenced by French Second-Empire designs. The decorative arched window and elaborate clock above the main entrance are best appreciated from a distance.

Palacio de Comunicaciones (Correos)

Plaza de Cibeles (91 521 65 00).
Metro Banco de España/bus all routes to Cibeles.
Open 8.30am-9.30pm Mon-Fri; 9.30am-9.30pm Sat; 8.30am-2pm Sun. **Map H7**

Recent arrivals in Madrid often refuse to believe that this extraordinary construction, dwarfing the Plaza de Cibeles and regularly compared to a sand castle or a wedding cake, can be just a post office. However, that's what it is. Madrid's main post office was designed in 1904 by Antonio Palacios and Joaquín Otamendi and completed in 1918, and is the best example of the extravagant style favoured by Madrid's elite at their most expansive. The design was influenced by Viennese art nouveau, but also features many traditional Spanish touches. Customers who come to buy stamps or post a parcel are treated to a grand entrance (with over-sized revolving door), a Hollywood film-set staircase, soaring ceilings, stained columns and grand marble floors. For details of mail services, *see chapter* **Directory**.

Museo de Escultura al Aire Libre

Paseo de la Castellana 41. Metro Rubén Darío/bus 5, 7, 16, 27, 45, 150. **Map H2**
An unconventional museum, this 1970s space alongside the Castellana by the junction with Calle Juan Bravo was the brainchild of engineers José Antonio Fernández Ordoñez and Julio Martínez Calzón. Designing a bridge across the avenue, they decided the space underneath would be a good art venue. Sculptor Eusebio Sempere convinced fellow artists or their families to donate their work, most imposing of which is the six-ton suspended cube *The Meeting* by Eduardo Chillida. Skateboarders use it a lot, too.

Nuevos Ministerios

Paseo de la Castellana 67. Metro Nuevos Ministerios/bus 5, 7, 14, 27, 40, 147, 150.
A seemingly endless, bunkerish building that contains a complex of government ministries, begun in 1932 and one of the largest government projects bequeathed by the Spanish Republic to Madrid. It was designed by a team led by Secundino Zuazo, chief architect of the Gran Madrid plan (*see chapter* **History**), in a monolithic '30s-rationalist style; then, after the victory of Franco, the same architect added to the still-unfinished building curving, complicated details more to the taste of the new regime. Inside it has a park-like garden, open to the public, that's often frequented by local office workers taking a break from the office.

Urbanización AZCA

Paseo de la Castellana 95 & Avda del General Perón. Metro Santiago Bernabéu, Nuevos Ministerios/bus 5, 27, 40, 126, 147, 150.
Known to some as 'Little Manhattan', this glitzy skyscraper development was first projected during the Franco regime's industrial heyday in the '60s, but gained extra vigour in democratic Spain's 1980s boom to become a symbol of Madrid yuppiedom. The most striking of its giant blocks are the circular **Torre Europa** and the **Torre Picasso**, designed by Japanese architect Minori Yamasaki in 1988 and, at 157m (515ft), Madrid's tallest building. Between them is Plaza Picasso, a well-maintained park. Originally built to lure business to a less traffic-ridden area of the city, the development now generates more than its share of traffic itself. Amid the office blocks, a chic shopping centre (**Moda**), restaurants and other facilities allow office workers to spend their whole day here without having to venture outside. As to the name, don't try to figure it out, as the letters AZCA apparently don't stand for anything at all.

Estadio Santiago Bernabéu

Paseo de la Castellana 144 (91 344 00 52). Metro Santiago Bernabéu/bus 27, 40, 43, 120, 126, 147, 150.
The temple of Real Madrid football club, designed in the '40s and named after the long-time chairman. A colossal grey structure, it resembles a stack of cans each larger than the next, with swirling stairwells at each corner. It has capacity for 105,000 fans. *See also chapter* **Sports & Fitness**.

The **Plaza de la Villa**, on Calle Mayor, began life as the Arab souk, and continued to be Madrid's main square until the creation of the Plaza Mayor. This early importance is marked by the fact that it still contains Madrid's city hall, the **Casa de la Villa**. In pre-Habsburg Madrid this was also the preferred place for residences of the local élite, one of which, the **Torre de los Lujanes**, is still there. With the third entirely different construction on the square, the **Casa de Cisneros**, they make up a compendium of the history of Madrid from provincial town to imperial capital.

The Calle Mayor was the main thoroughfare of Madrid for centuries. Cross-streets between Mayor and Arenal offer an odd mixture of bookbinders and picture-framers, liturgical outfitters and Galician restaurants. The western end of Mayor, near the Almudena and the Palacio Real, has several old palaces, an old church reserved for the use of the Army general staff, and **Casa Ciriaco**, one of Madrid's most famous restaurants (*see chapter* **Restaurants**). Back towards the Plaza Mayor, drop onto the iron-framed 1915 **Mercado de San Miguel** on Plaza San Miguel, the last market of its era still up and running in central Madrid (*see chapter* **Shopping**).

Calle Mayor runs out west into Calle Bailén, connected southwards to a splendid 1930s concrete viaduct offering wonderful views of the sierra and the Casa de Campo. However, its notoriety as a suicide point has led the town hall to discuss placing giant glass panels along it, which could ruin the view and maybe not do much for the suicide rate either. At the southern end of the viaduct is the hill of **Las Vistillas**, with more great views and cafés to observe them from, and the giant late-baroque church of **San Francisco el Grande**.

In the opposite direction, Calle Bailén runs up past the **Almudena** cathedral and the **Palacio Real** to dip through a tunnel under the now-pedestrianised **Plaza de Oriente**. Behind the Palacio Real, the delightful **Campo del Moro** gardens (*see page 60*) run down towards the river.

On the east side of Plaza de Oriente is Madrid's opera house, the **Teatro Real**, reborn in 1997 after a long, long renovation (*see chapter* **Music: Classical & Opera**). From here Calle Arenal, originally a stream bed, leads back to the Puerta del Sol. Off Arenal, in the alleyway next to the glitzy **Joy Eslava** disco that snakes around the church of **San Ginés**, there are some wooden bookstalls that have been bringing in the browsers since 1850, and the **Chocolatería San Ginés**, an institution for late-night revellers in need of sustenance (*see chapter* **Nightlife**).

Basílica de San Francisco el Grande

Plaza de San Francisco (91 365 38 00).
Metro Puerta de Toledo, La Latina/bus 3, 60, 148, C.
Open *Oct-May* 11am-1pm, 4-7pm, *June-Sept* 11am-1pm, 5-8pm, Tue-Sat. **Admission** 50ptas. **Map C9**

This huge, multi-tiered church between Puerta de Toledo and the Palacio Real is difficult to miss. A monastery on the site, reputedly founded by Saint Francis of Assisi himself, was knocked down in 1760; in its place Francisco Cabezas and later Francesco Sabatini built this neo-classical church from 1761 to 1784. Most challenging was the construction of the dome, with a diameter of 33m (108ft). So unusual (and potentially unstable) was it that it has recently needed extensive restoration work. Inside there is an early Goya, *The Sermon of San Bernardino of Siena* of 1781, and several frescoes by other artists. Visitors are not admitted during weddings.

Catedral de Nuestra Señora de la Almudena

C/Bailén 10, Plaza de la Armería (91 542 22 00). Metro Opera/bus 3, 25, 31, 39, 148. **Open** 10am-1.30pm, 6-8.30pm, Mon-Sat; 10am-2.30pm, 6-8.30pm, Sun. **Map C7/8**

If ever a project looked like it would last forever, this was it. For centuries, Church and State could not agree on whether Madrid should have a cathedral. When they did, in the 1880s, the building took 110 years to complete. In 1883 work began on a neo-Gothic design by the Marqués de Cubas, but this scheme went off course after only the crypt, accessible from Calle Mayor, was completed. Another architect, Fernando Chueca Goitia, took over in 1944, and introduced a neo-classical style. It has failed to attract any popular affection over the years, but it was finally finished in 1993 – such an achievement that it was marked by a visit from the Pope. Until 1870, when it was knocked down by liberal urban reformers, the site contained the church of Santa María de la Almudena, formerly the main mosque of Muslim Madrid.

Iglesia-Catedral de San Isidro

C/Toledo 37 (91 369 20 37). Metro La Latina, Tirso de Molina/bus 17, 18, 23, 31, 35, 65.
Open 7.30am-1pm, 6.30-8.30pm, Mon-Sat; 9am-2pm, 5.30-8.30pm, Sun, public holidays. **Map D8**

This giant church was built as part of the *Colegio Imperial*, centre of the Jesuit order in Spain, in 1622-33. The high-baroque design was by Pedro Sánchez (himself a member of the order), inspired by the mother church of the Jesuits, the Gesù in Rome. The façade was completed by Francisco Bautista in 1664. In 1767, after Charles III's dispute with the Jesuits (*see chapter* **History**), the church was dedicated to San Isidro and altered by Ventura Rodriguez to accommodate the remains of the saint and his spouse, brought from the Capilla de San Isidro (*see below*). It was Madrid's 'provisional' cathedral from 1885 until the completion of the Almudena in 1993.

Muralla Arabe (Arab Wall)

Cuesta de la Vega.
Metro Opera/bus 3, 31, 50, 65, 148. **Map C8**

Until the 1980s, this crumbling stretch of ninth-century rampart, only remaining relic of Madrid's Muslim founders, was virtually ignored by the city. As some recompense the area around it has now been renamed the **Parque Emir Mohammed I**. It's occasionally used as a venue in the summer arts festival (*see chapter* **Madrid by Season**).

Palacio Real (Palacio de Oriente)

Palacio de Oriente & C/Bailén (91 542 00 59).
Metro Opera/bus 3, 25, 39, 148. **Open** 9am-6pm Mon-Sat; 9am-5pm Sun, public holidays. **Admission** 850ptas; 350ptas students, under-16s, over-65s; *Wed only* free for EU citizens; *guided tours* 100ptas. **Map C7**

You are unlikely to catch sight of Spain's royal family here, as this 3,000-room official residence is only visited by them for occasional state functions requiring additional grandeur. The rest of the time the palace, commissioned by Philip V

The grand design of the **Basílica de San Francisco el Grande**.

Tales from the riverbank

Puente Reina Victoria, between San Antonio de la Florida and the Casa de Campo.

Madrid's river, the Manzanares, has often been disparaged. Quevedo called it 'a ditch learning how to be a river', and in the nineteenth century a visiting French aristocrat made the since much-repeated quip, upon seeing the regal Puente de Segovia, that since the city had such a fine bridge, then maybe it should now get a river. At the beginning of the twentieth century it was still being used for washing clothes, and older residents remember making the trek out to Puente de los Franceses, below Parque del Oeste, for a swim in its then-clean waters in the years after the Civil War. However, the river was neglected during the '50s and '60s, and became heavily polluted; in the '70s, the construction of the southern stretch of the M-30 inner ring road for several kilometres along its banks further added to its feel of abandonment.

However, the Socialist city administration of the early 1980s initiated a major clean-up, and since then a pleasant walk has been made available along a decent stretch of the river from the Puente del Rey, by the entrance to the Casa de Campo, all the way north to Puente de los Franceses. On the way there's an ideal stop off spot in the Asturian chicken-and-cider restaurant **Casa Mingo**, right by the Ermita de San Antonio (*see chapter* **Restaurants**). Further south, there are other less attractive riverside walks by Madrid's two historic bridges.

Ermita de San Antonio de la Florida

Glorieta de San Antonio de la Florida 5 (91 542 07 22). Metro Príncipe Pío/bus 41, 46, 75. **Open** 10am-2pm, 4-8pm, Tue-Fri; 10am-2pm Sat, Sun. Closed public holidays. **Admission** *Tue, Thur-Sat* 300ptas, 150ptas students, under-18s, over-65s; *Wed, Sun* free for EU citizens. **Map A4**

This plain neo-classical chapel was built by Felipe Fontana for Charles IV between 1792 and 1798. Situated a little out of the way, north of Príncipe Pío station on the Paseo de la Florida, outside the Parque del Oeste, it is famous as the burial place of Goya, and for the unique frescoes based on scenes of Madrid life he painted here in 1798. In contrast to the rather staid exterior, the colour and use of light in Goya's images are stunning; many consider them to be among his best work, and they were recently reborn for public view thanks to an exhaustive restoration programme carried out for the 250th anniversary of the artist's birth in 1996. Forming a pair with the Hermitage on the other side of a road leading into the park is a near-identical second chapel, built only in the 1920s in order to allow the original building to be left as a museum. There are free guided tours of the Ermita, in Spanish and English, at 11am and noon on Saturdays.

Puente de Segovia

C/Segovia. Metro Puerta del Angel/bus 25, 31, 33, 36, 39, 65, 138, C. **Map A8**
When travelling over this stone bridge by car it's hard to imagine that it was commissioned by Philip II from Juan de Herrera and completed in 1584, to make it easier for the King to get away to El Escorial (*see p225*). Below the Palacio Real, it's best appreciated from a distance, along the river's edge. As people have often noted, its elegant multiple arches make it much grander than the Manzanares flowing beneath it.

Puente de Toledo

Glorieta de las Pirámides. Metro Pirámides, Marqués de Vadillo/bus 23, 35, 36, 116, 118, 119.
South of the old city, this was only the second major bridge built over the Manzanares after the Puente de Segovia, and was constructed by Pedro de Ribera for Philip V in 1718-32. Its fine stonework has suffered from the fumes and noise thrown up by the M-30, which it straddles. However, restoration work was carried out in 1995, and the bridge itself is now closed to traffic; there's also a riverside park along the east side. It's a good place to see as part of a Sunday morning amble down from the Rastro along Calle Toledo and across to the very different neighbourhood on the west side of the river.

*Eternal contemplation in the **Plaza de la Paja**. See page 43.*

after the earlier Alcázar was lost to a fire in 1734, is open to view. The architects principally responsible for the final design, which reflects the taste of the Spanish Bourbons, were Italian – Giambattista Sacchetti and Francesco Sabatini, with contributions by the Spaniard Ventura Rodríguez. Filippo Juvarra, Philip V's first choice, had planned for a palace four times as large, but after his death the project became a little less ambitious. Completed in 1764, the late baroque-style palace is built almost entirely of granite and white Colmenar stone, and, surrounded by majestic gardens, contributes greatly to the splendour of the city.

Inside, you must keep to a fixed itinerary, but are free to set your own pace rather than follow a tour. The entrance into the palace is awe-inspiring: you pass up a truly vast main staircase, and then through the main state rooms, the Hall of Halbardiers and Hall of Columns, all with soaring ceilings and frescoes by Corrado Giaquinto and Giambattista Tiepolo. In the grand Throne Room there are some fine seventeenth-century sculptures commissioned by Velázquez, which were saved from the earlier Alcázar. Other highlights are the extravagantly ornate private apartments of the palace's first and most distinguished resident, Charles III, again decorated by Italians, especially the 'Gasparini Room' the King's dressing room, covered in mosaics and rococo stucco by Mattia Gasparini, and the 'Porcelain Room', similar to the one in Aranjuez, its walls covered entirely in porcelain reliefs. A later addition is another giant, the State Dining Room, redesigned for King Alfonso XII in 1880, and still used for official banquets. There are also imposing collections of tapestries, table porcelain, gold and silver plate and finally clocks, a particular passion of the little-admired King Charles IV. Also interesting, and with separate entrances off the palace courtyard, are the **Royal Armoury**, with a fine collection of ceremonial armour, much of which was actually worn by Charles V and other Habsburgs, and the engaging rooms of the **Royal Pharmacy**, one of the oldest in Europe, wholly dedicated to attending to the many ailments of

Spain's crowned heads for several centuries. The palace is closed to the public when official receptions or ceremonies are due, and it's a good idea to check before visiting. On the first Wednesday of each month the Royal Guard stages a ceremonial Changing of the Guard in the courtyard, at noon.

Plaza de Oriente

Metro Opera/bus 3, 25, 33, 39, 148. **Map C7**
Curiously, Madrid owes this stately square that seems ideally to complement the Palacio Real not to the Bourbon monarchs but to Spain's 'non-King', Joseph Bonaparte, who initiated the clearing of the area during his brief reign (1808-13). After his departure it was left as a dusty space for many years before being laid out in formal style in 1844. Most recently, it has been dug up again for years at a stretch while Calle Bailén has been sent into an underground tunnel. With the completion of this work the plaza is now fully pedes-trianised, and its avenues effectively extend up to the walls of the palace. At the centre of the square is a fine equestrian statue of King Philip IV that once stood in the courtyard of the Buen Retiro (*see chapter* **History**). It was designed by Velázquez and the sculptor Pietro Tacca, and engineered in Italy supposedly with the aid of Galileo. On the opposite side from the palace is Madrid's now fully functioning opera house, the **Teatro Real** (*see chapter* **Music: Classical & Opera**). Its final reopening in 1997 – after countless delays – has led to a certain revitalisation of the area's street- and nightlife, and the number of pavement cafés, all with a great view of the palace, is growing steadily. An ever more distant memory are the rallies Franco used to address here from the palace balcony, for which devotees were bussed in from all over the country.

Plaza de la Villa

Metro Opera/bus all routes to Puerta del Sol. **Map D8**
This historic square, the market square of Muslim and early medieval Madrid, contains three distinguished buildings all in different styles. Dominating it is the **Casa de la Villa** or

City Hall, designed in Castilian-baroque style by Juan Gómez de Mora in 1630, although financial problems prevented it being completed until 1695. The façade was also altered by Juan de Villanueva in the 1780s. It contrasts nicely with the **Casa de Cisneros**, which was built as a palace by a relative of the great Cardinal Cisneros in 1537. It was restored in 1910, and now also houses municipal offices. Opposite the Casa de la Villa is the simple **Torre de los Lujanes**, once the residence of one of Madrid's aristocratic families, from the 1460s. It is believed that King Francis I of France was kept prisoner in the tower by Charles V after his capture at the Battle of Pavia in 1525.

San Andrés & Capilla de San Isidro

Plaza de San Andrés 1 (91 365 48 71). Metro La Latina/bus 3, 17, 18, 23, 35, 60, 148. **Open** 8-9.30am, 6-7.30pm, Mon-Sat; 9am-2pm Sun. **Map C8**

The fifteenth-century **Capilla del Obispo** (Bishop's Chapel) on one side of this church in the heart of old Madrid is the best-preserved Gothic building in the city, with finely carved tombs of local aristocrats of the period. As with most of Madrid's medieval churches, other sections were rebuilt and made grander in later centuries. Most important is the baroque **Capilla de San Isidro**, built in 1657-69 by Pedro de la Torre to house the remains of the saint, which were later transferred to the **Iglesia-Catedral de San Isidro** (*see p46*). The rest of the church is sixteenth-century. Opening times may vary.

San Nicolás de los Servitas

Plaza San Nicolás (91 559 40 64). Metro Opera/bus 3, 25, 39, 148. **Open** 8.30am-2pm Mon; 8.30-9.30am, 6.30-8.30pm, Tue-Sun. **Map C7**

The oldest surviving church in Madrid, only a few minutes from Plaza de Oriente. The twelfth-century tower is one of only two *Mudéjar* towers, built by Moslem craftsmen living under Christian rule, in the city. Most of the rest of the church was rebuilt in the fifteenth and sixteenth centuries. To see it on days other than Monday, go to the priory behind the church on Travesía del Biombo and ask the monks there to open it for you. It's best to phone first if you can.

San Pedro el Viejo

Costanilla de San Pedro (91 365 12 84). Metro La Latina/bus 31, 35, 50, 65. **Open** 6-8pm daily. **Map D8**

The other *Mudéjar* brick tower in Madrid, from the fourteenth century. Again, the rest of the church is much later, rebuilt in the seventeenth century.

Sol & Gran Vía

The **Puerta del Sol** is where most of the streets (and many bus routes) of old Madrid converge, and where all newcomers from the rest of Spain come at least once to feel sure they've arrived. If you stop for a couple of minutes you can check out Madrid's totemic bear and strawberry tree (*madroño*) symbol, at the end of Calle Carmen, and the Tio Pepe sign over the eastern end of the square that has been there longer than practically any of its other fixtures, and so also ranks as a symbol.

Famously, people have come to the Puerta del Sol to find out what's going on. Until the 1830s the block between Calle Correo and Calle Esparteros was occupied by the monastery of San Felipe el Real, the steps and cloister of which were, in Habsburg Madrid, one of the recognised *Mentideros* – literally, 'Pits of Lies', or gossip-mills – where people came to pick up on the latest news,

anecdotes or scurrilous rumours. In a city with no newspapers, but where who was in or out of favour with the powerful was of first importance, they were a major social institution, and rare was the day when at least one of the great figures of Spanish literature such as Cervantes, Lope or Quevedo did not pass by here.

Today, a quarter of a million revellers turn out in the Puerta del Sol every New Year's Eve to douse themselves with spurting *Cava* and eat their lucky grapes, one for each chime of the clock (*see chapter* **Madrid by Season**). Just around the corner on Calle Tetuán is **Casa Labra**, famous for its zinc bar and tapas of *bacalao*, and as the place where the Spanish Socialist Party was founded in 1879 (*see chapter* **Tapas**). Sol is, too, where Napoleon's Egyptian cavalry, the Mamelukes, charged down on the Madrileño crowd on 2 May 1808, as portrayed in one of Goya's most famous and dramatic paintings.

The New Year's Eve clock rises out of Charles III's 1766 post office, the **Casa de Correo**, now the seat of the Madrid regional government. Under Franco it had much grimmer connotations as the Interior Ministry and police headquarters. In 1963 Julián Grimau, a sort of Communist Scarlet Pimpernel, 'fell' from an upper window, but was patched up for his date with the firing squad.

The area between Sol, Arenal, Alcalá and the Gran Vía forms central Madrid's main pedestrian axis and shopping centre, above all **Calle Preciados**. There are banks and shoe shops, stores such as **El Corte Inglés** and the **FNAC** and stacks of offices, as well as *cafeterías* and fast food temples for employees on their lunch break.

Running not quite alongside Preciados up to Gran Vía is **Calle Montera**, happily shabby, lined with mainly out-of-date shops and the main area for street prostitution in the city centre. At the top, parallel with Gran Vía, is Calle Caballero de Gracia, where the little nineteenth-century Oratory lays on special Masses for the working girls, many from the Dominican Republic, who operate along the street. Just north of Gran Vía, behind the Telefónica building on the south edge of Malasaña, lies Madrid's most recent hard-core zone. At the centre of it all is Calle Desengaño, which translates as 'disappointment'. Previously a haven for prostitution and sex clubs, this street is slowly picking up, as new cinemas in Plaza de Tudescos and low rents draw more people into the area. While seedy, these streets are not dangerous, and are heavily policed. Care should be taken walking around late at night, though, especially if you're on your own.

The area north and east of Sol is dominated, however, by its two great avenues, **Calle Alcalá** and the **Gran Vía**. Alcalá follows the centuries-old main route into Madrid from the east, and in the eighteenth century, when it was flanked by aristocratic palaces, was described as the grandest street in Europe. It is still pretty grand today, with a wonderful variety of early twentieth-century buildings, from the dignified **Banesto** building (no.14) to the cautiously modernist **Círculo de Bellas Artes**. There are also several fine older constructions along the street, such as the austere neo-classical Finance Ministry, built as the **Aduana** or Customs administration by Francesco Sabatini in 1761-9, and Pedro de Ribera's exuberantly baroque church of **San José**, of 1730-42. Opposite the latter, at the point where Alcalá and Gran Vía meet, there is the fairly recent addition of a sentimental statue of *La Violetera*, the heroine of the eponymous sentimental *zarzuela*, the theme of which was plagiarised by Charlie Chaplin in *City Lights*.

The Gran Vía is a child of this century, sliced through the old city – albeit with a rather rusty knife, for it took over 20 years – after 1910. Although an interloper, it has a style all of its own (*see page 55*). It completely transformed the core of old Madrid, with a new grand avenue full of bustle for banking, shopping, offices and, above all, cinemas. Love it or hate it, no one can deny that it's lively. On Sundays, it's packed with people queuing under the enormous hand-painted film posters around Plaza Callao.

To the north-west, the Gran Vía runs out into the sprawling space of the **Plaza de España**. South of the avenue, even though the streets are full of shops and shoppers, there are still corners of Habsburg Madrid tucked away, most notably the closed nunneries of the **Descalzas Reales** and the **Encarnación**.

Just north of the Encarnación, occupying the site of another convent, is the old, nineteenth-century **Palacio del Senado** (Senate), now made redundant by its back-to-back counterpart in granite and smoked glass by Santiago Goyarre. When it opened in 1991 the new Senate was loudly criticised not so much on architectural grounds as for the shameless perk it represents (with in-house swimming pool) for an upper house with even less of a political role than that in Britain.

Círculo de Bellas Artes

C/Alcalá 42 & C/Marqués de Casa Riera 2 (91 360 54 00). Metro Banco de España, Sevilla/bus all routes to Cibeles. **Open** *café* 9am-2am Mon-Thur, Sun; 9am-4am Fri, Sat; *exhibitions* 5-9pm Tue-Fri; 11am-2pm, 5-9pm, Sat; 11am-2pm Sun. **Admission** 100ptas. **Map G7**

Other Madrids

Madrid may be one of Europe's most homogeneous capitals, but its international migrant population is growing fast. In a little over 25 years the number of non-Spaniards known to be living here has tripled, from under 30,000 in 1970 to almost 95,000 in 1998. This is the official figure, and the true number of unregistered foreigners could be three or four times that. The city's face is becoming ethnically mixed, even though immigrants still make up barely two per cent of Madrid's population.

More affluent foreigners – Americans, Germans, Japanese – come here, of course, for a whole host of reasons, and from all over the world. Of economic migrants, the largest single group are Moroccans, followed by South Americans in general, people from the Dominican Republic, Filipinos and Poles. Madrid's most ethnically mixed neighbourhood is Lavapiés, where cheap, sometimes poor-quality housing, plus a tradition of attracting squatters and foreigners, have helped make the area home to West Africans and Chinese as well as Maghrebis and Dominicans.

Faced with ever-stronger walls around the core of fortress Europe, many people from North and West Africa fleeing poverty and war are prepared to try the hazardous crossing to Spain across the Straits of Gibraltar in rickety fishing boats, hoping then to disappear inside the country. For most of the Poles who make it here on tourist visas, Spain is seen as just a stopover – maybe a long one – on the way to Canada or the USA. They have little visible impact on the city, working mainly in construction or delivering butane gas door-to-door. Growing numbers of Romanians and Albanians are now filtering into Madrid from Italy, and can be found selling any of the several *Big Issue*-style magazines for the homeless that have sprung up.

Most Moroccans work in construction, but many West Africans eke out a living selling contraband tobacco on the streets. With local unemployment high, many African and South American women are pushed into prostitution, lining the avenues of the Casa de Campo at night, or working the streets off Gran Vía. Exaggerated publicity given to arrests of foreigners for drug dealing and mugging have exacerbated tension among a never-especially-tolerant Madrileño population, and police attitudes towards Arabs and Africans in particular are often openly racist. Black and brown readers should be aware that, if you don't look touristy enough, you can find yourself subjected to spot identity checks on the streets.

A place where people come and go, talking of Raúl and Rivaldo, the **Puerta Del Sol**.

Enormous windows giving on to the Calle Alcalá allow passers-by a look into one of Madrid's most stunning clubs, built in 1919-26 by Antonio Palacios. Fortunately, entry nowadays isn't restricted to members, provided you pay the very modest fee. As well as a beautifully airy main floor café, with a gracious pavement terrace, the Círculo offers a plethora of classes, exhibitions, lectures and concerts, plus an annual Carnival Ball. There is also a cosy, dark library. *See also chapters* **Cafés & Bars**, **Art Galleries** *and* **Music: Classical & Opera**.

Plaza de España

Metro Plaza de España/bus all routes to Plaza de España.
Map D5
This expanse at the end of the Gran Vía could be called the Franco regime's very own plaza, as it was mainly laid out in the 1940s and is flanked by two classic buildings of the type sponsored by the regime when out to impress, the '50s-modern Torre Madrid (1957) and the humungous mass of the Edificio España of 1948-53. The three statues in the middle – of Cervantes, Don Quixote and Sancho Panza – are by Teodoro

Anasagasti and Mateo Inurria, from 1928. The square around them is so large it can be a relaxing place to sit.

Real Monasterio de las Descalzas Reales

Plaza de las Descalzas 3 (91 542 00 59).
Metro Callao, Sol/bus all routes to Puerta del Sol.
Open 10.30am-12.45pm, 4-5.45pm, Tue-Thur, Sat; 10.30am-12.45pm Fri; 11am-1.45pm Sun, holidays.
Admission 650ptas; 250ptas students, under-16s, over-65s. *Wed only* free for EU citizens. **Map D7**
This atypical monastery was first built as a palace for Alonso Gutiérrez, treasurer of Charles V, and made into a convent by Charles' daughter Joanna of Austria when she herself became a nun. Rebuilt in 1556-64 by Antonio Sillero and Juan Bautista de Toledo, it is the most complete sixteenth-century building in Madrid. Behind its austere façade the interior is lavishly decorated, with a painted staircase, tapestries and a remarkable, long-forgotten collection of art. For further details, *see chapter* **Museums**.

Madrid's great white way

Fourteen streets disappeared forever when the Gran Vía was scythed out of the urban tangle in 1910 so that motor traffic could reach Cibeles from Calle Princesa. Intended to be a broad modern avenue, it got grander still when World War I made neutral Madrid a clearing house for international money. With the economy booming, developers and architects set out to embrace modernity as hard as they could, and to show that, if you wanted something impressive, they could provide it. In following decades, each 'generation' sought to keep up with the times and add their own stamp. The result is unique, and a walk up the Gran Vía reveals a fascinating collection of twentieth-century architectural eccentricities.

Spanish urban reformers had often compared Madrid unfavourably to Paris, and as the first address on the Gran Vía they got an entire Parisian building, the **Edificio Metrópolis**, designed by Jules and Raymond Février in 1905. It is offset by the stacked cupolas of the **Grassy** building (the one with the Piaget sign).

As you move away from Alcalá the buildings become taller, and grander. When the **Telefónica** building by the Gran Vía Metro stop went up in 1929 everyone was thrilled by how modern (ie un-

Spanish) it then seemed. At 81m (265ft) tall, it was nothing if not conspicuous, and as Madrid's first skyscraper it had a huge impact. It was designed by Ignacio de Cárdenas, with the help of a New York engineer called Louis Weeks.

The section of the street from Callao to the Plaza de España was completed under the Republic. On the corner of Calle Jacometrezo is Madrid's best art deco building, the 1932 **Edificio Carrión**, better known simply as the **Capitol**. Designed by Luis Martínez Feduchi and Vicente Eced, it is a classic of the style. The same section is also full of the Gran Vía's lavish 1920s movie palaces with their spectacular signs.

The last part of the Gran Vía is the work of the Franco era, when the Telefónica was finally upstaged by the **Edificio España** in the Plaza de España, from 1948-53. A baroque skyscraper, with all sorts of pseudo-Habsburg details, it sums up the contradictions of the regime – obsessed with 'eternal values', but desirous to show the world that it, too, could build a skyscraper as big as anyone's. It was designed by the brothers José María and Joaquín Otamendi, the latter of whom had worked with Antonio Palacios on the equally bizarre **Palacio de Comunicaciones**.

*What the **Plaza Santa Ana** is for. See page 59.*

Real Monasterio de la Encarnación

Plaza de La Encarnación 1 (91 547 05 10). Metro Opera, Santo Domingo/bus 25, 33, 39, 148. **Open** 10.30am-12.45pm, 4-5.45pm, Wed, Sat; 11am-1.45pm Sun, public holidays. **Admission** 425ptas; 225ptas students, under-16s, over-65s. *Wed only* free for EU citizens. **Map C6**

This understated monastery was built in 1611-16 for Margaret of Austria, wife of Philip III. Initially designed by Juan Gómez de Mora, it was damaged by fire in 1734, and rebuilt in a classical-baroque style in the 1760s by Ventura Rodríguez. It was opened to the public in the 1960s, but still houses a community of nuns, and is famous for its extraordinary relics room. For more details, *see chapter* **Museums**.

Huertas & Santa Ana

Spain has the greatest number of bars and restaurants per capita in the world, and you can get the impression that all of the 17,000-plus that there are in Madrid are crowded into the wedge-shaped swathe of streets between Alcalá and Calle Atocha. Oddly enough, this clearly delimited area has an identity problem, for the authorities can never agree on a name, but if anyone suggests a pub-crawl down Huertas, or a cooling jar in Santa Ana, it will always bring you – and about 15,000 others on any weekend – to the right place.

This was once the haunt of Madrid's Golden Age literary set, which explains the district's rather fussy alternative name, the *barrio de las letras* ('the district of letters'). Here were the theatres that provided them with a living, along with a fair few whorehouses and low dives. It still is Madrid's most distinctive theatre district. Close by but not too close lived the nobles who just might toss a couple

of ducats your way if you buttered them up in a sonnet. Otherwise there were feuds, libellous exchanges and duels to fall back on.

Lope de Vega's half-timbered house, the **Casa-Museo Lope de Vega** (*see chapter* **Museums**), with its sparse original furnishings and tiny garden, is on the street named after his bitter enemy, Cervantes. The author of *Don Quixote* lived around the corner on Calle León, but was probably buried in the Trinitarian convent on Calle Lope de Vega. Which seems deliberately confusing.

A reverential nod is in order to Madrid's **Ateneo** on Calle del Prado, the cultural institution that has been a major centre of discussion and thought at many times in its history, most notably in the years running up to the Republic of 1931. It has hosted heated *tertulias* lasting from three in the afternoon till early morning, in which ideas and polemics flew likes sparks from a forge. Today its strong point is its library, and it also has a good-value cafeteria (*see chapter* **Directory**).

In the old days, Ateneo members could find nearby any number of cafés with a suitably literary atmosphere. Nowadays the area is mostly turned over to bars and clubs. There are still a few old-style cafés, though, notably the genteel **Salón del Prado** (for all bars, *see chapters* **Tapas, Cafés & Bars** *and* **Nightlife**).

To the south, the area is bounded by the splendidly seedy Calle Atocha, with cheap *pensiones* and some gargantuan sex emporia. It is also home to the **Teatro Monumental** concert hall (*see chapter* **Music: Classical & Opera**) and to some

The Retiro

The Retiro is a jewel among parks. Covering nearly 122 hectares (300 acres), the gardens date from the 1630s, when they were laid out as part of the Buen Retiro palace of Philip IV, most of which was destroyed in the Napoleonic Wars (*see chapter* **History**). Charles III first opened sections of the gardens to the public in 1767, but it was only after the fall of Isabel II in 1868 that they became entirely free to the citizens of Madrid. After it became a park the Retiro acquired most of its many statues, particularly the giant 1902 monument to King Alfonso XII that presides over the lake.

Since becoming open to all, the Retiro has established a very special place in the hearts and habits of the people of Madrid. A Sunday morning stroll, especially before lunch, reveals just how much use is made of it. You will see multigenerational families watching puppet shows, dog owners and their hounds, children playing on climbing frames, vendors hawking everything from traditional wafers (*barquillos*) to etchings, palm and tarot readers, buskers from around the world, couples on the lake in hired boats, kids playing football, elderly men in leisurely games of *petanca* (boules), cyclists, runners and a good many bench-sitters who want nothing more than to read the paper. During the week it's much emptier, and it's easier to take a look at some of its 15,000 trees, the rose garden or the exhibition spaces. Inside the park you can always forget the city beyond the gates.

The Retiro also contains several interesting buildings. At the south end of the park is the **Observatorio Astronómico**, another of Charles III's scientific institutions, completed after his death in 1790. Beautifully proportioned, it is the finest neo-classical building in Madrid, designed by Juan de Villanueva. It still contains a working telescope, which can only be seen by prior request. One room is also open to the public. Also an important part of the Retiro are its fine exhibition spaces, the **Palacio de Cristal**, the **Palacio de Velázquez** and the **Casa de Vacas**. Built in the last century, they were all extensively renovated during the 1980s (*see chapter* **Art Galleries**).

The greatest curiosity of the park, though, is Madrid's monument to the Devil, Lucifer himself, in the moment of his fall from heaven. The statue, on the avenue south of the Palacio de Cristal and known as the **Angel Caído** ('Fallen Angel'), is unique, and featured in the film *El día de la bestia*, when the Devil appears in Madrid on New Year's Eve 1999.

Observatorio Astronómico
C/Alfonso XII 3 (91 527 01 07). Metro Atocha/bus all routes to Atocha. **Open** 9am-2pm Mon-Fri. **Map I9/10**

Parque del Retiro
Main entrance *Plaza de la Independencia (Puerta de Alcalá). Metro Retiro, Ibiza, Atocha/bus all routes to Retiro.* **Open** *Oct-Apr* 6.30am-10.30pm, *May-Sept* 6.30am-11pm, daily. **Map I/J7-9**

The Casa de Campo

Madrid is often promoted as the European capital with most parkland within its central area. Yet, aside from the Retiro, the first-time visitor is more likely to be struck by the absence of parks in the city centre. What they will have overlooked is the Casa de Campo, a sprawling 1,820-hectare (4,500-acre) woodland on the other, western side of the River Manzanares.

Once a royal hunting estate, the Casa de Campo was only opened to the public under the Republic in 1931, and its 'invasion' by the hoi polloi on 1 May that year (which was declared a holiday for the first time) was fondly remembered as symbolic of the new regime. Later, though, it became a key site for Franco's forces in the Civil War battle for Madrid, its valuable high ground being used to

shell the city centre and the university. Remains of trenches still exist.

Today, the Casa is home to the **Parque de Atracciones** funfair and the **Zoo** (*see chapter* **Children**), as well as, near Lago Metro, swimming pools and tennis courts (*see chapter* **Sport & Fitness**) and a lake ringed by cafés. There is also a pleasant **youth hostel** (*see chapter* **Accommodation**). Recently, this area has regained a lot of the attractiveness that it had lost in previous years. In 1997-8 all the restaurants around the lake were rebuilt, and although a bit more expensive than they used to be they still offer a splendid place for an outdoor lunch. The boating lake has been cleaned up and repaired, and it's again possible to hire row boats. Cyclists should

A delicious pleasure in a hot Madrid summer, the Casa's great lake.

heaving nightspots – **Angels** at no.38 and **Kapital** at no.125 (*see chapter* **Nightlife**).

Very different is the Carrera de San Jerónimo, which borders the north of the district. Part of the 'Ceremonial Route' of the Habsburg and Bourbon monarchs (*see chapter* **History**), it is one of the centres of official Madrid today. On one side is the **Congreso de los Diputados**, Spain's Parliament building, guarded by its regal bronze lions, while opposite is the **Hotel Palace**, to which politicians can pop to relax (*see chapter* **Accommodation**).

Further up the hill is **Lhardy**, the classic Franco-Spanish restaurant founded in 1839 (*see chapters* **Restaurants** *and* **Tapas**). Of its *castizo* charms, classy clientele and *cocido madrileño* much has been written; one need only note that a cup of consommé from its silver samovar makes an excellent restorative if the prices on the menu give you a coronary. North of San Jerónimo, behind the Congreso, is the grandish 1856 **Teatro de la Zarzuela**, the city's most characterfully distinguished music theatre.

note that nearly all the park's roads are closed to cars on Sundays until 2pm.

Once you stray away from the criss-crossing roads, much of the park is surprisingly wild, and it's possible to have a real country walk through its woods and gullies. A favourite way to visit is via the **Teleférico** cable car from Parque del Oeste (*see page 62*) which runs over the trees almost to the middle of the Casa, where there are viewpoints, an (admittedly undistinguished) bar-restaurant and picnic spots.

Couples seeking seclusion favour the Casa de Campo, by day and night, and the area by the Teleférico has been a gay cruising spot, although police have been cracking down on men hanging around there. In contrast, Madrid's *Partido Popular* city authorities seem near-set on turning the roads from Lago Metro to the Zoo, at night, into a semi-official prostitution zone, and some councillors have openly suggested 'cleansing' the city-centre of prostitutes and sending them all to the Casa to meet kerb-crawling punters – an idea opposed by prostitutes and all the other citizens who use the park.

The park also faces other pressures. As more car-owning citizens move to Madrid's western suburbs, more drivers use the Casa's roads as a rush-hour way into town. One suggestion is to close off all the park roads except the main two that run east-west into the city. Environmentalists, however, say it is precisely these through routes that are the problem, not the small, dead-end roads frequented only by picnickers, runners and cyclists using the park for its true purpose.

Casa de Campo

Metro Lago, Batán/bus 33, 41, 75/Teleférico.
Four special bus routes (Z-1 to Z-4) also run from the city centre to the Zoo on Saturdays, Sundays and public holidays.

To the south of Carrera de San Jerónimo several streets run back towards Huertas proper. On Calle Echegaray is **Los Gabrieles**, a drinking establishment sheathed in possibly the world's most photographed wall-to-wall tiles. An alternative with almost as good tiles is **Viva Madrid**, around the corner (*see chapter* **Cafés & Bars**).

Last but in no way least is the core of the district, **Plaza Santa Ana**. Like Plaza de Oriente, this popular square was bequeathed to Madrid by poor unappreciated Joseph Bonaparte, who tore down one more superfluous convent to do so. It's

a little quieter now than in the 1980s, since the conservative city administration has closed down the crafts market that ten years ago brought in the crowds every Saturday. Even so, the plaza is still a place where one can well hang out for an entire afternoon or three.

Here is the once-elegant **Hotel Reina Victoria**, the traditional bullfighters' hangout, and several fine bars such as **Cervecería La Moderna** (*see chapter* **Tapas**) and the **Cervecería Alemana** (*see chapter* **Cafés & Bars**), perhaps the best-known Hemingway haunt in Madrid. In the adjoining Plaza del Angel is **Café Central**, Madrid's best jazz club (*see chapter* **Music: Rock, Roots & Jazz**). On the eastern side of the plaza is the distinguished **Teatro Español**, on a site that has been a theatre continuously since 1583, when the Corral del Principe first opened its doors to the *Mosqueteros* (groundlings), whose reactions were so violent that they could force terrified playwrights to change plots in mid-play.

Congreso de los Diputados (Las Cortes)

Plaza de las Cortes (91 390 67 50). Metro Sevilla, Banco de España/bus 9, 14, 27, 37, 45. **Open** *guided tours only 10am-1pm Sat. Closed Aug & public holidays.* **Map G7**
Spain's *Cortes*, the Parliament, was built in 1843-50 by Narciso Pascual y Colomer on the site of a recently demolished monastery – something that has led to no end of problems, as the plot is too cramped to accommodate all the legislators' ancillary offices. A classical portico gives it a suitably dignified air, but the building is best distinguished by the handsome 1860 bronze lions that guard the entrance. Tourists are welcome on the very popular free Saturday guided tours. Given demand, it's best to phone ahead; groups of more than 15 can also book to visit on weekdays.

La Latina, Rastro, Lavapiés

South of Sol and the Plaza Mayor, between San Francisco el Grande and Atocha, the streets slope sharply downhill towards the *rondas* of Atocha, Valencia and Toledo. The districts within this area – commonly divided up by locals into La Latina, Rastro, Lavapiés and Embajadores – are the arch-repositories of Madrid's traditional *castizo* identity (*see chapter* **Madrid by Season**).

They used to be known as the *barrios bajos*, in the double sense of low-lying and full of low life – the closer to the river, the shabbier the surroundings. In imperial Madrid, most of the food brought to the city came in through the **Puerta de Toledo**, and many of the tasks that the upper classes wanted neither to see or smell, such as slaughtering and tanning, were concentrated here. Consequently, these districts became home to Madrid's first native working class. In the eighteenth century the *Majos* and *Majas* from these streets were admired by the intelligentsia for their caustic wit (*see chapter* **History**), and the tradition of sarcastic, uppity humour continues today.

La Latina takes its name from the nickname of Beatriz Galindo, teacher of Latin and confidante

Green acres

Madrileños are very attached to their parks, many of which were once royal gardens. The avenues of the Retiro and the great expanse of the Casa de Campo make up Madrid's most famous open spaces, but there are many more spread around the city. In addition, recent city authorities have created several fine new parks and open areas.

Campo del Moro

Paseo Virgen del Puerto (91 542 00 59).
Metro Príncipe Pío/bus 25, 33, 39, 46, 75, 138, C.
Open *Oct-Mar* 10am-6pm Mon-Sat; 9am-6pm Sun, public holidays; *Apr-Sept* 10am-7pm Mon-Sat; 9am-8pm Sun, public holidays. **Map B7**
Before or after a visit to the Palacio Real it's worth wandering round the pleasant formal garden below it, towards the river. It has two fine monumental fountains. The first, nearer the palace, is **Los Tritones**, originally made in 1657 for the palace in Aranjuez (*see p230*). The second, **Las Conchas**, is eighteenth-century and was designed by the architect Ventura Rodríguez. Both were installed here in the 1890s.

Capricho de la Alameda de Osuna

Paseo de la Alameda de Osuna.
Metro Canillejas, Campo de Naciones/bus 101, 105.
Open *Oct-Mar* 9am-6.30pm, *Apr-Sept* 9am-9pm, Sat, Sun, public holidays.
One of Madrid's most unusual parks, in a very unusual location, north of the Barcelona road between the Feria trade fair area, Parque Juan Carlos I and the airport. It's a formal French-style garden, designed by Marie Antoinette's gardener J-B Mulot for the Duchess of Osuna, a great hostess and friend of Goya, in the 1790s. Legends abound about the revels held there in the duchess's day; two of Goya's early macabre 'black paintings', the *Witches' Sabbath* and the *Witchcraft Scene* (both now in the **Museo Lázaro Galdiano**), were commissioned for her house here (long demolished). The gardens are wonderfully cool and peaceful, a romantic fantasy with an artificial lake with islands in the middle. In the early years of this century they fell into decay, while around them spread the semi-industrial sprawl between Madrid and the airport, until restoration work began in 1974. Nearby there is also a campsite (*see chapter* **Accommodation**).

Jardines de las Vistillas

C/Beatriz Galindo.
Metro La Latina/bus 3, 31, 50, 65, 148. **Map B/C8**
The biggest reason to head for these gardens, just south of the Palacio Real along Calle Bailén, is the view. Easily seen from this high open spot are the Almudena, the whole of the Casa de Campo and the peaks of the Guadarrama.

There's also a peaceful terrace bar, and the park is often used for neighbourhood events, concerts and dances during fiestas and in summer (*see chapters* **Madrid by Season** *and* **Cafés & Bars**).

Parque Juan Carlos I

Avda de Logroño & Avda de los Andes. Metro Campo de Naciones/bus 101, 105, 122.
This huge, state-of-the-art park, Madrid's newest green (and brown) space, lies between the airport and the **Feria de Madrid** trade fair centre. With time it should become one of Madrid's more attractive places, but so far it's been little used as it has taken a while for any trees to grow to provide necessary, user-friendly shade. That said, current draws include a series of different gardens within a circle of olive trees, an artificial river and other water features. *See also chapter* **Children**.

Parque del Oeste

Metro Moncloa, Argüelles, Príncipe Pío/bus 21, 46, 74, 82, 133. **Map A-C2-4**
A special method to reach this park is the **Teleférico** from the Casa de Campo (*see p62*). Once you've landed, it's easy to see why the park, designed by landscape gardener Cecilio Rodríguez in the 1900s, is considered one of the city's most attractive spaces. Particularly beautiful is **La Rosaleda**, the rose garden, magnificent in spring. The park formed part of the front line during the Civil War, and was virtually destroyed. Afterwards it was completely relaid, but you can still find some bunkers and gun emplacements. The Montaña del Príncipe Pío, at the south end of the park, is one of the highest points in Madrid, with wonderful views of the Palacio Real and the Casa de Campo. This was the site of the Montaña barracks, the Nationalists' main stronghold in Madrid at the start of the Civil War (*see chapter* **History**). It was later demolished, and the hill incorporated into the park. Bizarrely, it is now home to the **Templo de Debod**, a genuine Egyptian temple from the fourth century BC presented to Spain by the government of Egypt after it had been removed from its original site to make way for the Aswan Dam. Along the east side of the park is Paseo del Pintor Rosales, a popular place for outdoor cafés (*see chapter* **Cafés & Bars**); below the Teleférico stop a path leads to the river and the **Ermita de San Antonio de la Florida** with its Goya frescoes (*see p49*). The fountain below the Teleférico used to preside over the roundabout at Príncipe Pío station, but was moved into the park in 1994. In its place next to the station there is now the **Puerta de San Vicente** – an entirely new but reasonably convincing reconstruction of the eighteenth-century gate that once stood on this side of the city. After dark the park roads around the fountain have, like the Casa de Campo, become an area for prostitution, with some of the city's most flamboyant transsexuals offering a late-night spectacle, particularly at weekends.

---

to Queen Isabella. At the end of the fifteenth century she paid for a hospital to be built on the square that bears her name. Its site is now occupied by the **Teatro La Latina**, stronghold of traditional Spanish entertainment. The district is relatively quiet except during its grand fiestas, around the time of **La Paloma** in August (*see chapter* **Madrid by Season**).

On the eastern edge of La Latina is the **Rastro**, Madrid's time-honoured flea market (*see chapter* **Shopping**). It runs down to the Ronda de Toledo from **Plaza Cascorro**, with its monument honouring a young soldier raised in a nearby orphanage who volunteered for a suicide mission in Cuba in the 1890s. A cultural phenomenon, the Rastro is also a district with a strong identity, moulded by the centuries in which it has acted as an emporium for goods of all kinds. To avoid the crowds, and the pickpockets, see it on Sundays: the wicker furniture dealers will still be open, and so will the junk shops and purveyors of fine antiques.

If, on the other hand, instead of trying to make your way through the Rastro you head from Plaza Cascorro slightly eastwards down Calle Embajadores, you will see a truly outstanding slice of old Madrid. Embajadores and the near-parallel Calle Mesón de Paredes offer two of Madrid's most rewarding strolls. At the top of the latter is the **Plaza Tirso de Molina**, the main crossroads between these *barrios bajos* and the city centre proper, with a statue of the Golden Age dramatist whose name it bears. The plaza also houses the **Teatro Nuevo Apolo** (*see chapter* **Theatre**), good old-style bars and a range of urban fauna: left-wing groups with propaganda stalls on Sundays, winos, people looking for discount stores and sometimes drug-pushers at other times.

Calle Mesón de Paredes has acquired a new touch in the last few years thanks to the multi-coloured prints worn by Africans who have settled there. This street and the parallel Calle Amparo are packed with cheap jewellery wholesalers, and on Mesón de Paredes you can call in at a nineteenth-century Madrileño *taberna* in full working order, the 1830 **Taberna de Antonio Sánchez** (*see chapter* **Cafés & Bars**), but also find shops selling tropical fruit, an Arab tea house and Halal butchers.

Also on Mesón de Paredes is **La Corrala**, the city's best surviving example of an 1880s courtyard tenement, garnished as tradition requires with freshly washed sheets and underwear billowing from the balconies. After the demolition of Madrid's monasteries in the middle of the last century many streets in these districts were rebuilt with these distinctive open, balconied tenements. *Corralas* always faced an inner patio, multiplying the noise and lack of privacy that have never bothered Spaniards, and soon became one of the characteristic features of neighbourhood life. This one, at the junction with Calle Tribulete and restored in the '80s, can seem so carefully fixed up it looks more like a pastiche than the real thing. Your doubts disappear, however, if you spot one of the residents in shocking pink polyester dressing-gown and curlers calling to her neighbours from her balcony. In summer the building is used to present a season of Madrileño *zarzuela* (*see chapter* **Music: Classical & Opera**).

Few *corralas* survive, but to a remarkable extent these districts with their narrow streets, small shops and workshops still convey the essence of a distinctive local way of life that has changed little since the last century. A somewhat later example, but enclosed on all sides and so not easily visible from the street, is at Calle Embajadores 60.

The **Plaza de Lavapiés** is believed to have been the centre of Madrid's medieval Jewish community, expelled like all others in her dominions by the very pious Queen Isabella in 1492. The area is currently under restoration, but is still pleasantly shabby, and is once again host to a non-Spanish immigrant population, bringing shops and restaurants with them (*see page 52*). Lavapiés is also home to a lot of *guiris* – young Northern Europeans and Americans – and is undergoing something of a general revival, with a newly fashionable status and many new bars. This is the city's fringe theatre district: the pioneering **Sala Olímpia** on the plaza is currently being comprehensively rebuilt, but semi-professional and fringe companies have turned several older buildings, some of them former stables, into new venues (*see chapter* **Theatre**). Nearby there is also the **Filmoteca**, in the old art nouveau Cine Doré (*see chapter* **Film**).

South-east from Lavapiés, just before you emerge on to Glorieta de Atocha, you arrive at the **Centro de Arte Reina Sofía**, the opening of which has led to the appearance of small private galleries nearby (*see chapter* **Art Galleries**). Close by, filling a big stretch of Calle Santa Isabel, is the seventeenth-century **Convento de Santa Isabel**, sponsored, like the Encarnación, by Margaret of Austria, wife of Philip III, and one of the largest religious houses in Madrid to escape the liberals' axe in the last century.

Puerta de Toledo

Glorieta de la Puerta de Toledo. Metro Puerta de Toledo/bus all routes to Puerta de Toledo. **Map C10**
Now slightly swallowed up in the traffic at the meeting point of the old city and the roads in from the south-west, this plain neo-classical gate was one of the monuments commissioned by Napoleon's brother Joseph in his brief span as King of Spain. After his departure it was quickly rejigged to honour the return of the delegates from the Cortes in Cádiz, and then King Fernando VII.

Malasaña & Chueca

By day, Malasaña, between Calles Fuencarral and San Bernardo, is a quiet *barrio* that offers an eyeful of nineteenth-century Madrid: grannies watering their geraniums on wrought-iron balconies, idiosyncratic corner shops. By night, this is the epicentre of Madrid's bar culture, above all for the grungy, student crowd. Peaceful coexistence is possible between old and young since a lot of the time they never actually meet.

In completely another era this area was also the centre of resistance to the French on 2 May 1808. The name of the district comes from a 17-year-old seamstress heroine, Manuela Malasaña, shot by the invaders for carrying concealed weapons (her scissors), or for carrying ammunition to the Spanish troops – there are various different versions of her exploits. The name of the *barrio*'s main square, **Plaza Dos de Mayo**, also recalls that day. Where the square is today was then the Monteleón artillery barracks, from where the humble artillery captains

Daoíz and Velarde galvanised the resistance of the people. The last remaining part of the barracks, a gate, stands with a monument to the two men in the middle of the square.

In the 1980s this plaza gained a tough reputation because of petty crime and hard drug use. Malasaña, though, is one area where renovation schemes have been most successful: new businesses have opened, pedestrian access improved and buildings spruced up in vivid colours. The Plaza Dos de Mayo itself can be covered on Saturday and Sunday mornings with cans, bottles and more malodorous evidence of the previous night's partying, but once this has been cleaned up children cavort in the new play area, while a complete cross-section of the city enjoy a drink at its many *terrazas* (*see chapter* **Cafés & Bars**), even though nothing is done about the unpleasantly aggressive pigeons.

The cross-streets between San Bernardo and Fuencarral abound with bars and restaurants, as well as indications – such as the broad-arched doorways for carriages – that the nineteenth-century well-to-do once lived here. One of the most rewarding streets is **Calle San Vicente Ferrer**, with its jewellery shops and a delightful 1920s tile display advertising the long-defunct pharmacy Laboratorios Juanse. Other old ceramic signs on the adjacent **Calle San Andrés** feature a little boy proudly signalling that his chamber pot is full, and a dramatic reclining vamp. **Calle de la Palma** with its second-hand shops and **Calle Divino Pastor** with a range of craft and jewellery shops are equally worth a stroll.

The atmosphere gets more mobile as you approach the streets near Fuencarral that lead to the Gran Via, such as **Corredera Baja de San Pablo** and its continuation, the **Corredera Alta**. This is an area of cheap restaurants, wholesale produce dealers in white aprons, shops selling nothing but light bulbs, and working-class people who have known each other all their lives. Recent additions are club-style fashion shops selling imported and second-hand clothes, plus tattooists and body-piercers, especially towards or on Calle Fuencarral. The brick church at the corner of Corredera Baja de San Pablo and Calle Ballesta was built by Felipe III to cater for his Portuguese subjects in Madrid. Later it was set aside for German Catholic émigrés, and is still known as **San Antonio de los Alemanes**. It is difficult to see the interior today, as the church is rarely open.

On the eastern side of Malasaña in Calle Fuencarral is the **Museo Municipal**, formerly the eighteenth-century hospice, with an entrance by Pedro de Ribera done with great baroque brio (*see chapter* **Museums**). Just to the north, Fuencarral runs into the Glorieta de Bilbao, where you will find one of Madrid's very best cafés, the **Café Comercial** (*see chapter* **Cafés & Bars**).

Vantage points

With its narrow streets, cramped pavements and traffic congestion, Madrid can be claustrophobic at times, and it's natural to want to get above the urban tangle and take a broader view on things. In the middle of a mountain plateau, Madrid is a surprisingly hilly city, but the only building open to visitors expressly offering a spectacular view is the **Faro de Madrid**, Madrid's modern 'Lighthouse' in Moncloa.

The **Hotel Emperador** has the one rooftop pool open to the public (*see chapters* **Accommodation** *and* **Sport & Fitness**), far above the hurley-burley of the Gran Via. Travellers on the **Teleférico** across the Casa de Campo enjoy splendid views of Madrid's skyline from the west. The best time to go is near sunset, when the Palacio Real and Almudena are bathed in an orange glow. There is also a great vantage point inside the Casa at **Monte Garabitas**, a half-hour walk north of the Teleférico, with a view of the whole city. For views in the opposite direction, away to the Guadarrama in the north, the café at **Las Vistillas** is unbeatable, and wonderfully relaxing (*see chapter* **Cafés & Bars**).

Faro de Madrid

Avda de los Reyes Católicos (91 544 81 04).
Metro Moncloa/bus 16, 46, 61, 82, 83, 132, 133, C. **Open** *mid-Sept-May* 10.30am-2pm, 5.30-7.15pm, *June-mid-Sept* 11am-1.45pm, 5.30-8.45pm, Tue-Sun. **Admission** 200ptas; 100ptas 3-10s, over-65s. **Map B1**
If heights aren't a problem, the best way to get an overview of Madrid and its surroundings is from this tower, built for Spain's wonder year of 1992. It's even exactly 92m (302ft) high. Squeeze into the 12-person glass lift and before you know it you're atop the city with nearly a 360° view.

Teleférico de Madrid

Paseo del Pintor Rosales (91 541 74 50).
Metro Argüelles/bus 21, 74 to Casa de Campo.
Metro Lago/bus 33. **Open** *Oct-Mar* noon-dusk Sat, Sun, public holidays. *Apr-Sept* 11am-dusk daily. **Tickets** 515ptas return; 360ptas one-way; free under-3s. **Map B3**
If you have only ten minutes and 42 seconds to see Madrid, consider a ride in these six-person cable cars that connect the Casa de Campo and Parque del Oeste. The trip takes you right over the Casa de Campo, with great views of the Palacio Real, the Manzanares and the city skyline. It can carry 1,200 passengers each hour, so don't panic if there's a queue. Closing times vary with the sunset; also, there's often a break in service around 2-4pm, when, if you've got out to the Casa, you're expected to stay for lunch. *See also pp58-9, 60.*

Madrid may not seem to need a lighthouse, but it has one: the **Faro de Madrid**.

Big money

Long before Britain discovered lotteries, Spaniards were fanatical ticket-buyers. The best places to buy tickets for all the different national lotteries are the official designated outlets, *Administraciones de Lotería*, found on most shopping streets, and particularly around **Puerta del Sol**. You can also buy from street vendors, but if so use only those who have a clearly shown licence number. Lottery results can always be found in local papers, and are announced on TV. So, try your hand at the following – there are several more variations once you've got your toes wet:

Lotería Nacional The monthly national draw, with tickets 500ptas a pop; prizes can be 300 million pesetas. There are also several weekly draws.

Christmas Lottery (*El Gordo*/'The Fat One') The real biggie, with one of the largest payouts in the world. Tickets go on sale in September; the cheapest is a *décimo*, or tenth part, currently at 3,500ptas. Many people club together to buy tickets, and bars and shops often buy one for their regulars. The announcement of the winner, two days before Christmas, brings the country to a standstill.

ONCE Lottery Gambling in Spain does not only benefit the State. ONCE, the powerful charity that represents the blind and other disabled groups, is primarily lottery-funded, and sells 100ptas tickets through its phone box-like cabins, and the street vendors whose cries are another characteristic feature of Spanish life. Draws are made daily, and winning numbers announced on TV (Tele 5, 9.25pm) or in the next day's papers. A percentage of the winnings go to the seller, so you might feel more inclined to give a street vendor your money.

Chueca, the *barrio* between Fuencarral and Recoletos, has seen better days and worse. On the eighteenth-century Calle Hortaleza was the site of the *Recogida*, a refuge for 'public sinners' where women could be confined for soliciting on the street, or merely on the say-so of a male family member. Release was only possible through marriage or a lifetime tour of duty in a convent.

More recently, Chueca too had its reputation a few years ago as a junkie's haven, particularly the **Plaza de Chueca** itself. Its revival has been due in great part to the fact that is has been colonised by the gay community, and is now Madrid's gay village. With the growing crossover fashionable status of some gay venues among the hip non-gay crowd, Chueca is now booming, and the only limitation on the scene could be whether the plaza can actually hold any more people on some nights. As well as the gay scene, Chueca also has clubs such as **Torito**, and traditional bars and restaurants like the quaint *taberna* of **Angel Sierra** (*see chapters* **Cafés & Bars, Nightlife** *and* **Gay & Lesbian Madrid**).

Towards Recoletos, Chueca becomes more commercial and more upmarket. **Calle Barquillo** is full of electrical shops, while **Calle Almirante** and its cross-street **Conde de Xiquena** are an important fashion shopping zone. Off Almirante in Calle Tamayo y Baus is one of Madrid's main theatres, the **Teatro María Guerrero**, where Antonio Banderas made his first major stage appearance back in 1984 (*see chapter* **Theatre**).

The giant **Palacio de Justicia** is to the north on Calle Bárbara de Braganza. It was formerly the Convento de las Salesas, built in 1750-8 under the patronage of Queen Bárbara, wife of Fernando VI. It has housed law courts since 1870. Its refined classical baroque contrasts nicely with the frenzied art nouveau of the **Palacio Longoria**, a few streets away.

South toward Calle Alcalá is the **Plaza del Rey**, with the venerable 1580s **Casa de las Siete Chimeneas**, designed by Juan de Herrera, architect of El Escorial. Spain's Ministry of Culture now stands on the site of the Circo Price, a covered coliseum named after its expatriate founder impresario Thomas Price. As well as a permanent three-ring circus, it hosted *zarzuelas* from 1876 until it was torn down in 1969.

Sociedad General de Autores (Palacio Longoria)

C/Fernando VI 6 (91 349 95 14). Metro Alonso Martínez/bus 3, 37, 40, 149. **Map G4**
Given the extraordinary output of Catalan Modernist architects such as Gaudí in Barcelona at the beginning of the twentieth century, it is remarkable, to non-Spaniards at least, that there is not a single example of their work in Madrid. The only thing at all like it is this unusual building in Chueca, designed by José Grasés Riera in 1902 as a residence for banker Javier González Longoria. The façade looks like it was formed out of wet sand, moulded by an expert in giant cake decoration. If a building could be considered voluptuous, this would be it. It was once thought Catalan architecture had influenced Grasés, but Héctor Guimard and French art nouveau seem to have been a more direct source of inspiration. It is now owned by the Spanish writers' and artists' association. Until recently it kept its original character, but 1990s renovation has included some unattractive changes, particularly the green paint used for trim. Still, this is a treasure.

Salamanca & the Retiro

In the mid-nineteenth century, as it became evident that Spanish cities needed to expand beyond their old walls, attempts were made to ensure that this happened in an orderly way. Madrid and Barcelona had plans approved for *Ensanches* ('Extensions'; *see chapter* **History**). Carlos María de Castro's 1860 plan for Madrid envisaged the expansion of the city north and east in a regular grid pattern, with restrictions on building height and public open spaces at regular intervals and within each block, to ensure a healthy, harmonious urban landscape.

The problem was, however, that for a good while few of Madrid's middle classes seemed to have the money or the motivation to invest in such a scheme, and preferred to stay within the cramped, noisy old city. That Madrid's *Ensanche* got off the ground at all was due to a banker, politician and speculator notorious for his dubious business practices, the Marqués de Salamanca.

The marquis had previously built his own vast residence, now the **Banco Hipotecario**, on Paseo de Recoletos in 1846-50. It had the first flush toilets in Madrid, an amenity he later offered to residents in his new housing development. He spent one of several fortunes he made and lost in his lifetime on building a first line of rectangular blocks in the *Ensanche*, along the Calle Serrano. However, his ambitions and extravagance overstretched his resources, the apartments proved expensive for local buyers, and he went terminally bankrupt in 1867. Nevertheless, it is to the rogue Marqués, and not to the old Castilian university town, that Madrid's smartest *barrio* owes its name.

It was only after the Restoration of 1874 that Madrid's wealthy really began to appreciate the potential benefits of wider streets and residences with more class than the city's musty old neighbourhoods could supply. Once the idea caught on, however, the exodus proceeded apace, and the core of Salamanca was built up by 1900.

The wealthiest families of all built individual palaces along the lower stretch of the Castellana, in a wild variety of styles – French imperial, Italian Renaissance, neo-*mudéjar*. Only a handful of these extravagances remain – the Palacio de Linares, now the **Casa de América**, is perhaps the best preserved on the Castellana itself. Another good example is the palace of the Marqueses de Aboage at Calle Juan Bravo 79, now the **Italian Embassy**. Those who could not quite afford their own mansion moved into giant apartments in the streets behind. The *Barrio de Salamanca* has been the centre of conservative, affluent Madrid ever since.

Streets yield top designers (especially Calles Jorge Juan, Ortega y Gasset, Goya and segments of Serrano), art galleries and dealers in French wines, English silver or superior leather goods (*see chapter* **Shopping**). Salamanca also has its own social scene, based around Calle Juan Bravo, with shiny, smart, yuppie-ish bars and discos full of shiny, well-bred young folk discussing holidays. Towards the eastern end of Calle Goya there is a more affordable shopping area, as well as the **Palacio de Deportes**, venue for league basketball games (*see chapter* **Sport & Fitness**).

Art buffs are advised to head for the marble tower with attached sculpture garden at Calle Castelló 77, base for the **Fundación Juan March**'s first-rate collection of modern art. It also underwrites concerts of contemporary music and welcomes itinerant exhibitions (*see chapters* **Art Galleries** *and* **Music: Classical & Opera**). On and around Calle Claudio Coello, parallel to Calle Serrano, there is an abundance of private art galleries, and at the northern end of Serrano is the wonderfully eclectic **Museo Lázaro Galdiano**.

Salamanca abuts on to Madrid's overburdened lung, the **Retiro** park, originally part of a palace built by the Conde Duque de Olivares for Philip IV

to impress the world (*see chapter* **History**). The districts around and south of the Retiro are in some ways similar to Salamanca, but less emphatically affluent and more mixed, with more of a *barrio* feel.

Sights near the park include the imposing **Puerta de Alcalá**, by the north-west entrance in the middle of the traffic-surrounded Plaza de la Independencia, the Prado and the other museums nearby (*see chapter* **Museums**), and the church of **San Jerónimo el Real**. Further north-east is the city's glorious neo-*mudéjar* bullring, **Las Ventas**.

Just south-west of the park, right on Glorieta de Atocha, is one of the area's largest but lesser-known sights. One cannot but marvel at the magnificent misplaced grandeur of the **Ministry of Agriculture**, built in the 1880s by Ricardo Velázquez, the same architect who designed the delicate exhibition halls inside the Retiro itself. Further south-east along Paseo Reina Cristina is the dilapidated **Real Fábrica de Tapices** at Calle Fuentarrabia 2 (91 551 34 00), the tapestry factory for which Goya did several designs. This is no abandoned museum, but a faded yet still-going concern where dyeing and weaving are done as they were when it was founded in 1721. Skilled fingers are mostly kept busy maintaining the carpets of the Hotel Ritz, but you can also have work made to order yourself, for a very high price.

Puerta de Alcalá

Plaza de la Independencia. Metro Retiro/bus all routes to Plaza de la Independencia. **Map H/I6**
A short distance along Calle Alcalá from Cibeles, in the middle of another hectic traffic junction, stands this monumental neo-classical gate built for Charles III by his favourite Italian architect Francesco Sabatini to provide a grand entrance to the city. It was built in 1769-78, using granite and stone from nearby Colmenar. Like Cibeles, it is often used as a symbol of Madrid. Possible to miss in the daytime traffic, it is unavoidably impressive when floodlit at night.

Plaza de Toros de Las Ventas

C/Alcalá 237 (91 356 22 00).
Metro Ventas/bus 21, 53, 74, 146.
More than 22,000 spectators can catch a bullfight in this, Spain's largest arena, which was completed in 1929. Like most early twentieth-century bullrings it is in neo-*mudéjar* style, with much use of ceramic tiles in a design that could almost be called playful. Around it there is ample open space to accommodate the crowds and food vendors, so it's easy to get a good look at the exterior. It's not necessary to go to a *corrida* to see the ring from within, too, for when the bulls are back on the ranch concerts are held here (*see chapter* **Madrid by Season**), and alongside the ring there is the **Museo Taurino**. The bullfight season itself runs from May to October. *See also chapter* **Bullfighting**.

San Jerónimo el Real

C/Moreto 4 (91 420 30 78). Metro Banco de España, Atocha/bus 9, 10, 14, 19, 27, 34, 37, 45.
Open *Oct-June* 9am-1.30pm, 5.30-8pm, *July-Sept* 9am-1.30pm, 6-8pm, daily. **Map H8**
Founded in 1464 and then rebuilt for Queen Isabella in 1503, this church near the Retiro was particularly favoured by the Spanish monarchs, and even today is still used for state ceremonies. Most of the original building was destroyed in the Napoleonic Wars, however, and the present church is largely a reconstruction carried out between 1848 and 1883.

*Madrid's brave new business world, the **Feria de Madrid**. See page 68.*

North & west
Conde Duque, Moncloa, Argüelles

West of Malasaña lie the districts vaguely known as Argüelles and Moncloa, although it's not easy to distinguish where either begins and ends. In lay-out and feel, the streets between Calle San Bernardo and the Centro Conde Duque – an area sometimes called *Universidad*, although the university hasn't been there since the 1930s – are more similar to neighbouring Malasaña, with the same mix of old *tabernas*, rock bars, cafés and restaurants, than to the grid-pattern streets of Argüelles and Moncloa proper. These run up to the modern university area, and so form the main centre of student Madrid, with many shared flats, and plenty of bars and discos.

Not studenty at all is the **Palacio de Liria** on Calle Princesa, completed in 1783 and very much the private property of the Duchess of Alba, head of the only one of Spain's great aristocratic families to have held on to the greater part of their wealth through all the financial ups and downs of the last 150 years. Access to its hidden artistic treasures is only possible by written request (the waiting list is over a year long). Alongside it is the **Centro Cultural Conde Duque**, Pedro de Ribera's giant barracks for King Philip V's guard, built between 1717 and 1754, and wonderfully renovated by the Tierno Galván city administration in the '80s as a dynamic cultural centre (*see chapters* **Madrid by Season** *and* **Art Galleries**).

At the end of Calle Princesa, unmissable on the corner of the Paseo Moret, is one of the largest and most significant creations of the Fascist-kitsch architecture of the Franco regime, the **Ministerio del Aire**, the Air Ministry. In the first years of the regime Spanish artists were enjoined to return to eternal values, and take the Golden Age as a model in everything. The Ministry's architect Luis Gutiérrez Soto did just that, and built a brand-new Castilian-baroque (*see chapter* **Architecture**) building, an Escorial with electricity, between 1943 and 1957. Wags referred to it as the *Monasterio del Aire*. The regime had plans for other similarly retro-imperial constructions, but fortunately the state of the economy scotched them all.

Alongside the Ministry is Moncloa Metro station, and the departure point for many bus services to towns north and west of Madrid. Across the street rises the fake Roman triumphal arch Franco built himself as a prize for winning the Civil War, 20 years after its outbreak in 1956. More attractive is the **Faro de Madrid** observation tower (*see page 62*), a strange construction that looks like a visored helmet stuck atop a metal maypole.

Argüelles, properly speaking, is the grid of streets between Calle Princesa and Paseo del Pintor Rosales. The Paseo, above the **Parque del Oeste** (*see page 60*), is famous for its *terrazas*, open-air bars where all manner of folk can take the air and shoot the breeze all through the day and night.

Chamberí

Directly north of Malasaña is the *barrio* of Chamberí. This was one of the first working-class districts outside the walls to be built up and occupied in the second half of the nineteenth century. Consequently central Chamberí became one of the few areas outside the old city on the list of those generally considered to have genuine *castizo* character.

As befits a *barrio* with a proper identity, Chamberí has its own bar round, with rows of good (and relatively cheap) tapas bars around Calles Cardenal Cisneros and Hartzenbush (*see chapter* **Tapas**). There's also the pleasant, circular **Plaza de Olavide**, ringed with easygoing pavement cafés. On the north side of Chamberí, Madrid's water system, the **Canal de Isabel II**, occupies an ample tract of land. On Calle Santa Engracia, a neo-*mudéjar* water tower has been converted into a unique photography gallery, the **Sala del Canal de Isabel II** (*see chapter* **Art Galleries**).

Tetuán & the north

North of Chamberí are **Cuatro Caminos** and **Tetuán**, arranged along Calle Bravo Murillo, both modern, working areas. For the visitor the main point of interest is the local market, the **Mercado de Maravillas** at Calle Bravo Murillo 122, just north of Cuatro Caminos, the largest, liveliest and most colourful in the whole city. On Sunday mornings, too, a miniature 'rastro' gets going on Calle Marqués de Viana.

Across the Castellana, north-east of Nuevos Ministerios, is **El Viso**, an anomaly in high-rise Madrid. It was developed in the 1920s and 1930s as a model community on garden-city lines, on the fringes of the city at that time, and some of its two-or three-storey houses are museum-worthy examples of art deco architecture. The district has retained its desirable (and expensive) status.

South of centre

The *barrios* of southern **Embajadores**, **Delicias** and **Legazpi** occupy a triangular chunk of land just south of the old city, bordered by the Manzanares, the M-30 motorway and the rail lines from Atocha. Low rents attract a fair number of resident foreigners, despite the manic major roads around here. Conventional attractions are few – the **Museo Ferroviario** and the **Parque Tierno Galván**, with the **Planetario** (*see chapter* **Children**) – but the area contains the **Estación Sur** bus station, and two symbols of the city, the **Atlético Madrid** stadium and, alongside it, the **Mahou brewery**. It has long been said that the brewery will be moved at some time in the future, and the area may see other renovations.

Outer limits

Vallecas

Vallecas, out beyond the M-30 south-east of the city, was already an industrial suburb in the 1930s, and manages still to be one of the areas of Madrid with a firmest sense of its own identity. It doesn't lay much claim to being traditionally *castizo*, even though many of its residents came here as over-spill from the centre. Rather, to say Vallecas in Madrid is to suggest immediately the post-Civil War, post-'50s working class.

Vallecas is known for a strong sense of neighbourly solidarity. It has its own football team, the battling **Rayo Vallecano**, forever struggling to keep up with its money-laden neighbours (*see chapter* **Sport & Fitness**). Car stickers proclaim 'Independence for Vallecas' (spelt 'Vallekas' by hipper natives, who have their own punky sense of cool). It also has a very pleasant tree-lined main drag where generations mingle and hang out (officially **Calle Peña Gorbea**, known to *Vallecanos* as *El Búlevar*), more than enough to mark it out from the other areas around it, and Madrid's central wholesale market. There are some 'famous' problem areas near Vallecas, particularly around Entrevías, on its south side. This is the home of some of Madrid's largest Gypsy communities, some of whom live permanently on the edge, while others are quite prosperous. Even this area is being transformed, though, with the construction of Madrid's new regional assembly building, and a promised influx of civil servants.

The south

Carabanchel, Leganés, Getafe, Móstoles, Alcorcón – Madrid's southern industrial belt, virtually all of it built up from nothing since the 1960s. Areas still within the city such as Orcasitas blend into the towns of the *extrarradio*, the outskirts, and concrete flyovers and rows of tower blocks make up the urban landscape. **Usera**, to name but one, is a study in unplanned urban mess. Unemployment and hard drug use are serious problems. Yet the district's resolutely proletarian population are a sparky bunch, and some of the best hard rock groups in the vicinity came out of Usera, where they jammed in garages.

Central city dwellers sometimes come down here, too, for entertainment. **Alcorcón** holds its own flamenco festival (*see chapter* **Flamenco**), and nearby **Fuenlabrada** has a clutch of macro-discos popular with the teen crowd.

The northern suburbs

The northern and western *extrarradio* offers a radical contrast to the south. The thing to do for those with the necessary cash in Madrid in the last 20 years or so has been to adopt the Anglo-Saxon way of life and move out of city flats to house-and-garden developments in places like **Puerta de Hierro**, north of the Casa de Campo, which takes its name from the 1753 'Iron Gate' to the royal hunting reserve of El Pardo. The posh residences in this district, however, are no match for **La Moraleja**, off the Burgos road, a Beverly Hills enclave for executives and diplomats.

The growing districts to the east are not nearly so lush. The area along the A2 motorway towards the soon-to-be-expanded airport is intended to be Madrid's major commercial development zone, with the **Feria de Madrid** trade fair complex and the **Parque Juan Carlos I**. Oddly enough, the area already contains, swallowed up in the urban spread, one of Spain's most appealing and neglected eighteenth-century gardens, the **Capricho de la Alameda de Osuna** (*see page 60*), a delightful French garden with a river, islands and bridges, gurgling fountains, a temple to Bacchus, a neo-classical palace and endless parterre promenades.

Rides & tours

Above the ground

Medios Publicitarios Hinchables

C/Gutiérrez Solana 6 (91 563 39 94). Metro Santiago Bernabéu/bus 14, 43, 120, 150. **Open** *Sept-June* 9am-2pm, 5-8pm, *July-Aug* 9am-3pm, Mon-Fri.
Balloon trips over Madrid and the Guadarrama, by appointment only, departing from Villanueva del Pardillo, west of Madrid near Las Rozas. A flight of about two hours costs 20,000ptas, and longer trips can be arranged.

Trapsatur

C/San Bernardo 23 (91 541 63 20/21). Metro Noviciado/bus 147. **Open** 7.30am-9pm Mon-Sat; 7.30am-4pm Sun. **Credit** V. **Map E5**
Get a new view of Madrid and the Guadarrama with Trapsatur's flights in four-seater light aircraft (so bookings can only be made for groups of three), from Cuatro Vientos airfield south-west of the city. They are not allowed actually to overfly Madrid, but skirt the city on the way north. Flights over El Escorial last about 45 min and leave every 45 min, 9am-7pm daily; the cost per person is around 9,000ptas, Mon-Fri, and 6,500ptas Sat, Sun. There are also 1½-hour flights taking in Segovia. Transport is provided between the Calle San Bernardo office and Cuatro Vientos. *See also below* **Madrid Vision**.

Bus tours

For a quick overview of the city a bus tour can be a good bet, but the standards available in Madrid are pretty dull. All are in several languages, and are usually booked through hotels. **Madrid Vision** provides a cheaper and more flexible service.

Juliá Tours

Gran Vía 68 (91 559 96 05). Metro Santo Domingo/bus all routes to Gran Vía. **Open** 8am-8.30pm Mon-Sat; 8am-4.30pm Sun. **No credit cards. Map D6**
A well-known company offering the standard range of tours: bullfights, evening tours with flamenco shows and so on. Prices run from 2,750ptas to 13,200ptas. Also tours to towns near Madrid, for 5,000-10,700ptas (some with lunch).

Madrid Vision

Office *Avda Manoteras 14 (91 302 45 26/91 767 17 43).* **Route** *Telefónica-Plaza de España-Palacio Real-C/Bailén-C/Mayor-Puerta del Sol-Paseo del Prado-Atocha-Cibeles-C/Goya-Paseo de la Castellana-C/Serrano-Paseo de Recoletos-C/Alcalá-Telefónica.* **Office open** 7.30am-9pm Mon-Sat; 7.30am-4pm Sun. **Credit** V.
A tourist bus service with ten buses per day on a set route around all the major sights, with 14 stops en route, handy for getting a quick introduction to the city. With a full ticket you can get on and off the buses as many times as you wish during the same day; on board there are hostesses and a multilingual commentary through headsets. Tickets are bought on board. A full ticket costs 2,200ptas (2,900ptas for two days); a 1,700ptas one-day ticket entitles you to stay on the bus for the whole trip or get off at one stop, but not to re-board. Children aged 4-15 pay 40% less, and under-4s travel free; ticket holders are also entitled to discounts at a range of shops, restaurants and other attractions. The parent company **Trapsatur** (*see left*) also runs a variety of tours within Madrid.

Pullmantur

Main office: *C/Orense 16 (91 556 11 14). Metro Nuevos Ministerios/bus 5, 149, C.* **Open** 9am-1.30pm, 4.30-7.30pm, Mon-Fri; 9am-1.30pm Sat. **Credit** AmEx, DC, MC, V.
Bus terminal: *Plaza de Oriente 8 (91 541 18 05). Metro Opera/bus 3, 25, 33, 39, 148.* **Map C7**
A similar range of coach-with-guide tours as Juliá, at prices from 2,750ptas to 10,000ptas. Also much the same time-worn menu of tours of the classic towns around Madrid (Toledo, Segovia, Aranjuez and others), for 5,000-10,700ptas.

Walking tours

Descubre Madrid

(91 588 29 06/07). Metro Sol/bus all routes to Puerta del Sol. **Open** *Oct-June* 8.30am-2.30pm Mon, Tue, Thur, Fri; 8.30am-2pm, 4-6pm, Wed; *July-Sept* 8.30am-2.30pm Mon-Fri. **No credit cards. Map D8**
Run by the city tourist board, this service offers walking and bus tours covering every nook and cranny of Madrid, its architecture, literary life, little-known figures and so on. Most of the many itineraries on the list are available only in Spanish, but even if you don't speak much of the language they can be interesting, especially the ones that include sights and buildings otherwise difficult to get into. Prices are very reasonable: tours on foot cost 500ptas, by bus 1,000ptas.

Old Madrid Walking Tours

Tours depart from *Plaza Mayor, 3 (91 588 16 36). Metro Sol/bus all routes to Puerta del Sol.* **Tours** 10am (English), noon (Spanish) Sat. **Tickets** 500ptas; 400ptas students, 4-12s, over-65s. **No credit cards. Map D8**
Also run by the city office, these tours give the essential lowdown, in English, on Madrid's Golden Age heart, 'Madrid of the Austrias', starting from the tourist office in the Plaza Mayor. You are asked to meet at the office half an hour before the departure time; tours last about two hours.

Olé Spain Tours

Paseo de la Infanta Isabel 23 (91 551 52 94/939 175 792). Metro Atocha/bus all routes to Atocha. **Open** 10am-8pm Mon-Fri. **No credit cards. Map H10**
Formerly known as Fiesta Tours, this company takes city walks in English through the old city of Madrid, on request. Walks cost 2,500ptas per person and last four hours, covering the whole of Golden Age Madrid, with stops for drinks in a *taberna* (included in the price). Very near Atocha station, they also run tours to Toledo, Segovia and other places in the region, also on request, and are a very useful general information and travel agency, especially for budget accommodation and services in Madrid and throughout Spain.

Museums

Three of the world's great artistic treasure houses, priceless relics of ancient America – and many idiosyncratic, rewarding corners.

Already possessing the Prado and the Reina Sofía, Madrid pulled off a real coup in acquiring the Thyssen-Bornemisza collection in 1992, to complete an impressive trio of major museums. This 'Golden Triangle' – one of the threesome's several collective labels – has assured the city its place among the elite of European art capitals. However, visitors with more than just a few days to spare in Madrid who look beyond the great magnet of the 'Big Three' can also find many gems in other, far less famous collections.

Works by great Spanish painters such as El Greco, Goya or Velázquez as well as artists of the calibre of Dürer, Constable and Titian can also be found in the under-visited **Real Academia de San Fernando**, the astonishing **Museo Lázaro Galdiano**, the **Museo Cerralbo** or the superb monastery of the **Descalzas Reales**. Madrid's military museums, the **Museo del Ejército** and **Museo Naval**, have fascinating historical and artistic relics that can be of interest to anyone, and the **Museo de América**, closed to view for years prior to 1994, contains the finest collection of pre-Columbian artefacts anywhere outside the Americas. For railway fans there is the **Museo Ferroviario**, a museum that constantly renews itself, and anyone interested specifically in Madrid should take a look at the **Museo Municipal**.

The most important current development in the Madrid museum world is the controversial and far-reaching renovation programme at the **Prado** (*see pages 72-3*), which is finally gaining momentum. This will mean that several sections of the great jewel of Madrid museums may be closed off at some point in the next few years; the **Casón del Buen Retiro** annexe is already closed, and a temporary location for its nineteenth-century Spanish paintings has not been announced. This tends to undermine official assurances that none of the Prado's masterpieces will actually disappear from view during the great reconstruction. However, once completed the overall project could be spectacular.

Other Madrid museums also occasionally undergo very long-term restoration work (the Museo de América was a case in point): the **Museo de Carruajes** (Carriage Museum) next to the Palacio Real is another for which no reopening date is in sight at time of writing. In the smaller museums, standards of care and presentation range from impeccable to scandalous.

Museums of particular interest to children include the **Museo de Ciencias Naturales** and the **Museo Ferroviario**. For the **Museo de Cera (Wax Museum)** and a note on the future of the **Acciona** science museum, *see chapter* **Children**.

TICKETS & TIMES

The Spanish national museums (which includes all the majors, except the Thyssen) have a standard adult entry charge of 500ptas. There are discounts for students, and admission is free to everyone, Spanish or otherwise, under 18 or over 65 – something not appreciated by many foreign visitors, who assume they have to pay (ID may be required). It is also worth noting that admission to the national museums is free for everyone on Saturday afternoons and Sunday mornings (when they are often very full), and that some less frequented museums are still free at all times. Most museums do not accept credit cards.

Most museums are shut on Mondays, with the exception of the Reina Sofía, which closes on a Tuesday. Many of the national museums offer volunteer guides free of charge, but they rarely speak English. If you want a personal English-speaking guide you will nearly always have to pay. Only the major museums always have catalogues and so on in English; similarly, most exhibits are labelled only in Spanish, with a few exceptions such as the **Thyssen** and the **Museo Taurino**.

The mysterious *Paseo del Arte* ticket

The joint *Paseo del Arte* ticket gives entry to all of Madrid's 'Big Three' art palaces, the Prado, the Thyssen and the Reina Sofía, for 1,050ptas. After visiting one museum with the ticket you can visit the other two at any time within the same calendar year. This ticket was introduced with considerable publicity in 1995, but since then has been oddly unadvertised and hidden from view: only the Reina Sofía makes any mention of it in its brochures. However, it is available from the ticket desks at all three, you only have to ask. Each of these museums also has its own 'friends' tickets giving unlimited entry for one year, which are more expensive, and more widely publicised. *See also p42.*

Fine & decorative arts

Casón del Buen Retiro

C/Alfonso XII, 28 (91 420 26 28). Metro Banco de España, Retiro/bus all routes to Puerta de Alcalá.
Currently closed for renovation. Map H8

A five-minute walk from the main Prado, the Casón del Buen Retiro and adjacent **Museo del Ejército** (*see below*) are all that remain of Philip IV's Buen Retiro palace (*see chapter* **History**). Until recently the Casón housed the Prado's assembly of nineteenth-century Spanish art, but the building is now closed as part of the Prado renovation scheme. When it reopens it is likely to house a wider collection of Spanish art. If you can get to see it, Luca Giordano's ceiling fresco *The Order of the Golden Fleece* dominates the main salon, once Philip IV's ballroom.

Colección Permanente del Instituto de Crédito Oficial (ICO)

C/Zorrilla 3 (91 420 07 17). Metro Banco de España/ bus all routes to Plaza de Cibeles. **Open** 10am-7pm Tue-Sat; 10am-2pm Sun. **Admission** free. **Map G7**

The ICO, a State credit bank, began to invest in art in the 1980s, and inaugurated this exhibition space for its collection in 1996. It has three main parts – most important is Picasso's *Suite Vollard*, a milestone in twentieth-century prints, from 1927-37; there is also a fine selection of modern Spanish sculpture, and a well-chosen, if not daring, range of international painting from the '80s. The bank has bought little since the museum's inauguration, so changes come in the form of temporary shows.

Museo Cerralbo

C/Ventura Rodríguez 17 (91 547 36 46). Metro Plaza de España/bus all routes to Plaza de España. **Open** *Sept-June* 9.30am-2.30pm Tue-Sat; 10am-2pm Sun; *July & Aug* 10am-2pm Tue-Sat; 10.30am-1.30pm Sun. **Admission** *Tue, Thur-Sat* 400ptas; 200ptas students; free under-18s, over-65s. *Wed, Sun* free. **Map C4**

Feeding the artistic sensibility

To do Madrid's great art repositories justice you need to give each at least two hours of your time, so you'll probably want – and need – a break on the way. Each of the Big Three has its own café-restaurant, of differing degrees of attractiveness.

Cafetería del Museo del Prado

(91 330 28 00). **Open** 9.30am-6pm Tue-Sat; 9.30am-1pm Sun. **Average** 1,500ptas. **No credit cards.** **Map H8**
Often the best value of the three, with a pleasant bar and a self-service restaurant further inside. Dishes are well prepared and there's plenty of variety, with a range of salads and good sandwiches; for a larger meal, starters cost about 500ptas and main dishes around 800ptas. The café is only accessible from inside the museum.

Cafetería del Museo Thyssen

(91 429 27 32). **Open** 10am-7pm Tue-Sun. **Average** 1,500ptas. **Credit** AmEx, MC, TC, V. **Map G7**
This quiet, attractive restaurant offers fare that's a little more sophisticated than at the other museum cafés, with a partly Italian/international orientation in the menu. You can have anything from a simple baguette sandwich or *pincho de tortilla* to a full *menú del día* for around 1,500ptas; some dishes are pricey, but it's more comfortable than the other cafés and very pleasantly cool in summer, so it can be worth it. You can enter the café, in the basement, without going into the museum.

Cafetería del Reina Sofía

(91 467 50 62). **Open** 10am-8pm Mon, Wed-Sat; 10am-1pm Sun. **Average** 1,500ptas. **Credit** MC, V. **Map G10**
The plainest of the three, a straightforward basement bar with a more attractive restaurant at the back (open 1-4pm Mon, Wed-Sat only), although standards have improved in the last few years. The restaurant has a variety of *platos combinados* ('all-in-one' meals) and set menus for about 1,500ptas. Again, you don't have to pay the museum entrance fee to use the café.

OUTSIDE THE MUSEUMS

If on the other hand you prefer to step outside to get your refreshment, below are some places within a few steps of the 'Golden Triangle'. If

you're prepared to walk up the hill to Plaza Santa Ana, you'll also find a great many more bars and restaurants.

Cafés, bars & tapas

El Brillante *Glorieta del Emperador Carlos V 8.* **Map H9** Very near the Reina Sofía; great for a good-value fill-up, but not a place to linger, unless you get a table on the (busy) street outside (in place Mar-Nov). *See p130.*
La Dolores & **Los Gatos** *Plaza de Jesús.* **Map G8** Two classic tapas and *bocadillo* bars on a small back street plaza across the *paseo* from the Prado (up Calle Lope de Vega) and around the corner from the Thyssen. Both have a great atmosphere; the Dolores is more expensive. *See also p139* for **La Dolores** *and p136* for **Los Gatos**.
La Guagua Café *Paseo del Prado 26 (91 429 66 85). Metro Atocha, Banco de España.* **Open** 8am-11pm Mon-Fri; 9.30am-2pm Sat; 9.30am-11pm Sun. **No credit cards. Map G8** In the epicentre of the 'Golden Triangle', La Guagua offers freshly ground Colombian coffee, a range of sandwiches and cakes, and a suitably arty atmosphere.
La Platería *C/Moratín 49.* **Map G8** Decent tapas, charcuterie and *pulguitas* (rolls), and good breakfasts are offered at this small budget café. If your sightseeing is already over for the day, check out the commendable wine list. *See also p128.*

Restaurants

Cervantes Pizza Bar *C/León 8 (91 420 12 98). Metro Antón Martín/bus 6, 26, 32.* **Open** 11am-1.15am Sun-Thur; until 2.15am Fri, Sat. **Credit** AmEx, DC, MC, V. **Map F8** Walk a short way up Huertas and take a right at C/León to find the cheap and cheerful Cervantes, with 25 different pizzas, salads, pasta and home-made sweets.
Paradís Madrid *C/Marqués de Cubas 14.* **Map G7** Mid-priced modern Catalan food, behind the Banco de España and well placed for the Thyssen. *See also p117.*
La Vaca Verónica *C/Moratín 38.* **Map G8** A friendly casual favourite with good salads and pastas, and very near the Dolores and Los Gatos (*see above*) as well as the major museums. *See also p117.*
Viridiana *C/Juan de Mena 14.* **Map H7** The choice for gourmets in the museum area. *See also p124.*

Part of the opulent décor at the **Real Academia de San Fernando.** *See page 78.*

This sumptuous late nineteenth-century mansion houses the personal collection of its former owner Enrique de Aguilera y Gamboa, the seventeenth Marqués de Cerralbo. A man of letters, reactionary politician and fanatical collector, he travelled throughout Europe and Asia in pursuit of pieces to add to his collection, which he left to the Spanish State on his death in 1922. One curious feature of the museum stems from the fact that in his will the Marqués stipulated that the collection should be displayed exactly as he had arranged it – which means in a way that no museum curator would contemplate today, with paintings hung in three levels up the walls. Of the paintings, the major highlight is El Greco's *The Ecstasy of Saint Francis of Assisi*, but there are also works by Zurbarán, Alonso Cano and other Spanish masters. As well as the actual exhibits, a major attraction of the house is the opportunity it gives to see a near-intact aristocratic residence of the Restoration era, especially the centrepiece of the ground floor, presumably the domain of the Marqués' wife, the lavish ballroom. The upper level has a much more

masculine air, and this is where you find his astonishing collection of European and Japanese armour, weapons, watches, pipes, leatherbound books, clocks and other curiosities. Only some of the pieces are labelled. Guided tours in Spanish are available, but must be requested in advance.

Museo Lázaro Galdiano

C/Serrano 122 (91 561 60 84).
Metro Gregorio Marañón/bus 9, 12, 19, 51, 89. **Open** 10am-2pm Tue-Sun. **Admission** 400ptas; 200ptas students; free under-18s, over-65s. *Sat* free. **Map J1**
This extraordinary but still little-known private collection of 15,000 paintings and *objets d'art* is impressive in both size and scope. Like the **Museo Cerralbo** it is actually the former home of its founder and creator, in this case financier José Lázaro Galdiano (1862-1947), who amassed his eclectic collection over a period of some 70 years, from the age of 15 until he died. The monumental four-storey mansion and its fine gardens are a sight in themselves. *Continued on p78.*

The Prado

Madrid's most celebrated attraction extends along the city's loveliest tree-lined boulevard, the Paseo del Prado. The core of the museum, first opened in November 1819, is the Spanish royal art collection, supplemented by later purchases and works seized from religious houses following their dissolution in the 1830s. The royal collection itself reflects the shifting tastes and alliances of Spain's kings of the sixteenth and seventeenth centuries. Naturally, there is a comprehensive selection of works by the Spanish Court painters Diego de Velázquez and Francisco de Goya. Close ties with Italy, France and especially the southern, Catholic, Netherlands led to the presence of many superb works by Titian, Rubens and Hieronymus Bosch, among others.

Conversely, such choices caused some gaps in the collection. The monarchs' unfamiliarity with artists predating the High Renaissance is evident, and hostilities with England, Holland and other Protestant states also led to little representation of artists from these countries, although more recent acquisitions have made up for this to some extent.

Royal collecting began centuries before the museum was inaugurated, and in the 1500s Queen Isabella already possessed a large number of Flemish paintings. Under Charles V (1516-56) and Philip II (1556-98), Italian and Flemish painting still dominated the royal collections. Titian was favoured by both Kings. Philip II's eclectic taste led him to purchase several paintings by Bosch, among them one of the Prado's most popular, the enigmatically surreal triptych *The Garden of Earthly Delights*, which Philip kept in his bedroom at El Escorial. The white face beneath a hat in the 'Hell' panel is believed to be Bosch's self-portrait.

Philip IV (1621-65) commissioned several works from Rubens. The latter was contemptuous of Spanish painters until he saw the work of the young Velázquez, who would serve Philip IV as Court painter for nearly 40 years. Velázquez also supervised the acquisition of other works for Philip IV, adding to the collection nearly 2,000 paintings by Renaissance and seventeenth-century masters, including some by Van Dyck that had been in the collection of Charles I of England and were sold after his execution.

The 1734 fire that destroyed the old Alcázar of Madrid took with it over 500 works of art. However, more were bought or commissioned to replace these losses. The first Bourbon King of Spain, Philip V (1700-46), brought with him one

Goya: Saturn devouring one of his sons.

of the Prado's most extraordinary possessions, the *Tesoro del Delfín*, the 'Treasures of the Grand Dauphin'. The Grand Dauphin, eldest son of Louis XIV of France and father of Philip V of Spain, accumulated a massive art collection, part of which was left to Philip. The 'Treasure' consists mostly of sixteenth- and seventeenth-century Italian *objets d'art*, such as vases of rock crystal studded with semi-precious stones and fitted with gold and silver trimmings. This is scheduled to move to the Palacio del Buen Retiro at some point in the next few years.

The last monarch to add significantly to the royal collection was Charles IV (1788-1808), the employer of Goya, possibly the least respectful Court painter who ever lived. The neo-classical edifice by Juan de Villanueva that houses the Prado was built earlier for his father Charles III, originally to be a science museum. It was Spain's 'non-king', Joseph Bonaparte, who first thought of using it to exhibit the royal pictures, in what he wanted to call the *Museo Josefino*, after himself. Surprisingly, though, the restored Bourbon

Fernando VII, not a king usually known for any democratic impulses, kept the idea, and so the Prado was established, as one of the world's first public art museums.

ALL CHANGE

The Prado has been enduring renovation since the early 1980s, but changes have often been a little ad hoc. Its problem is that it has been bursting at the seams, with space to display only a fraction of its holdings. However, with the approval of a comprehensive plan in spring 1997 – and despite continual controversies, including a walkout by several of the most respected curators – some clear lines have finally emerged as to where the Prado should be going at the turn of the millennium.

The plan foresees a complete reorganisation of the collection, and the expansion of the Prado from two to five buildings. The main building is in the middle of refurbishing work; more than 25 rooms have already been renovated, and several new exhibition spaces inaugurated, most notably the 12 rooms opened in summer 1998 for the Dutch and Flemish schools. The **Casón del Buen Retiro**, which until recently has housed the Spanish nineteenth-century collection, is to have three new floors dug out of the earth, and will be dedicated to Spanish painting from the Middle Ages to the last century. Also foreseen is building work in the cloisters of the church of **San Jerónimo** (*see page 65*), which will be joined to the Prado by an underground passageway with shops, cafés and space for temporary exhibitions. The biggest changes will probably come in 2001-2, when the Prado is scheduled to take over the **Palacio del Buen Retiro**, currently the **Museo del Ejército** (whose fate remains a mystery). It should become an exhibition space for the sumptuous jewellery collections (such as the Treasures of the Grand Dauphin), some of the Court portraits and other parts of the royal collections.

Assurances have been given that while all this is happening none of the museum's most famous masterpieces will ever be withdrawn from view, but this could be difficult to sustain completely.

Highlights

The Prado contains such a high concentration of masterpieces that it is really impossible to do it justice in only one visit, or in just a brief survey. Also, its layout is quite confusing, although the free maps given out at the entrance do help, and future reorganisation should make for a more rational arrangement of its pictures. In the meantime, **due to the Prado renovation programme, the following information is inevitably subject to change**.

The main entrance is now the Puerta de Goya, at the north end, which brings you in via steps on to the first floor, where most of the large Spanish paintings are displayed. In the distance, past galleries to the left that contain the Prado's major Italian paintings, including Titian's portraits of Charles V and Philip II, you can spot Velázquez' *Las Meninas*, often described as the greatest painting in the world, because of its complex interplay of perspectives and realities. Velázquez paints himself at the left of the picture, supposedly painting a portrait of the King and Queen, who are seen bizarrely in a 'mirror' at the end of the room, but in whose place stands every spectator, watched forever by Velázquez, the little Infanta Margarita and other figures in the painting.

In the great hall at the centre of this floor are the massive state portraits painted by Velázquez of Philip IV and his Court, with their air of melancholic grandeur; also nearby is his wonderful *Surrender of Breda* (known in Spanish as *Las Lanzas*, 'The Lances'), which may in future move to the Palacio del Buen Retiro. There are also many religious paintings by El Greco, Zurbarán and other Golden Age masters.

Further on along the same floor are the eighteenth-century Spanish paintings and the main rooms devoted to Goya. Every stage of his career is superbly represented in the Prado: around 40 of the 60 light, carefree tapestry cartoons he designed for the royal palaces; his sarcastic portraits of the royal family and members of the aristocracy; and the renowned *Majas*. There are also his tremendous images of war, including the masterpiece *The Third of May*, depicting the executions carried out by the French in Madrid in 1808. Still more fascinating are the *Pinturas Negras* or 'Black Paintings', the turbulent images executed during his last years, usually shown on the floor below. Witchcraft, violence and historical drama combine in an astonishing array of monstrous images, many originally painted on the walls of his home, the *Quinta del Sordo*, between 1819 and 1823.

Also on the ground floor are the Prado's early Spanish, Flemish and German paintings, with Bosch, Brueghel the Elder and Dürer. Italian masters, with Raphael's *Portrait of a Cardinal* and Botticelli's *Story of Nastagio degli Onesti*, are back on the first floor with the main Spanish paintings. Elsewhere, almost unnoticed, you can find Rembrandt's *Artemisia*. *See also page 42.*

Museo del Prado

Paseo del Prado s/n (91 420 37 68). Metro Atocha, Banco de España/bus 9, 14, 27, 34, 37. **Open** 9am-7pm Tue-Sat; 9am-2pm Sun. Closed Mon. **Admission** 500ptas; 250ptas students; free under-18s, over-65s. *Sat & Sun 2.30-7pm free. Paseo del Arte Ticket 1,050ptas.* **Map H8** *Disabled: wheelchair access. Shop (9.30am-6.30pm Tue-Sat; 9.30am-1.30pm Sun).*

The Thyssen

The third point of Madrid's 'Golden Triangle' was completed with the official opening of the Thyssen-Bornemisza Museum on 10 October 1992. Widely regarded as the most important private collection in the world, it provides a rich complement and contrast to the different areas of art on show a short distance away in the Prado and the Reina Sofia.

Baron Hans-Heinrich Thyssen-Bornemisza's invaluable collection originally came to Spain on a nine-and-a-half-year loan, but later negotiations led to a purchase agreement for the 775 paintings, concluded in June 1993. No doubt the Baron's fourth wife, Carmen *Tita* Cervera, a former Miss Spain, influenced his final decision. More pivotal, however, was Madrid's offer to house it in the Palacio de Villahermosa, an early nineteenth-century pile that was empty and available at the time. It had been converted into offices in the 1960s, and so architect Rafael Moneo was able to give it an entirely new interior. This conversion, which cost over four billion pesetas (£21 million), is itself one of the most remarkable features of the museum. Terracotta-pink walls, skylights and marble flooring provide a luminous setting for the collection, and rarely is it possible to see old master paintings so perfectly lit.

This inimitable collection was begun by the present Baron's father in the 1920s. On his death in 1947, however, his 525 paintings were dispersed among his heirs. His son Baron Hans-Heinrich then set out to round the collection up once more, buying them back from his relatives, and took up his father's vocation with a passion, buying old masters until the 1960s, and then turning towards contemporary art. It was his desire to keep the collection together that led him to search for a larger home for his paintings, as his own Villa Favorita in Lugano in Switzerland could only accommodate about 300 pictures. Hence the attraction of the Villahermosa, although a part of the collection given to Spain, mostly early medieval and Renaissance works, is exhibited in the fourteenth-century Pedralbes Monastery in Barcelona.

The Collection

A visit to the Thyssen-Bornemisza affords an extraordinary lesson in the history of Western art. You begin at the top, on the second floor, with the thirteenth century and the early Italians (exemplified by Duccio di Buoninsegna's *Christ and the Samaritan Woman*), and work your way downwards through all the major schools until you reach the ground floor and the likes of Roy Lichtenstein's *Woman in Bath* (*see page 81*), or the basement café and Renato Guttuso's 1976 *Caffè Greco*. Alternatively, head for a favourite period, guided by the free plan provided.

The Thyssen-Bornemisza effectively fills in the gaps you may find in Madrid at the Prado or the Reina Sofia. Unlike either of the latter, it includes among its holdings a significant selection of German Renaissance works, seventeenth-century Dutch painting, Impressionism, German Expressionism, Russian Constructivism, geometric abstraction and pop art.

Detractors have alleged that the Thyssen is no more than a ragbag, a catch-all collection of every kind of style put together without discrimination or eye to quality. However, one of its great attractions is that, while it is extraordinarily broad in scope, it is also recognisably a personal collection directed by a distinctly individual taste, as seen in the wonderful room dedicated to early portraits, with works by Antonello da Messina and Hans Memling. Equally quirky is the section on early North American painting, including a Presumed *Portrait of George Washington's Cook* by Gilbert Stuart, and works by American artists rarely seen in Europe such as Thomas Cole, Frederick Remington and Winslow Homer.

And the museum does have its share of real masterpieces. Among the old masters, the works of Duccio, Van Eyck and Petrus Christus stand out. The museum's most famous painting is the Florentine master Domenico Ghirlandaio's idealised *Portrait of Giovanna Tornabuoni* (1488), in the portrait room.

Two rooms further on is Vittore Carpaccio's allegorical *Young Knight in a Landscape* from 1510, replete with symbols, and another of the gems of the collection. From among the masters of the Flemish School is the sublime *Annunciation* diptych by Van Eyck, more a three-dimensional sculptural relief than a painting. The German Renaissance is best represented by Albrecht Dürer, whose *Jesus among the Doctors* portrays an idealised, almost effeminate Christ pressed upon by diabolical doctors.

From the later sixteenth century and baroque there are superb paintings such as Titian's *Saint Jerome in the Wilderness*, Mattia Preti's unsettling *A Concert* and Caravaggio's wonderfully powerful *Saint Catherine of Alexandria* (*see page 81*).

Hotel Room 1931, *by Edward Hopper.*

There are also representative works by El Greco, Rubens, Guercino, Tintoretto and Jusepe Ribera, and a Bernini marble, *Saint Sebastian.*

The first floor, below, begins with several rooms of seventeenth-century Dutch pictures. There follows the most remarkably varied section of the museum, with such things as a sombre *Easter Morning* by Caspar David Friedrich, a Goya portrait of his friend *Asensio Juliá*, a great selection of Impressionists (Monet, Manet, Renoir, some Degas dancers, two beautiful and little-known Van Goghs, and Gauguin and Cézanne), and even Constable's 1824 *The Lock* – though not jumbled together, but carefully ordered and arranged. The collection is generally very strong in German art, with several rooms of Expressionists and great works by Kandinsky, Emil Nolde, Ernst Ludwig Kirchner, Otto Dix and Max Beckmann.

Also present, on the ground floor, are more familiar modern masters, such as Braque, Mondrian, Klee, Max Ernst and Picasso, in the shape of his 1911 *Man with a Clarinet* among other works. The last few rooms concentrate on the USA, with a fabulous Georgia O'Keeffe, *New York with Moon*, a *Hotel Room* by Edward Hopper and Robert Rauschenberg's *Express* from 1963, but also on show are *Large Interior, Paddington* by Lucian Freud and an early David Hockney, *In Memoriam Cecchino Bracci.*

At once personal and eclectic, and also fun, the Thyssen-Bornemisza collection allows you to contemplate a range of work that it would otherwise be physically impossible to reach – without unlimited time, travel privileges, and access to various private collections and museums. A full tour takes at least two hours. Before leaving, you have the opportunity to pay your respects to the giant, chocolate-box portraits of the Baron and *la Tita* themselves in the lobby, alongside companion pictures of the King and Queen of Spain on the same wall. *See also page 42.*

Museo Thyssen-Bornemisza

Palacio de Villahermosa, Paseo del Prado 8 (91 369 01 51). Metro Banco de España/bus 9, 14, 27, 34, 37. **Open** 10am-7pm Tue-Sun. Closed Mon. **Admission** 700ptas; 400ptas students, over-65s; free under-12s. *Paseo del Arte Ticket* 1,050ptas. *Temporary exhibitions* 500ptas; 300ptas students, over-65s. *Both* 900ptas; 500ptas students, over-65s. **Map G7** *Disabled: wheelchair access. Shop.*

The Reina Sofía

Two glass and steel lift-shafts stand out against the sombre façade of this building, which from 1781 until 1965 was the San Carlos hospital. Designed by British architect Ian Ritchie, the lifts provide uninterrupted dramatic views of Madrid while you ride up to any of its four exhibition floors. The rest of the centre is a little more low-key, but still a spectacular art space.

Madrid's national museum of modern art is housed in one of the largest buildings in the city, boasting all of 12,505sq m of exhibition space, an area that in Europe is surpassed only by the Centre Pompidou in Paris. The initial conversion of the old hospital was carried out between 1977 and 1986, when Queen Sofía first opened the new facility named after her. It was initially only a temporary exhibition space, and more thoroughgoing renovation – with the addition of the lifts – continued until 1990, when the building finally opened as a museum with a permanent collection.

Its great jewel is unquestionably Picasso's *Guernica*, his impassioned denunciation of war and fascism that commemorates the 1937 destruction of the Basque town of Guernica by German bombers supporting the Francoist forces in the Spanish Civil War – although some art historians have seen it more in formal terms, as a reflection on the history of Western painting, using elements taken from the work of the old masters. It has only been in the Reina Sofía, behind a bullet-proof glass panel on the second floor, since 1992, when it was transferred here from the **Casón del Buen Retiro** (*see page 69*) amid great controversy. Picasso had refused to allow the painting to be exhibited in Spain during the Franco regime, and it was in 1981 that it was finally brought to Madrid from the Museum of Modern Art in New York. The artist had intended that it should be housed in the Prado – of which the Casón was at least an annexe – and his family bitterly opposed the change of location. The acquisition of *Guernica* hugely boosted the prestige of the Reina Sofía, but the saga of its final resting place has continued: Bilbao, capital of the Basque province of Vizcaya (which contains the town of Guernica), has staked a claim on the picture for its Guggenheim museum (*see page 244*). As Picasso left the painting to the Spanish State, though, it is very unlikely that the Government will allow it to be moved again.

The rest of the permanent collection, much of which came from the old Museo Español de Arte Contemporáneo in Moncloa, has also not escaped controversy. The most common criticism is that,

while it contains works by just about all the major Spanish artists of this century – Picasso, Dalí, Miró, Juan Gris, Julio González, Tàpies and Antonio Saura are all here – the representation of individual artists is often patchy, with few major works. Complaints have also been made about the erratic coverage of non-Spanish art.

In response, an active acquisitions policy was adopted that filled some gaps in the display of Spanish art, and also created a growing collection of works by foreign artists. Additions made since the early '90s have included works by Donald Judd, Anish Kapoor, Bruce Nauman, Tony Cragg, Rosemarie Trockel and Julian Schnabel; another has been Picasso's 1928 *Figura*. Since the *Partido Popular* government came to power in 1996 (and given the demands made on the State arts budget by restoration at the Prado), greater limitations have been made on the purchasing budget of the Reina Sofía. Nevertheless, the amount of work that has already been amassed has made it a far more impressive collection.

The permanent collection is on the second and fourth floors; temporary exhibitions are presented on the ground (Floor 1) and third floors. On each of the permanent-collection floors there are additional rooms for the temporary display of works from the collection not normally on show. The second floor begins with a selection entitled 'A Change of Century', looking at the origins of modernism in Spanish art, and placing together

Basque sculptor Eduardo Chillida's Omar Khayyam Table II, *from 1983.*

rather haphazardly artistic currents from different parts of Spain – Basque painters such as Zuloaga, Regoyos and Echevarría, Catalan Modernists such as Rusiñol, Nonell and Casas – even though they have relatively little in common. Next is the first avant-garde, both Spaniards such as Joaquín Torres García and artists who worked in Spain such as Picabia and the Delaunays, followed by a room dedicated to Juan Gris. Shortly after that comes the major draw for most visitors, the rooms of Picassos. His work is divided into pre- and post-Civil War, with *Guernica* at its centre.

Miró, Julio González and Dali are also accorded rooms of their own. Paintings by the latter include *The Great Masturbator* and *The Enigma of Hitler*. Several of the works by Miró are from the last years of his life, in the 1970s. After a room on international surrealism (Ernst, Magritte) there follows one on Luis Buñuel, and then the final displays on this floor take you to the end of the Civil War in 1939, looking at Spanish art of the 1930s.

The fourth floor runs from Spain's post-war years up to the present day, starting with figurative art and the beginnings of abstraction in Spain, taking in Tàpies, Mompó, Oteiza, Palazuelo and Equipo 57. To provide international context there are also works by Bacon, Henry Moore and Lucio Fontana alongside Saura and Chillida. Later rooms feature pop art, figurative work by Arroyo, and minimalism, with pieces by Ellsworth Kelly, Dan Flavin and Barnett Newman.

The immense size of the building, with its large and tranquil inner courtyard, is a great advantage for the exhibition of monumental pieces. The garden has been given over to large installations in exhibitions, such as one in summer 1998 on Spanish industrial design (the garden served as a backdrop to street lamps, park benches and press kiosks). Plaza Sanchéz Bustillo, in front of the museum, is now thankfully no longer an ugly building site and has also been put to use – a train carriage, an aeroplane, a bus and a car were placed there during the same show. Inside, long halls, high-vaulted ceilings and masses of windows lend an airy, spacious feel to the museum.

The Reina Sofia also functions as a venue for many other activities, and has developed into a dynamic cultural centre. In its role as a space for major temporary exhibitions in contemporary art it has won universal praise, and purists hold that its temporary shows are far more important than anything on permanent display (except *Guernica*). Shows have included retrospectives on Lucien Freud, Spanish surrealism, Léger, Severo Sarduy and Eduardo Arroyo, as well as photography by Laszló Mogy and Duane Michals. It also acts as a base for Madrid's principal contemporary music centre, the **Centro para la Difusión de la Música Contemporánea** (*see chapter* **Music: Classical & Opera**), and has a library and archive of around 72,000 books, together with a photo archive and material on video, CD and other media, all focused on twentieth-century art and culture, plus an excellent book- and souvenir shop (*see chapter* **Shopping**).

Museo Nacional Centro de Arte Reina Sofía

C/Santa Isabel 52 (91 467 50 62). Metro Atocha/bus all routes to Atocha. **Open** 10am-9pm Mon, Wed-Sat; 10am-2.30pm Sun. **Closed Tue**. **Admission** 500ptas; 250ptas students; free under-18s, over-65s. *Sat & Sun 2.30-9pm free. Paseo del Arte Ticket 1,050ptas.* **Map G10** *Disabled: wheelchair access. Library. Shop.*

Untitled, by Donald Judd (1992).

Museo Lázaro Galdiano, *continued from p71*.
Unfortunately, the care and presentation of this venerable museum leave a great deal to be desired. In some rooms, lighting is limited to a chandelier, or comes only from shadowy curved recesses in vaulted ceilings. Also, the present lack of air-conditioning makes for an uncomfortable visit in the summer, even though some improvements have been made in this area. Among an abundance of religious gold and silverwork, ivory, jewellery, medals, fans and other decorative pieces, this highly personal collection boasts – unusually for Madrid – some fine works by English painters. Gainsborough, Ramsay, Reynolds, Constable, and Sir Thomas Lawrence can be seen alongside Flemish, Spanish and other paintings from various periods. There is even a soulful portrait of *The Saviour* attributed to Leonardo da Vinci. Almost an entire room is devoted to Goya, with two of his earliest macabre works or *Pinturas Negras* ('black paintings'), *El Aquelarre* ('The Billy-goat' or 'The Witches' Sabbath') and the *Escena de Brujería* ('Witchcraft Scene'); you should also look out for a Rembrandt and a couple of works by Hieronymus Bosch, half-hidden in a corner like many of the exhibits in the museum.
Disabled: wheelchair access.

Museo Nacional de Artes Decorativas

C/Montalbán 12 (91 532 64 99).
Metro Banco de España/bus all routes to Plaza de Cibeles.
Open 9.30am-3pm Tue-Fri; 10am-2pm Sat, Sun, public holidays. **Admission** 400ptas; 200ptas students; free under-18s, over-65s. *Sun* free. **Map H7**
Founded in 1871 primarily for teaching purposes, the National Museum of Decorative Arts consists of *objets d'art*, furniture and tapestries from all over Spain. Since 1932 it has been housed in a small palace overlooking the Retiro, formerly the home of the Duchess of Santoña. Of the 58 display rooms, the most prized is the tiled kitchen on the fifth floor, painstakingly transferred from an eighteenth-century Valencian palace. Its 1,604 painted tiles depict a typical domestic scene of that era, with a coterie of servants making tea for the lady of the house. The museum also contains a wealth of other curious objects, including the graphically shaped jewel cases from the 'Dauphin's Treasures', the rest of which are in the Prado, nineteenth-century dolls' houses, antique fans and an ornate sixteenth-century four-poster bedstead: one recent addition is a late eighteenth-century *secretaire* (writing desk) made for Prince Luis de Borbón by the Italian cabinetmaker Medardo Arnaldo. Guided tours are available, usually in Spanish only, if requested in advance.

Museo de la Real Academia de Bellas Artes de San Fernando

C/Alcalá 13 (91 522 14 91).
Metro Sevilla, Sol/bus all routes to Puerta del Sol.
Open 9am-2.30pm Sat-Mon, public holidays; 9am-7pm Tue-Fri. **Admission** 400ptas; 200ptas students; free over-65s, under-18s. *Sat, Sun* free. **Map E7**
Founded in 1794, the San Fernando Royal Academy of Fine Arts is the oldest permanent artistic institution in Madrid. The eclectic display collection is partly made up of works donated by aspiring members in order to gain admission to the academy. Its greatest possessions, though, are its works by Goya, an important figure in the early years of the institution, shown in a special room renovated for the 250th anniversary of the artist's birth in 1996. That year also marked the end of a five-year restoration plan – paintings are now organised in a logical way, each room has its most important work highlighted, lighting has been improved overall and the building now has air-conditioning. The Goyas include two major self-portraits, a portrait of his friend the playwright Moratín, a large portrait of Charles IV's hated minister Godoy, and *El Entierro de la Sardina* ('Burial of the Sardine'), a Carnival scene that already foreshadows his later, darker works. Another of the academy's prized possessions is Italian mannerist Giuseppe Arcimboldo's *Spring*, a playful portrait of a man made up entirely of flowers. It was one of a series on the four seasons painted for Ferdinand I of Austria in 1563: *Summer* and *Winter* are still in Vienna, but the whereabouts of *Autumn* is unknown. The academy also has a valuable collection of plans and drawings, such as those of Prado architect Juan de Villanueva, and an impressive collection of rare books. Outstanding is the second Latin edition of Dürer's Treatise on the *Proportions of the Human Body*. In the same building is the **Calcografía Nacional**, a similarly priceless collection and archive dedicated to engraving, fine printing and related topics, which has on show many of the original plates for the great series of etchings by Goya.
Disabled: wheelchair access.

Calcografía Nacional *(91 532 15 43)*. **Open** 10am-2pm Sat-Mon, public holidays; 10am-2pm, 4-8pm Tue-Fri. **Admission** free.

Museo Romántico

C/San Mateo 13 (91 448 10 45).
Metro Tribunal/bus 3, 37, 40, 149.
Open 9am-3pm Tue-Sat; 10am-2pm Sun, public holidays. Closed Aug. **Admission** 400ptas; 200ptas students; free under-18s, over-65s. *Sun* free. **Map G4**
This rather weather-beaten museum is slowly being restored. Until it is fully refurbished it will remain a fairly grimy reflection of nineteenth-century Romanticism in Spain, although its very neglect gives it a certain nostalgic charm. The period is evoked here through furniture, paintings, ornaments and memorabilia associated with various Spanish writers. There are also interesting early pianos. The museum is another set up by a private collector, the Marqués de Vega-Inclán, and the house, from 1770, is of interest in itself. Gracing its chapel is the museum's most valuable painting, Goya's luminous *Saint Gregory the Great*, showing the saint weighed down by his robes as he sits hunched over a book.
Disabled: wheelchair access. Guided tours.

Museo Sorolla

Paseo del General Martínez Campos 37 (91 310 15 84).
Metro Gregorio Marañón, Iglesia/bus 5, 16, 61.
Open 10am-3pm Tue-Sat; 10am-2pm Sun.
Admission 400ptas; 200ptas students; free under-18s, over-65s. *Sun* free. **Map H1**
The former home of Spain's foremost Impressionist painter, Joaquín Sorolla, is a must-see. Built for him in 1910, the mansion still exudes a very comfortable turn-of-the-century elegance, even though, like many Madrid old house-museums, it could now do with a lot more being spent on its upkeep. Visitors enter through the deliciously peaceful, Moorish-inspired garden, a haven for locals who just want to sit and contemplate the fountains. Inside, notice the skylights, essential elements in the home of an artist renowned for his iridescent, sun-drenched paintings. His studio contains a curious Turkish bed, decrepit but still in one piece, where he apparently used to take his *siesta*. Around the rooms are his collections, ranging from exotic to kitsch, including a very large collection of traditional Spanish ceramics. The ground floor has been preserved to give the visitor a feel of Sorolla's life, while the upper floor has been converted into a gallery. In his exquisite large portrait of the singer Ráquel Méller, her white dress shimmers with flecks of green, violet, ochre and pink. Beside it is a picture of Sorolla's family, lying on a sea of deep green grass. The few men as subjects are usually portrayed toiling away, while women and young boys are seen at play or rest. It's easy to dismiss Sorolla, for his leisured themes, and for producing pictures that are incorrigibly like greeting cards – as indeed they are used throughout the world – but few people fail to find his world at least a little seductive, or to admire his spectacular use of light.

*Ancient Mexico in the **Museo de America**.*

The monastery museums

Real Monasterio de las Descalzas Reales

Plaza de las Descalzas 3 (91 542 00 59).
Metro Callao, Sol/bus all routes to Puerta del Sol.
Open 10.30am-12.45pm, 4-5.45pm, Tue-Thur, Sat;
10.30am-12.45pm Fri; 11am-1.45pm Sun, public holidays.
Admission 650ptas; 250ptas students, children, over-65s. *Wed* free for EU citizens. **Map D7**

Those who chance upon this monastery-museum often feel amazed at their find, for few expect to come across such a place in the middle of one of Madrid's busiest shopping areas, close to the Gran Vía and the major stores. The *Descalzas Reales* (literally, 'the Royal Barefoot Sisters') is a convent, founded in 1564 by Joanna of Austria, the daughter of Charles V and sister of Philip II, and today is still occupied by an enclosed order of nuns. Founded with royal patronage, the Descalzas became the preferred destination of the many widows, younger daughters and other women of the royal family and high aristocracy of Spain who entered religious orders. For this reason it also acquired an extraordinary collection of works of art, given as bequests by the lofty novices' families – paintings, sculptures, tapestries and *objets d'art*. Equally lavish was the baroque decoration of the building itself, with its grand painted staircase, frescoed ceilings and 32 chapels, of which only some can be visited.

Various schools of art are represented here, but the largest non-Spanish contingents are Italian, with Titian, Luini, Angelo Narddi and Sebastiano del Piombo, and Flemish, with Brueghel (*The Adoration of the Magi*), Joos Van Cleve and Rubens. The Descalzas is also an exceptional showcase of Spanish baroque religious art, with important works by the sixteenth-century artists Gaspar Becerra, Miguel Barroso and Luis de Carvajal, while the seventeenth century is

represented by Zurbarán, Claudio Coello and Herrera Barnuevo. From another epoch, there is even a tiny painting attributed to Goya. In addition, as you walk round you can also catch glimpses of the nuns' courtyard vegetable garden, virtually unchanged since the convent was first built, and still closed to the public. The monastery had been seen by very few until the 1980s, and its restoration and opening to public view netted it the Council of Europe museum prize in 1988. It can only be visited with the official tours, and while the guides rarely speak English, the wealth of things to see easily makes up for this. Tours leave about every 20 min, and each tour lasts about 45 min. *See also p53.*
Shop.

Real Monasterio de la Encarnación

Plaza de la Encarnación s/n (91 547 05 10). Metro
Ópera, Santo Domingo/bus 25, 39, 148. **Open** 10.30am-12.45pm, 4-5.45pm, Wed, Sat; 11am-1.45pm Sun, public holidays. **Admission** 425ptas; 225ptas students, children, over-65s. *Wed* free for EU citizens. **Map C6**

Now occupied by only 17 nuns, this convent-monastery was once a *Casa de Tesoro* (treasury) connected to the nearby Alcázar via a passageway. However, the only part of the original convent building, commissioned by Philip III and his wife Margaret of Austria in 1616, that remains is the façade, since much of the rest was destroyed by fire in 1734. Though not as lavishly endowed as the **Descalzas Reales**, the Encarnación still contains a great many pieces of seventeenth-century religious art, with several rooms of fine paintings and sculpture, the most impressive of which is Jusepe Ribera's shimmering *chiaroscuro* portrait of *John the Baptist*. The Encarnación's most memorable room, though, is the *reliquario* (relics room). In its glass casements are displayed some 1,500 saintly relics, most of them in extravagantly bejewelled copper, bronze, glass and silver reliquaries. Most are bone fragments and/or former possessions of saints and martyrs. There's also the odd femur or two, draped in sashes and bedecked with jewels. This relics room has been said to be the most important in the Catholic world, because of the high artistic value of the reliquaries themselves, many of which are unique. On the altar dominating the room is a prized relic of a charred, burnt wooden Christ figurine, inside an ornate bronze and glass case. Even more amazing is the solidified blood of San Pantaleón, kept inside a glass orb. The blood reportedly liquifies each year from midnight on the eve of his feast day (27 July) until the stroke of midnight on the day itself, 28 July. The wait for this to happen has become an annual news item. *See also p56.*

Archaeology & anthropology

Museo Africano

C/Arturo Soria 101 (91 415 24 12).
Metro Arturo Soria/bus 11, 70, 114, 201. **Open** guided tour only 6.30pm Thur; 11.30am Sun. Call for appointment. Closed July-Sept. **Admission** free.

'Museum' is really too grand a term to describe this simply displayed collection of African artefacts. It has been assembled over more than 30 years by the Combonian Missionaries, an order founded by Italian priest Father Daniel Comboni. Its most prized hoard is its collection of tribal masks, but it also has unusual musical instruments to complement its knives, machetes, terracotta figures, gourds and implements used in traditional magic. There is also a fine collection of recordings of traditional African music. *Disabled: wheelchair access.*

Museo de América

Avda de los Reyes Católicos 6 (91 543 94 37).
Metro Moncloa/bus all routes to Moncloa. **Open** 10am-3pm Tue-Sat; 10am-2.30pm Sun, public holidays. **Admission** 500ptas; 250ptas students, free under-18s, over-65s. *Sun* free.

An oddly mixed experience. First the positives: Madrid's Museum of the Americas contains the finest collection of pre-Columbian American art and artefacts in Europe, a combination of articles brought back at the time of the Conquest or during the centuries of Spanish rule over Central and South America with later acquisitions and others donated by Latin American countries in the modern era. The museum fell victim to one of Madrid's longest-ever renovation programmes, lasting a full 12 years from 1982 to 1994. The reopening of its galleries, now beautifully lit and equipped, was eagerly awaited. The collection includes near-matchless treasures: there is the *Madrid Codex*, one of only four surviving Mayan illustrated glyph manuscripts anywhere in the world, discovered in a private collection in Madrid in the 1860s; the *Tudela Codex* and illustrated manuscripts from central Mexico describing the events of the Spanish Conquest; superb carvings from the Mayan city of Palenque, sent back to Charles III by the first-ever modern survey expedition to a pre-Hispanic American ruin in 1787; and the 'Gold of the Quimbayas', exquisite gold figures from the Quimbaya culture of Colombia, presented to Spain by the Colombian government. All the main pre-Columbian cultures are represented – further highlights include Aztec obsidian masks from Mexico, Inca stone sculptures and funeral offerings from Peru, and finely modelled, comical and sometimes highly sexual figurines from the Chibcha culture of Colombia, which give a vivid impression of the lives of their makers. There are also exhibits from the Spanish colonial period, such as the remarkable *Entry of the Viceroy Morcillo into Potosí* (1716) by the early Bolivian painter Melchor Pérez Holguín, a series of paintings portraying in near-obsessive detail the range of racial mixes possible in colonial Mexico, and a collection of gold and other objects from the galleons *Atocha* and *Margarita*, sunk off Florida in the eighteenth century and only recovered in 1988. The negative side of the museum is that, during the long years of closure the decision was taken to arrange the collection not in the apparently too-conventional way, by countries and cultures, but entirely thematically, so that rooms are dedicated to topics such as 'the family', 'communication' and so on, with artefacts from every period and country alongside each other. Some may find this approach stimulating, but some of the supposed 'connections' drawn between objects from different cultures and eras are frankly banal, and in general unless you already have some knowledge of the many pre-Columbian cultures it is frankly confusing and uninformative, and after all these years of waiting it seems an opportunity lost. Frustrating, but still a superb and intriguing collection.

Disabled: wheelchair access. Library & café open 9am-3pm. Shop.

Museo de Antropología/Etnología

C/Alfonso XII, 68 (91 539 59 95).
Metro Atocha/bus all routes to Atocha. **Open** 10am-7.30pm Tue-Sat; 10am-2pm Sun. **Admission** 400ptas; 200ptas students, free under-18s, over-65s. *2.30-7.30pm Sat, 10am-2pm Sun* free. **Map H10**
This three-storey edifice near the Retiro – officially called the Museo de Antropología, although confusingly it says Museo de Etnología on the building – makes for an attractive museum. The interior is structured around a grand open hall that allows a view of all levels, and each floor is devoted to a specific region or country. The first level has an extensive collection from the Philippines (a former Spanish colony), dominated by a 6m (20ft) long dugout canoe made from a single tree trunk. Among the bizarre highlights are a nineteenth-century Philippine helmet made from a spiky blowfish, shrunken human heads from Peru, and the skeleton of Don Agustín Luengo y Capilla, a resident of Extremadura who attracted scientific attention by being 2.25m (7ft 4in) tall. Even more enticing is an emaciated tobacco leaf-skinned mummy, said to have once been in Charles III's Royal Library. The latter two are to be found in the annexe to the first level. Temporary exhibitions can also be interesting.

Museo Arqueológico Nacional

C/Serrano 13 (91 577 79 12). Metro Colón, Serrano/bus all routes to Plaza de Colón. **Open** 9.30am-8.30pm Tue-Sat; 9.30am-2.30pm Sun, public holidays.
Admission 500ptas; 250ptas students; free under-18s, over-65s. *Sat & Sun 2.30-8.30pm* free. **Map I5**
One of Madrid's oldest museums, the Archaeological Museum was set up in 1867. It traces the evolution of human cultures from prehistoric times up to the fifteenth century, and the collection of artefacts includes finds from the Iberian, Celtic, Greek, Egyptian, Punic, Roman, Paleochristian, Visigothic and Muslim cultures. Remarkably, the great majority of them came from excavations carried out within Spain, illustrating the extraordinary continuity and diversity of human settlement in the Iberian peninsula. Some of the most interesting relics come from the area around Madrid itself, such as the 4,000-year-old neolithic campaniform (bell-shaped) pottery bowls found south of the city at Ciempozuelos. If you wish to do the whole museum you should start a visit from the basement, which holds paleontological material including skulls, tombs and a mammoth's tusks still attached to its skull. The ground floor holds the museum's most famous possession, the Iberian sculpture the *Dama de Elche*, an enigmatic figure whose true gender is a mystery. Further up, the usual definition of archaeology is stretched somewhat to include very interesting exhibits on post-Roman Visigothic and Muslim Spain, with wonderful ceramics and fine metalwork from Moorish Andalusia. In the front garden, steps lead underground to a reproduction of the renowned Altamira cave paintings in Cantabria. It is not very impressive, but since the actual caves have now been closed to visitors in order to preserve them from further deterioration this is probably the best you can do.
Disabled: wheelchair access.

Bullfighting

Museo Taurino

Patio de Caballos, Plaza Monumental de Las Ventas, C/Alcalá 237 (91 725 18 57). Metro Ventas/bus all routes to Ventas. **Open** *Mar-Oct* 9.30am-2.30pm Tue-Fri; 10am-1pm Sun; *Nov-Feb* 9.30am-2.30pm Mon-Fri. Call for times of bullfights. **Admission** free.
Its location beside the stables in the Las Ventas bullring makes this little museum easy to find – just let your nose lead you to it. If this fails, head towards the right side of the bullring entering from Calle Alcalá. It was renovated a few years ago, and only six bulls' heads remain from the original museum, which then seemed to be mostly a homage to the bull. The present museum celebrates more the man and the bullfight itself. It consists mainly of sculptures and portraits of famous matadors and *trajes de luces* (suits of lights), including the pink and gold outfit worn by the legendary Manolete on the afternoon of his death in the ring in 1947 (and the blood-transfusion equipment used in attempts to save him). Among the eighteenth-century paintings is a portrait of torero Joaquín de Rodrigo said to be by Goya, although this is often questioned. It's an old-fashioned, slightly shabby museum, although it is one of few in Madrid with labelling in both Spanish and English.

Literary & historical

Casa-Museo de Lope de Vega

C/Cervantes 11 (91 429 92 16). Metro Antón Martín/bus 9, 14, 27, 34, 37. **Open** 9.30am-2pm Tue-Fri; 10am-1.30pm Sat. **Admission** 200ptas. *Wed* free. **Map G8**
Spain's most prolific playwright and poet Félix Lope de Vega Carpio (1562-1635) spent the last 25 years of his life in this rather sombre three-storey house, oddly enough on a street now named after his rival Cervantes. The house itself is the

Lichtenstein and Caravaggio, two sides of the **Museo Thyssen-Bornemisza**. *See page 74.*

most interesting thing to see, as the furniture and ornaments, obtained from various sources, are approximations of Lope de Vega's inventory of his household rather than originals. Even the garden, though, contains the fruit trees and plants he detailed in his journals. If you are lucky, the guide you get on the obligatory guided tour will speak reasonable English, as nothing is labelled (catalogues and brochures are available at the entrance). The tour begins at the tiny chapel on the second floor. Lope de Vega, whose tumultuous life included numerous love affairs, scandals and service in the Spanish Armada, became a priest in 1614. His tiny alcove of a bedroom has a window that opens to the chapel so he could hear mass from his bed, as Philip II did at El Escorial. Curiously, just outside his alcove was the room where the women of the household met to sew and chat. It has no chairs, only a low platform with silk cushions propped round a brazier. In the children's bedroom on the top floor, you can see a quaint belt of amulets draping a small chair by a crib, of a type that was often given to children to ward off the evil eye. The house also holds within it 1,500 antique books, all from the sixteenth and seventeenth centuries.

Museo de la Ciudad

C/Príncipe de Vergara 140 (91 588 65 99). Metro Cruz del Rayo/bus 1, 29, 52. **Open** *mid-Sept-mid-July* 10am-2pm, 4-6pm, Tue-Fri; 10am-2pm Sat, Sun; *mid-July-mid-Sept* 10am-2pm, 5-7pm, Tue-Fri. **Admission** free.
Opened in 1992 in a new building in the north of Madrid near the Auditorio Nacional (*see chapter* Music: Classical & Opera), this museum seeks to show Madrid's history and future projects in store for the city. The collection, though, is patchy and the historical material inferior to that in the **Museo Municipal**. Informative but often heavy-going exhibits deal with the development of city services – the Metro, gas, water and so on. Its temporary exhibitions on Madrid-related topics are frequently more interesting than the permanent exhibits. *Disabled: wheelchair access. Library. Shop.*

Museo del Ejército

*C/Méndez Núñez 1 (91 522 65 99).
Metro Banco de España/bus 9, 14, 27, 34, 37.* **Open** 10am-2pm Tue-Sun. **Admission** 100ptas; 50ptas students, under-18s, over-65s. *Sat* free. **Map H8**

The Army Museum, a massive collection of military memorabilia, will eventually be transferred elsewhere – very possibly to Toledo's Alcázar – once the Prado takes over this historic building; this may happen in 2001 or 2002, although no dates have been fixed, and the museum's own administration still seems strangely unaware of what might be in store (*see pp 72-3*). In the meantime, it is still easy to visit this rambling collection, begun in 1803 and surprisingly sumptuous for a military museum. It holds such historic treasures as *La Tizona*, said to be the sword of the semi-legendary Castilian hero El Cid, and which, the story goes, he won in battle by slaying its owner King Bucar of Morocco. There is also a fragment of the cross planted by Columbus on his arrival in the New World. Toy soldier enthusiasts will be delighted with a whole room devoted to miniatures; even more curious is a room at the back dedicated to a handful of Spanish heroines, with romantic paintings of women such as seamstress Manuela Malasaña, killed by French soldiers in Madrid in 1808 when she tried to defend herself with a pair of scissors (*see p61*). Also, the building the museum occupies is one of the only remaining parts of the Buen Retiro palace (*see chapter* History), and its *Sala de los Reinos* ('Hall of the Kingdoms') retains most of its original decoration, some of it by Velázquez. The Army Museum is also one of few places in Madrid where these days you can still see a monument to General Franco. English-speaking guides can be arranged with a week's notice, for 7,500ptas. *Café. Disabled: wheelchair access. Library. Shop.*

Museo del Libro

Biblioteca Nacional, Paseo de Recoletos 20 (91 580 78 00). Metro Colón/bus all routes to Plaza de Colón. **Open** 10am-9pm Tue-Sat; 10am-2pm Sun, public holidays. **Admission** free. **Map I5**
Spain's national library, the **Biblioteca Nacional**, possesses such a wealth of printed matter that it has been described as the Prado of Paper. Over three million volumes make up its store of treasures, among them every work published in Spain since 1716, Greek papyri, Arab, Hebrew and Greek manuscripts, Nebrija's first Spanish grammar, bibles, and drawings by Goya, Velázquez, Rembrandt and many others. Given the precious and fragile nature of the texts, access has previously been limited to scholars, but in 1996 the administration opened this museum to allow the public

All of art's sides

MUSEO
THYSSEN-
BORNEMISZA

Pº del Prado, 8 - Madrid - Spain

*The impressively solid portal of the **Casa-Museo Lope de Vega**. See page 80.*

a glimpse of the library's riches. The displays are conceived as interactive, steering visitors through bibliographical history via state-of-the-art multimedia applications including laser shows, video and holographs. For more on access to the main library, *see p258*.
Disabled: wheelchair access.

Museo Municipal

C/Fuencarral 78 (91 588 86 72). Metro Tribunal/ bus 3, 37, 40, 149. **Open** *Sept-July* 9.30am-8pm Tue-Fri; 10am-2pm Sat, Sun; *Aug* 9.30am-2pm Tue-Fri; 10am-2pm Sat, Sun. **Admission** 300ptas; 150ptas children, over-65s. *Wed, Sun* free. **Map F4**
A primary highlight of Madrid's municipal museum is its façade and exuberantly ornate entrance by Pedro de Ribera, one of the finest examples of baroque architecture in Madrid. The building was first commissioned as a hospice, the *Hospicio de San Fernando*, and completed in 1722. The museum collection, inaugurated in 1929, traces the history of settlement in the area and the growth of Spain's capital

from the prehistoric age to the nineteenth century, with many unusual maps, manuscripts, paintings and artefacts, among them the oldest comprehensive map of Madrid, by Pedro Teixeira (1656). Fascinating, also, is an 1833 model of the city that occupies an entire room. There are also some noteworthy paintings, by Goya, Sorolla and Eugenio Lucas. In the patio there is a pretty baroque fountain, the *Fuente de la Fama* ('Fountain of Fame'), also by Ribera. Its good temporary shows are often an interesting complement to a visit. *Guided tours. Shop (9.30am-2pm, 4.30-8pm; Aug only morning).*

Museo Naval

Paseo del Prado 5 (91 379 52 99). Metro Banco de España/bus all routes to Cibeles. **Open** 10.30am-1.30pm Tue-Sun. **Admission** free. **Map H7**
Judging from the baritone hum of voices in the high-ceilinged rooms of this museum, most visitors are male. Amid its collection of navigational instruments, muskets, guns and naval war paintings are spoils from the expeditions of

Columbus and other early mariners. Glass displays enclose primitive weapons, some of which, like the swords lined with sharks' teeth from the Gilbert Islands, promise greater damage than their Western counterparts. The most impressive room is dominated by a huge mural-map that traces the routes taken by Spain's intrepid explorers: in front of it are two equally impressive giant globes, made by AP Coronelli in the late seventeenth century. The room also holds the museum's most valuable possession, the first known map of the Americas by a European. Dating from 1500, the parchment paper drawing by royal cartographer Juan de la Cosa is believed to have been made for Ferdinand and Isabella. *Guided tours. Shop.*

The natural world

Museo de Ciencias Naturales

C/José Gutiérrez Abascal 2 (91 411 13 28).
Metro Gregorio Marañón/bus all routes to Paseo de la Castellana. **Open** 10am-6pm Tue-Fri; 10am-8pm Sat; 10am-2.30pm Sun, public holidays. **Admission** 400ptas; 300ptas 4-14s, over-65s; *special exhibitions* 350ptas; 150ptas 4-14s, over-65s.
Don't confuse the street name with that of a larger street called José Abascal, which is on the other side of the Castellana from this museum. The Museum of Natural Sciences is made up of two buildings, behind a sloping garden. The building to the north was inaugurated in January 1994, and has one of the more dynamic and interactive displays in Madrid. The history of the earth and of all living creatures is illustrated via audio-visual presentations and hands-on exhibits, in imaginative, often child- and family-oriented displays. The second building contains a simpler, much more old-fashioned presentation of fossils, dinosaurs and geological exhibits. The two-level exhibition area is dominated by the replica of a Diplodocus, surrounded by real skeletons of a Glyptodon (giant armadillo), an Elephas antiquus (mastodon) and other extinct animals. The most distinguished skeleton here, though, is that of the Megatherium americanum, a bearlike creature from the pleistocene period unearthed in Luján, Argentina, in 1788. *Library (10am-6pm Mon-Fri). Shop.*

Museo Geominero

C/Ríos Rosas 23 (91 349 57 59).
Metro Ríos Rosas/bus 3, 12, 37, 45, 149. **Open** 9am-2pm Mon-Sat. **Admission** free.
The most striking thing about this geological and mining museum is the splendid stained-glass roof overhead – the best vantage point to see it is from beside the 450kg (992lb) block of rose-coloured quartz in the centre of the vast hall. Surrounding it above are three narrow exhibition floors, reached by a precipitous spiral staircase. The collection was begun in 1865, and is suitably old-fashioned.

Stamps & coins

Museo Casa de la Moneda

C/Doctor Esquerdo 36 (91 566 65 44).
Metro O'Donnell/bus all routes to O'Donnell.
Open 10am-2.30pm, 5-7.30pm, Tue-Fri; 10am-2.30pm Sat, Sun. **Admission** free.
Unless you're a coin collector, this museum will probably be of little interest, and the fact that some of its many rooms are poorly lit, if not in virtual darkness, doesn't help either. However, the size and scope of the collection, begun in the eighteenth century, place it among the most important in the world. The history of coins is represented in chronological order, and complemented by displays of seals, bank notes, engravings, rare books and medals. Temporary exhibitions are frequent here, such as a recent one on the Euro. *Guided tours. Shop.*

Museo Postal y de Telecomunicaciones

Palacio de Comunicaciones, C/Montalbán
(91 396 25 89). Metro Banco de España/bus all routes to Plaza de Cibeles. **Open** 9am-2pm, 5-7pm, Mon-Fri; 9am-2pm Sat. **Admission** free. **Map H7**
And one for stamp collectors. Although small, this museum contains a huge wealth of stamps from all over the world. There are also exhibits on the history of the post office and telecommunications, including antique switchboards, telephones, postmen's uniforms, seals, weighing machines and lion's-head mailbox slots from the nineteenth century. *Library (9am-2pm Mon-Fri).*

Transport

Museo del Aire

Carretera de Extremadura N-V, km10.5 (91 509 16 90).
Bus from Príncipe Pío to Alcorcón/by car Carretera de Extremadura/by train Cercanías line C-5 to Cuatro Vientos, then bus 139. **Open** 10am-2pm Tue-Sun. **Admission** 100ptas; free under-10s, over-65s.
Spain's air museum, on one side of the military airbase at Cuatro Vientos, on the south-west road out of Madrid, is a suitably gung-ho collection of historic aircraft, models, uniforms, photos and other relics from the Spanish and some foreign air forces. Some civil aircraft and artefacts are included, including a 1930s Autogiro, an early form of helicopter invented by the Spaniard La Cierva. Star attractions, though, are the De Havilland Dragon Rapide that was hired by Spanish aristocrats in England to fly Franco secretly from the Canaries to Spanish Morocco just before the Civil War in 1936, and a recently-added modern flight simulator. *Disabled: wheelchair access.*

Museo Angel Nieto

Avda del Planetario 4 (91 468 02 24). Metro Méndez Alvaro/bus 8, 102, 113, 148/by train Cercanías lines C-5, C-7b, C-10. **Open** 10am-2pm, 4.30-7pm, Tue-Fri; 11.30am-2pm, 4.30-7pm, Sat, Sun; *June-Sept* 11am-2pm, 5.30-8pm, Tue-Fri; 11.30am-2pm, 5.30-8pm, Sat, Sun. **Admission** 150ptas; 100ptas under-14s, groups.
In 1988 Madrid's city hall ceded this building, in the south of the city near the Planetario and the Parque Tierno Galván (*see chapter* **Children**), to sporting legend and local-boy-made-good Angel Nieto, 13-times world motorcycle champion in 50-250cc. The museum houses his personal memorabilia – everything to do with his career is here, including bikes, photos, trophies, press cuttings, helmets, gloves, and videos of him on the track. It could be fascinating and fun if you're a biker or a racing fan, although even then you might think Angel's ego is a tad overblown. *Shop.*

Museo Nacional Ferroviario (Antigua Estación de Delicias)

Paseo de las Delicias 61 (902 22 88 22/91 506 83 33).
Metro Delicias/bus all routes to Paseo de las Delicias. **Open** 9am-3pm Tue-Sun. Closed Aug. **Admission** 500ptas; 250ptas 412s, students, over-65s. *Sat* free.
Concealed behind the national railway offices is the elegant old station of Delicias, with ironwork by no less than Gustave Eiffel himself. Now disused, it houses the National Railway Museum, an evocative collection of old engines, impressive railway models and antique railway equipment and memorabilia. A recent addition is a collection of 180 ticket-inspectors' caps from every part of the world put together by a Spanish railway employee, many from now-defunct countries and rail lines. You can climb aboard, have a drink in an old restaurant car or watch historic film footage of Spanish railways. It's a particularly good museum for kids, with occasional children's theatre performances. *Café. Library. Shop.*

Art Galleries

Times are tough in the art marketplace, but there are still new currents flowing in Madrid's spectacular exhibition spaces and contemporary galleries.

Despite an inevitable rivalry with Barcelona and growing competition from other cities, Madrid maintains a position at the centre of the Spanish art scene. The fresh winds that blew in politics and society during the early 1980s brought a newly aroused interest in contemporary art, and as a result new galleries sprouted all over Madrid. Even some foreign gallerists, believing that Spain suddenly represented a vast new market, opened up spaces here. What they failed to realise was that Spanish art buyers were relatively new to the game, and generally only wanted to buy Spanish artists. Consequently, although many galleries have some notable foreign artists on their books, it's Spanish artists who predominate. Many are of unquestionable quality, but it needs to be said that there are others who are distinctly second-rate, and yet are given automatic display space purely because they are local.

By the early '90s the sector was oversized, and when recession hit Spain in 1993 a shake-out was inevitable. Gallery owners speak of a crisis that, if less acute now than a few years ago, refuses to go away. Some galleries have, indeed, gone under, and though new ones are constantly opening, not all survive. Others are worried about the potential consequences of any diversion to the Prado rebuilding fund of part of the Reina Sofía's purchasing budget for contemporary art, an important outlet for innovative private galleries.

It is not all doom and gloom, however: there are galleries that face up to the situation bravely, and instead of grumbling adopt an 'innovate or die' spirit, back new artists, forge links with galleries abroad and actively seek new buyers. Young artists still complain that the art scene is a closed world offering few opportunities: galleries, they claim, continue to show the same names over and over again. The Ministry of Culture holds an annual show every September in the former **Museo Español de Arte Contemporáneo** in Moncloa, which gives public exposure to a selection of around 20 young Spanish artists and helps them make contact with galleries outside Spain (check with tourist offices for dates and details). One recent and highly successful innovation is **PhotoEspaña**, a huge photographic jamboree first held in 1998 (*see page 9*). Photography and related art forms have been rapidly gaining ground throughout the Madrid art world.

One characteristic of the art scene here is that many galleries – commercial and public – are run by women, still referred to by local wags as *la mafia de las bragas* ('the knicker mafia'). A select group of women, among them Soledad Lorenzo, Juana de Aizpuru and the late Juana Mordó, have been the main movers in the developing art world, and wield their power knowingly.

The best source of information on what's on in private and public galleries is the free monthly magazine *Guiarte*, available from many galleries and (usually) all tourist offices. The *Guía del Ocio* and main newspapers also have gallery listings and reviews (*see pages 197-9*). Unless otherwise stated, admission to the following spaces is free.

Public spaces & foundations

Temporary exhibitions are also frequently held in the city's major museums (*see chapter* **Museums**).

Casa de América
Palacio de Linares, Paseo de Recoletos 2 (91 595 48 00). Metro Banco de España/bus all routes to Plaza de Cibeles. **Open** for exhibitions 11am-7pm Tue-Sat; *Palacio* 10am-noon Fri-Sun. **Admission** 300ptas; 150ptas under-14s, over-65s; *Palacio* free. **Map H6**
The Casa de América was opened in 1992 – Columbus' year – in the Palacio de Linares, an 1872 mansion, to showcase the arts of Latin America and promote cultural contacts between these countries and Spain. As well as exhibitions of artists from all the Latin American countries – established names and young unknowns – it offers music and theatre performances, talks and other events. There are also print and video libraries, a good bookshop and a very fine café-restaurant in the relaxing garden. New Latin American art has an attack and energy often lacking elsewhere, and is not to be missed. *Disabled: wheelchair access.*

Centro Cultural Casa de Vacas
Parque del Retiro (91 409 58 19). Metro Retiro/bus all routes to Puerta de Alcalá. **Open** 11am-3pm, 5-9.30pm, daily. **Map I7**
The Casa de Vacas, next to the boating lake in the Retiro, resembles nothing so much as a kind of suburban Spanish dream house. Run by the city, it houses an unpredictable variety of shows, often with younger audiences in mind, but it's worth checking out if you're in the park. A recent *National Geographic* photography show was a major hit.

Centro Cultural Conde Duque
C/Conde Duque 11 (91 588 58 34). Metro Noviciado, Ventura Rodríguez/bus 1, 2, 44, 133, C. **Open** 10am-2pm, 5-30-9pm, Tue-Sat; 10.30am-2.30pm Sun. **Map D3**

Des Garçons Sauvages, a 1998 group installation at **Helga de Alvear.** *See page 90.*

The Cuartel Conde Duque, a magnificent eighteenth-century edifice built as a barracks for Philip V's Guard by Pedro de Ribera, now functions as a multi purpose exhibition space, concert venue and base for a wide variety of other services. There are three big granite-walled galleries, and three huge patios showing sculpture. The centre stages about 12 large exhibitions a year, with both single artist and group shows. Historical shows also feature frequently.
Disabled: wheelchair access.

Centro Cultural de la Villa

Jardines del Descubrimiento, Plaza de Colón (91 575 60 80). Metro Colón/bus all routes to Plaza de Colón. **Open** 10am-9pm Tue-Sat; 10am-2pm Sun. **Map I4**
Go down the steps under the deafening but refreshing water cascade in the Plaza Colón, below the Columbus monument, and you come to the city authorities' only purpose-built cultural centre (rather than one recycled from an older building). It offers theatre, concerts, a café and a huge gallery space, where group shows of many important Hispanic artists are staged. *See also chapters* **Dance** *and* **Theatre.**
Disabled: wheelchair access.

Círculo de Bellas Artes

C/Marqués de Casa Riera 2 (91 360 54 00/ 902 422 442). Metro Banco de España/bus all routes to Plaza de Cibeles. **Open** *exhibitions* 5-9pm Tue-Sat; 11am-2pm Sat, Sun. **Map G7**
This great multi functional cultural and social centre, housed in its own fine building since 1926, could be compared to the ICA in London or the Kitchen in New York, but is older and larger than both. It continues to play a major part in every area of the arts in Madrid, and, apart from a theatre and concert hall and vast café, has four impressive exhibition spaces that show work in all media. *See also chapters* **Sightseeing, Cafés & Bars, Music: Classical & Opera** *and* **Theatre.**

Fundación Arte y Tecnología

C/Fuencarral 1 (91 531 29 70). Metro Gran Via/bus all routes to Gran Via. **Open** 11am-2pm, 5-8pm, Tue-Fri; 10am-2pm Sat, Sun. **Map E6**
The mega-rich, recently privatised national phone company, *Telefónica*, uses the big main space here to show selections from its permanent collection of Spanish art, including work by Eduardo Chillida, Luis Fernández, Miró, Picasso and Tàpies. It has recently been expanded with a new permanent show – criticised by some as incomplete – based around post-Civil War Spanish artists of the so-called Madrid and Paris Schools who went into either internal or external exile. A second space acts as a meeting point for art and technology, with shows of multimedia- and technology-based installations – wacky, sometimes weird, and never boring.

Fundación Banco Central Hispano

C/Marqués de Villamagna 3 (91 558 25 70/91 575 14 30). Metro Serrano/bus 5, 27, 45, 150. **Open** 11am-2pm, 5-9pm, Tue-Sat; 11am-2.30pm Sun. **Map I3**
The art foundation of the Banco Central Hispano has a collection of more than 800 works by Spanish artists, among them Broto, García Sevilla and Chillida. It also has a good gallery space for temporary shows of Spanish art.

Fundación la Caixa

C/Serrano 60 (91 435 48 33). Metro Serrano/bus 1, 9, 19, 51, 74. **Open** 11am-8pm Mon, Wed-Sat; 11am-2.30pm Sun. **Map I3**
The Catalan savings bank la Caixa is the largest and richest in Spain, and its cultural foundation's branch in Madrid is famous for its high-quality exhibitions. They often focus on twentieth-century Spanish artistic movements, although Whistler, Sickert and Japanese photographer Hiroshi Sugimoto have also been featured recently. The ultra-clean gallery space makes a perfect backdrop for contemporary art.

Fundación Juan March
C/Castelló 77 (91 435 42 40).
Metro Núñez de Balboa/bus 1, 29, 52, 74. **Open** 10am-
2pm, 5.30-9pm, Mon-Sat; 10am-2pm Sun. **Map K2**
Set up in 1955 by Juan March, one of Spain's richest men,
the Fundación March is one of the most important private
art foundations in Europe. It organises a large number of
art exhibitions each year, sometimes in collaboration with
other museums, galleries and private collectors. They are
regularly among the most interesting in Madrid. They are
presented in the Fundación's own space here in the capital,
as well as in other centres throughout Spain and abroad.
There are usually two major shows in Madrid each year,
generally retrospectives (lasting several months) of first-
rank artists such as Kandinsky, Picasso or Paul Delvaux
or lesser-known figures such as Amadeo de Souza-
Cardoso, plus group shows based on particular movements
or schools, including photography and other media. The
foundation's own collection contains over 1,300 works of
art by some of the best contemporary Spanish artists, some
of which are permanently exhibited in the Madrid building. The March is also a major patron of music (*see chapter* **Music: Classical & Opera**).
Disabled: wheelchair access.

Institut Français
*C/Marqués de la Ensenada 12 (91 319 49 63). Metro
Colón/bus all routes to Plaza de Colón.* **Open** 10am-1pm,
4-7pm, Mon-Fri; 10am-1pm Sat. **Map H4**
The French Institute in Madrid presents a varied programme
of exhibitions of painting, photography and sculpture by
artists from both sides of the Pyrenees, as well as occasional performances of dance, theatre and music.

Instituto de México en España
*Carrera de San Jerónimo 46 (91 369 29 44). Metro
Banco de España, Sevilla/bus all routes to Plaza de
Neptuno.* **Open** 10am-3pm, 5-7pm, Mon-Fri. **Map F7**
The official cultural centre of the Mexican Embassy
organises several short exhibitions each year of work by
Mexican artists, craftspeople and, frequently, photogra-
phers. In recent times interesting monographic exhibitions
have featured photographers Julio Mayo and Tina Modotti
and painter Esteban Arévalo.

Museo Nacional
Centro de Arte Reina Sofía
*C/Santa Isabel 52 (91 467 50 62). Metro Atocha/bus all
routes to Atocha.* **Open** 10am-9pm Mon, Wed-Sat; 10am-
2.30pm Sun. Closed Tue. **Admission** 500ptas, 250ptas
students, free under-18s, over-65s. *Sat & Sun 2.30-9pm*
free. *Paseo del Arte Ticket* 1,050ptas. **Map G10**
Despite the presence of *Guernica*, the Reina Sofía's
permanent collection is not necessarily always its main
attraction – often more exciting are the major travelling
exhibitions of international artists and important collections from around the world, which are shown on the
ground (called the first) and third floors of this vast building, the most impressive spaces in Madrid for works of art.
At any given time there are always at least three high-
quality shows at the centre covering painting, sculpture,
photography, prints and so on, making it one of Europe's
foremost exhibition venues for contemporary art. In addition, the building has a cinema, a well-stocked, large arts-
bookshop, a library, a restaurant and a café. For further
details, and information on the permanent museum
collection, *see pages 42, 76-7, 159 and chapter* **Music:
Classical & Opera**.
Disabled: wheelchair access. Library. Shop.

Museo Tiflológico
C/La Coruña 18 (91 589 42 00).
Metro Estrecho/bus 3, 43, 64, 126, 127. **Open** 11am-
2pm, 5-8pm, Tue-Fri; 11am-2pm Sat.

Run by the ONCE, the powerful Spanish organisation for
the blind and partially sighted, this centre presents regular exhibitions of work by visually-impaired artists (the
name is derived from the French word *tiphlologique*, for all
things connected with people with visual problems). In
contrast to the norm in most galleries and museums, work
here can be touched as well as seen, and is generally sculptural, three dimensional, rich in texture and highly tactile.

Palacio de Cristal
Parque del Retiro (91 574 66 14).
Metro Retiro/bus all routes to Puerta de Alcalá.
Open 11am-6pm Tue-Sun. **Map J8**
This beautiful glass and wrought-iron structure in the Retiro
has, sadly, fallen into disrepair in recent years and is slow-
ly undergoing restoration, which seems to be becoming inter-
minable – no reliable date can be given for its reopening.

Palacio de Velázquez
*Parque del Retiro (91 573 62 45). Metro Retiro/bus all
routes to Puerta de Alcalá.* **Open** Oct-Apr 10am-6pm
Mon, Wed-Sat; 10am-4pm Sun; *May-Sept* 11am-8pm Mon,
Wed-Sat; 11am-6pm Sun. **Map J8**
Built by Ricardo Velázquez for a mining exhibition in 1883,
this pretty brick and tile building amid the trees of the
Retiro is topped by large iron and glass vaults. Serving as
an annexe to the Reina Sofía, its galleries are wonderfully
airy, and it hosts very good touring shows. Recent exhibitions have included sculptures by Cristina Iglesias and
mixed work by Anselm Kiefer.

Sala de las Alhajas-Caja de Madrid
Plaza de San Martín 1 (91 379 24 61).
Metro Opera, Sol/bus all routes to Puerta del Sol.
Open 11am-2.30pm, 5-8pm, Tue-Sat; 11am-2.30pm Sun,
public holidays. **Map D7**
Run by the Fundación Caja de Madrid, part of the local
savings bank, the very centrally-located *Sala de las
Alhajas* ('Jewel Room') presents four major exhibitions
every season, and has become a significant artistic
reference point. Over the past few years it has hosted exhi-
bitions of Sol LeWitt, Max Ernst, Van Gogh, the Hague
School, and US artist Sam Francis.
Disabled: wheelchair access.

Sala del Canal de Isabel II
C/Santa Engracia 125 (91 445 20 00).
Metro Ríos Rosas/bus 3, 12, 37, 45, 149. **Open** 11am-
2pm, 5-9pm, Tue-Fri; 11am-2pm Sun.
A water tower, built in elaborate neo-*mudéjar* style in 1907-
11 and considered one of the finest pieces of industrial architecture in Madrid (*see p32*), has been restored and
imaginatively transformed into a unique exhibition space,
specialising in photography. Its shows are often world-class.

Commercial galleries

Madrid's art world has a particular geography.
Salamanca, above all Calle Claudio Coello, is the
traditional centre of the upmarket gallery trade. In
the past 20 years a number of newer galleries have
appeared across the Castellana, around Calle
Génova and in Chueca, mostly in the classier part
of the district close to Calle Almirante. Also, since
the '80s a crop of adventurous contemporary
galleries has emerged some way further south, in
Lavapiés and Atocha, clustered around the magnet
that is the Reina Sofía.

Most but not quite all private galleries close for
the whole of August.

Barrio de Salamanca

Guillermo de Osma

C/Claudio Coello 4, 1º (91 435 59 36).
Metro Retiro/bus all routes to Puerta de Alcalá. **Open**
10am-2pm, 4.30-8.30pm, Mon-Fri; noon-2pm Sat. **Map I6**
This influential gallery specialises in artists from the avant-
garde movements of 1910-40. Two of its shows – of
Barradas and Maruja Mallo – later transferred to major
State museums. It's an unusual, curious place, but it knows
what it's doing. The gallery only opens on Saturdays during some exhibitions.

Oliva Arauna

C/Claudio Coello 19 (91 435 18 08).
Metro Retiro, Serrano/bus 1, 9, 19, 51, 74. **Open** 11am-
2pm, 5-9pm, Tue-Sat. Closed Aug. **Map I5**
Open since 1985, this gallery has a strong interest in
sculpture, conceptual and minimal art, but also, most recently, in work in photography and video. Two of Spain's best

sculptors, Antoni Abad (who now dedicates himself mainly to video art) and José Herrera, show here, and it has also
shown Rosa Brun and several foreign artists such as
Norwegian Per Barclay, the German Marion Thieme, the
Chilean Alfredo Jaar and Brazilian Miguel Rio Branco. A
gallery that's consistently interesting.
Disabled: wheelchair access.

Tórculo

C/Claudio Coello 17 (91 575 86 86). Metro Retiro,
Serrano/bus 1, 9, 19, 51, 74. **Open** 5-9pm Mon; 10am-
2pm, 5-9pm, Tue-Fri; 10am-2pm Sat. **Map I5**
The Tórculo gallery, run by Carmen Ortiz, has been going
since 1979, putting on around 11 shows a year. Most of the
work shown consists of prints and original works on paper,
mainly by Spanish artists – look out for José Hernández,
Joaquín Capa and Manuel Alcorlo. The gallery also organises
a variety of other cultural activities – conferences, concerts
and literary discussions.
Disabled: wheelchair access.

Artistic get-togethers

Madrid hosts two well-established annual art
bazaars – completely different in scale – which
have in common that they both open up the art
scene, draw in the crowds and, in the case of
ARCO, put contemporary art on the front page.

ARCO

Feria de Madrid, Recinto Ferial Juan Carlos I (91 722
50 00/91 722 51 80/fax 91 722 57 98).
Metro Campo de las Naciones/bus 122. **Dates** 11-16
Feb 1999; 10-15 Feb 2000. **Open** 2-9pm Mon, Tue,
Thur; noon-9pm Fri-Sun. Closed Wed **Admission**
2,000ptas; 1,000ptas students Mon, Tue, Thur;
3,000ptas, 1,500ptas students Fri-Sun.
Madrid's *Feria Internacional de Arte Contemporáneo,*
known since its inception as ARCO, is one of the most
important contemporary art fairs in Europe, and was
launched in 1981. It was the first fully international event
of this kind to take place in Spain, and over the years has
earned the respect of the international art brigade, above
all during the late 1980s when it expanded massively.
State funding is no longer as lavish as it was during
Spain's boom years, but it is still a major annual event.
Originally held in the Casa de Campo, ARCO now takes
place at the gleaming **Feria de Madrid** trade fair site
(*see p264*). The number of galleries present each year
varies: 1993 and 1994 were lean years, but by 1996 numbers were back up to 188. Galleries from all over the world
exhibit here, but each year a specific country or area is
chosen for special focus – in 1997 it was Latin America,
with 32 galleries from the continent present. A section
devoted to electronic art titled *ArcoCyber* and featuring a
wide range of multimedia creations is a recent novelty, as
is an ongoing project to promote 'emerging art'. Another
development is the plan to make ARCO a meeting point
for private patrons and public institutions.
  ARCO provides a great opportunity to get a broad per-
spective on the international art market: it's open to professionals and to the general public, which has had the
noticeable effect of boosting Spanish interest in contemporary art and new forms of expression, and makes the
atmosphere less formal than at some similar events elsewhere. This has not led to any compromise in quality, but

Studying form at **ARCO**.

does mean that it's absolutely packed. The best time to
go is 2-4pm, when locals will normally be lunching. It's
also worth noting that all work is for sale. Check out what
you are interested in, then go back late on the final day
and make an offer. Many galleries prefer to sell work
cheaply than pack it up again for shipping back home. If
you need to have anything shipped, ARCO has an official
agent, **Transférex**, who will take charge of Customs for-
malities, packing, shipping and the reclaim of IVA (Value
added tax) for non-EU residents, on a sliding scale of fees.

Art Supermarket/American Prints

C/Claudio Coello 16 (91 577 91 55).
Metro Retiro/bus all routes to Puerta de Alcalá.
Open 5.30-9pm Mon, 11am-2pm, 5.30-9pm, Tue-Sat.
Admission free. **Map I5**
Normally a shop selling prints, posters and postcards
rather than a gallery, American Prints hosts an 'art supermarket' running several weeks from late November to
mid-January each year. The concept is quite special –
works by around 80 artists, mainly up-and-coming but
also including well-known names, are laid out like goods
in a supermarket, for customers to pick up a basket and
do their 'shopping'. Quality is variable, but you can find
some gems. Prices usually start at around 7,000ptas for
numbered prints.

Chueca & Calle Génova

Antonio Machón

C/Conde de Xiquena 8 (91 532 40 93).
Metro Chueca/bus all routes to Paseo de Recoletos. **Open**
11am-2pm, 5.30-9pm, Tue-Sat. Closed Aug. **Map H5**
Near the fashionable Calle Almirante shopping area, Machón
deals mainly with famous older artists such as Tàpies,
Antonio Saura and Bonifacio, but also hosts exhibitions of
younger Spanish artists. Another facet of the gallery's activities is the publishing of deluxe limited-edition books, which
have a literary, usually poetic, component and illustrations
by contemporary painters.

Dionís Bennassar

C/San Lorenzo 15 (91 319 69 72). Metro Tribunal/bus 3,
37, 40, 149. **Open** 10am-2pm, 5-9pm, Tue-Sat. **Map G4**
Firmly established in Mallorca, Dionis Bennassar has also
had a Madrid base since 1989. He primarily features young
painters and sculptors, without neglecting better-known
figures. This is also one of the few galleries to keep the
artistic flag flying in the August heat.

Elba Benítez

C/San Lorenzo 11 (91 308 04 68).
Metro Tribunal/bus 3, 37, 40, 149. **Open** 11am-2pm, 5-
9pm, Tue-Sat. Closed Aug. **Map G4**
In the courtyard of a nineteenth-century mansion, this
gallery opened in 1990 with the aim of introducing recent
foreign artists to Spanish audiences – particularly if they
had won international acclaim but remained unknown here.
Another intention was to assist rising young Spanish artists
to gain recognition. The fact that it has stuck to its brief
makes it one of Madrid's more interesting galleries – it has
guts. Artists to look out for are Ignasi Alballi, Fernanda
Fragateiro, Jürgen Partenheimer, Francisco Ruiz de Infante,
Francesc Torres, Dario Urzay and Valentín Vallhonrat.

Elvira González

C/General Castaños 9 (91 319 59 00). Metro Colón/bus
all routes to Plaza de Colón. **Open** 10.30am-2pm, 5-9pm,
Mon-Fri; 11am-2pm, 6-9pm, Sat. **Map H4**
A true professional, Elvira González deals mostly in modern
masters, among them Calder, Chillida, Léger and Picasso,
but she also promotes some current Spanish artists, with a
notable interest in minimalism and non-figurative painting.
Every exhibition held here is complemented by a special
print edition of the same artists' work.

Estampa

C/Justiniano 6 (91 308 30 30). Metro Alonso
Martínez/bus 3, 21, 37, 40, 149. **Open** 11am-2pm, 6-
9pm, Tue-Sat. Closed Aug. **Map H4**
A rather preciously run gallery that won its reputation by
producing limited editions of small artist-made objects, but
also deals in print editions. Juan Hidalgo, Juan Bordes and
Fernando Alamo are among those represented here.

Fúcares

C/Conde de Xiquena 12 (91 308 01 91). Metro
Chueca/bus all routes to Paseo de Recoletos. **Open** 11am-
2pm, 5-9pm, Tue-Sat. Closed Aug. **Map H5**
Norberto Dotor Pérez is a dedicated gallerist keen to promote
young Spanish artists. His exhibitions bring together the different generations of artists he represents, so you'll see
established local names such as Javier Baldeón, Ignacio
Tovar, Juan Ugalde and Abraham Lacalle along with the latest trends in the art world. The gallery plans to move to a
larger space in the summer of 1999.

Galería Juana de Aizpuru

C/Barquillo 44 (91 310 55 61).
Metro Chueca/bus 3, 37, 40, 149. **Open** 5-9pm Mon;
10am-2pm, 5-9pm, Tue-Sat. **Map H5**

Juana de Aizpuru, one of the powerful women who have
dominated the modern Madrid art world, opened her first
gallery in Seville in 1970, and this space in Madrid in 1982.
She has been a, if not *the*, driving force in the international
promotion of Spanish art, and **ARCO** (*see left*) was the result
of one of her initiatives. Aizpuru openings attract the whole
of the local art crowd, whether established or lesser-known.
Around a third of the work exhibited is by young Spanish
artists; otherwise shows mainly feature better-known figures
on the international scene such as sculptors Eva Lootz or
Franz West, painters such as Jiri Dokoupil and Sol LeWitt
and photographers Miroslaw Balka and Andres Serrano.

Galería Metta

C/Marqués de la Ensenada 2 (91 319 02 30). Metro
Colón/bus all routes to Colón, Recoletos. **Open** 11am-2pm,
5-9pm, Tue-Sat. Closed Aug. **Map H4**
Opened only in 1997, Metta has two fundamental aims – to
promote the young Spanish artists on its books at fairs and
galleries abroad, and to give exhibition space to foreign
artists in Madrid. A participating gallery in ARCO '98 (*see*
left), Metta also took part in PhotoEspaña with a show of still
photos by Dennis Hopper. Other names to look out for here
are Gilles Aillaud, Lamazares, Kiki Smith and Manolo Paz.

Galería Soledad Lorenzo

C/Orfila 5 (91 308 28 87). Metro Alonso Martínez/bus 3,
7, 21. **Open** 5-9pm Mon; 11am-2pm, 5-9pm, Tue-Sat.
Closed Aug. **Map H4**
One of the longest-established gallery owners in Madrid,
Soledad Lorenzo is traditional in her style of working, and
extremely powerful in the business. Her stable is made up
of established Spanish and foreign artists, from Miquel
Barceló and José María Sicilia to Julian Schnabel, Ross
Blechner and Anish Kapoor. As well as being the most pres-
tigious in the city, the gallery itself is a very beautiful space.

Marlborough

C/Orfila 5 (91 319 14 14).
Metro Alonso Martínez/bus 3, 7, 21. **Open** 11am-2pm, 5-
9pm, Mon-Sat. Closed Aug. **Map H4**
International dealers with branches in London, New York
and Tokyo. The Madrid gallery is in an ugly building, but
thanks to US architect Richard Gluckman, an art space specialist, has a stunning interior. Previously criticised for resting on its laurels, the Marlborough has in the last couple of
years offered an important show of contemporary Spanish
sculpture, as well as Scottish artist Stephen Conroy, hyper-
realist Richard Estes and graphic work by Ron Kitaj. The
gallery also took part in PhotoEspaña with French photographer Bernard Plossu and the Argentinian Humberto Rivas.

Masha Prieto

C/Belén 2 (91 319 53 71). Metro Chueca/bus 3, 37, 40,
149. **Open** 11am-2pm, 5-9pm, Tue-Sat. **Map G4**
A small space that tends to focus on the Spanish avant-garde
with, in the past, work by surreal *Movida* photographer Ouka
Lele, painter Patricia Gadea and the fascinating Angel
Bofarull. More recently there have been exhibitions by Din
Matamoro and the enjoyable Pablo Aizoiala, as well as a first-
ever show of work in colour by photographer Jaime Gorospe.

Moriarty

C/Almirante 5, 1º (91 531 43 65). Metro Chueca/bus all
routes to Paseo de Recoletos. **Open** 11am-2pm, 5-9pm,
Tue-Fri; 11am-2pm Sat. Closed July, Aug. **Map H5**
Founded by the dramatically named Lola Moriarty in 1981,
this gallery, originally in Calle Vergara, was a prime hangout and showcase for artists on the *Movida* scene, and as well
as holding exhibitions produced magazines and book
collections and promoted pop bands and other music groups.
A genuinely open space, Moriarty has continued its independent promotion of young artists. Some artists from the
early days, such as Alberto García-Alix and Mireia Sentis,

are still going and can be found here; other names to look out for in the gallery's interesting and wacky shows are Ana Navarrete, Chema Madoz, Javier Utray and Paloma Muñoz. *Disabled: wheelchair access.*

Sen

C/Barquillo 43 (91 319 16 71).
Metro Chueca/bus 3, 37, 40, 149. **Open** 11am-2pm, 5-9pm, Tue-Sat. Closed Aug. **Map H5**
Sen is dedicated to contemporary figurative art, promoting new and established artists. It's another gallery associated with slick, playful *Movida* artists such as Ceesepe, but other names to watch out for are Costus or Eduardo Sanz. It has recently expanded into the flat upstairs, and now has space in the basement for a permanent exhibition of sculpture. Sen also produces editions of graphic art and sculpture. *Disabled: wheelchair access.*

Lavapiés & the Reina Sofía

Cruce

C/Argumosa 28 (91 528 77 83). Metro Atocha/bus all routes to Atocha. **Open** 5-9pm Tue-Sat. **Map F10**
A relative newcomer to the Madrid arts scene, Cruce recently celebrated its fifth birthday. It's less a gallery as such than a centre for the promotion, production and presentation of a range of creative activities, run collectively by a group of young artists. It provides a space for meetings of ideas, workshops, book launches and exhibitions, often with audience participation, and joint projects have been carried out with galleries in other countries, notably one a couple of years back with the Stedelijk Museum in Amsterdam. Another recent initiative was its first 'Open', in autumn 1998, more or less a retrospective of Cruce's first five years.

Ediciones Benveniste

C/Relatores 20, 1° (91 429 80 09). Metro Tirso de Molina/bus 6, 26, 32, 65. **Open** 5-9pm Mon-Fri. **Map E8**
This functioning workshop/gallery, run by Danish-born master copperplate printer Dan Benveniste, has a relaxed feel that's quite different from the slightly snooty atmosphere found in many Madrid galleries. It's located on the first floor of an eighteenth-century convent, and the ample space is used to present four exhibitions a year, mainly of non-Spanish artists. Prints are also on sale. Call to check before visiting, as opening times are variable.

EFTI

Calle Fuenterrabia 4-6 (91 552 99 99). Metro Atocha Renfe/bus all routes to Atocha. **Open** 10am-2pm, 5pm-10pm, Mon-Fri; 11am-2pm Sat. Closed Aug. **Map J10**
Actually a photography school, EFTI also has a reasonably sized exhibition space consisting of two different rooms, and organises several shows of photography every year. The excellent Isabel Muñoz has featured here in recent times, as has fashion and advertising expert Miguel Oriola. Another annual feature are the Hoffman Prizes, which showcase work by a large number of young photographers.

Helga de Alvear

C/Doctor Fourquet 12 (91 468 05 06).
Metro Atocha/bus all routes to Atocha. **Open** 11am-2pm, 5-9pm, Tue-Sat. Closed Aug. **Map G9**
This gallery opened under its current name in January 1995 when Helga de Alvear, director and owner of the Galería Juana Mordó since 1980, decided to open her own space near the Reina Sofia. Founded by the late Juana Mordó, the forerunner had been dedicated to the diffusion and promotion of contemporary art, both Spanish and foreign, since 1964. It launched Spain's El Paso group and others of the same generation – Lucio Muñoz, Mompo, Zobel and Julio López Hernández – and introduced Botero, César, David Hockney and Kandinsky to the Spanish market in the '60s, Robert Motherwell and Miquel Conde in the '70s, and AR Penk and

*Work by Ouka Lele, as featured at **BAT**.*

Nam June Paik in the '80s. Helga de Alvear maintains the same spirit, and continually presents the most innovative and wide-ranging of work. *Disabled: wheelchair access.*

Elsewhere

Bassari

C/del Cristo 3 (91 541 33 60). Metro Noviciado, Ventura Rodriguez/bus 2, 147. **Open** 11am-2pm, 5.30-8.30pm, Mon-Fri; 11am-2pm Sat. **Map D4**
Named after an African tribe, Bassari aims to expand knowledge of African art and culture in Spain. Its three-monthly exhibitions feature different aspects of culture and ritual, an focus on a particular ethnic group or country. There's also a permanent exhibition of pieces, available for sale.

Estiarte

C/Almagro 44 (91 308 15 70).
Metro Rubén Dario/bus 7, 40, 147. **Open** 1.30am-2pm, 5-9pm, Mon-Fri; 10.30am-2pm Sat. **Map H2**
Specialists in printing and selling original graphics, mostly by contemporary artists. It represents many big names past and present – Miguel Barceló, Max Ernst, Calder, Chillida, Picasso, Piensa, José Maria Sicilia and Tàpies. A recent step has been to exhibit completely new work, always on paper.

Galería BAT – Alberto Cornejo

C/Rios Rosas 54 (91 554 48 10). Metro Rios Rosas/bus 5, 12, 45. **Open** 11am-2pm, 5-9pm, Tue-Sat.
Founded in 1986 and a little off the beaten track near Nuevos Ministerios, BAT promotes, publishes and shows a range of Spanish and international artists, especially graphic work. A regular participant in art fairs in Spain and abroad, the gallery has a large private collection with works by Chillida, Miró, Mompó, Picasso and Tàpies, as well as younger artists such as David Lechuga, Sadao Koshiba and Ouka Lele.

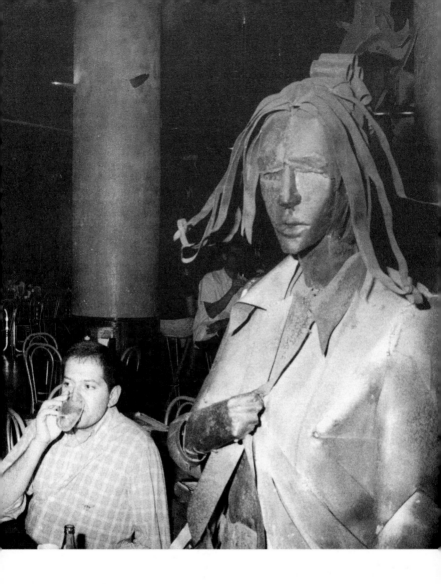

Eat, Drink, Sleep, Shop

Accommodation

From swish to spartan – beds for all budgets.

Finding somewhere to stay is never a real problem in Madrid. The city centre has plenty of mid-range and cheap hotels within walking distance of the artistic 'Golden Triangle' (the Prado, Thyssen and Reina Sofía). Finding something beyond character-less comfort without spending a fortune, however, is harder, but not impossible. At the top end of the price range, heavy hitters like the **Ritz** and the **Palace** remain jaw-droppingly luxurious, with service to match. It's the mid-range hotels, many part of chains, that tend to be well equipped but almost identical in style. The budget traveller looking for a clean, well-located place to sleep, on the other hand, catches some of the best bargains way down the scale in *hostales*, more and more owners of which are coming round to the idea of air-conditioning, a big asset in a city where temperatures regularly pass 40°C in summer. And there are still one or two quirky and well-priced gems to be found, such as the **Monaco** and the **París**. Away from the heart of town there is less to choose from, but there is a fair selection of mid-range business hotels around the Castellana and Salamanca.

Swimming pools are a desirable, if uncommon, luxury (*see page 105* **Splashing out**). If you're driving, try to find a hotel with garage parking. This will be safer and more convenient, as parking in central Madrid is severely restricted (*see page 252*).

STAR RATING, PRICES & DISCOUNTS

Hotel prices in Madrid, which for some time have dragged behind the rest of Europe, are fast catching up, but nevertheless there are still bargains to be had, right up to five-star establishments. Bear in mind, though, that the official star ratings from one to five, based on fairly arbitrary criteria, are not an entirely reliable guide. This can work in your favour, as four-star hotels can often have services equal to or better than more expensive five-stars. At the other end of the scale, anywhere called a hotel will normally have bathrooms in all rooms, whereas *hostales* and *pensiones* (terms that are virtually interchangeable) may not. The latter, usually, will also have only limited facilities in terms of bars, lounges and so on.

All hotel bills are subject to seven per cent IVA (Value Added Tax) on top of the basic price. A feature of Madrid hotels is that many upper-range establishments geared to business clients offer very user-friendly discounts at weekends, Christmas, during Easter Week and in August. Consequently, they may provide a much better deal all in all than places apparently further down the scale. Many hotels also reduce prices at certain other times of the year (often October-November), and it's always worth enquiring when booking about whatever special rates may be available.

The hotels and *hostales* listed here, apart from **Apartment hotels** and **Youth hostels**, are divided according to the **basic price of a double room at standard rates WITHOUT IVA**, which is normally quoted separately on bills. Given the frequency of discounts they should be taken as a **guideline** only. Prices quoted are per room, not per person, and do not include breakfast. The cheap bed and breakfast hotel doesn't really exist in Madrid. Most hotels will offer coffee and a roll as breakfast, but it's rarely included in the room price and the extra charge is often unreasonably expensive. Better to do like the city's natives and take breakfast in a local café.

If you arrive in Madrid without a room and don't feel like looking around yourself, the agencies listed here can make bookings for you. If you're staying for some time, and need information on renting a room longer-term, *see page 263*.

Brújula

C/Princesa 1, 6º (91 559 97 05). Metro Plaza de España/bus all routes to Plaza de España. **Open** *Oct-Mar* 9am-2pm, 4-7pm, *Apr-Sept* 9am-7pm, Mon-Fri. **Map D4**
A private agency (the name means 'Compass') that books rooms in hotels of all categories in Madrid and its region, and provides a map and directions on how to get there, for a fee of 250ptas (300ptas at any of the branches). It's often difficult to get through to the head office by phone, and easier to go to a branch in person.
Branches: Airport bus terminal Plaza de Colón (91 575 96 80). **Open** 8am-10pm daily. **Map I4**
Atocha station (91 539 11 73). **Open** 8am-10pm daily. **Map H10**
Chamartín station (91 315 78 94).
Open 7.30am-11pm daily.

Viajes Aira
(airport reservations desks)

Arrivals terminals 1 & 2, Barajas Airport (91 305 44 24/91 305 84 19). **Open** 8am-midnight daily.
Viajes Aira have two hotel reservations desks in the arrivals areas at Barajas. They do not deal with all hotels in Madrid, but mainly have rooms in the mid-range categories (about 7,000-13,000ptas a double). There is no booking fee. Once you've made your booking, you must find your way to the hotel yourself.
Head office *C/General Pardiñas 107 (91 562 26 14). Metro Avda de América/bus 12, 29, 52, C.* **Open** 9am-7.30pm Mon-Fri; 9am-1pm Sat. **Map K1**

Grand luxury (over 30,000ptas)

Hotel Eurobuilding

C/Padre Damián 23, 28036 (91 345 45 00/fax 91 345 45 76). Metro Cuzco/bus 11, 40, 150.
Rates *single* 26,500ptas; *double* 33,500ptas.
Credit AmEx, DC, EC, JCB, MC, £$TC, V.
The very name conjures up images of glossy modern blankness, but for business travellers this twin-tower, 600-room giant can't be beat. It's in a residential and business neighbourhood, with few tourists in sight. Almost every imaginable service and facility is offered, and there are superior indoor and outdoor pools for cooling down between conferences (both open to non-residents; *see chapter* **Sport & Fitness**). Apartment-size suites are available for any length of time.
Hotel services *Air-conditioning. Babysitting. Bar. Beauty salon. Business services. Car park. Conference facilities. Currency exchange. Disabled: room adapted for the disabled, wheelchair access. Fax. Fitness centre (gym/sauna/massge). Hairdresser. Interpreting services. Laundry. Lifts. Limousine service. Multilingual staff. Non-smoking rooms & floor. Restaurant. Swimming pool. Ticket agency.* **Room services** *Hairdryer. Minibar. Radio. Refrigerator. Room service (24hrs). Safe. Telephone. TV (satellite). Video.*

Hotel Palace

Plaza de las Cortes 7, 28014 (91 360 80 00/fax 91 360 81 00/website: www.palacemadrid.com). Metro Banco de España/bus 9, 14, 27, 37, 45. **Rates** *single* 40,000ptas; *double* 55,000ptas. **Credit** AmEx, DC, EC, JCB, MC, £$TC, V. **Map G8**
This colossal 440-room monster, which, along with the Ritz (*see below*), forms Madrid's duo of classic grand hotels, first opened its doors in 1913. It aims at – and mostly succeeds in – combining old world elegance with up-to-the-minute facilities such as the smart new fitness centre. The lounge areas and stunning lobby have maintained an air of real sumptuousness, and it has deliciously comfortable (and surprisingly reasonably priced) bars and restaurants, open to non-residents. It has a reputation as a place to let your hair down, and its bubbling, moving-and-shaking atmosphere keeps the crowds coming back. Take your pick from their glittering guest list – everyone from Mata Hari to Michael Jackson has stayed here. Staff are as smoothly professional as you would expect.
Hotel services *Air-conditioning. Babysitting. Bar. Beauty salon. Business services. Car park. Conference facilities. Currency exchange. Disabled: room adapted for the disabled, wheelchair access. Fax. Fitness centre. Hairdresser. Interpreting services. Laundry. Lifts.*

The Mónaco

Anyone with a sense of humour and an appreciation of kitsch will get a kick out of the Hotel Mónaco, a 38-room one-star in Chueca. It began life as an apartment block. In 1919, a year after its construction, the building was acquired by a French engineer, who had it completely redone as a home for his lover. Within a year, it had become a thriving brothel.

Right through to the late '50s, the building was the most fashionable house of ill repute in town. King Alfonso XIII held regular assignations in the most ornate of all the rooms, bringing with him a whole string quartet who accompanied the royal exertions discreetly from behind a curtain. Mussolini's son-in-law is said to have rented the whole place for three days in

1941, and many famous bullfighters have hung up their capes here.

In 1959 the building became the Hotel Mónaco, but all was not lost, and much of its fabulous décor has survived to this day. The intimate lobby of faux marble, peacock prints and worn leather furniture remains, as do the pink neon signs to the little cafeteria. The ambience is still quirky, too: the likes of French *Vogue* have staged photo-shoots in its rooms, but the Mónaco's owners make little of it (though the chatty staff might take you aside and tell you, 'This is not a hotel, it's a museum').

Some of the original fittings are not as well preserved as they could be, but many of the rooms are still wonderful. The King's room, no. 20, has a bathtub on a raised platform, dramatic paintings and a wall of mirrors behind the bed. So popular is it as a video backdrop that it's rarely available to guests. The bordello essence lingers in rooms such as no. 121, where fat cherubs dance round the ceiling between more mirrors than any anorexic would require, and Helen of Troy makes a painterly appearance in the bathroom. No. 123 has a huge ornate wooden canopy with mirror over the bed, while no. 127 is a riot of pink fabric-effect plaster walls and swagged curtains with a raised bath.

Despite its fame, the Mónaco is not expensive, and there are discounts for stays of one week or more. And in a city where hotels frequently offer only bland comfort, it's a definite gem. For hotel details, *see page 97* **Lower-mid**.

Limousine. Multilingual staff. Non-smoking floor/rooms. Restaurant. Ticket agency. **Room services** *Hairdryer. Minibar. Modem jack. Radio. Refrigerator. Room service (24hrs). Safe. Telephone. TV (satellite). Video (on request).*

Hotel Ritz

Plaza de la Lealtad 5, 28014 (91 521 28 57/fax 91 523 87 76/reserva@ritz.es). Metro Banco de España/ bus 9, 14, 27, 37, 45. **Rates** *single* 51,000ptas; *double* 58,000ptas; *suite* from 99,000ptas. **Credit** AmEx, DC, EC, JCB, MC, £$TC, V. **Map H7**

Madrid's most elite hotel was built in 1910 thanks to a personal intervention by King Alfonso XIII, who had been embarrassed during his wedding in 1906 because his official guests had not been able to find any hotel in the city of the standard they expected. Placed by several polls among the ten best hotels in the world, it's still gorgeous, right down to the hand-made carpets and fine linen sheets; the service is matchless; and the restaurant, serving Spanish and French cuisine, is superb. The rooms have all been renovated in their original belle époque style, and the hotel's garden terrace, a fashionable Madrid meeting point, is truly lovely. Smaller and more intimate than the Palace (158 rooms), the Ritz has tended to cultivate a more restrained, slightly stuffy image, but in the last few years this has changed, and it has welcomed the celebs it once shunned. Also, as well as the standard room prices there are advantageous weekend rates and occasional offers, making this oasis of luxury not as inaccessible as you might think.

Hotel services *Air-conditioning. Babysitting. Bar. Beauty salon. Business services. Conference facilities. Currency exchange. Fax. Garden. Fitness centre (gym/sauna/massage). Hairdresser. Interpreting services. Laundry. Lifts. Limousine service. Multilingual staff. Non-smoking rooms & floor. Restaurant. Ticket agency.* **Room services** *Hairdryer. Minibar. Radio. Room service (24 hrs). Safe. Telephone. TV (satellite). Video (on request).*

Hotel Santo Mauro

C/Zurbano 36, 28010 (91 319 69 00/fax 91 308 54 77/santomauro@itelco.es). Metro Rubén Darío/bus 5, 7, 40, 147. **Rates** *single* 35,000ptas; *double* 44,000ptas. **Credit** AmEx, DC, EC, JCB, MC, £$TC, V. **Map H3**

Built in the last century as an aristocratic palace, this hotel with just 36 rooms – each one different – is the last word in restrained chic. While the lounges, restaurant (in the beautiful old library) and bar have retained their original flavour, with high ceilings and marble fireplaces, the bedrooms have been slickly decorated in contemporary colours. It sits in a quiet, tree-filled area near Chamberi, with gracious gardens and a plain courtyard. Opened in the early '90s – previously it housed various embassies – it has welcomed Catherine Deneuve, Simon LeBon and other celebrities seeking luxury and privacy. The duplex rooms in the former stables are fabulous. Some rooms have a hydromassage bath.

Hotel services *Air-conditioning. Babysitting. Bar. Business services. Car park. Conference facilities. Currency exchange. Fax. Fitness centre (gym/sauna/ massage). Garden. Interpreting services. Laundry. Lifts. Limousine. Multilingual staff. Non-smoking floor/rooms. Restaurant. Safe. Swimming pool. Ticket agency.* **Room services** *Hairdryer. Minibar. Radio. Refrigerator. Room service (24hrs). Telephone. TV (satellite). Video.*

Hotel Villa Magna

Paseo de la Castellana 22, 28046 (91 576 75 00/fax 91 575 95 04/villamagna@hyattintl.com). Metro Rubén Darío/bus all routes to Paseo de la Castellana. **Rates** *single* 55,000ptas; *double* 60,000ptas. **Credit** AmEx, DC, JCB, MC, £$TC, V. **Map I3**

They say you get what you pay for, and here you pay for service: there isn't a single request you could dream up that the staff wouldn't rally round to fulfil. Business folk

Characters

Some complain that Madrid's hotels lack individuality, but look around and there are quite a few places not afraid to stick their head out.
Hotel Mónaco – fading decadence (*see p93*).
Hotel París – a riot of china and chandeliers, and wonky wooden floors.
Hotel Santo Domingo – hidden style near the Royal Palace and the Opera.
Hotel Santo Mauro – restrained chic; the library dining room is sheer heaven.
Hotel Tryp Ambassador – palatial elegance.

and affluent tourists flock to this modern 182-room hotel, as well as the stars – U2, Naomi Campbell and Madonna have stayed here. The exterior is plain, rooms are not remarkable, and the glitzy main floor is reminiscent of '70s Miami Beach chic, but it's very comfortable, and very conveniently placed for the Salamanca shopping area. It also houses an exceptional restaurant, the **Berceo-Le Divellec** (*see chapter* **Restaurants**).

Hotel services *Air-conditioning. Babysitting. Bar. Beauty salon. Business services. Car park. Conference facilities. Currency exchange. Disabled: room adapted for the disabled, wheelchair access. Fax. Fitness centre (gym/sauna/massage). Garden. Hairdresser. Interpreting services. Laundry. Lifts. Limousine. Multilingual staff. Non-smoking floor/rooms. Restaurant. Ticket agency.* **Room services** *Hairdryer. Minibar. Room service (24hrs). Safe. Telephone. TV (satellite). Video.*

Hotel Villa Real

Plaza de las Cortes 10, 28014 (91 420 37 67/fax 91 420 25 47/info@derbyhotels.es). Metro Banco de España/bus 9, 10, 14, 27, 45. **Rates** *single* 31,700ptas; *double* 39,600ptas. **Credit** AmEx, DC, EC, JCB, MC, £$TC, V. **Map G8**

When architects Fernando Chueca Goitia and José Ramos designed this intimate hotel of 115 rooms at the end of 1989, they set out to capture the feeling of its neighbouring competitors-to-be, the Palace and the Ritz (for both, *see above*). Refurbished again in 1998, it has a flavour of the past, with neo-classical embellishments in the lobby; the rooms do not have quite the same elegance, but the hotel is ideally situated for the main museums, Sol and Atocha.

Hotel services *Air-conditioning. Babysitting. Bar. Beauty salon. Business services. Car park. Conference facilities. Currency exchange. Disabled: room adapted for the disabled, wheelchair access. Fax. Hairdresser. Interpreting services. Laundry. Lifts. Limousine. Massage. Multilingual staff. Non-smoking rooms. Restaurant. Sauna. Ticket agency.* **Room services** *Hairdryer. Minibar. Radio. Room service (24hrs). Safe. Telephone. TV (satellite).*

Hotel Wellington

C/Velázquez 8, 28001 (91 575 44 00/fax 91 576 41 64/wellin@genio.infor.es). Metro Retiro/bus 1, 9, 19, 51, 74. **Rates** *single* 21,500ptas; *double* 34,250ptas. **Credit** AmEx, DC, EC, JCB, MC, £$TC, V. **Map J5**

A moment's walk from the Retiro and the chicest shopping area around C/Goya, this 288-room five-star is utterly swish. It has a handsome entrance and surprisingly intimate lobby, and attracts a faithful clientele of British and American executives. During San Isidro in May many bullfighters stay here, as it's the best-situated luxury hotel for Las Ventas bullring, and the basement houses a flamenco dance club.

Hotel services *Air-conditioning. Babysitting. Bar. Beauty salon. Business services. Car park. Conference facilities. Currency exchange. Fax. Hairdresser. Interpreting service. Laundry. Limousine. Massage. Multilingual staff. Restaurant. Sauna. Swimming pool. Ticket agency.* **Room services** *Hairdryer. Minibar. Radio. Room service (24hrs). Safe. Telephone. TV (satellite).*

Expensive (20-30,000ptas)

Gran Hotel Conde Duque

Plaza Conde del Valle Suchil 5, 28015 (91 447 70 00/ fax 91 448 35 69/condeduque@hotelcondeduque.es. Metro San Bernardo/bus 21, 147.
Rates *single* 16,000ptas; *double* 25,000ptas.
Credit AmEx, DC, EC, JCB, MC, £$TC, V. **Map E3**
The 143 rooms of this 40-year-old hotel were tastefully redesigned and rebuilt in 1992. Service is smooth, and travellers who are not too bothered about being close to the major museums will find the location refreshing, as it's on a small square on the fringes of Chamberí that's regularly full of students and local families socialising. Rare for Madrid, it looks attractive from the outside, too.
Hotel services *Air-conditioning. Babysitting. Bar. Business services. Car park. Conference facilities. Currency exchange. Fax. Interpreting services. Laundry. Lifts. Limousine service. Multilingual staff. Restaurant. Tearoom. Ticket agency.* **Room services** *Hairdryer. Minibar. Radio. Room service (24hrs). Safe. Telephone. TV (satellite).*

Gran Hotel Reina Victoria

Plaza de Santa Ana 14, 28012 (91 531 45 00/fax 91 522 03 07). Metro Sevilla, Sol/bus all routes to Puerta del Sol. **Rates** *single* 20,000ptas; *double* 25,000ptas.
Credit AmEx, DC, MC, V. **Map E8**
Overlooking a square that's a magnet for foreigners, tapas-seekers and the local night-time crowd (*see* chapters **Sightseeing, Cafés & Bars** *and* **Nightlife**), this 202-room hotel has a great history, having been a favourite put-up of bullfighters and their number one fan Ernest Hemingway in bygone days. The legendary Manolete's room is recreated within. Today, though, it relies heavily on its reputation.
Hotel services *Air-conditioning. Bar. Business services. Car park. Conference facilities. Currency exchange. Disabled: wheelchair access. Fax. Laundry. Lifts. Multilingual staff. Restaurant. Ticket agency.* **Room services** *Minibar. Radio. Room service (7.30am-5pm, 8.30pm-midnight). Safe. Telephone. TV (satellite).*

Hotel Emperador

Gran Via 53, 28013 (91 547 28 00/fax 91 547 28 17/ hemperador@sei.es). Metro Gran Via/bus all routes to Gran Via. **Rates** *single* 17,100ptas; *double* 21,300ptas.
Credit AmEx, DC, EC, MC, £$TC, V. **Map E6**
An immaculately maintained 50-year-old hotel that is ideally placed in the centre of town. Rooms are spacious, with original furnishings in impeccable shape, and surprisingly quiet, despite the traffic below. Bathrooms have been recently redone, and the staff are gracious. Its greatest plus, though, is its superb rooftop pool (*see* p105, and chapter **Sport & Fitness**). Although it has 241 rooms, you need to book early here, as it's popular, especially with Spanish stars. The area is not dangerous, but be careful with bags, particularly at night.
Hotel services *Air-conditioning. Bar. Beauty salon. Business services. Conference facilities. Currency exchange. Disabled: room adapted for the disabled, wheelchair access. Fax. Fitness centre (gym/sauna/ massage). Hairdresser. Interpreting services. Laundry. Lifts. Limousine service. Multilingual staff. Non-smoking floor/rooms. Swimming pool. Ticket agency.* **Room services** *Hairdryer. Minibar. Radio. Room service (7am-midnight). Safe. Telephone. TV (satellite).*

Hotel Santo Domingo

Plaza de Santo Domingo 3, 28013 (91 547 98 00/ fax 91 547 59 95/sdomingo@stnet.es). Metro Santo Domingo/bus all routes to Gran Via. **Rates** *single* 15,725ptas; *double* 22,175ptas. **Credit** AmEx, DC, JCB, MC, £$TC, V **Map D6**
Don't be put off by the murky salmon-coloured exterior of this 120-room former apartment block, or its sad sidestreet. It was taken over by the Barcelona Style chain four years ago, and inside is now all warm yellow walls, old paintings and statuary, as befits its four-star status. Though small, the bedrooms are individually styled and comfortable; fifth-floor rooms all have tiny balconies with great views over the rooftops to the city's green edges. In the heart of the sights, with Palacio Real around the corner and a shopping area two minutes away. Some rooms have a hydromassage bath.
Hotel services *Air-conditioning. Bar. Car park. Conference facilities. Currency exchange. Disabled: room adapted for the disabled, wheelchair access. Fax. Interpreting services. Laundry. Lifts. Limousine services. Multilingual staff. Restaurant. Ticket agency.* **Room services** *Hairdryer. Minibar. Radio. Refrigerator. Room service (7am-11.30pm). Safe. Telephone. TV (satellite). Video.*

Hotel Tryp Ambassador

Cuesta de Santo Domingo 5-7, 28013 (91 541 67 00/fax 91 559 10 40). Metro Opera, Santo Domingo/bus 25, 39, 44, 133, 147. **Rates** *single* 21,000ptas; *double* 26,250ptas.
Credit AmEx, DC, EC, JCB, MC, £$TC, V. **Map D7**
Hidden away in an unassuming backstreet close to the Opera House is this 181-room luxurious member of the Tryp chain, which used to be part convent, part palace. Plácido Domingo laid his head in suite 403 here after a hard night's singing at opening gala of the nearby opera house. Rooms are all different with plenty of light, and the hotel also has a plush atrium, classy bar and eating area. Don't miss the cool patio garden overseen by Curro the parrot. Helpful multilingual staff; four stars, but looks like five.
Hotel services *Air-conditioning. Bar. Conference facilities. Currency exchange. Fax. Laundry. Lifts. Multilingual staff. Non-smoking floor/rooms. Restaurant. Ticket agency.* **Room services** *Hairdryer. Minibar. Radio. Refrigerator. Room service (7am-midnight). Safe. Telephone. TV (satellite).*

Hotel Zurbano

C/Zurbano 79, 28003 (91 441 55 00/fax 91 441 32 24). Metro Gregorio Marañón/bus 12, 45, 147.
Rates *single* 19,400ptas; *double* 25,800ptas.
Credit AmEx, DC, EC, JCB, MC, £$TC, V. **Map H1**
In a quiet area west of the Castellana near Nuevos Ministerios, this 260-room hotel is divided between two buildings. Contemporary, bright and decorated with bleached wood and modern Spanish art, it's a good choice for anyone who prefers to be slightly off the tourist trail. Rooms are spacious, and the restaurant and bars are great, Metro and bus connections are a short walk away, and there are well-priced weekend rates.
Hotel services *Air-conditioning. Babysitting. Bar. Business services. Car park. Conference facilities. Currency exchange. Disabled: wheelchair access. Fax. Laundry. Lifts. Multilingual staff. Non-smoking floor/rooms. Restaurant.* **Room services** *Hairdryer. Minibar. Radio. Room service (24hrs). Safe. Telephone. TV (satellite). Video.*

Meliá Confort Galgos

C/Claudio Coello 139, 28006 (91 562 66 00/ fax 91 561 76 62/melia.confortgalgos@solmeliaes). Metro Núñez de Balboa/bus 9, 19, 51, 61.
Rates *single* 18,000ptas; *double* 29,825ptas. **Credit** AmEx, DC, JCB, MC, £$TC, V. **Map J2**

Fountains, mirrors, plants and piped music make up the lobby of this 357-room chain hotel on the north side of Salamanca, where the emphasis is firmly on the business customer. Rooms are fairly plain, and service professional. Its location is outside the main sightseeing area, but is well-placed for shoppers on one of Salamanca's most fashionable thoroughfares.
Hotel services *Air-conditioning. Babysitting. Bar. Car park. Conference facilities. Currency exchange. Fax. Interpreting services. Laundry. Lifts. Limousine service. Multilingual staff. Non-smoking floor/rooms. Restaurant. Ticket agency.* **Room services** *Hairdryer. Minibar. Radio. Refrigerator. Room service (24hrs). Safe. Telephone. TV (satellite).*

Upper-mid (13-20,000ptas)

Hotel Alcalá
C/Alcalá 66, 28009 (91 435 10 60/fax 91 435 11 05). Metro Príncipe de Vergara/bus all routes to C/Alcalá. **Rates** *single* 17,500ptas; *double* 18,600ptas. **Credit** AmEx, DC, EC, MC, £$TC, V. **Map K5**
Close to the Retiro, this could be one of the friendliest hotels in town, mostly down to the fact that many of the staff have worked here for years. Polished wood floors and fittings add to the warm atmosphere. The 146 rooms have been well refurbished, and inside rooms overlook an attractive courtyard garden. Stylish touches include one room on each floor fitted out by quirky fashion designer Agatha Ruiz de la Prada.
Hotel services *Air-conditioning. Bar. Car park. Conference facilities. Currency exchange. Fax. Laundry. Lifts. Multilingual staff. Non-smoking floor/rooms. Restaurant. Safe. Ticket agency.* **Room services** *Hairdryer. Minibar. Radio. Room service (24hrs). Telephone. TV (satellite).*

Hotel Aristos
Avenida de Pío XII 34, 28016 (91 345 04 50/fax 91 345 10 23). Metro Pío XII/bus 16, 29, 150. **Rates** *single* 15,800ptas; *double* 19,750ptas. **Credit** AmEx, DC, MC, V.
A distinctly chilly and business-like atmosphere reigns at this 25-room hotel, and it's not especially cheap; once inside, the rooms are functionally comfortable. Its appeal is its location, five minutes from the airport and the Feria trade fair, and 15 minutes from the city centre. There's also a decent restaurant next door.
Hotel services *Air-conditioning. Bar. Car park. Conference facilities. Currency exchange. Fax. Garden. Laundry. Lifts. Limousine service. Multilingual staff. Restaurant. Ticket agency.* **Room services** *Hairdryer. Minibar. Radio. Refrigerator. Room service (24hrs). Safe. Telephone. TV (satellite).*

Hotel Arosa
C/de la Salud 21, 28013 (91 532 16 00/ fax 91 531 31 27/arosa@hotelarosa.com). Metro Sol/bus all routes to Puerta del Sol. **Rates** *single* 12,730ptas; *double* 19,680ptas. **Credit** AmEx, DC, EC, JCB, MC, £$TC, V. **Map E7**
With Puerta del Sol and Gran Vía at opposite ends of the street, this 139-room hotel couldn't be more central. The immediate area can be a bit sleazy, but the street itself is quiet and the hotel entrance well protected. The spacious reception, restaurant and bar area on the second floor is a pleasant surprise. Rooms are clean, families are welcome, and the hotel is popular with British and American guests.
Hotel services *Air-conditioning. Babysitting. Bar. Car park. Conference facilities. Currency exchange. Fax. Laundry. Lifts. Multilingual staff. Restaurant. Ticket agency.* **Room services** *Hairdryer. Minibar. Radio. Room service (7am-11.30pm). Safe. Telephone. TV (satellite). Video.*

Hotel Carlos V
C/Maestro Vitoria 5, 28013 (91 531 41 00/fax 91 531 37 61/recepcion@hotelcarlosv.com). Metro Sol/bus all routes to Puerta del Sol. **Rates** *single* 11,020ptas; *double* 13,870ptas. **Credit** AmEx, DC, EC, JCB, MC, £$TC, V. **Map D7**
This hotel, with 67 unexceptional rooms, is in the pedestrianised shopping area north of Sol. The entrance is clean and bright, and there's an attractive second floor lounge and restaurant area. Go for the fifth floor rooms with balconies.
Hotel services *Air-conditioning. Bar. Car park. Currency exchange. Disabled: wheelchair access. Fax. Laundry. Lifts. Multilingual staff. Restaurant. Ticket agency.* **Room services** *Hairdryer. Minibar. Room service (8am-11.30pm). Safe. Telephone. TV (satellite).*

Hotel Opera
Cuesta de Santo Domingo 2, 28013 (91 541 28 00/ fax 91 541 69 23/hotelopera@sinis.net www.es.cotel). *Metro Opera/bus 3, 25, 39.* **Rates** *single* 9,500ptas; *double* 13,500ptas. **Credit** AmEx, DC, EC, JCB, MC, £$TC, V. **Map D7**
Facing the opera house, this unassuming three-star is themed accordingly. Smoked glass and wood panelling in the entrance give a business feel, and the 79 rooms are clean and well stocked, if not exciting. Plus points are location, on a quiet street next to the Palacio Real and Plaza de Oriente, with its stylish cafés; very friendly staff; and an adjoining restaurant that serves an above-average *menú del día* and at night boasts dinners accompanied by opera singers.
Hotel services *Air-conditioning. Bar. Conference facilities. Currency exchange. Disabled: room adapted for the disabled, wheelchair access. Fax. Interpreting services. Laundry. Lifts. Limousine service. Multilingual staff. Restaurant. Ticket agency.* **Room services** *Hairdryer. Minibar. Radio. Refrigerator. Room service (7.30am-midnight). Safe. Telephone. TV (satellite). Video.*

Hotel Suecia
C/Marqués de Casa Riera 4, 28014 (91 531 69 00/ fax 91 521 71 41/hotelsuecia@genio.infor.es). Metro Banco de España/bus all routes to C/Alcalá. **Rates** *single* 15,000ptas; *double* 18,800ptas. **Credit** AmEx, DC, EC, JCB, MC, £$TC, V. **Map G7**
In a peaceful section of the old city centre with good restaurants nearby, the Suecia ('Sweden') is also just minutes away from the Puerta del Sol and the museums. The rooms, 128 in all, are on the small side and fairly charmless, but there is a comfortable lobby and a seventh floor terrace that, while not huge, is a relaxing place for a nap and a sunbathe.
Hotel services *Air-conditioning. Bar. Car park. Conference facilities. Currency exchange. Fax. Laundry. Lifts. Multilingual staff. Non-smoking floor/rooms. Restaurant. Ticket agency.* **Room services** *Hairdryer. Minibar. Room service (7am-11pm). Safe. Telephone. TV (satellite).*

Residencia de El Viso
C/Nervión 8, 28002 (91 564 03 70/fax 91 564 19 65/ elviso@estanciases.es). Metro República Argentina/bus 7, 16, 19, 51. **Rates** *single* 9,000ptas; *double* 16,000ptas. **Credit** AmEx, DC, MC, V.
This art deco pink cube with tiny windows, in the leafy 1930s residential area of El Viso, was until recently a family home. It's now a 12-room hotel. The location makes it seem miles from the centre, but it takes only a few minutes to get there. Rooms don't quite live up to stylish art deco touches like the staircase, and some are a little shabby, but its best feature is the outside eating area and courtyard. Great for cool, quiet moments.
Hotel services *Air-conditioning. Babysitting. Bar. Conference facilities. Currency exchange. Disabled: wheelchair access. Fax. Garden. Laundry. Lifts. Limousine service. Multilingual staff. Restaurant. Ticket agency.* **Room services** *Hairdryer. Minibar. Room service (24hrs). Telephone. TV (satellite).*

Lower-mid (6-13,000ptas)

Hostal Madrid

*C/Esparteros 6, 2º, 28012 (91 522 00 60/fax 91 532 35
10). Metro Sol/bus all routes to Puerta del Sol.* **Rates**
single 5,000ptas; *double* 8,000ptas; *triple* 9,000ptas;
quadruple 10,000ptas. **Credit** MC, V. **Map D7**
An enterprising two-star *hostal* literally a few steps from Sol
and the Plaza Mayor. With 15 recently redecorated rooms,
all with bathrooms and TVs, it attracts a youngish clientele.
The owners are young and welcoming and provide drinks'
passes to clubs and a range of other information; guests are
also given keys so that they can come and go as they please,
and late-risers are never hustled out.
Hotel services *Air-conditioning.* **Room services**
Telephone. TV.

Hostal-Residencia Santa Bárbara

*Plaza de Santa Bárbara 4, 3º, 28004 (91 446 93 08/
fax 91 446 23 45). Metro Alonso Martinez/bus 3, 7, 21,
40, 149.* **Rates** *single* 5,750ptas; *double* 7,700ptas.
Credit MC, V. **Map H4**
Although a fairly ordinary *hostal* with rather drab furnishings, the Santa Bárbara, with two stars, is nevertheless clean
and well located, right on the plaza of the same name. All of
its 13 rooms have bathrooms.
Hotel services *TV lounge.* **Room service** *(daytime).*

Hotel Asturias

*C/Sevilla 2, 28014 (91 429 66 76/fax 91 429 40 36/
jcrodri@cestel.es). Metro Sevilla/bus all routes to
C/Alcalá.* **Rates** *single* 9,600ptas; *double* 12,600ptas.
Credit AmEx, DC, MC, £$TC, V. **Map F7**
Two hundred metres from Sol, this 170-room hotel, opened
in 1875, was renovated a few years ago. It's fairly down at
heel but decent value and popular with tourists, and the location is ideal for anyone keen to have the sights and nightlife
on their doorstep. Ask for an inside room, as the streets on
either side are noisy. Service is attentive.
Hotel services *Bar. Currency exchange. Disabled: room
adapted for the disabled, wheelchair access. Fax. Laundry.
Lifts. Multilingual staff. Restaurant.* **Room services**
Room service (24hrs). Safe. Telephone. TV.

The friendly **Hotel Alcalá**. *See page 96.*

Hotel Inglés

*C/Echegaray 8, 28014 (91 429 65 51/
fax 91 420 24 23). Metro Sevilla, Sol/bus all routes to
Puerta del Sol.* **Rates** *single* 7,700ptas; *double* 10,800ptas.
Credit AmEx, DC, MC, £$TC, V. **Map F7**
This 58-room hotel dating from 1853 is so clean and bright
you might be tempted to reach for your sunglasses as you
walk inside. Owned by the same family for some 30 years,
it has more character than many Madrid hotels. The rooms
overlooking the sometimes-hectic street are pleasant and
have lovely morning light; go for the inside rooms if you
want something quieter. Good value.
Hotel services *Bar. Car park. Currency exchange. Fax.
Laundry. Lifts. Multilingual staff. Fitness centre (gym).
Ticket agency.* **Room services** *Room service (7am-
11pm). Safe. Telephone. TV (satellite).*

Hotel Mónaco

*C/Barbieri 5, 28004 (91 522 46 39/fax 91 521 16 01).
Metro Chueca, Gran Via/bus 3, 40, 149.*
Rates *single* 7,000ptas; *double* 10,000ptas.
Map F6
An eccentric star among Madrid's many hotels. *See p93* **The
Mónaco.**
Hotel services *Air-conditioning. Bar. Fax. Laundry.
Lifts. Multilingual staff. Ticket agency.* **Room services**
Room service (8am-3pm). Safe. Telephone. TV.

Hotel Mora

*Paseo del Prado 32, 28014 (91 420 05 64/
fax 91 429 15 69). Metro Atocha/bus all routes to
Atocha.* **Rates** *single* 6,200ptas; *double* 7,200ptas. **Credit**
AmEx, DC, MC, V. **Map G8**
Built in the 1930s, this 62-room hotel has been renovated
quite recently, and is fresh, clean and bright. The entrance
is attractive, and, although everything else is a bit more functional, the place is often buzzing. It can be hard to get a room,
for not only is the Mora very good value, it's also opposite
the Prado and not far from Atocha station. Staff, however,
could work a little harder at being friendly.
Hotel services *Air-conditioning. Multilingual staff.*
Room services *Safe. Telephone. TV (satellite).*

Hotel París

*C/Alcalá 2, 28014 (91 521 64 91/fax 91 531 01 88).
Metro Sol/bus all routes to Puerta del Sol.*
Rates *single* 8,800ptas; *double* 11,800ptas.
Credit AmEx, DC, EC, MC, £$TC, V. **Map E7**
A riot of tacky china animals, velvet and crystal with super
friendly staff and right on Puerta del Sol. This 120-room hotel
remains a bargain, and has bags of character. Staff claim it's
the second-oldest hotel in the city, and it's been on the site
for at least a century. Rooms are wooden-floored (often
creaky) and sparsely furnished; not all have air conditioning, and exterior rooms are noisy, but a delightful interior
courtyard garden adds a breath of fresh air.
Hotel services *Air-conditioning. Bar. Currency
exchange. Disabled: room adapted for the disabled,
wheelchair access. Fax. Laundry. Lifts. Multilingual staff.
Non-smoking floor/rooms. Restaurant. Ticket agency.*
Room services *Radio. Room service (24hrs). Safe.
Telephone. TV. Video.*

Hotel-Residencia Don Diego

*C/Velázquez 45, 28001 (91 435 07 60/fax 91 431 42
63). Metro Velázquez/bus 1, 74, 89.*
Rates *single* 6,800ptas; *double* 9,000ptas.
Credit AmEx, DC, MC, V. **Map J4**
A strange arrangement, reached by a lift above private apartments with one forlorn man sitting downstairs at a scruffy
desk to represent the establishment. The 58 very basic rooms
are clean and, unusually, all have TV and air-conditioning.
Not pretty, not charming, but for budget travellers it would
be difficult to stay in this classy shopping district for less.

Hotel services *Bar. Fax. Laundry. Lifts. Limousine services. Non-smoking floor/rooms. Ticket agency.* **Room services** *Air-conditioning. Room service (8am-11pm). Safe. Telephone. TV.*

Hotel Santander

C/Echegaray 1, 28014 (91 429 95 51/ fax 91 369 10 78). Metro Sevilla, Sol/bus all routes to Puerta del Sol. **Rates** *single* 6,000ptas; *double* 7,500ptas. **Credit** MC, V. **Map F7**

An antique but well-maintained and cosy entrance lobby welcomes you into this charming old hotel of just 35 rooms, which is perfectly located between the Puerta del Sol and the Prado. With lots of high ceilings, generous bathrooms and individual furniture, this is something of a gem, and the corner room number 105 is particularly spacious and well lit. Some rooms face on to the Carrera de San Jerónimo and can be noisy, and the hallways are a bit dark, but the staff are very friendly, making the Santander far more likeable than many Madrid hotels.

Hotel services *Fax. Laundry. Lifts. Multilingual staff. Safe.* **Room services** *Room service (8am-7pm). Telephone. TV.*

Hotel Tirol

C/Marqués de Urquijo 4, 28008 (91 548 19 00/ fax 91 541 39 58). Metro Argüelles/bus 1, 21, 44, 74, C. **Rates** *single* 9,000ptas; *double* 11,250ptas. **Credit** MC, TC, V. **Map C3**

Reasonably priced, this 95-room hotel is in an area with relatively few hotels, conveniently placed for the Plaza de España, the university and the studentish Argüelles district. It is not the brightest or most characterful hotel you might find, but the rooms are spacious and clean, and reasonable prices make it good value.

Hotel services *Air-conditioning. Bar. Car park. Currency exchange. Disabled: wheelchair access. Laundry. Lifts. Multilingual staff. Ticket agency.* **Room services** *Room service (8am-midnight). Safe. Telephone. TV (satellite).*

Hotel Trafalgar

C/Trafalgar 35, 28010 (91 445 62 00/ fax 91 446 64 56). Metro Iglesia/bus 3, 16, 37, 40, 61. **Rates** *single* 7,900ptas; *double* 11,300ptas. **Credit** AmEx, DC, MC, £$TC, V. **Map F2**

In the middle of residential Chamberí, this 48-room hotel has plain, functional rooms that are a bit overpriced. Nevertheless, it's popular with guests who prefer to stay a little away from the heavily touristed areas of Madrid.

Hotel services *Air-conditioning. Bar. Currency exchange. Fax. Laundry. Lifts. Multilingual staff. Restaurant. Safe. Ticket agency.* **Room services** *Room service (8am-4pm). Telephone. TV.*

Budget (6,000ptas and under)

Like other Spanish cities, Madrid has areas where cheap hotels are bunched together. The most important is around Plaza Santa Ana and streets nearby such as Calle Cervantes, in the heart of the Huertas bar and nightlife area. There is another big cluster further north in Malasaña and Chueca, near the Calle Fuencarral. The hotels around the main train stations are generally not as pleasant as more centrally placed establishments at the same price.

Many basic hotels are in single apartments in blocks, where addresses will often be identified as *izq* (*izquierda*, left) or *dcha* (*derecha*, right) after the floor number.

Hostal Armesto

C/San Agustín 6, 1°, 28014 (91 429 90 31). Metro Antón Martín/bus 6, 9, 26, 32. **Rates** *single* 4,500ptas; *double* 5,600ptas. **No credit cards. Map G8**

A six-room hostel, with baths in each room, owned by a wonderfully friendly woman and her husband. It's right in the centre, handy for the Prado, Atocha and the Huertas bars. A treat for those with inside rooms is a view over the garden of an old palace next door, providing one easy way of conjuring up old Madrid.

Hostal Benamar

C/San Mateo 20, 2°, 28004 (91 308 00 92). **Rates** *single* 2,000ptas; *double* 3,200ptas; *triple* 4,900ptas. **No credit cards. Map G4**

Budget travellers wanting to be in the thick of the night action will be delighted by this airy, light *pensión* – a backpackers' favourite – between Chueca and Malasaña. The 22 sparklingly clean rooms all wash basins, but no baths, and there are four bathrooms. There's a TV lounge, and the friendly owner speaks some English.

Hotel Cervantes

C/Cervantes 34, 2°, 28014 (91 429 83 65/ fax 91 429 27 45). Metro Antón Martín/bus 9, 10, 14, 27, 34. **Rates** *single* 4,500ptas; *double* 6,000ptas. **Credit** V. **Map G8**

Just round the corner from the Armesto (*see above*), and equally close to the Huertas and Santa Ana bar scene. The 12-room hostel is bright and clean, and has a relaxed atmosphere kept up by friendly, helpful owners. All rooms have private baths, and firm beds.

Hotel services *Lifts. Room service (daytime). TV.*

Hostal Delvi

Plaza de Santa Ana 15, 3°, 28012 (91 522 59 98). Metro Sevilla, Sol/bus all routes to Puerta del Sol. **Rates** *single* 1,800ptas; *double* 3,500ptas. **No credit cards. Map F8**

Anyone who wants to be in the middle of things couldn't do better than stay on the Plaza Santa Ana itself. This pleasant and very cheap third floor *hostal* has eight rooms, all different in size. Some have showers, one has its own toilet, and some have space for three people. If you prefer a bit more peace and quiet, ask for a room facing the side street, away from the main square. The owner is friendly and obliging.

Hostal Filo

Plaza de Santa Ana 15, 2°, 28012 (91 522 40 56). Metro Sevilla, Sol/bus all routes to Puerta del Sol. **Rates** *single* 2,000ptas; *double* 3,500ptas; *double with bath* 4,500ptas. **No credit cards. Map F8**

Another *hostal* on Santa Ana; 20 high-ceilinged rooms have great furniture and lots of light. The owner seems grumpy, but is no dummy, and over the years has acquired just enough English to deal with his guests. Only four rooms actually face the square. Three rooms have bathrooms, but four toilets are shared by all guests. Some rooms are triples.

Hotel services *Air-conditioning. Drinks. Fax. Multilingual staff. Safe. Ticket agency.* **Room services** *Telephone.*

Hostal-Residencia La Coruña

Paseo del Prado 12, 3° dcha, 28014 (91 429 25 43). Metro Banco de España/bus 9, 14, 27, 37, 45. **Rates** *single* 2,500ptas; *double* 4,600ptas. **No credit cards. Map G7**

You'd have to camp inside the Prado – or put up at the Ritz – to get closer to the Goyas. The six clean rooms, with two shared bathrooms, have high ceilings, chandeliers and plain

With a plaza almost to itself, the **Gran Hotel Conde Duque**. *See page 95.*

furniture, and the friendly owners are clearly delighted to have guests. Also an easy walk from Santa Ana and Atocha, it's one of the best-value budget *hostales*, but closed in August. **Room services** *TV.*

Hostal-Residencia Gloria

C/Conde de Xiquena 4, 28004 (91 522 04 42). Metro Chueca/bus 27, 37, 45, 53. **Rates** *single* 2,000ptas; *double* 3,500ptas. **No credit cards. Map H5**
A tidy 14-room hostel some way from the main budget-hotel cluster, on a quiet street in fashionable, grungy Chueca. There are few facilities and it's a bit dark, but it's also very popular, and some guests have been staying here for years.

Hostal-Residencia Sud-Americana

Paseo del Prado 12, 6° izq, 28014 (91 429 25 64). Metro Banco de España, Atocha/bus 9, 14, 27, 37, 45. **Rates** *single* 2,600ptas; *double* 4,800ptas. **No credit cards. Map G7**
In the same building as the Coruña (*see above*) and sharing its great advantages as far as location is concerned. This charming hostel has eight rooms with some fantastic features: tasteful, vintage furniture; priceless chandeliers; high ceilings; and creaky wooden floors. Closed in August.

Hostal Retiro/Hostal Narváez

C/O'Donnell 27, 4° & 5°, 28009 (91 576 00 37). Metro Príncipe de Vergara/bus 2, 15, 28, C. **Rates** *single* 3,500ptas; *double* 5,300ptas. **No credit cards. Map K6**
You can practically roll out of bed and into the Retiro from these two *hostales*, one above the other, both run by the same family, and in a particularly untouristy area. The 30 rooms all have showers, and are bright and recently painted. **Hotel services** *Lifts. Multilingual staff.* **Room services** *Hairdryer. TV.*

Hostal Riesco

C/Correo 2, 3°, 28012 (91 522 26 92). Metro Sol/ bus all routes to Puerta del Sol. **Rates** *single* 3,600ptas; *double* 5,000ptas. **No credit cards. Map E7**

Built for a king, literally, Madrid's grand **Hotel Ritz.** *See page 94.*

Heavy on the decoration, this 22-room *hostal* just off Puerta del Sol is for those who really want to stay in the absolute centre of the city. All rooms have bathrooms, and several have balconies decorated with flowers. It has been run by the same family for 25 years, and the lady of the house, though sometimes severe, is efficient.
Hotel services *Air-conditioning. Lift.* **Room services** *Telephone.*

Hostal Rivera

Paseo de Santa María de la Cabeza 2, 3°, 28045 (91 527 37 17). Metro Atocha/bus all routes to Atocha. **Rates** *single* 2,500ptas; *double* 3,500ptas. **No credit cards. Map H9**
In a good spot for travellers arriving at Atocha by train, the Rivera is a small, family-run, friendly, no-nonsense sort of traditional *hostal*. It's also very near the Reina Sofía, and so not too far from Madrid's other main art palaces; the nine modestly-priced rooms all have washbasins, but share the same bathroom. There's no air-conditioning (naturally), but the Rivera, on the second floor of an old apartment block, stays relatively cool in summer. Some of the family speak English, and it's better than most Atocha cheap hotels.

Hostal Sil

C/Fuencarral 95, 3°, 28004 (91 448 89 72/ fax 91 447 48 29). Metro Bilbao/bus 3, 21, 40, 147, 149. **Rates** *single* 2,500-3,500ptas; *double* 5,500ptas. **Credit** MC, V. **Map F3**
This 21-room *hostal* at the most salubrious, northern, end of Calle Fuencarral is run by a middle-aged couple with occasional help from their English-speaking children. All the very well-kept rooms have air-conditioning and baths, and it offers excellent value for money.
Hotel services *Air-conditioning. Fax. Laundry. Multilingual staff. Ticket agency.* **Room services** *Telephone. TV.*

Hostal Valencia

C/Espoz y Mina 7, 4°, 28012 (91 521 18 45). Metro Sol/bus all routes to Puerta del Sol. **Rates** *single* 3,000ptas; *double* 4,500ptas. **No credit cards. Map E8**
This tiny hostel has a distinctly homely feel, helped along by the amiable young owner's attempts to jazz up the old apartment. The rooms, five doubles and one single, all with bathrooms, are comfortable and spacious, their walls washed

Awaiting the movers and shakers, the opulent **Hotel Palace.** *See page 93.*

in warm primary colours. Added extras include a fridge and washing machine for guests' use, and the street is well placed for Sol and Santa Ana.
Room services *TV.*

Hostal Villamáñez

C/San Agustín 6, 2°, 28014 (91 429 90 33). Metro Antón Martín/bus 6, 9, 26, 32. **Rates** *single* 4,500ptas; *double* 6,000ptas. **No credit cards. Map G8**
This hostel is on the floor above the Armesto (*see above*), bang in the centre of town. The eight rooms all have private bathrooms, plenty of plain, cheap furniture and air-conditioning, making it a good budget option for summer.
Hotel services *Safe.* **Room services** *Telephone. TV.*

Pensión Jaén

C/Cervantes 5, 3°; 28014 (91 249 48 58). Metro Antón Martín/bus 9, 10, 14, 27, 34. **Rates** *single* 2,700ptas; *double with shower* 4,300ptas; *double with bath* 4,500ptas. **No credit cards. Map F8**
The genial owners are the main plus at this tiny, basic *hostal* of just eight rooms in a fairly quiet spot on the Calle Cervantes, very close to the Plaza Santa Ana. All rooms have showers, and some have their own toilet and/or bath.
Hotel services *Safe.* **Room services** *Telephone. TV.*

Pensión Olga

C/Zorrilla 13, 28015 (91 429 78 87). Metro Sevilla, Banco de España/bus 9, 10, 27, 34. **Rates** *single* 4,100ptas; *double* 5,300ptas. **Credit** AmEx, MC, V. **Map G7**
With warmly decorated lounges that are invitingly comfortable after a day's sightseeing, this 20-room family-owned *hostal* offers slightly more sophisticated service than many in this bracket, although the rooms themselves are basic. It's well located on a quiet side street by the Cortes, midway between Sol and the Prado.
Hotel services *Safe.* **Room services** *Telephone. TV.*

Posada del Dragón

C/Cava Baja 14, 28005 (91 365 32 25). Metro La Latina/bus 17, 23, 35, 50. **Rates** around 950ptas per person. **No credit cards. Map D8**
Male travellers on a super-shoestring budget might just appreciate this dusty, 35-room place dating back to the last century – about the only survivor of the innumerable rough-and-ready *posadas*, a cross between a hotel and a lodging-house, that over the last 400 years have catered to the many who have arrived in Madrid seeking fame and fortune. Women, as is traditional, are not allowed. The rooms are either individual or shared, and there is one shared bathroom on each floor. There is no TV or telephone for residents' use, nor is any food served. Many of the long-term residents (at weekly rates) are elderly, down-at-heel and sometimes shady men. Few foreigners stay here, but it's certainly a part of old Madrid. Closed in August.

Apartment hotels

Apartamentos Juan Bravo

C/Juan Bravo 58-60, 28006 (91 402 98 00/ fax 91 309 32 28). Metro Diego de León/bus 26, 29, 52, 61, C. **Rates** *studios* from 35,000ptas per week; *apartments* from 45,000ptas per week.
No credit cards. Map L2
In a residential area on the eastern edge of Salamanca that's inconvenient for tourist attractions, these 300 apartments could do with refurbishment. The hallways are dark, and some of the fittings seem shoddy. None of that matters too much, though, come summer, as there's a great swimming pool at the back. A regular favourite with German visitors.
Hotel services *Air-conditioning. Car park. Fax. Laundry. Lifts. Multilingual staff. Swimming pool. Ticket agency.* **Room services** *Refrigerator. Safe. Telephone.*

The kids are alright

Children are generally made to feel very welcome in Madrid, and hotels are no exception; however, few have any special facilities beyond maybe a babysitting service. Nevertheless, the following are good places to head if you have sprogs in tow.

Hotel Arosa – families made very welcome.
Hotel Conde Duque – safe playpark right outside the door in a quiet plaza.
Hotel Emperador – a winner on two counts, with a rooftop pool and a babysitting service.
Hotel Eurobuilding – babysitting and a great pool.

Apartamentos Plaza Basílica

C/Comandante Zorita 27 & 31, 28020 (91 535 36 42/fax 91 535 14 97). Metro Santiago Bernabéu/bus 3, 5, 43, 149. **Rates** *studios 14,000ptas per night, 80,500ptas per week, 234,000ptas per month; one-bedroom apartment 19,600ptas per night, 108,000ptas per week, 330,000ptas per month; two-bedroom apartment 24,000ptas per night, 140,000ptas per week, 450,000ptas per month.* **Credit** AmEx, DC, MC, £$TC, V.
Built in 1989, this 80-apartment complex is professionally run and well appointed, although prices are bewilderingly high. However, it's conveniently located for anyone doing business in the financial district, or spending any time attending an event at the **Palacio de Exposiciones** (*see p264*). Rooms are coldly correct.
Hotel services *Air-conditioning. Bar. Car park. Currency exchange. Fax. Garden. Laundry. Lifts. Multilingual staff. Ticket agency.* **Room services** *Hairdryer. Minibar. Radio. Refrigerator. Safe. Telephone. TV (satellite). Video (on request).*

Youth hostels

To get a bed in one of Madrid's two official youth hostels it's usually necessary to reserve ahead, although if you feel like trying your luck you can turn up on the door to see what they have left for that night. Reservations must be made in writing 15 days in advance, and sent to the hostels themselves or to the **Instituto de Albergues Juveniles** *Central de Reservas, C/Alcalá 32, 28014 Madrid (91 580 42 16/fax 91 580 42 15)*, which also accepts reservations by fax. IYHF cards are required, and you can stay a maximum of three nights consecutively, and six nights in total during a two-month period.

There is a 1.30am curfew at both hostels, although if you want to stay out any later the staff are often prepared to be flexible and provide some means of getting back in. Doors reopen at 8am. Note that in summer Spanish youth hostels are often heavily booked by school parties, who tend to set the atmosphere.

Albergue Juvenil Casa de Campo

Casa de Campo, 28011 (91 463 56 99). Metro Lago/bus 31, 33, 39, 65. **Rates** (incl breakfast & IVA) *per person 1,300ptas, under-26s with youth card 950ptas.* **No credit cards.**
Groups of ten or more should book this hostel in advance, but individuals are welcome to turn up at the door. Its attraction is its location, in the middle of the Casa de Campo: a long way from the centre, but a great setting if you're into nature. The hostel has its own bar, and is quite comfortable and well maintained. All rooms have from two to six beds, and bathrooms are shared by two rooms. It's a bit of a walk from the Lago Metro station (to find it, walk along Paseo de los Castaños away from the lake, and look for signs for Albergue Juvenil). Prostitutes and kerb-crawlers congregate in this area at night, so ask about the best way of getting back after dark. Staff seem a little morose.
Hotel services *Café-bar. Disabled: block adapted for the disabled. Garden. Library. Laundry. Multilingual staff. Telephone. TV.*

Albergue Juvenil Santa Cruz de Marcenado

C/Santa Cruz de Marcenado 28, 28015 (91 547 45 32/fax 91 548 11 96). Metro Argüelles/bus 2, 21, 44, 133, C. **Rates** (incl breakfast & IVA) *per person 1,300ptas, under-26s with youth card 950ptas.* **Credit** V. **Map D3**
Individuals or groups of less than ten should write or fax to reserve at this hostel, which is in a quiet street in a student area near Argüelles, close to the Centro Cultural Conde Duque. The hostel is modern and quite well fitted-out, with 72 beds split between rooms for four to eight people with male- and female-only floors. Reception staff are matronly but friendly, and some speak a little English.
Hotel services *Disabled: rooms adapted for the disabled, wheelchair access. Garden. Lifts. TV.*

Campsites

There is a substantial number of campsites around the Madrid region, and towards the Guadarrama and Gredos mountains (*see chapter* **Trips Out of Town: The Sierras**). Although distances may be inconvenient, sites further away from the city are in more attractive locations and tend to have better facilities than those on the outskirts of Madrid. A full list is available from tourist offices; all sites are open all year.

Aterpe Alai

Carretera de Burgos (N-I), km 25, San Sebastián de los Reyes, 28700 Madrid (91 657 01 00). Bus 161, 166 from Plaza de Castilla to Fuente del Fresno. **Rates** *600ptas per person per night; 500ptas children; 600ptas per tent; 600ptas per car.* **No credit cards.**
This long-established campsite is 25km (16 miles) outside Madrid, north of the suburban town of San Sebastián de los Reyes. Open all year, it has shower facilities, small shops and a bar, but no swimming pool, a distinct drawback in summer.

Camping La Fresneda

Carretera M-608 between Soto del Real and Manzanares el Real (91 847 65 23). Bus 724 from Plaza de Castilla/by car M-607 north via Colmenar Viejo, then left on to M-608 (42km/26 miles). **Rates** *550ptas per person per night; 500ptas children; 550ptas per tent; 550ptas per car.* **Credit** AmEx, MC, V.
This high-grade campsite is about 45 min drive north of Madrid, just south of the fabulous rock formation known as La Pedriza, and 500m from the Embalse de Santillana, a reservoir where you can fish (with a licence). La Fresneda

has a laundry, two swimming pools, a tennis court and a small football pitch, and activities available include mountain bike hire, pony trekking and hiking trips with guides.

Camping Madrid
Carretera de Burgos (N-I), km 11, Madrid 28050 (91 302 28 35). Bus 129 from Plaza de Castilla/by car exit 12 from N-I. **Rates** 600ptas per person per night; 450ptas under-12s; 450-700ptas per tent; 600ptas per car; 450ptas per motorbike. **Credit** AmEx, MC, £$TC, V.
Recently renovated, this site is in the northern outskirts of Madrid and reasonably well connected by road with the centre, although difficult to reach by public transport. It's quite peaceful and nicely situated, and has a swimming pool, restaurant and bar, supermarket and free hot showers.

Camping Osuna
Avenida de Logroño s/n, 28042 (91 741 05 10). Metro Canillejas. Campo de Naciones/bus 101, 105. **Rates** 4,200ptas for two people per night. **No credit cards**.
The closest campsite to central Madrid, and the only one within reasonable distance of Metro stations. It's pleasantly situated amid pines in part of the eighteenth-century gardens of the **Capricho de la Alameda de Osuna** (*see p60*) and has a bar/restaurant, currency exchange, shop, playground, and 17 rooms available to rent in case you've forgotten your tent. However, it's also near the airport, and can be noisy.

Caravaning El Escorial
7.5km (4.5 miles) north of El Escorial on Carretera Guadarrama-El Escorial (91 890 24 12). Bus Herranz 664 from Moncloa/by car Carretera de La Coruña (N-VI/A6) to exit 2, Valle de los Caídos exit (52km/32 miles). **Rates** 650ptas per person per night; 650ptas per tent; 650ptas per car; plus 2,000ptas per plot. **Credit** AmEx, EC, MC, £$TC, V.
This luxury campsite, in the mountains about 45 min from Madrid, is set in 40 hectares (99 acres) of grounds and boasts four swimming pools and tennis, basketball and five-a-side football courts. Very popular with locals, it also has a decent restaurant, café-bar, a laundrette, supermarket and disco.

Soto del Castillo
C/Soto del Rebollo s/n, Aranjuez (91 891 13 95). Bus Aisa from Estación Sur/by car N-IV to Aranjuez Norte exit/by train Cercanías C-3 from Atocha. **Rates** 550ptas per person per night; 425ptas children; 475-600ptas per tent; 550ptas per car; 350ptas per motorbike. **Credit** MC, V.
In a bend of the Tagus near the Royal Gardens of Aranjuez, this site has a lovely setting, with plenty of shade. Facilities include a restaurant, supermarket, social club, children's park and swimming pool, and bikes and canoes can be hired. It's a short walk from Aranjuez, a little under an hour's drive from Madrid, and well served by public transport.

Splashing out

Because space within Madrid is tight, and many of its hotels are a few years old (at least), it's surprisingly hard to find places with swimming pools attached. The following make up the select few. You are more likely to find pools and similar facilities if you're prepared to resort to a campsite, or stay in towns outside Madrid such as **Aranjuez** or **El Escorial**.

Apartamentos Juan Bravo – rather like a Costa holiday development inside Madrid.
Hotel Emperador – a star among Madrid's hotel pools (*pictured*). The only mid-range hotel with a pool, and the only pool left in the city with a panoramic rooftop view.
Hotel Eurobuilding – pools indoors and out in this bland but facility-packed business hotel.
Hotel Santo Mauro – utterly palatial.
Hotel Wellington – more conventional luxury.

Restaurants

As Quentin Tarantino once noticed, 'Madrid, they eat at midnight there'. This is a city that takes its food seriously, at any time of day.

Anyone who wanders around the Madrid streets on a weekday lunchtime (that's after 2pm) or a Saturday evening can see at a glance that eating out is a central part of the city's life, a pleasure that's not to be skimped or passed over. Spaniards are well known for their love and enjoyment of their traditional dishes. Much less widely appreciated is the fact that Madrid's Japanese restaurants are considered among the best in the world outside Japan, or that Indian eateries now sit alongside traditional Madrileño establishments. In part, no doubt, this is due to the increasing globalisation of the world, but it also reflects the way in which Madrid attracts chefs from across Spain and around the world, while its residents – dedicated restaurant-goers – are increasingly on the look out for something new.

For all this growing variety, the best, most interesting food served in Madrid still tends to be Spanish. This does not imply any kind of limitation, for the range of Spanish cuisine – or cuisines – is enormous, and often not appreciated outside the country. They vary from the refined,

lighter dishes of Catalonia or the Basque Country – which can be hearty or nouveau – to the hefty roasts and stews of Castile, the fine fish and seafood of Galicia or the rice and vegetable dishes of Valencia and the Mediterranean coast. Madrid's own traditional dishes (*see page 111* **Stout stuff: *cocina Madrileña***) are humble food, with plenty of beans and lentils, and much use of offal. Worth looking out for – despite the city's distance from the sea – are fish and shellfish, which are outstandingly good here.

Madrid perhaps has not so much a restaurant culture as one of eating out and eating well. Spain is, after all, a country that has given snacking (as in tapas) near-equal status with full-scale dining, and restaurants as such are only part of a varied whole. For more eating places, *see chapters* **Tapas** *and* **Cafés & Bars**. For restaurants that are popular with a gay clientele, *see chapter* **Gay & Lesbian Madrid**, and for others favoured by bullfighting *aficionados, see chapter* **Bullfighting**; for places where you can eat a meal or snacks late at night, *see chapter* **Nightlife**.

Stoking the fires of Madrileño tradition at the **Posada de la Villa**. *See page 111.*

The Menu

For other ingredients and dishes more normally eaten as tapas (but which may also appear on restaurant menus), *see chapter* **Tapas**.

Basics

Primer plato (entrante) first course; **Segundo plato** second or main dish; **Postre** dessert; **Plato combinado** quick, one-course meal, with several ingredients served on the same plate; **Aceite y vinagre** oil and vinegar; **Agua** water; **Con gas/sin gas** fizzy/still; **Pan** bread; **Vino** wine (**tinto** red, **blanco** white, **rosado** rosé); **Cerveza** beer; **La cuenta** the bill.
Servicio incluído Service included. Propina tip.

Cooking styles & techniques

Adobado marinated; **Al ajillo** with olive oil and garlic; **Al chilindrón** (usually chicken or lamb) cooked in a spicy tomato, pepper, ham, onion and garlic sauce; **A la marinera** (fish or shellfish) cooked with garlic, onions and white wine; **A la parilla** charcoal-grilled; **A la plancha** grilled directly on a hot metal plate; **A la romana** fried in batter; **Al vapor** steamed; **Asado (al horno de lena)** roast (in a wood oven); **Crudo** raw; **En salsa** in a sauce or gravy; **Escabechado, en escabeche** marinated in vinegar with bay leaf and garlic; **Estofado** braised; **Frito** fried; **Hervido** stewed; **(en) Pepitoria** casserole dish, usually of chicken or game, with egg, wine and almonds; **Relleno** stuffed.

Huevos (Eggs)

Huevos fritos fried eggs (sometimes served with chorizo); **Revuelto** scrambled eggs; **Tortilla asturiana** omelette with tomato, tuna and onion; **Tortilla francesa** plain omelette; **Tortilla de patatas** Spanish potato omelette.

Sopas y potajes (Soups & stews)

Caldo (Gallego) broth of pork and greens; **Fabada** rich Asturian stew of beans, chorizo and morcilla; **Gazpacho** cold soup, usually of tomatoes, red pepper and cucumber; **Purrusalda** (Basque) soup of salt cod, leeks and potatoes; **Sopa de ajo** garlic soup; **Sopa castellana** garlic soup with poached egg and chickpeas; **Sopa de fideos** noodle soup.

Carne, aves, caza y embutidos (Meat, poultry, game & charcuterie)

Bistec steak; **Buey, vacuno** (cuts **solomillo**, **entrecot**) beef; **Butifarra** Catalan sausage; **Callos** tripe; **Capón** capon; **Cerdo** pork, pig; **Chorizo** spicy sausage, served cooked or cold; **Choto** kid; **Chuletas, chuletones, chuletillas** chops; **Cochinillo** roast suckling pig; **Cocido** traditional stew of Madrid (*see pxxx* Stout stuff: *cocina Madrileña*); **Codillo** knuckle (normally pig's); **Codornices** quails; **Conejo** rabbit; **Cordero** lamb; **Costillas** ribs; **Estofado de ternera** a veal stew; **Gallina** hen; **Faisán** pheasant; **Higado** liver; **Jabalí** wild boar; **Jamón ibérico** cured ham from Iberian pigs; **Jamón serrano** cured ham; **Jamón york** cooked ham; **Lacón** gammon ham; **Lechazo, cordero lechal** milk-fed baby lamb; **Liebre** hare; **Lomo (de cerdo)** loin of pork; **Morcilla** black blood sausage; **Pato** duck; **Pavo** turkey; **Perdiz** partridge; **Pollo** chicken; **Riñones** kidneys; **Salchichas** frying sausages; **Sesos** brains; **Ternera** veal (although in Spain it is slaughtered later than most veal, and so a bit more similar to beef).

Pescado y mariscos (Fish & shellfish)

Almejas clams; **Atún**, bonito tuna; **Bacalao** salt cod; **Besugo** sea bream; **Bogavante** lobster; **Caballa** mackerel; **Calamares** squid; **Camarones** small shrimps; **Cangrejo, Buey de mar** crab; **Cangrejo de río** freshwater crayfish; **Dorada** gilthead bream; **Gambas** prawns; **Kokotxas** (Basque) hake cheeks; **Langosta** spiny lobster; **Langostinos** langoustines; **Lubina** sea bass; **Mejillones** mussels; **Mero** grouper; **Merluza** hake; **Ostras** oysters; **Pescadilla** whiting; **Pescaditos** whitebait; **Pulpo** octopus; **Rape** monkfish; **Rodaballo** turbot; **Salmonete** red mullet; **Sardinas** sardines; **Sepia** cuttlefish; **Trucha** trout; **Ventresca de bonito** fillet of tuna; **Vieiras** scallops.

Verduras (Vegetables)

Acelgas Swiss chard; **Alcachofas** artichokes; **Berenjena** aubergine/eggplant; **Calabacines** courgettes/zucchini; **Cebolla** onion; **Champiñones** mushrooms; **Col** cabbage; **Ensalada mixta** basic salad of lettuce, tomato and onion; **Ensalada verde** green salad, without tomato; **Espárragos** asparagus; **Espinacas** spinach; **Guisantes** peas; **Grelos** turnip leaves; **Habas** broad beans; **Judías verdes** green beans; **Lechuga** lettuce; **Menestra** braised mixed vegetables; **Patatas fritas** chips; **Pepino** cucumber; **Pimientos** sweet peppers; **Pimientos de piquillo** slightly hot red peppers; **Pisto** mixture of cooked vegetables, similar to ratatouille; **Setas** forest mushrooms; **Tomates** tomatoes; **Zanahorias** carrots.

Arroz y legumbres (Rice & pulses)

Alubias, judías white beans; **Arroz abanda** rice cooked in shellfish stock; **Arroz negro** black rice cooked in squids' ink; **Fríjoles** red kidney beans; **Garbanzos** chickpeas; **Habas** broad beans; **Judiones** large haricot beans; **Lentejas** lentils; **Paella de mariscos** shellfish paella; **Pochas (caparrones)** new-season kidney beans.

Fruta (Fruit)

Arándanos bilberries; **Cerezas** cherries; **Ciruelas** plums; **Fresas** strawberries; **Higos** figs; **Macedonia** fruit salad; **Manzana** apple; **Melocotón** peach; **Melón** melon; **Moras** blackcurrants; **Naranja** orange; **Pera** pear; **Piña** pineapple; **Plátano** banana; **Sandía** watermelon; **Uvas** grapes.

Postres (Desserts)

Arroz con leche rice pudding; **Bizcocho** sponge cake; **Brazo de gitano** ice-cream or custard swiss roll; **Cuajada** junket (served with honey); **Flan** crème caramel; **Helado** ice-cream; **Leche frita** custard fried in breadcrumbs; **Membrillo** quince jelly (often served with cheese); **Tarta** cake; **Tarta de Santiago** sponge-like almond cake; **Torrijas** sweet bread fritters.

Quesos (Cheeses)

Burgos, Requesón white, fresh cheeses; **Cabrales** strong blue Asturian goat's cheese; **Manchego (tierno, anejo, semi, seco)** hard sheep's-milk cheese (young, mature, semi-soft, dry); **Tetilla** soft cow's milk cheese.

EATING HABITS

Madrid eating falls into two categories: lunch and dinner. Fewer and fewer Madrileños manage to get home for lunch, but they still expect home-style cooking for their midday meal, not just a sandwich on the hop. Restaurants, local bars and eating houses in office areas keep standards high to compete. Many offer *menú del día* set lunches (sometimes also available in the evenings) for 1,000-2,000ptas, usually with a choice of two or three dishes for each course, and often an exceptional bargain. Even gourmet restaurants have been forced to follow suit, and many now offer cut-price formulas. In the evenings set-price menus are much less common, prices are correspondingly a little higher, and people tend to pick and choose more.

Restaurant practicalities

Timing & booking Madrileños rarely lunch before two, and often have dinner after 11pm on hot summer nights, although 9-10pm is more usual at other times. It's advisable to book in higher-category restaurants, if rarely essential.
Children are welcome almost anywhere, if rather less so in the smarter business restaurants.
Prices, taxes, tips Thanks to the *menú del día* it is nearly always cheaper to eat lunch in restaurants rather than dinner. Dining can also be much cheaper, if less fun, if you stick to simple dishes rather than regional specialities. Bills include 7% IVA tax (VAT), which very occasionally is not included in the prices on the menu. Service is sometimes included in the bill (*cuenta*), but more often tipping is at your discretion. There is no percentage rule nor any absolute obligation to tip, but it will be welcomed, and it is reasonable to leave about 5-10%, up to and not over 500ptas.
Smoking Very few restaurants in Spain have no-smoking areas or tables. Normally, you just have to put up with it…
Sundays & holidays Despite growing flexibility in opening times, there are still relatively few city restaurants open on Sunday evenings, and many places will close for all or part of August. We've listed annual closing dates where possible, but during August it's a good idea to phone to check.
The vegetable question A tenet often observed in Spanish – above all Castilian – food is that, if an ingredient is good, it's best appreciated on its own, without any accompanying mush to obscure the flavours. However, a Castilian meal that consists of two pure-meat courses without a green leaf in sight can come as a shock to anyone accustomed to having vegetables provided automatically. In most restaurants, if you want greenery you should order it separately, as a first course or side salad, since main courses will normally come without vegetables (except perhaps *patatas fritas*, chips). For **vegetarian** restaurants, *see p115*.
Wines Virtually every restaurant in Madrid has an economically priced house wine, most commonly a Valdepeñas, from La Mancha – although there are now increasingly good-quality labels from this area. In cheap restaurants the house wine can be pretty poor, and locals often mix it with lemonade (*gaseosa*), if they don't just prefer beer. Of the quality wines, the products of Spain's best-known wine-growing region, Rioja, have in recent years often been surpassed by those of other areas, notably Navarra and Ribera del Duero. Also rapidly improving are Rueda and Basque Txacoli whites. For more on wines, *see chapter* **Shopping**.

Averages

Average prices listed are for a three-course meal consisting of a *primer plato* (starter), a main course (*segundo plato*) and a dessert (*postre*), without wine, beer or water. The set lunch menus given, however, do often include a drink.

Villa y Corte

El Alamillo

Plaza del Alamillo (91 364 07 33). Metro La Latina/ bus 31, 50, 65. **Lunch served** 1.30-4.30pm Fri-Sun. **Dinner served** 9-11.30pm Mon, Wed-Sat. **Average** 3,500ptas. **Credit** AmEx, MC, V. **Map C8**
Often overlooked in one of Madrid's most restaurant-packed areas, the Alamillo is ideal for that romantic dinner… Very well-presented food, based on Basque cuisine, but with an inventive, light touch. A tad pricey, but worth it.
Air-conditioning. Booking advisable.

Bar Salamanca

C/Cava Baja 31 (91 366 31 10). Metro La Latina/bus 18, 31, 35, 50, 65. **Lunch served** 1-4.30pm Wed-Sun. **Dinner served** 9pm-midnight Wed-Sat. **Set menus** 1,000ptas, 1,400ptas. **No credit cards. Map D8**
This tiny family-run restaurant south of the Plaza Mayor – surrounded by more expensive *mesones* (*see p111*) – offers great local dishes, with two good-value set menus. A candidate for the best *croquetas* and stuffed artichokes in town.

Casa Ciriaco

C/Mayor 84 (91 548 06 20). Metro Opera, Sol/bus all routes to Puerta del Sol. **Lunch served** 1.30-4.30pm, **dinner served** 8.30-11.30pm, Mon, Tue, Thur-Sun. Closed Aug. **Average** 2,500ptas. **Credit** DC, MC, V. **Map C8**
Over 70 years' worth of kitschy memorabilia and paintings donated by former clients hangs around the walls of this fine tavern, founded in 1917 and a meeting place of the intelligentsia in pre-Civil War days. From the staple Castilian fare, try the chicken *pepitoria*, trout *en escabeche*, the *cocido* on Tuesdays, and the paella served every Sunday. You can also sample fine Valdepeñas wine, with a meal or with tapas in the beautiful old tiled bar.
Air-conditioning. Booking advisable. Disabled: wheelchair access.

Casa Gallega

Plaza de San Miguel 8 (91 547 30 55). Metro Opera, Sol/bus all routes to Puerta del Sol. **Lunch served** 1-4pm, **dinner served** 8pm-midnight, daily. **Average** 4,000ptas. **Credit** AmEx, DC, JCB, MC, V. **Map D8**
This long-established Galician showcase is now quite pricey, but the quality of the food, particularly shellfish, is usually worth it. Apart from the seafood on ice in the windows, there are Galician standards – *caldo* (broth), *lacón con grelos* (gammon ham with greens) and a wide range of Galician wines. Great tapas are on offer, too, in the basement bar.
Air-conditioning. Booking advisable.
Branch: C/Bordadores 11 (91 541 90 55).

Casa Marta

C/Santa Clara 10 (91 548 28 25). Metro Opera/ bus 3, 25, 39, 148. **Lunch served** 1.30-4pm, **dinner served** 8pm-midnight, Mon-Sat. Closed Aug. **Average** 2,500ptas. **Set menu** 1,200ptas. **Credit** AmEx, DC, MC, V. **Map C7**
After 70 years as a tavern and tapas bar, Casa Marta was converted to a restaurant at the beginning of the '90s. Stews and hearty Castilian fare are the mainstay, and marvellously handled. How about a page out of *Don Quixote*, with *duelos y quebrantos*, the dish that the Don had every Saturday: *revuelto* (scrambled eggs), with *serrano* ham, chorizo, brains and sheep's stomach? Not for the faint-hearted.
Air-conditioning. Booking advisable.

El Estragón

Costanilla de San Andrés 10 (91 365 89 82). Metro La Latina/bus 31, 50, 65. **Lunch served** 1.30-5pm, **dinner served** 8.30pm-midnight, daily. **Average** 2,500ptas. **Set menu** 1,500-1,750ptas. **Credit** AmEx, DC, MC, V. **Map C8**

Recently opened, this pleasant vegetarian restaurant is a welcome addition to the newly restored Plaza de la Paja nearby, in the very heart of the oldest part of Madrid. With its good music, friendly service and quality food, it's no wonder it's so popular, especially with expats. A great place for meeting people.
Air-conditioning. Booking advisable.

Palacio de Anglona
C/Segovia 13 (91 366 37 53). Metro La Latina/bus 31, 50, 65. **Lunch served** 1.30-4pm daily. **Dinner served** 8.30pm-1am Sun-Thur; 8.30pm-2am Fri, Sat. **Average** 3,500ptas. **Credit** AmEx MC, V. **Map C8**
A large, three-level bar and restaurant with modern, vaguely trendy décor, young staff and imaginative, light, contemporary pasta, pizza and other internationally oriented dishes at very accessible prices. It's long been a particular favourite with students, wandering foreigners and late-night eaters, and is nearly always full till closing time.
Air-conditioning. Booking advisable.

La Taberna del Alabardero
C/Felipe V 6 (91 541 51 92). Metro Opera/bus 3, 25, 39, 148. **Lunch served** 1-4pm, **dinner served** 9pm-midnight, daily. **Average** 5,500ptas. **Gourmet menu** 5,500ptas. **Credit** AmEx, DC, JCB, MC, V. **Map C7**
Close to the Palacio Real and the opera house, this *Taberna* has a particular claim to fame in that it's owned by a priest, but its Basque food is of high standing as well. You can order

---

Top tables

The cooking of Madrid's finest restaurants reveals, in general, a mix of contemporary Spanish – especially Basque – and international – especially French – influences. Many of the most prestigious dining rooms are geared towards a business clientele, and filled by suited men at lunchtime. Jackets and ties may not be obligatory, except at **Zalacaín**, but casual travelling clothes and especially shorts are not acceptable. There are also first-class restaurants in some major hotels, above all the **Ritz** (*see chapter* **Accommodation**).
Berceo-Le Divellec
Fine cuisine from a Parisian chef.
Cabo Mayor Exquisite variations on Basque seafood in a delightful setting.
El Olivo
A great Franco-Spanish collaboration, and one of the best showcases in the world for fine olive oil.
Zalacaín Top of the range.
All in The Castellana, see right.
Casa Santa Cruz
Modern cuisine in a baroque chapel.
El Cenador del Prado
Innovative reworkings of Spanish traditions.
Lhardy Madrid's most venerable culinary landmark. *All in Huertas & Santa Ana, pp115-7.*
La Gastroteca de Stéphane y Arturo Chueca meets Parisian. *Malasaña & Chueca, p120.*
Viridiana Wonderful wines, and superior modern Spanish food. *Salamanca & the Retiro, p124.*
La Taberna de Liria
A little gem. *Conde Duque, p124.*

---

a selection of *raciones* at the bar, or enjoy a full meal at the tables further inside. The five-course gourmet menu is a real feast, and very good value.
Air-conditioning. Booking advisable. Tables outdoors May-Oct.

Taquería La Calaca
C/de las Fuentes 3 (91 541 74 23). Metro Opera/bus 3, 39, 148. **Lunch served** 1-4pm daily. **Dinner served** 8pm-1am Mon-Thur, Sun; 8pm-2.30am Fri, Sat. **Average** 2,000ptas. **Credit** AmEx, MC, V. **Map D7**
A dead-central Mexican café offering a dozen tequilas, a range of margaritas and specialities such as *pollo borracho* (literally, 'drunken chicken' – chicken stewed with chilli), tacos, *tamales* and *quesadillas*. Unfortunately, there are only small, high tables, without proper seating.
Air-conditioning. Booking advisable weekends.

El Tormo
Travesía de las Vistillas 13 (91 365 53 35). Metro La Latina/bus 3, 60, 148. **Lunch served** 1-4pm Tue-Sun. **Dinner served** 9-11pm Tue-Sat. Closed mid-July-mid-Sept. **Average** 3,000ptas. **No credit cards. Map C9**
A one-off foodie experience. Joaquín Racionero and his wife dish up fare from La Mancha (especially Cuenca), as made several centuries ago: *morteruelo* (hot game pâté), *guiso de cordero* (lamb stew), *ajoarriero* (salt cod and potato purée) and rice with honey. There are only five tables and a choice of menu, so it's best to go in a group to share dishes. Note also that they only open if they have prior bookings.
Booking essential.

The Castellana

The upper reaches of the Castellana, in the city's modern business district, are the location of several of Madrid's most prestigious restaurants. Further to the south in Recoletos, **Café Gijón** (*see chapter* **Cafés & Bars**) also serves full meals, with a good-value lunch menu.

Berceo-Le Divellec
Hotel Villa Magna, Paseo de la Castellana 22 (91 587 12 34). Metro Rubén Darío/bus all routes to Paseo de la Castellana. **Lunch served** 1-4pm, **dinner served** 8.30pm-midnight, daily. **Average** 7,000ptas. **Gourmet menu** 5,500ptas. **Credit** AmEx, DC, EC, JCB, MC, TC, V. **Map I3**
The Villa Magna is one of Madrid's best hotels, and has also gone to great trouble to establish one of the best restaurants in the city. French chef Jacques Le Divellec, whose Paris base has two Michelin stars, is an expert in seafood, and his cuisine is light, emphasising simple preparation and subtle sauces. Lobster with truffles is well worth a try, and sea bass baked in salt is divine. Little short of a gourmet paradise, and with a set menu for lunch and dinner, this is a treat one might justify for a last special evening in Madrid.
Air-conditioning. Booking essential. Disabled: wheelchair access.

Cabo Mayor
C/Juan Ramón Jiménez 37 (91 359 89 87). Metro Cuzco/bus 5, 40, 150. **Lunch served** 1.30-4pm Mon-Fri. **Dinner served** 9pm-midnight Mon-Sat. Closed Aug, Easter week. **Average** 7,000ptas. **Credit** AmEx, DC, JCB, MC, V.
Of the 1980s new-wave Spanish restaurants in the city, Cabo Mayor has matured most successfully. The mainly-seafood menu features modern Basque and northern Spanish dishes combining fish and vegetables in light but luxurious offerings such as a superb lobster salad. To follow, there are equally wonderful desserts. The slightly nautical interior is

Stout stuff: *cocina Madrileña*

Despite moves to broaden tastes, many of Madrid's residents love nothing better than to pile into an old-fashioned restaurant at least a few times each year for a lengthy meal of their own traditional hearty, powerful, wintery cuisine. The city's foremost dish is *cocido*, a kind of grand stew. In a real *cocido completo*, all the ingredients are cooked slowly together in the same pot, and then served as separate courses: first the broth and noodles, as a soup, then the vegetables (chickpeas, cabbage, leeks, turnips, onions and more), and finally the meat (beef, pig's trotters, chorizo, *morcilla*). As you might imagine, this is not a quick meal. Castilian roasts, *besugo a la madrileña* (sea bream in white wine and garlic), garlic soup and lentil stews also feature strongly. Classic places to find these dishes are the old *mesones* in or near Cava Baja, south of the Plaza Mayor. Despite their often-touristy look, much of the clientele is strictly local.

Also very Madrileño are offal dishes – *callos a la madrileña* (tripe in a hot tomato sauce, with chorizo and *morcilla*), *orejas* (pigs' ears), *sesos* (brains) and other things that other cultures shy away from – a long-standing tradition. They can be tried as tapas, and in offal shops such as **La Freiduría de Gallinejas** (*see chapter* **Tapas**).

La Bola Taberna

C/de la Bola 5 (91 547 69 30). Metro Opera, Santo Domingo/bus 3, 25, 39, 147. **Lunch served** 1-4.30 daily. **Dinner served** 9pm-midnight Mon-Sat. **Average** 3,500ptas. **Set menu** 1,900ptas. **No credit cards. Map D6**
This home to the city's most authentic *cocido* is still run – if no longer owned – by the family who founded it in the last century. The tiled interior is almost unchanged as well, as is the *cocido*, served only at lunchtime, and cooked completely in the traditional manner on a wood fire in big earthenware pots. Wash it all down with the good-quality house wine. Very popular.
Air-conditioning. Booking advisable. Disabled: wheelchair access.

La Botillería de Maxi

C/Cava Alta 4 (91 365 12 49). Metro La Latina/ bus 17, 18, 23, 35, 60. **Lunch served** 1-4.30pm, **dinner served** 8.30pm-midnight, Tue-Sun. Closed Aug. **Average** 2,500ptas. **Set menu** 1,100ptas. **No credit cards. Map D8**
A mecca for offal fans, with a sawdust-sprinkled tiled floor. A good *callos a la madrileña* has been known to convert fervent offal haters, and Maxi's is acknowledged as the best there is. If you really can't face it, there's also cheese, good *jamón serrano* and a simple set menu.
Tables outdoors.

Botín

C/Cuchilleros 17 (91 366 42 17). Metro Sol/ bus all routes to Puerta del Sol. **Lunch served** 1-4pm, **dinner served** 8pm-midnight, daily. **Average** 4,500ptas. **Set menu** 4,165ptas. **Credit** AmEx, DC, JCB, MC, V. **Map D8**
The most historic of the old taverns – and the most touristy – founded in the eighteenth century and still with its original wood-fired oven and tiles. A visit to this institution was an obligatory call for Hemingway and many other figures who have passed through Madrid. Specialities are Castilian roasts, rather than *cocido*.
Air-conditioning. Booking advisable.

Casa Lucio

C/Cava Baja 35 (91 365 32 52). Metro La Latina/bus 17, 18, 23, 35, 60. **Lunch served** 1-4pm Mon-Fri, Sun, **dinner served** 9pm-midnight, daily. Closed Aug. **Average** 5,500ptas. **Credit** AmEx, MC, DC, V. **Map D8**
The most reliable of the historic inns. A mixed political, artistic and business clientele comes here for Castilian roasts, *cocido*, occasional inventions such as *judías con faisán* (beans with pheasant), a sprinkling of Basque dishes, and... egg and chips. Service is brisk, and a reservation absolutely essential. To spot celebs, insist on a table in the main restaurant, not the annexe over the road.
Air-conditioning. Booking essential.

El Landó

Plaza de Gabriel Miró 8 (91 366 76 81). Metro La Latina/bus 31, 50, 65. **Lunch served** 1.30-4pm, **dinner served** 9pm-midnight, Mon-Sat. Closed Aug. **Average** 6,500ptas. **Credit** AmEx, DC, MC, TC, V. **Map C8**
Perhaps the least touristy of Madrid's traditional restaurants; pricey, but probably about as good as it gets, and without the affectation of places like Casa Lucio. Some diners go for a cholesterol orgy: egg and chips as a starter, maybe followed by tripe to die for. Then sit back and sip superb wines in the unhurried atmosphere.
Air-conditioning. Booking essential.

Malacatín

C/de la Ruda 5 (91 365 52 41). Metro La Latina/bus 17, 18, 23, 35, 60. **Lunch served** 1.30-5pm Mon-Sat. **Open also** 7.30-11pm for tapas. Closed July-Aug. **Set lunch** 2,500ptas. **No credit cards. Map D9**
People wax lyrical over the *cocido* at this century-old restaurant near the Rastro. It's made to order (you have to ring the day before) and served on wooden trestle tables. There are only two sittings, at 2.30pm and 3.30pm, or you can have tapas at the bar. If you decide to go the whole hog, you might well need a siesta afterwards. The price includes wine.
Air-conditioning. Booking essential.

Posada de la Villa

C/Cava Baja 9 (91 366 18 60). Metro La Latina/bus 17, 18, 23, 35, 60. **Lunch served** 1-4pm daily. **Dinner served** 8pm-midnight Mon-Sat. Closed Aug. **Average** 6,000ptas. **Credit** DC, MC, V. **Map D8**
Most picturesque of the old inns, with a domed oven and high-beamed roof. All the traditional Madrileño dishes are served, plus fine wood-roast lamb and suckling pig and now-rare traditional puddings such as *bartolillos* (small pastries filled with custard, then fried).
Air-conditioning. Booking advisable. Disabled: wheelchair access.

Viuda de Vacas

C/Cava Alta 23 (91 366 58 47). Metro La Latina/bus 17, 18, 23, 35, 60. **Lunch served** 1.30-4.30pm, **dinner served** 9.30pm-midnight, Mon-Wed, Fri, Sat. Closed Aug, Easter, Christmas. **Average** 2,500ptas. **Credit** AmEx, MC, V. **Map D8**
One of the most authentic of the old-town taverns, with its wood-oven, tiles, oak beams and spiral staircase. The excellent-value cooking features all the traditional standards, and is on a level with that of pricier rivals nearby.

pleasantly chic, the atmosphere is more relaxed than in many top-flight Madrid restaurants and as an extra attraction it has a neat pavement patio (evenings only) for summer. *Air conditioning. Booking essential. Tables outdoors June-Sept.*

La Doma
C/López de Hoyos 10 (91 564 16 16).
Metro Rubén Darío, Gregorio Marañón/bus all routes to Paseo de la Castellana. **Lunch served** 1-4.30pm, **dinner served** 9pm-midnight, daily. **Average** 3,500ptas. **Set menu** 1,700ptas. **Credit** MC, V. **Map I1**

In a city that loves its beef, but is highly demanding on quality, opening a new Argentinian restaurant is a challenge. La Doma, opened in 1997, has established a reputation for reasonable prices and fine-quality meat. The usual range of Argentine barbecue specialities is offset by Basque standards such as stuffed peppers, and a variety of fish dishes.

Hard Rock Café
Paseo de la Castellana 2 (91 436 43 40).
Metro Colón/bus all routes to Plaza de Colón. **Meals served** 12.30pm-2am daily. **Average** 2,000ptas. **Credit** AmEx, DC, JCB, MC, V. **Map I4**

Tour of Spain

As far as many Spaniards are concerned, there is not really such a thing as 'Spanish' food. Instead, every part of the country has its own distinctive cuisine, and its own treasured specialities; and, since the population of Madrid hails from all over Spain, its restaurants can almost form a culinary map of Iberia, with virtually every style represented. What follows is only a brief introduction to the most prominent of the Spanish cuisines.

Within this overall variety, there are some simple dishes that have more or less spread all over the country. Straightforward, often cheap dishes that don't fit into any one style – plain stews, or grilled fish – are often referred to as *comida casera*, home cooking. There are also restaurants that specialise in a type of food, particularly seafood. Basque, Galician and Catalan restaurants all feature seafood prominently; non-regional seafood specialists include **La Taberna de Abajo** and **La Trainera** (*see page 124*).

Andalusia
Andalusian restaurant standards are gazpacho, *pescadito frito* (flash-fried small fish) and *rabo de toro* (braised bull's tail). Also from this region and neighbouring Extremadura comes *jamón ibérico*, cured ham from the native Iberian breed of pig. Properly cured ham, from pigs fed on acorns to give the meat a distinctive earthy-sweet flavour, is an increasingly expensive luxury.
Restaurants: Don Paco *Sol & Gran Via, p114*; **La Giralda**; **El Rabo de Toro (Casa Díaz)** *Both in Salamanca & the Retiro, p123*.

Asturias
The northern region of Asturias, green and cool, is renowned for sturdy mountain food. *Fabada*, a rich stew of beans, onions, chorizo and black pudding (*morcilla*), is the classic dish; other specialities are strong cheeses, rice puddings and pastries, as well as fish soups and stews from the coast. Cider (*sidra*) rather than wine is the local drink, and the most traditional Asturian cider is coarse and strong.
Restaurants: Casa Lastra Sidrería *La Latina, Rastro, Lavapiés, p117*; **Fuente la Xana** *Malasaña & Chueca, p120*; **Casa Portal** *Salamanca & the Retiro, p123*; **Casa Mingo** *Keeping your cool, p121*.

Basque Country, Navarra, La Rioja
Basque cooking has long been recognised as the most sophisticated in Spain, and many of Madrid's finest restau-

rants also have Basque chefs (*see p110* **Top tables**). The Basque Country offers a superb, wide-ranging cuisine, with many highly original fish dishes, and seafood combinations using crab (*txangurro* in Basque). From inland Navarra and La Rioja come delicious vegetable dishes such as *menestra de habas* (broad beans and mixed vegetables in wine and herbs), fine meats, and freshwater fish options like *trucha a la navarra* (trout with ham).
Restaurants: El Alamillo; **La Taberna de Alabardero** *Both in Villa y Corte, p109*; **Asador Frontón** *La Latina, Rastro, Lavapiés, p117*; **Carmencita**; **La Castafiore** *Both in Malasaña & Chueca, p119*; **Centro Riojano** *Salamanca & the Retiro, p123*; **Currito** *Keeping your cool, p121*.

Castile
The food of Spain's central *meseta* is, like Madrileño cooking, stout stuff. Most famous are the wood-roasts of milk-fed lamb and suckling pig, most associated with Segovia (*see pp227-9*), and the superb Castilian lentil and bean stews. Also to be found, though, are less well-known specialities from specific areas such as Cuenca and the mountain plateau of El Bierzo in León.
Restaurants: Casa Ciriaco; **Casa Marta**; **El Tormo** *All in Villa y Corte, p109*; **El Buey**; **Mesón Prada a Tope** *Both in Sol & Gran Via, p114*; **El Puchero** *Malasaña & Chueca, p120*; **La Playa** *Chamberí, p124*.

Catalan & Mediterranean
Spain's Mediterranean coastline, from Catalonia through Valencia and the Balearic islands to Murcia, embraces sea and mountain. Catalonia is the source of some of the most inventive modern cooking in Spain, with light, varied dishes that mix together seafood, meat and vegetables to a degree rarely seen in Castile. The Mediterranean shoreline, above all Valencia, is also the home of the classic paella, although it is only one of hundreds of variations of meat and rice dishes found along the coast.
Restaurants: El Caldero; **Champagneria Gala**; **Paradís Madrid** *All in Huertas & Santa Ana, p115*.

Galicia
There are hundreds of Galician bar-restaurants around the city. Most have tapas bars at the front, and many are seafood *marisquerías*. As well as fish and shellfish, Galician standards are *caldo gallego* (a heavy broth of swiss chard, potatoes, gammon ham and chorizo), *lacón* (gammon ham) and *empanadas*, savoury pies with meat or fish fillings.
Restaurants: Casa Gallega *Villa y Corte, p109*; **Do Salmón** *Huertas & Santa Ana, p117*; **Ribeira Do Miño** *Malasaña & Chueca, p122*; **A Casiña** *Keeping your cool, p121*.

*Olive-maestro Jean-Pierre Vandelle proffers an aperitif at **El Olivo**.*

On a prime site by the Plaza Colón, with the usual interior filled with the rock memorabilia you'd expect, burgers just like they make 'em at your local HRC – and queues just as long. Full of young Spaniards in love with the US of A, and young Americans who like to 'travel' as little as possible. *Air-conditioning. Disabled: wheelchair access. Tables outdoors May-Oct.*

House of Ming

Paseo de la Castellana 74 (91 561 98 27). Metro Rubén Darío/bus all routes to Paseo de la Castellana. **Lunch served** 1.30-4pm, **dinner served** 8.30pm-12.30am, daily. **Average** 3,500ptas. **Set menu** 1,500ptas. **Credit** AmEx, MC, V. **Map I1**
One of Madrid's first Chinese restaurants, which has stayed true to its origins with fine-quality Peking cuisine. Highlights are Peking Duck, shrimp Wo Ba, and, rare in this city, dim sum. *Air-conditioning. Disabled: wheelchair access.*

El Olivo

C/General Gallegos 1, corner of Juan Ramón Jiménez 37 (91 359 15 35). Metro Cuzco/bus 5, 40, 150. **Lunch served** 1-4pm, **dinner served** 9pm-midnight, Tue-Sat. Closed Aug. **Average** 6,500ptas. **Set menu** 3,850ptas. **Gourmet menu** 5,850ptas. **Credit** AmEx, DC, JCB, MC, V.
It took a Frenchman to show off Spain's olives and their oil to their utmost advantage, but Madrileños have taken to Jean-Pierre Vandelle's olive-green dining room, with its trolley loaded with different oils and bar stocked with over 120 different sherries. Specialities include *salmón y mero* (salmon and grouper marinated in oil), salt cod cooked four different ways and a tasty *tarta de manzana* (apple tart). *Air-conditioning. Booking essential.*

Zalacaín

C/Alvarez de Baena 4 (91 561 59 35). Metro Gregorio Marañón/bus 12, 16, 40, 147. **Lunch served** 1.15-4pm Mon-Fri. **Dinner served** 9pm-midnight Mon-Sat. Closed Aug. **Average** 9,000ptas. **Gourmet menu** 11,500ptas. **Credit** AmEx, DC, JCB, MC, V.

Master chef Benjamín Urdaín and proprietor Jesús María Oyarbide run the best show in Madrid, only restaurant in the city with three Michelin stars. The setting is seamlessly luxurious, the seasonal, Basque-based cooking is superb, and the wine list includes an exceptional selection of fine Spanish vintages. It's as expensive as the clothing bills of the clientele, but at least with the '90s has come a set gourmet menu of five courses plus dessert (not cheap either, but worth it), so these days the main drawback to a visit could be the stuffy atmosphere and rather oppressive jacket-and-tie dress code. *Air-conditioning. Booking essential. Disabled: wheelchair access.*

Sol & Gran Vía

El Buey

Plaza de la Marina Española 1 (91 541 30 41). Metro Opera/bus 25, 39, 148. **Lunch served** 1-4pm, **dinner served** 9pm-midnight, Mon-Sat. **Average** 3,500ptas. **Credit** AmEx, DC, MC, V. **Map C6**
The centrepiece of the menu at this carnivores' haven is the superb beef fillet, *lomo de buey*, done any way, at 5,000ptas a kilo. Also to be had are a dozen first courses, two fish alternatives for the main course, and home-made desserts. *Air-conditioning. Booking advisable. Disabled: wheelchair access.*
Branch: La Trucha Marina C/General Díaz Porlier 9 (91 575 31 28).

Don Paco

C/Caballero de Gracia 36 (91 531 44 80). Metro Gran Vía/bus all routes to Gran Vía. **Lunch served** 2-4.30pm, **dinner served** 9.30-11.30pm, Mon-Sat. Closed Aug. **Average** 4,000ptas. **Set menu** 1,600ptas. **Credit** AmEx, DC, V. **Map F7**
Tucked away in a narrow street between Alcalá and Gran Vía, Don Paco is rightly considered one of the best Andalusian restaurants in the capital. Service is excellent, the atmosphere is very friendly, and the slightly-*Sevillano*

Vegetarianos

Madrid has never been a candidate for the world's most vegetarian-friendly city, but in the last few years the number of enjoyable vegetarian restaurants in town has increased rapidly, and all are well attended. Just about any bar-restaurant will also serve tortilla and salad, but with other choices it's worth remembering that a lot of vegetable dishes may come sautéd with ham, and lentil and bean stews might be made with a meat stock, so it's advisable to check when ordering.

Vegetarian restaurants

El Estragón *Villa y Corte, p109.*
Artemisa *Huertas & Santa Ana, p115.*
El Granero del Lavapiés
La Latina, Rastro, Lavapiés, p117.
Chez Pomme; La Granja; El Restaurante Vegetariano *All in Malasaña & Chueca, p119.*
La Galette *Salamanca & the Retiro, p123.*
EcoCentro *Chamberí, p124.*

décor has just the right balance of tiles and brickwork. Try the prawn omelette (*tortilla de gambas*), oxtail stew (*rabo de buey*) or sweetbreads (*mollejas*) in sherry. At lunchtime there's an excellent-value set menu at the bar.
Air-conditioning. Booking advisable.

Mesón Prada a Tope
Cuesta de San Vicente 32 (91 559 39 53).
Metro Plaza de España, Príncipe Pío/bus 39, 46, 75, 133, C. **Open** 10am-midnight. **Lunch served** 2-4pm, **dinner served** 8.30pm-midnight, Mon, Wed-Sun. Closed Aug. **Average** 2,500ptas. **Credit** V. **Map C6**
A small informal bar-restaurant down the hill towards the Campo del Moro from Plaza de España and the Palacio Real. Its specialities are the dishes of the tiny region of El Bierzo, between Castilla-León and Galicia: roasted red peppers with a spicy hot kick, *botillo* (a heavy sausage), *cerezas en aguardiente* (cherries in grain spirit), and excellent young wines in the cask or bottle.
Air-conditioning.

Musashi
C/Conchas 4 (91 559 29 39). Metro Callao/bus all routes to Plaza de Callao. **Lunch served** 1.30-4pm, **dinner served** 8.30-11.30pm, Tue-Sun. **Average** 2,000ptas. **Set menu** 900-1,200ptas. **Credit** JCB, MC, V. **Map D7**
A low-priced Japanese restaurant may sound like a contradiction in terms, but the Japanese eateries that have sprung up around Madrid take good advantage of the quality of fresh fish in the city. Just south of the Gran Vía lies Musashi, with little pretension to elaborate décor but attentive service and a good range of sushi for less than 2,000ptas, plus a special dish of the day for 1,000ptas.
Air-conditioning.

Robata
C/de la Reina 31 (91 521 85 28). Metro Gran Vía/bus all routes to Gran Vía. **Lunch served** 1.30-4pm, **dinner served** 8.30-11pm, Mon, Wed-Sun. **Average** 4,000ptas. **Set menu** 1,500ptas. **Gourmet menu** 4,000ptas. **Credit** AmEx, DC, MC, V. **Map F6**

A stylishly minimalist and modern Japanese restaurant just north of the Gran Vía with tatami rooms and sushi chefs at work behind an open bar. The evening gourmet menu of sushi with soya soup is not cheap, but high-quality and justifiably good value.
Air-conditioning.

Huertas & Santa Ana

Artemisa
C/Ventura de la Vega 4 (91 429 50 92).
Metro Sevilla/bus all routes to Puerta del Sol. **Lunch served** 1.30-4pm daily. **Dinner served** 9pm-midnight Mon-Sat. **Average** 2,500ptas. **Set menu** 1,250ptas. **Credit** AmEx, DC, MC, V. **Map F7**
One of the city's longest-established vegetarian eateries; it's always busy, perhaps due to a combination of a central location and low prices. Nevertheless, the cooking and the range of dishes on the menus – vegetarian staples such as organic gazpacho, vegetable curry or salads and pizzas – can be pretty routine.
Air-conditioning. Disabled: wheelchair access.
Branch: C/Tres Cruces 4 (91 521 87 21). **Open** 1.30-4pm, 9pm-midnight, Thur-Sun only.

El Caldero
C/Huertas 15 (91 429 50 44). Metro Antón Martín/bus 6, 26, 32. **Lunch served** 1-4pm daily. **Dinner served** 9pm-midnight Tue-Sat. **Average** 3,500ptas. **Credit** AmEx, DC, EC, JCB, MC, V. **Map F8**
One of a handful of restaurants in Madrid serving the food of Murcia, an interesting intermediate-point between Andalusia and Valencia. The star turns are good: *dorada* baked in a salt crust, and *arroz al caldero* (rice cooked in a rich fish and shellfish stock). First courses might be *habas con jamón* (broad beans with ham) or *salazones* (salt-dried tuna and roe, eaten cold). The restaurant is very good value, and has been recommended by readers.
Air-conditioning. Booking essential.

Casa Santa Cruz
C/de la Bolsa 12 (91 521 86 23). Metro Sol/bus all routes to Puerta del Sol. **Lunch served** 1.30-4pm, **dinner served** 8.30pm-midnight, daily. **Average** 4,000ptas. **Credit** AmEx, DC, MC, V. **Map E8**
This building was originally a chapel, part of a long-demolished eighteenth-century church, and later in its long life became Madrid's first stock exchange. Since it became and elegant and comfortable restaurant prices perhaps reflect the décor as much as the food, but it is a superb setting, and the restaurant's excellent fresh salads and light, modern versions of Madrileño dishes have a strong appeal for foreign taste buds.
Air-conditioning. Booking essential.
Disabled: wheelchair access.

El Cenador del Prado
C/del Prado 4 (91 429 15 61). Metro Antón Martín/bus 6, 9, 26, 32. **Lunch served** 1.30-4pm Mon-Fri. **Dinner served** 9pm-midnight Mon-Sat. **Average** 4,500ptas. **Gourmet menu** 3,500ptas. **Credit** AmEx, DC, MC, V. **Map F8**
The Herranz brothers produce imaginative, modern Spanish regional cuisine at their restaurant just off Plaza Santa Ana, with many interesting specialities such as *patatas con almejas* (potatoes with clams), and a *menú de degustación* (gourmet menu) at 3,500ptas. With a lush green conservatory and soothing décor, the restaurant has the feel of an oasis amid the busy Huertas streets. Service is also smooth, and despite the prestige of the restaurant the usual crowd is fashionable rather than formal.
Air-conditioning. Booking advisable.
Disabled: wheelchair access.

Champagneria Gala

*C/Moratin 22 (91 429 25 62). Metro Antón Martin/
bus 6, 26, 32.* **Lunch served** 2-4.30pm,
dinner served 9pm-1.30am, daily. **Average** 2,000ptas.
No credit cards. Map G8
This delightful, laid-back 'Champagnerie' specialises in
Catalan paellas and *fideuás*, a similar dish made with noodles
instead of rice: there are 14 of each to choose from, including
vegetarian options. Another distinction is its airy semi-glass-
covered garden patio at the back, filled with plants. Run by a
group of women, Gala is popular with women on their own,
and has also been greatly appreciated by *Time Out* readers.
The 'champagne' (Catalan *Cava*) includes the excellent
Vallformosa, and the even better Juvé i Camps.
Tables outdoors.

Donzoko

*C/Echegaray 3 (91 429 57 20). Metro Sevilla/bus all
routes to Puerta del Sol.* **Lunch served** 1.30-3.30pm,
dinner served 8.30-11.30pm, Mon-Sat. **Average**
3,000ptas. **Credit** AmEx, DC, JCB, MC, V. **Map F7**
Conveniently close to Plaza Santa Ana, this roomy Japanese
restaurant has all that you would expect: discreet décor, correct service and beautifully presented sushi and tempura.
*Air-conditioning. Booking advisable. Disabled: wheelchair
access.*

Lhardy

*Carrera de San Jerónimo 8 (91 521 33 85). Metro Sol/bus
all routes to Puerta del Sol.* **Lunch served** 1-3.30pm
daily. **Dinner served** 8.30-11pm Mon-Sat. **Average**
7,000ptas. **Credit** AmEx, DC, JCB, MC, V. **Map E7**
This landmark restaurant, opened in 1839, is credited with
having first introduced French haute cuisine into the culinary wilds of Madrid. Founder Emile Lhardy was supposedly enticed here by none other than *Carmen* author Prosper
Mérimée, who told him there was not another decent restaurant in the city. Today it's rated as much for its history and
belle époque décor as for the (very expensive) food. The
menu is as Frenchified as it has always been, although there's
also a very refined *cocido*, good game and *callos*, and an excellent, if pricey, wine list. *See also chapter* **Tapas**.
Air-conditioning. Booking essential.

Paradís Madrid

*C/Marqués de Cubas 14 (91 429 73 03).
Metro Banco de España/bus all routes to Plaza de Cibeles.*
Lunch served 1.30-4pm Mon-Fri. **Dinner served** 9pm-
midnight Mon-Sat. Closed Easter, Aug. **Average**
6,000ptas. **Credit** AmEx, DC, MC, V. **Map G7**
New-wave, light Catalan food: fish and seafood rices, *bacal-
là amb gambes* (salt cod with prawns), plus a selection of oils
and infusions. It has a stylish wine bar at the front, and prices
– especially the wines – reflect the smart setting. There is
also a Paradís in the very pretty garden of the Casa de
América on Plaza de Cibeles.
*Air-conditioning. Booking advisable. Disabled: wheelchair
access.*
Branch: Paradís-Casa de América Paseo de
Recoletos 2 (91 575 45 40).

Do Salmón

*C/León 4 (91 429 39 52). Metro Antón Martin/
bus 6, 26, 32.* **Lunch served** 1-4pm, **dinner served**
9pm-midnight, Tue-Sun. **Average** 3,000ptas.
Credit AmEx, MC, V. **Map F8**
Plain, straightforward but very good Galician food in an
unpretentious setting. Start with a plate of *tetilla* cheese or
entremeses and follow with *pulpo a feira* (octopus in sea salt,

*A relaxing garden in the middle of Madrid,
the* **Champagnería Gala**.

pepper and olive oil) or, for the ravenous, a *codillo* (boiled
shoulder of ham with potatoes, turnips and chorizo).
Carnivores love the *chuletón de buey*, a huge beef chop. The
house Ribeiro wine, drunk out of little white ceramic bowls,
is fine, but try the Albariño if you're feeling flush.

La Vaca Verónica

*C/Moratin 38 (91 429 78 27). Metro Antón Martin/
bus 6, 26, 27, 32, 45.* **Lunch served** 2-4pm Mon-Fri.
Dinner served 9pm-midnight Mon-Sat.
Average 3,500ptas. **Set menu** 1,900ptas.
Credit AmEx, DC, MC, V. **Map G8**
Hidden away at the bottom of Huertas, very conveniently
placed for the major museums, 'Veronica the Cow' has a
relaxed bistro feel. Interesting fresh pasta dishes, some with
seafood, imaginative salads and home-made desserts, plus
friendly service, have kept it popular for years. The full menu
can be a little pricey, but good-value set menus compensate.
Air-conditioning.

La Latina, Rastro, Lavapiés

Asador Frontón I

*Plaza Tirso de Molina 7; entry at C/Jesús y Maria 1
(91 369 16 17). Metro Tirso de Molina/bus 6, 26, 32,
35.* **Lunch served** 1-4pm daily. **Dinner served** 9pm-
midnight Tue-Sat. **Average** 5,000ptas.
Credit AmEx, DC, MC, V. **Map E8**
These two restaurants set up by former *pelota* star Miguel
Ansorena are the best-known Basque grills in Madrid. Their
fame is justified by first-class ingredients and grilling of
meat and fish refined to perfection. Don't be put off by the
giant-sized chops – they are served cut into strips that you
can share. The Pedro Muguruza branch has a broader menu.
Air-conditioning. Booking advisable.
Branch: C/Pedro Muguruza 8 (91 345 36 96).

Belmar

*C/Lavapiés 6 & C/Cabeza 12 (91 528 55 46).
Metro Tirso de Molina/bus 6, 26, 32.* **Meals served**
8am-1am daily. Closed Aug. **Average** 1,500ptas. **Set
menu** 1,000ptas. **No credit cards. Map E9**
A great budget bar-restaurant with half a dozen tables near
Tirso de Molina, serving a set menu and a selection of dishes from around the regions. If you cannot get a table, or don't
want a full meal, it also does good tapas.
Air-conditioning.

Casa Lastra Sidrería

*C/Olivar 3 (91 369 08 37). Metro Antón Martín, Tirso
de Molina/bus 6, 26, 32.* **Lunch served** 1-5pm Thur-
Tue. **Dinner served** 8pm-midnight Mon, Tue, Thur-Sat.
Average 3,500ptas. **Credit** AmEx, MC, V. **Map E9**
This hugely popular Asturian restaurant and cider house is
known for its massive portions. Recommended starters
include *fabes con almejas* (white beans with clams) and *chorizo a la sidra* (chorizo in cider); good mains are *entrecot al
cabrales* (entrecote with a powerful blue cheese sauce) and
merluza a la sidra (hake in cider) or, in winter, an excellent
fabada. Wash it all down with *sidra natural* (still cider) or
any of the wines from the extensive list. For dessert, try *arroz
con leche*, *carbayón* (made from almonds and sweetened egg
yolks) or baked apples. Expect queues at weekends.
Air-conditioning. Booking advisable.

El Granero del Lavapiés

*C/Argumosa 10 (91 467 76 11). Metro Lavapiés/bus 27,
34, C.* **Lunch served** 1-4pm daily. **Dinner served** 8.30-
11pm Fri, Sat. Closed mid-Aug. **Average** 2,000ptas. **Set
menu** 1,200ptas. **No credit cards. Map F10**
Though normally open only at lunchtimes, this is one of the
most popular restaurants among local vegetarians for its
simple, unfussy style, with an attractive, sunny dining room.

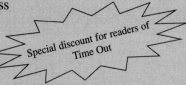

Asturian cider-drinking has its special rituals. **Casa Lastra Sidrería.** *See page 117.*

Food ranges from broccoli with carrot mayonnaise to *cardos con almendras* (cardoon, a type of edible thistle considered particularly healthy, with almonds).

La Pampa

C/Amparo 61 (91 528 04 49). Metro Lavapiés/bus 27, 34, C. **Lunch served** 1.30-4.30pm, **dinner served** 9pm-12.30am, Tue-Sun. **Average** 3,000ptas. **Credit** AmEx, DC, JCB, MC, V. **Map E10**
A carnivore's den (like most Argentinian restaurants), La Pampa also offers a full range of dishes and very sweet desserts. *Empanada de choclo* (maize pastry) and *pascualina* (a type of spinach pie) make interesting appetizers, and the hefty mains include *asado de tira* (a cross-the-ribs cut of steak). If your stomach can take it, finish with *dulce de leche* (condensed-milk toffee) or *milhojas* (millefeuille). Wines are stout and unsophisticated.
Air-conditioning. Booking essential weekends. Disabled: wheelchair access.

Soldemersol

C/Argumosa 9 (no phone). Metro Atocha, Lavapiés/bus all routes to Atocha. **Lunch served** 1-5pm, **dinner served** 8pm-midnight, daily. Closed mid-Aug-mid-Sept. **Average** 1,000ptas. **No credit cards. Map F10**
This tiled *económico* restaurant near the Reina Sofía is an institution among all in need of a cheap meal. Zalacaín it ain't, but the food is solid fare and offers a good choice, with vegetarian options. Service is friendly – two smiling brothers run the show, while an ancient lady, apparently their mother, can just be made out amid the steam of her kitchen. Try the cauliflower in batter, check out the kitsch water jugs and soak up the atmosphere. On Sunday lunchtimes arrive early, as after-Rastro crowds soon pack the place out.

El Viajero

Plaza de la Cebada 11 (91 366 90 64). Metro La Latina/bus 17, 18, 23, 35, 60. **Lunch served** 2-4.30pm, **dinner served** 9pm-12.30am, Tue-Sun. **Average** 3,500ptas. **Set menu** 1,400ptas. **Credit** AmEx, DC, MC, V. **Map D9**

El Viajero opened up in the heart of slightly trendy La Latina in 1994, and quickly became one of its most fashionable spots to eat. There's splendid meat from Uruguay, hormone-free – as is the *chorizo criollo*, a smoked sausage prepared on a charcoal griddle. Vegetarians need not feel left out, as there are also good pizzas and excellent pastas. After eating you can enjoy the spectacular views from its ultra-popular rooftop bar, or shoot some pool on the first floor. The restaurant gets crowded, so book or arrive early, especially to get a table on the roof. *See also chapter* **Nightlife**.
Booking advisable. Tables outdoors (roof terrace).

Malasaña & Chueca

Al-Jaima

C/Barbieri 1 (91 523 11 42). Metro Gran Vía/bus all routes to Gran Vía. **Lunch served** 1.30-5pm, **dinner served** 9pm-12.30am, Thur-Tue. **Average** 3,000ptas. **Set menu** 2,500ptas. **Credit** AmEx, DC, MC, V. **Map F6**
Run by a group of Moroccans and Spaniards from Granada, Al-Jaima offers North African food together with nominally Spanish dishes adapted from Moroccan cuisine. Excellent value, with the option (if you book) of eating from low Moroccan tables, seated on cushions.
Air-conditioning. Booking advisable.

Carmencita

C/Libertad 16 (91 531 66 12). Metro Chueca/bus 3, 37, 40, 149. **Lunch served** 1-4pm Mon-Fri. **Dinner served** 9pm-midnight Mon-Sat. **Average** 4,000ptas. **Set menu** 1,300ptas. **Credit** AmEx, MC, V. **Map G5**
Dating back to 1850, Carmencita's labyrinthine, old-world interior has been a favourite with the famous over the years, and continues to attract discreet gatherings of the well to do and well known. Not that that's the only reason to go there. The food is Basque-based these days, although plenty of traditional Madrileño fare such as clams with beans, partridge and squid still features on the menu.
Air-conditioning. Booking advisable.

Imaginative, modern food in a light, modern setting, **La Musa.** *See page 121.*

La Castafiore

*C/Barquillo 30 (91 532 21 00). Metro Chueca/
bus 37, 149.* **Lunch served** 2-4pm, **dinner served**
9.30pm-1am, Mon-Sat. **Average** 6,000ptas.
Set menus 1,550-2,600ptas. **Credit** AmEx, V. **Map H5**
La Castafiore's special 'formula' is its singing waiters: music
students and professionals blend in with real waiters, and
launch into an operatic aria at the drop of a hat. The menu
is short – a mix of simple but well-executed dishes from
Navarra, home ground of owner Javier Otero – but has
proved very popular. It's open all day as a normal café, tapas
bar or restaurant, but dinner with the promised accompaniment is served from 9.30pm.
*Air-conditioning. Booking essential. Disabled: wheelchair
access.*

Chez Pomme

*C/Pelayo 4 (91 532 16 46). Metro Chueca/bus 3, 37, 40,
149.* **Lunch served** 1.30-4pm, **dinner served** 8.30-
11.30pm, Mon-Sat. Closed Aug. **Average** 1,800ptas.
Set menu 1,000ptas. **Credit** V. **Map F6**
Chueca's only vegetarian restaurant, with a big gay clientele.
The menus have very much a home-cooking feel and, despite
a touch of the old macrobiotics, are more interestingly varied than those of some more basic and austere vegetarian
eating-places. The set menu is excellent value.
Air-conditioning.

La Chocolatería

*C/Barbieri 15 (91 521 00 23). Metro Chueca/
bus 3, 37, 40, 149.* **Lunch served** 1.45-3.45pm,
snacks and chocolate served from 6pm, **dinner
served** 9pm-1.30am, daily. **Average** 3,000ptas. **Set
menu** 1,800ptas. **No credit cards. Map F6**
Chueca's Chocolatería serves tasty, creative, well-prepared
dishes in a pleasant setting, and, unusually for a Madrid
restaurant, offers a choice of fresh vegetables that changes
daily and by season. Recommended are the *codillo en salsa
de ciruela* (pork knuckle in plum sauce) and *bacalao con
almendras* (cod with almonds); home-made sweets include

hojaldre de peras con toffee (pear pie with flaky pastry and
toffee sauce). As befits a *chocolatería*, it opens in the early
evening to provide snacks and thick hot chocolate.
*Air-conditioning. Booking advisable. Disabled: wheelchair
access.*

La Dama Duende

*C/de la Palma 63 (91 532 54 41/reservations
91 921 91 80). Metro Noviciado/bus 147.* **Dinner
served** 9pm-midnight Mon-Sat. **Average** 4,000ptas.
Credit MC, V. **Map E4**
A blend of inventive and traditional cooking, combined with
tasteful décor and a relaxed, neighbourhood atmosphere
have made this women's-run restaurant very popular. The
menu changes with the seasons: pheasant salad, cod fillets
in cream and ox medallions with onion jam are among the
delights. Lunch is served only for groups of from ten to 40
people (phone to reserve).
Air-conditioning. Booking advisable/essential for lunch.

Fuente la Xana

*Centro Asturiano, C/Farmacia 2 (91 522 42 18).
Metro Chueca, Tribunal/bus 3, 40, 149.* **Lunch served**
1.30-4pm daily. **Dinner served** 9-11.30pm Mon-Sat.
Average 3,500ptas. **Credit** MC, V. **Map G5**
There has been a restaurant on the second floor of the Centro
Asturiano, the official Asturian club, for many years, but
since new management took over in 1994 standards have
risen considerably. The menu offers a mix of traditional and
more innovative dishes, with particularly good fish soups.
Air-conditioning. Disabled: wheelchair access

La Gastroteca de Stéphane y Arturo

*Plaza de Chueca 8 (91 532 25 64). Metro Chueca/bus 3,
40, 149.* **Lunch served** 2-4pm Mon-Fri. **Dinner
served** 9-11pm Mon-Sat. Closed Aug. **Average**
5,000ptas. **Credit** AmEx, DC, EC, JCB, MC, V. **Map G5**
Stéphane Guérin's cooking is characterful modern French,
while her husband's front-of-house style is witty and very
Spanish, making this informal but very comfortable place

in Chueca interestingly offbeat. Favoured dishes include a black olive sorbet, skate cooked a variety of ways, and profiteroles with honey ice-cream. The wine list is one of the most varied and international in town.
Air-conditioning. Booking advisable.

La Granja
C/San Andrés 11 (91 532 87 93).
Metro Bilbao, Tribunal/bus 3, 21, 40, 147, 149. **Lunch served** 1.30-4.30pm daily. **Dinner served** 9pm-midnight Wed-Mon. **Average** 1,500ptas. **Set menu** 975ptas. **Credit** AmEx, MC, V. **Map E4**
With ultra-reasonable prices and a varied menu, La Granja is a great budget stop-off for vegetarians in Malasaña. Its paella, stuffed peppers and soya burgers are great, and there are also usually different home-made cakes to choose from. Very popular, so arrive early to get the full choice.

La Musa
C/Manuela Malasaña 18 (91 448 75 58).
Metro Bilbao/bus 21, 147, 149. **Open** 9am-midnight Mon-Thur; 9am-1.30am Fri; noon-1.30am Sat; noon-midnight Sun. **Average** 1,500ptas. **Set menu** 1,200ptas. **Credit** AmEx, DC, MC, V. **Map E3**
A light, bright and popular bar-restaurant with friendly young staff, a clean, plain-wood look and art work around the walls. The excellent, frequently changing fare consists of traditional Castilian/Spanish dishes with contemporary touches – a greater use of vegetables, more combinations of flavours – that make them lighter and maybe more appealing to non-Castilian taste buds. The set lunch menu offers a good-value choice usually of a fish or meat main course – maybe turkey *albóndigas*, or John Dory grilled in lemon; at the bar, similarly imaginative tapas are available. A very enjoyable place.
Air-conditioning.

Keeping your cool

When it's time to eat but still 80°F outside, where better to head than a *terraza*, perhaps the best expression of Madrid's Mediterranean mindset, a setting for open-air eating, music, socialising and general living for long months each summer. For visitors from colder climes, any chance to eat in the open air can be a treat, but, given the afternoon heat in mid summer, dinner is usually a better bet than lunch. Opportunities to eat outside are limited in the city centre: the Plaza Mayor is an obvious option, but the splendour of the setting is often offset by sub-standard food and service, and exploitative prices. Better than the rest is **El Soportal**, specialising in fish and meat grills.

Away from the centre and the crowds, **La Plaza de Chamberí**, in the square of the same name, offers good modern Spanish food and a very genuine atmosphere. A more classic place to eat al fresco in Madrid is **Los Porches** on Paseo del Pintor Rosales, with an (expensive) international menu and a leafy terrace with views of the Casa de Campo.

The Casa de Campo itself has some highly rated regional restaurants with garden terraces, and cleaner, cooler air than the city centre. In the park's exhibition area, **A Casinã** offers pricey but excellent Galician seafood dishes, while the Basque **Currito** has superb grilled fish and meats. Much cheaper are the cafés along the lake, especially popular in the early evening or for Sunday lunch. On the north-eastern edge of the park, across the river from San Antonio de la Florida, is the charming Colonia de Manzanares district, with a branch of **La Vaca Argentina** with tables beside the riverbank. This low-key, relaxed neighbourhood is an ideal place for a riverside stroll after eating, and just across the river by San Antonio itself is **Casa**

Mingo, a boisterous Asturian roast chicken and cider house that's one of the cheapest and most popular places to eat outdoors in Madrid.

Locations
A Casiña *Avda del Angel, Casa de Campo (91 526 34 25).* Metro Lago/bus 31, 33, 36, 39. **Open** 10am-midnight Mon-Sat; 10am-4pm Sun. **Average** 4,500ptas. **Credit** AmEx, DC, MC, V. *Air-conditioning. Booking advisable. Disabled: wheelchair access.*
Casa Mingo *Glorieta de San Antonio de la Florida 2 (91 547 79 18).* Metro Príncipe Pío/bus 41, 46, 75. **Meals served** 11am-midnight daily. **Average** 2,000ptas. **No credit cards. Map D4**
Currito *Pabellón de Vizcaya, Casa de Campo (91 464 57 04).* Metro Lago/bus 31, 33, 36, 39. **Lunch served** 1-4pm daily. **Dinner served** 9-11.30pm Mon-Sat. **Average** 6,500ptas. **Credit** AmEx, DC, MC, V. *Air-conditioning. Booking advisable.*
La Plaza de Chamberí *Plaza de Chamberí 10 (91 446 06 97).* Metro Iglesia/bus 3,16, 40, 61, 147. **Lunch served** 1-4pm, **dinner served** 9pm-midnight, Mon-Sat. **Average** 4,000ptas. **Credit** AmEx, MC, DC, V. **Map G2**
Air-conditioning. Booking advisable. Disabled: wheelchair access.
Los Porches *Paseo del Pintor Rosales 1 (91 548 13 36).* Metro Argüelles/bus 21, 44, 74, C. **Lunch served** 1-4pm, **dinner served** 8-30pm-midnight, daily. **Average** 6,000ptas. **Credit** AmEx, DC, MC, V. **Map B4**
Air-conditioning. Booking advisable.
El Soportal *Plaza Mayor 33 (91 366 39 66).* Metro Sol/bus all routes to Puerta del Sol. **Lunch served** 1-4pm, **dinner served** 8pm-midnight, daily. **Average** 4,000ptas. **Credit** AmEx, DC, MC, V. **Map D8**
Air-conditioning.
La Vaca Argentina *Ribera del Manzanares 123 (91 559 37 80).* Bus 41, 75. **Lunch served** 1-4.30pm, **dinner served** 9pm-midnight, daily. **Average** 3,500ptas. **Credit** AmEx, DC, MC, V.
Booking essential. Disabled: wheelchair access.
Branches: C/Bailén 20 (91 365 66 54); C/Caños del Peral 2 (91 541 33 18); C/Gaztambide 50 (91 543 53 83); C/Numancia 2 (91 311 69 45); Paseo del Pintor Rosales 52 (91 559 66 05)..

El Nueve

*C/Santa Teresa 9 (91 319 29 46). Metro Alonso Martínez/
bus 3, 21, 37, 40, 149.* **Lunch served** 1.45-4pm, **dinner
served** 9-11pm, daily. Closed Aug. **Average** 1,500ptas. **Set
menu** 1,050ptas. **No credit cards. Map H4**
On the edge of Chueca, the Nueve's been packing them in
for decades with cheap and plentiful food such as a full *cocido* and an Asturian *fabada* (bean stew).

Pizzería Mastropiero

*C/San Vicente Ferrer 34 (no phone). Metro Noviciado,
Tribunal/bus 3, 40, 147, 149.* **Dinner served** 8pm-1am
Mon-Thur, Sun; 8pm-2.30am Fri, Sat. **Average** 1,500ptas.
No credit cards. Map F4
A good, if cramped, Argentinian pizzeria in Malasaña. The
20 or so pizzas come small (750ptas) or large (1,500ptas), and
there are also pastries, quiches and cheap wine.

El Puchero

*C/Larra 13 (91 445 05 77). Metro Bilbao/bus 3, 37, 40,
149.* **Lunch served** 1.30-4pm, **dinner served** 9pm-
midnight, Mon-Sat. Closed Aug. **Average** 4,000ptas.
Credit AmEx, MC, V. **Map F3**
Checked tablecloths, white-aproned waitresses and a spread of
traditional dishes, with specials such as *capón relleno* (stuffed
capon), mark the style of this easily missed Castilian basement
restaurant. It also has good Ribera del Duero house wine.
Air-conditioning. Booking advisable.
Branch: C/Padre Damián 37 (91 345 62 98).

Restaurante Momo

*C/Augusto Figueroa 41 (91 532 71 62). Metro Chueca/bus
3, 40, 149.* **Lunch served** 1-4pm, **dinner served** 9pm-
midnight, daily. **Average** 2,500ptas. **Set lunch** 1,200ptas.
Set dinner 1,700ptas. **Credit** AmEx, DC, MC, V. **Map G5**
In the middle of the gay scene in Chueca, Momo attracts gays
and non-gays from around the district. It doesn't look cheap,
but its food – both simple fare and innovative culinary surprises – certainly is, especially if you stick to the set menus.
The place fills up at weekends, but if you haven't booked,
turn up, add your name to the waiting list, and go for a drink
in the square for half an hour. They won't forget about you.
Air-conditioning. Disabled: wheelchair access.

El Restaurante Vegetariano

*C/Marqués de Santa Ana 34 (91 532 09 27).
Metro Noviciado, Tribunal/bus 3, 40, 147, 149.* **Lunch
served** 1.30-4pm Tue-Sun. **Dinner served** 9-11.30pm
Tue-Sat. **Average** 2,000ptas. **Set menu** 1,000ptas.
Credit AmEx, MC, V. **Map E4**

The menu at the imaginatively named 'Vegetarian
Restaurant' – one of the most long-established vegetarians
in town – changes every three months, and features
interesting dishes such as roast Mediterranean vegetables
with houmous, and a good *sopa de pepinos* (cucumber soup).
The décor combines plain pine tables and hanging plants.
Air-conditioning. Booking advisable.

Ribeira Do Miño

*C/Santa Brígida 1 (91 521 98 54). Metro Tribunal/
bus 3, 40, 149.* **Lunch served** 1-4pm, **dinner served**
8pm-midnight, Tue-Sun. **Average** 3,500ptas.
No credit cards. Map E4
An extremely good-value, virtually undecorated Galician
marisquería, hung with nets, in a Chueca sidestreet. A
mariscada – shellfish platter – for two is 3,500ptas. There
are also a few cheap fishless dishes, and good Ribeiro house
wine. The restaurant has been liked and recommended by
several *Time Out* readers.
Air-conditioning. Booking advisable at weekends.

Salvador

*C/Barbieri 12 (91 521 45 24). Metro Chueca/
bus 3, 37, 40, 149.* **Lunch served** 1.30-4pm, **dinner
served** 9-11.30pm, Mon-Sat. Closed Aug. **Average**
4,000ptas. **Credit** AmEx, DC, MC, V. **Map F6**
In former times the artistic regulars of **Chicote** cocktail bar
(*see chapter* **Cafés & Bars**) often wandered over to eat at
this very traditional Castilian restaurant. The clientele is less
exotic these days, but the bullfight photos on the walls are
unchanged. The speciality is *rabo de toro* (bull's tail), but
other traditional dishes such as *gallina en pepitoria*, fried
merluza (hake) and *arroz con leche* are all excellent.
*Air-conditioning. Booking advisable. Disabled: wheelchair
access.*

Tienda de Vinos

*C/Augusto Figueroa 35 (91 521 70 12).
Metro Chueca/bus 3, 40, 149.* **Lunch served** 1-4.30pm
Mon-Sat. **Dinner served** 9.30-11.30pm daily. Closed
mid-Aug-mid-Sept. **Average** 1,500ptas.
No credit cards. Map H5
An eternally popular, regularly full budget bar-restaurant in
Chueca, still known to some as *El Comunista* because of its
role as a leftist meeting point years ago under Franco, serving traditional standards such as *estofado de ternera* (beef
stew) and grilled fish. Service is famously deadpan (don't
take it personally), and the food can be hit-and-miss, but the
great atmosphere, décor that's a real piece of old Madrid and
very friendly prices all make up for it.

Around the world

American

At the time of going to press a **Planet Hollywood**
was under construction in the former Galería del Prado
shopping mall, beneath the Hotel Palace on Paseo del
Prado (*see chapter* **Accommodation**). Already well in
place is the **Hard Rock Café** (*The Castellana, p113*);
several other US chains have outlets around the city.

Chinese

House of Ming *The Castellana, p114*; **Dinasty**
Salamanca & the Retiro, p123.
Indian Adrish *Conde Duque, p124.*
Italian Palacio de Anglona *Villa y Corte, p110.*

Japanese

Musashi; **Robata** *Both in Sol & Gran Vía, p115*;
Donzoko *Huertas & Santa Ana, p117.*

Latin American

For understandable reasons, Madrid has long hosted
many Latin American eating-places; less obviously
understandable is the fact that they tend to stay open
later than other places in town, and Argentinian
restaurants especially are handy for late-night eating
(*see also* **La Carreta**, *in chapter* **Nightlife**).
Taquería La Calaca *Villa y Corte, p110*;
La Doma *The Castellana, p113*; **La Pampa**;
El Viajero *Both in La Latina, Rastro, Lavapiés, p119*;
Zara *Malasaña & Chueca, p123*;
La Vaca Argentina *Keeping your cool, p121.*

Moroccan/North African

Al-Jaima *Malasaña & Chueca, p119*; **Al-Mounia**
Salamanca & the Retiro, p123.

No, I cannot be photographed enjoying cheap Cuban cocktails: **Zara**.

Zara

C/de las Infantas 5 (91 532 20 74).
Metro Gran Vía/bus all routes to Gran Vía.
Lunch served 1-5pm, **dinner served** 8-11.30pm, Mon-Fri. Closed Aug. **Average** 3,000ptas. **Set menu**
2,500ptas. **Credit** AmEx DC, MC, V. **Map F6**
Simple Cuban food and ace cocktails served beneath a pseudo-bamboo roof, for that touch of Caribbean colour. Forget the set menu and try the 'Typically Tropical' dishes such as *arroz a la cubana* (rice with tomato sauce and fried egg), banana omelette or *frijoles negros* (refried black beans). Very friendly service and amenable prices mean that queues are long, especially at night.
Air-conditioning.

Salamanca & the Retiro

Al-Mounia

C/Recoletos 5 (91 435 08 28).
Metro Banco de España/bus all routes to Plaza de Cibeles.
Lunch served 1.30-4pm, **dinner served** 9pm-midnight, Tue-Sat. Closed Aug. **Average** 6,000ptas.
Credit AmEx, DC, MC, V. **Map I5**
Ornate tiled décor, fine service and high culinary standards make this Moroccan restaurant a great place to eat. Meals run from the house aperitifs through salads, delicious *pastilla* (pigeon pie) and couscous, to a trolley of pastries and dried fruits. Note that it is on Calle Recoletos, a street running between the Paseo of the same name and Calle Serrano.
Air-conditioning. Booking advisable.

Casa Portal

C/Doctor Castelo 26 (91 574 20 26). Metro Ibiza/
bus 15, 26, 61, 63, C. **Lunch served** 1.30-5pm, **dinner**
served 8pm-midnight, Mon-Sat. Closed Aug. **Average**
4,000ptas. **Credit** MC, V. **Map K6**
This traditional Asturian restaurant, with fine cheeses piled in the window, has been serving *fabada* (including variants with partridge and clams), fish, shellfish, soups, tortillas and great cider for 50 years. Choose between the sawdust-strewn bar at the front or the more formal dining room behind it.
Air conditioning. Booking advisable.

Centro Riojano

C/Serrano 25, 1º (91 575 03 37). Metro Serrano/bus all
routes to Plaza de Colón. **Lunch served** 1.30-4pm,
dinner served 9-11.30pm, daily. **Average** 4,000ptas.
Set menu 2,500ptas. **Credit** MC, V. **Map I4**
Casual and unstuffy, this nineteenth-century dining room in the La Rioja regional club – which is in a first floor flat, and so easy to miss from the street – serves light, modern local cooking. The region's famed red peppers crop up in everything – roasted in a salad with anchovies and spring onions, or dried in *patatas a la riojana*, potatoes sautéed with peppers, onions, tomatoes and chorizo. The wine list, naturally, features many fine vintage Riojas.
Air-conditioning. Booking advisable.

Dinasty

C/O'Donnell 31 (91 431 08 47). Metro Goya/
bus 21, 29, 52, 53. **Lunch served** 1.30-4.30pm,
dinner served 8pm-midnight, daily. **Average**
4,000ptas. **Credit** AmEx, MC V. **Map K6**
One of a handful of decent Chinese eateries in Madrid. Very much a face of the new Chinese cuisine, Dinasty has opted for modern, minimalist décor, with a wide range of imaginative and well-presented dishes.
Air-conditioning. Booking advisable.

La Galette

C/Conde de Aranda 11 (91 576 06 41).
Metro Retiro/bus all routes to Puerta de Alcalá.
Lunch served 2-4pm, **dinner served** 9pm-midnight,
Mon-Sat. Closed Aug. **Average** 3,000ptas.
Credit AmEx, DC, JCB, MC, V. **Map I6**
The most plush of Madrid's vegetarian restaurants, with international dishes, some with oriental or Caribbean influences. There are meat and fish dishes for non-vegetarians.
Air-conditioning. Booking advisable.
Branch: C/Bárbara de Braganza 10 (91 319 31 48).

La Giralda

C/Claudio Coello 24 (91 576 40 69). Metro Serrano/bus
1, 9, 19, 51, 74. **Lunch served** 1-4pm daily. **Dinner**
served 9pm-midnight Mon-Sat. **Average** 5,000ptas.
Credit AmEx, DC, JCB, MC, V. **Map I5**

The quaint-ish décor of tiles and wine barrels of this Andaluz *taberna* is brand new and a bit brash, but the flavours of the bull's tail, fried fish and *salmorrejo* (thick gazpacho) are strong and good. It also has smaller branches, two next to each other in Chamberí, with great tapas. *Air-conditioning. Booking advisable.*
Branches: C/Maldonado 4 (91 577 77 62); C/Hartzenbush 12 & 15 (91 445 17 43).

El Rabo de Toro (Casa Díaz)

C/Ayala 81 (91 401 19 62). Metro Goya/bus 21, 26, 53, 61. **Lunch served** 1-4pm, **dinner served** 8.30pm-midnight, Mon-Sat. **Average** 2,500ptas. **Set lunch** 1,100ptas. **Credit** AmEx, DC, EC, JCB, MC, V. **Map L4**
Rough at the edges but honest, this family-owned Andalusian eating house buys bull's tail from around Spain to make its stew. This and fried fish are the specialities, but you'll find *jamón ibérico*, *merluza* (hake) and other choices on the menu, too. A good cheaper option in a pricey area. *Air-conditioning.*

La Trainera

C/Lagasca 60 (91 576 80 35). Metro Serrano/bus 1, 9, 19, 51, 74. **Lunch served** 1-4pm, **dinner served** 8pm-midnight, Mon-Sat. Closed Aug. **Average** 5,500ptas. **Credit** AmEx, DC, EC, MC, V. **Map J3**
Reportedly this seafood specialist was Francis Bacon's favourite restaurant on his trips to Madrid. It was set up by a wholesaler, and the fish and shellfish are selected with an expert eye. Prices are high, reflecting the Salamanca location, but, despite the upmarket clientele service, like the atmosphere, is surprisingly basic and brisk. *Air-conditioning. Booking advisable.*

Viridiana

C/Juan de Mena 14 (91 523 44 78). Metro Banco de España, Retiro/bus all routes to Puerta de Alcalá. **Lunch served** 1.30-4pm, **dinner served** 9pm-midnight, Mon-Sat. Closed Easter, Aug, Christmas. **Average** 7,000ptas. **Credit** AmEx, V. **Map H7**
A short walk from both the Prado and the Thyssen, hung with stills from Buñuel films, Viridiana offers excellent seasonal food (the menu changes weekly) backed up by a truly exceptional wine cellar, considered by some the best in Spain. Enjoy inventive combinations such as *cabracho con relleno de almejas* (scorpion fish stuffed with clams and dressed with olive oil) or *solomillo de buey con trufas negras* (steak with black truffles) at one of the few upper-range Madrid restaurants that genuinely doesn't care about dress. *Air-conditioning. Booking advisable. Disabled: wheelchair access.*

North & west
Conde Duque, Moncloa, Argüelles

Adrish

C/San Bernardino 1 (91 542 94 98). Metro Noviciado, Plaza de España/bus all routes to Plaza de España. **Lunch served** 1.30-4pm daily. **Dinner served** 8pm-midnight Mon-Thur, Sun; 8.30pm-1am Fri, Sat. **Average** 2,500ptas. **Set menu** 2,350-2,500ptas. **Credit** MC, V. **Map D4**
Not far from the Plaza de España, this Indian restaurant offers a menu that stretches beyond clichés. Chicken *chap* (a tandoori dish with almonds) and dried-fruit *kabli nan* are among the interesting dishes baked in the clay oven. *Air-conditioning.*

La Taberna de Abajo

C/Limón 16 (91 547 54 29). Metro Noviciado, Plaza de España/bus all routes to Plaza de España. **Lunch served** 1-5pm, **dinner served** 8.30pm-1.30am, daily. **Average** 2,500ptas. **No credit cards. Map D4**

Cheap eats

Eating cheaply and well in Madrid is never a problem, particularly at midday, when it's possible to get a *menú del día* for around 1,000ptas in many bar-restaurants. It is nearly always cheaper to sit down and eat, even à la carte, than to have tapas.

Budget restaurants
Bar Salamanca; Casa Marta
Both in Villa y Corte, see p109.
Belmar; Soldemersol
Both in La Latina, Rastro, Lavapiés, see p117.
La Granja; El Nueve; Pizzeria Mastropiero;
Tienda de Vinos
All in Malasaña & Chueca, see p119.

A very simple bar-restaurant near Centro Conde Duque, with a few tables, and shellfish stacked up behind glass at the bar. The speciality is *carabineiros*, red prawns – mainly boiled or *a la plancha* (grilled) – with bread and wine to go with them. *Air-conditioning.*

La Taberna de Liria

C/Duque de Liria 9 (91 541 45 19). Metro Ventura Rodriguez/bus 1, 2, 44, 133, C. **Lunch served** 1-3.30pm Mon-Fri. **Dinner served** 9.15-11.30pm Mon-Sat. Closed Aug. **Average** 5,000ptas. **Credit** AmEx, DC, JCB, MC, V. **Map D4**
Excellent, sophisticated cooking and a warm atmosphere are the twin attractions of this smart little restaurant off Calle Princesa. Young chef Michel López Castanier's menu reflects his Franco-Spanish origins, and might include beef in a rich basil sauce, fine pasta salads and Mediterranean-influenced fish dishes such as *dorada* (gilthead bream) in garlic and almonds; regulars on the dessert menu are his fabulously moreish sorbets. His wife Sonia is in charge front-of-house, and is very helpful in explaining anything that needs it. *Air-conditioning. Booking advisable. Disabled: wheelchair access.*

Chamberí
EcoCentro

C/Esquilache 4 (91 553 55 02). Metro Cuatro Caminos/bus all routes to Cuatro Caminos. **Meals served** 1am-midnight daily. **Average** 2,000ptas. **Set menu** 1,200ptas. **Credit** AmEx, DC, MC, V.
The enormous ground floor restaurant at this vegetarian centre offers a very wide choice of dishes. To drink there are organic wines, natural beers, and a selection of herb teas; the shop above has food, books, music and health and beauty products. *Air-conditioning.*

La Playa

C/Magellanes 24 (91 446 84 76). Metro Quevedo/bus 16, 37, 61, 149. **Lunch served** 1-4.30pm daily. **Dinner served** 8.30pm-midnight Mon-Sat. Closed Aug. **Average** 3,000ptas. **No credit cards. Map E2**
An old-fashioned family restaurant in Chamberí with very high-quality Castilian dishes, especially steaks, fast-cooked red-rare at your table. Ingredients are expertly selected, which means relatively high prices. The elderly white-jacketed waiters are from another age, but very charming. *Air-conditioning. Booking advisable.*

Tapas

Whether you're after a quick snack in a local bar or sophisticated delicacies, Madrid has tapas for all tastes and budgets.

Tapa is so broad a term as to make any precise definition almost impossible. According to the official Dictionary of the Spanish Royal Academy, a tapa is 'any portion of solid food that may accompany a beverage'. True, but since most of Madrid's 17,000 bars and cafés offer something to nibble on with a drink, then a tapa could be almost anything. A small plate of olives in the plainest of local bars is a tapa, as are the carefully built and usually pricey canapés offered in Salamanca. That's the point… tapas range from minimal snacks to expensive specialities, via many gastronomic styles.

The word tapa itself means a 'lid', and the custom comes from Andalusia, where traditionally a small dish was placed over a glass of wine to keep out the flies. Over time, small servings of food were placed on the lid to accompany the drink. It is thought tapas took root in Madrid after a royal decree ordered drinks always to be served with one as a way of reducing drunkenness in the city's taverns. Since then it has become a firm local habit and a culinary genre all of its own, with some bar-top cabinets resembling elaborate still-lifes.

Since Madrid's population includes so many non-natives, there are bars and tapas from every corner of Spain. Galician bars provide generous portions of octopus, prawns and seafood, traditionally with white Ribeiro wine served in little ceramic bowls. Asturian bars specialise in cider (*sidra*), theatrically poured from above the head to separate out sediment, accompanied by blood sausage, *morcilla*, or strong *cabrales* goat's cheese. Andaluz bars serve cold dry *fino* sherry with *mojama* (dry-cured tuna) or sardines. Madrid has its own specialities: *patatas bravas*, offal, such as pig's ears (*orejas*), tripe (*callos*) or sweetbreads (*mollejas*), plus snails in a hot sauce. Beer or vermouth on tap are alternatives to wine.

Eating tapas is a ritual with its own rules. It has its own verb, *tapear*. Opinions vary as to what a real tapas tour involves: according to legend, you have to visit as many bars as there are stations of the cross in a church (14, for those without the benefit of a Catholic education). This may seem a little excessive, but there *are* certain customs you might want to take into account. For example, if there's a group of you (from three to six is a good number), rounds should be paid for in strict rotation.

*Regulars know that the **La Casa de las Torrijas** has changed only in name. See page 126.*

As with most of life's essentials in Spain, there should be no hurrying involved. And be ready to do as locals do: many tapas come with throwaway material – olive stones, prawn husks: all involve plenty of contact with the fingers, and all can be dropped on the floor (except in upmarket places: check what other people are doing).

Tapas are a great way of trying new flavours, but these days the old custom of providing one free with each drink is far less common, and once you start sampling the cost soon mounts up. For other bars more suited to having coffee, drinking or a night out – but which also often serve tapas, since these divisions are never precise – *see chapters* **Cafés & Bars** *and* **Nightlife**. Few bars, except for one or two upscale places, accept credit cards.

Villa y Corte

Originally the classic district for a tapas tour, but now quite tourist-oriented. It still contains a few gems, if not many bargains. For seafood, try **Casa Gallega** (*see chapter* **Restaurants**).

El Almendro 13

C/Almendro 13 (91 365 42 54). Metro La Latina/ bus 17, 18, 23, 31, 35. **Open** 7pm-midnight Tue; 1-4pm, 7pm-midnight, Wed-Sun. **Map D8**

A neat bar that represents a touch of gentrification in the old Latina district. It has been skillfully restored and maintains an old Madrid feel, but with a newer, younger clientele. White wines, sherries and beer are the only drinks to go for, and the tapa you have to try is *pisto manchego* with fried eggs and bacon.

Casa Paco

Plaza de Puerta Cerrada 11 (91 366 31 66). Metro La Latina/bus 17, 18, 23, 31, 35. **Open** 1.30-4pm, 8.30pm-midnight, Mon-Sat. Closed Aug. **Map D8**

A classic old-town tavern with top-quality (if expensive) *Manchego* cheese and *jamón serrano*.

La Casa de las Torrijas, As de los Vinos

C/de la Paz 4 (91 532 14 73). Metro Sol/bus all routes to Puerta del Sol. **Open** 9.30am-4pm, 5-11.30pm, Mon-Thur; 9.30am-4pm, 6pm-midnight, Fri, Sat. Closed Aug. **Map E8**

A change that's maybe not a change. Since who-knows-when this historic old *taberna* near the Puerta del Sol had been *El Anciano Rey de los Vinos*, the 'Old Man King of Wines'. It was famed for its wines, and an unusual speciality – *torrijas* – bread soaked in wine and spices, coated in sugar and deep fried. Then, in 1998 it changed its name (*As de los Vinos* – 'Ace of Wines' – might be overdoing it slightly), and regulars held their breath: but not to worry, for everything else stayed the same. Plenty of alternatives to *torrijas* for those with less of a sweet tooth to stem the effects of the wine, such as fried *bacalao*, tripe and *albóndigas*, all at around 600ptas.

El Pulpito

Plaza Mayor 10 (91 366 21 88). Metro Sol/bus all routes to Puerta del Sol. **Open** 9.30am-1am daily. **Map D8**

A pleasant bar that's one of the least touristy on Plaza Mayor.

Tapas with ambitions

Since the mid-'90s, a new, more polished style of *tapeo* – tapa-sampling – has emerged in Madrid, with the opening of a whole series of bars, above all in the heart of the old city, that offer a similar combination of tradition and modernity. Generally calling themselves *tabernas*, they are rather like specialist wine bars, serving food but without reaching the status of restaurant.

Much care is taken to create a contemporary look that yet fits in with their historic surroundings: walls tend to be rag-rolled or sponged in pastel tones, or stripped down to plain bare brick, and lighting is intimate. Their food goes beyond the confines of more traditional tapas, attractively presented, at times quite original, and with a much greater care for fine ingredients. Most common item on the menu is the ubiquitous canapé, with a bewildering choice of toppings; wine lists are extensive, with, again, an emphasis on quality not seen in your neighbourhood bar, and this is where you can sample the best of recent Spanish wines. A drawback, of course, is the price: canapés start at 300ptas each and can easily cost double that, and wines are commonly upwards of 200ptas a glass (better to share a bottle).

Aloque

C/Torrecilla del Leal 20 (91 528 36 62). Metro Antón Martín/bus 6, 26, 32, 57. **Open** 7.30pm-1am Mon-Thur, Sun; 7.30pm-2am Fri, Sat. Closed Aug. **Map F9**

One new-style *taberna* that isn't in the La Latina bar zone. When this little bar opened up several years ago it was a pioneer in selling quality wines with home-cooked snacks, in a neighbourhood that's otherwise full of plain, humble bars, Lavapiés. A blackboard shows the wines of the day, from a huge potential range (over 200), that includes French as well as Spanish labels. The food on offer changes with the seasons to ensure freshness, but all year round there are excellent canapés such as *solomillo* (sirloin steak) with pepper sauce, or marinated salt cod. Also very good are the cheese pies.

La Corolla

C/del Almendro 10 (no phone). Metro La Latina/bus 17, 18, 23, 31, 35. **Open** midday-4pm, 8pm-midnight, Mon-Sat. **Map D8**

Friendly, lively and invariably crowded, this *taberna* is one of the latest to arrive on the scene and has a full range of Spanish wines ranging from a cheap but very drinkable Valdepeñas up to the most expensive Riojas and Riberas. Loads of canapés to choose from, with various combinations of cheese, anchovies, salmon and avocado.

Matritum

C/Cava Alta 17 (91 365 82 37). Metro La Latina/bus 17, 18, 23, 31, 35. **Open** 1-5pm, 8.30pm-midnight, Tue-Sun. No credit cards. **Map D8**

Despite the name ('The Little Octopus'), *pulpo* isn't always the best thing to have: try the *albóndigas* or *callos*. *Tables outdoors Mar-Nov.*

La Taberna de Cien Vinos
C/del Nuncio 16 (365 47 07). Metro La Latina, Tirso de Molina/bus 17, 18, 23, 31, 35, 50, 65. **Open** 1-3.45pm, 8-11.45pm, Tue-Sun. **Map D8**
The name ('100 wines') may be a bit of an exaggeration, but this lovely, plain stone *taberna* has a range that can't be far off, plus a good choice of *pinchos* and larger dishes.

La Torre del Oro
Plaza Mayor 26 (91 366 50 16). Metro Sol/bus all routes to Puerta del Sol. **Open** 11am-2am daily. **Map D8**
A little piece of Seville on the Plaza Mayor, just a bit touristy, with Sevillano tiles, bullfighting accoutrements on the walls and genuine Andaluz waiters who yell at each other and the punters with unflinching and manic glee, whether or not you understand a word. There's excellent *fino* sherry, and great prawns and *pescaditos* (whitebait) for around 1,000ptas. *Tables outdoors Feb-Nov.*

<h1>Sol & Gran Vía</h1>

Casa Labra
C/Tetuán 12 (91 531 00 81). Metro Sol/ bus all routes to Puerta del Sol. **Open** *bar* 9.30am-3.30pm, 6-11pm, Mon-Sat; 1-4pm, 8-11pm, Sun; *restaurant* 1.15-4pm, 8-11pm, Mon-Sat. **Map E7**
Founded in 1860, this *taberna*-restaurant was in 1879 the birthplace of the Spanish Socialist Party. It is also known for its *soldaditos de pavia* and great *croquetas*, and, as it's so busy at

lunchtimes, this is one of few bars where you pay as you order. The restaurant (not the bar) is shut on Sundays and holidays.

<h1>Huertas & Santa Ana</h1>

The best-known and most fashionable place for Madrileños to *tapear*, perhaps because it has the biggest range, from elegant to tatty.

Bar Viña P
Plaza de Santa Ana 3 (91 531 81 11).
Metro Sol/bus all routes to Puerta del Sol. **Open** 1-4.30pm, 8pm-12.30am, daily. **Map E/F8**
The place for *montados, gambas al ajillo*, asparagus, stuffed mussels, *almejas* and other *tapas* for about 1,000ptas a *ración*.

Las Bravas
Pasaje Matheu 5 (91 521 51 41).
Metro Sol/bus all routes to Puerta del Sol. **Open** 12.30-4pm, 7.30pm-midnight, daily. **Map E7**
If you only eat one tapa in Madrid, it has to be these *patatas bravas*. They claim to have invented them here, and as well as good they're also very cheap. Also fine *pulpo* and *orejas*. *Tables outdoors May-Sept.*
Branches: C/Espoz y Mina 13; C/Alvarez Gato 3.

Casa Alberto
C/Huertas 18 (91 429 93 56). Metro Antón Martín/bus 6, 26, 32. **Open** *bar* Sept-June 11.30am-12.30pm Tue-Sat; 11.30am-4pm Sun; *July & mid-Aug* noon-5pm, 8pm-12.30am, Tue-Sat. Closed two weeks Aug. *Restaurant* 1.30-4pm, 9pm-midnight, Tue-Sat. **Map F8**

A pleasant, warmly decorated *taberna*, Matritum (the Latin for Madrid) serves a selection of choice wines from Ribera del Duero, La Rioja, Penedès and Priorat, among others, and has excellent *raciones* as well as a range of canapés. The *croquetas*, with ham, prawns or Roquefort, are superb, as is the potato gratin with five cheeses and chickpeas with spinach.

Taberna Bilbao
Costanilla de San Andrés 8 (91 365 6125).
Metro La Latina/bus 17, 18, 23, 31, 35. **Open** 1-4pm, 8pm-midnight, daily (from 8.30pm, July-Aug). **Map C8**
Not exactly the cheapest but high on quality, Taberna Bilbao offers tasty Basque *tapas* and a huge range of wines. For a real taste of Euskadi, ask for a glass of *txacoli* (from the *taberna's* own vineyards) and a *ración* of *delicias de idiazábal* (smoked *idiazábal* cheese deep fried in a light batter). Other stars on the menu are *bacalao* (salt cod) in various ways, *cecina* and *zancarrones* – fillets of *morcillo* (stewing beef, not to be confused with *morcilla*) in a tomato and pepper sauce.

Taberna la Salamandra
C/Alfonso VI (91 366 05 15). Metro La Latina/bus 17, 18, 23, 31, 35. **Open** 1.30-4.30pm, 8.30pm-1am, daily. Closed last two weeks Aug. **Map C8**
An extremely pleasant *taberna*, La Salamandra takes its name both from the little lizard, iron reproductions of which lurk on the walls, and from the machine used to gratinée food, popularly know as a *salamandra*. Arguably the best canapé of the many on offer is the *solomillo con*

queso fundido, a mini sirloin steak with melted cheese served on lightly toasted garlic bread; the same cut of meat also comes with raspberry sauce, for something different, and warm salads are also excellent. Definitely a place for wine buffs, too.

La Taberna del Nuncio
Plaza de la Puerta Cerrada 7 (91 364 56 29).
Metro La Latina/bus 17, 18, 23, 31, 35.
Open noon-4pm, 7.30-12.30am, Mon-Thur, Sun; noon-4pm, 7.30-1.30am, Fri, Sat. **Map D8**
A new *taberna* that is a further annexe to the Café del Nuncio, itself divided into two parts (*see chapter* **Cafés & Bars**), thus completing the colonisation of the block. It offers a choice of hot canapés with toppings such as *morcilla*, or cold ones with tuna, crab, salmon, brie or anchovies. The choice of wines might seem a tad limited, but to compensate the house white is an excellent Rueda, and reds are reliable Riojas.
Tables outdoors Apr-Oct.

El Tempranillo
C/Cava Baja 38 (91 364 15 32). Metro La Latina/bus 17, 18, 23, 31, 35. **Open** noon-4pm, 8pm-1am, daily. Closed mid-end Aug. **Map D8**
In bullring ochre and bare brick, with photos of bulls on the wall and flamenco guitar on the sound system, El Tempranillo offers an impressive range of wines from nearly every Spanish region. The tapas and *raciones* are wicked too: try the *Boletus Edulis* of wild mushrooms in scrambled egg, the cheese and salmon salad or any of the cured meats.

Punto y Coma *may have gone posh, but its prices are still reassuringly low.*

Founded in 1827, Alberto's still retains its red-painted tavern façade from the nineteenth century, behind which you can choose from a fine range of freshly made tapas – *caracoles, calamares,* prawns – and some larger dishes.

Casa de Pontevedra

C/Victoria 2 (91 523 08 01). Metro Sol/bus all routes to Puerta del Sol. **Open** *restaurant* 10.30am-4.30pm, 8pm-midnight, daily. **Map E7**
A bar offering mainly Galician specialities, with great *pulpo a feira, empanadas, pimientos rellenos* (stuffed peppers) and Ribeiro and Albariño white wines.

Cervecería La Moderna

Plaza de Santa Ana 12 (91 420 15 82). Metro Sevilla, Sol/bus 6, 26, 32, 50. **Open** noon-12.30am Mon-Thur, Sun; noon-1.30am Fri, Sat. **Map E/F7**
A change from other bars on this square, La Moderna, as its name suggests, has no pretensions to antiquity. The décor is contemporary, and the tapas are great: there aren't many places in Huertas where they come topped with cumin, or offer such a wide choice of farmhouse cheeses (*quesos artesanales*). House wines are also a cut above those of most bars. The only hitch is that above-average quality means higher prices. *Tables outdoors May-Sept.*

La Fábrica

C/Jesús 2 (91 369 06 71). Metro Antón Martín/ bus 9, 10, 14, 27, 34, 37, 45. **Open** 11am-1am Mon-Thur, Sun; 11am-2am Fri, Sat. **Map G8**
This pleasant, roomy *taberna* at the bottom end of Huertas specialises in canapés, many topped with smoked fish or top-notch charcuterie. All can be ordered as straight tapas or as *raciones.* Wines hail from Rioja, Ribera del Duero and Penedès.

El Garabatu

C/Echegaray 5 (91 429 63 90). Metro Sevilla/bus all routes to Puerta del Sol. **Open** 8.30am-11.30pm Mon-Wed, Fri-Sun.
An Asturian bar-restaurant with great earthy tapas such as *chorizo a la sidra* (in cider), *fabada* and nose-bending *cabrales* cheese, and to go with it the necessary coarse Asturian cider.

El Lacón

C/Manuel Fernández y González 8 (91 429 36 98). Metro Sevilla, Sol/bus all routes to Puerta del Sol. **Open** noon-4pm, 8pm-midnight, Mon-Thur; noon-4pm, 8pm-1.30am, Fri-Sun. Closed Aug. **Map F8**

Down-to-earth Galician bar with excellent *pulpo, caldo gallego* (a meat and vegetable broth), mussels *a la marinera* and *empanadas.* It sometimes closes on Mondays.

Lerranz

C/Echegaray 26 (91 249 12 06). Metro Sevilla, Sol/bus all routes to Puerta del Sol. **Open** 1.30-4pm, 8.30pm-1am, daily. **Map F8**
A smartish tapas bar, with sometimes-snooty service, but which offers a very wide range from traditional country bread with various toppings to *pulpo con papas y ali-oli* and *ensalada mora,* and a set lunch menu for about 1,000ptas.

Lhardy

Carrera de San Jerónimo 8 (91 522 22 07). Metro Sol/bus all routes to Puerta del Sol. **Open** *bar* 9.30am-3pm, 5-9.30pm, Mon-Sat; 9.30am-3pm Sun; *restaurant* 1-3.30pm, 8.30-11pm, Mon-Sat. Closed Aug. **Map E7**
Madrid's most historic restaurant is also the aristocrat of tapas bars. Serve yourself consommé from the silver samovar, try the knock-out croquettes, or order *finos* and a hot pastryboat with kidneys (*barquitos de riñones*). Taking tapas at Lhardy's is a cheaper way of getting a look at this institution than eating in the restaurant. *See also chapter* **Restaurants**.

La Platería

C/Moratín 49 (91 429 17 22). Metro Antón Martín, Atocha/bus 9, 10, 14, 27, 34, 37, 45. **Open** 7.30am-1am Mon-Fri; 9.30am-1am Sat, Sun. **Map G8**
As well as serving quality tapas such as *jamón ibérico,* tuna steaks on toasted bread, charcuterie products and *pulguitas* (rolls), La Platería also offers breakfasts and *napolitanas.* The wine list is extensive: house wine is a young Ribera, but it also has *crianza* Riojas, Priorat, Penedès and cava.

Punto y Coma

C/del Príncipe 27 (91 420 14 49). Metro Sevilla, Sol/bus 6, 26, 32, 50. **Open** 10am-midnight daily. **Map F7**
On Plaza Santa Ana (despite the address), this big bar is one of the district's great standbys. The 'Semi-colon' was formerly a very straightforward tapas bar, but has recently joined the band of the slightly smartened-up. Nowadays, if you order red wine you'll be asked if you want Rioja or Valdepeñas, and the tapas are also more refined: stuffed peppers, curried quails, above-average *empanadas* and so on. It's still one of the best-value bars on the plaza, with all the bustling, friendly atmosphere a city tapas bar should have. *Tables outdoors May-Sept.*

Tapas technicalities

There are three basic sizes of tapas portion: a *pincho* (more or less a mouthful), a *tapa* (a saucerful or so) and a *ración* (a small plateful big enough to share). Some establishments also sell *medio raciones*. If there's a house speciality it's usually a good bet, but if there's something else you like the look of that isn't identifiable on the menu or the list behind the bar, just point to it. Bread – *pan* – normally comes automatically, but if not, you can always ask for it. In most places, as with other bar bills, you let a tapas bill mount up and pay it all together when you've finished, rather than when you order. It will usually be around 25 per cent more expensive if you sit at a table rather than eat at the bar.

For many other dishes more normally eaten as part of a full meal – but which may also appear as tapas – *see chapter* **Restaurants**.

Basics

Bocadillo sandwich in a roll or part of a French loaf; **Cazuelita** small hot casserole; **Montados** canapé-style mixed *tapas*, often a slice of bread with a topping; **Pincho/pinchito** small titbit on a toothpick, or mouthful-sized tapa; **Ración** a portion (small plateful), which you can sometimes order in halves; **Pulga** small filled roll; **Tabla** platter (of cheeses, cold meats); **Tosta** slice of toast with topping; **Una de gambas, chorizo, etc** one portion of prawns, chorizo, etc; **Por unidad** per item.

Carne, Aves y Embutidos (Meat, poultry & charcuterie)

Albóndigas meat balls; **Alitas de pollo** chicken wings; **Callos** tripe; **Cecina** dry-cured beef; **Chistorra** Navarrese sausage with paprika; **Chorizo** spicy sausage, eaten cooked or cold; **Criadillas** bulls' testicles; **Flamenquines** ham and pork rolls in breadcrumbs; **Oreja (de cerdo)** pig's ear; **Longaniza, fuet** mild but chewy, often herby salami-type sausages; **Mollejas** sweetbreads; **Morcilla** a black, blood sausage; **Pincho moruno** grilled meat brochette; **Riñones al Jerez** kidneys cooked in sherry; **Salchichón** large, fatty, soft salami-type sausage; **San Jacobo** fried ham and cheese escalope; **Sobrasada** soft Mallorcan paprika sausage;

Torrezno grilled pork crackling; **Zarajo** grilled sheep's intestine on a stick.

Pescado y Mariscos (Fish & shellfish)

Ahumados smoked fish; **Anchoas** salted conserved anchovies; **Anguilas** eels; **Angulas** elvers; **Berberechos** cockles; **Bienmesabe** marinated fried fish; **Boquerones en vinagre/fritos** pickled fresh anchovies; **Calamares a la romana** squid rings fried in batter; **Calamares en su tinta** squid cooked in their ink; **Carabineiros** large red ocean prawns; **Centollo** spider crab; **Chanquete** tiny Mediterranean fish, served deep fried; **Cigalas** crayfish; **Chipirones en su tinta** small Atlantic squid in their ink; **Chopito** small cuttlefish; **Croqueta de bacalao** salt cod croquette; **Fritura de pescado** flash-fried fish; **Gambas al ajillo** prawns fried with garlic; **Gambas en gabardina** prawns deep-fried in batter; **Huevas** fish roe; **Mojama** dried and salted tuna fish; **Navajas** razorshell; **Nécora** swimming crab; **Percebe** goose-neck barnacle; **Pulpo a feira/a la gallega** octopus with paprika and olive oil; **Quisquilla** shrimp; **Salpicón** cold chopped salad, often with shellfish; **Soldaditos de Pavía** strips of salt cod fried in batter; **Tigres** mussels filled with spicy tomato sauce and béchamel; **Zamburiñas** small scallops.

Vegetales (Vegetable tapas)

Aceitunas, olivas (adobados, rellenos) olives (pickled, stuffed); **Almendras saladas** salted almonds; **Pan con tomate** bread rubbed with fresh tomato and olive oil; **Patatas bravas** or **a la brava** deep-fried potatoes with hot pepper sauce; **Perdiz de huerta** lettuce hearts; **Pimientos de Padrón** fried, hot small green peppers; **Queso en aceite** cheese marinated in olive oil; **Setas** forest mushrooms.

Other tapas

Caracoles snails; **Croquetas** potato croquettes (may be with chicken, ham, tuna, and so on); **Empanada** flat pies, usually with a tuna filling; **Empanadilla** small fried pasties, usually with a tomato and tuna filling; **Ensaladilla rusa** salad of potatoes, onions, red peppers, usually tuna and maybe other ingedients in mayonnaise, now completely Spanish but still called a Russian salad; **Huevos rellenos** stuffed cold hard-boiled eggs; **Migas (con huevo frito)** fried breadcrumbs (with fried egg); **Pisto manchego** stir-fried vegetables mixed with meat, usually ham, and egg.

La Toscana

C/Ventura de la Vega 22 (91 429 60 31). Metro Sevilla/bus all routes to Puerta del Sol. **Open** 1-4pm, 8pm-midnight, Tue-Sat. Closed Aug. **Map F8**
Morcilla (black sausage) is a speciality at this typical Castilian bar, which has plenty of table space and *raciones* for around 1,000ptas. There are also good egg *revueltos*, and decent salads.

La Trucha

C/Manuel Fernández y González 3 (91 429 58 33). Metro Sevilla, Sol/bus all routes to Puerta del Sol. **Open** 12.30-4pm, 7.30pm-midnight, Mon-Sat. **Map F8**
A bar-restaurant with a wide range of tasty tapas and *raciones*, 'The Trout' is invariably packed at peak times. Most

dishes will set you back around 950ptas (for a *ración*), and there's also a *menú del dia*. A very enjoyable introduction to Madrid for new arrivals.
Tables outdoors July, Aug.

La Latina, Rastro, Lavapiés

One of the best areas for traditional, gutsy Madrileño tapas. The Rastro, another area full of bars, is most atmospheric (and busiest) on a Sunday morning: wandering around you'll find plenty of other good places as well as those listed here. Also worth trying is **Belmar** (*see chapter* **Restaurants**).

Bar Castilla

C/Mesón de Paredes 24 (91 467 54 56).
Metro Tirso de Molina/bus 6, 26, 32, 65. **Open** 9am–
midnight Mon-Fri, Sun. **Map E9**
One for *croqueta* fans: on a Sunday morning there's a choice
of over 100 kinds (nine for 450ptas) in this little bar, with
just six tables. Also a good place to try *chipirones en su tinta.*

El Brillante

Glorieta del Emperador Carlos V 8 (91 528 69 66).
Metro Atocha/bus all routes to Atocha.
Open 6am-1am daily. **Map H9**
On the edge of Lavapiés facing the busy Atocha roundabout,
this is one of a no-nonsense chain of big café-bars with quality food at swallowable prices. There's a huge variety of fresh
bread *bocadillos*, plus tapas and hot meals. An ideal daytime
call-in or starting point for a night's carousing, it's always
busy, especially in the early morning when it fills up with
recent arrivals from Atocha station and revellers ending the
night with hot chocolate and *churros.* It also has takeaway
snacks for train travellers. There are more branches around
the city; for addresses, check the phone book.
Tables outdoors Mar-Nov.

Café Melo's

C/Ave María 44 (91 527 50 54). Metro Lavapiés/bus 2,
26, 27, 32. **Open** 9am-2am Tue-Sat. Closed Aug. **Map E9**
An attractive little Lavapiés bar known for its delicious fresh
croquetas, zapatillas (sandwiches of Galician country bread,
cheese and ham) and *empanadas* with rich fillings.

Los Caracoles

Plaza de Cascorro 18 (91 365 94 39). Metro La Latina/
bus 17, 18, 23, 35, 60. **Open** 10am-4pm, 7-11.30pm,
daily. **Map D9**
Genial host Don Amadeo welcomes everyone to his bar at
the top of the Rastro, hugely busy on Sunday lunchtimes
and famous for its house speciality – snails, cooked traditional Madrileño-style in a rich broth with *chorizo* and paprika, a fast-disappearing local delicacy. If that doesn't appeal,
there are plenty of other tapas to choose from, and delicious
ice-cold beer or cheerfully cheap red wine to go with them.

Cayetano

C/Encomienda 23 (91 527 77 07). Metro La Latina,
Tirso de Molina/bus 17, 23, 26, 35. **Open** 9am-3.30pm,
7pm-midnight, Mon, Wed-Sun. **Map D9**
Another good Rastro stop off, this time for shellfish and
wine. Prawns in their shells will cost you about 1,300ptas.

La Freiduría de Gallinejas

C/Embajadores 84 (91 517 59 33).
Metro Embajadores/bus all routes to Embajadores.
Open 11am-11pm Mon-Sat. Closed Aug.
A haven for lovers of one of the fundamentals of Madrid's
traditional cuisine – offal. The city used to have many such
bustling, tiled fried-offal cafés, the local answer to the fish and
chip shop, but today they're hard to find. There's no better
place to sample the delights of deep-fried *mollejas* (sweetbreads), *entresijos* (stomach), *gallinejas* (lamb's chitterlings),
criadillas (bulls' testicles) and other delicacies. For dessert, try
the excellent freshly baked apples. The shop is on the southern stretch of Calle Embajadores, just outside the old centre.

Los Hermanos

C/Rodas 28 (91 468 3313). Metro La Latina, Puerta de
Toledo/bus 17, 18, 23, 35, 60. **Open** 7am-11pm Mon-Fri;
7am-5pm Sun. Closed Aug. **Map D10**
Right next to the Rastro, a bar with a strong neighbourhood
feel, generous complementary tapas and a huge range of
larger *raciones* such as *jamón de jabugo*, and Madrileño offal
dishes like *criadillas* and *callos*. On weekdays there is a *menú
del día* for 900ptas, and on Sundays one for 1,200ptas, but
expect to be packed with post-Rastro crowds.

La Mancha en Madrid

Miguel Servet 13 (no phone).
Metro Embajadores/bus 6, 27, 32, 57, 27.
Open 1-4.30pm, 8.30pm-1am, daily. **Map E10**
Popular with the *guiris* of Lavapiés, but also a meeting point
for that disappearing species the *progre*, the unique Spanish
mixture of hippie and lefty that grew out of the last years
of Franco. Great atmosphere, very well-served beer, reasonable wines, imaginative tapas – farmhouse cheeses, quality
ham and cold meats, and fish in *escabeche* – and walls fes-
tooned with posters and information about walks in the hills,
concerts, demonstrations and other activities.

La Taberna de Antonio Sánchez

C/Mesón de Paredes 13 (91 539 78 26). Metro Tirso de
Molina/bus 6, 26, 32, 65. **Open** noon-4pm, 8pm-
midnight, Mon-Sat; noon-4pm Sun. **Map E9**
Madrid's most historic and best-preserved *taberna*, founded
by a bullfighter in the heart of Lavapiés in 1830 and more or
less unchanged, from its classic zinc bar to the accoutrements
around the walls. Its owners have all been involved in the bullfighting world, and it still holds informal discussions between
critics, *toreros* and aficionados. It has also been patronised
by writers and artists, among them the painter Ignacio
Zuloaga, who left a fine portrait of the first Antonio Sánchez.
For all its fame, though, this is still very much a local place,
and the friendly owners are happy to chat about its history.
The superior tapas vary from *callos* to *morcilla* and smoked
fish *montados*, and full meals are also available.

La Taberna del Avapiés

C/Lavapiés 5 (no phone). Metro Tirso de Molina/
bus 6, 26, 32, 65. **Open** 12.30-3.30pm, 7pm-1am,
Mon-Thur; 12.30-3.30pm, 7pm-2am, Fri, Sat; 12.30-5pm
Sun. **Map E9**
Formerly a cocktail bar, but now offering a good selection of
charcuterie and imaginative tapas. Table service is attentive,
and the atmosphere is youthful and relaxed.

El Tío Vinagre

C/San Carlos 6 (91 527 45 93). Metro Lavapiés/bus 6,
26, 32, 50, 65. **Open** 8pm-1am Mon-Fri; 12.30-4pm, 8pm-
1am, Sat; 12.30-5pm Sun. Closed Aug. **Map E9**
Lavapiés' *castizo* charm has drawn in younger bar owners
in the last few years, and a trendier crowd than the old *barrio* norm. Run by a group of women, El Tío Vinagre is
notably female-friendly, and has good wines and unusual
tapas such as cod in olive oil, *cecina*, and chorizo and *cecina*
of venison (850ptas, 1,300ptas per *ración*).

Malasaña & Chueca

Malasaña and the streets that run across towards
Conde Duque (*see below*) make up one of the best
areas for good food and reasonable prices. Chueca,
now more a crazy night-dive centre, still has old-
fashioned restaurants, *tabernas* and tapas bars.

Batela

C/Silva 27 (91 522 14 42).
Metro Callao/bus all routes to Callao. **Open** 9am-2am
daily. Closed two weeks Aug. **Map D6**
Batela, just off Gran Vía, has nautical décor and a wide range
of good-value tapas. Oyster mushrooms and *bacalao al pil-
pil* (salt cod fried very hot in garlic and chilli) will both set you
back about 800ptas. To wash it all down there's excellent
Basque txacolin wine.

El Bocaíto

C/Libertad 6 (91 532 12 19). Metro Chueca/bus 3, 37,
40, 149. **Open** 1-4pm, 8-30pm-midnight, Mon-Fri;
8.30pm-midnight Sat. Closed Aug. **Map G5**

Madrileños rate this pricey tapas bar highly. Energetic, jokey waiters dish up *huevas* (fish roes), a variety of *revueltos*, pâtés, salads, pastries, mushroom kebabs and other unusual tapas. No seating, so it's not a place for leisurely eating.

Casa do Campañeiro
C/San Vicente Ferrer 44 (91 521 57 02). Metro Noviciado, Tribunal/bus 3, 40, 147, 149. **Open** 1.30pm-2am daily. **Map E4**
A Galician bar with wonderful tiles, traditional tapas – *pimientos de Padrón*, shellfish – and fine-quality wines.

Santander
C/Augusto Figueroa 25 (91 522 49 10). Metro Chueca/bus 3, 40, 149. **Open** 10.45am-4pm, 7-11pm, Mon-Sat. Closed Aug. **Map G5**
One of the largest assortments of tapas in Madrid, with around 100 to choose from, including *brandada* (salt cod and potato purée), stuffed mussels and a huge range of *montados* (canapés). Also well priced, from about 75ptas upwards.

El Timón
C/General Castaños 13 (91 308 01 22). Metro Colón/bus 21, 37. **Open** 10am-1am daily. **Map H4**
Lawyers from the Palacio de Justicia across the street flock to this smart nautical-style bar with a great range of tapas, all of them excellent – from shellfish to a salad of *pimientos*. The average price is 900ptas, and *fino* is 200ptas.

Salamanca & the Retiro

Upmarket – and prices reflect it – but there are some great, long-established bars, and the local clientele demand high standards. Tapas here are often more sophisticated than the earthy varieties common in the city centre.

Alkalde
C/Jorge Juan 10 (91 576 33 59). Metro Serrano/bus 1, 9, 19, 51, 89. **Open** 1-4.30pm, 8pm-midnight, daily. Closed Sat & Sun during July, Aug. **Map J5**
An old-fashioned Basque bar that's quite expensive, but has very good *chistorra*, *tortilla* with red peppers, *morcilla*, *jamón*, *empanadillas* and *chipirones en su tinta*.

Hevia
C/Serrano 118 (91 562 30 75). Metro Gregorio Marañón/bus 9, 16, 19, 51. **Open** 9.30am-1am Mon-Sat. Closed Aug. **Map J1**
A very upmarket but buzzy tapas bar near the Museo Lázaro Galdiano that uses excellent ingredients, which they'll put together in pretty much whichever canapé-combination you wish. Tapas are not cheap, but service by the white-jacketed waiters is great. The clientele are as plush as the locale. *Tables outdoors May-July, Sept.*

José Luis
C/Serrano 89-91 (91 563 09 58). Metro Núñez de Balboa/bus 9, 19, 51, 89. **Open** 9am-1am Mon-Sat; noon-1am Sun, public holidays. **Map J2**
A classic Salamanca bar with cocktail-type tapas from a menu largely unchanged since the '50s (smoked salmon tartare, melted Brie and pâté, small steak canapés and many mixed *montados*), delicious cakes and a yuppyish crowd. *Tables outdoors May-Sept.*
Branches: C/Rafael Salgado 11 (91 458 01 83); C/San Francisco de Sales 14-16 (91 441 20 43); Paseo de la Habana 4-6 (91 562 31 18).

Peláez
C/Lagasca 61 (91 575 87 24). Metro Serrano/bus 1, 74, 89. **Open** 10am-midnight Mon-Sat. Closed Aug. **Map J3**

An old bar in the middle of Salamanca where Luis Peláez has been turning out creative tapas – *huevas*, *montados*, *mojama*, smoked fish *tortillas* – for over 40 years. It's often packed with very noisy regulars, so be ready to fight your way to the bar.

North & west
Conde Duque, Moncloa, Argüelles

La Bilbaina
C/Marqués de Urquijo 27 (91 541 86 98). Metro Argüelles/bus 1, 21, 44, 133, C. **Open** 1-4pm, 7pm-midnight, Tue-Sun. Closed Aug. **Map B3**
Though its speciality is shellfish, this bar also has a great choice of other delights, ranging from *chistorra* to *lomo* marinated in olive oil.

La Fortuna
Plaza de los Mostenses 3 (91 547 30 98). Metro Plaza de España/bus all routes to Plaza de España. **Open** noon-midnight daily. **Map D5**
Visit this old-fashioned bar near the Plaza de España to sample bargain fine wines by the jug, fried *boquerones*, roast *chorizo* and bountiful supplies of meaty tapas.

Mesón Los Toledanos
Travesia de Conde Duque 6 (91 541 11 55). Metro Ventura Rodriguez, Noviciado/bus 1, 2, 44, 133, C. **Open** 7am-midnight Mon-Fri, Sun. Closed Aug. **Map D4**
A down-to-earth tapas bar near Cuartel Conde Duque with a great spread of *chipirones*, *caracoles*, very hot *chorizo*, marinated trout (*trucha en escabeche*) and other earthy dishes.

Chamberí

Another area with a tapas-round of its own – Calle Cardenal Cisneros and Calle Hartzenbush, near Glorieta de Bilbao, are lined with varied cheapish bars that are student favourites.

Bodegas La Ardosa
C/Santa Engracia 70 (91 446 58 94). Metro Iglesia/bus 3, 37, 149. **Open** 10am-3.30pm, 6-11pm, daily. Closed two weeks Aug. **Map G2**
Locals and buyers from the nearby market come in droves to this classic red-fronted *taberna*. It sells brilliant *patatas bravas*, marinated sardines, shellfish and lots of fried things.

Mesón do Anxo
C/Cardenal Cisneros 6 (91 446 17 43). Metro Bilbao/bus 3, 21, 147, 149. **Open** 9am-midnight daily. **Map F3**
A modern bar with a good range of tapas, among them wild mushrooms, fine *calamares* and, for the carnivores among you, grilled meat sold by weight.

Taberna 2
C/Sagasta 2 (91 532 21 43). Metro Bilbao/bus 21, 147, 149. **Open** 11am-3pm, 6pm-midnight, Mon-Thur; 11am-3pm, 6pm-2.30am, Fri, Sat. Closed Aug. **Map F3**
A good-value wine bar serving pungent Asturian *cabrales* cheese, and cheap *montados* of *sobrasada* (paprika sausage).

Taberna Los Madriles
C/José Abascal 26 (91 593 06 26). Metro Alonso Cano/bus 3, 5, 12, 37, 149. **Open** 11am-4pm, 7pm-12.30am, Tue-Sun.
Imitating the old-style Madrid *taberna*, Los Madriles is all white tiles adorned with photographs of regular customers – as children. The range of tapas is not huge but very choice: the *gambas al ajillo* are great, and the *callos* (tripe) as enjoyable for those who've acquired the taste. The star snack is *pincho los madriles*, of red pepper and anchovies.

Cafés & Bars

From Mediterranean to metropolitan, Madrid's watering holes are the essence of the city.

A coffee, a beer, a sandwich or something cold… whatever you're in need of, the café or bar (the difference in names often doesn't matter) is an integral part of a Madrileño's daily life. The city sustains a remarkable number of such places, sometimes more than one on every street corner. They range from the most basic, tending to the needs of a few dozen locals in forgotten *barrios*, to the internationally known – with prices to match.

With so many to choose from, it's impossible for any brief list to be exhaustive. They are grouped here by area, but in any given district you'll find a range of options. In fact, wherever you are in the city, you never need walk more than a hundred metres or so to find food, drink and shelter from the summer heat or winter cold. Madrileños spend a huge amount of time out of their homes, and much of it sitting in bars. There's no better way to get a feel for the city and its people than by sitting in a café, just looking on or listening to people.

Virtually all the places listed here serve food of some kind, and many are open late. However, for other bars where the emphasis is more emphatically on food, *see chapter* **Tapas**. For places that you would more likely visit in a late-night tour of the city, *see chapters* **Nightlife** *and* **Flamenco**. For an explanation of any of the drinks mentioned, *see page 134* **Bar codes**.

Many bars keep only roughly to 'official' opening times, and those listed here should be taken as guidelines (dates when places change to summer schedules are particularly variable). Most neighbourhood bars close around midnight, but on Fridays and Saturdays they may open until 1am or so. In the centre all bars tend to stay open later, and if you're caught between nightspots they offer a cheap way to keep up alcohol and food intake.

Villa y Corte

The historic heart of Madrid has dozens of old-fashioned tiled *tabernas*, relaxing cafés, straightforward bars, and, recently, a growing number of upscale tapas and wine bars (*see chapter* **Tapas**).

Café de los Austrias

Plaza de Ramales (91 559 84 36). Metro Opera/bus 3, 25, 39, 148. **Open** *9am-1.30am Mon-Thur; 9am-3am Fri, Sat; 5pm-midnight Sun.* **Map C7**
Given the tendency for older cafés to disappear beneath competition from other types of hostelry, this re-creation of a turn-of-the-century café – actually only a few years old – on

The ultimate in spacious cafés: the **Círculo de Bellas Artes.** *See page 135.*

Terracing

Madrid summers increasingly tend to drive people into air-conditioned interiors by day, but there are still some fine places around the city in which to pause and enjoy some shade. It's after dark that the urge to sit outside and watch the world go by makes most sense to locals. No summer evening is complete without a sampling of the city's open-air *terraza* bars, most of which are open May to October. Some new-style *terrazas* are at their busiest after midnight (*see chapter* **Nightlife**). For open-air dining, *see chapter* **Restaurants**.

Malasaña's grungy but refurbished **Plaza Dos de Mayo** boasts at least ten *terrazas* with open-air tables most of the year round. The **Plaza de las Comendadoras**, at the western end of Calle de la Palma, hosts the **Café Moderno**, fake art deco but quietly elegant, and **Taquería de Birra**, a Mexican restaurant that has no problem with serving just a drink. A good place to meet up if you're going to events at the Centro Conde Duque (where the bars inside are pretty poor).

The oldest part of the city, west of the Plaza Mayor, offers several opportunities for stop offs. Heading west from a perhaps obligatory (but expensive) stop in the cafés of the **Plaza Mayor** you can take in the **Plaza Conde de Barajas**, a tiny square often overlooked by the crowds nearby. Carry on across Calle Segovia to the two halves of **Café del Nuncio**, at either end of the Escalinata del Nuncio, an alley of steep steps that's one of the most picturesque streets in old Madrid. Nearby too is **Kairos**, an attractive modern bar (*see page 133*). Down the hill of Calle

Segovia there are more outdoor cafés in Plaza de la Cruz Verde, particularly **Café del Monaguillo**. From there, a walk along Calle de la Morería brings you to **Las Vistillas**, a bar that's run with absolutely no concern for fashions or trends but has a superb location looking out over the Casa de Campo all the way to the Guadarrama.

The **Retiro** and **Casa de Campo** both contain many small cafés around their lakes. At the eastern end of the Teleférico, above Parque del Oeste, there is also the **Paseo del Pintor Rosales**, another favourite spot with *terrazas* open by day and night. In the centre, **Café Gijón** and **El Espejo** (*see pages 133-5*) have *terrazas* on Recoletos that maintain a dignified old-world charm. Note that wherever you are, in the same way that you pay extra if you're served at a table inside a bar, you will pay more again for the privilege of sitting outside.

Locations

Café Moderno *Plaza de las Comendadoras 1 (91 522 84 61). Metro Noviciado/bus 21, 147.* **Open** *approx Sept-June* 6pm-2am Mon-Thur, Sun; 6pm-3am Fri, Sat; *June-Sept* noon-midnight daily. **Map D3**
Café del Nuncio *C/Nuncio 12 & C/Segovia 9 (91 366 08 53). Metro La Latina/bus 31, 50, 65.* **Open** 12.30pm-2.30am daily. **Map D8**
Café del Monaguillo *Plaza de la Cruz Verde 3 (91 541 29 41). Metro La Latina /bus 31, 50, 65.* **Open** 5.30pm-2.30am daily. **Map C8**
Taquería de Birra *Plaza de las Comendadoras, 2 (91 523 28 06). Metro Noviciado/bus 21, 147.* **Open** 8pm-midnight daily. **Map D3**
Las Vistillas *C/Bailén 14 (91 366 35 78). Metro Opera/bus 3, 148.* **Open** 11am-1am Mon-Thur, Sun; 11am-3am Fri, Sat. **Map C8**

---

the site of a former nunnery is welcome. It's big, with windows looking out onto two old streets, Calles Amnistia and Santiago, and the plaza alongside, added to marble tables and prints of monarchs along the walls.

De 1911

*Plazuela de San Ginés 5 (91 366 35 19).
Metro Opera, Sol/bus all routes to Puerta del Sol.*
Open 6pm-2am daily. **Map D7**
Not far from Sol, the tiny Plazuela de San Ginés is a haven of tranquillity. This is one of the nicest bars on the square, so named because, well, it opened in 1911. Inside, it has been finely refurbished with hand-painted tiles, and can offer a selection of beers from around the world, together with excellent speciality and Irish coffees.

Kairos

C/del Nuncio 19 (91 364 01 25). Metro La Latina/bus 17, 31, 50, 65. **Open** 8pm-3am daily. **Map D8**
Just off Calle Segovia is this well-designed, pleasant bar with a faithful local clientele, fine cocktails and excellent coffee, wines and beers. It's small on the inside, but there's an upstairs balcony that's ideal for a relaxing coffee. *Tables outdoors (May-Oct).*

La Madriguera

C/Santiago 3 (91 559 33 45). Metro Opera/bus 3, 25, 39, 148. **Open** 9.30am-4.30pm Mon; 9.30am-midnight Tue-Thur; 9.30am-2am Fri, Sat; noon-8.30pm Sun. **Map D7**
'The burrow', run by a group of women, combines several functions in one space – a relaxing café, a restaurant with innovative food, a music venue, exhibition space and bookshop. The café is comfortable, and the dining area at the back is a pleasant tiled room, which often hosts photography shows. In the basement there is a small performance space.

The Castellana – Recoletos

The Paseo de Recoletos, above Plaza de Cibeles, is one of Madrid's classic café venues.

Café Gijón

*Paseo de Recoletos 21 (91 521 54 25).
Metro Banco de España/bus all routes to Cibeles.*
Open 7am-2am daily. **Map H6**
Madrid's definitive literary café, opened in 1888. It maintains its literary connections with an annual short story prize, and

Bar codes

Deportment

The civilised tradition that you only pay when you are ready to leave is still the norm in bars in Spain, and rarely abused. Spaniards generally respect queues and wait their turn, and you'll find it easy to get a waiter's ear with a brisk *oiga* (literally, 'hear me', a perfectly polite way of attracting someone's attention).

In busy bars Madrileños tend to get their drinks down quickly. Added to the fact that in the centre there are entire streets given over to bars, this means that at night people often move from place to place, have a drink and then move on. Settling in to one place is something more usually done in cafés, or in summer at outdoor *terrazas*.

Tipping is discretionary. Change is usually returned in a small dish, and regardless of the amount spent it's unusual to leave over 100ptas. Most people just leave a few coins. Also, in neighbourhood bars, olive stones, toothpicks, the tissue-type napkins (*servilletas*) available along the bar and other disposables are customarily thrown on the floor.

Coffee & tea

For breakfast, most people have a *café con leche*, a largish, milky coffee, which at that time of day comes in a cup. At later times it will often be smaller and served in a glass, and if you want a cup you should ask for a *taza grande*. A plain black espresso is a *café solo*; the same with a dash of milk is *un cortado*, while *un americano* is a *solo* diluted with twice the normal amount of water. With a shot of alcohol, a *solo* becomes a *carajillo*. A true Madrileño *carajillo* is made with coffee, sugar, some coffee beans and brandy in a glass (*un carajillo de coñac*), which is then set alight on top so that the mixture gets mulled a little; a *carajillo* can also be just a solo with a shot of *coñac*, and you can equally ask for a *carajillo de whisky*, de *ron* (rum), de *anís* or anything else you fancy. Also popular are Irish coffees (*café irlandés*) and a variety of other mulled spirit-and-cream combinations, labelled generically *cafés especiales*. Decaffeinated coffee is *descafeinado*.

The quality of coffee in bars varies enormously. It tends to arrive at medium temperature, and if you want it really hot you should remind the waiter *que esté bien caliente, por favor*. In summer a great café alternative is *café con hielo*, iced coffee, usually with a slice of lemon.

Tea in bars is usually awful, as most places have little idea how to prepare it. Very popular, however, are herb teas, *infusiones*, such as *menta* (mint) or *manzanilla* (camomile).

Beer

Wine may be more traditional in Spain, but in terms of quantity *cerveza* has overtaken it as the national drink. Draught beer (*de barril*) is served in *cañas*, a measure around ¼ litre (in bars people often ask for *una caña, dos cañas*, and so on) in tall glasses called *tubos*, or in a *doble*, which is around ½ litre. Some places even serve *pintas* (pints). Bottled beer is usually served in *tercios* (⅓ litre) or *botellines* (1/5 litre).

Spain produces some good-quality beers. In Madrid, the favourite by far is the local brand Mahou, with two basic varieties, green label and the stronger red label. A darker Mahou beer (*negra*) is also increasingly available. Other common brands worth a try are Aguila and Cruzcampo. Quite a few bars now also stock imported beers, but they are nearly always a good deal more expensive than Spanish brands.

Wines, spirits & other drinks

All bars have a sturdy cheap red (*tinto*) on offer, and usually a white (*blanco*) and rosé (*rosado*). A traditional but disappearing drink is *tinto con sifón*, red with a splash of soda. If you fancy a better wine, then most bars listed here will have at least a decent Rioja, and probably *Cava*, Catalan sparkling wine. Good wines, however, are often expensive in bars that do not have wine as a speciality. Sherry is *jerez*. The type virtually always drunk in Spain is a dry *fino*, served very cold. A good fuller-bodied variety is *palo cortado*. Sweet sherries have traditionally been only for export.

Red vermouth (*vermút*) with soda is another Madrid tradition, usually as an aperitif, and has recently come slightly back into fashion. For a powerful after-dinner drink, try Galician *orujo*, a fiery spirit similar to grappa or schnapps, which comes plain (*blanco*) or *con hierbas*, with a luminous green colour. Other *digestivos* include *Patxarán*, a fruity almond-flavoured liqueur from Navarra, and the more Castilian *anís*, the best of which hails from Chinchón (*see p232*) and available dry (*seco*) or sweet (*dulce*).

Non-alcoholic drinks

Low- and alcohol-free beers (Laiker, Buckler, Kaliber) have carved an important niche in the market, and other favourites for non-alcohol drinkers are the Campari-like but booze-free Bitter Kas, and plain tonic water (*una tónica*), with ice and lemon. Fresh orange juice, *zumo de naranja*, is widely available, but strangely expensive in a country with so many oranges. Trinaranjus is the best-known Spanish bottled juice brand; favourite flavours are orange, pineapple (*piña*) and peach (*melocotón*). *Mosto* is grape juice, served in small glasses, sometimes with ice and a slice. A great and unappreciated Spanish speciality, though, are its traditional summer refreshers: most unusual is *horchata*, a milky drink made by crushing a root called a *chufa*. It has to be drunk fresh, from a specialised shop, as it curdles once made. The same places also offer *granizados* – crushed ice with fresh lemon, orange or coffee – which when properly made are fabulous. Mineral water (*agua mineral*) can be ordered anywhere, either fizzy (*con gas*) or still (*sin gas*).

Food

At any time of day, you can accompany your coffee or drink with something to eat. For breakfast, many places have traditional *churros* or *porras*, sweet deep-fried sticks of batter, or fresh pastries such as croissants, *napolitanas* (soft, glazed pastries filled with egg custard), *sobaos* (a buttery sponge from Santander) or *madalenas* (sponge cakes). To soak up your ritual *caña*, even bars that do not have any special display of tapas offer such things as a *pinchito de tortilla*, a little piece of potato omelette, sometimes for free. For more on bar food, *see chapter* **Tapas**.

Tobacco

A cigarette is probably still an automatic accompaniment to a drink for a majority of Spaniards. In bars, cigarettes (*cigarros*) are sold in machines. Spaniards differentiate between black tobacco (*tabaco negro*) and international-style light tobacco (*rubio*). If you want to pass for a native, try Ducados or their stronger brothers Habanos, full-flavoured black tobacco. Popular Spanish *rubio* brands are Fortuna and Nobel. Marlboro, Camel and Winston are also popular.

Hemingway really was here: **Chicote.**

has tried to keep the *tertulia* tradition (*see chapter* **History**) alive with rather formalised gatherings of writers, film makers, bullfighters and so on. A decent-value set menu is served at lunchtime. Get a window seat if you can, or stand at the bar, which as well as the literati attracts an in-off-the-street crowd of concierges and office workers. Outside it has a pleasant (but expensive) terrace bar for the summer.
Tables outdoors (Mar-Nov).

El Espejo
Paseo de Recoletos 31 (91 319 11 22). Metro Colón/bus all routes to Plaza de Colón. **Open** 9am-2am daily. **Map H6**
Not nearly so historic, although it may look it: opened in 1978, 'the Mirror' set out to be the art nouveau bar Madrid never had, with positively Parisian 1900s décor. Its terrace bar on the Paseo occupies a splendid glass pavilion reminiscent of a giant Tiffany lamp. Fashionable and comfortable, it has excellent tapas at reasonable prices, particularly the *croquetas* and *tortilla*.
Tables outdoors (May-Oct).

Sol & Gran Via

In the central shopping district there are some of Madrid's finest cafés from the pre-Civil War years.

Bar Cock
C/de la Reina 16 (91 532 28 26). Metro Gran Via/ bus all routes to Gran Via. **Open** *Sept-June* 7pm-3am daily; *July-Aug* 9pm-4am Mon-Sat. **Map F6**
Not strictly Sol-side of the Gran Via, but one of three cocktail bars that form a tiny city-centre triangle (the others being **Chicote** and **Del Diego**). Post-1am, this is the most moddish of the trio. Dark wood-panelled walls and a high-beamed ceiling give it a subdued air, and it competes with the best in attracting the media, theatre and fashion crowd.

Café del Círculo de Bellas Artes
C/Alcalá 42 (91 360 54 00/902 422 442). Metro Banco de España/bus all routes to Cibeles. **Open** 9am-2am Mon-Thur, Sun; 9am-3am Fri, Sat. **Map G7**
A few years ago the Circulo (*see also chapters* **Sightseeing**, **Art Galleries** *and* **Music: Classical & Opera**) began to charge a nominal 100ptas for non-members to use its elegant but informal café overlooking Calle Alcalá. It's well worth this slight extra cost, to be able to sit and read or chat for a few hours in spacious, airy surroundings amid Antonio Palacios' grand '20s décor, one of the best places to carry on a *tertulia* in modern Madrid. There are also tasty tapas.
Tables outdoors (May-Oct).

Chicote
Gran Via 12 (91 532 67 37). Metro Gran Via/ bus all routes to Gran Via. **Open** 8am-3am Mon-Thur; 8am-4am Fri, Sat. **Map F6**

The doyen of Madrid cocktail bars, with the city's best 1930s art deco interior, and famous for never having closed during the Civil War. The seats are also original, which means that you could be sitting where old Hemingway and the rest of the international press gang spent their days sheltering from the artillery shells flying down the Gran Via. Since then, Grace Kelly, Ava Gardner and about every Spanish writer, actor and artist of the last 60 years have passed through too. The cocktail range is impressive, but expect to pay close to 1,000ptas in the evenings (prices are cheaper before 5pm). The waiters are gentlemen from another epoch. Grab one of the alcove tables, and savour a treat to remember.

Del Diego
C/de la Reina 12 (91 523 31 06). Metro Gran Via/ bus all routes to Gran Via. **Open** 7pm-3am Mon-Thur; 7pm-4am Fri, Sat. **Map F6**
Founded by former Chicote waiter Fernando del Diego, this bar has a younger clientele and a lighter style than is associated with traditional *coctelerias*. The atmosphere is convivial, and the cocktails are something else. Ask for a Diego: vodka, kirsch, peach, lime and crushed ice.

Huertas & Santa Ana

The *guiris'* favourite (*see page 36*), relaxed back streets that offer a respite from touristed bars on the Castellana, or the crowds at Sol.

Casa Pueblo
C/León 3 (91 429 05 15). Metro Antón Martín/ bus 6, 26, 32, 57. **Open** *Sept-June* 7pm-2am; *July-Aug* 9pm-2am Tue-Sun. **Map F8**
A perfect re-creation of a 1900 bar/café, Casa Pueblo has been offering quietly formal but relaxed service to regulars for over 15 years. Excellent jazz on tape and a live pianist after midnight help make it one of Madrid's most pleasant watering holes.

Cervecería Alemana
Plaza de Santa Ana 6 (91 429 70 33). Metro Antón Martin, Sol/bus all routes to Puerta del Sol. **Open** 10.30am-12.30am Mon, Wed, Thur, Sun; 10.30am-2am Fri, Sat. **Map E/F8**
Built in 1904 and based (loosely) on a German bierkeller, the Alemana still serves beer in steins, if you ask for it. Hemingway used to drink here when in Madrid, and the old place is still much as it was then. Although on the tourist trail, it's still a locals' bar, particularly on Sunday mornings when it offers peace and an ideal setting to browse the paper.

Cervecería Santa Ana
Plaza de Santa Ana 10 (91 429 43 56). Metro Antón Martin, Sol/bus all routes to Puerta del Sol. **Open** 11.30am-2.30am daily. **Map E/F8**
Slightly overshadowed by the Alemana next door, the Santa Ana is plainer to look at but still has good beer, including draught Guinness and Belgian bottled beers. There are no tables inside, and in the evenings places at the bar are highly sought after. Good cheese, pâté and tapas are on offer.
Tables outdoors (May-Oct).

Los Gabrieles
C/Echegaray 17 (91 429 62 61). Metro Sevilla, Sol/bus all routes to Puerta del Sol. **Open** 12.30pm-2am Mon-Thur, Sun; 12.30pm-3.30am Fri, Sat. **Map F8**
With an even more impressive tiling job than its near-neighbour **Viva Madrid** (*see p136*), Los Gabrieles is an institution. Until the '70s it was a brothel, run by gypsies, with rooms in the now-inaccessible cellar that saw them all come and go, so to speak. It then became a bar, and at the height of its popularity during the *Movida* years it attracted all the city's beautiful and famous. More recently it has started to become a pick-up place for rich kids, as reflected in the prices.

Café de Ruiz *is one of the most comfortable Malasaña meeting-places. See page 138.*

Los Gatos

*C/de Jesús 2 (91 429 30 67). Metro Antón Martín/
bus all routes to Neptuno.* **Open** noon-1am Mon-Thur;
noon-2am Fri, Sat. **Map G8**
Fortunately overlooked on most tourist trails despite its very
handy location at the bottom of Huertas, not far from the
Prado and the Thyssen, this veteran is a companion to near-
neighbour **La Dolores** (*see p139*). Popular with the bullfighting fraternity (among many others), it retains the feel
of a local bar, with excellent tapas and good, frothy beer
served at amiably down-at-heel tables.

Naturbier

*Plaza de Santa Ana 9 (91 429 39 18). Metro Antón
Martín, Sol/bus all routes to Puerta del Sol.* **Open** 11.30am-
2am Mon-Thur, Sun; 11.30am-3am Fri, Sat. **Map E/F8**
Neighbour to Cervecerías Alemana and Santa Ana on the
plaza, Naturbier's special attraction is that it is one of the few
places in Madrid that brews its own beer, following traditional German recipes. Always very popular with students
and foreigners.
Tables outdoors (May-Oct).

Reporter

*C/Fúcar 6 (91 429 39 22). Metro Antón Martín/bus 6,
26, 32, 57.* **Open** 11am-2am Mon-Thur; 11am-3.30am
Fri; 6pm-3.30am Sat, Sun. **Map G9**
Splendid cocktails and fruit juices are the major draws of
this trendy, stylish Huertas cocktail-café, with low-volume
jazz and occasional photo shows. It also serves tapas and
meals in the afternoon.

El Salón del Prado

*C/del Prado 4 (91 429 33 61). Metro Antón Martín/bus
6, 9, 26, 32.* **Open** 2pm-2am Mon-Thur; 2pm-3am Fri,
Sat; 2pm-1am Sun. **Map F8**
Elegance itself, and easily among Madrid's best cafés. In the
middle of the Huertas/Santa Ana area, the Salón del Prado
is one of the best spots around for a coffee, better still an Irish
one, in the late afternoon or early evening after a hard day's
touring and eating. The service is formal, but also friendly,
and children are welcome. On Thursday nights there are
chamber music concerts (except in July-Sept).

La Venencia

*C/Echegaray 7 (91 429 73 13). Metro Sevilla, Sol/bus all
routes to Puerta del Sol.* **Open** 1-3pm, 7.30pm-1.30am
daily. **Map F8**
Cheerfully down at heel, the Venencia is worthy of a film set,
with peeling sherry posters from no-one knows when, barrels alongside the bar and walls burnished gold by decades
of tobacco smoke. It serves nothing but sherry, from dry fino
to robust *palo cortado*, accompanied by olives or *mojama*
(dry-cured tuna).

Viva Madrid

*C/Manuel Fernández y González 7 (no phone). Metro
Sevilla, Sol/bus all routes to Puerta del Sol.* **Open** 1pm-
2am Mon-Thur, Sun; 1pm-3am Fri, Sat. **Map F8**
One of Madrid's best-known bars, a favourite with visitors
and residents. A little expensive, but worth it for the interi-
or, with vaulted ceiling, whirring fans, beams, and fabulous
painted tiles of Madrid scenes from the 1900s. A classic place
to start off a bar crawl.

La Latina, Rastro, Lavapiés

Currently undergoing a smartening up, Madrid's
barrios bajos still boast some of the most authentic old-style bars, mixed in with designer joints.

La Clave

*C/Calatrava 6 (91 366 48 38). Metro La Latina, Puerta
de Toledo/bus 17, 18, 23, 35, 60.* **Open** 9pm-1am Mon-
Thur, 9pm-2.30am Fri, Sat; 9pm-1.30am Sun. **Map C9**
An ideal way to plug into the arts scene. As much a gallery
as a café, this place also hosts *tertulias*. The owners even
publish their own arts magazine. The coffee's not bad, either.

El Chiscón

C/Lavapiés 48 (no phone). Metro Lavapiés/bus 6, 32, 65.
Open noon-4pm, 8pm-2am, daily. **Map E9**
Very much part of the recuperation of Lavapiés, and its
inexorable conversion over the years into a trendy, increasingly moneyed area. The walls and corners are piled high

with old pictures, lamps, and knick-knacks, and Chiscón offers a distinctive ambience as much as anything else – it's popular round the clock.

El Eucalypto

C/Argumosa 2 (no phone). Metro Lavapiés/bus 6, 26, 32, 57, 27. **Open** noon-midnight daily. **Map F10**
Eucalyptus offers one of Madrid's better *mojitos*, a terrific choice of tropical fruit drinks, non-alcoholic cocktails and alcoholic milkshakes. The real appeal, though, is in sitting out on the ad-hoc terrace on what's become known as the 'Costa Argumosa' of outdoor bars. Even in the depths of winter, though, space can be found inside for a taste of summer.

Montes

C/Lavapiés 40 (91 527 00 64). Metro Lavapiés/bus 6, 26, 32, 57, 27. **Open** noon-4pm, 7.30pm-midnight, Tue-Sat; 11am-4pm Sun. Closed Aug. **Map E9**
An authentic neighbourhood bar where genial owner César has been catering to the finer palates of Lavapiés for decades. It's a walk-in-off-the-street joint, with little more than standing room, where recently arrived Brits, Americans and other foreigners soaking up the atmosphere rub shoulders with local regulars. The wine selection is excellent, and the fresh tapas (some on the house) include fine *jamón de pato* and good anchovies and *cabrales* cheese.

Nuevo Café Barbieri

C/Ave María 45 (91 527 36 58). Metro Lavapiés/bus 6, 26, 32. **Open** 3pm-2am Mon-Thur, Sun; 3pm-3am Fri, Sat. **Map E/F9**

After years of shabby decline, the Barbieri was taken over in the 1970s by a cooperative who partly restored its columned interior to its former glory. It's retained a certain seedy quality, though, despite attracting a young clientele. Newspapers and magazines on the bar make it an excellent spot to while away an afternoon, and it's a good place to go on your own. *Tables outdoors (May-Oct).*

El 21

C/Toledo 21 (91 366 28 59). Metro La Latina/bus all routes to Plaza Mayor. **Open** noon-3.30pm, 7-11pm, Mon-Thur, Sun; noon-3.30pm, 7pm-midnight, Fri, Sat. **Map D8**
A perfect stop-off near the Rastro, the 21 and its marble countertop seem locked in a time warp. No sign identifies the bar from the street, and most of the time it's filled with elderly locals, although a young crowd arrives at night and weekends. The owner, a definite candidate for the hostess with the mostest, receives all with unflagging hospitality.

Malasaña & Chueca

Chueca has seen an explosion of cafés and bars since the mid-'90s as its streets have been cleaned up and it has become Madrid's gay village.

Café Comercial

Glorieta de Bilbao 7 (91 521 56 55). Metro Bilbao/bus 3, 21, 40, 147, 149. **Open** 8am-1am Mon-Thur, Sun; 8am-2am Fri, Sat. **Map F3**

This sporting *vida*

Aren't satellites wonderful? Thanks to the demands of a growing British and Irish community hungry to keep up with the feats of their sporting heroes (sometimes), coupled with the internationalisation of soccer, there are now plenty of pubs around Madrid where it's possible to follow English league football – especially – and other sports on TV.

The demands of the sports-viewing drinker can be few, but some bars have caught on better than others when it comes to keeping the customer satisfied. For example: at what height do you put the telly, and do you want sitting areas and something to eat as you watch Coventry City overwhelm Man U? One of the most popular of the current plague – beg pardon, trend – of Irish pubs is **The Quiet Man**, with at least four screens and pub food. The only problem is that there's not much seating space, and the TVs – the daft oblong Panavision type – are way above head height. The food, though, is good. **O'Neill's** is a roomy place on two floors that turns over the whole basement for big British and Irish games, with rows of seats and a nice little bar. It also lays on sandwiches. **Anyway** and **Anyway Too** are faithful recreations of an ordinary, slightly down-at-heel English pub,

complete with quizzes. Food is limited, but they take their football (seen on normal-size TVs) seriously.

Bo Finn is a newish, smartish Irish pub in Salamanca where you can scoff international cuisine as you watch the All-Ireland hurling championship; **Molly Malone's** in Malasaña and the massive **Irish Rover** on Avenida de Brasil have a number of nooks and snugs with TVs available.

Locations

Anyway *C/Viriato 64 (91 448 64 08). Metro Iglesia/bus 3, 5, 16, 61.* **Open** noon-2am Mon-Thur; noon-2.30am Fri; 4pm-2.30am Sat; 4pm-2am Sun. **Map G1**
Anyway Too *C/Las Fuentes 9 (91 548 37 72). Metro Ópera/bus 3.* **Open** 11am-2am Mon-Thur; 11am-2.30am Fri; 4pm-2.30am Sat; 4pm-2am Sun. **Map D7**
Bo Finn *C/Velázquez 97 (91 411 40 79.) Metro Núñez de Balboa/bus 16, 19, 51.* **Open** midday-1am Mon-Thur, Sun; midday 2am Fri, Sat. **Map J1**
The Irish Rover *Avda de Brasil 7 (91 555 76 71). Metro Santiago Bernabéu/bus 5, 43, 126, 149.* **Open** 11am-2.30am Mon-Thur, Sun; 11am-3.30am Fri, Sat.
Molly Malone's *C/Manuela Malasaña 11 (91 594 12 01). Metro Bilbao/bus 21, 147.*
Open 1pm-2.30am Mon-Thur; 1pm-3.30am Fri, Sat; 5pm-2.30am Sun. **Map F3**
The Quiet Man *C/Valverde 44 (91 523 46 89). Metro Tribunal/bus 3, 40.*
Open *Sept-June* 1pm-3am daily; *July-Aug* 6.30pm-3am Mon-Thur; 1pm-3am Fri-Sun. **Map F5**

An institution, one of the city's ever-popular meeting points. With heavy wooden tables and leather-lined seats, its mirrored interior attracts all kinds of people, from huddled bunches of students and would-be literary types to elderly local residents who have been taking breakfast there since before the Civil War. Bring a newspaper, and settle in. *Tables outdoors (May-Oct).*

Café Isadora

C/Divino Pastor 14 (91 445 71 54). Metro Bilbao/bus 3, 21, 40, 147, 149. **Open** 4pm-2am daily. **Map E/F3**
Books and a variety of old prints line the walls, giving this Malasaña café a relaxed, literary feel. Opened in the late 1970s, it has a black and white tiled interior and chunky, dark wood furniture. Their collection of different kinds of *Patxarán* (*see p134* **Bar codes**), many individually made, is worth examining, and the coffees are excellent.

Café Manuela

C/San Vicente Ferrer 29 (91 531 70 37). Metro Tribunal/bus 3, 40, 149. **Open** 7pm-2am daily. **Map E4**
A Malasaña café that was a hive of activity for the early-'80s scene and is still going strong in post-*Movida* times. An obligatory stop-off on the local round, with elegant art nouveau décor, a full range of coffees and varying entertainment through the week.

Café de Ruiz

C/Ruiz 11 (91 446 12 32). Metro Bilbao/bus 3, 21, 40, 147, 149. **Open** 1pm-3am Mon-Thur, Sun; 1pm-4am Fri, Sat. **Map E3**
An amiably old-fashioned feel and very comfortable seats make this Malasaña café, a *Movida* meeting point in its time, a pleasant spot to kill a few hours or retreat from the night-time grunge. Fine coffee, milkshakes (*batidos*), large, elaborately made *carajillos* (*see p134* **Bar codes**), cocktails and even Havana cigars can all be mulled over while reading the papers or eavesdropping on the next table.

El Maragato

C/San Andrés 14 (no phone). Metro Tribunal/bus 3, 40, 149. **Open** 2-4pm, 7.30pm-midnight, daily. Closed Aug. **Map F4**
While it cannot boast any ornate traditional tiles, this pleasantly scruffy little bodega facing Plaza Dos de Mayo has a lot of history behind it. It's been in the same family since the 1880s, the wrinkled old boy who serves the drinks still writes the tab in pencil on the marble bar-top, and prices are ridiculously low; at the back there's a dining room where the budget-concious can enjoy a *menú del día* for 700ptas. Lately, it has become popular with Malasaña's young crowd.

Net Café

C/San Bernardo 81 (91 594 09 99). Metro San Bernardo/bus 21, 147. **Open** 10am-2am Mon-Thur; 11am-3am Fri, Sat; 11am-2am Sun. **Map E3**
Madrid's home for netties. Eight terminals, in tables under thick glass screens so you have somewhere harmless to rest your glass, are spread around the tastefully decorated bar. Another Internet café in Madrid is **La Ciberteca**, Avda del General Perón 32 (91 556 56 03). Metro Santiago Bernabéu/bus 3, 5, 43, 149. **Open** 9am-3pm

El Parnasillo

C/San Andrés 33 (91 447 00 79). Metro Bilbao/bus 3, 21, 40, 147, 149. **Open** 3.30pm-3am Mon-Thur, Sun; 3.30pm-3.30am Fri, Sat. **Map F3**
A smart Malasaña café with a relaxed atmosphere, pleasant, almost classical décor and a full range of alcohol-boosted coffees and cocktails, especially *caipirinhas* and Cuban *mojitos*. Frequented since the '70s by writers, artists, journalists and intellectuals, it was very much at the centre of Madrid and Malasaña's post-Franco cultural renewal, to the point that it was once bombed by a far-right terrorist group. Don't panic, though – there's no danger of that happening now.

El Son

C/Fernando VI 21 (91 308 04 29). Metro Alonso Martínez/bus 3, 37, 40, 149. **Open** 8.30am-2am Mon-Fri; 8.30pm-3am Sat. Closed Aug. **Map H4**
Rum-lovers' paradise. 'The Sound' offers some 90 labels from Cuba, Venezuela, Nicaragua, Colombia, Dominican Republic, Barbados, Guatemala, Haiti and Jamaica. Resisting the lure of kitsch tropical décor, the owners have done the bar out in Barcelona design-bar style; music, though, is pure Latino – salsa, merengue, cumbias. Try Cuban Paticruzado or Haitian Barbancour, and offset the effects with Colombian coffee.

Salamanca & the Retiro

The capital's smartest area prides itself on being ahead in refinement when it comes to places for a drink or a tapa. The area south of Goya, down the east side of the Retiro, is more down-to-earth.

Café del Arte

C/Alcalá 113 (no phone). Metro Príncipe de Vergara, Retiro/bus 15, 29, 52, 146. **Open** 7am-10.30pm daily. **Map J5**
A good stopping-off point after a hectic afternoon's Salamanca shopping, the Café del Arte looks onto the Retiro, and its classic café design is complemented by regular art exhibitions.

Café y Té

C/Goya 18 (91 578 29 67). Metro Velázquez/bus 1, 21, 53, 74. **Open** 6am-1.15am Mon-Thur, Sun; 6am-3am Fri, Sat. **Map J4**
A very American-looking café chain that started out in Barcelona. The design, with a half-on-the-street, half-inside feel, makes it very much a quick stop-off, but a fine selection of coffees and attentive service from the uniformed waiters are temptations to stay on a bit longer and read the paper. *Tables outdoors (May-Oct).*

Balmoral

C/Hermosilla 10 (91 431 41 33). Metro Serrano/bus 1, 9, 21, 53, 74. **Open** *Sept-July* 12.30-3pm, 7pm-2am; *Aug* 8pm-2am Mon-Sat. **Map I4**
The Balmoral keeps itself to itself. However, behind its slightly daunting exterior you will find not only a bizarre Scottish theme (tartan carpet, the Monarch of the Glen and hunting prints), but also a clientele ranging from crusty older locals to bikers. Plus excellent cocktails and impeccable service, even if prices are a bit steep.

El Botánico

C/Ruiz de Alarcón 27 (91 420 23 42). Metro Banco de España/bus all routes to Plaza de Cibeles. **Open** 8am-11pm daily. **Map H8**
A world away from the tourist trail of the Prado, which it sits directly behind (you can see the museum from the terrace, as well as the Jardín Botánico). The customers who frequent its roomy interior, decorated with old bicycles and the like, mainly hail from the wealthy Retiro *barrio* around it. *Tables outdoors (May-Oct).*

Conde Duque/Argüelles

Bordering Malasaña, the district around Cuartel Conde Duque has some great idiosyncratic bars.

El Cangrejero

C/Amaniel 25 (91 548 39 35). Metro Noviciado, Plaza de España/bus all routes to Plaza de España. **Open** 12.30-3.30pm, 7pm-12.30am, Thur-Tue. Closed Aug. **Map D4**

Over 60 years old, the Cangrejero is a Madrileño secret, off the tourist trail near the Cuartel Conde-Duque. A big part of its success is its superbly kept beer: with a thick, frothy head and ice cold, and a wonderful accompaniment to the bar's excellent mussels. No-nonsense formica tables and a comically gruff owner add to the charm.

Carpe Diem
Plaza Conde de Toreno 2 (91 559 77 02).
Metro Noviciado, Plaza de España/bus all routes to
Plaza de España. **Open** 11.30pm-5.30am Fri, Sat; 3pm-8pm Sun. **Map D4**
A bar with wider social objectives. Seven per cent of takings go to the funding of 'popular kitchens' in Peru, channelled through the Spanish aid organisation Intermón, and the bar is intended also to serve as a meeting point for other alter-

native and humanitarian organisations. A pleasant place, playing international and Spanish pop and, at weekends, salsa and merengue.

El Maño
C/de la Palma 64 (91 521 50 57). Metro Noviciado/
bus 147. **Open** 7pm-midnight Mon-Wed; noon-3.30pm, 7pm-midnight, Thur-Sun. **Map D4**
For years this bodega was a pleasant, scruffy-ish place serving cheap wine, beer and simple tapas to a local clientele. More recently, as this side of town has gone a little upmarket, El Maño hasad a lick of paint and diversified its fare. House wine is only 100ptas a glass, and there are Riojas, Raimats and Cavas from 250ptas. Tapas worth trying are own-made pâté and the platter of *ahumados* (smoked fish); no outside tables, but wide doors open right on to the street.

On the tiles

Two things identify Madrid's most characterful, most traditional bars: tiles and zinc. Colourful tiles around the walls, and zinc counters awash with water on the bar, to rinse the glasses. Plenty of these great 'tile bars' remain, you just have to know where to look…
See also **La Taberna de Antonio Sánchez**, *in chapter* **Tapas**.

El Anciano
C/Bailén 19 (91 559 53 32).
Metro Opera/bus 3, 25, 39, 148. **Open** 10am-3pm, 5-11pm Thur-Tue. Closed Aug. **Map C8**
Dating back to the 1900s, this bar by the C/Bailén viaduct was originally a sister to El Anciano Rey de los Vinos (*see chapter* **Tapas**). Kept much as it was 50 years ago, extremely simple, it serves decent beer and wines and good tapas. A great place to go for a drink after visiting the Palacio Real.

Angel Sierra
C/Gravina 11 (91 531 01 26).
Metro Chueca/bus 3, 40, 149. **Open** 10.30am-4pm, 7.30-11pm, Thur-Tue. Closed Aug. **Map G5**
There was a time when Madrid was filled with *tabernas* like this one, looking on to the Plaza de Chueca, with tiled walls, zinc bar top, overflowing sink and glasses stacked on wooden slats. The thing to have is vermouth and a splash, with an anchovy and olive tapa.

Bodega de la Ardosa
C/Colón 13 (91 521 49 79). Metro Tribunal/bus 3, 40,
149. **Open** 12.30-3.30pm, 7-11.30pm, daily. **Map 1/E5**
The tiled *taberna* meets the Irish theme bar: the décor of this Malasaña bar combines Spanish tiles and Goya with posters from Irish pubs, and it was one of the first in Madrid to serve Guinness. Also a fine selection of other imported beers.

Casa Camacho
C/San Andrés 21 (91 531 35 98). Metro Tribunal /bus
3, 40, 149. **Open** 10am-midnight daily. **Map E/F4**
This family-run bodega, opened in 1928 and located right in the very centre of Malasaña, is a popular meeting point for locals and for groups of all ages before they go on to other bars in the district. With vermouth and beers on tap and cheap wine and spirits, Camacho's services most needs of passers-by. Going to the toilet is an experience,

Truly Madrileño: **Bodega Gerardo**.

and requires a certain level of agility – you have to duck under the bar and slip through the doorway at the back, not forgetting to say hello to Granny Camacho who sits in the next room.

La Dolores
Plaza de Jesús 4 (91 429 22 43). Metro Antón
Martín/bus all routes to Paseo del Prado. **Open** 11am-1am Mon-Thur, Sun; 11am-2am Fri, Sat. **Map G8**
Dating back to the '20s, this bustling, attractive Huertas bar is very well placed for the big museums and attracts a clientele divide mainly between the overspill from the district's night-haunts at weekends and office workers who come in at lunchtime or after work in the week. Beers are reasonably priced, but the tasty, tempting tapas are a little expensive.

Vinos/Bodega Gerardo
C/Calatrava 21 (91 365 36 46).
Metro Puerta de Toledo/bus all routes to Puerta de
Toledo. **Open** noon-4pm, 7.30-11.30pm, Mon-Fri; noon-4pm Sat, Sun. **Map C9**
'Vinos' is what you'll see outside, but this old-time bar is known locally as Gerardo's. It's the place to be during La Paloma in August (*see chapter* **Madrid by Season**), but even at other times it's an essential part of the La Latina neighbourhood, serving excellent sausage, ham and cheese, fine seafood and anchovies and well-chilled vermouth.

Sweet nothings

In among its alcohol-outlets Madrid also has cafés that specialise in teas, cakes and summer coolers. Some *chocolaterías* – serving thick, hot chocolate – are also favourite stop offs on the Madrileño night-time round (*see chapter* **Nightlife**).

Bruin
Paseo del Pintor Rosales 48 (91 541 59 21). Metro Argüelles/bus 21, 74. **Open** *mid-Sept-June noon-8pm, July-mid-Sept 10am-2am, daily.* **Map B3**
One of Madrid's oldest, best-known ice-cream parlours, ideally placed near the Teleférico (*see p62*). Over 20 different flavours, and ice-cream cakes, *granizados* and horchata.

Café Viena
C/Luisa Fernanda 23 (91 559 38 28). Metro Ventura Rodríguez/bus 1, 2, 44, 74, C. **Open** 8am-2am Mon-Sat; 4pm-2am Sun. **Map C4**
This ornate, velvet-draped, gilt-covered café specialises in Irish and similar coffees, hot chocolate and cakes. Another feature of the café is its very popular Monday-night 'Lyrical' sessions, when singers perform opera and *zarzuela* favourites.

Compañía Infusionera de las Indias
C/de las Minas 1 (no phone). Metro Noviciado/bus 147. **Open** 5pm-midnight daily.
For a wide choice of teas from all over Asia and a laidback, not to say chilled-out, atmosphere, try this hippieish tea house at the quieter end of Malasaña. In its spacious rooms you'll find carpets, cushions, armchairs and relaxing music.

Embassy
Paseo de la Castellana 12 (91 576 00 80). Metro Colón/bus all routes to Plaza de Colón. **Open** *Sept-June 9am-1am daily; July-Aug 9am-1am Mon-Sat.* **Map I4**
For a real traditional English tea, such as the English are supposed to enjoy, this 1930s tearoom is the place to come. Popular with prosperous Salamanca residents, especially store-cruising ladies, it has dozens of teas, and even little diamond-shaped cucumber sandwiches. For something stronger, try one of the cocktails. You can also enter through the shop entrance at Calle Ayala 12.

Oliveri
Paseo de la Castellana 196 (91 359 77 19). Metro Cuzco, Plaza de Castilla/bus 5, 27, 40, 147, 149, 150, 150. **Open** 8am-1am daily.
When this café first opened in the '60s there were still sheep grazing in fields around it at the top of the Castellana, and it was a favourite stop off for ice-creams during Sunday walks. Remarkably, it has managed to survive the surrounding space has filled with apartment and office blocks. With a front garden, it's popular with locals by night and office workers by day. *Tables outdoors (May-Oct).*

Viena Capellanes
C/Princesa 73 (91 543 10 10). Metro Argüelles/bus 1, 44, 133, C. **Open** 7.15am-9.15pm daily. **Map C3**
The Viena chain of cake and pastry shops is scattered throughout Madrid, but this branch has counter and table service for on-the-spot sampling of its delicious snacks and coffee. For other addresses of other branches, pick up a napkin.

Nightlife

It's 4pm in Madrid, and there's no one on the streets. They're all waiting till it's dark to come out.

Pounding the Madrid streets can wear you out.

Traffic jams are building up around the city centre, the pavements are jammed, entrances to the Metro are thronged with people. Madrid is once more steeling itself for the onset of its regular dusk to dawn street party. It's another weekend, and Europe's most nocturnal capital is going out.

The first thing that differentiates Madrid is the extent to which nightlife – even in winter – happens in public, on the street. On the pavements grungy slackers brush past eager ravers, while a dressy office-party crowd compete for attention with colourful ageing punks. Main streets are sluggish rivers of red tail lights and gridlocked taxis, a regular ritual in Madrid's 4 to 5am rush hour.

Where other cities tend to hide their sociability behind pub and club doors and licensing laws, Madrileños love to wander the streets, watching each other, pausing to chat or simply drink. Malasaña, especially, often resembles a bizarre street carnival, in that the studenty kids who have made the district their own spend much of their time hang-

ing around on the pavements rather than going into bars, where they'd have to shell out more money. Instead, they roll joints in doorways, and gather in big groups that literally pack the streets around Plaza Dos de Mayo. *Calimocho* is the favourite tipple of Malasaña, a sickly-sweet concoction of cheap red wine and cola, and as well as bars the area has little corner shops that sell the basic ingredients, so that kids can mix themselves industrial-size measures of the stuff in plastic bottles on the street.

The weather plays its part in this street life, but more crucial is Madrileños' love of seeing and being seen, of participating in a cast of thousands and meeting a random assortment of people. To veterans of the Madrid night things have calmed a bit since the highwater mark of '80s hedonism. The current city council has shut down some clubs, and in some areas local residents are pressing for further action against noisy revellers. Any visitor, however, is likely to wonder where all this is happening, for in the busiest night-time areas

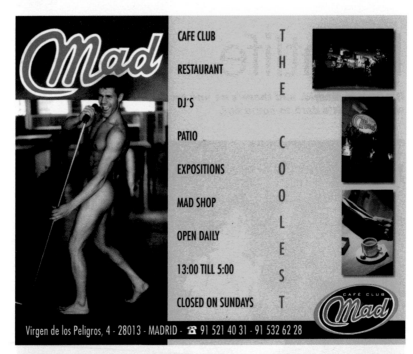

Taking the night air: *terrazas*

Whenever the heat arrives Madrileños head for the open air tables of the city's many late-night *terrazas*. Certain parts of Madrid have become particularly associated with them. Often they are open plazas, conveniently traffic free. Other *terrazas*, though, are to be found in more unlikely settings like the central reservation of the Paseo de la Castellana, which is hardly relaxing but buzzes on summer nights in time to raucous '80s pop.

Among the best areas for night-time *terrazas* are the **Plaza Dos de Mayo**, the **Plaza de Chueca**, hub of the gay scene, **Plaza de la Cebada** and **Calle Argumosa** in Lavapiés. Places on the Castellana tend to be glitzier, with dressy punters and more expensive drinks. These terrazas tend to run only from May to mid-September, but many smaller places are more flexible, and may pull out their tables whenever there's a heatwave.

Bavaro

Paseo del Prado, next to Jardín Botánico (no phone). Metro Atocha/bus all routes to Atocha.
Open noon-4am daily. **Map H9**
A leafy *terraza* situated between the Atocha roundabout and the palatial Ministry of Agriculture. Pink neon lights

welcome fun seekers to its many tables, which fill up as soon as temperatures begin to soar.

Bolero & Boulevard

Bolero *Paseo de la Castellana 33 (no phone)*;
Boulevard *Paseo de la Castellana 37 (91 435 54 32).
Metro Rubén Darío/bus 3, 25, 33, 39, 148, N1, N20.*
Open *May-Sept* approx 7pm-3/4am daily. **Map I2**
Arising out of the greenery in the centre of the Castellana like chic settlements in the jungle, these two big *terrazas*, separated by a few hundred metres, are in many ways two halves of the same bacchanalian beast. The atmosphere is stunningly frivolous, a crush of coquettish people, chatting through blaring Euro pop and eyeing up their peers. Regular launch parties, fashion shows and wild speciality nights – drag queen beauty contests, all sorts of daft competitions – provide the more restrained with an excuse to join the party.

La Vieja Estación

Estación de Atocha, Avda Ciudad de Barcelona, s/n (91 539 93 30). Metro Atocha/bus all routes to Atocha. **Open** *May-Sept* 10pm -5am daily.
Admission 1,000ptas Fri, Sat only. **Map H10**
A 'multi *terraza*' impressively placed in a gorge-like dip next to Atocha station, with no neighbours to inhibit loud music. It boasts an Argentinian restaurant, loads of bars, a karaoke space and a misnamed Chill Out room, playing the same frantic music as elsewhere. It's a fun place despite its theme-parkish feel, but expensive, since on top of the weekend entry fee drinks, once inside, have prices that are well above average.

the streets seem as full as ever, and in some ways the successive city 'crackdowns' could be seen as case studies in bureaucratic impotence. Madrileños simply do not pay attention to local by-laws the way Northern Europeans generally do.

Geography

Beyond the charms of the street lies a diverse array of bars and clubs: cosy liquor locales, Irish pubs, trippy chill-out bars, dance halls, salsa venues and indie and house clubs. Madrid's attitude to musical fashions is tolerant – underground sounds co-exist with dressy discos, Latin American dance and world music command the same respect as rave and dance culture.

The key to sampling night-time Madrid is mobility. People don't stay in one place for long, but keep on the move, ducking in and out of bars in a never-ending search for the perfect night. What might seem like impatience is really a healthy curiosity for what's going on elsewhere, a desire not to miss out on any of the fun.

Despite the size of the city, the main nightlife areas are manageable villages within it, for, if you're going to check out a whole string of places in one night it's best if they're within walking distance of each other. Huertas, Malasaña and Chueca are the three great 'hubs' of the nightly round, each with its own identity. Put very broadly, **Huertas** is both the smartest and the most mixed of the three, the most popular with out-of-towners, *guiris* (*see p36*) and other recent arrivals in Madrid, and the one where you're most likely to hear Spanish music, whether flamenco or camp Spanish pop. **Malasaña** attracts the youngest, grungiest crowd – they have to be, to spend so much time sitting on the pavement – and its bars are the most rock-orientated, although its northern part, around Alonso Martínez, has a more middle-of-the-road feel. **Chueca** is Madrid's gay village (*see chapter* **Gay & Lesbian Madrid**), but has also become a place to be for Madrid's trendiest, most stylish night owls of all sexual persuasions. Big club venues are often in 'intermediate' areas – such as around **Sol** – where they can be reached easily from several of the main 'village' drags.

Lavapiés is a rather more hip overshoot of Huertas, and another up and coming part of town is the cluster of bars near **Conde Duque**, around Calles de la Palma and Amaniel, which is similarly a more innovative overspill from Malasaña. Other areas include the *pijo* districts (*see below*) of **Salamanca** and Avenida de Brasil, way up the **Castellana**, and the cheap and tacky **Argüelles** and Moncloa, full of students getting off their faces before their parental curfews take effect.

Rules of engagement

From about 8pm to midnight the weekend belongs to teenagers, but as they head off home a slightly older crowd arrives, and the real thing gets underway. Bars fill up between midnight and 1am, peak time being from 2 to 4am. The fun continues into daylight hours, and after hours clubs (*see below*) allow the serious reveller to carry on well into the following afternoon. Otherwise, if you decide to call it a day,

one of the great rituals of the Madrid nights is to go for a nightcap/breakfast of thick hot chocolate and *churros*, sticks of sweet batter (*see p155*).

Loose Spanish licensing laws mean that the distinction between a bar and a club, charging admission, is often academic. Many night-time bars have a dance floor of some sort, and similarly some of the larger venues may not charge on entry, and function just as bars, on quiet nights. Equally, there's no given hour for moving on to a club, and it's quite possible to drink and dance till dawn without ever going anywhere bigger than small bars. Venues with admission normally cost about 800-1,500ptas, which usually also includes a *consumición*, a first drink, either spirits, beer or a soft drink.

Dress codes are pretty loose, although some venues have a ban on trainers (sneakers). Madrid-by-night comes to a virtual stop in August and the weeks either side of it, when only some venues stay open. The rest of the time, Friday and Saturday are the biggest nights of the week, of course, but there's a school of thought that sees Thursday as Madrid's best night out. It's a popular night, but there's enough room to move around in for everyone to be happy.

Something else that lifts the atmosphere of nocturnal Madrid above mere exuberance and into the level of camaraderie is the absence of physical threat. People are rarely aggressive, and even doormen are often personable folk, rather than the psychos in suits employed in other countries.

Club one-nighters are becoming steadily more common (*see p148*), but they still represent only one part of a very varied whole. Two venues listed in this chapter, **But** and **Reflejos**, are old-style glitzy dance halls, where you can dance pasadobles or salsa to a live band. Another possibility offered by Madrid – popular with teens – is all night (11pm-8am) disco and splash-around sessions offered from June to September at the **AquaMadrid** waterpark (*see p179*). Different kinds of special event are the **International Parties** in the opulent setting of the **Palacio de Gaviria** on most Thursday nights from September to June, aimed directly at the thousands of young foreigners living or studying in Madrid. While hardly cutting edge, they can be good ways of meeting a wide range of people (Spaniards as well as *guiris*), and fun. The organisers, **Forocio** (91 522 56 77), can provide information on forthcoming events.

Terms to know

calimocho red wine and cola (*see p143*)
caña standard, small glass of beer, around ¼ litre
combinado any spirit and soft drink mix, which often will cost the same as beer
cuba libre rum and coke
gintonic yes, a gin and tonic
marcha energy, movement, excitement. What night owls go out looking for, or maybe wanting to work off. You can say of a good place *tiene mucha marcha*, and walk out of somewhere because *le falta marcha* (it hasn't any). People who carry it with them are *marchoso/a*
pijos wealthy and well-brushed young people who go to well-brushed and expensive nightspots. Salamanca is the archetypal *pijo* area of Madrid, but there are others. *Pijos*, of course, are never cool

After hours

Madrid's hopping 'after' venues are spread around the city.
Davai *Sol & Gran Vía, p149.*
Bar de la Comedia, *Huertas & Santa Ana, p149.*
But; Goa, *both in Malasaña & Chueca, p152.*
Arena; Midday, *both in Conde Duque/Argüelles, p154.*
Space of Sound, *Chamartín, p155.*

Villa y Corte

Kathmandú

C/Señores de Luzón 3 (91 541 52 53). Metro Sol/bus all routes to Puerta del Sol. **Open** 11pm-5am Thur; 11pm-6am Fri, Sat. **Admission** *average* 600ptas incl 1 drink. **Map C7**
Distinctive orange lights signal one of Madrid's most consistently reliable venues for good dance music and a young, hip crowd. For a small fee you can savour an imaginative mix of acid jazz and deep house, career around the dancefloor (cleverly cooled by an overhead stream of cold air), or relax in its sweaty back room, awash with conversation and resinous smoke. Still the club to beat.

Manzanares clubland

Madrid is at a crossroads in its relationship with dance culture. Things expanded rapidly in the mid-'90s, with clubs like Kathmandú and Bali Hai introducing a generation to drum'n'bass, deep house and techno. More recently, things have reached a plateau, and in some cases regressed – Bali Hai has closed, and there are mutterings of discontent among DJs and promoters about the conservative tastes of Spanish youth. It's true that for a big city Madrid has a limited dance music scene, and rock and pop dominate the airwaves. Even so, the position is more positive than people like to admit, with a talented crew of local DJs coming through with their own distinctive styles.

Despite all the cynicism, Madrid has something that a lot of clubbers would kill for – a small, committed network of venues, DJs and clubbers devoted to the cause. Better still, the scene is very lacking in the sort of commercialism prevalent elsewhere. Clubs and bars open because of the owners' belief in what they're doing, rather than through a desire for a merchandising empire. And compared to places where dance music is already firmly established there's a greater excitement and intimacy. Once you've found the key places it's easy to meet people, talk to DJs, and find out about events.

The best way to check out what's going on is to pick up the free magazine *AB*, available in many of the street fashion shops in Malasaña (*see pages 160-1*); alternatively, drop into *AMA Records* (*see page 171*), pick up fliers and talk to the friendly gang, some of whom speak English. It's also worth looking out for the re-emergence of the Jazzin' Club DJ collectives, who have connections with AMA, but are currently taking a breather.

Below is one idea of how to squeeze the weekend until the pips squeak; of course, it's in the nature of the beast that new places are always opening, while others can just as suddenly close...

Thursday
11.15pm After dinner at **Soldemersol** (*see p119*) stroll up to **El Mosquito** to sample the chilled out drum'n'bass and friendly people.
12.15am Down to suave **La Trocha** for *caipirinhas* before popping up the hill to **Kasbah**, where cool sounds and the psychedelic ambience soon exercise the desired effect.
2.30am Wander over to **Cardamomo** for a bit of salsa sensuality.
3.30am Suitably carnivalled out, grab a cab up to **Nature** for a dose of trancey fluoro-mayhem.
6am Stumble into the street thinking about trees in Brazil. It's only 6.30 when you get home. Early.
Friday
11pm Decide to see what's going on in Chueca. Swagger into **La Bardemcilla** for cinematic

refreshments and celluloid charm. Order a *ración* of *huevos de oro* to keep going.
11.45pm Looking for a bit more action, head round the corner to **Star's**, where there's still room to sit down and appreciate the pumping house music.
12.30am Still peckish, so wander up to **La Carreta** for a no-nonsense bit of Argentinian meat and a healthy bottle of house Rioja.
1.30am Saunter over to Alonso Martínez, and think about going into **Kingston's**, but in the end can't resist the reggae vibrations of **Big Bamboo**.
2am Flag down a cab and head towards **Kathmandú** for some excruciatingly funky house.
3.30am Wander up to the Gran Vía and into **Soma**.
5am Discover **Davai** around the corner, and decide to give it a go.
6am When Davai shuts join the crowd that's heading across Plaza de España to **Arena** for a stretch of after hours indulgence.
8.30am Can't swing that feather boa any longer, and decide to call it a day. Catch the Metro home.
Saturday/Sunday
1am Breeze into **Café de la Palma** for a while to have a tranquil drink.
1.45am Nearby, find **Radar** resounding to quality techno, and enjoy its trippy lights.
3am Motor down to **Soul Kitchen** in a taxi, quickly slip on a basketball top and then get on down to the muscular hip hop.
4am Wander down to the incandescently funky **El Sol**.
6am Walk to the nearby **Chocolatería San Ginés**, for much needed intake of *chocolate con churros*.
7am Rejuvenated, arrive at **Goa** and join the queue. Wait patiently with the chatting ravers before hitting the already-packed floor.
10.30am Move on to **Midday**, where recently-risen ravers supplement the well-worn night-time clubbers.
1pm Take a cab up to **Space of Sound**, where things are only just starting to kick off.
2.30pm Incapable of dancing anymore, slope off to the Metro. Awake from an intense dream on the train to discover you're at the end of the line in Aluche.
4pm Give up, and get cab home. Collapse into bed, and remain unconscious for two days until landlady breaks down door and administers emergency first aid.

The Castellana

Living

Avda de Brasil 7 (no phone). Metro Santiago
Bernabéu/bus 5, 43, 149, N20. **Open** 11.30pm-5.30am
Thur-Sat; 11.30pm-3.30am Sun.
In the heart of *pijo* country, this is as close as you'll get to a
dance club in this part of Madrid. The music's extremely loud,
the lights are very bright, but it could bring dance music to
the Castellana at last. There's a dress code (no trainers).

Moby Dick

Avda de Brasil 5 (91 555 72 81).
Metro Santiago Bernabéu/bus 5, 43, 126, 149, N20.
Open 10pm-5am Mon-Sat.
During the week this is a venue for live music, but at weekends it often hosts DJ sessions leaning to reggae and rap. It's
a cross between a bar and a club, dark, packed and very hot
inside, with a *guiri* and Spanish clientele. *See also page 206.*

Sol & Gran Vía

Davai

C/Flor Baja 1, corner Gran Vía 59 (91 547 57 11).
Metro Plaza de España/bus all routes to Plaza de España.
Open 11pm-5am daily; *after hours* 9am-2pm Sun.
Admission *average* 700ptas. **Map D5**
A landmark on the Madrid club scene when it opened in
1997, Davai began as home to the Jazzin' Club, one of the
more progressive DJ crews in the city, but lately has moved
away from their drum'n'bass agenda to a more populist
house message. Even so, it still attracts a crowd up for a
night of hedonistic abandon, under the tutelage of DJs Tribe
and Joker. They describe their musical proclivities as tech-
house and techno-soul, but are not averse to other sounds as
well. If the killer tunes get too much there's a chill out space,
and a balcony with strategic views of the dance floor.

Joy Eslava

C/Arenal 11 (91 366 37 33). Metro Ópera, Sol/bus all
routes to Puerta del Sol. **Open** 11.30pm-5am Mon-Thur;
11.30pm-6am Fri, Sat. **Admission** 1,500ptas Mon-Thur;
2,000ptas Fri, Sat, incl 1 drink. **Map D7**
Is this a disco or what? In an 1850s theatre in the centre of
Madrid, this is probably the city's most famous nightspot:
the music changes slightly, but otherwise it remains the same
ostentatiously glitzy disco, decked out in velvet and gold and
attracting an untrendy crowd – men in smart suits and
jewelled ladies out on the town. Flamenco shows and salsa
act as brief interludes amid commercial dance music. Careful
where you sit – some tables are reserved for important folk.

Palacio de Gaviria

C/Arenal 9 (91 526 60 69/91 526 60 70).
Metro Sol/bus all routes to Puerta del Sol. **Open** 11pm-
5.30am Mon-Sat; 9.30pm-2am Sun. **Admission** *average*
2,000ptas incl 1 drink. **Map D7**
Believe the hype, this place is a real nineteenth-century
palace, a beautiful space that's open to anyone with a decent
pair of shoes and a well-stocked wallet. A broad staircase
leads you up to the first floor landing, and once there you
have the run of a dozen or so rooms, all furnished in appro-
priately baroque style. Oriental rugs cover the oak floors,
chandeliers hang from the frescoed ceilings and antique
paintings line the walls, and most of the rooms indulge a different musical style. The club also hosts popular **international nights** on Thursdays, except in summer (*see pxxx*).

El Sol

C/Jardines 3 (91 532 64 90).
Metro Gran Vía/bus all routes to Gran Vía. **Open** 1.30-
5.30am Tue-Sat. **Admission** 1,000ptas. **Map E7**

The elder statesman of Madrid's clubs. On weekend nights
it's a funk phenomenon that warms up late but, once hot,
radiates an infectious party atmosphere. By 3.30 it's packed
with sexy young things losing it to a varied mix of funk, acid
jazz and hip hop. Solar powered fun – if you're beginning to
tire, it could be just the alternative energy source you're looking for. El Sol also hosts a varied mix of live music, often
before the club sessions (*see p206*).

Soma

C/Leganitos 25 (no phone).
Metro Plaza de España/bus all routes to Plaza de España.
Open 11pm-5.30am Tue-Sat. **Map D6**
Soma is a word that means much to local techno fans.
Minimalistic electronica coelesces with more acidic numbers
to form a tapestry of techno unrivalled elsewhere in Madrid.
Downstairs dimly lit tunnels wind between the two chill out
bunkers, where DJ Cocó spins down-tempo techno. It's a
unique place, eschewing musical fads to focus on sounds that
attract a dedicated alternative following. It used to be pretty much a sauna, but has recently acquired air-conditioning.

Huertas & Santa Ana

Alhambra

C/Victoria 9 (91 521 07 08).
Metro Sol/bus all routes to Puerta del Sol. **Open** 10am-
2am Mon-Thur, Sun; 10am-4.30am Fri, Sat. **Map E7**
A popular place playing traditional Spanish music and salsa
to an exuberant crowd. Very late on Saturdays it sometimes
plays *bacalao*, dull Spanish early '90s techno.

Bar de la Comedia

C/Príncipe 16 (91 521 51 64). Metro Sevilla, Sol/
bus all routes to Puerta del Sol. **Open** 7pm-4am Mon-
Thur, Sun; 7pm-5am Fri, Sat; *after hours* 5am-9am Sun.
Admission 1,000ptas incl 1 drink. **Map F8**
A crowded, fast-paced joint playing rap, rock and funk to a
20-something crowd. It's mingling and drinking at the front,
while dancing, if you can carve out a space, goes on at the
back. A special feature is an ever-present barmaid who's a
dead ringer for Uma Thurman's character in *Pulp Fiction*.

Begin the Beguine

C/Moratín 27 (no phone).
Metro Antón Martín/bus 6, 26, 32. **Open** 8pm-2.30am
Mon-Thur, Sun; 8pm-3.30am Fri, Sat. **Map G8**
A cocktail den with a musty wooden interior, lined with
dusty bottles, that makes a cosy environment in which to
imbibe the tropical concoctions it serves up. Chocolate and
pineapple are prominent ingredients, and while they're not
cheap (from 700ptas), they're big enough to share.

La Boca del Lobo

C/Echegaray 11 (91 429 70 13). Metro Sevilla, Sol/bus all
routes to Puerta del Sol. **Open** 11pm-5am daily. **Map F7**
Three levels of retro ambience in a steamy, smokey cellar,
everyone's idea of a Bohemian-intellectual dive. A student
favourite since the '60s, La Boca has rejuvenated itself several times. Musically, it could be in New Orleans, Memphis
or Buenos Aires anytime between the 1930s and now, but its
soul seems to be in the '50s. There's a bar in the foyer, a
dance floor upstairs where the wizened owner plays his
favourite records, and a cellar where those who don't know
their mambo, tango or rock'n'roll can hide their blushes.

El Burladero

C/Echegaray 19 (91 420 21 84). Metro Sevilla, Sol/bus all
routes to Puerta del Sol. **Open** 8pm-3.30am daily. **Map F8**
A packed two-storey locale off Santa Ana that's regularly
full of couples swinging each other round to flamenco, shouting *olé* and clapping. On the upper floor it's calmer, and
there's a bit more supping space.

Cardamomo

C/Echegaray 15 (91 369 07 57). Metro Sevilla, Sol/bus all routes to Puerta del Sol. **Open** 9pm-4am daily. **Map F8**
If you've got no more than a passing interest in flamenco or salsa this is an essential stop. The dancing varies from eye-catchingly sensual to reassuringly clumsy, leading to a natural question: is rhythm innate or learnt? No one here gives a fig about such theoretical niceties, and the friendly *gitano* flavour ensures the music cannot be resisted for long.

Kapital

C/Atocha 125 (91 420 39 64/91 420 29 06). Metro Atocha/bus all routes to Atocha. **Open** *afternoon session* 6pm-midnight Fri-Sun; *night session* midnight-6am Thur-Sat. **Admission** 2,000ptas. **Map G9**
Madrid's superclub, Kapital is a 'total entertainment experience' boasting seven floors of disco decadence. It's a deliberately big, gadget-laden place – there's a cashpoint and a shop selling Kapital merchandising, and drinks can only be obtained at the bar by handing over a ticket bought from one of many vending machines. The ground level hosts the main dancefloor, a wide open space filled by a mixture of ages dancing to the latest house tunes, impressively illuminated by state of the art lasers and backed by podiums where scantily-clad dancers writhe provocatively. Up above there's a series of balconies, a karaoke bar, cinema and two more dance floors, including one on the third and '70's disco on the fifth. Right at the top of the building there's a *terraza*, complete with palm trees and a retractable roof that's opened when the weather warms up. At 2000ptas to get in, it's not cheap, but it's an experience. To kap it's mega-disco feel it has special 'early' sessions (ending at midnight) aimed at teens.

Kasbah

C/Santa María 17 (no phone). Metro Antón Martín/bus 6, 26, 32. **Open** 9pm-2.30am daily. **Map F8**
The green door doesn't seem to offer much, but push it open and you're plunged into a dark cave dotted with coloured lights, psychedelic installations, and surreal murals. Kasbah is one of the hippest joints in town. At the forefront of Madrid's fledgling dance culture, it offers an eclectic vision with nights devoted to lounge listening (Thursday) and chill out (Sunday) as well as its trademark deep house and techno. It attracts a charmingly subversive crowd, sporting cool threads, laidback minds and the occasional Saint Bernard. At weekends the narrow interior makes for crowded frugging, but during the week intimate seating arrangements make Kasbah prime chatting territory.

Matador

C/de la Cruz 39 (no phone). Metro Sol/bus all routes to Puerta del Sol. **Open** 7pm-2.30am Mon; noon-2.30am Tue-Sun. **Map E8**
A camp temple to all things stereotypically Spanish, playing gypsy rumba and other Andalusian stuff and equipped with a lifesize, sequinned matador hanging from the ceiling. The bar is only small, and the mixed clientele of natives and *guiris* often spills out onto the street.

Salón de Té Damasco

C/Infante 4 (91 369 09 36). Metro Antón Martín/bus 6, 26, 32. **Open** 6pm-1amWed; 6pm-2am Thur; 6pm-4am Fri, Sat; 6pm-midnight Sun. **Map F8**
A sweet smelling Arab bar that offers teas and syrups as well as the intriguing, possibly intoxicating charms of various differently flavoured pipes to smoke.

Salón de Té Sherazade

C/Santa María 16 (no phone). Metro Antón Martín/bus 6, 26, 32. **Open** 8pm-2.30am daily. **Map F8**
A smarter, more ornate interior than Damasco, with prices to match, and a spacious open-plan area at the back where people sit on the floor Buddha-style. Expect to pay around 1,600ptas for a pipe.

Suristán

C/de la Cruz 7 (91 532 39 09). Metro Sol/bus all routes to Puerta del Sol. **Open** 10pm-5.30am daily. **Admission** 1,000ptas. **Map E7**
A buzzing space that's mainly a live venue devoted to world music, but which after gigs offers DJ sessions with a similarly wide range. The crowd is racially diverse and universally friendly. Somewhere to warm your ears, and broaden your own musical horizons. Admission is not always charged outside of concert times. *See also chapters* **Music: Rock, Roots & Jazz** *and* **Flamenco**.

Torero

C/de la Cruz 26 (91 523 11 29). Metro Sevilla, Sol/bus all routes to Puerta del Sol. **Open** 11pm-6am Tue-Sat. **Map E8**
Two straightbacked doormen bar the way to this famous Santa Ana nightspot. Getting in is free, their job is to weed out the trainer-clad riff-raff from the dressy majority. It's worth making the effort, though, as not many bars can compete with its full-on party atmosphere, or its celebrity visitors. On the opulent ground floor the best Latin sounds hold sway, while in the cellar things rock to a more housey beat.

La Trocha

C/Huertas 55 (no phone). Metro Antón Martín/bus 6, 26, 27, 32, 45. **Open** 7pm-2.30am Mon-Thur, Sun; 7pm-3.30am Fri, Sat. **Map G8**
Smooth jazz and even smoother drinks make this an ideal place to raise the moral tone of your night. There's no beer on tap, and everyone seems to drink *caipirinhas*. Sink back into the sofa, sip your smooth cocktail and check out your elegant neighbours, while pretending to gaze at the black and white prints on the walls. Genuinely refreshing.

La Latina, Rastro, Lavapiés

Down

Ronda de Toledo 1 (no phone). Metro Puerta de Toledo/bus all routes to Puerta de Toledo. **Open** 11pm-5am daily. **Admission** *average* 1,000ptas. **Map D10**
Originally based in Malasaña, Down has lately begun to use a space in Puerta de Toledo, next to the **Café del Mercado** (*see p207*), and has put the new premises to good effect with several dance floors and a hanging garden. Sadly the move hasn't resulted in much more room for the punters – it's been packed since day one – but the dance music menu is still up to scratch. Some sessions are still held in the old venue.
Branch: C/de las Minas 20 (no phone). **Map E4**

Kappa

C/del Olmo 26 (no phone). Metro Antón Martín/bus 6, 26, 32. **Open** 8pm-2am Tue-Thur, Sun; 8pm-3.30am Fri, Sat. **Map F9**
Named after the Greek letter rather than overpriced sportswear, this small, stylish place offers a safe haven from boisterous crowds and raucous music. The decor is warm, the ceilings high and the cushions deep, and the crowd are a wide, gay and non-gay mix. Playing a soothing mix of ambient and trip hop, it's a great place to sit down and chat.

El Mosquito

C/Torrecilla del Leal 13 (no phone). Metro Antón Martín/bus 6, 26, 32. **Open** 8pm-2.30am Mon-Sat; 6pm-2.30am Sun. **Map F9**
'Musical and political' is how its friendly owner likes to describe this mixed gay- and non-gay bar in Lavapiés. Leaflets on the walls advertising demonstrations, exhibitions and performances make evident its commitment to gays, squatters and film and theatre groups; its musical claims are based on the quality of its various DJs, and monthly fliers can be picked up detailing who's playing what style when. Standard sounds include drum'n'bass, funk and techno.

Flamenco? No, it's the hip hop fans at **Soul Kitchen**.

El Viajero
Plaza de la Cebada 11 (91 366 90 64).
Metro La Latina/bus 17, 18, 23, 35, 60. **Open**
bar 1-4.30pm, 9pm-3am, Tue-Sun. **Map D9**
For those in the know this second-floor rooftop *terraza* is the place to be at night as soon as things hot up. The views, elegant balcony and cool bar make it a cut above the usual street cafés, and it attracts a hip, youthful crowd. Below, there's cool music and a pool table in the bar, and Uruguayan and international food in the restaurant (*see p119*).

Malasaña & Chueca

La Bardemcilla
C/Augusto Figueroa 47 (91 521 42 56).
Metro Chueca/bus 3, 40, 149. **Open** *lunch served* noon-4.30pm Mon-Fri; *dinner served* 8pm-3am Mon-Sat.
Average 1,500ptas. **Set menu** 1,250ptas.
Credit AmEx, DC, MC, V. **Map G5**
This superior film bar in the centre of Chueca is owned by the Bardem clan, and run by Mónica, sister of Javier – one of Spain's current leading actors, and star of *Jamón Jamón* and Almodóvar's *Live Flesh*. By day it's a restaurant, but by night it becomes a film buff's bar serving themed *raciones* such as *croquetas Jamón Jamón*. It's no Planet Hollywood, as the interior's tastefully done and discretely adorned with photos of famous movie figures and the Bardem family's oeuvre. An interesting stop for fans of Spanish cinema.

Big Bamboo
C/Barquillo 42 (91 562 88 38).
Metro Alonso Martínez/bus 3, 37, 40, 149, N19. **Open** 10pm-6am Tue-Thur; 10pm-7am Fri, Sat. **Map H5**
A great place to listen to reggae. Most people are too busy getting together and feeling alright to notice, but the pictures on the wall are worth inspecting: as well as the usual celebration of His Bobness, there's amusing artwork showing rastas in incongruous settings. Its distinctly primitive open plan toilets are compensated for by cheap cocktails, such as Big Bamboo Passion: rum, vodka and cinnamon. It fills up between midnight and 12.30am, and thereafter it's packed.

But
C/Barceló 11 (91 446 42 31/91 448 06 98).
Metro Tribunal/bus 3, 40, 149, N19. **Open** 10.30pm-5am Mon, Tue, Thur; 7pm-5am Wed & Sun; midnight-5am Fri, Sat. *after hours* 5-10am Sat, Sun. **Admission** 1,000-1,500ptas incl 1 drink. **Map G4**
Not a club, a real dance hall – but whatever your prejudices about such places But is a pleasant surprise, more downtown Buenos Aires than Come Dancing. It's a big place, swirling with great music and filled with a lively crowd of all ages. The dancing's surprisingly good, and the moves range from rag time to rumba, polka to pasodoble. For the inexperienced there are also classes, including special children's lessons. Trainers are not allowed. But also has another identity, in that it hosts the **Heat** after hours sessions.

Corto Maltés
C/San Andrés 11 (no phone). Metro Tribunal/bus 3, 40, 149, N19. **Open** 9pm-3.30am daily. **Map F4**
With a great location right on Plaza Dos de Mayo, this colonnaded bar has a warm, balmy feel to it. Its real strength, though, is its music, which remains resolutely dance orientated in a *barrio* over-endowed with guitar-fixated rock bars. At weekends DJs play a seamless mix of trip hop, house and techno at noise levels still conducive to conversation.

Flamingo Club/Soul Kitchen/Goa
C/Mesonero Romanos 13 (91 532 15 24). Metro Callao, Gran Vía/bus all routes to Callao. **Map E6**
Main nights: Soul Kitchen midnight-5.30am Wed, Sat.
Admission 1,500ptas incl 1 drink.
Goa 6-10am Sat, Sun. **Admission** 1,000ptas incl 1 drink.
The Flamingo is not a club in itself, but an important venue for Madrid's repertoire of one-nighters. It hosts a range of nights at different times, but an important 'regular' is **Soul Kitchen** on Wednesdays and Saturdays, a welcome change in a city where black culture often seems disconcertingly absent. There are as many black faces as white, baseball caps and basketball wear is the order of the night and the music is a blend of hip hop and swingbeat. The icicles that hang above the dancefloor are an unfortunate reminder of how much like a kitchen it is. Still, if you can't stand the heat…

Cabarets

Amid its many other traditions, Madrid has long had a certain liking for vaguely decadent live shows.

Berlin Cabaret

Costanilla de San Pedro 11 (91 366 20 34).
Metro La Latina/bus 31, 50, 65, N13, N14.
Open 11pm-5am Mon-Thur, Sun; 11pm-6am Fri, Sat. **Admission** normally free. **Map C3**
This strange mixture of yuppy disco and lewd cabaret is an eye-opening introduction to the crude comedy and inane audience participation beloved of some Spaniards. At around 1am the mainstream music halts and the dancefloor clears, to make way for a drag queen who is met by a chorus of gross abuse. Her task is to embarrass the hecklers and regale everyone with tales from the sexual battlefield. Even if you don't fully understand the language, it's an entertaining experience, at least as a one-off.

Café del Foro

C/San Andrés 38 (91 445 37 52). Metro Bilbao/bus 3, 21, 40, 147. **Open** 7pm-3am Mon-Thur, Sun; 7pm-4am Fri, Sat. **Performance** 10pm. **Map F3**
This friendly place in Malasaña is reassuringly unchanging, hosting magic acts, hypnotists, stand-up comics, singer-songwriters and sometimes more elaborate theatre groups. Also an enjoyable music venue, mainly featuring Latin bands (*see p207*).

Candilejas

C/Bailén 16 (91 365 55 45).
Metro Opera, La Latina/bus 3, 39, 148, N13, N15.
Open 8.30pm-3am Tue-Thur, Sun; 8.30pm-5am Fri, Sat. **Admission** *average* 1,000ptas incl 1 drink. **Map C7**
For 18 years this small theatre has gone it alone, determined to preserve its artistic independence. The company's mission is to offer an alternative to what they see as the anaesthetic effect of television. They know how to have a laugh, too. Resident drag artist Absurdino is a versatile and intelligent stand up, poetry reader and storyteller; he/she is joined by sidekick Ninetto, and eccentric stage acts often inspired by literature. Having some ear for Spanish idiom adds a great deal to appreciation of the acts, but some are fairly visual.

Houdini

C/Fuencarral 21 (91 521 06 70).
Metro Gran Vía/bus all routes to Gran Vía.
Open 8.30am-3am daily. **Admission** *average* 1,000ptas incl 1 drink. **Map F5**
Not exactly a nightclub, not really a cabaret, Houdini is a temple of magic, a few steps from the Gran Vía. It has a permanent exhibition of objects connected with the occult, from kitsch portraits with moving eyes to shrunken heads and voodoo accoutrements. In the basement theatre, every kind of magic-related show can feature on the bill.

Just as central to the scene is **Goa** after hours on weekend mornings. From 6am until mid-morning the dark interior pulses to progressive house, in a session that's equally popular with a gay and straight crowd. It's probably the most popular of Madrid's after hours gigs, and you may have to queue to get in. Make sure to bring your shades –

that daylight thang can be a real drag when you come out. Later on Sunday nights the Flamingo hosts the **Shangay Tea Dance** (*see p194*).

Kingston's

C/Barquillo 29 (91 521 15 68).
Metro Chueca, Alonso Martínez/bus 3, 37, 40, 149, N19.
Open 11pm-5am daily. **Map H5**
A place that likes to think of itself as a cut above other music bars in the area: the owner has dropped reggae from the playlist, explaining it only attracted dopeheads. It now starts off with soul, moving to a funkier beat as the night progresses, and the pleasantly decorated interior attracts a slick, smartish crowd. Put your hands in the air and reach for the sky – the blue ceiling is daubed with fluffy clouds.

Maravillas/Galax

C/San Vicente Ferrer 35 (no phone). Metro Tribunal/bus 3, 40, 149, N19. **Open** 9pm-3.30am Tue-Sat. **Map E4**
A favourite of indie fans, Maravillas plays the best guitar-based music in town, specialising in Britpop and US indie bands, with some big beat and funk thrown in (but definitely no heavy metal, despite the Malasaña location). Entrance policy varies: there's sometimes an 800ptas charge, but most of the time it's free. Thursdays it hosts **Galax**, an innovative look at electronic music with DJs given freedom to indulge their own passions (highlights have included a night of Kraftwerk remixes, if that's your cup of strudel).

Mission Cleimd

C/de la Palma 29 (no phone). Metro Tribunal/bus 3, 40, 149, N19. **Open** 9pm-3am daily. **Map E4**
Dark Malasaña bar showing music videos mainly by Britpop and big beat acts. Notice how, whenever a Prodigy vid comes on, all the boys give their attention to the screen, while the girls hardly notice the depraved action and carry on talking. A suitable anteroom for Maravillas.

El no. 1

C/de las Minas 1 (no phone). Metro Noviciado/bus 147.
Open 6pm-2am Mon-Sat; 5pm-2am Sun. **Map E4**
If you're in need of a bit of calm this place is as mellow as it gets. A languid *tetería* just off Calle del Pez, it offers comfort and rejuvenation in the form of teas, fruit juices and cocktails, and living-room upholstery – big sofas and inviting armchairs. It's on two levels (upstairs is lighter, downstairs ultra violet), never very full, and has friendly service.

Pachá

C/Barceló 11 (91 447 01 28). Metro Tribunal/bus 3, 40, 149, N19. **Open** 11.30pm-5am Wed-Sat. **Admission** *average* 1,500-2,000ptas incl 1 drink. **Map G4**
Though related musically to its Ibiza namesake, Pachá is owned by the same people who run Joy Eslava. Inside it's big and camp, echoing to garage divas and house favourites and inspired by sensual dancers up on the stage. Populist in the best sense of the word, and open till late.

El Pez Gordo

C/del Pez 6 (no phone). Metro Noviciado/bus 147.
Open 7pm-2.30am daily. **Map E4**
The Fat Fish isn't flash but has an understated elegance. It boasts a good selection of wines and tapas, displayed on big blackboards at the bar. The loyal local clientele ensures the atmosphere's relaxed and friendly, making it a perfect place to try some different wines or have a pacharán or two.

Star's Café

C/Marqués de Valdeiglesias 5 (91 522 27 12). Metro Banco de España/bus all routes to Cibeles. **Open** 9.30pm-3am Mon-Thur; 9.30pm-4am Fri, Sat. **Lunch served** 2-4pm Mon-Sat, **dinner served** 8.30pm-12.30am Mon-Fri. **Average** 2,000ptas. **Set menu** 1,400-1,900ptas. **Credit** AmEx, DC, MC, V. **Map G6**

The jewel in Chueca's mixed gay-fashionable crown, this 'dance café', with its big windows overlooking the street, has the feel of a vantage point from which to view the night. Inside it's equally chic, all yellow paint, Grecian columns, high ceilings, neat tables and chairs, and the odd sofa for the weak and infirm. A great, very stylish venue, with bouncy, high-NRG house to keep the people happy. *See also p191.*

Speakeasy

C/Fernando VI 6 (no phone). Metro Alonso Martinez/bus 37, N19. **Open** 9.30pm-3.30am daily. **Map H4**
This three-level place lets women in free, so it's predictably packed to the rafters with thrifty girls and hopeful boys. There's a big dancefloor where people try and groove to naff Spanish pop, while below it there's a pub-style bar with pool and table football; the first floor is quieter and more intimate. Perennially popular with a noisy, young crowd.

Torito

C/Pelayo 4 (91 532 77 99). Metro Chueca/bus 3, 40, 149, N19. **Open** 10pm-5am daily. **Map G5**
A small, intimate Chueca bar playing only Spanish music. There's lots of interesting clutter to look at around the bar, and the owners couldn't be more friendly. Plus it has a pool table at the back.

La Vaca Austera

C/de la Palma 20 (91 523 14 87). Metro Tribunal/bus 3, 40, 149, N19. **Open** 8.30pm-3.30am Mon-Sat. **Map E4**
Another Malasaña bar offering rock music, pool and a friendly environment. It's also light enough to see who you're talking to, which may or may not be a good thing.

La Vía Láctea

C/Velarde 18 (91 446 75 81). Metro Bilbao, Tribunal/bus 3, 21, 40, 149, N19. **Open** 7.30pm-3am daily. **Map F4**
Remember the days when rock music ruled the world? No? Well you ought to get out more, specifically to Malasaña's 'Milky Way', where the past is chronicled in rockcentric terms: memorabilia, newspaper cuttings and lurid posters. It's always packed in the basement, but there's a bit more room to swing a cat upstairs. Wednesday and Thursday offer (blasphemy) DJ sessions and Brazilian sounds, respectively. Normally, needless to say, it plays rock from the '70's, '80's and '90's. Known in some circles as The Woodstock Bar.

Salamanca & the Retiro

Teatriz

C/Hermosilla 15 (91 577 53 79). Metro Serrano/bus 1, 21, 53, N1, N4. **Open** 9pm-3am daily. **Admission** normally free. *Restaurant* **Lunch served** 1.30-4.30pm, **dinner served** 9-12.30am, daily. **Average** 6,000ptas. **Credit** AmEx, DC, MC, JCB, V. **Map I4**
Madrid's principal 1980s design bar and restaurant, this former theatre, rejigged by Philippe Starck, offers two separate, carefully sculpted bars. One is discreet, with tables hidden away and surrounded by brilliantly-lit installation art; the second is in the same space as the dining room, and lives up to its name, a spectacular high-ceilinged hall with velvet curtains enclosing the old stage. Drinks aren't cheap, and it attracts a very smart Salamanca clientèle. Best of all, though are its toilets, surrounded by frosted glass, steel and mirrors, mirrors and more mirrors. Those the worse for wear shouldn't attempt them alone.

Conde Duque/Argüelles

Arena

C/Princesa 1 (91 547 66 85). Metro Plaza de España/bus all routes to Plaza de España. **Open** 6am-noon Sat, Sun. **Admission** 1,000ptas incl 1 drink. **Map D4**

A big club just off Plaza de España, which generously offers those unwilling to go home the opportunity to carry on dancing. DJ Jabato starts his sets gently with some ambient stuff, moving onto jazzy house before reaching a smooth plateau of tech house. It boasts one of the biggest dance floors in the city, which can seem desolate early on, but by 7.30am it's usually packed. At other times it often hosts live gigs.

Café de la Palma

C/de la Palma 62 (91 522 50 31). Metro Noviciado/bus 147. **Open** 4pm-3am Mon-Wed, Sun; 4pm-4am Thur; 4pm-5am Fri, Sat. **Admission** *concert nights average* 1,000ptas. **Map E4**
Currently Madrid's hottest bar, La Palma offers three separate spaces. The front bar has a cosy pub feel, behind it there's an 'alternative' room without chairs where everyone sits stoically on the floor, and on one side a passage leads off into a long hall with a classic café look, dotted with little tables. The owner's have managed to create a multi-faceted bar that is smart without being at all *pijo*, hip without being intimidating. It's popular during the week, and crowded at weekends, but always retains a sense of space, and gathers together an interesting mix of people. It's also an enterprising music venue (*see p205*).

Fresh

C/Alberto Aguilera 54 (no phone). Metro Argüelles/bus 1, 21, 44, C. **Open** 11pm-7am daily. **Admission** *average* 1,000ptas incl 1 drink. **Map C3**
A kangaroo makes an eye-catching logo outside, and the theme continues within, although no one seems to know if there is any significance to it. Fresh occupies an unlikely position – formerly the home of Deep, a much lamented acid-jazz club – an island of noise amid residential calm, and is open very late. It offers pretty stolid mainstream dance music, but that doesn't trouble the flirtatious student crowd.

Midnight/Nature/Midday

C/Amaniel 13 (91 547 25 25). Metro Noviciado, Plaza de España/bus 147, N16, N17, 18. **Map D4**
Main sessions: **Nature** midnight-6am Thur. **Admission** *average* 1,000ptas.
Midday 9am-3pm Sun. **Admission** *average* 1,000ptas.
This venue no longer hosts its earlier Midnight sessions on Fridays and Saturdays, but slightly confusingly that's the only name normally visible over the door. No matter, it continues as the home of two of the most irreplacable sessions for dedicated Madrileño clubbers. **Nature** is where sparks fly on a Thursday night. Kicking trance, thumping beats and a chemically-enhanced public make for one of the wildest club nights in Madrid, with music that builds relentlessly up and up until it seems like the place is going to explode.
Midday is just as much a name that strikes fear into lesser clubbers, Madrid's classic Sunday social. While others are asleep or maybe at Mass, a hardy band of hedonistic souls are dancing the day away to a wicked selection of progressive house. Operating at this time it's an interesting phenomenon – some people have obviously been going since midnight, others appear freshly showered and pristinely dressed, having just got up. Once inside its dark throbbing womb, Sunday lunch seems a strange and distant concept.

Radar

C/Amaniel 22 (no phone). Metro Noviciado, Plaza de España/bus all routes to Plaza de España. **Open** 8pm-4.30am daily. **Map D4**
The most underground of Madrid's music bars. Its owner, a bespectacled techno-baron called Seve, is devoted to non-commercial, futuristic music. Radar, however, indulges several different specialist audiences – Wednesday: noise, industrial, experimental; Thursday: accessible techno; Friday: electronica; Saturday: a mixture of dance genres. The bar itself is a purist's heaven – minimalist, never too packed and home to musicians and aficionados of fringe sounds.

Dancing's not frowned upon, but the music is more a vehicle for cerebral motion than high jinks. So leave your sequinned tops and whistles at home and bring along a penchant for Kraftwerk. You might meet robots in the toilets.

Reflejos
C/Galileo, 7 (no phone). Metro San Bernardo/bus 2, 21, 61, N18. **Open** 8pm-3.30am Thur-Sun. **Map D3**
A spot of Latino colour amidst the quiet of Calle Galileo, a dance hall with a touch of sleaze. The mischievous Peruvian owner has turned it into an eclectic celebration of all things South American – dance, cuisine, shows and that famous indigenous ritual, um, stripping. On Thursdays there are dance lessons, Fridays see live salsa, Saturdays recorded dance music, and on Sunday there's Latino food available, and shows to go with it.

Siroco
C/San Dimas 3 (91 593 30 70).
Metro San Bernardo/bus 21, 147, N19. **Open** 9.30pm-3am Tue-Thur; 10pm-5.30am Fri, Sat. **Map E4**
More of a club than a bar, although it's a close run thing. Its varied music policy takes in everything from '70s disco

and '90's rock to tech house, breakbeat and **Ridim**, Thursday's weekly hip hop mélange. It's easy to miss out on good music here, which is sometimes not well advertised, so keep a look out for what's coming up. It also hosts live gigs (*see p206*).

Elsewhere

Space of Sound
Estación de Chamartín (91 733 35 05/ 902 104 028). Metro Chamartín/bus 5, 80, N20. **Open** 7am-noon Sat, Sun.
It may be built over a railway station, but this club looks and feels most like an airport terminal. The stark interior has a wide dance floor, flanked on one side by rows of airport lounge seats, where club victims can be seen sleeping off the effects of the night, although how they manage to blot out the incredibly loud and monotonous music is another thing. It doesn't fill up for hours, but with such static, uninvolving *bacalao* (crude Spanish techno), it's not surprising that people only come here when more danceable places shut their doors.

Late/early eating

With so many people wandering around the streets at night, Madrid naturally has plenty of places where night owls can stave off attacks of the hungers. Representing a great Spanish tradition of late-night indulgence are *churrerías* and *chocolaterías*, places where you can fill up with delicious, warming, freshly-made cups of hot chocolate and sweet cakes to dunk in them as the sun comes up.

Bar Farras
C/Mayor 28 (no phone).
Metro Sol/bus all routes to Puerta del Sol. **Open** 8am-4am Mon-Fri; 2pm-8am Sat, Sun. **Map D7**
Nothing fancy, but this little bar, overseen by its plump, jovial owner Julio, turns out good *bocadillos* and *raciones* into the night for an assorted mix of taxi drivers, ravers and insomniacs. With a mean *lomo* sandwich, this makes a perfect refuelling stop on the way from Huertas or Chueca to the Kathmandú.

Bar Estocolmo
C/de la Palma 72 (no phone). Metro Noviciado/bus 147. **Open** 8pm-2.30am daily. **Map E4**
'How d'you like your phallic imagery, sir?' If it's in the form of glossy photos of pork then this is your place. A lone Swedish flag flutters outside the 'Bar Stockholm', but it's the explicit colour pics that draw in the passer-by, with their depictions of Danish sausages, pittas and Carlsberg. In fact, the only Swedish thing about it is the Absolut vodka it serves, in various flavours. With good high-fat fare, this is a fine place to launch a pre-emptive strike on that hangover.

La Busca
C/Huertas 74 (no phone). Metro Antón Martín/bus 6, 26, 32. **Open** 9am-2.30am Mon-Thur; 9am-3.30am Fri; 11am-3.30am Sat, Sun. **Map G8**
A recently-opened Huertas bar that's a good late-night call-in for bocadillos, beers and morish canapé-style tapas.

La Carreta
C/Barbieri, 10 (91 532 70 42).
Metro Chueca/bus 3, 40, 149, N19. **Lunch served** 1-5pm, **dinner served** 8.30pm-5am, daily. **Average** 3,500ptas. **Credit** AmEx, MC, V. **Map F6**
This Argentinian restaurant in Chueca serves pasta, fish and lamb, and some of the best steak you'll ever eat. On Fridays and Saturdays between midnight and 4am it presents shows that including dancing, tangos and stand up comics, which you can enjoy while you chew your *churrasco*.

Chocolatería Muñiz
C/Calatrava 3 (no phone).
Metro Puerta de Toledo/bus 3, 17, 18, 23, 41, 60, 148, C. **Open** 6.30pm-11am daily. **Map C9**
A classic little place that's been there forever, an ideal stop off in La Latina for something warming on the way home from all-night partying.

Chocolatería San Ginés
Pasadizo de San Ginés 11 (91 365 65 46).
Metro Opera, Sol/bus all routes to Puerta del Sol.
Open 7pm-7am daily. **Map D7**
A Madrid institution, serving *churros y chocolate*, deep fried batter and thick hot chocolate through the city nights since 1894. Watching people it's easy to be struck by the incongruity of the scene, with blue-rinsed old ladies sitting beside sweaty ravers, until you see they're united in the common cause of dunking their *churros* into the chocolate. By about 4am it's full of people refuelling in this traditional Madrileño way, although alcohol is available if you need stronger stuff.

Laidy Pepa
C/San Lorenzo 5 (no phone). Metro Chueca, Tribunal/bus 3, 40, 149, N19. **Open** 11pm-5am daily. **Average** 1,500ptas. **No credit cards. Map G4**
This little place opens late and stays relatively empty for the first few hours, but once the bars and clubs begin to shut the hungry hordes arrive demanding plates of its decent, filling pasta dishes.

Shopping

Clubwear or plaster saints, original jewellery, fine booze or handmade shoes: Madrid's mosaic of merchandise offers an endless variety.

In little more than a decade, Madrid has left the commercial backwaters and become a shopper's playground. A late-'80s consumer boom, coupled with other changes such as a middle-class shift to the suburbs and a fast-increasing number of women in work, have all impacted on Madrileño shopping habits. The weekly stock-up at the hypermarket has become common, as has buying fashion on credit. The result has been a boom in out-of-town hypers and city shopping malls. Fears that this would lead to a decline in Madrid's mass of idiosyncratic small shops have not been groundless, but while many have gone under there are still enterprising people setting up new businesses that offer a degree of variety and personal attention that the big stores cannot match.

Where to go

The area around **Calle Preciados**, between Sol and Gran Via, is still the area most Madrileños consider the city's shopping heart, but it is by no means the only one. To the east of the centre, well-heeled **Salamanca**, especially Calles Serrano, Velázquez and Goya and the streets in between, is a hive of activity, with some of the smartest stores. Moving west across the Castellana, the **Calles Almirante** and **Conde de Xiquena** in **Chueca** are two streets with designer shops side by side. **Calle Barquillo**, meanwhile, is replete with hi-fi centres, and further into Chueca there are many gay-oriented shops. Chueca, **Calle Fuencarral** and **Malasaña** to the west form Madrid's big centre for cheap, and second-hand club fashion (*see pp160-161* **On the street**).

Calle Orense, just north of Nuevos Ministerios, has a shopping area, around the AZCA business zone, while further out in Barrio del Pilar is the massive **La Vaguada** mall. A very different shopping experience can be had at the **Rastro** (*see p167*), the Sunday flea market, in the old centre.

Sunday opening: an ongoing discussion

Until the late 1980s, only bakeries, *pastelerias* (cake shops) and shops around the Rastro could open on Sundays. The advent of hypermarkets and malls brought demands for changes in the law to allow them to trade on Sundays as well, but this aroused fierce opposition from small traders, fear-

For books, mags and vids, **Fnac**'s got the knack.

ful of being unable to compete unless they abandoned their only day off. The current situation is a truce, and may or may not change in future. Regulations vary in each of Spain's autonomous regions: in Madrid 'large spaces' (big stores and malls) can open on eight Sundays and four other holidays each year. Sundays chosen usually include all four prior to Christmas, and the first in other months (opening days are well advertised). Shops selling 'cultural goods', such as **Vip's**, **Fnac** and **Crisol**, can open every Sunday.

Sales & tax refunds

Sales run through January, February, July and August. IVA tax (VAT) depends on the classification of the product – 7 per cent on most products, 16 per cent on some classed as luxuries – but in many stores non-EU residents can request a Tax-free Cheque on purchases of over 15,000ptas, which can be cashed at the airport on departure to reclaim VAT. Shops in the scheme have a 'Tax-Free' sticker by their doors.

One-stop shops

See above regarding **Sunday opening**.

El Corte Inglés

C/Preciados 1-4 (all branches 91 418 88 00). Metro Sol/bus all routes to Puerta del Sol. **Open** 10am-9.30pm Mon-Sat. **Credit** AmEx, DC, MC, £TC, $TC, V. **Map E7**
A Spanish institution if ever there was one, this retailing giant has long been the most complete department store in the country, and stands alone after swallowing rival Galerías Preciados in 1995. There are over 60 outlets throughout Spain, between stores and hypermarkets (called **Hipercor**). They provide virtually everything you might need, plus multilingual staff to help out lost foreigners and many useful services such as key-cutting and shoe repair. Most branches also have good food supermarkets. Some branches specialise: Castellana 85 is for things for children, toys,

After hours

For 24-hour pharmacies, *see page 257.*

7-11

C/San Bernardo 33 (no phone). Metro Noviciado. **Open** 24 hours daily. **No credit cards.**
General stores for non-sleepers and those who have simply forgotten something. General provisions, booze, newspapers and magazines. There is a large number of 7-11 branches around Madrid, particularly at petrol stations.

Vip's

Gran Vía 43 (91 559 66 21). Metro Callao, Santo Domingo/bus 1, 44, 74, 133, 148. **Open** 9am-3am daily. **Credit** AmEx, DC, MC, V. **Map D6**
The most central branch of the immensely succesful Vip's chain, which has others all over town. They are multi purpose emporia, bland but handy, offering things you might need late at night or on a Sunday afternoon: restaurants (ever more diverse, usually with a pizzeria and almost always with a kids' menu), cafés, supermarkets (pricey), books, cosmetics, records, videos, toys, film processing and newsstands. Among the books there are generally some in English.
Central branches include C/Serrano 41; C/Velázquez 84, 136; C/Fuencarral 101; Glorieta de Quevedo 9.

sports, hardware and DIY, and also has a whole floor devoted to computers and IT; Serrano 47 has mainly fashion, shoes, jewellery and cosmetics; and Fuencarral 118 sells books, CDs and videos.
Main branches: Paseo de la Castellana 71, 85; C/Princesa 42; C/Goya 76; C/Raimundo Fernández Villaverde 79; C/Fuencarral 118; C/Serrano 47; Centro Comercial La Vaguada; **Hipercor** Centro Comercial Méndez Alvaro; more branches in suburbs.

Fnac

C/Preciados 28 (91 595 61 00).
Metro Serrano/bus 44, 75, 133, 146, 147. **Open** 10am-9.30pm Mon-Sat; noon-9.30pm Sun, public holidays.
Credit AmEx, MC, £$TC, V. **Map E7**
Not really a complete one-stop shop, but this huge French-owned emporium has an enormous range of books, CDs, videos, magazines, Spanish and foreign newspapers, computers and software, mostly at discount prices and displayed in a convenient, ultra-modern fashion. There is a limited stock of books in English and French, a photo-developing service and a ticket agency (*see chapter* **Services**).

Marks & Spencer

C/Serrano 52 (91 520 00 00).
Metro Serrano/bus 1, 9, 19, 51, 74. **Open** 10am-9pm Mon-Sat. **Credit** MC, TC, V. **Map J2**
M&S is well established in Madrid and successful with Spaniards as well as British residents and visitors, who will be pleased to know that store cards from back home can be used here, as can gift vouchers.
Branches: Centro Comercial La Vaguada (91 730 38 74); Centro Comercial 'Centro Oeste' (Las Rozas); 'Parque Corredor' mall, Torrejón.

Centros Comerciales/Malls

See above regarding **Sunday opening**.

ABC Serrano

C/Serrano 61 (91 577 50 31). Metro Rubén Darío/bus 5, 9, 14, 27, 51. **Open** 10am-9.30pm Mon-Sat. **Map J2**
A chic Salamanca mall behind the ornate façade of the building that once housed the ABC newspaper. Inside it has five levels with fashion, design, gift and crafts shops, plus cafés, restaurants and ample services. Its rooftop summer terrace bar, **Top Madrid** (open till 3-4am), is popular with a well-heeled crowd. There's also a huge number of parking spaces.

Centro Comercial Arturo Soria Plaza

C/Arturo Soria 126 (91 759 76 32). Metro Arturo Soria/bus 11, 70, 120, 122, 201. **Open** 10am-9pm Mon-Sat; 10am-8pm Sun.
A comprehensive mall, less frantic than La Vaguada: inside you'll find a supermarket, florist, clothes, software, a Body Shop and several places to eat. As a radical step, it has baby-changing facilities in both the women's and men's toilets.

Centro Comercial La Vaguada

Avda de Monforte de Lemos 36 (information 91 730 10 00). Metro Barrio del Pilar/bus 49, 83, 128, 132. **Open** 10am-10pm daily; *leisure area only* 10am-3am, Mon-Sat.
Madrid's biggest mall – about 350 outlets, including a **Corte Inglés** (*see p157*), plus an entertainments floor (cinemas, a disco, a bowling alley and a mini-fairground). A drawback is its location, a long way from the centre.

El Jardín de Serrano

C/Goya 6-8 (91 577 00 12).
Metro Serrano/bus 9, 19, 21, 51, 53. **Open** 10am-10pm Mon-Sat; 10am-9pm Sun. **Map L4**
A small but ultra-chic mall. The 20 or so shops mainly offer high-fashion clothes and accessories.

Antiques

There are fascinating concentrations of antiques shops, galleries and *almonedas* (auction houses, but which also sell in the normal fashion) around the Rastro, with stock ranging from junk to real oddities. There is also a clutch of antique shops in Huertas, around Calle del Prado. The main area to head for expensive, luxury antiques is Salamanca. Streets such as Claudio Coello, Serrano, Velázquez and Jorge Juan contain around 50 prestigious shops.

Galerías Piquer

C/Ribera de Curtidores 29. Metro Puerta de Toledo/ bus 3, 17, 23, 35, C. **Open** 10.30am-2pm, 5-8pm, Mon-Fri; 10.30am-2pm Sat, Sun. **Map D9**
Twenty different antique shops in one space. Opening times may be different for the various shops.

Nuevas Galerías

C/Ribera de Curtidores 12.
Metro La Latina/bus 17, 18, 23, 35. **Open** 9am-2pm, 5-8pm, Mon-Sat; 9am-2pm Sun. **Map D9**
There are 11 different antique shops in this arcade. Opening times may differ in the various shops.

Bookshops

Fnac (*see page 157*) has an excellent general book selection. A centre of the traditional book trade is the **Calle de los Libreros** ('Booksellers' Street') off Gran Vía, with many specialist bookshops. For travel and map shops, *see page 235*.

La Casa del Libro Espasa Calpe

Gran Vía 29 (91 521 21 13). Metro Gran Vía/bus all routes to Gran Vía. **Open** 9.30am-9.30pm Mon-Sat.
Credit AmEx, DC, JCB, MC, £$TC, V. **Map F6**
Madrid's most comprehensive bookshop, this five-storey monster has a publishing house, a good English section and plenty of English teaching materials.
Branch: C/Maestro Victoria 3 (91 521 48 98).

Crisol

C/Juan Bravo 38 (91 423 82 80).
Metro Diego de León/bus 26, 29, 52, 61, C.
Open 10am-10pm Mon-Sat; 11am-3pm, 5-9pm, Sun, public holidays. **Credit** AmEx, DC, MC, V. **Map L2**
A bookshop with a bit of everything, and an efficient book-finding service. There are good English-language, foreign press and record sections, and it has a concert ticket agency.
Branches: C/Goya 18; C/Serrano 24; Paseo de la Castellana 154; C/Galileo 110; Paseo de la Habana 5.

Librería Aldeasa

Centro de Arte Reina Sofía, C/Santa Isabel 52 (91 467 84 87). Metro Atocha/bus all routes to Atocha.
Open 10am-8.45pm Mon, Wed-Sat; 10am-2.15pm Sun. **Credit** AmEx, DC, MC, V. **Map G10**
This shop in the Reina Sofía has an international range of coffee-table type books on art and photography, with others that are more theoretical. Also for sale are posters, postcards and innovative art-related design items, along with Reina Sofía souvenirs.

Librería de Mujeres

C/San Cristobal 17 (91 521 70 43).
Metro Sol/bus all routes to Puerta del Sol. **Open** 10am-2pm, 5-8pm, daily. **Credit** V. **Map D7**

The only specialised women's bookshop in Madrid, with its own publishing house, *Horas y Horas*. The children's books section is particularly good.

English-language books

Booksellers

C/José Abascal 48 (91 442 79 59). Metro Ríos Rosas/ bus 3, 12, 37, 149. **Open** 9.30am-2pm, 5-8pm, Mon-Fri; 10am-2pm Sat. **Credit** AmEx, DC, V.
As well as a full range of English-language literature, press from both sides of the Atlantic and everything an English teacher might need, Booksellers has a fine children's section and a range of videos in English. Staff are helpful, although, maybe because this is now Madrid's only solely English-language bookshop, service seems to have slipped a little of late.

The International Bookshop

C/Campomanes 13 (91 541 72 91).
Metro Opera, Santo Domingo/bus 3, 25, 39, 500.
Open *Sept-July* 10.30am-2.30pm, 4.30-8.30pm, Mon-Fri; 10.30am-3pm Sat; *Aug* 11am-3pm Mon-Sat.
No credit cards. Map D7
This popular, mainly second-hand bookshop buys and sells books in English, French, German, Italian, Portuguese and Spanish. Included are classics, bestsellers, travel guides, biographies, poetry, drama, history and sports. There's also a noticeboard advertising rooms to let, language classes and other services, mostly offered by and for resident foreigners.

Second-hand & rare books

Bookshops dealing in rare and antique books are concentrated around C/Huertas. A great place to find cheap second-hand books is the **Cuesta de Moyano**, the street that runs up to the Retiro alongside the Jardín Botánico (**Map H9**). It has a line of kiosks selling second-hand books, from rare editions to recent remainders. There are some open all week, but they're busiest on Sunday mornings. If you're in town for San Isidro, check out the **Fería del Libro Antiguo y de Ocasión** (Old & Rare Books Fair; *see pp8-9*).

Librería del Prado

C/del Prado 5 (91 429 60 91). Metro Antón Martín/bus 6, 9, 26, 32. **Open** 10am-2pm, 5-8pm, Mon-Fri; 10am-2pm Sat. **Credit** MC, V. **Map F8**
Books from the eighteenth and nineteenth centuries, and manuscripts, postcards and the like. Prices are reasonable.

Children

Clothes

Children's clothes are expensive in Spain. Adult chains such as **Zara** (*see p163*) also have imaginative children's lines.

C&A

C/Bravo Murillo 202 (91 570 32 05). Metro Estrecho/ bus 3, 43, 66, 124, 127. **Open** 10am-9pm Mon-Sat. Closed Aug 1.30-5.30pm. **Credit** MC, TC, V.
Possibly the best deals in kids' clothes and shoes anywhere in town, with exceptionally good bargains during sales.

Max Kinder

C/Carretas 19 (91 522 80 50).
Metro Sol/bus all routes to Puerta del Sol. **Open** 10am-2pm, 5-8.30pm, Mon-Sat. **Credit** MC, V. **Map E8**
The kiddies' version of the fashion store Max Moda (opposite at no.8) has a good range of trendy kidswear for ages from three months up to 16 years. Prices are often very reasonable, and there are frequently end-of-line items on sale.

On the street

With the explosion of international club culture in Madrid in the mid-'90s, the kids who go for it have taken on the trappings as well. While a few years ago the mere suggestion that stylish clothes could be second-hand would have been a joke in itself, Spanish kids now hunt out cheap clubwear with relish. Consequently there are now many little shops selling imported fashion (mainly from London or Amsterdam) and accessories, shades and jewellery. Mainly in Malasaña, especially Calle Fuencarral, they come and go with alarming frequency, not unlike the club scene they supply.

Most recently new ones have emerged in other neighbourhoods, often slightly more upmarket and selling newer, pricier first-hand stuff by named brands. Malasaña itself has recently seen the opening of the first big investment in the scene, **Mercado Fuencarral** at Calle Fuencarral 45, a three-floor complex with over 50 shops, cafés, art spaces, a cinema, hang out spots and so on.

Amano

C/Bordadores 3 (91 548 02 36). Metro Opera, Sol/bus all routes to Sol. **Open** Sept-May 10am-2pm, 4.30-8.30pm, Mon-Sat; June-Aug 10am-2pm, 4.30-8.30pm, Mon-Fri. **Credit** MC, V. **Map D7**
In a street otherwise noted for religious relics – not in the main Malasaña drag – this shop has a neo-hippie-ish but clubby feel, with wickerwork on the walls and lots of tie-dyed clothes. Jeans, dresses and knitwear make up the bulk of the stock, but there is a small range of accessories. Apart from the Spanish label Albania, clothes are mainly imported from London.

Buggin

C/Fuencarral 74 (91 522 31 21).
Metro Tribunal/bus 3, 37, 149. **Open** 11am-2pm, 5-9pm, Mon-Sat. **Credit** MC, V. **Map F4**
Originally in the Rastro, Buggin moved to the streetwear heartland a while back. A DJ's cabin provides funky rhythms while you look at the stuff on the shelves. Desso, Dickies, Freshjive, Diesel and Buggin's own make are all featured labels.

Oshkosh B'Gosh

C/Castelló 48 (91 577 73 06).
Metro Velázquez/bus 1, 21, 53, 74. **Open** 10am-2pm, 5-8pm, Mon-Fri; 10am-2pm Sat. **Credit** MC, V. **Map K4**
For parents who want their kids to look ultra-trendy, and can spare a peseta or two, Oshkosh offers a cute range of dungarees and denims for babies and kids up to age 14.

Prénatal

C/Fuencarral 17 (91 521 64 24).
Metro Gran Via/bus 3, 40, 146, 149. **Open** Sept-June 10am-1.45pm, 5-8pm, July-Aug 10am-1.45pm, 5-8.30pm, Mon-Sat. **Credit** AmEx, DC, MC, V. **Map E6**
Everything for parents and kids from pregnancy wear up to clothes for children of about eight: prams and pushchairs, Moses baskets and cots, feeding bottles and toys. It's quality stuff, but at a price. There are several other branches throughout the city.

Chill Out

C/Martin de los Heros 17 (91 542 34 06).
Metro Plaza de España, Ventura Rodriguez/bus 1, 2, 44, 74, 133 C. **Open** 10.30am-2pm, 5.30-9pm, Mon-Sat. **Credit** AmEx, MC, V. **Map C4**
Funky little shop with psychedelic décor (fuchsia walls and a green fake fur counter), selling club and street wear, mainly by Dickies and Lois, and Lee Cooper trousers. Also a good collection of colourful tops for girls, and wacky accessories.

Glam

C/Fuencarral 35 (91 522 80 54). Metro Chueca, Gran Via/bus 3, 40, 149. **Open** 10am-2pm, 5-9pm, Mon-Sat. **Credit** AmEx, DC, JCB, MC, V. **Map F5**
One of the best and most popular of the British-style club- and streetwear shops that have sprung up around Malasaña in the last few years, Glam by name and nature has an exciting, daring range of fashion, at non-hostile prices. Belts, sunglasses and many other accessories complete the range.
Branch: C/Hortaleza 62 (91 521 38 61).

Loreak Mendian

Plaza Carlos Cambronero 5 (91 523 58 11).
Metro Callao, Noviciado/bus 3, 40, 149.
Open 5-9pm Mon; 11am-2pm, 5-9pm, Tue-Sat. **Credit** AmEx, EC, MC, V. **Map E/F5**
Basque designer Loreak Mendian and his team, with shops in San Sebastián and Bilbao, have jumped on the streetwear bandwagon with their own stylish lines, including some very cool T-shirts. Other names stocked include Carhartt, 2-CKEP, Kanabeach, Droors and trainers by DC. Skaters and surfers come here for their gear. Downstairs there is a separately-run record store with the latest in dance sounds.

No Comment

C/Fuencarral 39 (91 531 19 57). Metro Chueca, Gran Via/bus 3, 40, 149. **Open** 10.30am-2.15pm, 5-9pm, Mon-Sat. **Credit** AmEx, MC, TC, V. **Map F5**
You can't miss the fluorescent green and orange front of this shop, and the clothes inside aren't sober either. Million Dollar, BTKA and Standard de Luxe are among the lines, and you can also stock up on hair dyes and other extras, or, for an unforgettable souvenir of Madrid, get a tattoo or a piercing.

Toys

The largest toy and games store in Madrid is the Paseo de la Castellana 85 branch of **El Corte Inglés** (see p157).

Bazar Mila

Gran Via 33 (91 531 87 28). Metro Callao/bus all routes to Callao. **Open** Sept-June 9.30am-8.30pm, July-Aug 10am-9pm, Mon-Sat. **Credit** AmEx, DC, JCB, MC, V. **Map E6**
A very traditional toy shop with a window stuffed with gigantic teddies and pandas, as well as train sets, modelling kits and dolls' houses. Lots more inside, too.

Imaginarium

C/Núñez de Balboa 52 (91 577 33 55). Metro Núñez de Balboa, Velázquez/bus 1, 21, 74. **Open** 10am-2pm, 5-8.30pm, Mon-Sat. **Credit** AmEx, MC, V. **Map J3**
A toy shop with a difference – there are no war toys, and the

No Comment. *Nuff said.*

Odd!
*C/León 35 (91 429 05 70). Metro Antón Martín/bus
6, 26, 32, 57.* **Open** 10.30am-2pm, 5.30-9pm, Mon-
Fri. **Credit** AmEx, MC, V. **Map F8**
A funky little shop in Huertas (a change from
Malasaña) run by four brothers and sisters. The bright,
hip clothes for men and women, some brought from
Britain, come at good prices.

Other locations
Flip *C/Mayor 19 (91 366 44 72). Metro Sol/bus all
routes to Puerta del Sol.* **Open** 10am-2pm, 5-9pm,
Mon-Sat. **Credit** AmEx, EC, MC, V. **Map D7**
Shangri-la *C/de la Palma 24 (91 531 72 49).
Metro Noviciado, Tribunal/bus 3, 40, 147, 149.*
Open 11am-2pm, 5.30-8pm, Mon-Fri; 11am-2pm Sat.
Closed Aug. **Credit** AmEx, DC, JCB, MC, V.
Map E4
Tamburi & Hereza *C/Fuencarral 43 (91 532 04
58). Metro Chueca, Tribunal/bus 3, 40, 149.*
Open 11am-2pm, 5-9pm, Mon-Sat. **Credit** AmEx,
JCB, MC, V. **Map F5**

emphasis is on educational and interactive games and toys
for young children. There are branches in many local malls.

Puck
*C/Duque de Sesto 30 (91 575 07 43).
Metro Goya, Príncipe de Vergara/bus 2, 15, 28, C.*
Open 4.30-8pm Mon; 10am-1.30pm, 4.30-8pm, Tue-Sat.
Closed Aug. **Credit** MC, V.
Wooden toys and dolls' houses for assembly at home.

Cosmetics & perfumes

Perfumerías are to be found on about every street
in Madrid, and major stores naturally carry a full
range of cosmetic and beauty products. Here are
two that are a little more unusual.

Manuel Riesgo
*C/Desengaño 22 (91 531 19 56). Metro Gran Vía/bus all
routes to Gran Vía.* **Open** 9am-1.30pm, 4.30-7.30pm,
Mon-Fri; 10am-1.30pm Sat. Closed mid-Aug. **Credit** V.
Map E6
A vision of how shopping used to be done: this incredible
shop has some 25,000 products (pigments, essences, oils,
waxes and the like) for use in the fields of beauty, pharma-
ceuticals and art.

Néctar Beauty Shops
*Centro Comercial Laurel, C/Princesa 47 (91 548 06 17).
Metro Argüelles/bus 1, 21, 44, C.* **Open** 10am-8.30pm
Mon-Sat. **Credit** AmEx, DC, JCB, MC, V. **Map C3**
Spain's answer to the Body Shop, with environmentally
friendly shampoos, bath oils, soaps, skin creams and so on.
Several more branches around Madrid.

Design & household

Aldaba
*C/Belén 15 (91 308 38 33).
Metro Chueca/bus 3, 37, 40, 149.* **Open** *Sept-June* 10am-
2pm, 5-9pm, *July-Aug* 10am-2pm, 6-9pm, Mon-Sat.
Credit AmEx, DC, MC, V. **Map G4**
A roomy shop just on the trendy side of Chueca, with a good
selection of lamps, household items and ornaments.

BD Ediciones de Diseño
*C/Villanueva 5 (91 435 06 27). Metro Retiro,
Serrano/bus 1, 9, 19, 51, 74.* **Open** 9.30am-1.30pm,
4.30-8pm, Mon-Fri; 10am-1.30pm Sat. Closed Aug.
Credit AmEx, DC, MC, V. **Map I5**
A high-style design shop much frequented by designers
and architects themselves, who come to see furniture and
other work by Spanish designers such as Oscar Tusquets
and international figures such as the Memphis group.
Often wonderful to look at (although some people feel
they've rested on their '80s laurels for the last few years),
and suitably expensive.

Casa
*C/Castelló 36 (91 575 20 86). Metro Velázquez/bus 21,
29, 52, 53.* **Open** 10am-2pm, 5-8.30pm, Mon-Sat. **Credit**
AmEx, MC, V. **Map K4**
A Portuguese chain selling bright, imaginative ranges of
kitchen and tableware, furnishings and other accessories for
the house.
Branches: C/San Bernardo 2; C/Comandante Zorita 12.

Gastón y Daniela
*C/Velázquez 42 & 47 (91 435 24 21). Metro
Velázquez/bus 1, 9, 19, 51, 74.* **Open** *July-Sept* 10am-
2pm, 5-8.15pm, *July-Aug* 10am-2pm, 4.45-8pm, Mon-Sat.
Credit AmEx, DC, MC, V. **Map J4**
The best in Madrid for high-quality fabrics, curtain materi-
als, chair coverings and so on, with many beautiful designs.
The Calle Hernani branch, near Cuatro Caminos, has ends of
lines from the plusher shops in Salamanca.
Branches: C/Velázquez 47; C/Hernani 68; C/Núñez de
Balboa 53.

La Oca
*Ronda de Toledo 1 (91 366 35 31). Metro Puerta de
Toledo/bus all routes to Puerta de Toledo.* **Open** 10am-
2pm, 5-8.30pm, Tue-Sat; 11.30am-3pm Sun. **Credit**
AmEx, MC, V.
This designer kitchen and household emporium by the
Rastro is next to a failed mall, Mercado Puerta de Toledo,
but has managed to survive alone. The range is substantial, from the inevitable Starck lemon squeezer to carpets,
lamps, and sofas. It's a great place for browsing, and often
has goods on sale.

Pamuk

*Plaza Dos de Mayo 6 (91 521 04 94). Metro Bilbao,
Tribunal/bus 21, 147, 149.* **Open** 10am-2pm, 5-9pm,
Mon-Sat. **Credit** MC, V. **Map E4**

Friendly and individual, Pamuk offers an eclectic selection
of articles for the home from around the world. Good quality products from India, China, Pakistan, Indonesia, Africa
and Andean countries fill the ample space, from folding
Indian screens and batik cloths to rugs, armchairs and sofas.

Fashion

Many fashion stores, such as **Mango** and **Zara**,
are now classed as 'large spaces', and so open on
some Sundays. *See page 156* **Sunday opening**.

Designers

If you're in the mood to splash your cash, head for Calle
Ortega y Gasset: you'll find **Gianni Versace** (91 577 37 88)
at no.10, the more affordable **Kenzo** at no.15 (91 435 65 93)
and **Giorgio Armani** (91 576 10 36) at no.16; **Emporio
Armani** (91 575 14 37) is nearby at Calle Claudio Coello 77.

Adolfo Domínguez

*C/José Ortega y Gasset 4 (91 576 00 84). Metro Núñez de
Balboa/bus 1, 9, 19, 51, 74.* **Open** 10.15am-2pm, 5-8.30pm,
Mon-Sat. **Credit** AmEx, DC, JCB, MC, V. **Map I3**

Adolfo Domínguez won his fame by bending the rules and
dressing Spanish trendsters and politicians alike in simple,
comfortable and original clothes. For the last few years his
lines have been a bit sober (and you can get sick of his trademark mousey browns), but are still very stylish.
Branch: C/Serrano 96.

Agatha Ruiz de la Prada

*C/Marqués de Riscal 8 (91 310 44 83).
Metro Alonso Martínez, Rubén Darío/bus 5, 7, 14, 27,
150.* **Open** 10am-2pm, 5-8pm, Mon-Fri; 10am-2pm Sat.
Credit AmEx, MC, V. **Map I3**

A product of the *Movida* scene, Agatha Ruiz manages to sell
to her public the kind of off-the-wall couture that seems made
only for the catwalk and those who walk on it. Circus motifs
are a favourite; she also has a range of accessories.

Jesús del Pozo

*C/Almirante 9 (91 531 3646).
Metro Chueca, Colón/bus 3, 37, 40, 149.* **Open** 11am-2pm, 5-8pm, Mon-Sat. Closed two weeks in Aug, and Sat
pm in Aug. **Credit** AmEx, MC, TC, V. **Map H5**

Designer Jesús del Pozo's exquisite locale has a feeling of
spaciousness, the clothes exude sober beauty, and the range
covers shirts, trousers, tops, dresses, suits and wedding
dresses, plus a range of accessories and cosmetics.

María José Navarro

*C/Conde de Xiquena 9 (91 523 47 98). Metro Banco,
Chueca, Colón/bus 3, 37, 40, 149 and all routes to
Recoletos.* **Open** 10.30am-2pm, 5-8.30pm, Mon-Sat. Closed
last two weeks Aug. **Credit** AmEx, MC, V. **Map H5**

Aimed at professional, independent women, María José
Navarro's clothes – mainly dresses and trouser suits – are
classic but modern, stylish, unfussy and practical with an
emphasis on greys, blacks and dark blues.

Pedro Morago

*C/Almirante 20 (91 521 66 28). Metro Chueca,
Colón/bus 3, 37, 40, 149 & all routes to Recoletos.*
Open 10.30am-2pm, 5-8.30pm, Mon-Sat. Closed Sat pm
in Aug. **Credit** AmEx, DC, MC, V. **Map H5**

Purveyor of trendy togs to the city's style-conscious footballers and many famous faces from the world of cinema,

Pedro Morago carries on a crusade against the conservative
dress habits of Spanish men with his sleek jackets. Check
out that cloth.

Robbert Max

*C/Columela 2 (91 431 23 87). Metro Retiro/bus 2, 9, 15,
19, 20, 28, 51.* **Open** 10am-1.45pm, 5-8.45pm, Mon-Sat.
Credit AmEx, EC, MC, TC, V. **Map I6**

Classy and slightly formal, but modern, Robbert Max's
clothes look equally good in a suit-and-tie work situation or
out on the town at night. Men's suits and shirts are a speciality; the women's line, aimed at 30-plus professionals, is
similarly stylish.
Branch: C/Milaneses 3 (menswear only, 91 542 35 88).

Sybilla

*C/Jorge Juan 12 (91 578 13 22). Metro Retiro,
Serrano/bus 1, 9, 19, 51, 74.* **Open** 10am-2pm, 4.30-
8.30pm, Mon-Fri; 11am-3pm, 5-8.30pm, Sat. Closed Aug.
Credit AmEx, DC, JCB, MC, V. **Map J5**

Sybilla, once labelled the *maga* (sorceress) of Spanish design,
was a celebrity figure of the *Movida*. Since then her international take-off has not been as spectacular as might have
been expected; however, she still produces exciting ranges
of accessories, shoes and bags and striking but wearable
clothes, all available in her Madrid shop.

Vacas Flacas

*C/Claudio Coello 24 (91 575 64 83). Metro Serrano/bus
1, 21, 74, 89.* **Open** 10am-2pm, 5-9pm, Mon-Sat. Closed
Aug. **Credit** AmEx, DC, JCB, MC, V. **Map J4**

'Skinny Cows' is a shop run by two young designers in
which all the clothes and accessories are made from old
stock that has been recycled, chopped up or rearranged –
dresses made from ties sewn together, or handbags made
entirely from zips. The décor itself is a mish mash of
recycled materials.

Fashion stores

Ararat

*C/Almirante 10 & 11 (91 531 81 56).
Metro Chueca/bus 5,14, 27, 37, 45.* **Open** 11am-2pm, 5-
8.30pm, Mon-Fri; *July-Aug* 11am-2pm, 5.30-9pm, Mon-Sat.
Credit AmEx, DC, JCB, MC, TC, V. **Map H5**

Innovative clothes for women by Spanish and international
designers (Bamboo, Equipment, Marina Spadafora) make
this one of the most attractive shops on Almirante. Also good
men's and kid's ranges (**Ararat Junior**). It's not cheap,
however.

Asuntos Internos

*C/Fuencarral 2 (91 532 32 99). Metro Gran Via/bus all
routes to Gran Via.* **Open** 10.30am-2pm, 5.30-9pm, Mon-Sat. **Credit** AmEx, DC, JCB, MC, V. **Map E6**

'Internal Affairs' has Armand Basi, Diesel and Charles
Jourdan clothes for men on the ground floor, while the basement contains underwear and swimwear by such names as
Amadeus, Nikos, Olaf Benz, Hom, Armani and Guess.

Blanco

*C/Mayor 14 (91 366 44 26). Metro Sol/bus all routes to
Puerta del Sol.* **Open** 10am-9pm Mon-Sat, first Sun of
month except Aug. **Credit** AmEx, DC, MC, V. **Map E7**

A fun shop with daring styles in women's clothes, shoes,
belts and bags, at very accessible prices.
Branch: Centro Comercial La Vaguada; C/Alcalá 300.

Caracol Cuadrado

*C/Justiniano 8 (91 308 47 46). Metro Alonso Martínez/bus
21.* **Open** 10.30am-2pm, 5-8.30pm, Mon-Sat. **Credit** AmEx,
MC, V. **Map H4**

For those who want to find designer rags at knock-down
prices, this could be the place. Caracol Cuadrado has many

end-of-lines by names like Moschino, Armani, Versace, Dolce
& Gabbana and so on for much less than anywhere else.
Branch: C/General Pardiñas 22 (91 576 30 30).

Ekseption

*C/Velázquez 28 (91 577 43 53). Metro Velázquez/bus 1,
9, 19, 51, 74.* **Open** 10.30am-2.30pm, 5-9pm, Mon-Sat.
Credit AmEx, DC, JCB, MC, TC, V. **Map J4**
Gaultier, Dolce & Gabanna and Sybilla are just some of the
names to be found in this imaginatively designed boutique.
Women's clothes only, plus a good selection of shoes.
Branch: C/Concha Espina 14.

Solana

*C/Bravo Murillo 14 (91 447 16 74).
Metro Quevedo/bus 16, 37, 61, 149.* **Open** 10.30am-2pm,
5-9pm, Mon-Sat. **Credit** AmEx, DC, MC, V. **Map E1**
Aimed at teens and twentysomethings, Solana's lines are
trendy and sexy, such as mini-skirts and skimpy tops in flu-
orescent colours that demand sunglasses just to look at them.
In winter, expect black. Also shoes, boots and accessories.
Branches: Puerta del Sol 6; C/Arenal 9;
C/Alberto Aguilera 60.

Mid-range

Mango

*C/Princesa 75 (91 543 54 20). Metro Argüelles/bus 1,
21, 44, 133, C.* **Open** 10.30am-8.30pm Mon-Sat. **Credit**
AmEx, DC, MC, V. **Map C2**
Immensely popular with trendy teens and young working
women, one of the big successes of Spanish retailing, the
Mango chain has a full range of smart and casual wear that
looks good and doesn't cost a bomb.
Branches: C/Princesa 68; C/Bravo Murillo 114; C/Goya
83; Centro Comercial La Vaguada; C/Hermosilla 22.

Massimo Dutti

*C/Princesa 79 (91 543 74 22).
Metro Argüelles/bus 1, 21, 44, 133, C.* **Open** Sept-July
10am-8.30pm, *Aug* 10am-2pm, 5-8.30pm, Mon-Sat.
Credit AmEx, DC, MC, V. **Map C2**
Despite the name, this isn't Italian – it's run by a young Span-
iard who began selling shirts all at one price, and now sells
a whole range of fashionable but good-value menswear.
There are several more branches around Madrid.

Zara

*C/Princesa 45 (91 541 09 02).
Metro Argüelles/bus 1, 21, 44, 133, C.* **Open** 10am-
8.30pm Mon-Sat. **Credit** AmEx, DC, MC, V. **Map C3**
Zara has more than 100 branches all over Spain and abroad.
Whatever top designers produce each season, Zara copies at
a fraction of the price within a few weeks, and men, women
and small kids are all catered for. Check buttons, zips and
seams, though, when buying. Look in the phone book for
branches around the city.

Second-hand

Second-hand clothes culture has not usually had much
appeal in Spain, but lately trendy second-hand shops have
been much more noticeable in Malasaña (*see p160* **On the
street**). Otherwise, try the **Rastro** (*see p167*).

Camaleón Usados

*C/Arenal 8 (91 523 21 63). Metro Sol/bus all routes to
Puerta del Sol.* **Open** 10am-9pm Mon-Sat, first Sun every
month except Aug. **Credit** AmEx, DC, MC, V. **Map D7**
A smartish classic clothes shop where you can find second-
hand Levi's for around 3,000ptas, original American '40s
baseball and biker's jackets, and jeans recycled into dresses. Also new jeans and jackets at fairly standard prices.
Branch: C/Postas 1.

Pepita is Dead, *poor thing.*

Estraperlo

*C/Gravina 3 (91 319 74 79). Metro Chueca/bus 3, 40,
149.* **Open** 5.30-8.30pm Mon; 11am-2.30pm, 5.30-8.30pm,
Tue-Sat. **No credit cards. Map G5**
A tiny shop in Chueca with clothes and accessories from the
'60s and '70s. Particularly good is the selection of coats and
jackets in leather and suede.

Pepita is Dead

*C/Doctor Fourquet 10 (91 528 87 88). Metro Atocha/bus
all routes to Atocha.* **Open** 11am-2pm, 5-8.30pm, Mon-
Sat. **Credit** DC, MC, V. **Map G9**
This little shop around the corner from the Reina Sofía is run
by alternative designer Cristina Guisado, with a very personal touch. Originally she sold only her own designs, but
now has new and second-hand '60s and '70s clothes and a
selection of household bits and pieces from the same era.

Fashion accessories
Lingerie & underwear

Corsetería La Latina

*C/Toledo 49 (91 365 46 22). Metro La Latina/bus 17,
18, 23, 35, 60.* **Open** 10am-1.30pm, 5-8pm, Mon-Fri.
Closed Aug. **Credit** AmEx, DC, MC, V. **Map D9**
Corsets, bras, girdles and suspenders for a race of giants. For
many years people walking along Calle Toledo have been
unable to resist pulling up in front of the window display in
sheer amazement.

¡Oh, qué Luna!

*C/Ayala 32 (91 431 37 25). Metro Serrano, Velázquez/bus
1, 74.* **Open** 10am-2pm, 5-8.30pm, Mon-Fri; 11am-2pm, 5-
8.30pm, Sat. **Credit** AmEx, DC, MC, V. **Map J3**
Very stylish, sexy underwear, nightwear and dressing
gowns for men and women, as well as sheets and bedlinen.
Branches are to be found in various malls in the suburbs.

Woman's Secret

*C/Velázquez 48 (91 578 09 21). Metro Velázquez/bus 1,
9, 19, 51, 74.* **Open** Sept-June 10.15am-8.30pm Mon-Sat;
July-Aug 10.15am-2pm, 5-8.30pm, Mon-Sat. **Credit**
AmEx, DC, EC, MC, V. **Map J4**
An excellent choice of good-quality underwear at very good
prices, and also a range of skincare products. Several more
branches around the city.

Ancient staples: ham and cheese

The range of names, sizes, shapes and prices of Spanish *embutidos* (a generic term for just about anything crammed into a skin and cured) and *fiambres* (cold meats) is amazing. There are also great variations in quality. The difference in price between *jamón serrano* (cured ham) at about 2,500ptas per kilo and *jamón de jabugo* at over 8,000ptas stems from the fact that the latter comes from pigs fed on a diet of acorns and has been cured carefully and entirely naturally for at least a year, while a lot of cheaper *serrano* is produced 'industrially'. More expensive still is *jamón ibérico* (the best is *pata negra*, 'black foot'), also acorn-fed but from the native Iberian breed of pig. These products have *denominaciones de origen* like fine wines; the same applies with the best chorizo and cured *lomo* (loin), which begin at around 4,500ptas a kilo. Others to look out for are *chorizo cular*, and *salchichón*, especially *a la pimienta*, smothered in black pepper. *Longaniza* is a hard, thin *embutido*, best when flavoured with herbs. Equally worth trying are *mojama*, dry-cured tuna, and *cecina*, dry-cured beef.

Then there are the blood sausage or black puddings, *morcilla* and the Catalan *butifarra negra*. *Morcilla de Burgos* comes stuffed with rice, whereas the thinner *morcilla de Asturias* is just blood and a little fat. Both are great fried or stewed.

Cheese/*Quesos*

Cheeses to look for

Manchego The 'standard' Spanish cheese, and as there is so much of it, quality varies hugely. It ranges from *tierno*, young and mild (even *mantecoso*, buttery), to *añejo*, fully mature. Another difference is between *Manchego semi*, semi-soft and quite creamy, and *seco*, hard and dry. An *añejo seco* is pretty strong. Some Manchego is cured (*curado*) in oil for upwards of two years, and very tangy indeed. Normal prices go from around 1,400ptas per kilo to about 3,000ptas.

Burgos, Villalón, Requesón Similar to cottage cheeses, and often eaten as dessert. They are usually quite cheap.

Cabrales A must for fans of really strong cheeses. From Asturias, made with a mix of sheep's and goat's milk and matured in caves, it's blue-veined, creamy in texture and almost spicy in taste. Good ones cost about 2,000ptas a kilo.

Idiazábal Made from pure sheep's milk in the Basque Country, smoked or unsmoked (the smoked variety can be recommended). Upwards of 1,500ptas a kilo.

Mahón A normally mild, creamy cow's milk cheese from Menorca, although there are slightly stronger *añejo* versions. Pay about 1,500ptas for a decent one.

Where to buy

In **La Cebada** market there is a very good cheese stand, no.20/21, **Magerit**.

Jamonería Ferpal

C/Arenal 7 (91 521 51 08). Metro Sol/bus all routes to Puerta del Sol. **Open** *Sept-July* 9.45am-8.45pm, *Aug* 9.45am-2pm, 5.30-9pm, Mon-Sat. **Credit** MC, V. **Map D7**
Right in the city centre, and with as good a selection as you will find anywhere of *embutidos*, hams and cheeses.

Mozzarella

C/Hortaleza 49 (91 532 49 35).
Metro Chueca, Tribunal/bus 3, 40, 149. **Open** 10am-2pm, 5-8.30pm, Mon-Fri; 10am-2pm Sat. Closed Aug.
Credit AmEx, MC, V. **Map G5**
A small shop crowded out with different cheeses, mainly from France, Switzerland and Italy. They also stock ever more cheeses from Spain (the little-known regional cheeses are fabulous), and a range of pâtés and fresh pasta.

Museo del Jamón

Carrera de San Jerónimo 6 (91 521 03 46/91 531 57 21). Metro Sol/bus all routes to Puerta del Sol.
Open 9am-midnight Mon-Sat; 10am-midnight Sun, public holidays. **Credit** MC, V. **Map E7**
The five branches of the 'Ham Museum' around the city centre are not the cheapest place to stock up on Spanish hams and cheeses, but the most spectacular. You can sample their huge stock at the bar or in their giant restaurants.

El Palacio de los Quesos

C/Mayor 53 (91 548 16 23).
Metro Opera, Sol/bus all routes to Puerta del Sol.
Open *Nov-Apr* 9am-2.30pm, 5-8.30pm, Mon-Sat. *June-Sept* 9am-2.30pm, 5.30-8.30pm, Mon-Fri; 9am-2.30pm Sat. **No credit cards. Map D8**
After the Museum of Ham, visit the Palace of Cheese. This fine old shop also has great wines and other delicacies.

Shoes & leather

An institution are the *zapaterías de muestrarios* – shops specialising in end-of-line footwear, where good-quality, top-name shoes cost from 5,000ptas. There are about 20, mostly around Calle Augusto Figueroa in Chueca. There are several more upscale shoe shops in or around Calle Almirante.

Antigua Casa Crespo
C/Divino Pastor 29 (91 521 56 54). Metro San Bernardo/bus 21, 147, 149. **Open** Sept-Apr 10am-1.30pm, 4.30-8pm, Mon-Fri; *May-mid-Aug* 10am-1.30pm, 5-8.30pm, Mon-Fri; 10am-1.30pm Sat. Closed late Aug.
No credit cards. Map E3
The most famous espadrille shop in Madrid, with every kind of traditional *alpargata*, in every size, in a shop that is itself a museum piece.

Camper
C/Ayala 13 (91 431 43 45).
Metro Serrano/bus 1, 9, 19, 51, 74. **Open** 10am-8.30pm Mon-Sat. **Credit** AmEx, DC, MC, V. **Map I3**
Camper shoes combine comfort with a rugged, chunky, casual style. There are branches in several shopping malls: check the phone book.

Los Guerrilleros
Puerta del Sol 5 (91 521 27 08). Metro Sol/bus all routes to Puerta del Sol. **Open** 9.30am-2pm, 4.30-8.30pm, Mon-Sat. **Credit** AmEx, MC, V. **Map E7**
A bargain-basement store that's known for its very silly sign (given the prices): 'Don't buy here, we're very expensive!' It's actually dead cheap, but sometimes momentarily stylish.
Branches: C/Montera 25; Plaza de Lavapiés 5.

Loewe
C/Serrano 26 & 34 (91 577 60 56).
Metro Colón, Serrano/bus all routes to Plaza de Colón. **Open** Serrano 26, 9.30am-2pm, 4.30-8.30pm, Serrano 34, 9.30am-8.30pm, Mon-Sat. **Credit** AmEx, DC, EC, JCB, MC, TC, V. **Map I4**
A world-famous Spanish leather goods company with superb-quality bags, suitcases and other accessories, as well as classic coats and jackets for men and women.
Branches: Gran Vía 8; **Hotel Palace**, Plaza de las Cortes 7.

Florists

Madrid does not have a central flower market. Gypsies set up stalls on street corners and at Metro stations (one of the biggest and best is outside the Calle Génova exit of Alonso Martínez Metro). Also recommended is **Center Blumen** – there's a branch in the Centro Comercial La Vaguada (*see page 157*), which is open every day (91 739 20 38).

Ana Millán
C/Hortaleza 55 (91 522 32 83). Metro Chueca/bus 3, 40, 149. **Open** 10am-1.45pm, 5-8pm, Mon-Fri; 10am-2pm Sat. Closed Aug. **Credit** AmEx, MC, V. **Map G5**
Say it with flowers or… undies. Ana Millán is a fully functioning florist that also sells sexy men's and women's underwear. A curious combination that works.

Martín Floristas
corner of C/San Sebastián & C/Huertas (91 429 13 32). Metro Antón Martín, Sol/bus 6, 26, 32, 57.
Open 10am-2pm, 5-8pm, Mon-Fri; 10am-2pm Sat. **Credit** AmEx, MC, V. **Map E8**

A rare construction for central Madrid – a one-storey building with garden – in a privileged location near Plaza Santa Ana. For more than a century this family business has provided Madrileños with cut flowers, floral arrangements and plants for indoors and out.

Food & drink
Chocolates, cakes & sweets

Casa Mira
Carrera de San Jerónimo 30 (91 429 88 95).
Metro Sevilla/bus all routes to Puerta del Sol. **Open** *Nov-Jan* 9.30am-2pm, 4.30-9pm, daily; *Feb-Apr, Oct* 10.30am-2.30pm, 5.30-9pm, daily; *May-July, Sept* 10.30am-2.30pm, 5.30-9pm, Mon-Sat. Closed part of July & Aug. **No credit cards. Map F7**
Going for almost 150 years, Casa Mira is a specialist in *turrón* (a type of nougat), an inseparable part of a Spanish Christmas. There's also a big selection of chocolates, marzipan, cakes and a few savouries, including *empanadas* (pies).

La Duquesita
C/Fernando VI, 2 (91 308 02 31).
Metro Alonso Martínez, Chueca/bus 37. **Open** 9.30am-2.30pm, 5-9pm, Tue-Sat; 9.30am-2.30pm Sun. Open Mon in Dec, Jan. Closed Aug. **No credit cards. Map G4**
This fabulous little *pastelería* hasn't changed much since it started in 1914 (it is sometimes used for period-piece filming), and sells wonderful chocs and seasonal cakes, with a huge range of *turrones* in the pre-Christmas period.

Horno San Onofre
C/San Onofre 3 (91 532 90 60). Metro Gran Vía/bus 3, 40, 46, 146, 149. **Open** 9am-9pm Mon-Sat; 9am-8pm Sun. **Credit** AmEx, DC, MC, V. **Map E6**
This fine old establishment is not to be missed. Everything is baked on the premises, including seasonal cakes (*torrijas* at Easter, *turrones* at Christmas, *Roscón de Reyes* for 6 January). The *tarta de Santiago* (a traditional sponge cake) is excellent, as are savouries such as *empanada gallega*.
Branches: Tahona San Onofre C/Hortaleza 9; **Horno La Santiaguesa** C/Mayor 73.

El Madroño
C/Caravaca 10 (91 527 68 43). Metro Lavapiés/bus 6, 26, 27, 32, 57. **Open** 10am-2pm, 6pm-midnight, Tue-Thur, Sun; 10am-2pm, 6pm-2am, Fri, Sat. **No credit cards. Map E9**
Perhaps the most original cake shop of all, this Lavapiés establishment serves its own liqueur, *Licor del Madroño* (a delicate, strawberry-ish invention) and cakes made from such unlikely ingredients as spinach and beetroot.

La Mallorquina
Puerta del Sol 8 (91 521 12 01). Metro Sol/bus all routes to Puerta del Sol. **Open** 9am-9.15pm Mon-Sat. Closed mid-July & Aug. **No credit cards. Map E7**
A splendid slice of local life that's been going strong for 50 years. On the ground floor is a bustling pastry shop, with a stand-up café for baked-on-the-premises cakes and savouries. Above, there's a table-service café regularly full of *señoras* chatting over excellent coffee and the best *napolitanas* in town.

El Riojano
C/Mayor 10 (91 366 44 82). Metro Sol/bus all routes to Puerta del Sol. **Open** 9am-2pm, 5-9pm, *Sept-June* daily; *July-Aug* Mon-Sat. **Credit** MC, V. **Map D7**
Since 1885 this delightful *pastelería* has been serving cakes, pastries, glacé fruits and seasonal goodies to Madrileños. All are made in the traditional way, and the presentation and all-original décor are marvellous.

Delicacies

See also page 164 **Ancient staples: ham and cheese.**

A Lareira

C/Fernando El Católico 78 (91 543 74 80).
Metro Argüelles, Moncloa/bus 16, 44, 61, C.
Open 9am-2.30pm, 5-8.30pm, Mon-Fri; 9am-2.30pm Sat.
Closed Aug. **Credit** AmEx, DC, JCB, MC, V. **Map C2**
A bewildering range of products from northern Spain: powerful cheeses from Cantabria and Asturias, crisp Ribeiro and Albariño white wines and *Orujo* (a very strong grain spirit) from Galicia, *morcillas* and chorizos from León, and many kinds of honey. Try the *hogazas* (huge loaves from Galicia).

Cuenllas

C/Ferraz 3 (91 547 19 64). Metro Plaza de España,
Ventura Rodríguez/bus 74. **Open** 9am-2pm, 5-8.30pm,
Mon-Fri; 9am-3pm Sat. **Credit** AmEx, MC, V. **Map C5**
Not really for those on a tight budget, but an excellent selection of charcuterie and smelly cheeses from Spain and abroad, pasta shells in all colours, grappa from Italy, French brandy, Scotch whisky, pâtés and much more besides.

Grape juice

Some labels and recent vintages to look out for from the principal Spanish wine regions.
Cava (Catalan sparkling wine):
Labels: Castell de Vilarnau (*brut* and *brut nature*),
Juvé i Camps Reserva Familia, Louis Vernier *brut.*
Segura Viudas *brut* and *brut reserva.*
Galician whites (Albariño & Ribeiro):
Crisp, young white wines. **Labels:** Albariños:
Condes de Albarei ('97), Martín Códax ('97); Ribeiro:
Vilerma ('95).
Navarra: Good years: '89, '93, '97.
Labels: Guelbenzu (good quality-price ratio,
particularly for '93), Chivite, Ochoa ('97), León
Marzot ('97), Piedemonte Albero ('97).
Penedès: Most important Catalan wine region, for
reds and whites. **Good years:** '93, '96.
Labels: Jean-Leon ('89), Gran Caus ('89), Albet i
Noya ('97), Can Vendrell ('97); the products of
Bodegas Torres are all reliable.
Priorat: A rising Catalan wine region, with very
good strong reds. **Labels:** Clos Martinet, Clos de
l'Obac, De Muller, Negre Scala Dei ('97).
Ribera del Duero: Good years: '88, '89, '94, '95,
'96. **Labels:** Vega Sicilia Gran Reserva ('85),
Pesquera ('94), Pago de Carraovejas ('94),
Viña Pedrosa ('97).
Rioja: Good years: '87, '91, '94, '95, '96.
Labels: Cosme Palacio ('94), Marqués de Griñón
('94), Barón de Ley (*reserva*, '91), Artadi Pagos
Viejos ('92), Campillo (*rosé*, '95), Javier San Pedro
Rández ('97), Valdemar ('97).
Rueda: Fine whites. **Good years:** '87, '96.
Labels: Marqués de Riscal, Mantel Blanco.
Txacolí (Chacolí): A young Basque wine, slightly
similar to Portuguese *vinho verde,* that has
improved enormously in the last few years. **Good
years:** '97. **Labels:** Agarre, Akarregi, Basa-Lore.
Valdepeñas: A near-universal restaurant wine in
Madrid. **Good years:** '89, '93, '95, '96.
Labels: Albali (good price-quality ratio), Casa de la
Viña ('97), Señorío de los Llanos.

La Dehesa

C/Argensola 21 (91 319 14 50).
Metro Alonso Martínez/bus 3, 37, 40, 149. **Open** 11am-
2pm, 5-8.30pm, Mon-Fri; Sat am only. Closed two weeks
in Aug. **Credit** AmEx, MC, V. **Map H4**
As well as fine wines and liqueurs, this smart shop on the north side of Chueca specialises in select Spanish and imported products. Charcuterie, fine cheeses, smoked meats and fishes, caviar, pâtés, extra virgin oils, vinegars, pastas and various types of rice are just some of the products on display in this attractive, tempting little place.

Mallorca

C/Serrano 6 (91 577 18 59). Metro Retiro, Serrano/bus
all routes to Plaza de la Independencia. **Open** 9.30am-
9pm daily. **Credit** AmEx, DC, JCB, MC, V. **Map I6**
The Mallorca shop-cafés, dotted around Madrid, are multi-purpose gourmet establishments where you can call in for a coffee and a cake, have a drink and a quick meal or pick up every kind of luxury foodstuff. Their delicatessens have a great choice of cakes and sweets, plus excellent charcuterie and ready-prepared dishes and fine cheeses, wines and *cava.* Beautiful presentation, too, although prices are to match. There are branches all over town; a few are listed below.
Branch: C/Velázquez 59 (91 431 99 09); C/Ortega y Gasset 8 (91 431 60 60); C/Comandante Zorita 39 (91 553 51 02).

Patrimonio Comunal Olivarero

C/Mejía Lequerica 1 (91 308 05 05).
Metro Alonso Martínez, Tribunal/bus 3, 21, 37, 40, 149.
Open 10am-2pm, 5-8pm, Mon-Fri, 10am-2pm Sat. Closed
Aug. **Credit** MC, V. **Map G4**
Every kind of olive oil: a vast range from all over Spain, including several that are sold only through this shop, at all grades and in quantities from two-litre bottles up to five-litre tins.

Supermarkets

Madrid's booming hypermarkets are mostly around the edge of the city, on the A2, A6 and M-30, and accessible only by car. If you're mobile and need to stock up, look for advertising for **Alcampo, Continente, Jumbo** and **Pryca.** Smaller city-centre supermarkets can cover most short-term needs. Branches of **El Corte Inglés** (*see p157*) have good (if pricey) supermarkets. *See also p156* **Sunday opening.**

Expresso

C/Bravo Murillo 16 (91 447 37 71).
Metro Quevedo/bus 16, 37, 61, 149. **Open** 9.30am-9pm
Mon-Sat. **Credit** MC, V. **Map F3**
A little more upmarket than other supermarkets in central Madrid, Expresso stocks imported items such as German beers, French, Italian and other cheeses and English tea – at a price. There are many branches around town.

Simago

C/Valencia 2 (91 467 42 08). Metro Lavapiés/bus 27, 34,
C. **Open** 9am-9pm Mon-Sat. **Credit** MC, V. **Map F10**
Simago food supermarkets always have good offers, and other sections offer kids' clothes, underwear and a big range of cheap household goods. Several branches around Madrid.

Vegetarian & health foods

Central Vegetariana

C/de la Palma 15 (91 447 80 13). Metro Tribunal/bus 3,
40, 147, 149. **Open** 10am-2pm, 5-8pm, Mon-Fri; 10am-
1.30pm Sat. Closed Aug. **Credit** MC, V. **Map E4**
Organic food, herbal medicines and natural cosmetics.

The Rastro

Browsing the stalls at Madrid's biggest crowd-puller, the Rastro.

Thought to date back five centuries, the Rastro, Madrid's teeming flea market, is a must – even if you're not a shopper, the show that develops here every Sunday is something to be seen. Keen marketgoers arrive before the rush, say around 7am, to watch the stalls being set up. It really gets going about 9am, and from 10am to 2pm it's shoulder-to-shoulder all the way down **Calle Ribera de Curtidores**. It's as much a mass hang out point as a place to buy and sell, although most people at least try to look as if they're after something.

The market is a rambling affair, and while it has traditionally been centred on Ribera de Curtidores, it is spreading outwards all the time. Stalls sprawl down Ribera de Curtidores from the main square, the **Plaza de Cascorro**, which serves as a good meeting point. Stalls towards the top mainly offer clothes and cheap jewellery, but down the hill and in the surrounding streets you can buy anything from spare car parts to a TV remote control, from real and fake antiques to '50s furniture, from second-hand clothes to the latest in bondage gear. Clothes, camping equipment, books old and new, porno films and comics, religious relics, prints, paintings, birds and lots of plain junk are all bought and sold here. Despite its image as a flea market, there are fewer second-hand goods than cheap, fairly new ones. Ribera de

Curtidores sells mostly commercial goods, while streets to the right, looking downhill, have second-hand clothes and furniture. Some parts have a reputation for fencing stolen goods. Haggling is usually restricted to very expensive items, or very cheap stuff.

Along the Rastro streets there are also permanent shops, such as the antiques galleries (*see page 159*), which are also open during the week. Other shops worth finding are **Marihuana** in Plaza del Cascorro, for groovy stuff in black, **El Transformista**, Calle Mira el Río Baja 18, for '50s designs and furniture, and **Marmota**, across the street at no.13, for second-hand clothes.

By about 1pm, the crowds have become pretty immobile, and in summer it's also very hot. This is when it's time to repair to one of the district's many bars, which get packed out (*see chapter* **Tapas**).

The Rastro is not a dangerous place, but it *is* a pickpocket's paradise. This is the one place in Madrid where they are most active: so, don't look careless or carry open bags or a wallet in a back pocket, and be aware if somebody seems to be sticking too close behind you in the crowd.

El Rastro

C/Ribera de Curtidores. Metro La Latina, Puerta de Toledo/bus 17, 18, 23, 35, 60, 148, C. **Open** dawn-approx 2pm Sun, public holidays. **Map D9-10**

Quality, Value, Service

MARKS & SPENCER

Serrano, 52. Tube: Serrano

El Linar

C/Huertas 5 (91 429 64 25). Metro Antón Martín/bus 6, 26, 32, 57. **Open** *Sept-June* 10am-8.30pm Mon-Fri, 10am-2pm Sat; *July-Aug* 10am-2pm, 5.30-8.30pm, Mon-Fri. **Credit** AmEx, DC, MC, V. **Map G8**

A full range of wholefoods and environmentally friendly cosmetics, cleaning materials and literature.

Wine & drink/*bodegas*

A *bodega*, literally a cellar, can be anything from an old tavern to a superbly stocked wine shop.

Almacén de Licores David Cabello

C/Cervantes 6 (91 429 52 30). Metro Antón Martín/bus 6, 26, 32, 57. **Open** 9.30am-2.30pm, 5-9pm, Mon-Fri; 9.30am-2.30pm, 6.30-8.30pm, Sat. **Credit** AmEx, DC, MC, TC, V. **Map G8**

This *bodega* wasn't designed with the comfort of the customer in mind – it's often hard to get in the door, such is the confusion of bottles, crates and red-nosed locals. Once across the threshold, however, the effort is worthwhile, as there's an incredible selection of wines (including 500 table wines) and spirits. Prices – chalked up outside – are extremely reasonable.

Bodegas Lafuente

C/Luchana 28 (91 448 13 52). Metro Bilbao/bus 3, 21, 40, 147. **Open** 10am-2pm, 5-8.30pm, Mon-Sat. **Credit** V. **Map G2**

Laid out like a supermarket, this cavernous wine and spirits store has a prodigious range of Spanish and foreign labels, sometimes at near-wholesale prices. It's self-service, but the staff know their stock, and are very helpful. **Branch:** C/San Bernardo 10 (91 521 25 39).

Mariano Aguado

C/Echegaray 19 (91 429 60 88). Metro Sevilla, Sol/bus all routes to Puerta del Sol. **Open** 9.30am-2pm, 5.30-8.30pm, Mon-Fri; 9.30am-2pm Sat. Closed Aug. **No credit cards. Map F8**

The name of this quiet, slightly solemn establishment only appears embossed in the doorstep, so it's easy to miss. It is partly oriented to the serious wine connoisseur, and always has lesser-known but good-quality wines from Rioja and Navarra, as well as a good selection of whites from Rueda from around 295ptas.

Mariano Madrueño

C/Postigo de San Martín 3 (91 521 19 55). Metro Callao/bus all routes to Plaza de Callao. **Open** 9.30am-2pm, 5-8pm, Mon-Fri; 10.30am-2pm Sat. Closed Aug. **Credit** MC, V. **Map D7**

This fabulous *bodega*, with wrought-iron columns and carved wooden shelves, is over 100 years old. Its selection of wines and spirits is enormous, drawn from all over Spain.

*Smashing plates at **Cántaro**.*

Regina Vini

C/Francisco de Rojas 1 (91 593 33 66). Metro Bilbao/bus 3, 21, 37, 40, 147. **Open** 10am-2pm, 5.30-8.30pm, Mon-Sat. **Credit** MC, V. **Map G3**

This smart, spacious place is a relative newcomer to the trade, but is already giving the older establishments a run for their money. It boasts an impressive stock of wines (in the cellar, with an especially good choice of reds) and spirits (on the ground floor). The staff are both knowledgeable and helpful.

Ceramics & crafts

El Arco de los Cuchilleros

Plaza Mayor 9, bajos (91 365 26 80). Metro Sol/bus all routes to Puerta del Sol. **Open** 11am-8pm Mon-Fri; 11am-9pm Sat, first Sun of month except Aug. **Credit** AmEx, MC, V. **Map D8**

An attractive small craft, jewellery, glass and gifts shop with an interesting selection of modern craftwork. It also has a gallery space that hosts innovative exhibits by Spanish craftworkers and designers. Despite its location, just off the heavily touristed Plaza Mayor, prices are extremely reasonable.

El Bazar de Doña Pila

C/Divino Pastor 31 (91 522 59 19). Metro San Bernardo/bus 21, 40, 147. **Open** 10am-1.30pm, 5-8.30pm, Mon-Sat. **Credit** AmEx, DC, JCB, MC, V. **Map E3**

One of the first shops of its kind in Madrid, this place started its life selling Mexican crafts, but it now stocks a more varied, very eye-catching range that includes papier-mâché figures, original ceramics, neo-classical busts, stylish glass, and board games, all by craft designers from Spain and many other countries. It also hosts occasional exhibitions of original work.

Cántaro

C/Flor Baja 8 (91 547 95 14). Metro Plaza de España, Santo Domingo/bus all routes to Gran Via & Plaza de España. **Open** 10am-2pm, 5-9pm, Mon-Sat. **Credit** AmEx, MC, V. **Map D5**

Conveniently situated just off the Gran Via, Cántaro sells a large range of traditional ceramic products from practically every Spanish province. Discounts are given for large purchases and commissions for specific work are accepted.

Casa Julia

C/Almirante 1 (91 522 02 70). Metro Chueca. **Open** 10am-2pm, 5-8.30pm, Mon-Fri; 10.30am-2.30pm, 5-8.30pm, Sat. **Credit** MC, V. **Map H5**

On the corner of Almirante and Barquillo, this enormously varied shop, spread over three floors, is full of decorative *objets* from Spain, Africa, Asia and elsewhere. Sculptures, ornaments, cloths and lamps are among the most outstanding items on sale, but there's also jewellery and smaller gifts. Recently it has begun to stock a lot of Spanish crafts, especially ironwork, as well as handmade furniture from Java.

Kantharos

C/Divino Pastor 6 (91 593 11 33). Metro Bilbao/bus 21, 147. **Open** 10.30am-2pm, 5-10.30pm, Mon-Fri; 10.30am-2pm Sat. Closed two weeks Aug. **Credit** AmEx, DC, JCB, MC, V. **Map E3**

This shop was once a *taberna*, and later a herbalist. Today it's a fascinating little store run by an art historian who specialises in convincing reproductions of antique and historic knick-knacks. Among the objects to be found on its shelves are jewellery, hip flasks, picture frames, candlesticks, clocks, mirrors, brass mortars and pestles and (genuine) antique maps.

The market/*el mercado*

The market is for those who want to shop for food the traditional way, who like hustle and bustle and are prepared to try out phrases like '*¿Quién da la vez?*' or '*¿Quién es el último/la última?*' – both mean 'Who's the last in the queue?' There's always an astounding range of quality and prices. The assault on the senses comes from colourful displays of fruit and vegetables, wet fish stands, delicatessens piled high with odorous cheeses and all manner of pork products, and hawkers in the doorways with bags of garlic bulbs at 100ptas.

Markets

Among the more interesting of the markets in the city are **La Cebada** – ugly to look at, but very good price-wise; **La Paz** in Salamanca, which has the most varied selection in central Madrid; **Maravillas**, in Tetuán, the biggest of them all, with a near-unbeatable range of fresh fish, and **San Miguel**, which, although very central, is of most interest for its architecture.

All markets are open from around 9am-2pm and 5-8pm Mon-Fri, and 9am-2pm Sat.

Antón Martín *C/Santa Isabel 5 (91 369 06 20). Metro Antón Martín/bus 6, 26, 32, 57.* **Map F9**

La Cebada *Plaza de la Cebada s/n (91 365 91 76). Metro La Latina/bus 17, 23, 35, 60.* **Map D9**

Chamartín *C/Bolivia 9 (91 459 49 48). Metro Colombia/bus 7, 14, 16, 29.*

Maravillas *C/Bravo Murillo 122 (91 534 84 29). Metro Alvarado/bus all routes to Cuatro Caminos.*

La Paz *C/Ayala 28 (91 435 07 43). Metro Velázquez, Serrano/bus 1, 9, 19, 51, 74.* **Map J3**

San Miguel *Plaza de San Miguel (91 548 12 14). Metro Sol/bus all routes to Puerta del Sol.* **Map D8**

Luna Creciente

C/Divino Pastor 22 (91 593 86 07).
Metro San Bernardo/bus 21, 40, 147. **Open** 11.30am-2pm, 5-9pm, Mon-Fri; 11.30am-2pm Sat. Closed Aug.
Credit AmEx, MC, V. **Map E3**
'Crescent Moon' offers an eclectic range of crafts from Asian countries, particularly South-east Asia – such as Indonesian figu-rines and batiks – along with an extensive selection of silver jewellery and fine handmade metalwork from Afghanistan.

Quetzal

C/Mayor 13 (91 365 11 69). Metro Sol/bus all routes to Puerta del Sol. **Open** 10am-2.30pm, 4.30-9pm, Mon-Sat. **Credit** AmEx, DC, JCB, MC, TC, V. **Map D7**
Madrid's foremost purveyor of Guatemalan products and textiles, plus clothes and crafts from the rest of Central and South America.

Specialities various

La Casa de la Ecología

C/de la Palma 34 (91 532 59 29).
Metro Noviciado, Tribunal/bus 3, 40, 147. **Open** 9am-2pm, 5-8pm, Mon-Fri; 10am-2pm Sat. Closed two weeks Aug. **No credit cards. Map E4**
This little Malasaña shop specialises in recycled paper products, and even sells a DIY paper-recycling kit. It also develops environmentally conscious software, and intends to go on-line with cyber-info for the ecologically concerned.

Condoms & Co

C/Colón 3 (no phone).
Metro Tribunal/bus 3, 40, 149. **Open** 11am-2pm, 5-9pm, Mon-Sat. **No credit cards. Map F5**

Not quite a condom-only emporium, because, according to the owner, 'You can't live on condoms alone'. So, as well as a full assortment of sheaths, the shop also has in stock a selection of streetwear, and sometimes holds small art exhibitions.

Galeán

C/Carretas 31 & 33 (91 521 18 94).
Metro Sol/bus all routes to Puerta del Sol. **Open** 9.30am-1.30pm, 5-8pm, Mon-Fri; 10am-2pm Sat. **Credit** EC, JCB, MC, TC, V. **Map E8**
Calle Carretas has its share of eccentric shops, and this one is a classic example: every possible type of oilcloth (popular in Spain as hard-wearing table coverings), some with engaging designs, combined with a bizarre range of orthopaedic and exercise equipment.

Macarrón

C/San Agustín 7 (91 429 68 01). Metro Antón Martín/bus 9, 19, 27, 37, 45. **Open** 9am-1.30pm, 4.30-8pm, Mon-Fri; 10am-1.30pm Sat. Closed Aug & Sat during Sept. **Credit** AmEx, DC, MC, V.
The official art materials supplier to the Círculo de Bellas Artes, patronised in its day by Dalí and Picasso. The staff are helpful, friendly and very well informed.

Sobrinas de Pérez

C/Postas 6 (91 521 19 54).
Metro Sol/bus all routes to Puerta del Sol. **Open** 9.30am-1.30pm, 4.30-8pm, Mon-Sat. Closed Sat pm Aug. **Credit** AmEx, DC, EC, MC, TC, V. **Map E7**
Everything in a religious vein: since 1867 this small but crammed establishment, one of several similar shops around Sol, has been selling model baby Jesuses, crucifixes, candles, prints and Bibles. Even if you don't buy anything, check out the fabulous display.

Music

The **Fnac** (*see page 157*) houses a comprehensive record store. There are also plans to open a **Virgin Megastore** on Calle Hortaleza (Map G5-H4).

AMA Records

C/Espíritu Santo 25 (91 521 34 89).
Metro Tribunal/bus 37, 149. **Open** 11am-2pm, 5-9pm, Mon-Fri; 5-9pm Sat. **Credit** AmEx, MC, V. **Map E4**
A small shop in Malasaña, AMA stocks the latest in dance music and is a favourite destination for local DJs. As it's also run by DJs, it has the hottest info on the underground party and club scene, plus plenty of magazines on music and club culture.

El Flamenco Vive

C/Conde de Lemos 7 (91 547 39 17).
Metro Opera/bus 3, 25, 39. **Open** 10.30am-2pm, 5-9pm, Mon-Sat. **Credit** AmEx, DC, JCB, MC, V. **Map C7**
As well as a good selection of flamenco CDs and tapes, this shop, 'Flamenco Lives', stocks books on the genre (some of them in English), and flamenco clothing and other paraphernalia.

Mad House Projects

C/de la Palma 21 (91 593 28 47).
Metro Tribunal/bus 3, 40, 149. **Open** 10.30am-2pm, 5-9pm, Mon-Sat. **Credit** AmEx, DC, EC, MC, V. **Map E4**
Specialising in multi-national imports, MHP has the full whack of dance sounds: house, techno, ambient, hip hop, trip hop, jungle, psychedelic Goa, funk and all the rest. Friendly, laid-back service.

Madrid Rock

Gran Vía 25 (91 523 26 52).
Metro Gran Vía/bus all routes to Gran Vía. **Open** 10am-10pm daily. **Credit** AmEx, MC, V. **Map E6**
The biggest general record store in Madrid, with a very complete selection of all styles of music. It often has good clear-out offers, and also sells tickets for many rock concerts, particularly in major venues (*see p176*). There are several other branches around the city.

Manzana

Plaza del Carmen 3 (91 521 40 61). Metro Sol/bus all routes to Puerta del Sol. **Open** 10.15am-2pm, 5-8.30pm, Mon-Sat. **Credit** AmEx, DC, MC, V. **Map E7**
An excellent selection of Latin music (salsa, cumbias, merengue) as well as goodish jazz, blues and world music sections. Also – rare these days – a lot of stuff on vinyl.

Musical instruments

There are several small shops selling fine handmade guitars and other instruments around the Huertas area.

Garrido Bailén

C/Bailén 19 & C/Mayor 88 (91 542 45 01).
Metro Opera/bus 3, 25, 39, 148. **Open** 10am-1.30pm, 4.30-8.15pm, Mon-Fri; 10am-1.45pm Sat. **Credit** AmEx, DC, EC, JCB, MC, TC, V. **Map C8**
Possibly the world's best musical instrument shop. It stocks everything from tiny ocarinas to Alpine horns, modern electronic keyboards and drum machines, along with every kind of traditional Spanish musical instrument.

Guitarrería F Manzanero

C/Santa Ana 12 (91 366 00 47).
Metro La Latina/bus 17, 18, 23, 35, 60. **Open** 10am-1.30pm, 5-8pm, Mon-Fri; *July* 10am-1.30pm Mon-Fri. **Credit** AmEx, DC, EC, MC, TC, V. **Map D9**
The very friendly Félix Manzanero has been making all kinds of guitars (beginners', semi-professional and professional) for around 45 years. Fans will also love the display of old and rare string instruments.

Photographic

For fast-developing shops, *see chapter* **Services**.

Aquí

Plaza Santa Ana 1 (91 532 62 09).
Metro Sevilla, Sol/bus all routes to Puerta del Sol. **Open** 9am-2pm, 5-8pm, Mon-Fri; 9am-2pm Sat. **Credit** AmEx, DC, EC, MC, TC, V. **Map E/F8**

AMA good DJ, I am. Spinning the tunes at **AMA Records**.

Olé, and all that

There's no getting away from it – Spain is a true treasure trove of kitsch, from lurid 1960s postcards to plastic bulls with velveteen hair. They just keep on producing the stuff. However, in among it all it *is* possible to find traditional craftwork that will merit more than a snigger when you show it off back home.

Almirante 23

C/Almirante 23 (91 308 12 02). Metro Chueca/bus 5, 14, 27, 37, 53. **Open** 11am-2pm, 4.30-9pm, Mon-Sat. **Credit** AmEx, DC, JCB, MC, V. **Map H5**
Basically a living room, this wonderful tack and junk shop specialises in old postcards and prints.

Almoraima

Plaza Mayor 12 (91 365 42 89). Metro Sol/bus all routes to Puerta del Sol. **Open** 10.30am-2.30pm, 4-8pm, Mon-Fri; 10.30am-2.30pm Sat. Closed Jan-Mar. **Credit** AmEx, DC, MC, TC, V. **Map D8**
Traditional fans of all descriptions and for all tastes.

Caramelos Paco

C/Toledo 52 & 55 (91 365 42 58). Metro La Latina/bus 17, 18, 23, 35, 60. **Open** 11am-3pm Sun; *Sept-June* 9.30am-2pm, 5-8.30pm, Mon-Sat; *July-Aug* 9.30am-2pm, 5-8.30pm, Mon-Fri; 9.30am-2pm Sat. **Credit** MC, V. **Map D9**
All manner of boiled sweets, including replicas of hams, sausages, figurines and giant lollipops. If you're worried about your teeth, just take a photo of the wonderful window display.

La Casa de los Chales

C/Maiquez 3 (91 409 72 39). Metro Goya, O'Donnell/bus 2, 28, 30, C and all routes to Felipe II. **Open** 9.30am-2pm, 5.30-8.30pm, Mon-Sat. **Credit** AmEx, MC, V.
Originally selling fabrics, this shop now specialises in *mantones de Manila*, traditional fringed and embroidered shawls, as well as more conventional wraps. Shawls come in all colours, and the price range is enormous. They are mainly embroidered by hand in lace, crêpe or georgette; more spectacular models come in velvet, organdie and lamé.

La Casa de las Escayolas

C/León 5 (91 429 48 50). Metro Antón Martin/bus 6, 26, 32, 57. **Open** *Sept-June* 9.30am-2pm, 5-8.30pm, Mon-Sat; *July-Aug* 10am-2pm, 5-8.30pm, Mon-Fri. **Credit** AmEx, MC, V. **Map F8**
A shop dedicated to the plaster statue trade. Pick up your scale-model reproduction of Michelangelo's *David*, and paint him bright pink in the comfort of your own home. Nearby at no.19 is the similar **Escayolas Inma**, its permanent rival.
Branches: C/Cervantes 3; C/Fernández de los Ríos 25.

Casa Jiménez

C/Preciados 42 (91 548 05 26). Metro Callao/bus all routes to Plaza de Callao. **Open** 10am-1.30pm, 5-8pm, Mon-Sat. Closed Aug & Sat pm July. **Credit** AmEx, DC, JCB, MC, TC, V. **Map E7**
The most famous shop in Madrid (and Spain) specialising in *mantones* and *mantillas* – traditional lace and embroidered shawls. Superb, beautiful pieces of workmanship cost from 5,000ptas. They're also surprisingly wearable.

Guantes Luque

C/Espoz y Mina 5 (91 522 32 87). Metro Sol/bus all routes to Sol. **Open** 10am-1.30pm, 5-8pm, Mon-Sat. **Credit** V. **Map E8**
An astonishing range of gloves, and only gloves, in all styles and at all prices. In the same family for over a century, Luque can boast famous clients such as Spanish

A professional centre selling films, renting equipment and so on; other branches are more geared to the amateur, with a good developing service. Over 12 branches around town.

Fotocasión

C/Carlos Arniches 22 (91 467 64 91).
Metro Puerta de Toledo/bus all routes to Puerta de Toledo. **Open** 4.30-8.30pm Mon; 9.30am-2pm, 4.30-8.30pm, Tue-Fri. **Credit** JCB, MC, V. **Map D10**
A treasure trove for professional and amateur photographers and camera collectors. Owner José Luis Mur is a walking encyclopaedia on anything and everything relating to cameras; he also has great offers on spare parts, new equipment and second-hand cameras, and a large stock of just-past-the-date films and materials.

Sports

Deportes Legazpi

C/Ribera de Curtidores 8 & 15 (91 527 04 37). Metro *La Latina/bus 17, 18, 23, 35, 60.* **Open** 10am-2pm, 5-8pm, Mon-Sat; 10am-2pm Sun. **Credit** MC, V. **Map D9**
A general sports shop on the Rastro that's especially hot on bargain prices for outdoor and mountain sports equipment.

Fútbol Total

C/Eloy Gonzalo 7 (902 442 433). Metro Quevedo/bus 16, 61, 149. **Open** 10.30am-2pm. 5-8.30pm, Mon-Sat; Closed Sat pm July, Aug. **Credit** AmEx, JCB, MC, V. **Map F2**
Maybe the only souvenir shop you need. A full choice of Spanish, Portuguese, Italian and English Premier league shirts, plus some from elsewhere, in a mecca for the football-loopy. Plus all kinds of other kit, videos, stickers and badges, books (in Spanish) and other memorabilia.

Stamps & coins

Every Sunday the Plaza Mayor is taken over by an avid mass of stamp and coin collectors buying, selling and eyeing each others' wares. It has also become a Sunday-morning attraction for anyone on a stroll about the city centre, whether or not they share a fascination with tarnished old pesetas, stamps of all nations and early twentieth-century share certificates. The market has diversified too, and there are now traders selling anything and everything, including old magazines, second-hand books, postcards, badges and old former-Soviet bloc military regalia – even phonecards are beginning to appear. In short, just about anything collectable is here.

Stamp & Coin Market

Plaza Mayor. Metro Sol/bus all routes to Puerta del Sol. **Open** approx 9am-2pm Sun. **Map D8**

Tobacco & smoking

Estancos (tobacco shops; *see page 261*) are found all over town; cigarettes are also sold in vending machines in bars.

La Mansión del Fumador

C/Carmen 22 (91 532 08 17). **Open** 10.30am-1.30pm, 4.40-8.30pm, Mon-Sat.
Credit AmEx, V. **Map E7**
No tobacco, but well stocked with articles such as cigar-cutters, lighters, humidifiers, pipes, ashtrays and the like.

---

showbiz divas Sara Montiel and Rocio Jurado and the bullfighter Espártaco.

Objetos de Arte Toledano

Paseo del Prado 10 (91 429 50 00).
Metro Banco de España/bus 9, 14, 27, 34, 37.
Open 9.30am-8pm Mon-Sat. **Credit** AmEx, DC, JCB, MC, TC, V. **Map G7**
If you're going to the Prado, pop into this shop (*pictured below left*) selling everything from flamenco dolls to full-size suits of armour, as well as Lladró porcelain and pearls by Majorica. Across the way in Paseo del Prado you can get the kitsch ultimate – a poster of a *torero* or a flamenco singer with your name on it.

Rhesa

Gran Via 57 (91 547 18 35).
Metro Santo Domingo/bus all routes to Gran Via.
Open 9.45am-1.30pm, 5-8.30pm, Mon-Sat. **Credit** AmEx, DC, EC, MC, TC, V. **Map D6**
Selling tack much in the line of Objetos de Arte Toledano, Rhesa also doubles up as a photo developers, and has a Spanish music section in the basement. Schlock on sale includes a wonderful line in ceramic reproductions of the Puerta del Sol, and Quixotic memorabilia such as tin hats as worn by the windmill-jouster himself. Bullfight posters with your name are printed on the spot, naturally.

Seseña

C/de la Cruz 23 (91 531 68 40). Metro Sol/bus all routes to Puerta del Sol. **Open** 10am-2pm, 4.30-8pm, Mon-Fri; 10am-2pm Sat. **Credit** AmEx, DC, EC, JCB, MC, TC, V. **Map E8**
A long-established business that's the only one left in the city specialising in traditional Madrileño capes. Ideal for the aspiring dandy. They're beautifully made, wonderfully warm, and expensive.

Services

Need a laundrette on Christmas day? There's one in town. Run out of cocktails at 5am? The city can deliver.

The world of services in Madrid is one where the traditional sits side by side with hi-tech, and the little guy pits his wits against the multinational. One pleasant aspect of life in any *barrio* is the profusion of small *locales* offering a huge range of services, from cobblers who fix shoes the way they used to (while muttering about the poor quality of modern footwear) to laser photocopying and scanning of texts on to disk. Threatening these businesses – and many are going to the wall – are all-under-one-roof chains such as **El Corte Inglés** (*see page 156*), which offer a multitude of services from heel-bars and key-cutting to e-mail and fax, all convenient, fast and, usually, cheap.

Servicio a domicilio means someone will deliver it, collect it or come to your house to repair it. *En el acto* means they do it while you wait. For car and bike hire, *see page 252*.

Clothes & accessories

Cleaning, repairs, shoe repairs

Truly self-service *lavanderías* (laundrettes) are hard to find. Although their machines are automatic, in most there will be an attendant who will probably assume that male customers want her to do their washing for them, for a small extra charge, and will often proceed as if this is the case without asking. *Tintorerías* are mainly dry-cleaners, but also offer other clothing care services (including repairs) and sometimes take in laundry. Every market and most *barrio* streets have a shoe repairer – look for *rápido* or *reparación de calzados* signs.

Calzados LG

Gran Vía 11 (91 531 82 73). Metro Gran Vía/bus all routes to Gran Vía. **Open** 9.30am-2pm, 4.30-8pm, Mon-Fri; 9.30am-2pm Sat. **Credit** AmEx, MC, V. **Map F7**
Skilled artisan shoemakers LG have a full repair service. **Branch:** C/Lope de Rueda 57 (91 573 30 30).

Lavaquick

C/Cardenal Cisneros 82 (91 447 04 22). Metro Iglesia, Quevedo/bus 3, 16, 37, 61, 149. **Open** 10am-3pm, 5-9pm, Mon-Fri; 10am-3pm, 5-7pm, Sat; 11am-3pm Sun. **No credit cards. Map F2**
Unbeatable opening times (365 days a year) and reasonable prices are the best thing about this laundrette, which has coin operated machines and other services such as dry-cleaning and ironing. Up to 5 kg costs 500ptas, up to 7 kg 700ptas. Opening times may change in the future, and there is the possibility of credit card facilities being added.

Tinte Rapi-Seco

C/Gaztambide 35 (91 543 30 32). Metro Moncloa/bus 2, 16, 44, 61, C. **Open** 8.30am-8pm Mon-Fri; 8.30am-2pm Sat. **No credit cards. Map C1**
A good dry-cleaner with opening hours more convenient than most. There's a discount of 10% if you pay in advance. A suit costs 810ptas, a quilt 1,250ptas.

Tintes Saigon

C/León 14 (91 429 49 85). Metro Antón Martín/bus 6, 26, 32. **Open** 9am-2pm, 5-8pm, Mon-Fri; 9am-2pm Sat. Closed mid-Aug. **No credit cards. Map F8**
Family-run Tintes Saigon is friendly, economical and very conveniently located in the middle of *pensión*-land. Jackets cost 750ptas, a dress 800ptas and suits or overcoats 1,250ptas. The owners also have plans to open a fully automatic coin-op laundrette nearby.

Tu Hermosa Lavandería

C/Don Felipe 4 (91 523 32 45).
Metro Tribunal/bus 3, 40, 149. **Open** 10am-9pm Mon-Sat. **No credit cards. Map F4**
Clean, pleasant and with piped music, 'Your Beautiful Laundrette' is an unusually bright and efficient laundrette that serves local residents and *pensión*-dwellers alike. A wash of up to 7kg costs 600ptas; a giant machine that can take up to 16kg of clothes costs 1,500ptas. Dryers are 100ptas for a five-minute cycle. Just don't expect to see Daniel Day-Lewis come out from the back with his mop and bucket.

Dress & costume hire

Cornejo

C/Magdalena 2 (91 530 55 55).
Metro Tirso de Molina/bus 6, 26, 32, 65. **Open** Sept-June 9am-2pm, 3-6pm, July-Aug 8am-3pm, Mon-Fri.
No credit cards.
Dress yourself up as Napoleon or Cleopatra, or find that gorilla suit you've always wanted at this historic costume-hire shop. The stock is enormous, and prices start from 8,000ptas for a weekend (Friday to Monday). Should you be swept away at the party, Cornejo also hires out wedding dresses and formal attire. There are several similar (but smaller) shops along the same street, Madrid's special party-equipment thoroughfare.

Fiestas Paco

C/Toledo 55 (91 365 27 60). Metro La Latina/bus 17, 18, 23, 35, 60. **Open** Oct-June 9.30am-2pm, 5-8.30pm, Mon-Sat; 11am-3pm Sun; July-Sept 9.30am-2pm, 5-8.30pm, Mon-Fri; 9.30am-2pm Sat. **Credit** MC, V. **Map D9**
Stock up on masks, disguises, decorations, tricks, jokes and goodies at this supermarket of silliness. Staff can also put you in touch with clowns, magicians and many other kinds of entertainer.

Menkes

C/Mesonero Romanos 14 (91 532 10 36). Metro Callao/bus all routes to Callao. **Open** 9.30am-2pm, 4.30-8.30pm, Mon-Sat. **Credit** AmEx, DC, MC, V. **Map E6**

Spanish regional costumes for hire starting from 8,500ptas for three days, and also an enormous choice of fancy dress. A theatrical costumier more than just a hire shop, it also provides made-to-measure flamenco dresses and shoes, and beautifully made ballet shoes.

Embroidery

Carmelitas Descalzas de Aravaca
Carretera de Aravaca a Húmera km 1.5 (91 307 18 74). Bus Llorente 657 from Moncloa, 563 from Aluche. **Open** *Sept-June* 10am-noon, 4-7pm, *July-Aug* 10am-1pm, 5-8pm, Mon-Fri. Closed Easter. **No credit cards.**
Few things could be more in keeping with one time-honoured conception of Spain than having a favourite piece of clothing hand-embroidered by the Barefoot Carmelite nuns. You must take the article to the convent, where you can choose the style of work you want done, and then pick it up in a few days. Designs, as one might expect, are traditional. Prices vary but are very low for the quality of the work.

Leather goods & watch repairs

Aldao
Gran Vía 15 (91 521 69 25). Metro Gran Vía/ bus all routes to Gran Vía. **Open** 9.30am-1.30pm, 5-8.30pm, Mon Fri; 9.30am-1.30pm Sat.
Credit AmEx, DC, MC, V. **Map F7**
A jeweller's, silversmith's and watch-seller. You can hand in broken watches at both branches, although Calle Velázquez (closed in August) is the specialist in repairs.
Branch: C/Velázquez 43 (91 431 46 50).

Restauraciones Peña
C/Ave María 8 (91 369 39 97). Metro Antón Martín/ bus 6, 26, 32. **Open** 9.30am-1.30pm, 4.30-8pm, Mon-Fri; 9.30am-1.30pm Sat. Closed Aug.
No credit cards. Map F9
All kinds of leather goods – bags, cases, clothes – repaired, cleaned or restored, quickly, cheerfully and with great skill.

Electrical repairs

Abatel
C/Angosta de los Mancebos 8 (91 366 70 99). Metro La Latina/bus 3, 31, 50, 65, 148. **Open** 9am-2pm, 4-7pm, Mon-Fri; 9am-noon Sat. **No credit cards. Map C8**
Specialists in video repair who also fix stereos and other electrical goods. There is no call-out charge.

Food & drink delivery

Since the 1980s Madrid has been crazy for home delivery. So, if you can't raise the energy to leave your hotel…

Motopaella
(91 459 20 10). **Open** 1-4pm, 8-11.30pm, daily. **No credit cards.**
Freshly cooked paella in around an hour. A chicken paella for three to four people costs 2,995ptas, a seafood one 3,125ptas and a mixed one 3,575ptas.

No cocine
(91 577 44 68).
Open 12.30-4pm, 8.30pm-midnight, Mon-Fri; 1-4pm, 8.30pm-midnight, Sat, Sun. **Credit** AmEx, MC, V.
This company, whose name means 'Don't cook', has deals with over a dozen restaurants – American, Chinese, Mexican, Japanese, Italian, Moroccan, Indian and Peruvian among

them – and will deliver from any of them to the customer in just 45min for 350ptas on top of the cost of the meal. Minimum order is 1,500ptas.

Telecubata
(91 447 76 65). **Open** 7pm-3am Mon-Thur, Sun; 7pm-5am Fri, Sat, public holidays. **No credit cards.**
You're planning a party or a tête-à-tête in your *pensión* room, and you suddenly realise the essential cocktails are missing. Never fear, Telecubata (a *cubata* is a rum and Coke) will speed to the rescue with a party pack of booze, ice, mixers, soft drinks, plastic cups and, yes, condoms. Prices vary but are reasonable, starting at 875ptas for a bottle of spirits; minimum order is 1,500ptas. They also send crisps, olives and the like if you really want to impress your invitees.

Telepescaíto
(91 767 05 13). **Open** 11am-4pm, 7.30pm-midnight, daily; *July-Aug* Closed Mon. **Credit** MC, V.
Flash-fried whitebait (950ptas), *pipirrana* (tuna salad) and other Andalusian dishes, plus chilled *fino* if you wish, to your door. The drawback is that it's based in north Madrid, far from the centre, so can take a while to arrive. It may open Mondays in summer in future. Minimum order 2,500ptas.

Telepizza
(91 539 41 03/902 122 122).
Open 10am-1am daily. **No credit cards.**
The idea's American, the food's Italian, but this success story is pure Spanish. Leo Fernández built an empire of 100 outlets in five years – he says the secret's in the dough. There are branches all over town; call the above number to find out the phone number of your nearest one.

Tele Sushi
(91 533 08 82).
Open noon-4pm, 8pm-midnight, daily. **No credit cards.**
A basic sushi selection can be delivered to your door anywhere in Madrid for 1,500ptas.

Hair & body care

Hairdressers

Alta Peluquería Vallejo
C/Santa Isabel 22 (91 527 44 48). Metro Antón Martín/bus 6, 26, 32. **Open** 9am-2pm, 4.30-8.30pm, Mon-Fri; 9am-1.30pm Sat. **No credit cards. Map G9**
A traditional gentlemen's barber's. It's friendly, cheap (1,100ptas) and offers good basic cuts.

Jofer
C/Galileo 56 (91 447 51 60). Metro Quevedo/bus 2, 12, 16, 61. **Open** 8am-10pm Mon-Sat. **Credit** V. **Map D2**
Reasonably priced unisex salons that also have beauty and sunbed treatments. A men's cut costs around 1,400ptas; women pay upwards of 3,000ptas. At the training school, supervised apprentices are let loose on your locks; you pay just 400ptas. There are more branches around the city.
School: Taller de Peluqueros
C/Madera 5 (91 522 59 90).

Sally Whitmore/mobile hairdresser
(91 859 50 35).
Vidal Sassoon-trained and formerly of Trevor Sorbie's London salon, Sally Whitmore is an English hairdresser who will travel anywhere in the Madrid area. Often booked up, she recommends calling at least 48 hours ahead to avoid disappointment. Minimum charge per visit is 3,000ptas; women's cut and blow costs from 5,000ptas; men's 3,000ptas; children's (under 12) 1,000ptas. Also perms and highlights.

Tattoo

Travesía de Belén 3 (91 319 61 57).
Metro Chueca/bus 3, 37, 40, 149. **Open** 2-9pm Mon-Fri;
noon-4pm Sat. **Credit** MC, V. **Map H4**
Despite the name, this is a hairdresser's – and a trendy one
at that. A wash and cut for women will be about 5,000ptas;
for men, 2,500ptas.

Tattooing & body piercing

No Comment (*see page 160* **On the street**) also
offers tattooing and piercing.

Santa Ana

C/Torrecilla del Leal 6 (91 527 76 11).
Metro Antón Martín/bus 6, 26, 32, 57.
Open 11.30am-2pm, 5-9pm, Tue-Sat. Closed some days
Aug. **No credit cards. Map F9**
Boss Richi and his fellow body-artists will tattoo or pierce
any part of your body for a reasonable price. A basic small
tattoo costs about 5,000ptas, a navel ring or stud is around
5-6,000ptas. There may be credit facilities in future.

Tatuajes Públicos y Privados

C/Pizarro 15 (91 521 34 33). Metro Noviciado/bus 147.
Open 4.30-10pm Mon-Fri. **No credit cards. Map E5**
Based in the back room of a large shop otherwise occupied
by hairdresser Miguel – who's also worth a visit – two guys
named Angel do tattoos to any design, worked out between
themselves and the customer. Service is efficient, clean and
friendly, and prices start at around 5,000ptas.

Opticians

General Optica

C/Velázquez 49 (91 575 21 95). Metro Serrano,
Velázquez/bus 1, 9, 51, 74. **Open** *Sept-June* 9.30am-2pm,
3-8.30pm, Mon-Sat; *July-Aug* 10am-2pm, 5-8.30pm, Mon-
Fri. **Credit** AmEx, DC, MC, V. **Map J4**
Glasses, contact lenses and other products all come with a
year's guarantee, and there are frequent special offers for
students and pensioners. They have a wide range of contact
lens solutions.
Branches: C/Carmen 22 (91 521 00 65); C/Preciados 22
(91 522 21 21); C/Serrano 54 (91 435 08 13); Avda de la
Albufera 115 (91 437 60 55).

Photography, photocopying, fax

Most stationers (*papelerías*) or printers
(*imprentas*) have fax and photocopying
machines. Specialist copy shops are the cheapest
option for copying, but some larger Metro
stations also have photocopiers. For camera
shops, *see chapter* **Shopping**.

Foto Sistema

Gran Vía 22 (91 521 20 63). Metro Gran Vía/bus all
routes to Gran Vía. **Open** 9.30am-8pm Mon-Fri; 9.30am-
2pm Sat. **Credit** AmEx, DC, MC, V. **Map F6**
A good-quality fast developing service, with more branches
around central Madrid.

Reprografía Moreno

C/Fernando el Católico 88 (91 543 41 61).
Metro Moncloa/bus all routes to Moncloa.
Open 9am-2pm, 4.30-8pm, Mon-Fri; 9.30am-1.30pm Sat.
No credit cards. Map C2
A large specialist copy shop that can do enlargements, colour
copying and so on, and much used by students.

Ticket agencies

Sales of tickets for concerts, theatres and so on
have become a more competitive business in
Madrid with the entry into the field of savings
banks, a trend that began in Catalonia. The most
important is the **Tel-entradas** operation of the
Caja de Cataluña, but **la Caixa** bank has
Servicaixa machines in some of its branches,
through which you can buy some tickets with a
credit card (also by phone, 902 33 22 11), and
Cajamadrid has a phoneline for sales by credit
card (902 48 84 88). However, so far the latter two
only carry tickets for a limited range of events.
Concert and other tickets are also sold at branches of **El Corte Inglés** (91 379 80 00 for ticket info,
902 40 02 22 for credit card sales) and **Crisol** bookshop (*see chapter* **Shopping**).

Fnac

C/Preciados 28 (91 595 61 00). Metro Callao, Sol/
bus all routes to Callao, Sol. **Open** 10am-9.30pm
Mon-Sat; noon-9.30pm Sun, public holidays.
Credit AmEx, DC, MC, £$TC, V. **Map E7**
The ticket desk in the foyer of this music and book super-
store sells theatre and concert tickets at list price, with no
extra commission. *See also chapter* **Shopping.**

Madrid Rock

Gran Vía 25 (91 523 26 52). Metro Gran Vía/bus all
routes to Gran Vía. **Open** 10am-10pm; *ticket sales* 10am-
3pm, 4.30-9pm, daily. **Credit** AmEx, MC, V. **Map F6**
This record shop is one of the city's main outlets for rock and
pop gig tickets. *See also chapter* **Shopping.**

Tel-entradas/Caja de Cataluña

Main branch: Paseo de Recoletos 15
(Tel-entradas 902 38 33 33). Metro Banco de
España/bus all routes to Cibeles. **Open** *office* 9am-1pm
Mon-Fri; *phoneline* 24 hours daily. **Map H5**
Caja de Cataluña savings bank has a ticket-sales service
through which you can obtain tickets for most main Madrid
theatres, some alternative venues and many concerts. There
is no commission fee. Tickets can be bought at any Caja
branch (the phone book has a full list) or by credit card with
the Tel-entradas phone line. Tickets booked by phone must
be collected at the venue just before the performance.

TEYCI

C/Goya 5-7 (91 576 45 32). Metro Colón, Serrano/
bus all routes to Plaza de Colón. **Open** 9.30am-2pm, 4-
8pm, Mon-Thur; 9.30am-8pm Fri, Sat; 9.30am-4pm Sun.
Closed Aug. **No credit cards. Map I4**
A traditional ticket agency with tickets for theatre, opera,
bullfights, football and most other events in Madrid, except
rock gigs, but with a substantial 20% commission.

Travel agents

For **TIVE**, the official student and youth travel
agency, *see page 265*.

Viajes Zeppelin

Plaza de Santo Domingo 2 (information 91 542 51 54).
Metro Santo Domingo/bus all routes to Callao. **Open** 9am-
8pm Mon-Fri; 10am-1pm Sat. **Credit** MC, V. **Map D6**
The best place to look for cheap European charter deals and
long-haul youth fares. Popular, so you may have to queue,
but service is fast and friendly.

Arts & Entertainment

Children

Waterslides and train rides... kids have fun in Madrid, even though they may not exactly be spoilt for choice.

In Spain, as in most Latin countries, babies are universally cooed over, and children are both seen and heard. Strange, then, that facilities specifically for children are so few in this country. This has little to do with the decreasing birthrate – Spain now has one of the lowest in the world – as this is a relatively new phenomenon. It's more to do with the traditional place that kids have in Spanish society: they are treated just like everyone else, and the idea of separate menus and areas for children is unthinkable. They eat the same as adults, and roam around as they wish. Hence, there is little pressure for special children's facilities to improve.

That said, things *are* gradually changing. And there's plenty of entertainment: summer, when the waterparks are open, is an especially good time for kids in Madrid, but you can find plenty of other things to keep the little terrors occupied at any time of the year.

Eating out

Bringing children to Madrid, whether for a holiday or a longer stay, means accepting a change in routine. Lunch is not eaten before 2pm, and dinner is after 9pm, making the *merienda* (tea) at 5pm or 6pm necessary. Accordingly, children go to bed much later than their Anglo-Saxon counterparts – around 10pm in the school year. In summer, this timetable – with a *siesta* during the afternoon heat – makes perfect sense, and it is not uncommon to see whole families eating out or at the funfair at midnight.

You can take your child to almost any restaurant in Madrid, but few, with the exception of **Vip's** (*see p157*), provide children's menus (or high chairs – so it's a good idea to take a buggy with you). Most will do a plain hamburger (*hamburguesa*), meatballs (*albóndigas*), chips (*patatas fritas*) and other simple dishes for kids on request. Places with child-friendly un-Spanish food include the **Hard Rock Café** (*see p113*), the **Irish Rover** (*see p137*) and all the international fast-food chains. For pizza and food delivery, *see p175*.

Sights & attractions

Of the 'Big Three' museums the **Reina Sofía** (*see pages 76-7*) is most likely to have exhibits that engage young imaginations, particularly in its temporary shows, and the **Palacio Real** (*see page 46*) impresses most children with its sheer size and opulence. The **Faro** ('lighthouse') observation tower in Moncloa (*see page 62*) is also fun. Check with tourist offices on the current state of **Acciona-Museo Interactivo de la Ciencia**, a child-friendly interactive science museum north of Madrid in Alcobendas. It is currently under renovation, and officially due to reopen in spring 1999.

Acuárium de Madrid

C/Maestro Victoria 8 (91 431 81 72). Metro Callao, Sol/bus all routes to Puerta del Sol. **Open** 11am-2pm, 5-9pm, daily. **Admission** 575ptas; under-12s 375ptas. **Credit** (for large groups only) MC, V. **Map E7**
The ground floor of this bizarre private establishment is a pet shop, specialising in tropical fish. The basement levels hold a fascinating collection of fish, reptiles and spiders.

IMAX Madrid

Parque Tierno Galván (91 467 48 00). Metro Méndez Alvaro/bus 62, 102, 148. **Shows** 11am-1pm, 4-9pm, Mon-Thur; 11am-1pm, 4pm,-midnight Fri; 11am-2pm, 4pm-midnight, Sat; 11am-2pm, 4-9pm, Sun. **Admission** 850-1,400ptas. **Credit** AmEx, MC, V.
A giant-format cinema near the Planetario (*see below*), in the same park. Unfortunately, as with other IMAX cinemas around the world, virtually all the films shown on the seven-storey-high screen are wildlife spectaculars, and of limited interest. There's also a café, restaurant and shop. Tickets can also be bought by phone via Servicaixa (902 33 22 11).

Museo de Cera (Wax Museum)

Paseo de Recoletos 41 (91 308 08 25). Metro Colón/bus all routes to Plaza de Colón. **Open** 10.30am-2.30pm, 4.30-8.30pm, Mon-Fri; 10am-8.30pm Sat, Sun, public holidays. **Admission** 900ptas; 600ptas 4-12s, over-65s. *Tren del Terror* 500ptas; *Virtual Reality* 400ptas. **No credit cards. Map I4**
A mixed-bag of scenes, from historical figures to a motley crew of current celebrities (mainly Spanish) with the inevitable horrible crimes and gory 'Tortures of the Inquisition'. Some are lifelike; others (Margaret Thatcher) laughably grotesque (OK, so lifelike in their way). It's not well labelled, so you might need to shell out for the glossy colour guide. Recent innovations include the *Tren del Terror* (tacky but popular), and the Virtual Reality Simulator.

Planetario

Parque Tierno Galván (91 467 38 98). Metro Méndez Alvaro/bus 62, 102, 148. **Shows** *mid-Sept-mid-June* 9.30am-1.45pm, 5-7.45pm, Tue-Fri; 11am-1.45pm, 5-9pm, Sat, Sun, public holidays; *mid-June-mid-Sept* 11am-1.45pm, 5-7.45pm, Tue-Sun, public holidays. **Admission** 450ptas; 200ptas 2-14s, over-65s. **No credit cards.**
Madrid's planetarium is in this relatively new park. The display is modern but in Spanish only, and even many native kids find it long, wordy and dull. Shows last around 50 minutes. The playground outside could be its saving grace.

Parks & gardens

With a thriving street culture and space at a premium, the city's squares automatically double as playgrounds. The standard of facilities for children within parks varies enormously, but improvements have been made in recent years. The central part of the **Paseo del Prado** has a safe set of wooden climbing frames and slides, and one of the city's best play areas is just inside the **Plaza de Independencia** entrance to the **Retiro**. Further afield, the **Plaza de Chamberí** and **Plaza Dos de Mayo** both have sandy play areas for toddlers (although early on Saturdays and Sundays Dos de Mayo tends to be covered in remains of the previous night's revels, until the cleaners arrive). **Plaza del Conde del Valle de Suchil**, also in Chamberí, has a newly installed play area, and further north in **Avda de Brasil** (Metro Cuzco), there is a great adventure playground. Also, on Sunday mornings **Calle Fuencarral** above Glorieta de Bilbao is closed to traffic, offering a 'safe area' for bikes and skateboards. Another option is **Parque Tierno Galván** near Méndez Alvaro, with an IMAX cinema and a planetarium (*see above*).

A favourite park ride is the **Teleférico** cable car between Casa de Campo and Parque del Oeste (*see page 62*). For more on parks, *see pages 57-60*.

Casa de Campo

Metro Lago, Batán/bus 31, 33, 39, 41, 75.
Locals tend to cluster along the southern edge of this enormous area of rough parkland, the site of major attractions such as the **Parque de Atracciones** and the **Zoo** (*see below*). There's also the boating lake with its cafés, and the swimming pools (*see chapter* **Sport & Fitness**). Be warned, though, that, particularly to the west of the lake, due to night-time prostitution in the park, you can come across a variety of discarded 'refuse' during the day. To the north towards the **Teleférico** you leave crowds and cars behind for rolling land that's ideal for walking, jogging or mountain biking. Best time for picnics is spring, when the flowers are out – in summer it's too hot, and the grass is dry and spiky.

Parque Juan Carlos I

Avda de Logroño, Avda de los Andes, Carretera de Barcelona (91 721 00 79). Metro Campo de las Naciones/bus 122. **Open** *catamaran & train* 6.30-9.30pm Tue-Fri; 11.30am-2pm, 6.30-9.30pm, Sat, Sun.
Admission 300ptas adults; 200ptas children.
Twice the size of the Retiro, Madrid's newest park offers several attractions for children and has recently become more accessible with a new Metro station. An artificial river offers fishing and rides on a catamaran, a train takes you on a tour, play areas are spread around the park and during the long, hot summer nights there are *son et lumière* spectacles at the fountains (*June-Sept* 10.30pm-midnight, Thur-Sun).

*Puppets in the **Retiro**. See page 180.*

Parque del Oeste

Metro Moncloa, Príncipe Pío/bus 21, 46, 74, 82, 133. **Map A/B1-5**
Sloping down towards the Manzanares, this is a beautiful shady park. For children its major attraction is as the starting point of the **Teleférico** cable car. End the round trip with an ice-cream at **Bruin**, or in summer join other families for an evening stroll along Pintor Rosales and refreshment at one of the many *terrazas* (*see pp133, 141*).

Parque del Retiro

Metro Retiro, Ibiza, Atocha/bus all routes to Retiro. **Map I/J7-9**
Madrid's best-loved park has many attractions for kids, most of all the boating lake. Around it you'll find street performers, puppet shows, fortune tellers and waffle vendors. There are shady cafés and tame red squirrels, and sports facilities in the south-west corner. In summer look out for concerts, and weekend shows in the puppet theatre (*see below*).

Outings

As well as the zoo and funfair, in the last few years Madrid has acquired a new answer to its summer heat: waterparks. Most rides are suited to older kids, but there are usually special sections for smaller children. For conventional pools, *see page 218*.

AquaMadrid

Carretera de Barcelona (N-II), km 15.5, San Fernando de Henares (91 673 10 13). Bus 281, 282, 284, 285 from Avda de América/by train Cercanías C-1, C-2, C-7a from Atocha to San Fernando. **Open** *June-Sept* noon-8pm Mon-Fri; 11am-8pm Sat, Sun, public holidays.
Admission *Mon-Fri* 1,300ptas; 950ptas under-12s; *Sat, Sun, public holidays* 1,600ptas; 1,200ptas under-12s.
Half-day (after 4pm) *Mon-Fri* 1,000ptas; *Sat, Sun, public holidays* 1,350ptas. **Credit** MC, V.
The oldest of Madrid's waterparks, near the airport in San Fernando de Henares, may be smaller than its competitors, but it's still pretty big and busy. Its lures include giant water slides, a large lake/main pool, a toddlers' pool, cafés, restaurants and – an added attraction for teens and upwards – occasional all-night disco and dip sessions.

Aquasur

Carretera de Andalucía (N-IV) km 44, Aranjuez (91 891 60 34). Metro de América (Metro Méndez Alvaro) to Aranjuez/by train Cercanías C-3 from Atocha to Aranjuez. **Open** *June-Sept* 10.30am-9pm daily. **Admission** *Mon-Fri* 900ptas; 500ptas 2-6s; *Sat* 1,100ptas; 700ptas 2-6s; *Sun, public holidays* 1,300ptas; 900ptas 2-6s. **Credit** MC, V.
More than just a waterpark, Aquasur is a whole complex outside Aranjuez (*see p230*), with all kinds of fun things for children of all ages, including mini-golf, a western fort, a mini-zoo, a picnic area and karaoke. Water comes in the form of a giant pool with five slides, and a special children's pool.

Aquópolis

Avda de la Dehesa, Villanueva de la Cañada (91 815 69 11). Bus 627 from Moncloa to Villanueva de la Cañada; also free buses from Cuesta de San Vicente (Metro Plaza de España) & Estación Sur (Metro Méndez Alvaro)/By car Carretera de La Coruña N-VI, Las Rozas-El Escorial exit. **Open** *June-Sept* noon-9pm daily.
Admission *Mon-Fri* 1,700ptas; 1,150ptas 4-10s; 1,200ptas over-65s; *Sat, Sun, public holidays* 1,875ptas; 1,250ptas 4-10s; 1,300ptas over-65s. **Credit** MC, V.
This giant complex towards El Escorial (*see p225*) is one of the largest waterparks in Europe, with the usual adventure lakes, wave machines and water slides – only much bigger. There are food outlets, but it's more fun to take a picnic.

Parque de Atracciones

*Casa de Campo (91 463 29 00/91 526 80
30/reservations 902 38 33 33).*
*Metro Batán/bus 33, 65 & special bus from Metro
Estrecho, Pacífico & Ventas Sun, public holidays.* **Open**
Oct-June noon-11pm Mon-Fri, Sun; noon-1am Sat. *July-
Sept* noon-1am Mon-Fri, Sun; noon-2am Sat. **Admission**
entrance only 575ptas; *incl 2 rides* 975ptas; *under-7s incl
4 rides* 975ptas; *SuperNapy (all-inclusive ticket)* 2,200ptas;
1,225ptas under-7s. **No credit cards.**
A perennial favourite, this rambling funfair offers more than
40 rides, from the gentlest merry-go-round to the stomach-
churning Top Spin. Additions made in recent years include
Los Rápidos, a white water rafting ride, and *Los Fiordos* (The
Fjords), an uphill boat ride followed by a terrifying 15m (50ft)
drop and enormous splash. There's also an open-air auditorium, which hosts Spanish and Latin singers and pop bands
in summer. The fair gets packed on summer nights, and you
may have to queue, but it's worth waiting for the best rides.

Parque Mágico

Paseo de la Virgen del Puerto s/n (91 365 61 71).
*Metro Pirámides, Marqués de Vadillo/bus 17, 18, 23, 34,
36, 50, 116, 118, 119.* **Open** *mid-Sept-June* 5-9pm Mon-
Fri; noon-10pm Sat, Sun and public holidays; *July-mid-
Sept* 6.30pm-11pm Mon-Fri; noon-2.30pm, 6.30-11pm Sat,
Sun till midnight. **Admission** *one ride* 200ptas, *five rides*
700ptas (800ptas on Sat), *unlimited rides* 1,800ptas; 20%
discount Mon. **No credit cards.**
A small funfair near the Puente de Toledo that cannot match
the Parque de Atracciones, but nonetheless offers lots of fun
and rides for children aged between two and 12. Attractions
include a shark, 'Formula 1' go-karts, bumper boats and
bouncy castles. There's also a bar with a *terraza*.

Planeta Welby

Avda de España s/n, Majadahonda (91 634 47 22).
*Bus 651, 652, 653 from Moncloa to Majadahonda/
by car Carretera de la Coruña N-VI.* **Open** 5pm-midnight
Mon-Thur; 5pm-1am Sat; noon-midnight
Sun, public holidays. **Admission** 200ptas under-12s;
pulsera (ticket for activities plus hot dog) 1,100ptas Mon-
Fri; *pulsera* (ticket for activities only) 1,500ptas Sat, Sun,
public holidays. **No credit cards.**
A family leisure park in Majadahonda, in the north-western
suburbs, with a mini golf course, bumper boats, a maze, a
roller coaster, roundabouts, bouncy castles and *son et
lumière* show. There's also an educational farm, a restaurant
with international food (and a special children's menu), a
burger restaurant and several bars.

Safari de Madrid

*Aldea del Fresno, Carretera de Extremadura N-V,
km 32 (91 862 23 14). By car N-V to Navalcarnero, then
M-507 to Aldea del Fresno.* **Open** 10.30am-sunset daily.
Admission 1,600ptas; 1,000ptas 3-12s.
No credit cards.
This safari park, around 40km (25 miles) from Madrid, can
only be visited by car, as the chief attraction is a tour of the
park area where bears, monkeys, lions, rhinoceroses,
giraffes, elephants and tigers all roam around freely.
Admission also includes entry to snake and reptile houses,
a tropical aviary and shows featuring lion taming and birds
of prey; during July and August, there's also a swimming
pool, a lake with pedalos, a go-kart track, mini-motorbikes
and a giant slide.

Sport Hielo

*Estación de Chamartín, C/Agustín de Foxà (91 315 63
08). Metro Chamartín/bus 5, 80.* **Open** 5-9pm Thur; 5.30-
10.30pm Fri; 11.30am-2pm, 5.30-10.30pm, Sat, Sun, public
holidays. **Admission** (incl rental of skates) 1,000ptas
Thur; 1,300ptas Fri-Sun; 1,000ptas Sat, Sun morning.
No credit cards.

One of only four ice-skating rinks in the greater Madrid area,
and by far the most convenient. Children from three years
upwards are admitted; safety helmets (available for hire)
may be made obligatory for children in the near future.

Tren de la Fresa (Strawberry Train)

*Estación de Atocha (902 228 822). Metro Atocha
RENFE/bus all routes to Atocha.* **Open** *Apr-July & Sept*
depart from Atocha 10am Sat, Sun, public holidays
(return from Aranjuez 6.30pm). **Tickets** 3,100ptas;
1,900ptas 4-12s. **Credit** MC, V. **Map H10**
Recreate a favourite outing of Madrileños of a century ago
– travelling by steam train to Aranjuez to enjoy its palaces,
gardens and the fresh produce of its riverside orchards,
notably the strawberries (*fresas*) for which the town is
famous. The historic engine and coaches depart from Atocha
on weekend mornings and roll south at a leisurely pace,
returning in late afternoon; entry is included to the palaces
and gardens of Aranjuez. Hostesses on the train wear period
costume, and travellers get to sample some of those juicy
strawbs. The trip is extremely popular in May and June, but
you can book tickets through travel agents, RENFE offices
or the Museo Nacional Ferroviario (*see p84*). For more on
Aranjuez, *see p230*.

Zoo-Aquarium de la Casa de Campo

*Casa de Campo (91 512 37 70). Metro Batán/
bus 33, 65; special buses Sun, public holidays from
Metros Pacífico, Ventas & Estrecho.* **Open** 10.30am-9pm
daily (box office closes at 6pm). **Admission** 1,590ptas;
1,280ptas under-8s. **No credit cards.**
Madrid's zoo has over 2,000 animals, covering 150 species
of mammal and 100 types of bird, including 29 endangered
ones. Highlights include a parrot show and the dolphinari-
um, and among the recently added attractions are a giant
tank of mean-looking sharks and an immense net within
which birds of prey can fly freely. There's also a children's
section and a train ride. Snack bars are dotted about the zoo.

Theatre

Many fringe theatres fill the Saturday and Sunday
early evening slot with children's productions.
Montacargas, **Cuarta Pared**, **Sala Triángulo**,
El Canto de la Cabra, **Pradillo** and **Teatro
Lara** all have children's programmes, in Spanish
(for theatre details, *see chapter* **Theatre**). Also,
there are several local theatre groups that regularly stage productions in English, some of which
are for kids (*see page 222*).

Sala San Pol

Plaza de San Pol de Mar (91 541 90 89).
Metro Príncipe Pío/bus 41, 46, 75. **Performances** 6pm
Sat, Sun, public holidays. Closed July-Aug.
Admission 975ptas. **No credit cards.**
Madrid's official children's theatre, home to the company La
Bicicleta. They are very professional, and there's no
skimping on production costs.

Teatro Municipal de Títeres del Retiro

*Parque del Retiro. Metro Retiro/bus all routes to Puerta
de Alcalá.* **Performances** 7pm Sat, Sun, public holidays.
Titirilandia in Aug 7.30pm, 9pm, 10.30pm, Fri-Sun,
public holidays. **Admission** free. **Map I7**
This open-air puppet theatre in the Retiro has shows every
weekend throughout the year. In summer, as part of the
Veranos de la Villa (*see p9*) it offers extra shows as part
of the *Titirilandia* festival, featuring puppet companies from
around the world. Puppetry-related exhibitions are also held
in summer at the nearby **Casa de Vacas** exhibition space.

Events & fiestas

Many of Madrid's *fiestas* and festivals include activities for children. **Christmas** is full of possibilities. The traditional Spanish Christmas decoration is the *Belén* or nativity scene, and kids love the annual *Exposición de Belenes* at the **Museo Municipal** (*see page 83*). It's equally traditional for Spanish children to leave out a shoe to receive their presents from the Three Kings, on the night of 5 January. On **Reyes**, the next day, the Kings' arrival is celebrated with a spectacular procession of giant floats from their helicopter landing point in the Retiro, along Calle Alcalá to Sol and Plaza Mayor. Crowds are huge, and the 'Kings' throw out sweets to children along the route.

During **Carnaval** in February special children's carnivals are organised all around the city. Every year on the second or third Sunday of April, **Calle Bravo Murillo** between Cuatro Caminos and Plaza Castilla is taken over by thousands of kids and their parents, and filled with bouncy castles, puppet shows, firemen spraying foam, handicrafts workshops, candy floss stalls and the like. There are also plenty of events for children in **San Isidro** and, on a smaller scale, at the summer **Verbenas**. Tourist offices have programme details. *See also chapter* **Madrid by Season**.

Childcare & babysitters

For Spanish working mothers childcare often comes in the form of granny. There is a growing number of *guarderías* (crèches/nurseries), but only a few are public, and places are hard to come by. There are more private *guarderías*, which offer daily care for children from as young as three months. Many provide activities in English, although they are directed at Spanish-speaking children. If you're staying in Madrid for a while it's worth going to the nearest playground at the end of the school day: this is the best way to make friends and get recommendations on babysitters or *guarderías*. For short-term needs, check also the local English-language press (*see pages 198-9*).

Children's parties
(mobile 929 324 619).
Bilingual actress-choreographer Heidi Méndez offers kids' entertainment with a difference. Instead of letting the children just watch the clowns, she gets them involved in theatre-based games with music, dance and improvisation.

Centro Infantil Nenos
C/Uruguay 21 (91 416 98 22). Metro Colombia/ bus 7, 16, 29, 51, 52. **Open** 10am-1.30pm Mon; 10am-1.30pm, 4.30-9pm, Tue-Fri; 11am-2pm, 4.30-9pm, Sat, Sun. Closed Aug. **Admission** 750ptas per hour; 6,000ptas 10 hours. **Credit** MC, V.
A drop-off centre with indoor play area (with bouncy castles and play-pools), a range of related services, and a bar for parents. Children are left under experienced supervision; the atmosphere is pleasant, and it's used a lot by resident English speakers. It also has a list of reliable babysitters.

El Descanso de Mamá
C/Condes de Torreanaz 4 (91 574 39 94). Metro O'Donnell/bus 2, 28, 30, 71, C. **Open** 24 hours daily. **Credit** V.
A 'children's hotel' where you can leave a child for any length of time from a few hours to several weeks. It's bright and modern, and children are looked after and entertained by fully trained staff. Prices vary depending on requirements.

Escuela Infantil Olavide
C/Gonzalo de Córdoba 22 (91 593 24 69). Metro Quevedo/ bus 3, 37, 16, 61, 149. **Open** 7.30am-9.30pm Mon-Fri; *Aug* 7.30am-6pm Mon-Fri. **No credit cards. Map F2**
This *guardería* serves locals and foreign residents, and takes babies and pre-school children. They can be left for anything from a few hours to a full day, with meals provided. Staff are very professional, and some speak English. Phone for rates.

Gorongoro
Avda de Felipe II 34 (91 431 0645). Metro Goya/bus 2, 15, 29, 30, 43, 56, 61, 63, 71, C. **Open** *schooldays* 4.30-8.30pm, *non-schooldays* 10.30am-2.30pm, 4.30-8.30pm. **Admission** over-4s, 350ptas per 30 min; under-4s 250ptas per 30 min. **No credit cards. Map L4/5**
An indoor play park for kids aged four to 11, Gorongoro takes children by the hour or for longer sessions, and is especially useful for parents who are shopping in or around the nearby **Corte Inglés** (*see p157*). It also organises childrens' parties. Kids under four must be accompanied by an adult.

St George's Church
C/Núñez del Balboa 43 (91 576 51 09). Metro Serrano, Velázquez/bus 1, 9, 19, 51, 74. **Map J4**
A meeting point for Madrid's English-speaking community. A playgroup meets on Wednesdays at 10am. There's a noticeboard that's a good place to find details of babysitters – a reliable one is Chris (91 726 72 89).

Bullfighting

Gaudy, noisy, existential drama, or just blood in the afternoon – the corrida's fans and its haters will never share common ground.

Probably the one thing most people in the world know about Spain is that there is bullfighting. It is the activity that most sets the country apart, for good or ill. Foreigners have long been fascinated or repelled by it, regarding it as a symbol of the country's dark, exotic, mysterious nature.

It is, certainly, the extreme, dramatic spectacle so admired by writers like Hemingway; it can also be very vulgar, with lots of noise, raw humour and primary colours. Many Spaniards, for their part, see bullfighting as a regrettable hangover from a Spain locked into a tedious stereotype, something they'd rather not be associated with.

And yet, bullfighting has been intertwined with the country's culture for centuries, and is something from which it cannot easily be disentangled. It is thought to have originated in the Bronze Age Minoan civilisation in Crete. In Castile and Andalusia the bull is an ever-present symbol in traditional folklore, and bullfights of some kind have been held since at least the Middle Ages. Like sports that are an integral part of a nation's life such as cricket or baseball, it has inspired a vast amount of literature, from ultra-detailed press reports to one of the greatest works of modern Spanish poetry, García Lorca's *Llanto por Ignacio Sánchez Mejías*, an elegy for a bullfighter friend of the poet killed in the ring in 1934.

For years it was suggested that bullfighting was dying out. Not a bit of it. The 1990s has seen it more in vogue than ever, and combined with modern marketing techniques to boot. At the ring, you're likely to bump shoulders and rub knees with every strata of Madrid society, from the beret-wearing old villager to fashion models and young business types with slicked-back hair and sharp suits. Young *toreros* fill the gossip sheets and are promoted like pop stars, and in some cases (Jesulín) even make (regrettable) records.

One problem with bullfighting is in saying exactly what it is. It's not a sport, as there is no competition involved. It's more of a ritual, with certain set requirements.

How it is viewed by those who have grown up with it or become addicted to it is naturally very different from the way it's seen by those who simply find it revolting. One cultured *aficionado* has said that a *corrida* is a combination of *arte, ética y estética* – art (the skill the bullfighter needs), ethics (he must face up to the risk, and give the bull

plenty of chance to catch him, and if he doesn't will not be asked back) and aesthetics (the grace in movement that wins the greatest praise from the hyper-critical crowd). To put it another way, a bullfight is the ultimate fulfilment of the old English sporting adage that it ain't the winning but the taking part. Barring occasional incidents, the outcome is highly predictable, but it is how the final victory is achieved, with what degree of courage, skill, cunning and even elegance, that is all important. A long-established Spanish expression of admiration is to say that somebody did something *a la torera* – with no other resources than nerve, flair, style, and not a little cheek.

Of course, you could say this is nothing but the sort of stuff that comes out of the end of a bull by the tail. But, aside from such considerations, what keeps most *aficionados*, Spanish and foreign, coming to the ring is that they find there's no other spectacle that gives them such a buzz, that's so gripping and even spine-chilling. For, in order for a *corrida* truly to be a demonstration of grace under pressure, there has to be a real element of danger for the bullfighter at every stage, no matter how formalised, or even corny, the event may appear.

THE PLAN OF THE *CORRIDA*

A bullfight is a complicated affair, and if you go to one it's advisable to have an idea of what you are going to see first. The main type of bullfight is the *corrida*, with the matador, or *torero*, on foot. Although its rules and rituals are now regarded almost as holy writ they were only established in the eighteenth century, when this relatively proletarian form of bullfighting first became dominant. The bullfights staged in the Plaza Mayor in imperial Madrid were mainly of the old aristocratic type, on horseback. Called *rejoneo*, this is still practised today, but though very skilled it is not regarded highly by hard-core *aficionados*.

Every aspect of the bullfight is determined by fixed rules, from the opening parade to the role of the *Presidente* of the *corrida* (in Madrid, usually a police inspector), who directs the various stages of the event by waving a series of different-coloured handkerchiefs. The *corrida* itself is divided into six 15-minute-long sections, with three *toreros* alternating and killing two bulls each.

And while the bullfight goes on, for two hours or more, the running commentaries from fans munching on their tortilla *bocadillos* while the wine is passed back and forth, the raucous abuse they yell at the *torero* or the bull-breeder's mother, the cries of the beer and whisky hawkers and the lively pasodobles from the resident brass band, ensure a thoroughly festive spirit.

Fighting bulls, *toros bravos*, weigh between 500 and 600 kilos (1,100-1,300lb), and are reared semi-wild on large ranches. They should have as little contact with a human on foot as possible before their entrance into the ring. At midday before the fight they can be seen in the *apartado* outside the ring, when they are put into individual pens. When finally released from confinement into the ring, the animal's natural instinct is to charge and remove or kill all that moves before him. At this point the bull is too fast and strong for the bullfighter to be able to kill it in the strictly prescribed manner. It has to be weakened, and for the *torero* to get close enough he has to try to bring it under his control with the skill of his capework.

Each quarter-hour fight is divided into three sections called *tercios* (thirds). The first begins with the *torero* making *pases* or movements with a large pink cape to test out the temperament, strength and speed of the animal. This can seem one of the most innocent parts of the *corrida*, as if the two were playing. It is actually very dangerous, for at this point the bull still has all its strength.

Next, still in the first *tercio*, lance-wielding *picadores* appear on heavily-padded horses, inciting the animal to charge and then stabbing it in its neck muscle to force it to lower its head. This is a part of the fight most condemned by those opposed to bullfighting. For *aficionados*, however, it's crucial in gauging the bull's spirit, on the basis of whether it returns to charge the *picador* and his horse despite having been spiked and felt pain.

The next *tercio* involves the *banderillas*, long, multi-coloured barbed sticks. The *torero* and his three assistants run towards or receive the charging bull, and then stab the *banderillas* into the back of its neck. This is perhaps the most spectacular part of the bullfight, and one of the bloodiest.

Finally, in the last third, comes the *faena de muleta*, the bullfighter's period alone with the bull, when he demonstrates his artistry in dominating the beast by making it follow a smaller red cape, the *muleta*. The bull is wounded and weakened, but for this same reason is much more unpredictable. This culminates, after the traditional dedication of the bull to someone in the crowd, in the kill, the one moment when the ring falls silent. A 'good' kill, in which the sword is plunged in through a two-square-inch area between the shoulder blades and into the heart with precision, causing the bull to drop in seconds, will be received rapturously by the crowd. In contrast, matadors will be booed and heckled deafeningly if the animal is seen to suffer through bungled attempts to get the sword in the right place.

More than in any other spectacle the crowd plays a vital part in bullfighting. They complain and criticise constantly. It is only through the crowd's insistent waving of white handkerchiefs that a *torero* is presented with the prized ear or, better, the tail of the bull he has killed. Likewise, if the bull has displayed remarkable courage, the crowd can demand it be pardoned and granted a regal life back on the ranch thereafter. If they think a bull is not up to scratch they can also insist it be taken away, with green handerkerchiefs.

THE STARS

If a good kill is far from guaranteed, a good bull-fight is also hard to come by, although for the first-time visitor this may not matter as it takes some experience to distinguish a good from a bad one. For those involved, a truly good bullfight is as elusive as any masterpiece: the big names of the moment are more likely to give value for money, but it's notoriously impossible to guarantee.

Among current leading figures of the corrida are the spectacular Colombian **César Rincón**; **Joselito**, generally thought of as the best of the younger generation; and the teen-star **Jesulín de Ubrique**, who attracted worldwide attention with his women-only fights where his fans could throw their underwear at him. Older *aficionados* who despise such flashiness prefer the austere **Enrique Ponce**, and a grand old man of the ring, **Curro Romero**, whose many eccentrically sub-standard performances only add to his legend when he suddenly hits form. As a traditionalist Ponce refuses point-blank to share a bill with one of the most publicised of modern bullfighters, **Cristina Sánchez**, the first woman to have a real impact in the *corrida* in years. Her abilities are unquestioned, but some say that a woman in the ring misses the whole ritualistic point of the thing.

Some critics put the lack of good fights down to other factors. Bullfighting is now very much a part of modern Spain, moving billions of pesetas each year. There is much talk of 'decaffeination', with star *toreros* accused of using their influence to get ranchers to breed weaker, more easily managed bulls, and stories of horn-shaving (to make the bulls shy of attacking the bullfighter) and other devious practices. These complaints, though, are not new, and similar stories have been heard almost ever since bullfighting was invented. Anyone wishing to know more on the history of bullfighting should visit the **Museo Taurino**, alongside the bullring (*see page 80*).

Going to the Toros

Corridas are held at Las Ventas every Sunday from March to October, at 7pm. During the **Feria de San Isidro**, from May into June, and the **Feria de Otoño**, beginning in late September, fights are held every day. San Isidro is also preceded by another fair, the **Feria de la Comunidad**, which includes several *novilladas* for novice bullfighters.

Tickets go on sale only two days in advance, and it is difficult to get an idea much in advance of which *toreros* will appear on a given day. Some agencies sell tickets, with commission (*see p176*), but most people buy them at the ring. There are many grades of ticket – the main division is

If you're sitting in sol, you'll need a hat.

between the cheap *sol* (sun) and *sombra* (shade), but some intermediate seats are *sol y sombra*. Sitting in *sol* in midsummer can be very uncomfortable, and it's worth paying to be in the shade. The best seats, which are very expensive, are in *sombra* near the front, the *barrera*. You get a pretty good view from any point, but probably the best price-comfort ratio is in *sol y sombra* about halfway up. Wherever you sit, at whatever price, rent a cushion as you go in, or the cramped stone seats will give you pains for days afterwards. They also come in handy for joining in as the crowd showers insults and other things on a below-par bullfighter.

Plaza de Toros de Las Ventas

C/Alcalá 237 (91 726 48 00/91 356 22 00). Metro Ventas/bus 21, 38, 53, 106, 201. **Box office** *Mar-Oct* 10am-2pm, 5-8pm, Thur-Sun. **Tickets** 1,000-12,000ptas. **No credit cards.**

Bull bars

It's worth arriving early for a bullfight, especially any involving big-name *toreros*. Outside the ring, thousands will be milling around: touting for tickets, looking at the souvenirs, and taking in the atmosphere. Many of the *aficionados*, once they've got their tickets, will head off to escape the hot sun and chat about this or that capeman's form in one of the many bars around Las Ventas, which have become almost as much a part of the bullfighting experience as the ring itself.

Aside from offering a chance to soak up the atmosphere, these bars offer excellent-value *rabo de toro* – bull's tail stew – in their lunch menus. During the season, the animal used will be one that has been publicly sacrificed a couple of days earlier in the plaza. Given that, prior to their date with destiny, fighting *toros de lidia* spend their whole lives running wild over vast grazing lands, the meat is of exceptional quality. These bars will also prepare for you that all-important *bocadillo* wrapped in silver paper, without which the bullfight would not be complete.

Just west of the ring, on or near Calle Francisco de Navacerrada, are three unassuming bars that are favourite rallying points for pre- and post-bullfight fans: **El Paseíllo, El Burladero**, and **El Bríndis**. Back on Calle Alcalá itself is **Los Timbales**, easy to spot with its tiled exterior depicting bullfighting scenes. A few doors down is the **Cervecería La Monumental**, specialising in excellently served beer. Across Alcalá in Calle Alejandro González is a splendidly old-fashioned bar, **La Tienta**, unchanged since the 1950s, that's always crowded with locals before a *corrida*. On the cross-street, C/Pedro Heredia, is **Donde Leo**, a bar and restaurant where impromptu *tertulias* linger on after dinner, especially during San Isidro.

Metro Ventas/bus 21, 38, 53, 106, 201.

El Paseíllo *C/Francisco de Navacerrada 58;* **El Brindis** *C/Francisco de Navacerrada 60;* **El Burladero** *C/Cardenal Belluga 13;* **Los Timbales** *C/Alcalá 227;* **Cervecería La Monumental** *C/Alcalá 225;* **La Tienta** *C/Alejandro Gonzalez s/n;* **Donde Leo** *C/Pedro Heredia 22.*

All bars are open appoximately 7am-midnight daily.

Bull fairs around Madrid

Villages and towns in the surrounding region also hold *corridas* every Sunday during the season. Many also hold bull fairs, with bullfights daily, during their annual *fiestas*. These small-town fairs often include an *encierro*, in which young bulls are run through the streets first thing in the morning, as in the most famous of such events, Pamplona's San Fermín. They are pretty manic, with a good deal of drink taken, and anyone wanting to try the full Hemingway-esque experience should be prepared for a fair few bruises, and also keep in mind that an *encierro* always involves a very real risk.

Bull fairs

The fair in **Valdemorillo**, to the north west, offers the earliest bullfights of the year, in February, a rare opportunity to see a *corrida* in freezing cold. Most spectacular *encierro* near Madrid is in **San Sebastián de los Reyes**; most prestigious fair is the one in **Colmenar Viejo**. Dates vary slightly each year; further information is available from town halls. **Aranjuez** *(91 891 74 42). For travel details, see pp231-2.* **Ferias** end May & early Sept. **Chinchón** *(91 894 00 84). For travel details, see p232.* **Feria de Agosto** mid Aug. **Colmenar Viejo** *(information 91 845 00 53). Bus 721 from Plaza Castilla.* **Feria de Agosto** late Aug. **Manzanares el Real** *(91 853 00 09). Bus 724 from Plaza Castilla.* **Feria de Agosto** early Aug. **San Sebastián de los Reyes** *(91 652 62 00). Bus 152, 154 from Plaza Castilla.* **Feria de Agosto** late Aug. **Valdemorillo** *(91 897 73 60). Bus 641, 642 from Moncloa.* **Feria** early Feb.

Dance

Times are tough and the future uncertain, but the dance scene in Madrid continues to offer a lively, varied menu.

Madrid is home to two major dance companies, the *Compañía Nacional de Danza* and the *Ballet Nacional de España*, specialists in Spanish dance (for which, *see page 210*). The city also has a wide range of schools teaching a great diversity of styles, which regularly produce new talent.

When dynamic dancer-choreographer Nacho Duato (who hung up his own shoes in 1996) took over the *Ballet Lírico*, he renamed it *Compañía Nacional de Danza* and embraced a more contemporary style. The influence of Jiri Kylian, Duato's mentor at the Nederlands Dans Theater, is clearly discernible. Committed to touring, the company only appears two or three times a year in Madrid, and it was not until the **Teatro Real**'s second season that Duato's *Romeo y Julieta*, his first full-length work, could grace the stage of the city's most important new venue. The Real's apparently lukewarm commitment to dance, and a reduction in programmes at the **Teatro de la Zarzuela** – only one stint by the *Ballet Nacional* in 1998-9 – has meant that the greater exposure hoped for with the opening of the Real has not materialised.

Astutely stepping into the gap left by Duato in classical ballet, Victor Ullate's *Ballet de la Comunidad de Madrid* has taken a more traditional tack with *Giselle*, *Les Sylphides* and *Don Quijote*. Its excellent dancers can be seen in short seasons at the **Teatro de Madrid** or the **Albéniz**. Summer is a good time to look for classical dance, as the *Ballet Nacional de Cuba* comes annually to the Albéniz, and there are visits by Eastern European companies.

DANCE POLITICS

Dance, however, is heavily affected by the political climate. Funding for the showpiece companies looks safe, but for the rest the panorama is confusing. The governing *Partido Popular* is committed to austerity, with culture a prime victim. Grants are fewer and smaller, and a further complication is a dispute between Spain's regions and the Culture Ministry over the allocation of grants, which at times has paralysed funding. Even before this began, dance has always been the Cinderella of Spanish arts, and while Madrid has a passionate public, there is no venue exclusively dedicated to it. Major performances and touring productions have arrived under the umbrella of festivals, whose once-lavish budgets are also subject to cuts.

The situation for contemporary dance is not easy, but its exponents soldier on with admirable energy and enthusiasm. Two outstanding groups are the lively *10 y 10* and hard-working *Provisional Danza*, who appeared in the 1998 Dance Umbrella in London. Initiatives by independent choreographers include *La UVI*, an ad hoc choreographers' association which runs showcases titled *Desviaciones* ('Deviations') at **Cuarta Pared**, combining dance and performance art. Other interesting developments are the mix of dance, theatre and humour in works such as *Estado Hormonal* (*pictured*), recently at the **Pradillo**, or the fusion of flamenco and contemporary forms in the work of the *Arrieritos* company or the *Nuevo Ballet Español* (*see page 210*). Another facet is dance for young audiences, especially by Enrique Cabrera's *Aracaladanza* company.

A truly local modern style is difficult to pin down. Limón and Bausch remain prime influences, and contact improvisation and release work are increasingly present. Choreographers to look out for include María José Ribot, Francesc Bravo and his company *Rayo Malayo*, Denise Perikidis, Teresa Nieto, Blanca Calvo and Laura Kumin.

Spain is also near-unique in Europe in having its own indigenous dance tradition. For Spanish Dance, *see page 210*, in *chapter* **Flamenco**.

Dance venues

The **Teatro Real** and **Teatro de la Zarzuela** present major Spanish and international dance companies, although it is not foremost in their programmes (*see above, and chapter* **Music: Classical &**

Opera). Several theatres host dance: **Cuarta Pared** and **Sala Triángulo** provide space for young contemporary groups, and the **Teatro Lope de Vega** and **Teatro Nuevo Apolo** host international companies (for all, *see chapter* **Theatre**). One formerly significant dance venue, the Sala Olimpia in Lavapiés, is being rebuilt and will not reopen before 2000 (at least). Venues used in festivals include the **Centro Cultural Conde Duque**, the **Círculo de Bellas Artes**, the **Institut Français** and **Museo Reina Sofía** (for all, *see chapter* **Art Galleries**). *Except where indicated box offices do not take credit cards, but tickets can also be bought by card through savings banks (see page 176).*

Centro Cultural de la Villa

Jardines del Descubrimiento, Plaza de Colón (91 575 60 80). Metro Colón/bus all routes to Plaza de Colón. **Box office** 11am-1.30pm, 5-8pm, Tue-Sun. **Tickets** *Sala 1* 1,300-2,500ptas; *Sala 2* 1,000ptas. **Map I4**
This mid-size city auditorium presents smaller ballet companies, Spanish dance and contemporary work. It's very comfortable, but sight lines from the sides are poor. Tickets through Tel-entradas. *See also chapters* **Art Galleries** *and* **Theatre**.

Teatro Albéniz

C/de la Paz 11 (91 531 83 11). Metro Sol/bus all routes to Puerta del Sol. **Box office** 11.30am-1pm, 5.30-9pm, Tue-Sun. **Tickets** 1,700-3,500ptas; group discounts. **Credit** V. **Map E8**
The main venue for the **Festival de Otoño** and the theatre closest to the heart of the local dance community. The stage is a bit cramped for ballet, but good for middle-scale work. Tickets through Cajamadrid. *See also chapter* **Theatre**.

Teatro de Madrid

Avda de la Ilustración s/n (91 740 52 74/91 730 17 50). Metro Barrio del Pilar/bus all routes to Barrio del Pilar, La Vaguada. **Box office** 5-9.30pm Wed-Sun. **Tickets** 1,000-3,000ptas; discounts groups, and Wed, Sun.
This modern theatre in the north of the city seems tailor-made for dance. Built by the city, it's run by a private company, but they have kept a policy of featuring Spanish and international dance companies, including a good deal of Spanish Dance. Tickets also through Cajamadrid. *See also chapter* **Theatre**.

Teatro Pradillo

C/Pradillo 12 (91 416 90 11). Metro Concha Espina/bus 16, 29, 52, 122. **Box office** 1 hour before performance Wed-Sun. **Tickets** 1,500ptas; 800ptas under-12s.
An intimate studio theatre with a good space for dance: programmes have frequently been highly praised. It also presents theatre for adults and children, including puppet shows and English-language theatre. Tickets through Tel-entradas.

Dance events

See also the **Veranos de la Villa** and **Festival de Otoño** (*see pages 9-10*).

Día Internacional de la Danza

Information Asociación de Profesionales de la Danza (*see below*). **Dates** 29 April-1 May.
International Dance Day, 29 April, is celebrated with a Gala at the **Teatro Albéniz**. The programme over the next two days features about every figure in dance in Spain today.

Madrid en Danza

Information Comunidad de Madrid (012/91 580 27 09). **Dates** early May-mid-June.
Begun in 1986, this festival originally showcased contemporary dance, but now features ballet, and has spread beyond the **Albéniz** and the **Pradillo** to several more venues in Madrid and surrounding towns. *See also p7.*

Certamen de Coreográfia de Danza Española y Flamenco

Information Producciones Maga (91 547 69 79). **Dates** July.
Held over three days in July at the **Albéniz**, this competition is a great opportunity to spot new trends and talents in the somewhat traditional world of Spanish Dance.

Certamen Coreográfico de Madrid

Information Paso a Dos, C/Tutor 18 (91 547 69 79/ 91 365 70 37). **Dates** late Nov.
A national platform for new work in contemporary dance and ballet. It has been held at the Sala Olimpia, and a venue for 1999 and 2000 is still to be decided.

Classes & information

Asociación de Profesionales de la Danza/Asociación Cultural por la Danza

C/Atocha 105 1° A (91 420 30 32). Metro Atocha/bus 6, 26, 32. **Open** 10am-1.30pm, 4-6pm, Mon-Fri. **Map G9**
The Asociación de Profesionales represents the interests of the dance community, and organises a wide variety of courses and events; the Asociación Cultural produces a bi-monthly magazine, *Por la Danza*. Both are invaluable sources of information, especially at adult and professional level.

Carmen Roche

C/del Roble 22 (91 579 08 05). Metro Tetuán/bus 3, 66, 124. **Open** 9.30am-10pm Mon-Fri.
Very well-regarded school with an across-the-board range of classes for students of all levels: classical, Spanish, contemporary, jazz, ballroom, sevillanas. Also exercise classes.

Centro Coreográfico La Ventilla/ 10 y 10 Danza

C/Carmen Montoya 12 (91 315 32 72). Metro Ventilla, Valdeacederas/bus all routes to Plaza de Castilla. **Open** 10am-4pm Mon-Fri.
The new, renovated studio is the base of the *10 y10* company, directed by Pedro Berdayes and Mónica Ründe. There is a contemporary class at 10-11.30am daily, costing 700ptas, or 5,000ptas for a ten-class card valid for a month. Afterwards the company itself rehearses, and students can often stay and watch. Rehearsal space is available for hire.

Centro de Danza Karen Taft

C/Libertad 15 (91 522 84 40/91 532 13 73). Metro Chueca/bus 3, 40, 149. **Open** *Oct-June* 9am-10pm Mon-Fri; *July-Sept* intensive groups 9am-10pm Mon-Thur. **Map G5**
One of the foremost schools in Spain, with classes in classical and modern techniques, as well as flamenco and tap. It also houses the Isabel Quintero school for Spanish Dance.

Estudio de Carmen Senra

C/Apolonio Morales 11 (91 359 16 47). Metro Plaza de Castilla/bus 14, 150. **Open** 10am-10pm Mon-Fri.
Madrid's most important studio for contemporary dance, offering classes in a variety of styles, including jazz, flamenco, ballroom and pre-dance for children.

Estudios Amor de Dios

C/Fray Luis de León 13 (91 530 16 61). Metro Embajadores/bus all routes to Plaza de Embajadores. **Open** 10am-10pm Mon-Fri; 10am-3pm Sat.
The nerve centre of Madrid's flamenco dance scene, packed with students eager to learn from prestigious artists. Twelve studios of varying sizes offer classes in all the Spanish styles and techniques, or are available to rent by the hour.

Film

Affordable prices, a wide range of cinemas showing films undubbed and a revival of Spanish cinema make Madrid a great city for movie-goers.

Spaniards go to the cinema a lot. Hollywood blockbusters, predictably, top the crowd ratings, and most Spaniards still prefer to see foreign imports dubbed into Spanish. But, perhaps surprisingly, there is an ever-increasing audience for films shown in their original language, with subtitles. The growth in specialist 'original version' moviehouses has been dramatic in the last decade, with the city now boasting over ten of them.

Home-grown cinema has its ups and downs. Like the rest of the planet, it has been forced to adjust to the reality of tastes moulded by the onslaught of adroitly marketed Hollywood product, which has captured over 70 per cent of the local market. It's not all bad news, though: after the lean years of the '80s, the 1990s have seen a revival in Spanish cinema, which for the moment – within the limitations of any non-Hollywood industry nowadays – seems to have found its feet, balancing commercial and artistic interests. Private TV, particularly Canal +, has joined the State RTVE in financing film production, while Europudding co-productions, especially with France and Italy, are seen as one way to combat Hollywood.

In the meantime, a new generation of *auteur* directors has emerged with such talents as Alejandro Amenábar, Agustin Yáñez, Chus Gutiérrez, Enrique Gabriel, Salvador Garcia Ruiz and Pablo Llorca, who mostly write and direct their own, low-budget projects. Outside Spain Pedro Almodóvar is still the country's best-known director, although his star has been waning a little at home, as the camp formula that saw its apotheosis in such films as *Women on the Edge of a Nervous Breakdown* a decade ago has worn a bit thin. However, his 1997 picture *Live Flesh* (*Carne Trémula*) was a welcome new departure indicating that he hasn't lost his film-making creativity.

Sadly, Spain is not very interested in the cinema of its Latin American cousins, and films from the continent that make it here tend to be co-productions, or international box-office successes such as *Like Water for Chocolate*.

Venues

The Gran Via is Madrid's archetypal movie-avenue: massive first-run cinemas line the street, and their extraordinary publicity hoardings, hand-painted for each film, are one of the sights of the city. Some are divided into multiplexes, others carry on in their original 1-2,000-seater form, and all attract capacity houses on Sunday nights for the dubbed international blockbusters they mostly screen.

When a film is shown in its original language, with Spanish subtitles, this is indicated by the letters **VO** (*versión original*) in newspapers and on cinema publicity. Specialist VO cinemas (and the official film theatre, the **Filmoteca**, which only shows films in VO) are listed below.

Mercifully, all the cinemas listed have air-conditioning.

Tickets & times

Newspapers and the *Guia del Ocio* (*see chapter* **Media**) are reliable sources of cinema schedules. In the same way that they eat late, Madrileños tend to go to the movies later than is the norm in many other countries: the most popular screenings are at around 10-10.30pm, and 8pm shows are usually much easier to get into. The busiest day is Sunday, when it's advisable to buy tickets in advance or at least arrive in very good time for 8pm and 10pm shows. Several VO cinemas also have late (after midnight) shows on Fridays and Saturdays. Ticket prices are relatively low; in addition, some cinemas charge lower prices for the first show in the afternoon, and many have a reduced-price day, the *dia del espectador* (filmgoer's day) once a week, usually on Monday or Wednesday.

Credit card pre-booking has not arrived in Madrid cinemas, and although more of them now sell numbered seats up to a week in advance, long queues and getting into one's seat at the last minute are still the norm.

Gran Vía picture palaces

Acteón

C/Montera 29 & Plaza del Carmen 7 (91 522 22 81). Metro Sol, Gran Via/bus all routes to Puerta del Sol. **Open** box office 4-10.45pm Mon-Thur, Sun; 4pm-12.45am Fri, Sat. **Tickets** 750ptas; 550ptas Wed except public holidays. **Map E7**
A smart new multiplex showing mainly low-budget Spanish independents, and a fair number of imports. Beware, though – they're nearly always dubbed.

Callao

Plaza de Callao 3 (91 522 58 01). Metro Callao/ bus all routes to Plaza de Callao. **Open** box office 4-10.15pm daily. **Tickets** 750ptas. **Map D6**
An established 1920s landmark, its façade looming over the Plaza de Callao. It seats around 1,000, and modern refurbishment means it's comfortable and welcoming.

Capitol

Gran Via 41 (91 570 66 33). Metro Callao/bus all routes to Plaza de Callao. **Open** box office 4.15-10.15pm Mon-Thur, Sun; 4.15pm-12.45am Fri, Sat. **Tickets** 750ptas; 550ptas Wed except public holidays, also over-65s, students Mon-Fri except public holidays. **Map D6**
A classic cinema from the heyday of the Gran Via. Big comfy seats, giant screen, terrific sound. The only problem is that the flick is usually a dubbed Hollywood import.

Looks interesting, but I preferred his older stuff... Alphaville.

Gran Vía

Gran Vía 66 (91 570 66 33). Metro Santo Domingo, Plaza de España/bus all routes to Plaza de España. **Open** *box office* 4.30-10.30pm daily. **Tickets** 750ptas; 550ptas Wed except public holidays; 550ptas over-65s, students Mon-Fri. **Map D5**
Old world elegance – the Gran Vía's sparkling splendour is crowned by a dozen chandeliers, some of Bohemian crystal. It still has just one, 1,000-seater auditorium, and there are no plans to convert it into a multiplex.

Palacio de la Música

Gran Vía 35 (91 521 62 09). Metro Callao/bus all routes to Plaza de Callao. **Open** *box office* 4-10.15pm daily. **Tickets** 750ptas; 550ptas Wed except public holidays. **Map E6**
A grand old cinema dating back to the 1930s. Gilded balustrades and carved relief surfaces add to the opulence of this 2,000-seater former concert hall.

Palacio de la Prensa

Plaza de Callao 4 (91 521 99 00). Metro Callao/bus all routes to Plaza de Callao. **Open** *box office* 4-10.15pm daily. **Tickets** 750ptas. **Map D6**
A massive '40s cinema, the Palacio has been transformed into a very comfortable three-screen multiplex.

VO cinemas

Alphaville

C/Martín de los Heros 14 (91 559 38 36). Metro Plaza de España, Ventura Rodríguez/bus all routes to Plaza de España. **Open** *box office* 4-11pm Mon-Thur, Sun; 4pm-1am Fri, Sat. **Late shows** *begin* 12.30-1am Fri, Sat. **Tickets** 725ptas; 500ptas Mon except public holidays. **Map C4**
This four-screen has established a loyal following since it opened in 1977. Its basement café was an in-vogue meeting point in its '80s heyday, as a venue for experimental screenings and performances by theatre and musical acts. A screen in the café acts as a reminder of these efforts to create an alternative space, and it's still sometimes used to host off-the-wall initiatives. Nowadays, though, people are more likely to come here for the Italian chef's tasty apple strudel.

Bellas Artes

C/Marqués de Casa Riera 2 (91 522 50 92). Metro Banco de España/bus all routes to Plaza de Cibeles. **Open** *box office* 4.15-10.30pm daily. **Tickets** 750ptas; 525ptas Mon except public holidays. **Map G7**

Originally a theatre, the Bellas Artes was made into a cinema in 1937. In 1970 it pioneered the screening of foreign films in their original language, and was among the first cinemas to provide film notes. Today it boasts Dolby sound and the latest equipment, but is probably the only cinema in Madrid where a vendor still walks the aisles selling popcorn and drinks. There's also a café and film souvenir shop.

California

C/Andrés Mellado 53 (91 544 00 48). Metro Moncloa/bus 2, 12, 16, 61, C. **Open** *box office* 4.15-10.15pm daily. **Tickets** 650ptas Mon,Tue, Thur, Fri; 750ptas Sat, Sun, public holidays; 550ptas Wed except public holidays. **Map C1**
This 500-seater near the university screens mostly commercial films, but also some less-standard fare, and encourages students to use it for English-teaching purposes.

Lumière

Pasaje Martín de los Heros, C/Princesa 5 (91 542 11 72). Metro Plaza de España/bus all routes to Plaza de España. **Open** *box office* 4-10.15pm Mon-Thur, Sun; 4pm-12.30am Fri, Sat. **Late shows** *begin* midnight-1am Fri, Sat. **Tickets** 500ptas Mon-Fri; 700ptas Sat, Sun, public holidays. **Map D4**
A modern two-screen showing a mix of both dubbed and VO, mainstream and other movies. The early evening shows are usually more child-oriented than ones after 8pm.

Luna

C/Luna 2 (91 522 47 52). Metro Callao/bus all routes to Plaza de Callao. **Open** *box office* 4-10.30pm daily. **Tickets** 650ptas Mon, Tue, Thur, Fri; 750ptas Sat, Sun, public holidays; 550ptas Wed except public holidays. **Map E6**
This once run-down cinema has taken on a new lease of life as a VO house, with an interesting selection of imported cinema. The area around is a bit sleazy, although the growing Chinese community is smartening things up.

Multicines Ideal

C/Doctor Cortezo 6 (91 369 25 18). Metro Tirso de Molina/bus all routes to Puerta del Sol. **Open** *box office* 4-11pm Mon-Thur, Sun; 4pm-12.45am Fri, Sat. **Late shows** *begin* 12.30-1am Fri, Sat. **Tickets** 750ptas; 550ptas Mon except public holidays. **Map E8**
An eight-screen multiplex that programmes a mix of Spanish films, international box-office hits and art-house movies in VO. Very popular with both locals and foreigners.

Princesa

C/Princesa 3 (91 541 41 00). Metro Plaza de España/bus all routes to Plaza de España. **Open** *box office* 3.45-11pm Mon-Thur, Sun; 3.45pm-1am Fri, Sat.

Late shows *begin* 12.45am Fri, Sat. **Tickets** 750ptas; 550ptas over-65s, students first show Mon-Fri except public holidays. **Map D4**
Part of the Renoir chain, this ultra-modern six-screen shows VO foreign and Spanish films. One of the most comfortable cinemas, with plush seats, wide screens and Dolby sound.

Renoir (Plaza de España)
C/Martín de los Heros 12 (91 541 41 00). Metro Plaza de España, Ventura Rodríguez/bus all routes to Plaza de España. **Open** *box office* 4-10.30pm Mon-Thur, Sun; 4pm-12.45am Fri, Sat. **Late shows** *begin* 12.45am Fri, Sat. **Tickets** 750ptas; 550ptas over-65s, students first show Mon-Fri except public holidays. **Map C4**
The enterprising Renoir chain has three VO multiplexes in Madrid, and plans for more. The first, the Plaza de España five-screen, opened in 1986. It lays on film notes and good late-night screenings.

Renoir (Cuatro Caminos)
C/Raimundo Fernández Villaverde 10 (91 541 41 00). Metro Cuatro Caminos/bus all routes to Glorieta de Cuatro Caminos. **Open** *box office* 4-10.30pm Mon-Thur, Sun; 4pm-12.45am Fri, Sat. **Late shows** *begin* 12.45am Fri, Sat. **Tickets** 750ptas; 550ptas over-65s, students first show Mon-Fri except public holidays.
Another very comfortable Renoir VO multiplex, with tables, chairs and fold-down seats along the walls in the foyer for bearable queuing. High ceilings allow for four large screens.

Rosales
C/Quintana 22 (91 541 58 00). Metro Argüelles, Ventura Rodríguez/bus 1, 44, 74, 133, C. **Open** *box office* 4-10.30pm daily. **Tickets** 700ptas; 500ptas Mon & first show Tue-Fri; 750ptas Sat, Sun, public holidays. **Map C3**
The Rosales opened in 1969, and now specialises in art-house films in VO. The 360-seat cinema sometimes stages theme weeks featuring, for example, a celebrated director or French or Italian cinema, and always gives out film notes.

The Filmoteca

Filmoteca Española (Cine Doré)
C/Santa Isabel 3 (91 369 11 25). Metro Antón Martín/bus 6, 26, 32. **Open** *box office* 4-10.45pm daily; *bar-restaurant* 1pm-1am Tue-Sun; *bookshop* 4.30-10.30pm Tue-Sun. **Tickets** 225ptas; 1,700ptas for 10 films. **Map F4**
Founded in 1953, Madrid's official film theatre has lately expanded its role in restoring and preserving the heritage of Spanish cinema. As well as its very likeable cinema (one of the oldest in the city), it has a good bookshop and very popular bar-cafés. Films are shown in the open air in the rooftop bar each summer. The Filmoteca has access to the archives of other countries to feed its series on classic directors, individual genres or the cinema traditions of different countries, and foreign films shown here are always in VO.

Open-air movies

Fescinal (Cine de Verano)
Parque de la Bombilla, Avda de Valladolid (91 541 37 21). Metro Príncipe Pío/bus 41, 46, 75. **Open** *July-Sept* from 10.15pm daily. **Tickets** 500ptas; 400ptas over-65s, students; free under-5s.
As part of the city's **Veranos de la Villa** festival (*see chapter* **Madrid by Season**), films are shown in an open-air venue, with a double bill nightly through the summer. Most films screened are fairly mainstream, but more unusual fare is also included, and some are shown in VO. The giant screen is set up in the Parque de la Bombilla, by the river a little north of San Antonio de la Florida, a site that can be a good few degrees cooler than the rest of the city

Of Latin lovers…

Spaniards are proud of Antonio Banderas. Never before has a Spanish actor become so internationally ubiquitous. Press and TV never tire of informing readers and viewers that the simmering sex-god, currently married to Melanie Griffith and the star of Hollywood hits such as *The Mask of Zorro, The Mambo Kings* and *Evita*, is the boy from nowhere. Born in Málaga, the young Banderas moved to Madrid, where he caught the eye of Pedro Almodóvar.

Despite his 'Latin lover' tag of today, Banderas started out playing serious roles, and his performance in Almodóvar's *The Law of Desire* (1987) ranks as one of the most sensitive in recent Spanish cinema. To his credit he has maintained a degree of balance over in Hollywoodland, and avoided complete type-casting (in part because he's been in so many films it's been hard to pin him down). Nevertheless, the fact he was offered (and turned down after death threats) the role of Kemal Ataturk suggests that he might end up a latter-day Anthony Quinn – a universal ethnic.

Banderas' success, coupled with the frustrations of a national cinema that is not exactly an export-oriented product, has led others to follow in his footsteps. Two former Almodóvar stablemates, Victoria Abril and Carmen Maura, have firmly established themselves as Euroactresses, with star presence in France. So far they have not been tempted by Hollywood: their accents are too strong for anything other than 'sexy Latins', and the parts simply aren't there.

Spanish directors, on the other hand, are increasingly eager to make the move across the ocean, with Oscar-winning Fernando Trueba and Chus Gutiérrez setting stories in America. Others now bypass Spain completely and make cinema essentially for the international market, albeit with a Spanish feel. Alejandro Amenábar, the young director who shot to success with his first film, *Tesis* (*Thesis*), has been looking to remake his follow-up *Abre los Ojos* (*Open Your Eyes*) in the US.

Gay & Lesbian Madrid

It's a paradox: Madrid politicians talk about crackdowns on clubs and call for everyone to go home, but the gay scene is booming as never before.

Madrid's gay scene – its *ambiente* – has come a long way in recent years. Indeed, it has blossomed to such an extent that many visitors rank it as one of the most enjoyable in the world. The uniformity often found in other cities with regard to dress codes and music is simply not here. People of all ages, shapes and sizes go out at night with one thing in common: a desire to have fun. This lack of exclusivity is what sets the Madrid scene apart.

CHUECA AND OTHER CONTINENTS

You can't talk about gay and lesbian Madrid without talking about Chueca, now established as the centre of Madrid gay life. Sure, there are gay clubs, shops and cafés elsewhere in the city, but this *barrio* has the biggest concentration of gay businesses, clubs, restaurants, cafés, shops and bookstores, and, most of all, gay streetlife, especially around the Plaza de Chueca itself. Chueca has its critics as well as its fans. The idea of a gay-lesbian ghetto divides the gay population: some feel it is a starting point from where an accepted gay life can grow, others feel that it closes the doors to full acceptance (as ghettos tend to do).

Thanks in large part to the influx of gay businesses, though, Chueca is now considered by some analists to be the district with the fastest economic growth in Madrid. Gay venues exist in harmony with traditional fruit shops, markets and newsstands, just as gay and straight neighbours do, and by day it's a peaceful, pretty ordinary *barrio*. It's in the evening that bars and clubs open their doors and the place fills up, and on weekend nights, above all, it can be hard to find a table for dinner or a coffee, or to find a space to squeeze through the crowds in the plaza. The variety is what makes Chueca most interesting: the different styles of people, the variety of venues, the possibility of meeting up with people you know, the different energies on the street.

Chueca is busy at any time of year, but really comes alive during **Gay Pride week**, around 28 June, International Gay Pride Day. The district explodes into a festive parade of hundreds of people of all ages and sexual tendencies, with concerts, competitions (fancy a race in stilletos?), free *sangria* dished out on the street, and social and gay-related seminars organised by clubs, shops, and neighbourhood associations, particularly the **COGAM** (*see below* **Contacts & information**). High point of the week is the Gay Pride parade (on Saturday), when thousands of gay men and women take part in a colourful and festive march from Puerta de Alcalá to the Puerta del Sol, with its quota of social-political demands. The week ends on Sunday with a mass picnic in the Retiro.

LIFE'S PATTERN

Gay nightlife in Madrid follows more or less the same formula as that of the rest of the population. While the places listed below cater mainly to a gay or lesbian clientele, many gay people in Madrid do not go out exclusively to gay places, and when they do visit them they may often be accompanied by straight friends. Rigorous social separatism is not a Spanish custom. This easygoing 'crossover' tendency has been further encouraged by the boom in Chueca, which has seen the 'gay district' also become popular with a trendy straight crowd. There are some venues with an established gay popularity that are listed in other chapters: for **Chez Pomme** and **Restaurante Momo**, *see chapter* **Restaurants**; for **Kappa** and **El Mosquito**, *see chapter* **Nightlife**.

The ways gays relate to each other can also be different from those of more northerly countries. Flirting is much more important among Spaniards (of all tendencies) than Anglo-Saxons, and can last the best part of an evening. Similarly, eye contact is very common in Spanish culture, so when someone eyes you up, it might not necessarily mean anything, or then again it might.

Cafés, bars & restaurants

Except where indicated, venues do not accept credit cards. For **Medea**, **La Rosa** and **Urania's**, *see page 196* **Lesbian Madrid**.

A Brasileira

C/Pelayo 49 (91 308 36 25). Metro Chueca/ bus 3, 40, 149. **Lunch served** 1-5pm, **dinner served** 9pm-2am, Mon-Sat. **Average** 1,500ptas. **Credit** AmEx, MC, V. **Map G5**
A tiny, cosy restaurant in Chueca serving great, interesting Brazilian cuisine.

Café Acuarela

C/Gravina 10 (91 570 69 07). Metro Chueca/bus 3, 37, 40, 149. **Open** *mid-Sept-mid-June* 3pm-2am Mon-Thur; 3pm-4am Fri, Sat; *mid-June-mid-Sept* 4pm-2am Mon-Thur; 4pm-4am Fri, Sat. **No credit cards. Map G5**
This little café is very special, an ideal place for a quiet drink. The décor is an eclectic mix of baroque and countless other styles, and the place is filled with sofas, café tables, angels, flowers and candles. The waiters are cute, the crowd is great, and it's also popular with gay and straight women.

Café Figueroa

C/Augusto Figueroa 17 (91 521 16 73). Metro Chueca/bus 3, 40, 149. **Open** noon-1am Mon-Thur; noon-2.30am Fri, Sat. **Map G5**
Madrid's oldest gay café. It's still a good place to start the evening, huddle together on a cold night or shoot pool upstairs.

Café La Troje

C/Pelayo 26 (no phone). Metro Chueca/bus 3, 40, 149. **Open** 5pm-2am daily. **Map G4**
A great café – service is excellent, the décor cosy and welcoming, the music is good and the crowd amiable. There are also interesting monthly changing art exhibitions. Not surprisingly, it's very popular.

Ciberespacio

C/Pelayo 42 (91 308 14 62). Metro Alonso Martínez, Chueca/bus 3, 21, 37, 40, 149. **Open** noon-2am daily. **Map G5**
The first gay cyber coffee house in Madrid. So, if you haven't found true love in the real world, you can always try your luck on the Net.

Gula Gula Madrid

Gran Vía 1 (91 522 87 64). Metro Gran Vía/bus all routes to Gran Vía. **Lunch served** 1-4.30pm daily. **Dinner served** 9pm-1.30am Mon-Wed, Sun; 9pm-2.30am Thur-Sat. **Average** 2,000ptas, **buffet** 1,500ptas. **Credit** AmEx, MC, DC, V. **Map F2**
The two Gulas are among the most popular bar-restaurants in Madrid with gay men, lesbians and a straight crowd. The Gran Vía branch – the second to open – is housed in an impressive building, and the smaller, original Gula also has striking décor. As well as good, contemporary food and good-looking waiters, they present a variety of shows. **Branch**: Gula Gula C/Infante 5 (91 420 29 19).
Air-conditioning. Booking essential.

Sarrasín

C/Libertad 8 (91 532 73 48). Metro Chueca/bus 3, 37, 40, 149. **Lunch served** 1-4pm, **dinner served** 9pm-midnight, Mon-Sat. **Set lunch** 1,200ptas. **Set dinner** 1,700ptas. **Credit** MC, V. **Map G5**
A very trendy and popular Chueca restaurant, with good food at easily swallowable prices. The décor is an added bonus, and it can be highly recommended.
Air-conditioning. Booking essential. Disabled: wheelchair access.

La Sastrería

C/Hortaleza 74 (91 532 07 71). Metro Chueca/ bus 3, 40, 149. **Open** 10am-2am Mon-Thur; 10am-3am Fri; 11am-3am Sat; 11am-2am Sun. **Map G4**

A big café that's one of the best decorated in Madrid, catering to gays and lesbians alike. A good place for dinner, a coffee after dinner or a last drink before you head off home.

Star's Café

C/Marqués de Valdeiglesias 5 (91 522 27 12). Metro Banco de España/bus all routes to Plaza de Cibeles. **Lunch served** 2-4pm Mon-Sat. **Dinner served** 8.30pm-12.30am Mon-Fri. **Average** 2,000ptas. **Set meal** 1,400-1,900ptas. **Credit** AmEx, DC, MC, V. **Map G6**
Madrid's first dance-café, a 'mixed' venue with great décor, serving breakfast, lunch or dinner, coffee and drinks. A wonderful place, popular, friendly, with attractive waiters and waitresses, and good music – at night you can strut your stuff on the dancefloor. *See also chapter* **Nightlife**.
Air-conditioning. Booking advisable.

XXX Café

corner of C/Clavel & C/Reina (91 532 84 15). Metro Gran Vía/bus all routes to Gran Vía. **Open** 9.30am-1.30am Mon-Thur; 9.30am-2.30am Fri, Sat; 4pm-1.30pm Sun. **Map F6**
This beautifully decorated place is the first gay café in Madrid to have big windows on to the street, so you can check out what's going on from outside before you venture in. It also stages excellent cabaret at weekends.

Clubs & *discobars*

The countless bars, *discobars* (with a dancefloor, but which don't charge on the door) and discos in Madrid open, close and change names with alarming frequency. The city's nightlife is becoming a little more sedate during the week (with fewer people venturing out, and places closing around 2am), but at weekends the scene can still last the full 48 hours, depending on your stamina. Madrileños still love to tour the bars and discos, so you might find yourself in a place that's semi-empty one moment, and packed to the gills the next. A feature of most of the venues that are really exclusively gay is that they have backrooms. Safe sex is accepted practice these days.

Admission prices to clubs can be unpredictable, and those listed should be taken as guidelines only.

Blanco y Negro

C/Libertad 34 (91 531 11 41). Metro Chueca/bus 3, 40, 149, N1, N19, N20. **Open** 8pm-5am daily. **Map G5**
A Madrid classic. There are two floors – the top one has strip shows and is favoured by older men looking for young ones, while the bottom floor has a disco.

Cruising

C/Pérez Galdós 5 (91 521 51 43). Metro Chueca/bus 3, 40, 149, N16, N17, N18. **Open** 7.30pm-12.30am daily. **Map G5**
This disco/club is another gay classic. Upstairs is a quiet pub area and a little theatre-like room showing porn films. Downstairs there's a large dancefloor and various backrooms. The place could do with a paint job, but its scruffiness is part of the charm. Women are allowed upstairs.

Eagle

C/Pelayo 30 (no phone). Metro Chueca/bus 3, 40, 149. **Open** 10am-3am daily. **Map G4**
The closest in Madrid to a real leather bar, and quite seedy. Uniforms, military fatigues and boots are de rigueur. Prices are keen. It has recently started to open for breakfast, and to admit women in the early evening; From 10pm it's men-only.

FLAMINGO
M U L T I C L U B

ONE DISCO FIVE SESSIONS
UNA DISCO CINCO SESIONES

SOUL KITCHEN MADRID
THE BEST FUNKY 'N' SOUL SESSION OF MADRID
La mejor sesión funky/soul de Madrid.

WEDNESDAYS AND SATURDAYS NIGHT
00:00 to 5:00 A.M.
Miércoles y Sábados noche, de 12 a 5 horas, a.m.

DARK HOLE - *GOTHIC CLUB*

FRIDAYS AND SATURDAYS, 20:00 TO 00:00 HOURS.
Viernes y Sábados tarde, de 8 a 12 horas.

Shangay
SHANGAY TEA DANCE
LIVE ACT - DISCO MUSIC - GAY SESSION

EVERY SUNDAY NIGHT   21:00 to 2:00 A.M.
Todos los Domingos noche, de 9 a 2 horas, a.m.

DISCO INFERNO - *LATIN HOUSE - JAZZ HOUSE*

FRIDAYS NIGHT 00:30 to 5:00 A.M.
Viernes noche, de 12:30 a 5 horas, a.m.

GOA AFTER CLUB
NUMBER ONE AFTER CLUB MADRID

FRIDAYS, SATURDAYS AND EVE HOLY DAY
6:00 to 10:30 A.M.
Viernes, Sábados y vísperas de fiesta, de 6 a 10:30 a.m.

MESONERO ROMANOS, 13 (ESQ. GRAN VIA, 34) 28013 - MADRID - SPAIN
http://www.interocio.es/goa   *(/shangay, /darkhole, /soulkitchen, /discoinferno).

Art Work: OnlyOcio +34 91 541 35 00

There are bars that aren't in Chueca. **El Mojito**.

Goa After Hours

Flamingo Club, C/Mesonero Romanos 13 (91 531 48 27).
Metro Callao, Gran Vía/bus all routes to Gran Vía.
Open 6-10am Sat, Sun. **Admission** 1,000ptas (incl one
drink). **Map E6**
The best after-hours place for those who just can't get
enough fun. Technically speaking a mixed night, but it's a
real gay favourite. *See also chapter* **Nightlife**.

Heaven

C/Veneras 2 (91 548 20 22). Metro Callao, Santo
Domingo/bus all routes to Plaza Callao.
Open midnight-6am Mon-Fri; 8pm-6am Sat, Sun.
Admission 1,000ptas (incl one drink). **Map D6**
Three floors, each different: a quiet pub-like area on the top
floor, a show area in the middle and house dancefloor on the
lower floor. Especially popular at weekends, when it's some-
times quite mixed.

LL Bar

C/Pelayo 11 (91 523 31 21). Metro Chueca/bus 3, 40,
149, N16, N17, N18. **Open** 6pm-3am daily. **Map G4**
Two floors with drag and striptease shows at weekends. The
lower floor has a backroom with porn videos.

La Lupe

C/Torrecilla del Leal 12 (91 527 50 19). Metro Antón
Martín/bus 6, 26, 32, 57, N14. **Open** *Sept-May* 4pm-
2.30am, *June-Aug* 10pm-2.30am, daily. **Map F9**
An off-Chueca bar that attracts a crowd of mostly youngish
gay men and women who come here to get away from the
trendier venues of the gay 'heartland'. Good music, great
prices, shows on some days during the week, and it's also
open in the afternoon for coffee.

El Mojito

C/Olmo 6 (no phone). Metro Antón Martín/bus 6, 26, 32,
57. **Open** *Sept-June* 9pm-2.30am Mon-Thur, Sun; 9pm-
3.30am Fri, Sat; *July, Aug* 10pm-2.30am Mon-Thur, Sun;
9pm-3.30am Fri, Sat. **Map F9**
Outside of the main Chueca scene, this bar, along with La
Lupe and El Mosquito (*see chapter* **Nightlife**), forms part of
an alternative gay circuit. Good music and great *mojitos*
(Cuban cocktails of rum, lemon and mint).

New Leather Bar

C/Pelayo 42 (91 308 14 62). Metro Chueca/bus 3, 40,
149, N16, N17, N18. **Open** 8pm-3am daily. **Map G5**
A classic hangout. Two floors with dancing downstairs,
and a big backroom with lots of surprises. The erotic
parties on Thursday, Friday and Saturday usually include
strip shows.

Priscilla

C/San Bartolomé 12 (no phone).
Metro Chueca, Gran Vía/bus 3, 40, 149. **Open** 10pm-
6am Mon-Thur; 10pm-8am Fri, Sat. **Map F6**
The younger brother of the Why Not? (*see below*): less crowded, but the music is just as good and the crowd just as much
fun. Décor, though, is nothing to write home about.

Refugio

C/Doctor Cortezo 1 (91 369 40 38).
Metro Tirso de Molina/bus 6, 26, 32, 57, N14. **Open**
midnight-6am Mon-Thur; midnight-7am Fri, Sat.
Admission 1,200ptas (incl one drink). **Map E8**
A very popular disco-cave, famous for foam parties. It also
hosts tea dances and 9pm-2am on Sundays there are cabaret
shows. A good-looking crowd, and wonderful waiters.

The friendly and definitely trendy **Serge K**. *See page 195.*

Rick's

C/Clavel 8 (no phone).
Metro Gran Via/bus 1, 2, 3, 40, 74, 149, N16, N17,
N18. **Open** 11pm-5am daily. **Map F6**
One of Madrid's best gay clubs, though drinks are pricey.
Weekend nights are the best, with great music and a drop-dead-gorgeous crowd. Women are also welcomed.

Rimmel

C/Luis de Góngora 2 (no phone).
Metro Chueca/bus 3, 40, 149, N16, N17, N18.
Open 7pm-3am daily. **Map G5**
A small place with two large screens, one with music videos,
the other showing porn films. Women get a frosty 'welcome'.

Shangay Tea Dance

Flamingo Club, C/Mesonero Romanos 13 (91 531 48 27).
Metro Callao, Gran Via/bus all routes to Gran Via.
Open 9pm-2am Sun. **Admission** 1,000ptas (incl one
drink). **Map E6**
Another session at the Flamingo (like **Goa**, *see above*) that's
an absolute wow on the gay scene. Great disco music and
the best 'tea dance' in Madrid, together with different shows
every weekend. *See also chapter* **Nightlife**.

Strong Center

C/Trujillos 7 (91 541 54 15). Metro Opera/bus 3, 25, 33,
44. **Open** midnight-7am Mon-Thur, Sun; midnight-9am
Fri, Sat. **Admission** 1,000ptas (incl two drinks Mon-Wed, Sun, one drink Thur-Sat). **Map D7**
The seediest club in Madrid. A huge place with a big dance-floor (usually empty), and supposedly the largest backroom
in Spain (invariably packed).

Tábata

C/Vergara 12 (91 547 97 35). Metro Opera/bus 3, N13,
N15. **Open** 10pm-5am daily. **Map C7**
Tábata attracts a good-looking mixed crowd and plays pop,
disco and dance music.

Topxi

C/Augusto Figueroa 16 (909 028 971).
Metro Chueca/bus 3, 40, 149, N16, N17, N18. **Open**
6pm-2.30am daily. **Map G5**
A buzzing 'Happy Hour' (6-10pm), a backroom and porn
videos are the reasons why Topxi is popular. An old
favourite with gay men, where women are not admitted.

Troyans

C/Pelayo 4 (91 521 73 58).
Metro Chueca/bus 3, 40, 149, N16, N17, N18. **Open**
9pm-3am Sun-Thur; 8pm-4am Fri, Sat. **Map G4**
One of the few bars in Madrid consistently hosting leather
parties – on the first Thursday of every month. Fairly seedy,
but a classic venue. Sunday night has a nude party in the
back area, and there's a backroom downstairs. Women are
not admitted.

Why Not?

C/San Bartolomé 6 (91 523 05 81).
Metro Chueca, Gran Via/bus 3, 40, 149, N16, N17, N18.
Open 10pm-6am Mon-Thur; 10pm-8am Fri, Sat.
Admission 1,000ptas (incl one drink).
A seriously happening club, so much so that it can get
uncomfortably crowded at the weekend. The music is great
– '60s, '70s and '80s – as are the waiters, and the prices of
drinks are not extortionate. Not exclusively gay, and filled
with a fun, mixed crowd.

Accommodation

Hostal Hispano

C/Hortaleza 38, 2ºA (91 531 48 71/fax 91 521 87 80).
Metro Gran Via/bus all routes to Gran Via. **Rates** *single*
3,475ptas; *double* 4,815ptas. **Credit** EC, MC, V. **Map G5**
A small, simple hostal in the centre of town, right next to the
main gay area, and very cheap. The clientele are mainly (but
not exclusively) gay.

Hostal Odesa

C/Hortaleza 38, 3º (91 521 03 38). Metro Gran Via/
bus all routes to Gran Via. **Rates** *single* 3,000ptas; *double*
4,000ptas. **Credit** DC, EC, MC, V. **Map G5**
Madrid's first *hostal* aimed at the gay community – both men
and women. It's small, but very clean and pleasant.
Room services *Telephone. TV.*

Hostal Sonsoles

C/Fuencarral 18 (91 532 75 23). Metro Gran Via/bus all
routes to Gran Via. **Rates** *single* 3,500ptas; *double*
4,500ptas. **Credit** DC, MC, V. **Map E6**
A quaint but comfortable new *hostal*, perfectly placed for the
Chueca bar and club scene.
Room services *Radio. Telephone. TV.*

Shops

Berkana
C/Gravina 11 (91 532 13 93). Metro Gran Via/ bus 3, 40, 149. **Open** 10.30am-2pm, 5-8.30pm, Mon-Sat. **Credit** V. **Map G5**
In the heart of Chueca, this is the first gay/lesbian bookshop in Madrid, a wonderful place with a great assortment of newspapers, a wide range of books (some in English), T-shirts, videos and postcards. Staff are helpful and friendly.

Condoms & Co
C/Colón 3 (no phone).
Metro Tribunal/bus 3, 40, 149. **Open** 11am-2pm, 5-9pm, Mon-Sat. **No credit cards. Map F5**
As well as condoms of all shapes, sizes and flavours, this shop also sells men's clothing.

Hiedras Peluqueros
C/Colón 4 (91 521 49 84).
Metro Tribunal/bus 149. **Open** 10am-8pm Mon-Fri; 10am-6pm Sat. **No credit cards. Map F5**
A trendy hairdresser's in the middle of Chueca.

OVLAVS
C/Augusto Figueroa 1 (91 522 73 27).
Metro Chueca/bus 3, 40, 149. **Open** 10.30am-2pm, 4-9pm, Mon-Sat. **Credit** AmEx, DC, MC, V. **Map G5**
A new shop that's one of the funkiest places for the latest clubwear. Clothes are pricey, but good quality, and the staff are very attractive, which can be a good excuse to pop in.

Serge K
C/San Gregorio 3 (91 319 04 53).
Metro Chueca/bus 3, 40, 149. **Open** 10.30am-3pm, 4.30-8pm, Mon-Fri; 10.30-3pm Sat. **Credit** MC, V. **Map G4**
One of the trendiest hairdresser's in Chueca, Serge K also does piercing and tanning. A very friendly place.

Sex Shop Barco 43
C/del Barco 43 (91 531 49 88).
Metro Tribunal/bus 3, 40, 149. **Open** 10am-2pm, 5-10pm, Mon-Sat. **No credit cards. Map F5**
The only exclusively gay sex shop in Madrid.

Soho
C/Galileo 32 (91 593 45 61).
Metro San Bernardo/bus 2, 21. **Open** 10.30am-2pm, 5-8.30pm, Mon-Sat. **No credit cards. Map D1**
Specialises in body piercing, but also sells a selection of street- and clubwear.

Trilogía
C/Gravina 17 (91 522 63 03).
Metro Chueca/bus 3, 37, 40, 149. **Open** 11am-2pm, 5-9pm, Mon-Sat. **No credit cards. Map G5**
Hip underwear, swimming gear, presents and belts, watches and so on, for men and women.

Xiquena Peluqueros
C/Marqués de Monasterio 5 (91 319 66 59).
Metro Chueca/bus 37, 149. **Open** 10am-6pm Mon-Fri. **No credit cards. Map H5**
In Chueca (where else?), this is one of the best hairdresser's catering to the gay community.

XXX
C/San Marcos 8 (91 522 17 70).
Metro Chueca/bus 3, 40, 149. **Open** noon-2pm Sat; Sept-June noon-2pm, 5-8.30pm, Mon-Fri; July, Aug noon-2pm, 5.30-9pm, Mon-Fri. **No credit cards. Map F6**
Stylish men's underwear, and the Barquillo branch a few streets away also stocks undies for women.
Branch: C/Barquillo 41 (91 310 38 60).

Encounters

Outdoors
Parks in Madrid are, like those in most cities, conducive to casual encounters. Be warned, though, that night-time cruising can be dangerous. Madrid's largest park, the **Casa de Campo**, has been turning into the city's largest outdoor sex area. There's a gay area by the *Teleférico* cable car, but the police have been more intrusive lately. The **Retiro** has a gay area during the day (particularly in the afternoon) behind the Chopera sports centre. At night, it shifts to Calle Alfonso XII and the Paseo del Prado near Calle de Los Madrazo. **El Obelisco**, the obelisk in front of the Ritz in Plaza de la Lealtad, is a popular, quite safe night-time location, particularly in the early hours until about 5am.

The **Parque de Atenas** near the Puente de Segovia and the Manzanares, beside the Campo del Moro, is another night-time cruising area that's probably the safest in the city. One of Madrid's favourite year-round cruising areas, strangely enough, has been around the **Las Ventas** bullring and the nearby car park: not much goes on during the day, but it's safe at night. Otherwise, very popular among gays on summer days are the city's **swimming pools**, especially those in the Casa del Campo, La Elipa, and La Vaguada, with nudist areas (for pool details, *see page 218*).

Saunas
Men *C/Pelayo 25 (91 531 25 83).*
Metro Chueca/bus 3, 40, 149. **Open** 3.30pm-8am daily. **Admission** 1,000ptas. **Map G4**
A small sauna, lacking facilities (there are only dry and steam saunas), but handily placed in the centre of Chueca. Popular, especially on Sundays.
Paraíso *C/Norte 15 (91 522 42 32).*
Metro Noviciado/bus 147. **Open** 3pm-1am daily. **Admission** 1,400ptas. **Map E4**
An excellent, spotlessly clean sauna. Massage, UVA baths and a bar.
Príncipe *C/Príncipe 15 (91 429 39 49). Metro Sevilla/bus all routes to Puerta del Sol.* **Open** 10am-1am daily. **Admission** 1,500ptas. **Map F7**
Recently reopened and nicely renovated. It's clean, and has a good range of facilities, including massage, dry and steam bath, bar, video room and backroom. Recommended.

Contacts & information

Gay groups
Club Gay Service *(91 542 30 41).*
Open by appointment 11am-2pm, 5-8pm, Mon-Fri. The city's only contact service.
COGAM (Coordinadora Gay de Madrid)
C/Fuencarral 37 (91 522 45 17). Metro Chueca, Tribunal/bus 3, 40, 149. **Open** 5-9pm Mon-Fri. **Map F5**.
The largest gay and lesbian organisation in Madrid. It organises Gay Pride week, campaigns for gay rights, and offers help on health issues, leisure activities and anything to do with the gay community.
Comité Ciudadano Antisida de Madrid *(91 523 43 33).* **Open** 10am-6pm Mon-Fri. Confidential and anonymous information about AIDS.
Gai Inform *(91 523 00 70).*
Open 5-9pm daily. Information service on homosexuality, relationships, health, tourism, leisure activities, legal and psychological help.
MSC Madrid *PO Box 18213, 28080 Madrid (no phone).*
A leather organisation, offering information every Saturday and during Leather Night at Troyans (*see above*).
Rosa que te quiero Rosa *(91 394 28 28).*
The gay and lesbian organisation of the Complutense University, based in room 500 in the Faculty of Political Science on the Somosaguas Campus.

Health care

For general health care and specialist HIV/AIDS (*SIDA* in Spanish) services, *see pages 256-7*.

Nexus

(91 522 45 17). **Open** for phone calls 5-9pm daily.
A health-advice organisation that forms part of **COGAM** (*see above*), and is always very helpful.

Publications

Revista Mensual

The most complete local gay magazine, with information about clubs, hotels, shops, and so on all over Spain. Available from most newsstands in central Madrid, and some clubs.

Shangay Express

A newspaper on gay life in Madrid that's given out free in many clubs, cafés, **Berkana** bookshop (*see above*) and other shops. A good way to find out about the latest activities in town.

Lesbian Madrid

Years ago the separation between gays and lesbians in Madrid was very clear. Today, most gay associations are run by both men and women, and Chueca is shared by gays and lesbians alike. Several important community facilities and businesses such as **Berkana** (*see above*) are joint ventures run by gays and lesbians.

While Madrid's gay and lesbian scenes have each grown a lot in recent years, the lesbian *ambiente* continues to be less showy than its male counterpart. As with the male scene it is less exclusive than its equivalents in many other cities, and many of its venues cater not only to a lesbian clientele but to gay men and straight people as well. Some of the most popular *terrazas* on Plaza de Chueca are run by lesbian clubs.

One of the biggest changes that has occurred in lesbian Madrid can be seen by comparing the secretiveness of past years and the openness of today. Nowadays the lesbian community has a noticeably laid-back attitude, and an apparent lack of political orientation, both of which attract the attention of foreign lesbians. This doesn't mean, though, that lesbians in Madrid don't feel that there are rights to be won; it's just that the fight for lesbian rights doesn't colour all lesbian life, in the same way that gay rights activism doesn't colour gay life, either.

See also above **Gay Madrid** for hotels, shops and services relevant to lesbians as well as gays.

Cafés, restaurants & clubs

For venues that are also popular with gay men and straight women, especially **Café Acuarela**, **La Lupe** and **El Mojito**, *see above* **Gay Madrid**; for **Kappa** and **El Mosquito**, *see chapter* **Nightlife**.

Ambient

C/San Mateo 21 (no phone). Metro Tribunal/bus 3, 40, 149. **Open** 8pm-5am Tue-Thur, Sun; 9pm-5am Fri, Sat. **Map G4**
Tasty pizza and good music. There's a pool table and a noticeboard where you can find out what's going on, plus occasional parties. The décor is warm and relaxed.

El Barberillo de Lavapiés

C/Salitre 43 (no phone).
Metro Antón Martín, Lavapiés. **Open** 9pm-2.30am Tue-Thur, Sun; 9pm-3.30am Fri, Sat. **Map F9**
A pleasant café, away from Chueca in Lavapiés, that's a good place to have an early drink or a coffee after dinner.

Escape

C/Gravina 13 (no phone). Metro Chueca/bus 3, 37, 149. **Open** midnight-5am Thur; 1-6am Fri, Sat. **Map G5**
This club/disco opened as a lesbian venue, but has since become highly mixed. It still has very good music, and a friendly crowd.

Medea

C/de la Cabeza 33 (no phone). Metro Antón Martín, Tirso de Molina/bus 6, 26, 32, 57. **Open** 11pm-5am Tue-Sun. **Admission** 1,000ptas (incl one drink). **Map E9**
A classic lesbian hangout with a sizeable, loud disco, cabaret, a pool table and a young crowd. Men are allowed in if accompanying gay women. Usually packed at weekends.

La Rosa

C/Tetuán 27 (no phone).
Metro Sol/bus 3, 5, 15, 20, 51, 52, 53, 150. **Open** 11pm-6am daily. **Admission** 800ptas (incl one drink). **Map E7**
This elegantly decorated club hosts popular Thursday night cabaret; at other times there's good music and a relaxed crowd. Men can join the fun if they're accompanied by lesbians.

Truco

C/Gravina 10 (91 532 89 21). Metro Chueca/bus 3, 40, 149. **Open** 8pm-2.30am Sun-Thur; 9pm-5am Fri, Sat. **Map G5**
Amid the men's venues on Plaza de Chueca, this women's disco-pub-*terraza* has become enormously popular with a lively crowd. The music is loud, there's a fun buzz, and it has a pool table: gay men and straight people are all welcome.

Urania's (COGAM Café)

C/Fuencarral 37 (91 522 45 17).
Metro Chueca, Tribunal/bus 3, 40, 149. **Open** 5pm-midnight Mon-Thur, Sun; 5pm-1am Fri, Sat. **Map F5**
A café run by the gay and lesbian association COGAM (*see above* **Gay groups**). A pleasant place for a drink, and to find out what's cooking on the political or social side of the scene.

Lesbian groups

Most organisations are shared by gay men and women (*see above* **Contacts & information**) but specifically lesbian groups are listed here. All three operate from the **Centro de la Mujer** women's centre (*see also p266*).

Centro de la Mujer

C/Barquillo 44 (91 319 36 89).
Metro Chueca/bus 3, 37, 40. **Map H5**
Colectivo de Feministas Lesbianas de Madrid *Meets* 4-8pm Mon-Fri. An organisation that deals with feminist issues from a lesbian point of view.
CRECUL (Comité Reivindicativo Cultural de Lesbianas) *Meets* 8.30-10.30pm Thur, Fri. CRECUL focuses on social issues concerning lesbians, and also has a lesbian contact service, *Ellas*.
Info Lesbi *(91 319 16 90).* A telephone service for lesbians, providing information on anything and everything related to the lesbian community (closed Aug).

Media

Columnists and commercials, sport and celebrities, brain-dead TV and wordy political debate: the media map.

Press

Madrid's street-corner kiosks offer a vast array of magazines, papers, part works and, in some cases, books. This is despite the fact that only around ten per cent of Spaniards actually buy a daily newspaper (the figure is higher in major cities).

Most newspapers are tabloid in size, but not in outlook. What there is of sensationalist journalism, *prensa amarilla* ('yellow press'), is relatively tame, and mostly confined to the gossip magazines, the *prensa del corazón* (literally, 'press of the heart'), a field in which Spain is a world leader. The most common style in newspapers is a rather humourless mix of political reporting – with much verbatim quoting of politicians – detailed local coverage, and a litany of traffic accidents, forest fires (every summer) and freaky crimes. Extensive, often erudite coverage of sports, arts and entertainment is another standard. No Spanish paper would feel complete, either, without big-name columnists, given ample space in which to pontificate on matters of the day.

The news-hungry should not miss the newspaper libraries in the **Hemeroteca Municipal** and **Biblioteca Nacional**, with good selections of the Spanish and international press (*see page 258*).

Newspapers

ABC

Extraordinarily old-fashioned and archly conservative, ABC might seem to be no more than a leftover from the Franco years, but this paper is still the preferred reading of Madrid's most solidly established citizens. It takes some getting used to the curious format (unchanged since the 1920s, with the cover and first few pages all photos, and the rest almost uninterrupted text, with line drawings) and the leaden, very correct style of language; however, it has a very highly regarded arts supplement on Mondays, and its journalists have a reputation for a greater degree of basic professionalism (such things as checking facts, or listening to interviewees) than is shown by their more modern brethren on other papers.

Diario 16

D16 looks and reads like a more middle-of-the-road version of *El Mundo* (*see below*), to whom it lost its most prominent journalists a few years ago. No balls but plenty of bulls – full colour gore from the *corrida* is a speciality, and sports coverage in general a strongpoint. It survives – so far – despite falling circulation and serious financial problems.

La Farola & La Calle

Magazines sold on the street by homeless people, similar in concept to Britain's *Big Issue*. *La Farola* is the most solid, with some interesting articles; *La Calle* is more ephemeral.

Marca & As

The two most important – in Madrid – of the many titles devoted to sport, the national obsession. *Marca* is, in fact, frequently the bestselling daily paper, its circulation regularly surpassing that of *El País*. Football, basketball, cycling and the rest are all reported with statistical zeal and hysterical headlines, but most attention naturally goes to Madrid's major football clubs, Real and Atlético. Freed from having to deal with regular news, the sports papers are the only ones here to use tabloid techniques and puns in headlines.

El Mundo

This paper made its name by unearthing many of the corruption scandals that corroded the previous Socialist government, stories that were passed over for far too long by its rival *El País*. Its criticism of Felipe González and his governments was ferocious, unremitting and often highly personalised, but led its editor Pedro J Ramirez, formerly with *Diario 16*, to claim that *El Mundo* is to Spain what the *Washington Post* was to America in the '70s. Since the election in 1996 of a conservative *Partido Popular* government to which the paper had given open support, however, the role of *El Mundo* has changed, as the paper has become visibly blander and more passive. To some extent, in fact, *El Mundo* and *El País* seem to have changed places, to the extent that in 1997 Ramirez was hit by scandals of his own, both political –around his willingness to act as a PP mouthpiece – and sexual. Among *El Mundo*'s (too) many star columnists, the acerbic if self-adoring Francisco Umbral stands out, and Carmen Rigalt's society column is witty. There's good sports coverage, and an arts magazine, *La Luna*, and a listings supplement, *Metrópoli* (*see below*), both come with Friday's edition. It also often has interesting supplements on Madrid matters, on Sundays.

El País

Founded in 1976 shortly after Franco's death, *El País* soon established itself as required reading for the liberal middle classes, becoming synonymous with democratic Spain. It has built up a reputation for being competent, if rarely exciting, but has excellent international news coverage, and an informative daily Madrid supplement. Under the Socialist administrations from 1982 to 1996 its government-friendly reputation earned it the nickname *Boletín Oficial del Estado* (the real *Boletín* is the official gazette, in which new laws are published), and it was accused of downplaying Socialist scandals. However, the PP victory in 1996 was just the kick *El País* needed. Its chairman Jesús Polanco has been involved in a head-to-head battle with the government over the company's attempts to expand into satellite TV, and the paper itself has become more challenging, lively and questioning. *El País* carries a range of supplements: Friday's edition has the arts and listings magazine *Tentaciones* (*see below*); a high-quality culture pull-out comes on Saturdays; and Sunday's *País* has a glossy magazine, and is good for job ads.

Foreign newspapers

Most kiosks around Sol, Gran Via, Calle Alcalá and the Castellana, and all Vip's stores (*see chapter Shopping*), have a decent selection of European newspapers the day after publication at the latest. The *International Herald Tribune*, *USA Today* and many British papers arrive the same day.

Ten years after

Now that the country has entered the digital and satellite era – with the addition of Via Digital to the pre-existing subscriber service Canal+ – Spanish television could be said to have come of age. Sadly, the dominant pattern ever since the opening up of private television at the end of the '80s, when two new national channels – Antena 3 and Tele 5 – appeared together with publicly funded regional stations (such as Telemadrid), has been one of an ever-greater, ever-duller conformity. 'Reality' shows, football six nights a week, American imports, game shows and Latin American and home-made soaps that make *Neighbours* look like *Brideshead Revisited* are the staple diet. The amount of advertising has reached world-record levels, to the extent of rendering many programmes truly unwatchable.

When the new channels appeared, they were not given a brief requiring them to dedicate space to minority groups, or to producing drama, documentaries or film. Similarly, television contributes very little to forming a new generation of technicians and writers and directors who could, in turn, revitalise the film industry.

With the advent of pay TV, the old argument of greater choice is being wheeled out. Yet neither Canal + nor Via Digital has any remit to produce its own programmes; instead, Via Digital looks set to be a slightly downmarket version of Canal +, based on a lazy, cheap formula of imported US sitcoms, Hollywood movies dubbed into Spanish, sport and a smattering of (imported) nature series.

The impact of the *Partido Popular* government on television has been less than many people expected. One set of influences has been replaced by another in RTVE news. The launch of Via Digital, which is owned by the recently privatised phone company *Telefónica*, was pushed through by the PP partly as a way to make life difficult for the Socialist-supporting media boss Jesús Polanco, head of both Canal+ and *El País*. The seeds of the present mediocrity of television, though, were all sown under the Socialists in the '80s and early '90s.

Admittedly, Spanish television is now very similar to that found in many other parts of the world. In many ways, its consolidation into a supposedly more balanced and sophisticated animal runs parallel to the country's political process; it is unlikely that, were there ever to be another general strike, television would be able, as it did under the Socialists in 1989, simply to not report the event on the day's news. Nevertheless, the optimism that characterised Spain during the emergence from dictatorship 25 years ago has given way to self-satisfied conservatism and apathy, and this change is exemplified perhaps nowhere better than on TV.

Classified ads

Both *El Mundo* and *El País* have extensive small ads sections, especially on Sunday. The best place to look for or to place ads, though, for flats and also for courses, if you want to break into the local music scene, and so on, is the magazine *Segundamano*, published on Mondays, Wednesdays and Fridays. To bag the bargains, buy each edition and start calling as early as possible. Ads can be placed free at any of its offices around the city. *Mercado de Trabajo*, published on Fridays, is another magazine devoted solely to job ads. *The Broadsheet* and *In Madrid* (*see below*) also have useful classified pages.

Magazines

¡Hola!, Pronto, Diez Minutos & Semana

Your gateway into Spanish life, or at least into conversations in bus queues or at the hairdressers'. *La prensa del corazón*, 'the press of the heart', is a quintessentially Spanish invention, giving beautiful people the chance to show off their beautiful homes, babies, boy/girlfriends, operation scars and weddings, and to explain to a waiting public how much better they are feeling after coming to terms with childbirth, divorce, a boob job or corruption trial. It's an ongoing national soap opera, with a cast of thousands. *¡Hola!*, fairy godmother of the genre, started in 1944 and is still leader of the pack. Its unchanging format has of course been exported to Britain in the ineffable *Hello!*, and there are plans for a French version, too.

Music & style magazines

Rock de Lux A well-written, long-running monthly that covers a wide range of music including the more esoteric extremes, but also appeals to a wide audience.
Undersounds An excellent music monthly that's great for information on Madrid's buzzing club scene (*see chapter* **Nightlife**). Mainly sold in record shops and at festivals.

English-language magazines

There are four local English-language magazines, which are fairly widely available in Madrid.
The Broadsheet Running since the 1980s, but recently relaunched in a glossy, full colour A4 format, *The Broadsheet* is a free monthly magazine available from a few kiosks in the city centre but mainly from tourist offices, pubs and other anglophone businesses, language schools, VO cinemas and shops around the city. Its straightforward writing offers a good introduction to Madrid, with stories on political and social events, plus listings information, features on the capital's attractions and classified pages.
Guidepost A weekly (not free) published by the American Club (*see p264*), with Spanish business news and classifieds.
In Madrid A free monthly found in pubs, restaurants, bookshops, universities, language schools and tourist offices, with information on what's on, articles, events, reviews and classifieds. More basic than the *Broadsheet*.
Lookout A magazine sold throughout Spain, with pieces on Spanish life, food and law for expats, and classified ads.

Listings magazines

Guía del Ocio
Published every Friday, with cinema, arts and entertainment listings, and the best galleries section of the listings mags. However, Madrid social life often works by word of mouth, and it misses out on some events or last-minute changes.

Metrópoli
A complete magazine, free with *El Mundo* on Fridays. It has full film listings, good reviews of exhibitions, and enterprising coverage of clubs, bars and restaurants. *Metrópoli* also frequently has interesting features about Madrid.

Tentaciones
The arts and entertainment pull-out free with Friday's *El Pais*. Its event listings for Madrid are more limited than *Metrópoli*'s, but it has more information on other parts of Spain and features and interviews on current fashions, trends and styles, with a certain obsession with Hollywood and multi-national glitz.

TV & radio

TV
Madrid lags behind Barcelona in establishing a meaningful local TV channel. The *Comunidad*'s **Telemadrid** has rarely sought to establish a very distinctive identity, and apart from that the only free alternatives to the national channels (two State and two private, although all carry advertising) are the abysmal Canal 39 and Canal 7, both of which border on the farcical. Some non-Spanish films and shows on **TVE 1**, **TVE 2** and especially **Telemadrid** can be received in their original language on stereo TV sets; look for *VO* in listings and the *Dual* symbol at the top of the screen.

TVE 1 (La Primera)
The flagship channel of the State broadcaster RTVE, professional if predictable. Since the arrival of private TV in 1989 it has built up its frothy entertainment-quotient in a bid to match the excesses of its competitors; politically, its news programmes are notoriously subject to 'influence' from above (the Socialists before '96, PP since then).

TVE 2 (La Dos)
RTVE's 'minority channel' this may be, but it scarcely goes in for innovative programming. The arts, documentaries, education, children's shows and sport make up the fairly stolid mix; consolation comes every night after midnight when classic films are shown in the original language, with Spanish subtitles.

Antena 3
Superficially more serious than its rival Tele 5, the private Antena 3 has overtaken TVE 1 as the most-viewed channel. Secret of its success is an emphasis on 'family entertainment', peppered with odd bits of late-night salaciousness. Its evening 'news' slot, presented by the ineffable José María Carrascal, is a model of sanctimonious bias (or bigotry, if you prefer).

Tele 5
Colourful, commercial and crass – Tele 5 has been a byword for tackiness, and barged its way into the ratings when private channels first appeared in 1989. More recently, the public taste for so many gorgeous young presenters, audience-participation shows and legions of bimbos seemed to be waning, and the station has said it wishes to be more serious – though this has not always been reflected on screen. We can thank Tele 5 for launching the host of revelation-reality-sex and violence talk shows begun by Pepe Navarro, which now dominate late-night TV (having been eagerly picked up by other channels as well).

Telemadrid
Like every other autonomous region, Madrid has its own TV station. Telemadrid is cheerful and upbeat, and good for local news and live league football on Saturday nights. Films on the channel can sometimes be received in English (*see above*).

Canal +
A classier-than-most channel available only to subscribers with a decoder, although many hotels, bars and cafés now receive it. Like the associated channel in France, its mainstays are recent movies (which can be viewed undubbed) and sports – above all league football, for the exclusive rights to which Canal Plus (written Canal +) has been ready to pay out huge sums. It also has a very popular football-chat show, *El Día Después* on Monday nights, with former Liverpool man Michael Robinson, and non-sports programmes include documentaries, music and comedy. Canal + also shows US ABC news daily at 8.05am (not codified, and so accessible to non-subscribers).

Satellite & cable
Madrid now has access to digital satellite television through Via Digital and Canal Satellite, owned by Canal + (*see above*) and *El Pais*. The two are in strong competition, both offering a similar package for around 4,000ptas a month, and so far neither has found enough subscribers. A merger between them to create a Murdoch-style monopoly seems a likely outcome.

Radio
The field is still dominated by **Radio Nacional de España** (RNE); the alternative for news is **SER** (91.7 FM, part of the *El Pais* group), **La Cope** (100.7 FM) and **Onda Madrid**. Music lovers are best served by **RNE-3**. The **BBC World Service** can be found until midnight on 12095 kHz on short wave.

Stations
RNE-1 (88.2 FM) *Radio Uno* is where you can hear plenty of (sometimes intelligent) chat. A more bouncy, sometimes silly local talk station is **Onda Madrid** (101.3 FM).
RNE-2 (96.5 FM) Classical music station – an oasis of calm. **Sinfo Radio** (104.3 FM) is similarly serene.
RNE-3 (93.2 FM) A pop music channel that gets more alternative after dark. Rocky and ravey, plus gig details.
RNE-5 (90.3 FM) A rolling news station with full bulletins every hour.

Music: Classical & Opera

Some said it would never happen – Madrid has its grand opera back.

A milestone in the history of classical music in Madrid was passed on 11 October 1997. At long last, ten years after its closure for thoroughgoing renovation and just as long a time of political mud-slinging, cock-ups, false starts and embarrassment for every institution involved, the **Teatro Real**, the city's showpiece, state-of-the-art opera house, opened its doors and ushered in a new era.

The cost had long since gone into orbit, and finally totalled 21,000 million pesetas (£88 million, or $140 million). Many heads had rolled along the way, miles of column space had been devoted to the matter in the press, but, there it was, a splendid edifice which would finally put Madrid on the operatic circuit and complete the city's set of prestigious music houses. The first season had its ups and downs, and after so much time and expense critics inevitably watched the Real's every move. Reviews ranged from acid to acclamatory. Still in its infancy, the Real promises much, and with it Madrid has the resources to offer a full, diverse range of quality music to a hungry public.

During Spain's 1980s boom much was already done to put Madrid on the musical map. The **Auditorio Nacional**, opened in 1988, is another lavish and expensive project that gave the city's musical life a fundamental boost by providing, for the first time, high-standard modern facilities for the performance of symphonic and chamber works. During the years of the Real's closure, opera fans had to make do with productions at the **Teatro de la Zarzuela**. Now freed of its operatic duties, the theatre has returned to the genre from which it takes its name (*see page 202*), for which it's ideally suited.

Many expected that 1992, Madrid's year as European City of Culture, would see the city's consecration on the international stage, topped off by the inauguration of the Real. In the event, it was still a building site, and the year seemed more like the beginning of a musical recession. Economic problems from 1993 onwards brought a drop in grants, sponsorship, commissions and audiences. Contemporary music was hard hit, after a decade of progress. Since 1996 the music world has also been coming to terms with the austerity policies of the *Partido Popular*, pledged to encouraging

*At last... the **Teatro Real**. See page 203*

private funding for the arts, in a context in which, apart from the ever-present (and indispensable) savings banks such as the Caja de Madrid, business has rarely shown consistent interest in sponsorship. The interest generated by the Real, it is fondly hoped, will bring a change in this situation.

Tickets & programmes

The main state theatres, the **Auditorio Nacional**, the **Teatro de la Zarzuela**, the **Comedia**, the **María Guerrero** and the currently-closed **Olimpia** (for the latter three, *see chapter* **Theatre**), have a joint ticketing system which makes it possible to buy tickets for all these venues at any one of them. Tickets for large-scale concerts at the Auditorio Nacional are often hard to come by: in many cases most tickets are only available to subscribers with season tickets for a specific concert series, and the number on public sale is limited. Season tickets bring significant reductions, and are recommended if you are planning a longer stay. Tickets for the ONE's lower-price Sunday morning concerts go on sale the same day or shortly in advance, and are in great demand (*see below* **Auditorio Nacional**).

As with theatres, tickets for many music venues can be bought with a credit card through savings banks (*see p176*). The one most active in the music field is **Cajamadrid** (**902 48 84 88**), which handles tickets for the **Auditorio**, the **Zarzuela**, the **Teatro Real** and several other venues.

The **Teatro Real** does not come within the state theatre scheme. Again, there has a season ticket system, and tickets on public sale for some productions have been very scarce, a growing cause for complaint among music fans. Tickets officially go on sale 30 days in advance of the performance, at the box office and through Cajamadrid. There is a special phone number for credit card bookings from abroad (34 91 558 87 87). The main auditorium is divided into seven zones (A-G), with widely differing prices; some of the cheapest seats (in F and G) have very limited vision. Prices also vary considerably between productions, and as in most opera houses are much higher for premières.

Concert seasons are packed into the October to June period; in summer, festivals take over (*see below, and p9*). Local listings magazines (*see p199*) are not always comprehensive on classical music, and it's worth picking up programme leaflets at individual theatres and tourist offices.

Orchestras & ensembles

Grupo Círculo

Founded in 1983 and based at the **Círculo de Bellas Artes** (*see below*), this 11-strong group has as its musical director José Luis Temes, one of Madrid's most distinguished contemporary musicians. The group's continuity is an indication of its members' determination and strong sense of inspiration. They divide their time between performances and recording of Spanish contemporary music, featuring works by modern composers of international renown such as Cristóbal Halffter and Luis de Pablo, and younger, lesser-known names.

Orquesta Nacional de España & Coro Nacional de España

The flagships of Spanish classical music over the last 50 years. Their triple obligations of attracting public attention, creating basic repertoires and simultaneously enlarging them into new areas have often been too much to bear. Initially formed in 1938 in Barcelona, then capital of the Spanish Republic, the orchestra was re-created two years later in Madrid after the Nationalist victory. Recently it has been marked by internal strife, and some music fans suggest that it needs a good, forceful conductor in order to perform up to scratch. Musicians, whose role is complicated by their position as state employees, went on strike in 1993 for the first time in the orchestra's history, and the director, Italian Aldo Ceccato, left the following year. Since then the ONE has performed under guest musical directors, most frequently the Austrian Walter Weller, but also including Antoni Ros Marbà and even Yehudi Menuhin. Currently there is still no permanent director, although Rafael Frühbeck de Burgos holds the position of Director Emeritus and clearly has much to say in its running. The National Choir also saw the departure of its director, Adolfo Gutiérrez Viejo, although in this case a replacement has been appointed, the German Rainer Steubing. Orchestra and choir have an excellent home in the Auditorio Nacional, but funding cuts exacerbate the occasional disarray.

Orquesta y Coro de RTVE

Born out of the need to perform music for broadcasting, the Spanish Radio and Television Orchestra began concert performances in the 1960s. Instrumental in its origins was Ernesto Halffter, one of the finest modern Spanish composers and uncle of Cristóbal Halffter. It has made magnificent recordings of Spanish works, and a very successful *Antología de la Zarzuela*. It moved into the **Teatro Monumental** (*see below*) in 1988, and had Romanian Sergiu Comissiona as director from 1990 to 1998, giving it a rare continuity which it is hoped will continue under new director Enrique García Asensio. The varied repertoire covers romantic classics, Spanish works and contemporary music.

Orquesta Sinfónica de Madrid

Unencumbered by extra-musical problems, this orchestra was founded in 1903. Its most famous director was the violinist Enrique Fernández Arbós, appointed in 1905 and in place for 30 years, who dominated the pre-war period so much that the orchestra became known as the *Arbós*. Despite several attempts to revive the orchestra's fortunes, it was not until 1981 that it fully recovered from the disintegration caused by the Civil War. That year saw its controversial appointment as resident orchestra at the **Teatro de la Zarzuela** (*see below*), a move opposed by Madrid's two other major orchestras. It justified the vote of confidence, and recently has taken up temporary residence at the Teatro Real, although it still occasionally performs elsewhere.

Trio Mompou

Based in Madrid, and so-named as a tribute to the late Catalan composer and master pianist Frederic Mompou, this contemporary chamber ensemble is highly regarded at home and abroad. Mompou himself once remarked on the 'quality and exquisite musicality of their performances', and their repertoire comprises over a hundred works by almost every Spanish composer of this century as well as some from elsewhere. An important facet of their activity is the presentation of totally new work. Highly recommended.

Venues

The **Real Academia de Bellas Artes de San Fernando** (*see page 78*) hosts free chamber concerts in its grand eighteenth-century building at noon on most Saturdays from October to May, which are broadcast on RNE-2 radio. It also sometimes hosts other concerts.

Auditorio Nacional de Música

C/Príncipe de Vergara 146 (91 337 01 00). Metro Cruz del Rayo/bus 1, 29, 52. **Open** *box office* 5-7pm Mon, 10am-5pm Tue-Fri, 11am-1pm Sat, also Cajamadrid. Closed Aug. **Main season** Oct-June. **Tickets** *ONE concerts* 800-4,200ptas Fri, Sat; 550-2,200ptas Sun; other concerts vary. **Credit** AmEx, DC, MC, V.

The inauguration of this ugly building in 1988 put Madrid on the itineraries of the most important international conductors, soloists and orchestras, attracted by a new symphony hall rivalling the Berlin Philharmonie and Amsterdam Concertgebouw in capacity (2,000-plus in the main hall). Home to the **Orquesta Nacional de España** and its associated choir and the impressive **Joven Orquesta Nacional de España** youth orchestra, it has, despite outward appearances, symphonic and chamber music halls that are light, comfortable and have pretty good acoustics (although strangely they are sometimes better in the circle than the stalls). It hosts an intensive concert programme in the relatively short October-June season, with performances virtually every night except Sundays and Mondays. Most are structured in regular seasons or concert series, run in parallel. The centrepiece season features the ONE with international guest conductors and soloists, with concerts at 7.30pm on Fridays and Saturdays and 11.30am on Sundays. Tickets for Sunday concerts are cheaper and go on sale just one hour in advance; some extra tickets are also made available four weeks in advance, and a noticeboard outside the Chamber Hall indicates which concerts still have tickets available. Another season (very difficult to get into for non-season ticket holders), from October to May and currently titled *Orquestas del Mundo*, features international ensembles of the standing of the King's Consort, the Warsaw Symphony or the French National Orchestra. There is also a regular season of two concerts per month sponsored by the private *Asociación Filarmónica de Madrid*, featuring major international artists and open to non-members (but at a higher price), and many one-off concerts through the year. The main events in the 692-seat chamber hall (the *Sala de Cámara*) are the seasons *Cámara y Polifonía* – 'Chamber and Polyphony' – on Tuesdays and Thursdays from October to June, and *Liceo de Cámara*, featuring a varied chamber programme on different nights of the week. Chamber works receive less attention from Madrid music-goers, so finding tickets is usually less of a problem.

Círculo de Bellas Artes

C/Marqués de Casa Riera 2 (91 360 54 00/902 422 442). Metro Banco de España, Sevilla/bus all routes to C/Alcalá or Cibeles. **Season** Sept-June.
Tickets prices variable. **Map G7**
Among its many activities the Circulo is an important contemporary music centre, acting as base for the **Grupo Círculo**, hosting concerts of the **Centro para la Difusión** de la Música **Contemporánea** and international groups and welcoming an ever-wider range of music from the **Festimad** pop and new music festival (*see p7*) to jazz, new age, *fados* and other styles. *See also chapters* **Sightseeing**, **Cafés & Bars**, **Art Galleries** *and* **Theatre**.

Teatro Calderón

C/Atocha 18 (91 369 14 34).
Metro Sol, Tirso de Molina/bus 6, 26 32, 65. **Open** box office 11am-2pm, 4pm-9pm, daily, also Cajamadrid.
Main Season Sept-July. **Tickets** 3,000-9,000ptas; 2,000-7,000ptas Tue. **Credit** AmEx, MC, V. **Map E8**
If tickets are unavailable at the Real – as is often the case – opera fans have the alternative of coming to this theatre, which, under José Luis Moreno, has presented an imaginative regular season for three years now and plans to continue in the foreseeable future.

Madrid's own tunes: *Zarzuela*

Madrid is the home of *zarzuela*, Spain's very own form of light opera. Its distant origins are in the Golden Age, in the entertainments staged for King Philip IV at the hunting lodge of La Zarzuela outside Madrid. Real *zarzuela* in its recognisable, commercial, form, however, developed from the 1830s onwards. It is comparable to the contemporary German *singspiel* or Viennese operetta, but with a distinctively Spanish musical idiom.

At the end of the last century *zarzuelas* dominated the world of entertainment in Madrid, and there were often ten different productions playing in the city at the same time. Their plots dealt not with great themes or heroic figures, but instead offered very identifiable, usually comic, sometimes slightly bawdy scenes of local life. *Zarzuelas* played a great part in establishing the *castizo* mythology of working-class Madrid (*see page 8*), with stories of street-corner romances between flat-capped *chulos* and flashing-eyed, razor-tongued *chulapas* in flowered shawls, set in the tenements and markets of La Latina and Lavapiés. The world of *zarzuela* also became part of this mythology itself, since singers like the baritone Emilio Mesejo or the soprano La Pastora entered the jet set of the era, and it was the height of fashion for young aristocrats to have *las tiples*, the girls of the *zarzuela* chorus, as lovers.

The *zarzuela* repertoire is huge, and includes some fine, sometimes subtle music. Tomás Bretón's *La Verbena de la Paloma*, Pablo Sorozábal's *La del Manojo de Rosas,* Ruperto Chapí's *La Revoltosa* and Lorente and Serrano's *La Dolorosa* are some of the classics. New *zarzuelas* were produced right up until the 1930s, and it was only the Civil War and its aftermath, with the body-blows they dealt to Madrid's traditional culture, that saw a final decline in the genre's popularity and creativity.

More recently *zarzuela* has struggled against the contempt of many serious music-lovers, and the accusation that it is opera's poor relation. It has also been dismissed as just plain corny and kitsch. Nevertheless, it is one of Spain's, and above all Madrid's, most distinctive cultural forms, it retains a keen following, and there is considerable official interest in ensuring it survives. An enthusiastic supporter is Plácido Domingo, son of *zarzuela* singers, who has successfully recorded collections of *zarzuela* songs.

Where to find it

Madrid's *zarzuela* season is in summer, from June to September. The **Auditorio Nacional** and **Teatro de la Zarzuela** each stage at least one production each year. Three other venues also stage *zarzuelas* every summer – the **Centro Cultural de la Villa**, **Teatro Albéniz** and **Teatro de Madrid** (*see chapters* **Dance** *and* **Theatre**). One of the most popular ways to catch a production, though, is in the traditional, open-air setting of La Corrala. *Zarzuela* buffs may also hear it sung in a handful of bars in the city.

La Corrala

C/Tribulete 12 & C/Sombrerete 13 (no phone).
Metro Embajadores, Lavapiés/bus all routes to
Embajadores. **Information** 010. **Season** July, Aug.
Box office one hour before performance.
Performances 10pm Tue-Sun. **Tickets** *average* 2,000ptas. **No credit cards. Map E10**
This 1882 building is the best surviving example of the corridor-tenements that were once found throughout working-class Madrid (*see p61*), and which formed the backdrop to many a popular *zarzuela*. Since its restoration in 1979 it has been used to stage *zarzuela*, effectively in a real-life setting. Only one production each year – usually one of the classics of the genre – during a short, month-and-a-half season. This event has become a fixture of the Madrid summer scene, and to cap the nostalgic atmosphere some of the audience turn up in genuine 1890s *castizo* costume.

Teatro Monumental

C/Atocha 65 (91 429 81 19). Metro Antón Martín/bus 6, 26, 32. **Open** *box office* 11am-2pm, 5-7pm, daily. **Season** Oct-April. **Ticket** 1,200-2,200ptas; *season tickets* 7,900-15,800ptas. **No credit cards. Map G9**

In no way comparable to the Auditorio, the Zarzuela or the Real in facilities, this theatre has as its main function that of recording concerts by the **RTVE** orchestra and choir for broadcasting – which it does very well. It's a reasonably-priced venue, which offers orchestral concerts, opera and *zarzuela*, and opens to the public for rehearsals for free on Thursday mornings (you must call first and put your name on a list, as demand from school groups is high). Among the concert series of the RTVE orchestra is a contemporary season, *Música del Siglo XX*, from October to April.

Teatro Real

Plaza de Oriente (91 516 06 60/91 516 06 06). Metro Opera/bus 3, 25, 39, 148. **Open** *box office* 10am-1.30pm, 5.30-8pm, Mon-Sat, also Caja Madrid. **Season** Sept-July. **Tickets** *opera average* 2,000-15,000ptas; *concerts from* 800ptas. **Credit** AmEx, DC, MC, V. **Map C/D7**

Finally open, and possibly the most technologically advanced opera house in Europe. First inaugurated in 1850, the Real has had many ups and downs in its history, and was in a pretty run-down state by the 1980s, so there was little disagreement with its closure for renovation in 1987. After all the time and money invested since then, as the project mushroomed, the theatre's management is now set on proving that the wait was worthwhile. One of the building's main boasts is the splendid, horseshoe-shaped main hall, which, it is claimed, could contain the the entire Telefónica building from the Gran Vía. The stage itself is a real feat of engineering, with a series of platforms built on a waterwheel principle so that up to six sets can be in use swung into place at any one time. The acoustics are so good that sound quality is practically the same everywhere in the hall. Décor is accordingly lavish: the elliptical main foyer, with columns in fine wood, gives a feel of monumental roominess in what is in fact a limited space. The restaurant, café and other spaces are equally impressive.

At present the semi-private foundation that runs the theatre has a two-year mandate to prepare the ground for the future. The theatre still has no permanent orchestra, choir or ballet company, and the management has committed itself to making firm decisions in this area by the end of the 1998-9 season. In terms of actual productions so far, critics have been sharp to pick up on perceived failings both in artistic policy and the general running of the theatre. Unanimously acclaimed, though, have been productions – by invited companies from Brussels and Paris – of Britten's *Peter Grimes* and Janacek's *The Cunning Little Vixen*, and the Pina Bausch company's *Carnations*, although the latter was not a hit with the conservative Madrid public, many of whom left in the interval. The 1998-9 season saw a new, home-grown *Aida* that was reasonably well-received, and scheduled for later in the year are *La Bohème*, *Carmen*, Massenet's *Werther*, with Alfredo Kraus, and Philip Glass's *O Corvo Branco*, which is sure to raise polemic. The problem for many music lovers has simply been that of getting into the place, since tickets have often been as scarce as the proverbial gold dust.

Teatro de la Zarzuela

C/Jovellanos 4 (91 524 54 00). Metro Sevilla, Banco de España/bus all routes to Plaza de Cibeles. **Open** *box office* noon-5pm daily (noon-8pm performance days), also Caja Madrid. **Season** Sept-July. **Tickets** *average* 1,200-4,500ptas. **Credit** AmEx, DC, MC, V. **Map F7**

A theatre with a chequered history. Designed on the lines of Milan's Scala, this beautiful building was opened in 1856, in an attempt to boost the prestige of *zarzuela*. It was ravaged by fire in 1909, but rebuilt. Callas sang here in 1958, and an annual opera festival began in 1964. It was declared a national monument in 1994. For ten years from 1987 it was Madrid's official opera house, but now, unshackled of that

responsibility can again dedicate more resources to *zarzuela*, as well as ballet and an interesting range of smaller-scale operatic work (chamber pieces and very modern works) not found at the Real. Its current musical director is Miguel Roa, but many other conductors make guest appearances. The theatre also hosts the *Ciclo Lied*, an annual series of Lieder concerts with artists of the calibre of Anne-Sofie Von Otter, Olaf Bär, Thomas Hampson, Thomas Quasthoff, Bryn Terfel and Teresa Berganza. It runs from October to late April.

Institutions

Centro para la Difusión de la Música Contemporánea

Museo Nacional Centro de Arte Reina Sofía, C/Santa Isabel 52 (91 467 50 62). Metro Atocha/bus all routes to Atocha. **Season** Oct-June. **Map G10**

Founded in 1983, this innovative music centre has been based at the **Reina Sofía** (*see pp76-7*), since 1987. In its early stages the pressure of battling against musical conservatism nearly finished off its founder, composer Luis de Pablo, who left after only two years. However, thanks to his work the centre became established as the city's main focus for contemporary music. It gives 30 or so commissions annually to Spanish and foreign composers, which are premièred in two or three concerts each month, on Wednesdays in the chamber hall of the **Auditorio Nacional**, on Sunday mornings in the **Círculo de Bellas Artes** and in some other venues.

Fundación Juan March

C/Castelló 77 (91 435 42 40). Metro Núñez de Balboa/bus 9, 19, 29, 52. **Main season** Oct-June. **Map K2**

The Fundación March, a major player in many areas of the arts in Spain (*see chapter* **Art Galleries**), has provided financial support for musical creation and research since 1955. The small concert hall is in constant use, and its free concerts at noon on Saturdays and Mondays and 7.30pm on Wednesdays, featuring a variety of styles and genres, are recommended. The Foundation also organises concerts for young people, and has an extensive music library.

Festivals & other venues

The main festivals in Madrid that feature classical music are the **Veranos de la Villa** and **Festival de Otoño** (*see pp9-10*). In addition, Madrid offers many other opportunities to see concerts in unique and historic venues, sometimes for free. Open-air concerts are held in city-funded cultural centres such as the **Centro Cultural Conde Duque** (*see chapter* **Art Galleries**). For information, consult tourist offices or the 010 phoneline (*see p261*). A small festival within the framework of the Festival de Otoño that is held out of town in **Aranjuez** (*see pp230-2*) is **Música Antigua de Aranjuez**, featuring early music and chamber groups from many countries. Information is available on the *012* line or from the promotors, **CP Conciertos** (91 447 64 00).

There are bars for most occasions in Madrid, and some host good music. **Café Viena** has sessions every Monday where opera and *zarzuela* singers perform (*see p141*).

La Fídula

C/Huertas 57 (91 429 29 47). Metro Antón Martín/bus 6, 26, 32, 65. **Open** 6pm-3am Mon-Thur, Sun; 6pm-4am Fri, Sat. July, Aug opens at 9pm. **Admission** free. **Map F8**

La Fídula, in the heart of the Huertas bar district, is a 'café-concert', presenting small concerts – quartets, trios, soloists, singers – most nights of the week from September to June, and at weekends in summer. The performers are mostly music students, but often extremely good, and it's pleasant just as a bar. The musical menu is also increasingly diverse, and it's possible to catch jazz and tango as well these days.

Music: Rock, Roots & Jazz

Cuban, African, Jazz... and Spanish. Madrid's music scene has wide horizons, and sends out some fascinating cross-currents.

After a few years in the doldrums, Madrid's live music scene perked up again in the mid-'90s, regaining a lot of the vibrancy it had shown ten years earlier. Music had suffered from a (perhaps apparent) post-*Movida* depression, as well as from the (very real) zeal of the *Partido Popular* city hall in pushing through a policy of earlier closing times and closing down venues for minor irregularities, all to clamp down on a supposed wave of immorality said to have flowed from the deliberate laxity of earlier Socialist administrations.

Even today, the PP Ayuntamiento still gives only lukewarm support to non-classical or non-ultra-mainstream music in the city. However, in spite of the best efforts of Mayor Alvarez del Manzano and his cronies to encourage what they see as Spanish and traditional, a stealthy music revolution has been taking place in Madrid, thanks in large part to the efforts of several modest-sized venues with eclectic, freeranging programming policies that deliberately set out to encourage interest in a complete diversity of musical styles. In the face of the relative absence of large venues, it is these smaller places that have taken on the job of breathing new life into the music scene.

Thanks to the imaginatively open programmes of venues like **Suristán**, previously overlooked – often non-Spanish – types of music are in vogue: whereas salsa was once looked down upon, flamenco was what their Andalusian grandparents listened to and African music was simply ignored, all are now enjoying unprecedented popularity. Today, if one word can sum up the atmosphere it is the fruitful concept *mestizaje*, Spanish for 'crossbreeding' or 'intermixing'. Flamenco, rock, Arab or Cuban music can all feature on different nights, and all have influence on local musicians.

This free-flowing mixing has been reflected in two parallel trends – expanding creativity on the part of Spanish artists, and an explosion in musicians from outside Spain regularly playing in Madrid. Cuba is dear to the heart of many Spanish music fans, and one of the most vibrant elements in the current scene is the wealth of talent from the island that visits frequently, from the nonagenar-ian Compay Segundo to the versatile young band Habana Abierto. A similar phenomenon has occurred with African artists, so that groups such as Afrika Lisanga, Bidinte, Las Hijas del Sol and Rasha have become well-known on the circuit.

Spanish musicians themselves have become increasingly open to outside influences, while at the same time looking to their own roots without many of the neuroses that sometimes characterised previous generations. Flamenco, still basking in the fashionable status it has acquired in the '90s, is still perhaps the most exciting current within Spanish music (*see chapter* **Flamenco**). In pop-rock, *mestizaje* is evident in innovative acts such as Amparanoia from Granada, who combine bluesy vocals with a Caribbean feel and tunes that run from Mexican *rancheras* to languid Cuban *boleros*.

The **Festimad** festival each May (*see page 7*) has done a lot to encourage local indie groups. Sharing top of the bill in 1998 were Massive Attack and a local indie group, Dover, who sing in English. There are several more strongly Anglo-influenced bands in the city as well, such as Sexy Sadie and Australian Blondes.

JAZZ & OTHERS

Madrid has a vibrant jazz scene, with a devoted, long-standing public: there are only around five main venues that function throughout the year, but two of them – **Café Central** and **Clamores** – are absolutely top-notch. The music also has its moment during the autumn **Festival Internacional de Jazz**, which attracts a good many heavyweights from the international circuit.

Another kind of music that has been enjoying a revival is that of *cantautores*, Spanish singer-songwriters, more associated with the politicised '60s and 70s. A new generation of performers has revitalised the genre, adding rock, pop and Latin rhythms, and a wealth of smallish locales such as the **Café de la Palma** give a stage to singers like Ismael Serrano, Pablo Bicho and Jorge Drexler.

Spain also, of course, still has – perhaps more than most non-English speaking European countries – its own bustling, traditional commercial music scene, *canción española*, music more to the taste of the local authorities. It thrives on in the face of international competition, and older performers such as Rocío Jurado or Isabel Pantoja can be heard belting out their dramatic tunes on radios in shops and cafés all over Madrid, as well as at venues such as the **Parque de Atracciones** or **Teatro La Latina** (*see page 221*). The boundaries of the genre – especially between it and flamenco – are always flexible, however, and there are also younger rock-influenced artists such as Rosario and Azúcar Moreno (a duo of two sisters), acts that are both massively popular.

Venues/programmes

Madrid continues to suffer from a shortage of medium-sized, centrally located music venues, but the situation has improved with the appearance of several venues with good facilities scattered around the city such as **La Riviera**, **Suristán**, **Sala Caracol** and **Moby Dick**. Big stadium concerts take place at Atlético Madrid's home, the **Vicente Calderón**, or the **Palacio de los Deportes** (*see page 213*). Another venue which has seen top names recently is the **Palacio de Congresos** in the Castellana (*see page 264*), and the bullring, **Las Ventas**, makes an excellent outdoor concert space, used particularly during festivals (*see chapters* **Madrid by Season** *and* **Bullfighting**).

In the *Movida* years, Malasaña was the most happening *barrio* for live music, but venues have now sprouted up in many parts of the city. Entrance to small venues is often free, or costs only a few hundred pesetas, with *consumición* (one drink) included. Venues that do not charge entry generally expect to make their money at the bar, so drinks cost more than they would elsewhere. Many places combine live gigs or cabaret with DJ sessions, and similarly, many venues listed in *chapter* **Nightlife** sometimes host live music: two that present live acts most frequently are **La Boca del Lobo** (pop-rock, singer-songwriters) and **Arena** (pop-rock, some techno, indie bands).

Many gigs are sponsored by radio stations such as **Cadena Ser** or **Onda Cero**, which often give away promotional tickets. The *Guía del Ocio* and the *Metrópoli* supplement of *El Mundo* (*see page 199*) both have listings of upcoming gigs, although they're not always comprehensive. Otherwise, concert information comes on flyposters and in fanzines, usually free from bars and music and fashion shops (*see pages 160-1, 171*). Magazines to look for include *What Music?*, *Novedades*, *AB* and the irregular *Undersounds*. For ticket agencies, *see page 176*. Venues do not normally accept credit cards at the door.

Rock/world music

Al'Laboratorio

C/Colón 14 (91 532 26 69). Metro Tribunal/bus 3, 40, 149. **Open** 9pm-3am Tue-Thur, 9pm-6am Fri-Sun. **Admission** *average* 500ptas. **Map F5**

Country & Western décor combines with pop music at this lively, if dingy, two-floor Malasaña local. You won't find any big names here on Thursday, Friday and Saturday nights, but Al'Lab declares 'a passion for music' and encourages young groups, organising 'battle of the bands'-style contests.

Café de la Palma

C/de la Palma 62 (91 522 50 31). Metro Noviciado/bus 147 **Open** 4pm-3am Mon-Wed, Sun; 4pm-4am Thur; 4pm-5am Fri, Sat. **Admission** *concert nights* 1,000ptas. **Map E4**

Very popular, this bar has three separate areas, one of which serves as a performance space for a wide range of artists.

High on the list are Madrid's new generation of singer-songwriters, but Cuban groups often play and the flamenco-crossover fraternity are well represented as well. Tuesday nights brings story-telling (*cuentacuentos*), without music.

Chesterfield Café

C/Serrano Jover 5 (91 542 28 17). *Metro Argüelles/bus 1, 2, 21, 44, 133, N18.* **Open** noon-3.30am daily. **Map C3**

Opened in 1997, with razzmatazz Americana décor, the Chesterfield is part of an ersatz-American chain that began in Paris and has now reached Moscow. Apart from offering food (Tex-Mex and Italian) and snacks at all times, the café, on two floors, hosts live gigs from Wednesday to Sunday at 11.30pm. Bands play mostly deeply innovative basic boogie rock: among the first artists billed were none other than hepcats Keanu Reeves and John 'you are the pits' McEnroe.

La Coquette

C/de las Hileras 14 (no phone). *Metro Opera, Sol/bus 3, 25, 39, 500, N13, N15.* **Open** 8pm-2.30am daily. **Map D7**

Known as the Blues Bar, because that's what it is – Madrid's only bar dedicated to blues. Swiss-Spanish owner Albert has quite a record collection, and purists won't be disappointed. Old-school blues bands play from Tuesday to Thursday, and if you don't mind snogging students and hash smoke, you can enjoy well-intentioned if a bit ersatz Spanish harp-wailing. Drinks cost about 150ptas extra during performances.

Davai

C/Flor Baja 1 (91 547 57 11). Metro Plaza de España/bus all routes Plaza de España. **Open** 11pm-5am daily. **Admission** *concert nights* 700ptas. **Map D5**

Davai was opened only in 1997 as a club with a mission, to become the focal point of Madrid's cutting-edge club and music scene, a ground-breaking meeting point for musicians and fans. It offered a range of club sessions with underground, garage, house, funk, acid jazz through the week, and also live gigs with pop-rock, world music, flamenco-pop and other styles. However, only a year after inauguration it seems to have lost its sense of direction: the DJ and club menu has become much more pedestrian, and the mostly pop-rock live programme – now with gigs Thursday to Saturday nearly every week – is unpredictable. *See also chapter* **Nightlife**.

Downtown

C/Covarrubias 31. Metro Alonso Martínez/bus 3, 37, 40, 147, 149, N19. **Open** 10pm-2am Mon-Thur, Sun; 10pm-3.30am Fri, Sat. **Map G3**

Just a short walk up from the Glorieta de Bilbao, close to the Plaza de Chamberí, Downtown has a tiny stage to host the best of Madrid's blues bands on Fridays and Saturdays, and an authentic, bluesy bar-room feel the rest of the week.

Honky Tonk

C/Covarrubias 24 (91 445 79 38). *Metro Alonso Martínez/bus 3, 37, 40, 147, 149, N19.* **Open** 9pm-5am daily. **Map G3**

Going strong for nearly a decade, and with a restaurant attached, the Honky Tonk, forming something of a pair with Downtown, offers local country, blues and rock acts every night of the week. The clientèle are mainly 30-plus: it fills up after 2am and, while no strict dress code applies, if there's a queue the smartish have a better chance of getting in.

Maravillas

C/San Vicente Ferrer 35 (91 523 30 71). *Metro Tribunal, Bilbao/bus 3, 40, 149, N19.* **Open** 9am-3.30am Tue-Thur, Sun; 9am-6am Fri, Sat. **Admission** usually free; 800ptas some concerts. **Map E4**

An 'alternative pop' club in the heart of Malasaña that usually offers live music (especially grunge, indie and Britpop-influenced bands) on Fridays and Saturdays. Watch out for posters announcing forthcoming gigs. On non-gig nights, you can hear international indie sounds, and, usually, ambient and trance on Thursdays. The crowd is pretty young.

Moby Dick/The Irish Rover

Avda de Brasil 5-7 (91 556 72 81/91 555 76 71).
Metro Santiago Bernabéu/bus 5, 43, 126, 149, N20.
Open *Moby Dick* 10pm-5am Mon-Sat; *The Irish Rover* 11am-2.30am Mon-Thur, Sun; 11am-3.30am Fri, Sat.
Decked out in fairly kitsch nautical-theme décor, with port-hole windows and bottles dangling in nets, **Moby Dick** alternates between being a nightspot frequented by the *pijo* crowd and a live music joint several nights a week, with performances of pop, blues and rock. Many of the English-speaking bands on the Madrid circuit play here. Attached to it (Avda de Brasil 7) is **The Irish Rover**, a huge Irish theme pub with regular live Irish, folk and Country music, and occasional theatre productions in English. Two *terrazas*, one out front and a garden at the back, shared by both bars, add an extra dimension in summer. *See also chapter* **Nightlife**.

La Riviera

Paseo Bajo de la Virgen del Puerto s/n,
near Puente de Segovia (91 365 24 15).
Metro Príncipe Pío/bus 25, 31, 39, 138, C, N15, N16.
Open midnight-6am Tue-Sun. **Admission** 1,500ptas; *concerts average* 2,500-5,000ptas. **Map A8**
A disco next to the Manzanares, the Riviera is also Madrid's best bigger-than-club size music venue, with good acoustics and several bars decorated in different styles. Part of its roof opens up in the summer, creating a very large *terraza*. The crowd tends to be trendy 20- and 30-somethings, and recent concerts have included Blur, Patti Smith, Manu Dibango, Neneh Cherry, the Soweto String Quartet, Marilyn Manson, Ali Farka Touré and Massive Attack. It also attracts top salsa bands, and is often used for new record presentations, big PR functions and so on.

La Sala

Avda Nuestra Señora de Fátima 42 (91 462 77 89).
Metro Carabanchel/bus 17, 35, N14.
Open 7pm-5am daily. **Admission** 1,000ptas.
Definitely not in the city centre, since this bar-venue is in the deeply unfashionable proletarian suburb of Carabanchel, but it's worth seeking out. It's really two bars in one: at street level it's a typical Madrid bar, with pool table, videos, pinball machines and loud music; above is a completely different setting, a purpose-built venue holding around 300 people, with excellent sound, lighting and atmosphere. There are live bands most nights of the week, Spanish rockers in the main, but playing a range of styles.

Sala Caracol

C/Bernardino Obregón 18 (91 527 35 94).
Metro Embajadores/bus all routes to Embajadores.
Open 9pm-3am Wed-Sun. **Admission** *average* 1.500-3,500ptas, incl one drink.
Once one of Madrid's foremost specialist flamenco venues, Caracol took a radically different tack in 1996. They still usually have a pure-flamenco night once a week (Wednesday or Thursday), but otherwise follow **Suristán** (*see below*) in presenting a multi-varied, multi-ethnic range of music from across the world. African and Cuban music figure high on the agenda, but most recently rock in all its forms has carved out a niche. Cornershop and Catatonia have both visited.

Siroco

C/San Dimas 3 (91 593 30 70).
Metro San Bernardo, Noviciado/bus 21, 147. **Open** 9.30pm-3am Tue-Thur; 10pm-5.30am Fri, Sat.
Admission *average* 1.500ptas. **Map E4**
An unpretentious little place, with a bar upstairs and disco in the basement, that hosts local bands of the rock/pop/funk/indie persuasion, and is often frequented by A &R

types. It even has its own record label. Also very much a place to be as a club, with resident DJs offering many different styles of music. *See also chapter* **Nightlife**.

El Sol

C/Jardines 3 (91 532 64 90). Metro Gran Vía/bus all routes to Gran Vía. **Open** 1.30am-5.30am Tue-Sat.
Admission *average* 1,000ptas. **Map E7**
One of the melting pots of the *Movida* in the 1980s, this popular venue attracts Spanish and international acts of all styles (pop, funk, punk, rock, world music...), thanks to its excellent acoustics and the proximity of the stage to the audience. It's a bit tatty, but in a likeable way, and open very late. DJs play often funk-oriented sessions at other times, so expect to queue at weekends. *See also chapter* **Nightlife**.

Suristán

C/de la Cruz 7 (91 532 39 09). Metro Sevilla, Sol/bus all routes to Puerta del Sol. **Open** 10pm-5.30am daily.
Admission 1,000ptas. **Map E7**
This medium-sized venue with ethnic décor was unique in Madrid when it opened in 1994 in its pioneering approach to live music. Practically every night of the week you can experience a different musical style – from African music to rock, singer-songwriters, Brazilian and Cuban artists. Flamenco is a permanent speciality. Acoustics are good, but get there early for a decent view, as the place packs out, and it doesn't have the best layout. (Recorded) music is as varied as the amiable, likeably mixed crowd. *See also chapters* **Nightlife** *and* **Flamenco**.

Vapor Blues

C/Doctor Esquerdo 52 (91 504 21 50). Metro Sainz de Baranda/bus 2, 30, 56, 71, 143. **Open** 11am-4am daily.
A pub-like bar, a little off the beaten track, with a small room at the back which from Thursday to Sunday hosts pretty serious local r&b and blues exponents. Look out for Ñaco Goñi or Francisco Simón, who are always good.

Jazz

Café Central

Plaza del Ángel 10 (91 369 41 43).
Metro Antón Martín, Sol/bus all routes to Puerta del Sol. **Open** 2pm-3.30am daily. **Admission** *supplement on first drink on concert nights* 700-1,500ptas. **Map E8**
This beautiful high-ceilinged café/bar just off Plaza Santa Ana was a mirror shop until its conversion in the early '80s. Since then it has built a reputation as Madrid's best jazz venue, and one of the best in Europe. Leading international and Spanish performers (George Adams, Don Pullen, Jorge Pardo, Bob Sands) play in a relaxed atmosphere; the wonderful Cuban bolero queen Lucrecia also appears regularly.

Café Populart

C/Huertas 22 (91 429 84 07). Metro Antón Martín/bus 6, 26, 32. **Open** 4pm-2.30am Mon-Thur, Sun; 4pm-3.30am Fri, Sat. **Admission** *supplement on first drink on concert nights* 250-1,000ptas. **Map F8**
A short walk from the Central, this former pottery shop puts on a range of music from pure jazz and blues to salsa and reggae. There are two sets nightly, at 10.30pm and 1am, and the atmosphere's nicely relaxed and friendly, although if you really want a good view you need to get there early.

Clamores

C/Alburquerque 14 (91 445 79 38). Metro Bilbao/bus 3, 21, 37, 149, N19. **Open** 7pm-3am Mon-Thur, Sun; 7pm-4am Fri, Sat. **Admission** *supplement on first drink on concert nights* 500-1,000ptas. **Map F3**
This premier jazz club – substantially bigger than others in Madrid – hosts a sometimes bizarre range of events that have included tango and karaoke nights. The crowd, though, are

*Blowing horns at the **Café Central**.*

good-natured and jazz-knowledgeable. Two other features to mention – clients play ludo (yes, ludo) in the early evening, and it claims to have Madrid's biggest selection of *cava*. Even so, Clamores still finds time to host a properly satisfying jazz programme, as well as other kinds of music from pop to soul, blues, reggae and various Latin American styles, especially musicians from the seemingly endless Cuban talent mine. A frequent performer is Compay Segundo, aged over 90, who played on 'Buenavista Social Club' with Ry Cooder.

Colegio Mayor San Juan Evangelista

C/Gregorio del Amo 4 (91 534 24 00). Metro Metropolitano/bus 132, F, C. **Concerts** usually Oct-June 10.30pm Fri, Sat; 8pm Sun. **Admission** 1,000-2,500ptas. The music club in this student residence (open to, and long popular with, non-students) in the Ciudad Universitaria has over many years established a reputation as one of Madrid's most discerning jazz venues. It also presents concerts of classical and world music, and a festival of flamenco (*see chapter* **Flamenco**). The administration do not go out of their way to sell themselves, so it's necessary to keep a lookout for for posters advertising gigs.

Dizzy Jazz

Calle de la Luz 8, Las Matas (91 636 02 30/91 635 65 54) Cercanías C-8, C-10 to Las Matas/bus 622 from Moncloa. **Open** 9pm-midnight Tue-Thur, Sun, 9pm-3am Fri, Sat. A long way from town on the way to the Guadarrama, Dizzy Jazz is a welcoming little spot worth visiting if you're in the sierra. A frequent performer is Brazilian Jayme Marqués.

Segundo Jazz

C/Comandante Zorita 8 (91 554 94 37). Metro Nuevos Ministerios, Cuatro Caminos/bus 3, 43, 149, C, N19, N20. **Open** 7pm-4am daily. **Admission** *supplement on first drink on concert nights* 600ptas. A mixed bag: '60s nights on Mondays, live jazz from Tuesday to Saturdays (unknowns midweek, names on the local scene and some international acts Fridays and Saturdays) and *cantautores* on Sundays.

Triskel Tavern

C/San Vicente Ferrer 3 (91 523 27 83). Metro Tribunal/bus 3, 40, 149, N19. **Open** 10am-3am, Aug 7pm-3am, daily. **Map F4**
A popular Malasaña Irish pub that hosts a regular Tuesday night jazz jam (about 11pm) with resident bands, and has also presented some very strong guest performers, among them Jorge Pardo and Arturo Sándoval. As you might expect, Irish music often features on other nights (*see also page 137*).

Latin

For more Latin clubs, slightly less likely to feature live bands, *see chapter* **Nightlife**.

Café del Foro

C/San Andrés 38 (91 445 37 52). Metro Bilbao, Tribunal/bus 3, 21, 147, 149, N19. **Open** 7pm-4am Fri, Sat. **Admission** *average* 1,500ptas incl one drink. **Map F4**
This cabaret club, in an old shopping arcade in Malasaña, is just the right side of cutesy, with an imitation star-lit sky painted above the stage. As often in Madrid, acts cover an eclectic range: magicians, hypnotists and comedians on Sunday and Monday nights, then it's salsa and merengue most of the week, although singer-songwriters, cabaret, theatre groups and pop bands also appear.

Café del Mercado

Ronda de Toledo 1 (inside Mercado Puerta de Toledo), (91 365 87 39). Metro Puerta de Toledo/bus all routes to Puerta de Toledo. **Open** 10pm-4am daily. **Admission** *average* 1,000ptas incl one drink. **Map D10**
The café is located in the failed Mercado Puerta de Toledo development, an attempt to create a swish, ultra modern shopping complex in a former fish market, but is unaffected by the problems around it. After a layoff of a year due to licensing problems, owner Seju Monzón once again lays on

The Abdu Salim Trio, recent headliners at **Café Populart**. *See page 206.*

one of the most varied and interesting menus of Latin music in the city – maybe merengue, salsa, bolero and chachachá. Like a lot of the best places in town, it doesn't usually get going until well after midnight.

Galileo Galilei

C/Galileo 100 (91 534 75 57). Metro Canal, Quevedo/ bus 2, 12. **Open** 6pm-3am Sun-Thur, 6pm-5am Fri, Sat. **Admission** 500-2,000ptas.

A sister club of **Clamores** (*see above*), Galileo Galilei presents all manner of artists from singer-songwriters to salsa bands, as well as occasional magic acts and stand up comedy. In April the *Feria de Sevilla* comes to Madrid and fills the place with sevillanas, *fino* sherry and lots of shouting.

Oba-Oba

C/Jacometrezo 4 (no phone). Metro Callao/ bus all routes to Plaza de Callao. **Open** 11pm-6am daily. **Admission** 1.000ptas. **Map D6**

This friendly, thumping Brazilian bar pumps out samba until the sun comes up, with live music most nights of the week, and is packed with a good-time crowd from about 1am onwards. It's a cosy place, with wonderful *caipirinhas*.

La Tolderia

C/Caños Viejos 3 (91 366 41 72). Metro La Latina/bus 3, 31, 65, 148, N13. Open 11pm-4am Tue-Sat. **Admission** *average* 1,000ptas. **Map C8**

Latin American folk – not dance – music from throughout the continent is performed for a serious but appreciative audience. Some big names have appeared here over the years, among them Chavela Vargas and Mercedes Sosa. There are three or four acts, between about 12.30 and 3am. Not a place to let your hair down, and not cheap either.

Outdoor venues

In summer, Madrid comes alive after dark and out of doors. Balmy evenings and original and often inspired locations can make this the best time of year to enjoy live music. The courtyards of the **Centro Cultural Conde Duque** (*see chapter* **Art Galleries**) make great performance spaces, usually as part of festivals (*see below*). Very popular for salsa and other dance bands during San Isidro is the park of **Las Vistillas** (*see page 60*).

Hipódromo de la Zarzuela

Carretera de La Coruña (N-VI), km 7.8 (91 307 01 40). Bus from Moncloa all routes to Aravaca/by car N-VI to El Pardo exit. **Open** *June-Sept* 9pm-5am Fri, Sat. **Admission** free; *concerts* from 500ptas.

Madrid's racecourse now only functions as a music venue, since race meetings have been suspended. It's big enough to have hosted a Jean-Michel Jarre muzak extravaganza; the summer music programme is eclectic, but worth checking out.

Parque de Atracciones

Casa de Campo (91 463 29 00). Metro Batán/bus 33. **Open** *see page 180.* **Admission** *entrance to the park only* 575ptas.

All the fun of the fair and spectacular sunsets to boot. Summer gigs by Spanish family favourites and local rock bands are free with the entry ticket. Rides, though, cost more. *See also page 180.*

Festivals

San Isidro, the **Veranos de la Villa** and a good many more of Madrid's annual events feature good live music. The **May Day** celebrations and **Festimad** in May, the **Fiesta Africana** in Getafe in July and the **Fiestas del Partido Comunista** in September are all good opportunities to see a wide range of locally based bands. For festivals named, *see chapter* **Madrid by Season**. A Madrid event that has been growing is **Reggae on the River** in June, which regularly attracts Jamaican and UK-based artists. In 1998 it was held in a field outside Cobeña, near Alcobendas northeast of Madrid, but venues can change from year to year. For information, try calling (91 562 88 38).

Festival de Jazz de Madrid

Information: *Colectivo Promociones Jazz (91 447 64 00).* **Dates**: Oct-Dec.

In November, when other cities are beginning to feel the cold, Madrid is blowing hot. The Jazz Festival, which has come at the end of the general **Festival de Otoño** (*see p10*), has been steadily growing in stature. In addition to the usual venues, during the festival theatres and auditoria open their doors to respected jazz musicians from the world over.

Flamenco

Flamenco may be archetypically of the south, but Madrid is its modern capital – it's here that new talent makes its mark, and new forms emerge.

Flamenco is Spain's most distinctive art form, one of the things, like bullfighting, that makes the country's culture so unique. It is also something that has been widely misunderstood and caricatured, at home and abroad.

The swirling dresses, furious footwork and clattering castanets often served up to unwary tourists at hefty prices are no more than a sad parody of the real thing. Many Spaniards, too, have often seen flamenco music and dance as part of a hackneyed, kitschy and uncreative folkloric culture that they would rather get away from. Under Franco, decaffeinated flamenco was an integral part of the régime's self-promotion campaigns, and even after the end of the dictatorship, flamenco, associated with the poor south and timeless tradition, still seemed out of step with the new Spain's rush to prosperity and infatuation with all things modern. And, since the strongholds of the music are still very much among Spain's Gypsy communities, a degree of racism also played its part.

At the beginning of the '80s there were almost no venues in Madrid regularly featuring quality live flamenco. This trend has been completely turned around in the last 15 years. A major factor has been a startling coincidence of new and imaginative talent – above all guitarists Paco de Lucía and Tomatito, and the singer Camarón de la Isla, one of the most extraordinary voices of this century, whose death at only 41 in 1992 was a national catastrophe. They helped vindicate the music's finest traditions while continually breaking new ground, attracting entirely new audiences to flamenco. New venues opened their doors, spearheading a flamenco resurgence. Today, the music is fashionable, concerts are well attended and young people show up in large numbers.

Most flamenco venues today feature both traditional performers and what's called *nuevo flamenco*, New Flamenco. This has developed out of the innovations of Paco de Lucía and Camarón and the subsequent experiments of young musicians, often themselves from Gypsy families – where they absorbed the music with their mothers' milk – but also open to a whole range of other musical influences. They are ready to blend traditional styles with blues, pop, jazz, rock, folk, salsa, Latin American styles and Arab music, and experiment with such unflamenco-like instruments as

saxophones and electric bass. Far from succumbing to crossover blandness, though, much of New Flamenco still has an unmistakable Gypsy edge.

The flamenco world has a deep sense of tradition, and *aficionados* argue endlessly over whether this kind of fusion represents a real advance for the music, or simply its dilution – even though the line has always been vague between flamenco and Spanish popular music in general, and many artists have long been happy to flit between both. Another point at issue is how far flamenco can ever be open to *payos* (the Spanish Gypsy word for all non-Gypsies). The results of *nuevo flamenco* are uneven, but no one can deny that this opening up of flamenco can produce highly original, fresh and dynamic sounds, making it far the most exciting music being produced in Spain today.

THE ESSENCE: *CANTE*

The origins of flamenco can be traced back more than 500 years to the folk songs of Arab Andalusia. The late-medieval Gypsy immigration into Spain was, of course, the major factor in the development of the music, but it also combines elements of Indian chants, Spanish-Jewish folk music and Middle Eastern, oriental and Latin American musical traditions and religious influences.

The essence of flamenco is the *cante jondo* or 'deep song': a voice, a guitar, a story to tell, and an audience to share in the telling. The guitar and singing are often accompanied by dancing, but good *cante* can always stand on its own. Guitar (always acoustic) and singer (the *cantaor* or *cantaora*) establish a taut communication, based on subtle rhythmic improvisation within the contours of the different styles, called *palos*. There are a great many of them, all richly inter-related, and differentiated by their intricate rhythmic patterns, chord structures, lyrical content and regional origin – *alegrías, bulerías, siguiriyas, soleares, tarantos, tientos, malagueñas, tangos* and *fandangos* are only the best-known.

Musicians play and sing within these recognised styles, but a real flamenco performance is still the most utterly spontaneous and improvised of music, each one unique and unrepeatable. The audience plays a crucial part in the success of each performance. More than silence, what is demanded is rapt surrender to the artists' travails. *Cantaor* and guitarist always start quite cold, and it is only after a couple of songs that they really begin to get going, as in any conversation. Side-performers and the audience can accompany the more rhythmically intense *palos* with intricate hand-clapping and shouts of *¡olé!*, though this is probably better left to the initiated.

The emotional repertory is far-ranging: from tender desperation to joyful celebration, a miner's lament, songs that speak of love, of solitude, of despair, of dire foreboding. Even the most ecstatic of *alegrías*, though, never seems to break away completely from the deep sense of pain and anguish that marks all *cante jondo*. Nor is the stark tragedy of a *siguiriya's* deathly brooding ever without some element of cathartic relief.

Raw and honest, flamenco is an audacious music, full of risks and improvisation. Singers rely

Hot taps: Spanish dance

Spain is unique in Europe in possessing an entirely indigenous dance tradition that covers the range of sophistication from pure folk dance to highly studied and refined techniques. The differences in styles can be hard to distinguish for newcomers, but even so, devotees can dispute passionately whether this or that movement is within the never-quite-defined tradition.

Flamenco is only one of four major categories. The others are *escuela bolera*, developed in the eighteenth century, using castanets, *danza folclórica*, regional folk dances from all over Spain, and *danza estilizada*, often called *Ballet Español* or Spanish Ballet, a theatricalised hybrid combining elements from all other styles, and usually to music by Spanish classical composers.

Spanish dance styles enjoy huge commercial success outside Spain, and periodically produce superstars such as Joaquín Cortés, who, although he has faded slightly from view lately, performs in Madrid about once a year. The polished and spectacular *Ballet Nacional de España* also spends its time touring, and only appears in Madrid for a short spell each year, usually in the **Festival de Otoño**. Some theatres, such as the **Centro Cultural de la Villa** and the **Teatro de Madrid**, regularly host short seasons by other companies (*see page 186*). Very worth catching is the *Nuevo Ballet Español*, an exciting company led by two of the best current male dancers, Angel Rojas and Carlos Rodriguez, who present traditional flamenco forms through modern eyes. For schools of Spanish dance, *see page 186*.

TABLAOS & SALAS ROCIERAS

Where people are most likely to see Spanish dance, though, is at a flamenco show, a *tablao*, which is also where flamenco artists earn their bread and butter in between theatrical performances. There are several in Madrid, but those below are the ones where you are most likely to catch genuine, intense performances. As well as the show, you can dine or just have a drink; both are appallingly expensive, but if you stay till closing time you may get your money's worth of flamenco dance and music. The fun really starts about midnight, when most tourists go off to bed and the major artists appear; until then you may just get the kitsch jollity of the *cuadro de la casa* (the house musicians and dancers).

Also, as well as watching a Spanish dance show you can join in, by making for a *sala rociera* or Andaluz dance club for a bout of *sevillanas* and the odd *rumba*. Note, though, that Seville's elegant dance is complex; if you want some prior preparation, many schools offer classes (*see page 186*).

Al Andalús
C/Capitán Haya 19 (91 556 14 39). *Metro Santiago Bernabéu/bus 5, 43, 149, 150*. **Open** 10.30pm-6am Mon-Sat; shows start 11pm, 1.30am. **Admission** free. **Credit** AmEx, MC, V.
With *sala rociera* décor reminiscent of a *caseta* at the *Feria* in Seville, this place offers a brassy live show, but best of all is watching the mainly middle-aged public throw themselves into *sevillanas* till dawn. There is a minimum bar/tapas charge of 2,000ptas, Mon-Thur, 3,000ptas, Fri-Sat.

Almonte
C/Juan Bravo 35 (91 563 25 04). *Metro Núñez de Balboa/bus 29, 51, 52, 61*. **Open** 9pm-6am daily. **Admission** free, average bar/tapas 1,500ptas. **Credit** AmEx, DC, MC, V. **Map K2**
On two floors, this *sala rociera*-disco in Salamanca and is packed with upmarket trendsters letting their hair down. No live show, just pricey drinks, tapas and *sevillanas*.

Café de Chinitas
C/Torija 7 (91 547 15 01). *Metro Santo Domingo/bus 44, 133, 147*. **Open** 9pm-2am Mon-Sat; show starts 10.30pm. **Admission** *dinner & show* 9,500ptas; *drink & show* 4,300ptas. **Credit** AmEx, MC, V. **Map D6**
With a plushy, nostalgic ambience evoking its nineteenth-century namesake, this is Madrid's most luxurious *tablao*, with a good *cuadro* of 10 performers and regular appearances by prestigious guest artists.

Corral de la Morería
C/de la Morería 17 (91 365 84 46). *Metro La Latina/bus 17, 23, 35, 60*. **Open** 9pm-2am daily; show starts 10.45pm. **Admission** *dinner & show* 10,000ptas; *drink & show* 4,200ptas. **Credit** AmEx, DC, JCB, MC, V. **Map C8**
Another of Madrid's more serious *tablaos*, smaller and more rustic in style. Apart from the *cuadro*, the show often features respected senior figures of the Madrid flamenco scene.

An electric night at **Casa Patas**. *See page 212.*

on plaintive wails, stifled sobs and throaty murmurs to recount tales of personal or collective tribulation. In its most inspired moments, when what *aficionados* call the *duende* – an untranslatable word roughly meaning 'spirit' or 'enchantment' – possesses performer and listener alike, the effect can be stunning; a primal emotion, an atavistic river of tears, seems to flow through the artists. Commanding performers can envelop the most varied of audiences with a sense of common humanity and shared fate.

RISING STARS & OTHER FIGURES

As a result of the flamenco resurgence Madrid, more than anywhere in the south, is now the best place in Spain to hear good flamenco. A sample, and only that, of names to watch out for in the traditional field are José Menese, Mariana Cornejo, Maite Martín, Chano Lobato, Fernanda de Utrera, Agujetas and Chaquetón, among singers. The many fine younger singers include Ginesa Ortega and Duquende, but the flamenco sensation of recent years is Niña Pastori, heavily influenced by Camarón (*see page 212*). Leading guitarists are Paco de Lucía, Tomatito, Juan Habichuela and his brother Pepe, Gerardo Núñez, Rafael Riqueni, Enrique de Melchor and Vicente Amigo.

Divisions between traditional and New Flamenco are never as precise as some people make out, and many musicians, like Paco de Lucía and Tomatito, work freely between both camps. Best-known of New Flamenco groups is Ketama, who combine flamenco with jazz, rock and salsa. The best flamenco/rock fusion group has been Pata Negra, whose leader Rafael Amador included blues legend BB King on his 1996 solo release *Gerundina*. Other acts to look out for are the jazz/flamenco mix of saxophonist-flautist Jorge Pardo and pianist Chano Domínguez, the flamenco-reggae experiments of La

Barbería del Sur (most detested of all for flamenco traditionalists), and singers El Potito, Ramón el Portugués, El Lebrijano and Enrique Morente, who aroused passions with his 1997 album *Omega*, fusing flamenco and hard rock. Despite the furore in purist circles, the record was well received critically, and brought him a new audience.

Venues

For anyone new to flamenco, the easiest introduction will be a session in a club such as **Suristán** or **Casa Patas**. The venues listed here mainly feature music and singing, although dancers may appear. For venues where dance is the main attraction, *see left*. Concert listings are found in local papers and listings magazines (*see page 199*). Note that, since spontaneity is the essence of flamenco, timekeeping is often imprecise.

As well as these venues, look out for flamenco nights in theatres and music venues, or outdoors in summer. **Colegio San Juan Evangelista** schedules major flamenco shows five or six times a year. Other venues with flamenco include the **Café del Foro**, **Caracol** and **Clamores** (for all, *see chapter* **Music: Rock, Roots & Jazz**).

Candela

C/del Olmo 2 (91 467 33 82). Metro Antón Martín/ bus 6, 26, 32. **Open** 10pm-4.30am Mon-Thur, Sun; 10pm-5.30am Fri, Sat. **Map F9**

Although it does not programme live music, this bar is a cornerstone of the Madrid flamenco scene, simply because every flamenco artist seems to go there at some point in their off hours. Consequently, it tends not to fill up before 2am, and often keeps going long after the official closing time. The after-hours jam sessions in the grotto-like cellar are legendary. Unfortunately, they tend to be by 'invitation' only, but if you are lucky enough to get asked in the results are likely to be memorable. Also, Candela is a good contact point for meeting guitarists willing to give private lessons.

Niña Pastori

Still only 20 in 1998, Niña Pastori sang with Camarón as a child, and took the flamenco world by storm in her mid-teens. Following the best-selling albums *Entre dos puertos* and *Eres Luz*, she is now taking flamenco further than ever, to new audiences and venues. Writer Nuria Barrios has interviewed Niña Pastori several times.

Is flamenco a birthright?
Yes, and if you have it then you're flamenco in everything, singing, playing, eating…

What makes a flamenco, being Gypsy, or Andalusian?
Both. But, with respect, Andalusian Gypsies are different. Everything. It's a way of life, of being. An Andalusian gypsy will always find a way to express him or herself, in whatever. But in the end… if you've got it inside, it'll come out. You've only got to look at Duquende, from Barcelona… his singing is incredible, too much.

What do you think about people who say that innovations like yours are killing cante jondo?
I couldn't care less what 3,000 purists think. Because my records have sold to 100,000 people. I want my music to reach everybody, and if that means that a 15-year-old girl who normally listens to Madonna, and who doesn't know anything about flamenco, listens to me, then that's a step forward.

Are you frightened that one day your fame will run out?
No. Because I know who I am and what I do. I'm ready for the times when things don't go so well. Sooner or later I'll take time out and get on with my life. But I know that deep down I'm an artist, and that I only know how to do one thing. I'm not that interested in money. The important thing is to live to a ripe old age and die singing.

Casa Patas

C/Cañizares 10 (91 369 04 96). Metro Antón Martín, Tirso de Molina/bus 6, 26, 32, 65. **Open** noon-5pm, 8pm-2am, Mon-Thur; noon-5pm, 8pm-3am, Fri, Sat. Closed Sun. **Performances** 10.30pm Mon-Thur; midnight Fri, Sat. **Admission** 1,700ptas. Mon-Thur; 2,500ptas. Fri, Sat. **Credit** AmEx, DC, MC, V. **Map E8**
A pioneer of the flamenco upswing, a big, comfortable bar with a club space at the back where flamenco shows are staged most nights of the week. Patas presents some of the best traditional flamenco singers and dancers in Madrid, plus *nuevo flamenco* groups. It has established itself as the city's most important flamenco specialist, and another meeting point for Madrid's 'flamenco family'. Dancers and musicians both feature in its shows. The tapas are good, but pricey.

Peña Flamenca Chaquetón

C/Canarias 39 (91 671 27 77). Metro Palos de la Frontera/bus 6, 8, 45, 55, 102. **Open** *performances only* 11pm Fri. **Admission** 2,000ptas.
A *peña*, one of the small, non-profit-making clubs where *aficionados* stage flamenco recitals for their own delectation in a warm, intimate setting. Chaquetón is the dean of Madrid *peñas*, a citadel of orthodoxy that's highly respected among performers. Despite its small size, it manages to line up some of the best artists in the country. Do not be scared off by the 'members only' (*solo socios*) sign on the door; flamenco lovers of all kinds are welcome, although we wouldn't recommend showing up with a tour bus. Also, do not go expecting food, tapas, comfortable seats or colourful décor. With only a bare selection of drinks, no waiters, and poor ventilation, it's not for the comfort-seeker, the tobacco-weary or the casual listener. But it's often the best bet in Madrid for hearing pure *cante jondo* at its finest among genuine *aficionados*.

La Soleá

C/Cava Baja 27 (91 365 33 08). Metro La Latina/bus 17, 31, 35, 50, 65. **Open** 8.30pm-2am daily. **Map D8**
This tiny bar, in the middle of Madrid's best-known traditional restaurant area, has a house guitarist who is willing to accompany anyone wishing to test their luck in the art of flamenco singing. Anything can happen (and usually does if you visit often enough): you may be treated to a stirring recital by an outstanding artist who happens to come by, or an inspired amateur, or you may have to suffer through some direly inept droning. The only sure thing is the good-natured atmosphere amid which it all takes place.

Suristán

C/de la Cruz 7 (91 532 39 09). Metro Sevilla, Sol/bus all routes to Puerta del Sol. **Open** 10pm-5.30am daily. Flamenco 11pm Wed. **Admission** 1,000ptas. **Map E7**
One of the most innovative music venues in Madrid, Suristán programmes virtually every kind of music, but dedicates one night each week to flamenco, usually Wednesdays. The performers are mostly younger artists, in traditional and *nuevo flamenco*, and the audience runs through music followers of all sorts to traditional flamenco enthusiasts. This atmosphere and mix makes it one of the best places to appreciate the range of modern flamenco (it's also very cheap). Check before going, as concert days can vary. *See also chapters* **Nightlife** *and* **Music: Rock, Roots & Jazz**.

Festivals

Like other arts, flamenco in Madrid has suffered under the PP *Ayuntamiento*. The city used to have half a dozen festivals a year, but this has narrowed down to two fixed events. In **February** or **March** comes the week-long **Festival Flamenco Cajamadrid**, usually, but not always, in the Teatro Albéniz: the emphasis is on artists linked to Madrid, focussing each year on a particular performer. The Círculo de Bellas Artes generally hosts parallel activities (exhibitions, seminars on flamenco themes). In **April**, the Colegio San Juan Evangelista puts on the **Festival Flamenco por Tarantos**, which attracts artists from all over the country. Flamenco concerts, often in open-air venues, are also included in city festivals such as **San Isidro** and the **Veranos de la Villa** (*see pages 8-10*). For venue details *see chapters* **Music: Rock, Roots & Jazz** *and* **Theatre**.

Smaller events pop up during the year, many organised by Flamenco Cultyart (91 553 25 26), who always have up to date information on other festivals. Spain's most important purely flamenco festival, though, is the **Bienal** in Seville. The next one takes place in early September 2000; for information, contact Seville 95 421 83 83.

Sport & Fitness

When football's driving you crazy, Madrid has many other places where you can work up a sweat, shoot some billar or cool off by the pool.

Spain's permanently semi-hysterical sports press – represented in Madrid by *Marca* and *As* – has had plenty of reasons for printing its screaming headlines in recent years. The triumphs of Arantxa Sánchez, Carles Moya and many more in tennis, Miguel Induráin's five consecutive Tours de France and Abraham Olano's recovery of the domestic cycling crown in the 1998 Tour of Spain invariably won them a front-page title of *¡Héroes!* The 22 Olympic medals won in Barcelona '92, the further 17 in Atlanta, the under-21 football team's achievements and Real Madrid's European Cup victory over Juventus have all been sources of pride. After all that, the dismal failure of the national team in France '98, on the other hand, spread gloom throughout the land and earned them a *¡Venios ya!* ('Come on home now') from one indignant paper.

Perhaps inspired by the feats of the *héroes*, more Spaniards than ever before now also take part in some form of sport. Facilities are not abundant in central Madrid, but anyone who really wants to take exercise of some kind doesn't have to look too hard to find a place to jog, a tennis court, a gym or a swimming pool. For information on sports that can be sampled in the mountains and countryside around Madrid, *see pages 240-1*. Note that, unless stated, **credit cards** are not accepted by the venues listed.

Spectator sport

Athletics/*atletismo*

Sports authorities in Spain have been keen to demonstrate that their successes in recent Olympics were not just a flash in the pan. Hence the huge investment made in the stadium in Canillejas, in eastern Madrid. Indoor events are also held in the **Palacio de Deportes** (*see below* **Basketball**), in particular the *Trofeo Memorial Cagigal* international meeting each February.

Estadio de la Comunidad de Madrid

Avda de Arcentales s/n (91 580 51 80/012 information line). Metro Las Musas/bus 38, 48, 140.
This striking stadium, inaugurated only in 1994, has world-class facilities. Several important national athletics events are held here annually, along with occasional international meetings. There is also an indoor hall and several other facilities. The stadium is also sometimes known as the *Estadio de Canillejas* or the *Estadio Olímpico de Madrid*, since Madrid's *Ayuntamiento* has hopes to use it as a base to make a bid for the 2008 Olympics.

Maratón Popular de Madrid

Information MAPOMA (91 366 97 01).
Date last Sunday in April.
Madrid's marathon is more of a fun run than an outing for serious runners, and as such is very well attended. The course usually finishes in the Retiro or Plaza de Cibeles. The previous Sunday there is another popular road race, the **20 Kilómetros de Madrid**, organised by the Agrupación Deportiva Maratón (91 521 79 83).

Basketball/*baloncesto*

A booming sport in Spain, second only to football among teenagers. Madrid has two teams that play at the top of the Spanish league and in European competitions, **Estudiantes** and **Real Madrid** (a division of the football club). Both play at the **Palacio de Deportes**, which is also used for many other indoor sports.

Palacio de Deportes de Madrid

Avda de Felipe II (91 401 91 00/012 information line). Metro Goya/bus 30, 56, 71, C. **Open** *ticket office* 11am-2pm, 5-8pm, daily, depending on match.
Average 1,000-3,000ptas.
The season runs from September to early May, but really hots up in April with the league play-offs, when one of the Madrid teams almost inevitably clashes with one of their great rivals from the Barcelona area.
Clubs *Estudiantes* (91 562 40 22);
Real Madrid (91 398 43 00).

Football/*fútbol*

Madrid has two First Division football clubs, **Atlético Madrid** and **Real Madrid**, and another, **Rayo Vallecano**, that regularly flits in and out of the top flight. Matches are usually played at 5pm on Sundays during the September-May season, although they are increasingly held on Saturday evenings (at 8.30pm) as well, and there are also often midweek cup or European games. Tickets are available from the clubs and, with commission, from some ticket agencies (not, as yet, savings banks; for agencies, *see page 176*). Shirts and fan-junk can also be bought at sports shops such as **Fútbol Total** (*see page 173*). *See also page 214* **Foreign bodies**.

Atlético de Madrid

Estadio Vicente Calderón, Paseo de los Melancólicos s/n (91 366 47 07/shop 91 365 38 31). Metro Pirámides/bus 17, 36, 50, 118, 119. **Ticket office** 11am-2pm, 5-8pm, daily; continuously from 11am on match days.
Tickets 1,000-12,000ptas.

Atlético's stadium on the banks of the Manzanares has room for 60,000, and is often more animated than the Bernabéu. The basic ticket (which, for most non-European games, will be 2,500ptas) gives you a decent view from the upper stands behind either goal. Converts can pick up an *Atleti* shirt from the stadium shop for a whopping 9,980ptas. Tickets usually go on sale from the Wednesday before the match.

Rayo Vallecano

Nuevo Estadio de Vallecas, Avda del Payaso Fofó s/n (91 478 22 53/shop 91 477 73 57). Metro Portazgo/ bus 54, 58, 103, 136. **Ticket office** 5.30-8.30pm daily, depending on match. **Tickets** 1,000-3,500ptas; 500ptas children. **Credit** MC, V.

The 20,000-capacity stadium where Rayo's loyal followers ponder once more whether their team will ever get back into the First Division (they have never survived there more than two seasons together). Admitting their difficulties in competing with their bigger neighbours, Rayo often play Sunday games at noon rather than clash at 5pm. The club shop has Rayo shirts (pretty cool, and rather like a Red Stripe beer can) for a modest 6,500ptas.

Real Madrid

Estadio Santiago Bernabéu, C/Concha Espina & Paseo de la Castellana (91 398 43 00/shop 91 458 69 25). Metro Santiago Bernabéu/bus 5, 14, 27, 120, 150. **Ticket office** 6-9pm daily, depending on match. **Tickets** 2,000-6,000ptas.

This giant stadium was enlarged a few seasons ago, but from the 1998-9 season its capacity has been reduced to 85,000, due to the installation of seats in the terraces. It is often used for cup finals and internationals. Avoid the south end, *Fondo Sur*, the main base of Real's small neo-fascist hooligan element. As the stadium is so huge, any ticket for less than 4,000ptas (or around 5,000ptas for European games) may only get you a poor view. Pick up an official shirt for 8,995ptas from the shop, **Todo Real Madrid**, next to the stadium. *See also p45.*

Motor sport

Circuito del Jarama

Carretera de Burgos N-I, km 27, San Sebastián de los Reyes (91 657 08 75). Bus 171 from Plaza de Castilla to Ciudad Santo Domingo/by car N-I to Fuente del Fresno.
This track formerly hosted the Spanish Grand Prix, but in 1992 the race moved to the Catalunya circuit near Barcelona. The track's calender of events is therefore now rather diminished, and isn't fixed, but there are still several motorcycling meets every year, and for real motor-freaks the European Truck Racing Championship in early October.

Other events

Chess The *Torneo Magistral* tournament, category 16 in the international ratings, is traditionally held each May, but the organisers are planning to hold it later in future, probably in October. The tournament takes place in the Auditorio de la ONCE, Paseo de la Habana 208.
Information Federación Madrileña de Ajedrez (91 477 27 22). **Open** 6-9pm Mon-Fri.
Cycling *La Vuelta de España* (the Tour of Spain) makes its way around the country during September, and ends on the third weekend of the month in Madrid with a last stage of five laps of the Castellana, between Plaza de Castilla and the Estadio Bernabéu. The progress of the tour is fully covered throughout the three weeks in the sports press – *Marca* and *As*.
Golf The *Open de España* (Spanish Open) is often held at some point from April to June at the **Club de Campo** (*see below*). The venue can change, so check ahead.

Foreign bodies

Spanish football followers (that is, most of the country) are disconcerted, and more than a touch disenchanted. Two problems, thought by many to be interlinked, are currently being debated in a nation where Bill Shankly's famous comment that football was much more than a matter of life and death has long been a bit of an understatement.

The national team's shameful showing in France '98 is one. Spain had set off across the Pyrenees theoretically as one of the favourites, but coach Javier 'if you want entertainment go to the cinema' Clemente showed a greater fear of losing than ambition to win. Afterwards, his bull-headed refusal to resign sparked off a genuine national crisis, but in his defence he blamed the squad's plight on the invasion of foreign players in the Spanish league.

Pariah as he is, Clemente did have a point. The Bosman ruling has had a major impact on a league awash with TV revenue. Still more players from EU countries are tempted by Spanish clubs, leaving 'foreigners' slots to be occupied by (relatively) cheap Brazilians, Yugoslavs and others. Consequently, at the beginning of the 1998-9 season 43 per cent of players in the 'League of the Stars' (*Liga de las Estrellas*, as the Spanish league has taken to publicising itself) were non-Spanish. The results are there for anyone to see – the first big Real Madrid-Barcelona clash of the season involved all of six Spaniards, only four in the initial line-ups. This, many say, is undermining the national game, and forcing talented Spanish players to seek their fortune abroad.

Another worry is the spectre, or promise (depending on which viewpoint you take), of a European superleague. Whichever solution is finally adopted (the UEFA's expanded Champions' League or the Berlusconi dog's-breakfast alternative), the main impact on Spanish football will be to reinforce an already hierarchical situation. Automatic candidates for any such competition are Real Madrid and Barcelona. Both could use the extra revenue generated to strengthen their stranglehold over a domestic league that for years has been far too much of a two-horse race. The effects on the national team could be disastrous as well, as the big two stock up on quality players just in case to maintain their squads ready for big games and keep talent sitting on the bench, while becoming more reluctant to release players for national duty.

In the meantime, while the 'League of the Stars' may not always be stellar, it does produce plenty of thrills and spills. **Real Madrid**, the aristocrats of Spanish football, have always been the team to beat. The occupants of the vast Bernabéu stadium boast 27 Leagues, 17 Cups, seven European Cups, and many other titles. The early '90s was a lean period, with only a couple of trophies to celebrate, and a boardroom coup followed in '95-6 in which chairman Ramón Mendoza was deposed by his (former) friend and business associate Lorenzo Sanz. Some immensely costly signings (despite the club's fantastic debts) – Mijatovic, Suker, Seedorf, Roberto Carlos and former Milan coach Fabio Capello – were a huge gamble. Capello's efficient but boring team won the 1997 league, and he returned triumphant to Italy; Jupp Heynkes was then called in to prepare the assault on the Champions' League, and the victory in 1998 ended an anxious 30-year wait to bring home a coveted seventh European Cup. This, though, was not enough to save Heynkes' neck, and Sanz replaced him with the ex-Dutch national coach Guus Hiddink.

Atlético de Madrid, *El Atleti*, is not short on silverware either: nine Leagues, nine Cups and a Cup-Winners' Cup. The '95-6 double-winning season was the greatest in its history. Architect of the campaign Serbian coach Radomir Antic

has since left, along with most of the players involved, but Atlético's prestige as Spain's number three club has at least been restored. Their mouthy and ever-controversial chairman, construction magnate Jesús Gil, has delegated most functions to his infinitely more sensible son these days, something Atlético fans are deeply thankful for, and Arrigo Sacchi is now in the driving seat. Juninho, Kiko, Jugovic and the young José-Mari are the current idols of the red-and-whites (such as those pictured *above*), at least until the Gils get sick of them.

Down in Division Two, **Rayo Vallecano** are a bit like the Crystal Palace of Madrid football. A symbol of identity for proletarian Vallecas, this modest bunch are currently struggling to regain First Division status (in order that they can just as swiftly lose it again, as tradition demands). Despite having another eccentric chairman, Jerez financier José María Ruiz Mateos (executive decisions are delegated to his equally barmy wife, Doña Teresa), Rayo are a true neighbourhood club. They generally play on Sunday mornings to avoid competition with Atlético, Real and… Sunday lunch. A fun atmosphere is assured. Local rivalry at this level comes in the form of the unimaginatively named **Atlético B** and, from the industrial belt, the battling **Leganés**, with a spanking new stadium.

For more on how to see a game, *see left*.

And the other lot... Real fans demand to be included in the European Superleague.

Active sport

Sports centres/*polideportivos*

Madrid boasts 45 city-run *Polideportivos* (sports centres). At any of them you can pick up a map and a guide to the facilities available at each municipal centre. Some offer a lavish range of activities, including pools and tennis courts; others are just a gym and little else.

All the centres have the same basic entrance fees, but there may be extra charges for some facilities. The most central place to obtain a leaflet and further information is **La Chopera** in the Retiro.

Estadio Vallehermoso

Avda de las Islas Filipinas 10 (91 534 77 23/012 information line). Metro Canal, Guzmán el Bueno, Rios Rosas/bus 2, 12, 44. **Open** 8am-9.30pm, *swimming pool* 11am-8pm, daily. **Admission** *swimming pool* 410ptas Mon-Fri; 510ptas, Sat, Sun, public holidays.
This athletics stadium and multi purpose sports centre is run by the *Comunidad de Madrid*, and has an indoor sports hall, gym, a football pitch and an open-air swimming pool. It's also good for jogging, and the Parque de Santander, across the street, is pleasant as well.

Instituto Municipal de Deportes

Palacete de la Casa de Campo, Puente del Rey (91 463 90 50). Metro Lago, Príncipe Pío/bus 25, 33, 39, 46, 138. **Open** 8am-3pm Mon-Fri.
The central administration for all the city sports facilities, which will provide additional information on request.

Parque Deportivo La Ermita

C/Sepúlveda 3 (91 470 01 11). Metro Puerta del Angel/bus 17, 25, 138, 500. **Open** 9am-11pm Mon-Fri; 10am-8pm Sat; 10am-3pm Sun. **Admission** *squash, tennis* from 1,915ptas per 30 min; *swimming pool* 1,600ptas per day Mon-Fri; 1,400ptas per day Sat, Sun; .
This enormous private sports centre caters for just about every need, and you don't have to be a member to go. As well as offering racquet courts and an open-air pool, it has a gym and weights room and indoor sports halls. The centre also offers a range of sports tuition (such as tennis lessons), particularly for children, with multi-sport programmes and activities outside the city during summer. Charges for most facilities (apart from the pool) rise considerably after 1.30pm.

Polideportivo de la Chopera

Parque del Retiro (91 420 11 54). Metro Atocha/bus all routes to Atocha. **Open** 8am-10pm daily. **Admission** varies according to facilities used. **Map I8**
Near the entrance to the Retiro behind the Museo del Prado, this attractive centre has a gym, full-size, 11-a-side football pitches (sand surface) and courts for five-a-side games, tennis and basketball.

Billiards & pool/*billares*

Club Academia de Billar Guarner

Paseo de las Delicias 31, 6° (91 528 55 94). Metro Palos de la Frontera/bus all routes to Atocha. **Open** 5.30pm-1.30am Mon-Thur, Sun; 5.30pm-2.30am Fri, Sat. **Tables** 900ptas per hour; 1,000ptas after 10pm Fri, Sat.
This 'academy' offers two-week courses in Spanish billiards, otherwise known as *carambola*. There are nine pool tables, a full-size snooker table – one of very few in Madrid – and two *carambola* tables. It's slightly different from the usual smoke-filled pool hall, with sofas, armchairs and even a TV. There's also a 'happy' hour (5.30-6.30pm Mon-Fri), when pool tables can be hired for 500ptas.

Bowling/*boleras*

Bowling Azca

Paseo de la Castellana 77 (91 555 76 26). Metro Nuevos Ministerios/bus all routes to Nuevos Ministerios. **Open** 8am-1am Mon-Thur, Sun; 8am-3am Fri, Sat. **Games** *before 6pm* 350ptas, *after 6pm* 475ptas, Mon, Tue, Thur, Sun; 350ptas all day Wed; *before 6pm* 475ptas, *after 6pm* 600ptas, Fri, Sat. **Credit** V.
Although it's located in the heart of the business district, within the AZCA complex (*see p45*), this well-equipped 16-lane bowling alley has a pleasantly relaxed atmosphere, and attracts a varied public.

Canoeing/*remo*

Lago Casa de Campo

Casa de Campo (91 464 46 10). Metro Lago/bus 31, 33, 36, 39, 65. **Open** 9am-dusk daily. **Boat hire** 550ptas per 45 min, 1-4 people; large boat 150ptas per person.
The lake in the Casa de Campo, where you can just hire a boat (*see pp58-9*), is also used by three canoe clubs, Alberche, Canal and Ciencias. Weekly courses and canoes for hire for experienced canoeists are offered.

Cricket

There is indeed an MCC, the Madrid Cricket Club. They play regularly against the 14 other clubs, mainly of expats, based around Spain. Further information is available from Martín De Careaga, President of the MCC and the *Asociación Española de Cricket*: write to C/Descubridores 27, bloque 8, 1ºB, Tres Cantos, 28760 Madrid (91 803 82 56).

Football/*fútbol*

English Football League

The EFL began over ten years ago, and now includes teams that are mixed-nationality or wholly Spanish (or Peruvian) as well as others from language schools. Games are played on Sundays from around noon until 5-6pm at the **Colegio del Niño Jesús**, a large school with excellent facilities just east of the Retiro (Metro Ibiza, Sainz de Baranda/**Map K8**). A weekly broadsheet, *The Pink'Un*, keeps everybody informed about results and gossip, and there's even a website, http://ourworld.compuserve.com/homepages/robraabe. Teams are often looking for new players, so if you fancy your chances, call league secretary Dave Weston (91 844 37 69).

Golf

Golf clubs around Madrid tend to be quite exclusive, and are expensive for non-members.

Club de Campo Villa de Madrid

Carretera de Castilla, km 2 (91 357 21 32). Bus 84 from Moncloa. **Open** 9am-dusk daily. **Rates** *Mon-Fri* 1,825ptas club entry, plus 6,550ptas course fee; *Sat, Sun* 3,650ptas club entry, plus 12,400ptas course fee.
The best-equipped course in the Madrid area, with 36 holes and a driving range. Not suprisingly, it's very expensive. The lavishly equipped country club also offers squash, tennis, clay pigeon and range shooting, hockey pitches, polo, horse riding and a swimming pool. Rental of clubs will cost an additional 2,600ptas.

RACE (Real Automóvil Club de España)

Carretera de Burgos (N-I), km 28, San Sebastián de los Reyes (91 657 00 11).
Bus 166, 171 from Plaza de Castilla/by car Carretera de Burgos to Fuente del Fresno. **Open** 9am-dusk daily.
Rates *Mon-Fri* 5,500ptas; *Sat, Sun* 10,500ptas.
Near the Jarama racetrack *(see above)*, the Spanish auto club *(see p252)* has a golf and country club that is a little less expensive than some. However, you have to be a member or a member's guest in order to play. There's also a good pool.

Gyms & fitness centres/*gimnasios*

Some hotels have agreements with private health clubs for guests to use their facilities.

Bodhidharma

C/Moratines 18 (91 517 28 16). Metro Embajadores/bus all routes to Embajadores. **Open** 8am-11pm Mon-Fri; 9am-2pm, 6-10pm, Sat; 10am-3pm Sun. **Rates** 9,300ptas per month; 22,700ptas for 3 months (2 days per week £ Sat, Sun free). **Credit** AmEx, MC, V.
A well-equipped mixed health club with sauna, weights, exercise machines and aerobics and martial arts classes.

Training Gym

C/Don Ramón de la Cruz 67 (91 402 26 48). Metro Lista/bus 1, 16, 26, 74. **Open** *Sept-June* 9am-10pm, *July, Aug* 10am-9pm, Mon-Fri. **Rates** *average* 5,000ptas.

This unisex health club offers a weights room, and classes ranging from aerobics to ballet, *sevillanas* and other dance forms. Membership rates vary according to the facilities you use, and dance classes are more expensive than others.

Votre Ligne

C/Lagasca 88, 1º (91 576 40 00).
Metro Núñez de Balboa/bus 1, 74. **Open** 8.30am-9.30pm Mon-Fri; 10am-2pm Sat. **Rates** *annual* 108,000ptas; *monthly* 15,000ptas **Credit** AmEx, MC, V. **Map J3**
A lush women-only facility where Madrid's bodies beautiful go to make sure things stay that way. As well as a gym and aerobics classes, there are weights machines, a sauna, jacuzzis, a pool, massage, beauticians and several other services. The associated **El Presidente** club offers similar luxury for men. Both offer special rates for members in summer.
Branches: C/Juan Ramón Jiménez 45 (91 359 14 36). Metro Cuzco, Plaza de Castilla/bus all routes to Plaza de Castilla; **El Presidente** (men only) C/Profesor Waksman 3 (91 458 67 59). Metro Santiago Bernabéu/bus 5, 27, 40, 150.

Horse riding/*hípica*

For information on schools that offer riding and trekking trips into the Guadarrama mountains to the north of Madrid, *see page 240*.

Escuela de Equitación Soto de Viñuelas

C/del Caballo s/n, Carretera de Colmenar Viejo, km 21 (91 804 37 73). Bus 712, 713, 723 from Plaza de Castilla/by car Carretera de Colmenar Viejo to Soto de Viñuelas/by train Cercanías C-1, C-7b to Tres Cantos. **Open** 10am-2pm, 5-9pm, Tue-Sun. **Rates** *lesson* 2,500ptas; 2,000ptas children; *1-hour hire* 2,000ptas.
A school to the north of Madrid that offers beginners' and more advanced courses for all ages from six years upwards. Membership is not required. Trekking is not available.

Jogging & running/*footing*

There is a set jogging route in the **Retiro** *(see page 57)*, with recommended exercises marked at stops along the way, although you can easily go whichever way you want. More rural is the **Casa de Campo** *(see pages 58-9)*, an excellent place to jog because the air quality is better. In summer, the ideal time to go is first thing in the morning (certainly before 9am), as the freshness and contrast to the heat later in the day is wonderful. If you like longish straight runs, try the **Parque del Oeste** *(see page 60)*. If you fancy your chances in the marathon, *see above* **Spectator sports**.

Roller skating/blading/*patinaje*

A favourite area for rollerbladers and skateboarders in Madrid is the eastern side of the **Retiro**, on and around the Paseo de Fernán Núñez **(Map J8)**. More hyper-urban locations that offer plenty of concrete ramps and similar are found at various points along the Castellana, especially in the **AZCA** complex and the **Museo de Esculturas al Aire Libre**, both regularly full of boarders and skaters *(see page 45)*. Back in the centre, Calle Fuencarral **(Map F3-5)** is closed off to traffic on Sunday mornings, and makes another popular place for skaters.

El Patín de Oro

Paseo de los Pontones 17 (91 517 25 69). Metro Puerta de Toledo/bus all routes to Puerta de Toledo. **Open** 10.30am-2pm, 5-8.30pm, Mon-Fri; 10.30am-2pm, 5-7pm, Sat. **Price** 1,500ptas; *deposit (refundable)* 15,000ptas. **Credit** MC, V.
The most central of the very few shops renting out in-line skates in Madrid. Helmets, knee-pads and so on are available, but only for sale, not for hire.

Squash

Palestra

C/Bravo Murillo 5 (91 448 98 22).
Metro Quevedo/bus 16, 37, 61, 149.
Open 7.30am-11.30pm Mon-Fri; 9am-11pm Sat, Sun.
Rates 1,500 per 30 min. **Credit** AmEx, MC, V. **Map E2**
Quite central, Palestra is a general gym that also has squash courts and is open from sunup to sun down for squash players with a crowded agenda. Membership is not required.

Swimming pools/*piscinas*

A city hundreds of miles from the nearest beach and with summer temperatures reaching 40°C is naturally well equipped with swimming pools. Public pools in Madrid are run by the city (*Ayuntamiento*) or the regional authority (*Comunidad de Madrid*, CAM), and each body has its own separate pricing and ticket systems. For more facilities that have pools attached, *see above* **Sports centres**.

There are also several waterparks around Madrid, which are fun for kids, and sometimes open at night in summer (*see chapter* **Children**). For more hotels with pools, *see page 105*.

City-run open-air pools

Open *Casa de Campo* 1 May-mid-Sept; *other pools* 15 May-mid-Sept, 10.30am-8pm daily. **Admission** 500ptas; 225ptas under-16s; 125ptas over-65s; *voucher for 20 admissions* 7,500ptas; 3,250ptas under-16s; 850ptas over-65s.
The best – and most popular – of the public pools are the ones in the Casa de Campo (*see pp57-9*), where there is an indoor pool (closed July-Aug), and three open-air pools: Olympic standard, a children's pool and one intermediate-size. Like the other city pools, it is attractively equipped and landscaped, with several cafés. Topless sunbathing is allowed, and there is an informal gay area. The pools get very crowded at weekends, but are usually more relaxed during the week. In addition to the municipal pools listed below there are several more, mostly around the outskirts. Leaflets available at city sports centres (*see above*) have details.
Piscinas Casa de Campo Avda del Angel s/n (91 463 00 50). Metro Lago/bus 31, 33, 36, 39.
Barrio del Pilar C/Monforte de Lemos (91 314 79 43). Metro Barrio del Pilar/bus 134, 137.
This pool has a nude sunbathing area.
Concepción C/José del Hierro (91 403 90 20). Metro Barrio de la Concepción, Quintana/bus 21, 48, 146.
La Elipa Parque de La Elipa, C/O'Donnell s/n (91 430 35 11). Metro Estrella/bus 71, 110, 113.
In one of Madrid's newest parks, this pool and sports centre has water chutes and a nude sunbathing section.
Moratalaz C/Valdebernardo s/n (91 772 71 21). Metro Pavones/bus 8, 32, 71.

City-run indoor pools

Open 8am-7pm Mon-Fri; 10am-9pm Sat, Sun, public holidays. Closed Aug. **Admission** 500ptas,; 225ptas under-16s; 125ptas over-65s; *voucher for 20 admissions* 7,500ptas; 3,250ptas under-16s; 850ptas over-65s.

The city also has several indoor pools, most of them open all year except for August (hours for some pools may vary). Full information is available from sports centres (*see above*). Chamartín is Olympic-standard, and the pool with the best facilities; La Latina is the only city pool in central Madrid.
Chamartín Plaza del Perú s/n (91 350 12 23).
Metro Pío XII/bus 16, 29, 150.
La Latina Plaza de La Cebada 1 (91 365 80 31).
Metro La Latina/bus 17, 18, 23, 35, 60. **Map D9**

Canal de Isabel II

Avda de las Islas Filipinas 54 (91 533 96 42).
Metro Ríos Rosas/bus 2, 3, 37, 149. **Open** 8am-10pm daily. **Admission** *swimming pool* 460ptas Mon-Fri; 510ptas Sat, Sun; 235ptas under-14s, over-65s daily; *voucher for 20 admissions* 6,900ptas.
Run by the CAM, this lovely complex, well located and easily accessible in north-central Madrid, has an Olympic-size swimming pool, a special children's pool, tennis courts, and a pleasant bar and restaurant.

Hotel Emperador

Gran Vía 53 (91 547 28 00). Metro Gran Vía/bus all routes to Gran Vía. **Open** *June-Sept* 11am-9pm daily. **Admission** *average* 1,500ptas.
Credit AmEx, DC, MC, V.
One of the most spectacular pools in Madrid, on the roof of the Emperador hotel, but open to non-residents. Undo all the good work in the café-restaurant, also on the terrace, which has fabulous views over central Madrid. *See also p95.*

Hotel Eurobuilding

C/Padre Damián 23 (91 345 45 00).
Metro Cuzco/bus 5, 27, 40, 150.
Open *June-Sept* 11am-8am daily. **Admission** 3,500ptas.
Credit AmEx, DC, JCB, MC, TC, V.
Another hotel with excellent indoor and outdoor pools that are open to non-residents, but expensive. *See also p93.*

Piscina Club Stella

C/Arturo Soria 231 (91 359 16 32). Metro Arturo Soria/bus 11, 70, 120, 122, 201. **Open** *June-mid-Sept* 11am-8pm daily. **Admission** *Mon-Fri* 850ptas; 500ptas children; *Sat* 1,000ptas; 550ptas children; *Sun & public holidays* 1,200ptas; 600ptas children.
An attractive, well-equipped private swimming club that is open to non-members.

Tennis/*tenis*

Many city and private sports centres (*see above*) have clay or tarmac courts for hire. At municipal *polideportivos*, court hire is 650ptas per hour plus 150ptas reservation fee. Top-notch private clubs such as the **Club de Tenis de Chamartín** (C/Federico Salmón 2; 91 345 25 00) are members-only, though you can always opt for the 13,000ptas temporary monthly membership if your budget won't stretch to the 150,000ptas annual fee.

Disabled sports facilities

The city sports institute is slowly adapting all its *polideportivos* to allow full access for disabled users, but this programme will not be completed for some time. The majority of indoor swimming pools have been adapted, while most outdoor pools already have ramps and will gradually be given full-access changing rooms in the next few years.

Theatre

A classic tradition, a flow of major international names and an enterprising fringe mean that Madrid's vibrant theatre scene is back on the up.

Theatre goes back a long way in Madrid. The tradition was begun by the classic Golden Age dramatists Lope de Vega, Tirso de Molina and Calderón de la Barca, and continued through the centuries by great playwrights such as Zorrilla, Valle-Inclán and García Lorca. Works by all of these heavyweights, and many more from other countries, are staple fare in Madrid theatres.

In the last two decades theatre has made great strides in the city and, despite apparently bleak prospects in terms of official backing for the performing arts, the outlook for the commercial theatre and the independent fringe seems promising. The 1998-9 season began with an array of nearly 100 new productions in Madrid. The good news doesn't stop there: the creation of new venues, the presence of prestigious companies from Spain and abroad and a handful of internationally acclaimed actors and directors have brought a degree of optimism that had not been felt for some time.

Spain has no national theatre company as such, but the *Centro Dramático Nacional*, based at the magnificent **Teatro María Guerrero**, and *Compañía Nacional de Teatro Clásico*, specialised in the Golden Age and based at the **Teatro de la Comedia**, fill this gap to a certain extent.

Musicals enjoy mixed fortunes here. The **Teatro Nuevo Apolo** had a great success with *Les Misérables*, but more recently *West Side Story* fizzled out after a short run. A promising new player in the same game is the **Teatro Lope de Vega**.

Theatres, seasons & tickets

The city's top theatres are the **María Guerrero**, the **Comedia**, and the **Español**, while the award-winning **La Abadía** now challenges their hegemony. The main season runs from September to June, but many theatres now continue working in summer, presenting open-air works as part of the **Veranos de la Villa** festival. Concern about the future of theatre in the **Festival de Otoño** seems for the moment to be groundless, although rumours persist that a festival held a few years back, the International Theatre Festival in spring, may be revived to replace it. Another event that was one of the liveliest parts of the Autumn Festival, the 'Alternative Theatre' gathering at **Sala Triángulo**, now runs independently in February and March. For more on festivals, *see chapter* **Madrid by Season**. The **Círculo de Bellas Artes** holds a festival in November.

Theatres are usually closed on Mondays, although some programme other events. The *Guía del Ocio* and *El Mundo*'s Friday supplement *Metrópoli* carry listings (*see p199*), as does *El País' Tentaciones*, although its information is less complete. Many theatres have a *dia del espectador* ('theatre-

goer's day', usually Wednesday) when prices are reduced, and many offer children's shows (*see chapter* **Children**).

The State theatres – the Comedia, María Guerrero, Sala Olímpia, Teatro de la Zarzuela and Auditorio Nacional (*see chapter* **Music: Classical & Opera**) – have a joint ticketing system whereby tickets for all can be bought at any one of them. Tickets for other theatres can be purchased ahead from box offices, and in most cases can also be bought in advance through savings bank ticket operations (*see p176*), such as the **Tel-entradas** of Caja de Cataluña (24-hour phoneline 902 38 33 33), or **Cajamadrid** (24-hour phoneline 902 48 84 88). Phone sales must be with a credit card.

Unless indicated otherwise, however, the theatre box offices listed do not accept credit cards themselves.

Mainstream theatres

The **Sala Olímpia**, previously known for its avant-garde work but more recently incorporated into the *Centro Dramático Nacional*, is being completely rebuilt, and is not due to open before 2000.

Centro Cultural de la Villa

Jardines del Descubrimiento, Plaza de Colón (91 575 60 80/91 575 64 96). Metro Colón/bus all routes to Plaza de Colón. **Box office** 11am-1.30pm, 5-8pm, Tue-Sun. **Tickets** *Sala 1* 1,300-2,500ptas; *Sala 2* 1,000ptas. **Map I4**

A spectacular, very comfortable venue in Plaza Colón. It offers concerts, children's theatre and, in the largest of its three halls, quality popular theatre by living Spanish playwrights. It also stages a Latin American festival every autumn, and *zarzuela* in summer (*see chapter* **Music: Classical & Opera**). *See also chapters* **Art Galleries** *and* **Dance**.

Círculo de Bellas Artes

C/Marqués de Casa Riera 2 (91 360 54 00). Metro Banco de España, Sevilla/bus all routes to C/Alcalá or Cibeles. **Box office** 11.30am-1.30pm, 5pm until performance, Tue-Sun. **Tickets** 1,300-3,500 ptas. **Map G7**

A multifaceted arts centre that hosts much more than theatre, the Círculo was once home to Valle-Inclán's company. Today it offers several interesting theatre productions a year,

Golden oldies

Pacy, vibrant, closely linked to the politics of the time and entertaining, the *comedias* of Spanish Golden Age theatre can be light-hearted and serious, humorous and tragic all at the same time. Dealing with classic themes of love, intrigue, honour and revenge, they still have a universal appeal today. As well as the *comedias*, other forms of Golden Age drama were *autos sacramentales*, shorter, symbolic religious dramas, sometimes performed in the open air during religious festivals, and *entremeses* (interludes), short one-act pieces performed as curtain-raisers to longer works.

Three writers dominate Golden Age theatre – **Lope de Vega** (1562-1635), **Tirso de Molina** (1584-1648) and **Calderón de la Barca** (1600-81). The inevitable comparisons with Shakespeare are not overly helpful – the rapid turnover of plays in Madrid (and very low pay per play) meant that new pieces had to be turned out quickly, which led to a greater formalisation of plot and structure.

Lope de Vega, for example, claimed to have written 1,500 plays, although 800 is probably a more realistic estimate. He established the basic structure of the *comedia* in his *El Arte Nuevo de Hacer Comedias* (1609), laying down a set mix of characters, action and situations to ensure mass appeal. His output included historical dramas, comedies and tragedies, written in verse with great wit and verve, and his greatest works, such as *Fuenteovejuna* and *El Perro del Hortelano*, are full of earthy originality and poetic insight.

Tirso de Molina's work had a stronger religious element, although a wicked sense of humour comes through in plays like *El Vergonzoso en Palacio*. He is also credited with the first major treatment of the Don Juan story, in *El Burlador de Sevilla*.

Although he penned comedies (*La Dama Duende*), Calderón de la Barca is generally known for plays of a more serious nature. Along with Don Juan, perhaps the most famous single character in Golden Age drama is Segismundo, from his *La Vida es Sueño* ('Life is a Dream'), a complex meditation on the nature of reality. After 1651 Calderón wrote solely for Philip IV's Court theatre in the Buen Retiro (*see page 15*). The elaborate *autos sacramentales* he created for the King are among the best in the genre, full of powerful rhetoric.

The past few years have seen a resurgence in Golden Age drama in Madrid, with new life being breathed into the classics through

imaginative productions at independent and fringe venues as well as at the major official theatres. Credit should especially be given to the late director Pilar Miró, who brought the Golden Age to a much younger and wider audience with her film of Lope's *El Perro del Hortelano*, keeping faithfully to the original verse.

Great survivors: historic theatres

In addition to the living heritage of the plays themselves, not far from Madrid there are two beautiful historic theatres, both remarkable survivors from the early eras of Spanish drama. For an authentic experience of Spanish classic drama, an evening at the **Corral de Comedias** (*pictured*), a uniquely preserved seventeenth-century *corral* theatre (an open courtyard, rather like a Shakespearean theatre, only square) in the town of **Almagro** in La Mancha, is a must. The *corral* was restored in 1950, and since 1977 has hosted an annual festival in July and August, featuring Spanish classics and near-contemporary international works performed by the *Compañia Nacional de Teatro Clásico*, other Spanish groups and foreign companies. Additional performing spaces in the town include the San Juan hospital and the Dominican cloister. Equally fascinating is the **Real Coliseo de Carlos III**, an exquisite little eighteenth-century theatre built for King Charles III near the monastery at **El Escorial** (*see p225*). It too is used as an occasional venue for classic drama, opera and chamber concerts.

Too far from Madrid to be visited in a day, **Mérida**, in Extremadura, has an original Roman theatre that hosts the annual **Festival de Teatro Clásico de Mérida** every July-August. For information call 943 33 00 07/943 33 03 12.

Corral de Comedias de Almagro

Festival Internacional de Teatro Clásico de Almagro (926 86 00 46)/Madrid office C/Príncipe 14, 1º izq (91 521 07 20). Tickets also through Tel-entradas. **Dates** July-Aug. **Tickets** *approx* 1,700-2,300ptas. **Getting there:** *By bus* AISA from Estación Sur, 2 buses daily; *by car* N-IV south, at Puerto Lápice turn on to N-420 for Almagro (190km/118 miles). **Where to stay:** Parador de Almagro (926 86 01 00), or the cheaper Don Diego, C/Ejido de Calatrava 1 (926 86 12 87).

Real Coliseo Carlos III

C/Floridablanca 20, San Lorenzo de El Escorial (91 890 44 11). **Information** from El Escorial (91 890 15 54) & Madrid tourist offices. **Getting there:** *see p226.*

plus dramatised readings, opera and puppet shows for children. There's also a November theatre festival for young companies and directors from all over Spain (information 91 537 36 70). In the same building is the **Teatro Bellas Artes** (91 532 44 37/38), which, despite a few resounding flops recently, sometimes comes up with a good production.

Teatro de la Abadía
C/Fernández de los Ríos 42 (91 448 16 27/e-mail abadia@ctv.es). Metro Quevedo/bus 2, 16, 61. **Box office** 5-9pm Tue-Thur; 5-10pm Fri, Sat; 5-8pm Sun. **Tickets** 1,900-3,000ptas; discounts under-26s, students, over-65s. Tue, Wed. **Credit** V. **Map D1**
One of Madrid's newest (1995) and most beautiful theatres, the Abadía has already received major awards. Among the outstanding productions performed in its two spaces have been works by Valle Inclán, Cervantes, Shakespeare, Brecht, Lorca and Ionesco, and Steven Berkoff has played here. There are also poetry recitals and one-act operas, and the theatre has a strong commitment to training new actors.

Teatro Albéniz
C/de la Paz 11 (91 531 83 11). Metro Sol/bus all routes to Puerta del Sol. **Box office** 11.30am-1pm, 5.30-9pm, Tue-Sun. **Ticket** 1,700-3,500ptas, discounts under-26s, groups. **Credit** V. **Map E8**
The Albéniz stages a wide variety of quality drama, and is the principal venue for the **Festival de Otoño** (*see p10*). It also hosts opera and dance. *See also chapter* **Dance**.

Teatro de Cámara
C/San Cosme y San Damián 3 (91 527 09 54). Metro Antón Martín, Lavapiés/bus 6, 26, 32. **Box office** 30 min before performance, Tue-Sun. Closed Aug. **Tickets** 1,500ptas; 1,000ptas over-65s. **Map F9**
A small but highly regarded independent repertory theatre presenting worldwide drama by major writers, with a particular interest in Russian works. Chekhov is a mainstay.

Teatro de la Comedia (Compañía Nacional de Teatro Clásico)
C/Príncipe 14 (91 521 49 31). Metro Sevilla, Sol/bus all routes to Puerta del Sol. **Box office** 11.30am-1.30pm, 5-8pm, daily. **Tickets** 1,300-2,600ptas. **Credit** AmEx, DC, MC, V. **Map F8**
Classic Spanish theatre at its best. Under director Adolfo Marsillach the *CNTC*, dedicated to preserving the heritage of Golden Age theatre, became one of the best-respected and most vital Spanish companies. He resigned in 1996 (one of many leading artistic figures who felt they couldn't work in the new climate under the PP), and was succeeded by Rafael Pérez Sierra. There are usually three productions a year, plus occasional French or English plays of similar epochs.

Teatro Español
C/Príncipe 25 (91 429 62 97). Metro Sevilla, Sol/bus all routes to Puerta del Sol. **Box office** 11.30am-1.30pm, 5-7pm, Tue-Sun. **Ticket** 200-2,300ptas; 50% discount Wed. **Map F8**
This site has housed a theatre since 1583, when the Corral del Príncipe, in which many of Lope de Vega's works were premièred, opened its doors. The current theatre, which replaced it in 1745, is the most beautiful in Madrid. It now presents mainly twentieth-century Spanish drama, along with new work and international classics, plus occasional children's productions such as one of *The Jungle Book*.

Teatro Lara
Corredera Baja de San Pablo 15 (91 521 05 52). Metro Callao/bus all routes to Plaza de Callao. **Box office** 11.30am-1pm, 5pm until performance, Tue-Sun. **Tickets** 1,400-3,000ptas; discounts groups. **Map F5**
After being closed for many years, this jewel of nineteenth-century theatre architecture was rescued and reopened in

1996, with its original décor restored. The Lara saw the première of many works by Valle Inclán, Jacinto Benavente and Falla (*El Amor Brujo*). Since reopening, it has offered a wide mix, including Edward Albee's *Three Tall Women*. Try to take the kids to one of the excellent children's matinées here.

Teatro La Latina
Plaza de la Cebada 2 (91 365 28 35). Metro La Latina/bus 17, 18, 23, 35, 60. **Box office** 11am-1pm, 6-8pm, Tue-Sun. **Tickets** 1,500-2,500ptas; discounts under-18s, over-65s, groups. **Map D9**
Specialising in revivals of '30s Madrileño comedies, this big revue theatre often has the 'indestructible' Lina Morgan in star roles, and stalwarts of the kitsch Spanish entertainment world in the audience. Dance is a recent feature.

Teatro Lope de Vega
Gran Vía 57 (91 548 70 91). Metro Callao, Santo Domingo/bus all routes to Callao. **Box office** 11am-1pm, 5pm until performance, Tue-Sun. **Tickets** 2,500-6,000ptas. **Credit** V. **Map D6**
Originally a theatre, then a cinema, the Lope de Vega recently returned to its former state to specialise in musicals – *Man of la Mancha*, a big hit, and a full-scale production of *Grease*. It also hosts major international classical ballet companies.

Teatro de Madrid
Avda de la Ilustración s/n (91 740 52 74/91 730 17 50). Metro Barrio del Pilar/bus all routes to Barrio del Pilar, La Vaguada. **Box office** 5-9.30pm Wed-Sun. **Ticket** 1,000-3,000ptas; discounts groups, and Wed, Sun. **No credit cards.**
A modern public theatre built by the city council far from the centre, but with lavish facilities. It presents a mixture of ballet, Spanish dance and high-budget drama, and children's shows, especially around Christmas. *See also chapter* **Dance**.

Teatro María Guerrero (Centro Dramático Nacional)
C/Tamayo y Baus 4 (91 319 47 69). Metro Colón/bus all routes to Plaza de Colón. **Box office** 11.30am-1.30pm, 5pm-until performance, Tue-Sun (advance sales only until 6pm). Closed July-Sept. **Tickets** 2,200-2,600ptas. **Credit** AmEx, MC, V. **Map H5**
The base for Spain's *Centro Dramático Nacional*, which presents international and contemporary Spanish drama in high-quality productions with top-class Spanish performers. However, it too has fallen victim to political changes, and the entire top brass of the CDN resigned or were removed in 1996. The 1998-9 season saw a prestige production by Peter Brooke of his *Je suis un phénomène*. The 1885 theatre has a beautiful interior, and a thorough renovation scheme (including provision of wheelchair access) was recently completed.

Teatro Marquina
C/Prim 11 (91 532 31 86). Metro Banco de España, Colón/bus all routes to Plaza Colón & Plaza Cibeles. **Box office** 11.30am-1.30pm, 5.30pm until performance, Tue-Sun. **Tickets** average 2,800ptas. **Map H5**
After a complete refurbishment, in 1997 the Marquina reopened with Nuria Espert, a *grande dame* of the Spanish stage. In the '98-9 season it has housed Yasmina Reza's worldwide hit *Art*, directed by and starring the prestigious Catalan actor Josep Maria Flotats.

Teatro Nuevo Apolo
Plaza de Tirso de Molina 1 (91 369 06 37/902 115 018). Metro Tirso de Molina/bus 6, 26, 32, 65. **Box office** 11.30am-1.30pm, 5-8pm, Tue-Sun. **Tickets** 1,500-5,000ptas; 50% discount under-14s. **Credit** V. **Map E8**
Madrid's venue for big musical spectaculars: recent shows have been *West Side Story* (a flop), Gospel singer Queen Esther Marrow and Catalan company Dagoll Dagom with a (very loose) version of *The Pirates of Penzance*.

Also worth checking out are the productions staged at **Teatro Pradillo** (*see chapter* **Dance**).

El Canto de la Cabra

C/San Gregorio 8 (91 310 42 22).
Metro Chueca/bus 3, 40, 149. **Box office** 1 hour before performance, Thur-Sun. **Tickets** 1,000-1,500ptas; discounts under-26s, unemployed, groups. **Map G4**
One of the more experimental venues, 'The Goat's Bleat' programmes work by contemporary Spanish and foreign writers. With a capacity of 70, it is cosy and intimate. In summer there are outdoor performances in the adjoining square.

Cuarta Pared

C/Ercilla 17 (91 517 23 17). Metro Embajadores/bus all routes to Embajadores. **Box office** 1 hour before performance. Closed Aug. **Tickets** 700-1,200ptas.
A reasonably sized venue (capacity 170) that presents quality contemporary productions and some excellent dance. It also houses theatre workshops, courses and children's plays.

Ensayo 100

C/Raimundo Lulio 20 (91 447 94 86). Metro Iglesia/bus 3, 37, 40, 147. **Box office** 2 hours before performance, Fri-Sun. **Tickets** 700-2,100ptas. **Map G2**
The fare here is generally intellectual, and the attitude totally professional; the inaugural work was a series of monologues by the company's director, Argentinian Jorge Eines, based on stories by Borges. Some English theatre has been staged here too, and it has even organised *tertulias* on the relationship between football and art.

In English

English-language productions may be very much a minority interest within the Madrid theatre scene, but they're well attended by resident Anglos and curious Spanish audiences alike, and have been praised by critics in recent years. Productions usually involve a mixture of professional and amateur actors. The three main groups are the **Madrid Players**, the city's longest-standing group, with an excellent annual pantomime; **ACT** (American and Classical Theater), formerly the White Light Company; and the **Transatlantic Theatre Company**, which stages performances alternately in English and Spanish, and has also branched out into bilingual adaptations. None of them has a permanent base – productions tend to be staged in fringe theatres, particularly **Sala Triángulo.**
ACT Leslie Freschet 91 457 92 22
Madrid Players Thisbe Burns 91 413 50 34/ e-mail madridplayers@hotmail.com
Transatlantic Theatre Company Ramón Camin 91 420 13 52/e-mail transat@ctv.es
The International Bookshop (*see p159*) plans to sell tickets for Madrid Players performances; otherwise, look for posters around pubs, or check out *The Broadsheet* (*see p198*).

Madrid's comedy centre, **Teatro Alfil.**

El Montacargas

C/Antillón 19 (91 526 11 73).
Metro Puerta del Angel/bus 31, 33, 39, 65, 138.
Box office 30 min before performance, Fri-Sun. **Ticket** 1,200ptas; 800ptas under-12s Sun.
This sparky cultural association on the west bank of the river hosts kid's shows (Sunday, 6pm), *café-teatro* (cabaret) and a range of workshops and other activities as well as its theatre programme, which is suitably unpredictable.

Sala Mirador

C/Doctor Fourquet 31 (91 539 57 67).
Metro Atocha, Lavapiés/bus all routes to Atocha.
Box office 1 hour before performance, Wed-Sun. **Tickets** 1,500-2,500ptas. **Map G10**
Worth visiting for the unique entrance alone: an oldfashioned Madrid patio. Productions are varied, and have included dance, children's shows and Joe Orton.

Sala Triángulo

C/Zurita 20 (91 530 69 91). Metro Lavapiés/bus all routes to Embajadores. **Box office** 30 min before performance, Fri-Sun. **Tickets** 800-1,400ptas. **Map F9**
One of the best fringe venues, the Triángulo has hosted almost every theatrical movement at some point, and is a good showcase for new writing and young actors. Look out for the *Muestra de Teatro Alternativo* in late winter-early spring, an international festival of avant-garde theatre, and the regular children's shows and *café-teatro* (cabaret).

Teatro de las Aguas

C/Aguas 8 (91 366 96 42). Metro La Latina/ bus 17, 18, 23, 35, 60. **Box office** 1 hour before performance, Thur, Fri, Sat. **Map C9**
A tiny space that has not been going long, and has made its niche with a mix of small productions. Look out for Englishlanguage shows: Albee's *Zoo Story* is a recent example.

Teatro Alfil

C/del Pez 10 (91 521 45 41). Metro Callao/bus 147. **Box office** 1 hour before performance, Tue-Sun. **Ticket** 1,000-2,000ptas; discounts students, groups. **Map E5**
The Alfil has survived several attempts to close it down, and since 1996 has been under new management. So far, the risky programming seems to be paying off – one good sign is the *Festival Internacional de Teatro de Humor*, held so far for two successful edition in spring 1997 and '98. Comedy and stand-up comedians are increasingly the mainstay here.

Teatro Estudio de Madrid

C/Cabeza 14 (91 532 64 47). Metro Tirso de Molina/bus 6, 26, 32, 65. **Box office** 1 hour before performance, Fri-Sun. Closed Aug. **Tickets** 1,200ptas. **Map E9**
A tiny fringe theatre (capacity 50) that makes a suitably intense venue for solo shows or two-handers. Short pieces by Dario Fo are a regular feature.

Trips Out of Town

Getting Started

Pardon me boy, is that the Guadarrama choo-choo?

By bus

Most of the companies that run inter-city coach services to and from Madrid now operate from the new **Estación Sur de Autobuses**, C/Méndez Alvaro (Metro and *Cercanías* Méndez Alvaro). It is some way south-east of the city centre; to get into the centre by Metro, take line 6 (grey) one stop to Pacífico, and change onto line 1 (pale blue). A single phone line (**91 468 42 00**) handles all enquiries, but many companies have their own lines. If the main number is engaged and you have a local Yellow Pages, look up *Autocares*: ads often show the companies' routes. At the station itself there is a computer information system to tell you which companies serve which destinations.

However, buses for many places listed in these chapters – especially some closer to the city within the *Comunidad de Madrid* – don't depart from the Estación Sur but from their companies' own depots or terminal points around the city, close to the main highways to their destinations.

For regional buses to routes north and north-east of Madrid, use the **Plaza Castilla** terminal; for the north-west, the streets around **Moncloa** Metro; and for the south-east, around Avda del Mediterráneo, next to **Conde de Casal** Metro. The Continental Auto company's buses to the north (Burgos, Basque Country, Soria) currently leave from a depot at C/Alenza 20 (91 533 04 00; Metro Cuatro Caminos), but in late 1999-2000 this station will be closed and they and some local services will transfer to another new terminal at **Avenida de América**. Further details of current services are available from tourist offices and, for buses within the *Comunidad*, on map 4 of the *Consorcio de Transportes* series. Some popular routes are listed below. Local tour companies also offer guided trips to many destinations. For details, *see page 68.*

Avila (94km/59 miles): Larrea Est. Sur (91 539 49 00).
Chinchón (45km/28 miles): La Veloz Avda del Mediterráneo 49 (91 409 76 02). Metro Conde de Casal.
Cuenca (165km/103 miles) & Salamanca (215km/ 134 miles): Auto-Res C/Fernández Shaw 1 (information 91 551 72 00). Metro Conde de Casal/bus 14, 26, 32, 56, 143.
To El Escorial (50km/31 miles): Autocares Herranz C/Fernández de los Rios, corner C/Isaac Peral (91 890 41 22). Metro Moncloa/bus all routes to Moncloa.
To Segovia (90km/56 miles): La Sepulvedana Estación Sur (91 539 58 13) & Paseo de la Florida 11 (91 530 48 00). Metro Principe Pio/bus 33, 39, 46, 75, C.
To Toledo (70km/44 miles): Empresa Galeano Continental Estación Sur (91 527 29 61).

By car

The infamous six roads, numbered in Roman numerals N-I to N-VI, which are the driver's sole normal way out of Madrid, can all be reached from the M-30 or the outlying M-40 ring road. For the eastern **Guadarrama** and the **Sierra Pobre**, the N-I (Carretera de Burgos) is the main road. For **Guadalajara**, take the N-II Barcelona road, and for **Chinchón**, the N-III towards Valencia. The N-401 to **Toledo** can be reached from either the M-30 or the N-IV, and the route toward **El Escorial**, **Segovia**, **Avila** and **Salamanca** is the N-VI north-west, the Carretera de La Coruña. For more on driving and car hire, *see page 252.*

Driving around Madrid can be an appalling experience at times when the whole city decides to go somewhere. On some weekends there are bottlenecks as far as Talavera de la Reina, 120km out on the N-V. For safety and/or your sanity's sake avoid leaving the city on Friday evenings. The real teeth-grinder is the return trip on Sundays: dead in the water from mid-afternoon till well past midnight. Immense back-ups and a substantial crop of accidents are also dismally predictable on long weekends and at the beginning and end of August.

By train

Alcalá, **Aranjuez**, **El Escorial** and many towns towards the Guadarrama are on the *Cercanías* local rail network (*see Map page 287*). At main RENFE (Spanish Railways) stations *Cercanías* platforms are signposted separately. Services to other destinations leave from the main line stations, **Chamartín** and **Atocha**, although many trains also stop between them at **Nuevos Ministerios** and **Recoletos** *Cercanías* stations. Some towns, especially those on *Cercanías* lines, have frequent rail services; for others, particularly **Segovia**, buses are quicker and more frequent. For **RENFE information**, call **91 328 90 20** (English spoken). For more on rail services, *see pages 249-50.*

Avila: 16 trains daily from Chamartín or Atocha. Journey time for *Regional-Exprés* services 1½ hours.
Aranjuez: *Cercanías* C-3 from Atocha; at least 2 trains each hour, 5.30am-11.30pm, more at peak times.
El Escorial: *Cercanías* C-8a from Atocha, Chamartín, frequent services.
Salamanca: 3 trains a day from Chamartín, Mon-Thur, Sat; 4 on Fri, Sun. Journey time 3½ hours. All Salamanca trains pass through Avila, so the two can be combined in one longish overnight.

Around Madrid

Madrid is circled by a ring of palaces and historic towns offering cuisine, fresh air, architectural treasures and a glimpse of rural Spain.

Still a relatively compact city, Madrid offers old-world towns and unspoiled countryside within 40km (25 miles) of the Puerta del Sol. The areas north and west have the most spectacular landscapes, with the three main Sierras (*see page 235*). The country to the south and east is flatter and less dramatic, but full of fascinating places – among them Aranjuez, Chinchón and, above all, Toledo. As well as having whole streets full of architectural gems, historic centres like Toledo, Segovia and – a little further away – Avila still retain the pleasant feel of living, functioning towns.

El Escorial

Take it as you will: Philip's folly, the forbidding barracks of fanaticism, a megalomaniac's monument to himself. Foreigners have never thought much of this immense monastery-mausoleum, dreamt up by the same king who gave us the Invincible Armada. Any number of writers have seen it virtually as the Inquisition raised in stone. But, if you visit with an open mind, it's hard not to conclude that this is one of the most extraordinary structures ever built by man.

The statistics are staggering: 2,675 windows, 1,200 doors, 16 inner courtyards, 15 miles of passageways and 86 staircases. Its architects, Juan Bautista de Toledo and Juan de Herrera, built it on a rectangular pattern to represent the gridiron on which the martyr Saint Laurence roasted to death. What makes it so imposing is the monumentality and coldness of all that Guadarrama granite and the un-Spanish frugality of ornamentation.

Philip II – dour, devout and shy – required a resting place for his father where a community of

*The peppery buttresses of **Segovia** Cathedral. See page 227.*

monks could pray for the eternal repose of his lineage. He also needed somewhere to go to commune privately with God the Father – the two father figures were a little mixed up in his mind. Hence, he chose to combine a palace (a very bare, unhedonistic one), a monastery and a royal tomb in one. All but two Spanish sovereigns and their consorts (with one exception, only heir-bearing queens were admitted) lie in the jasper, gold and marble mausoleum under the altar of the enormous basilica.

Philip's austere private apartments are above the altar of the vast grey basilica, with a *jalousie* window so he didn't miss Mass when bedridden. Otherwise, he amused himself with his art collection, including a huge El Greco and works by Bosch, Titian and the Flemish masters (the best pictures are now in the Prado, but several, including Titian's *Last Supper* and El Greco's *The Adoration of the Name of Jesus*, are still at El Escorial). He could also browse beneath the barrel-vaulted ceiling of the magnificent library, whose 50,000 volumes rival the Vatican's holdings.

After the Spanish Habsburgs inbred themselves to extinction, their Bourbon successors made little use of the Escorial, except for hunting-mad cuckold Charles IV. The **Palacio de los Borbones**, the apartments that he had remodelled to his taste – light, airy, and in a fluffy neo-classical style completely at odds with the gloomy corridors of Philip's palace – contain many superb tapestries designed by Goya and his contemporaries. This area had been closed for restoration for years, but can now be visited with guided tours on certain days. Outside the main monastery in the gardens, the restorers have arrived at Charles IV's pretty summerhouse the **Casita del Príncipe**, which is now closed. Another eighteenth-century building that contrasts completely with the monastery is the dainty **Real Coliseo** theatre (*see chapter* **Theatre**) in the town, added by Charles III.

The monastery is in **San Lorenzo de El Escorial**, a 2km (1¼-mile) walk (or bus ride) uphill from the train station, in **El Escorial** proper. San Lorenzo is also a fine base for walks into the Guadarrama mountains; for routes, *see page 237*.

Information

Getting there: *by bus* Herranz **661** and **664** from Moncloa to San Lorenzo (55 min), departures at least every ½ hour 7.15am-10pm (9am-9.30pm Sat; 9am-11pm Sun, holidays). Last return 9pm (8pm Sat, 10pm Sun, holidays); *by car* N-VI/A6 to Guadarrama, then turning left (south) onto M-600; *by train* Cercanías C-8a, 27 trains from Atocha 5.48am-11.33pm, Mon-Fri; every hour Sat, Sun. Last return 10.17pm daily.
Trains run to El Escorial, not to San Lorenzo and the monastery, so the bus is more direct.
Monasterio de San Lorenzo de El Escorial
(91 890 59 02/3/4): **Open** *Oct-Mar* 10am-5pm, *Apr-Sept* 10am-6pm, Tue-Sun. Closed Mon. **Admission** 850ptas; 350ptas 5-16s, students, over-65s; *Wed* free for EU citizens; *guided tours* 100ptas extra.
Palacio de los Borbones: Guided tours only 4pm, 5pm, 6pm Fri; 10am, 11am, noon, 5pm, 6pm Sat.

Admission 500ptas; 350ptas 5-16s, students, over-65s. Reservations essential, at least 24 hours in advance.
Where to eat: Fonda Genara *Plaza San Lorenzo 2 (91 890 43 57/91 890 33 30).* A pretty, comfortable restaurant entered via a likeable bar in a street-level arcade very near the monastery, with good-value Castilian fare. The dining room is adorned with period furnishings and old playbills from the Real Coliseo. **Horizontal** *Camino Horizontal (91 890 38 10).* High up behind San Lorenzo, in the Abantos district, this restaurant offers outdoor eating in summer and a warm welcome in winter. **Parilla Príncipe** *C/Floridablanca 6 (91 890 16 11).* Very central, an eighteenth-century palace with a hotel on the upper floors and a classic blend of sierra home cooking and fish dishes available below.

El Valle de los Caídos

The 'Valley of the Fallen', Franco's vast monument (officially) to the dead on his own side in the Spanish Civil War, lies a little north of El Escorial off the Guadarrama road. It may theoretically commemorate all the nationalist war dead, but you won't find here any imposing lists of names, as in most collective war memorials; in the whole place the only names shown are two, those of Franco himself and José Antonio Primo de Rivera, the rich boy founder of the Falange, conveniently dead (and so no rival to the dictator) long before the mausoleum was begun. It is thus, really, nothing other than one of the most megalomaniac monuments ever created by one man to himself, worthy of Hitler, Stalin, or Ceaucescu.

Opinions differ as to whether Franco had already decided that this should be his final resting place when he had chain gangs of Republican prisoners labour for a decade to quarry this giant cavern out of the rock. Nobody knows how many died in the process, but it must be a bitter irony to their families to think they rest for eternity alongside the dictator beneath a basilica laden with gargantuan examples of unadulterated kitsch so dear to the totalitarian mindset, topped by a 152m-(500ft-) high stone cross, visible for 50km. Inside, it's one huge, converging tunnel, each chamber slightly smaller than the last and ending finally in the tomb, with effects worthy of a Hollywood horror movie set. The whole thing is so bizarre you can almost forget to dislike it. If you want the total fascist experience, go on 18 July, anniversary of the 1936 military uprising, or better still on 20 November, Franco's deathday.
Getting there: *by car* N-VI/A6 to Guadarrama exit.
El Valle de los Caídos: Open *Oct-Mar* 10am-6pm, *Apr-Sept* 9.30am-7pm, Tue-Sun. Closed Mon and some holidays. **Admission** 650ptas; 250ptas 5-16s, over-65s.

El Pardo

Just 6km (4 miles) north of Madrid, the village of El Pardo has managed to avoid becoming a dormitory adjunct to the capital, and retains an air of rural calm. Not far from the Palacio de la Zarzuela, main residence of the royal family, it houses many barracks and other military installations. It's best known to Spaniards, though, for the **Palacio de El Pardo**, long the residence of General Franco.

Like Aranjuez and the Escorial, the palace was one of the ring of royal residences that surrounded Madrid. The hunting estate of El Pardo was what first attracted the Emperor Charles V to Madrid; a palace was built there for Philip II, but it was damaged by fire and rebuilt by Francesco Sabatini in the eighteenth century. Fernando VI made much use of it as a hunting lodge. Since Franco's passing it has been used to house foreign heads of state on official visits, but part of the palace is open to the public. There are fine displays of Spanish tapestries, some designed by Goya, and also Franco's cabinet rooms; the *Generalísimo's* plain, gloomy office gives an immediate insight into the dry little man who ran Spain for four decades. The ornate theatre, built for Charles IV's Italian wife María Luisa, is where film buff Franco used to watch flicks with his chums before deciding on their suitability for the great unwashed.

Whether because many people assume it is closed to the public, or because of its Francoist associations, El Pardo is the least visited of the royal residences. Outside in the fresh air, the palace can best be savoured from a distance. This is not as easy as one would wish, as much of the magnificent surrounding parkland is closed to the public. It's a superb stretch of hills and woodland, remarkably untouched due to its royal/dictatorial status, and extremely rich in bird- and wildlife such as deer and imperial eagles. Game features prominently in the village's popular restaurants.

Information

Getting there: *by bus* Alacuber SA **601** from Moncloa, services every 10-15 min 6.30am-midnight daily. Last return at 12.30am. Journey time 25 min; *by car* M-30 to El Pardo-M-40 exit, then C601.
Real Palacio de El Pardo *(91 542 00 59)*: **Open** *Oct-Mar* 10.30am-5pm Mon-Sat; 9.30am-1.30pm Sun; *Apr-Sept* 10.30am-6pm Mon-Sat; 9.30am-1.40pm Sun. Closed during official visits. **Admission** 650ptas; 250ptas 5-16s, students, over-65s; *Wed* free for EU citizens.
Where to eat: El Gamo *Avda de la Guardia 6 (91 376 03 27)*. Next to the palace and a string of other game-centred restaurants, El Gamo stands out for the quality of its food. Rabbit and snail stew, local venison and scrambled eggs with wild mushrooms and seafood are specialities. **La Marquesita** *Avda de la Guardia 29 (91 376 03 77)*. An open fire and the feel of an old hunting-lodge make this a fine winter stopoff. Roast venison, or pies of wild asparagus and langoustines, can provide an ideal lingering lunch.

Segovia

Despite the hordes of tourists and Madrileño day-trippers who take over the place in summer, and on Sundays throughout the year, Segovia is still very much its own town. Wander the back streets up towards the Alcázar, and you'll find atmospheric corners, and bars frequented only by locals.

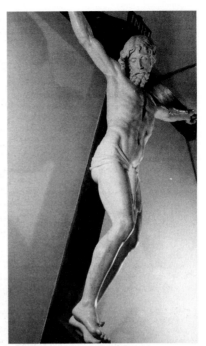
Art and baroque faith: **El Escorial**.

The Roman **Aqueduct** comes first, since all approaches to the old city, high on a bluff over the diminished Eresma river, bring you almost within touching distance of its double-decker span. The unsightly braces around some of its 163 arches were put up when the whole thing seemed about to collapse due to erosion caused by exhaust fumes. It was probably built early in the second century AD – no date was recorded by Roman contemporaries. As is evident, the rough-hewn blocks mesh perfectly without benefit of mortar. Generations of guidebooks have reported that it still carries water, but it hasn't done so for years.

Steps ascend the wall where the Roman span splices into the hill, or you can spiral up the streets that channel traffic up and down. Buttresses flying brazenly, the **Cathedral** stands to the left of the arcaded Plaza Mayor. It looks like a graceful piece of medieval Gothic, but was actually built in this anachronistic style to replace a predecessor destroyed in the *Comunero* rising of 1521.

Second only to eating yourself silly, the attraction of Segovia is in wandering the narrow streets between the **Plaza Mayor** and the **Alcázar**, especially those on the outer ramparts with views over the vast dry plains of Castile. From the northeast-

Paradors
of virtue

None of the 84 *Paradores Nacionales* dotted around Spain and its islands is in Madrid itself. However, both **Alcalá de Henares** and **Chinchón** boast fine examples of this state-run chain of luxury hotels, with a policy of taking over the most historic building in town – castles, monasteries, palaces – or, failing that, one with the best views of it. All *Paradores* have been beautifully restored and fitted with high-standard facilities. Rather than just a room for the night, a stay in a *Parador* can make a trip a real experience.

Further from the city but still within easy reach are the *Paradores* in **Sigüenza** (a medieval castle), **Segovia, Avila, Gredos, La Vera, Oropesa, Toledo** and **Salamanca**. In the south there are others at **Córdoba** and **Carmona**, outside Seville.

Paradores are not budget hotels (naturally), but with a bit of planning, and at the right time of year, a stay in one can be a not-too-expensive treat. Rates vary depending on the location – Gredos is around 15,000ptas a night, while Segovia weighs in at 22,000ptas. However, discounts of 20 per cent apply on the price of a room if you stay on a half-board basis for two nights or more, and a voucher book is available giving five nights' stay for around 60,000ptas (£260, if booked from the UK).

Reservations: *Central de Reservas, C/Requena 3 (91 516 66 66/fax 91 516 66 57/www.parador.es). Metro Opera/bus 3, 25, 33, 39, 148.* English spoken.

In the UK: **Keytel International** *402 Edgware Road, London W2 1ED (0171 402 8182/fax 0171 724 9503).* **In the USA & Canada**: **Marketing Ahead** *433 Fifth Ave, New York, NY 10016 (1 212 686 9213/toll-free 1 800 223 1356/fax 1 212 686 0271).*

fle-iron studs on its façade, is found amid the downhill shopping streets south of the cathedral.

The **Alcázar** juts out where the city's rocky plinth forms a sharp natural prow, its ramparts making an acute angle over the abyss into which a negligent nursemaid once dropped a fourteenth-century heir to the Castilian throne. Its towers and turrets give it a flamboyantly un-Spanish fairy tale look – a perfect model for all Disney castles – but the attractive bits weren't added until the nineteenth century. Only quite recently has the Army (which owns the place) got round to filling its chambers with a rather haphazard selection of weaponry, armour, tapestries and works of art, so paying visitors would have something to see.

So much for the scenery. What hordes of city-folk come to Segovia to do on a weekend, though, is to eat. The city is the capital of Castilian cuisine, and roasts of lamb and suckling pig are the star dishes for Sunday lunch in Segovia's traditional *mesones*, their walls covered with photos of distinguished former clients. It used to be that Segovia had the best piglets and surrounding towns – Torrecaballeros, Pedraza and especially Sepúlveda – saw to the lambs, because that's where they grazed. Insatiable demand on the part of day-trippers from Madrid has rendered this particular generalisation obsolete, and also impacted a little on the quality of the cooking at weekends.

Spaniards like their meat crisp on the outside, excruciatingly tender but well done within (no pink lamb, ever). The best Segovia piglets are *lechones*, nurtured with the milk of barley-fed mothers, and no more than 21 days old when they go into a brick baker's oven. The late Cándido (*see below* **Where to eat**) originated the stunt whereby the pork is sliced with the edge of a plate to show how tender it is.

Lamb is also eaten young, and sometimes suckled by two ewes to produce a superior quality meat. As a rule, a good quarter-lamb serving two is cooked cavity-side up in a dry earthenware dish rotated according to a secret ritual. Some roasters baste their lamb with pork drippings, but eschew herbs, garlic or salt so as not to interfere with the flavour of the smoke from ilex, oak and other fragrant woods. Don't expect *any* vegetables to eat with it; that would be to insult the meat.

If you have a car, you might want to continue north-east along the N110 to **Pedraza**, a classically beautiful medieval town with castle and arcaded main square that is much favoured by wealthy Madrileños as a weekend retreat.

Information

Getting there: *by bus* La Sepulvedana from Estación Sur or Paseo de la Florida 11. 12 buses daily 6.30am-9pm. Last return 8pm Mon-Sat, 9pm Sun. Journey time (direct services) 1¼ hours; *by car* N-VI/A6 to Guadarrama, then N603; or Navacerrada road from Guadarrama (slow mountain road); *by train* from Atocha or Chamartín, 9 trains daily, but a slow trip.

ern flank, you can just make out a Romanesque gem, the **Vera Cruz** church, built by the Templars with loot from the Crusades. It's a long walk out there, but well worth a close look.

Within the old town, **San Esteban** church is easy to spot because of its striking belltower and segment of cloister. A dozen more churches and convents from the twelfth to the sixteenth centuries are likewise within reach. **San Millán** is first-rate Romanesque, with an elaborate carved wooden ceiling, but often overlooked. As for secular buildings, the **Casa de los Picos**, with waf-

Tourist office: *Plaza Mayor, 10 (921 46 03 34)*. **Open** 10am-2pm, 5-8pm, daily.
Where to eat: **Cándido** *Plaza Azoguejo 5 (921 42 81 03)*. Where Orson Welles wolfed down a roast piggy entire and called out for more. It's now very touristy, and the cooking is no better and no worse than elsewhere, only more expensive. Go for pork, not the lamb. If you can't stand the sight of another roast, try the trout.
Mesón del Duque *C/Cervantes 12 (921 43 05 37)*. Castilian cooking with a tendency to fanciness. Only quarter-lambs served. Everyone gets a cholesterol-dissolving slug of brandy on the house. **Restaurante José María** *Cronista Lecea 11 (921 46 11 11)*. Consistently good; the best roast lamb in town, and excellent *cochinillo* (suckling pig). The earthy Ribera del Duero house red is exactly right, as are the prices.
Where to stay: **Los Linajes** *C/Dr Velasco 9 (921 46 04 75)*. In a thirteenth-century palace on a steep street edging the knoll: beamed ceilings, antiques in the rooms, a cosy bar in the cellar, and a lush patio.

La Granja & Ríofrío

About 11km (7 miles) from Segovia, back towards Madrid on the N601, lies **La Granja de San Ildefonso**, the former hunting estate where Philip V built a scaled-down version of the palace where he spent his childhood, Versailles, to remind him of home. His wife Isabella Farnese, equally out of place in Madrid, added many Italianate touches.

The King liked gardens – even though he was told that a French garden would never take in the harsh sierra – and classical statuary by the hundredweight, arranged around splashing fountains. He imported trees and plants from his dominions to 'improve' the mountain pine groves – look out for the giant California sequoia towering outside the chapel, in semi-tropical company. Nature runs ahead of the current maintenance budget, which gives the gardens an appealing unkempt edge. Nymphs and goddesses cavort in every shaded corner, but nowadays normally without cascades of spray around them, because of the drought.

The palace itself is notable for a glittering collection of cut-glass chandeliers, and one entire wing displaying a mere selection of Spanish and Flemish tapestries from the five linear miles of wall hangings purportedly in the royal collections.

From the grounds of La Granja there's a spectacular hike up and over the top of the sierra to El Paular and Rascafría *(see page 238)*.

Information
Getting there: *by bus* La Sepulvedana from Estación Sur or Paseo de la Florida 11, one bus 9.30pm Sun only, with return at 7.30pm; *by car* N-VI to Collado Villalba, then N601.
Palacio Real de La Granja de San Ildefonso *(921 47 00 19)*: *Palace* **Open** *Apr, May* 10am-1.30pm, 3-5pm, Tue-Fri; 10am-6pm Sat, Sun, holidays; *June-Sept* 10am-6pm Tue-Sun; *Oct-Mar* 10am-1.30pm, 5-7pm, Tue-Sat; 10am-2pm Sun, holidays. **Admission** 650ptas; 250ptas 5-16s, students, over-65s.
Gardens **Open** *Oct-May* 10am-6pm, *June-Sept* 10am-9pm, daily. *Fountains* operate *June-Sept* at 5.30pm Sat, Sun. **Admission** 325ptas; 200ptas 5-16s, over-65s.
Both *Wed* free for EU citizens.

Where to eat: **Restaurante Zaca** *C/Embajadores 6 (921 47 00 87)*. Open only for lunch, and it's essential to book. A family-run restaurant in business since 1940, with 'home-style' cooking: chunky casseroles, braised ox tongue and the like. No roasts, and huge portions.

Ríofrío

The palace of Ríofrío has cause to feel slighted; despite their proximity, the day is just not long enough to see La Granja and move on to this pure-Italian residence, built for Philip V's widow Isabella Farnese in 1754. She built it smack in the middle of the best deer-hunting country near Madrid, so later sovereigns also came to this beautiful estate to blast away to their hearts' content.

If hundreds of antlered skulls are to your liking, the hunting museum might appeal. You can also see the chambers where a heartbroken King Alfonso XII nursed his grief after Mercedes, his bride of a few months, died while still in her teens.
Getting there: *by car* the palace is south-west of Segovia, on a side road between the N110 and N603 (90km/56 miles from Madrid); *by train* Segovia trains (*see above*) stop at La Losa, about 2km (1¼ miles) from Ríofrío.
Palacio de Ríofrío *La Losa (921 47 00 19)*.
Open *Oct-May* 10am-1pm, 3-5pm, *June-Sept* 10am-6pm, Tue-Sun. **Admission** 650ptas; 250ptas 5-16s, students, over-65s. *Wed* free for EU citizens.

In the gardens of **Aranjuez**. *See page 230.*

Alcalá de Henares

Alcalá de Henares lies 31km (19 miles) east of Madrid along the N-II Barcelona road. Although its name is Arabic in origin (*Al-khala Nahar*, the Moorish city-fort located here), excavations have shown that this privileged site on the banks of the Henares river has been home to homo sapiens since paleolithic times. Carthaginians, Romans and Visigoths all settled here before the Moors arrived.

Now an industrial city of 50,000 people, Alcalá once rivalled Madrid in cultural importance thanks to its university, founded in 1498 by Cardinal Cisneros, Queen Isabella's mentor and the most influential leader the Spanish Church has ever had. The Universidad Complutense (*Complutum* was the Roman name for the city) was one of the most important in Europe; one of its greatest achievements was the Polyglot Bible, commissioned by Cisneros, a colossal work of scholarship with the text shown in a range of languages. Cervantes was also born in Alcalá, in 1547. When the university was moved to Madrid in 1836 the city began a decline that was only reversed in the 1960s. It now has a new university, opened in 1977 in an attempt to bring back some of the ambience that made it special for over three centuries.

This effort has paid off, and Alcalá is an interesting place to spend an afternoon. Many of its historic churches were damaged in the Civil War, but are still worth visiting. The heavily restored sixteenth-century **San Justo** stands on the site where Alcalá's two child saints, San Justo and San Pastor, were supposedly murdered. However, the University buildings and adjacent **Colegios Mayores** are the most popular sights. The University is justly famous for its Renaissance façade; the *Colegios*, built as student residences, now house hotels, restaurants and schools.

After 7pm, the pedestrianised Calle Mayor fills with locals taking their evening stroll. On the street is the **Casa Natal de Cervantes**, a reconstruction of his birthplace. Next door is the **Hospital de Antequena**, opened in 1493, with a typical Castilian patio courtyard at the back. The **Capilla de San Ildefonso**, housing the marble tomb of Cisneros (although not his remains) is also of note, as is the fifteenth-century **Capilla de Oidar**. Now used for exhibitions, it contains a reconstruction, pieced together from the same stones, of the Roman font in which Cervantes is said to have been baptised. The **Casa Consistorial** (town hall) is also worth a visit. On display inside are a copy of the Polyglot Bible and Cervantes's birth certificate, and rare editions of *Don Quixote*.

Information

Getting there: *by bus* Continental Auto **223** from Avda de América, buses about every ¼ hour 6.15am-11pm Mon-Sat, less frequent Sun; *by car* N-II/A2, 25 min; *by train* Cercanías C-2, C-7a; at least 5 trains per hour each way 5.10am-11.30pm daily.
Tourist office: *Callejón Santa María 1 (91 889 26 94).* **Open** *Sept-June* 10am-2pm, 4-6.30pm, daily; *July, Aug* 10am-2pm, 5-7pm, Tue-Sun.
Where to eat: Hosteria del Estudiante *C/de los Colegios 3 (91 888 03 30).* Traditional Castilian food in a fascinating setting – a Golden Age students' hostel; **Reinosa** *C/Goya 2 (91 889 00 42).* A good alternative.
Where to stay: El Bedel *Plaza de San Diego 6 (91 889 37 00).* In the centre of the city, but quiet.

Guadalajara & the Alcarria

Arriaca to the Romans, this city was called *Wad-ilh-hajra* or 'River of Stones' by the Moors, a name later hispanicised as Guadalajara. Conquered by the Christians in 1185, it rose to a peak of prestige and wealth in the sixteenth and seventeenth centuries, thanks to the Mendoza family. One of them built the city's main monument, the Gothic-*mudéjar* **Palacio del Infantado**. Its *Patio de los Leones* and façade are outstanding for their carving.

Guadalajara also has several fine churches. The thirteenth-century **Santa María** is the oldest; **San Ginés** contains many Mendoza tombs; and **San Nicolás** is famous for its baroque altar. **Santiago** (fourteenth-century), on the other hand, is a magnificent example of the Gothic-*mudéjar* style.

The towns and villages of the surrounding region, the **Alcarria**, make pleasant day trips from Madrid if you have a car. The Alcarria is a rugged region of low mountains and valleys, once one of the pockets of rural isolation and remoteness that existed only a short distance from Madrid. **Pastrana** (85km/53 miles from Madrid, 45km/28 miles from Guadalajara) is one of the highlights of the southern Alcarria. This historic town is now home to only a few thousand people, but was once an important Roman city, and in the seventeenth century still had a population of almost 20,000. The best way to enjoy Pastrana is to walk through its winding, cobbled streets and admire the old, grey-stone houses of the village. The **Colegiata** museum is worth a visit, and there are several good restaurants to choose from.

Information

Getting there: *by bus* Continental Auto from Avda de América 34 (91 533 04 00) to Guadalajara, buses hourly or 1½-hourly 7am-10pm Mon-Fri, 9am-10pm Sat, Sun; local services run from Guadalajara to Pastrana; *by car* N-II/A2 to Guadalajara (56km/35 miles); then N320 and C200 for Pastrana; *by train* Cercanías C-2 from Chamartín to Guadalajara, trains every 15-30 min 5am-11.30pm.
Tourist office: *Plaza Mayor 7 (949 22 06 98).*
Where to eat: Casa Victor *C/Bardales 6, Guadalajara (949 21 22 47).* Good-quality traditional Castilian fare.

Aranjuez & Chinchón

Just 45km (28 miles) south of Madrid, Aranjuez is an oasis in the arid plains of central Spain. Famous for its royal palace, asparagus and giant strawberries, it sits in a wide valley formed by the Jarama and Tajo (Tagus) rivers. The area has been inhabited since prehistoric times, and has seen Romans and Moors come and go. Aranjuez reached its greatest splendour, however, between the seventeenth and nineteenth centuries, when its palace served as the official spring residence of the Kings and Queens of Spain and their Court.

The mixed baroque and classical **Real Palacio** and its gardens have dominated town life for centuries. When the Court came to town in the spring, the village's population of 6,000 increased four-fold. Built for Philip II in the 1560s, the palace was greatly enlarged in the 1770s by Charles III, who had Francesco Sabatini add a further two wings. Despite all this architectural fiddling, it is surprisingly harmonious. Inside are lavish salons (the Throne Room, the Dress Museum, the extraordinary Porcelain Room) filled with treasures. The gardens that inspired Rodrigo's *Concierto de Aranjuez* lie between the palace and the Tagus, and are wonderful places for a stroll. Some sections (the **Jardín de la Isla**,

the **Jardín del Príncipe**) were laid out in the sixteenth century. A restoration programme has done wonders to return flora and fountains to their original splendour.

The **Casita del Labrador** is worth a visit by itself. In the middle of the gardens, this rococo fancy was built in 1803 as an indulgence for silly King Charles IV. Inside are painted ceilings, tapestry-lined walls, and porcelain and marble floors, some embedded with Roman mosaics brought from Mérida in Extremadura. The *Casita* can only be visited with guided tours: places are limited, and in great demand at weekends, so book ahead or get there early to reserve a slot for the same day.

Information

Getting there: *by bus* Autominibus **423**, **423a** from Estación Sur, hourly 8am-10pm Mon-Fri; 8am-9pm Sat; 9am-10pm Sun. Last return 7pm Mon-Sat, 8pm Sun; *by car* N-IV/A4; *by train Cercanías* C-3 from Atocha, trains every 15-20 min 5-9am, every ½ hour until 11.55pm, Mon-Fri, with a reduced service (within the same times) at weekends. Last return 11.34pm. For a special treat, especially for families, the steam-powered 'Strawberry Train' (*Tren de la Fresa*) covers the 45km at a leisurely

*Walls with memories: the synagogue of **Santísima María la Blanca**, Toledo. See page 234.*

pace on summer weekends and holidays (for details, *see* chapter **Children**).
Tourist office: *Plaza del Puente (91 891 04 27)*. **Open** *Oct-June* 10am-1pm, 3-5pm; *July-Sept* 10am-2pm, 4-6pm, Tue-Sun.
Real Palacio de Aranjuez: *(91 891 13 44)*. **Open** *palaces* 10am-6.15pm Tue-Sun; *gardens Oct-Mar* 10am-7.30pm, *April-Sept* 8am-8.30pm, daily. **Admission** *palace* 650ptas; 250ptas under-14s, students, over-65s. *Casita del Labrador (guided tours only)* 500ptas; 250ptas under-14s, students, over-65s. *Casa de Marinos* 325ptas; 225ptas under-14s, students, over-65s. *All* Wed free for EU citizens. *Gardens* free.
Where to eat: Casa José *C/Abastos 32 (91 891 14 88)*. A delightful little restaurant regarded by many as the finest south of Madrid, presenting international cuisine given a skilfully distinctive slant with fresh local produce, such as asparagus and strawberries. It's in the centre of the town, near the main square. Aranjuez has many more restaurants. **El Molino de Aranjuez**, *C/Príncipe 21 (91 892 42 33)*, has traditional Castillian fare, served amid period furniture; **Casa de Comidas Gobernador**, *C/del Gobernador 57 (91 891 65 76)*, is a decent budget choice.

Chinchón

A short distance east of Aranjuez and 45km (28 miles) out of Madrid lies Chinchón, one of the most picturesque towns in the province. It's a popular weekend getaway for Madrileños, who fill its typical *mesones* for lunch and dinner, despite their rather shaky price/quality ratio.

Winters are cold in this part of Castile, and Chinchón is known for its *anís*, an aniseed spirit popular with Spanish workers for getting their motors running on frosty mornings. It's most famous, though, for its grand town square, the **Plaza Mayor**. An oft-filmed and unforgettable setting for bullfights during local fiestas in June and late August, the plaza is a giant amphitheatre ringed by three-storey, wooden balcony-lined houses that are centuries old. The whole is overlooked by the impressive façade of the town church, originally the Chapel of the Counts of Chinchón.

Mesones abound in this town of fewer than 5,000 inhabitants. Prices, menu and quality are similar in all of them, and only the décor and settings change. Several of the most popular have tables on balconies overlooking the Plaza Mayor. Others have splendid dining rooms lined with *tinajas*, the baked-clay casks formerly used for storing wine, or impressive wine cellars (*bodegas*, or *cuevas* as they are called in Chinchón) where you can try the strong red several metres underground.

A good place to sample *anís* is at the splendid **Parador**, in a former convent. Even teetotallers (and non-residents) will enjoy a walk through its Moorish-style gardens graced with pomegranates, roses and hidden fountains. The ruins of a medieval castle, last burned by Napoleon's troops and more recently used as an *anís* distillery, can be seen (from the outside) on a hill west of the town.

Information

Getting there: *by bus* La Veloz **337** from Avda del Mediterráneo 49, buses every hour on the hour 7am-10pm Mon-Fri, 8am-9pm Sat, and every 1½ hours 9am-10.30pm Sun. Last return 7.30pm, Mon-Sat, 9pm Sun. Journey time about 1 hour; *by car* N-III or N-IV, then N300.
Where to eat: Mesón de la Virreina *Plaza Mayor 28 (91 894 00 15)*: eat roast lamb and bean stews while enjoying the view over the magnificent plaza. There's also excellent *pisto* and sweet pepper salad. Other good *mesones* are **Mesón La Cerca** *C/Cerca 9 (91 893 55 65)*; **Mesón Cuevas del Murciélago** *C/Quiñones 29 (no phone)*; **Mesón Cuevas del Vino** *C/Benito Hortelano 13 (91 894 02 85)*; **Venta de Reyes** *Ronda de Mediodía 18 (91 894 00 37)* is a café-bar with garden that's open daily, but has full meals only on weekends.
Where to stay: Parador Nacional de Turismo *C/Generalísimo 1 (91 894 08 36)*. Set back from the main square, the parador has a beautiful seventeenth-century dining room where you can sample its specialities of venison with truffles and very sweet eggy puddings.

Toledo

It would be fair to say that Toledo is one of the most seen but least understood cities in the world. Almost every day of the year, thousands of tourists fill its streets, making getting around by car almost impossible. Although impressed by the magnificence of it all, these same visitors usually fail to look behind the Imperial City's austere brick façade and tourist shops to uncover the human side of this crossroads of history.

Toledo, 70km (43 miles) south of Madrid, bears little relation to its late-coming neighbours. Madrid did not even exist when Toledo was capital of Visigothic Spain (AD 567-711). Aranjuez was a sleepy village until the Court decided it was a nice place to spend spring in the 1560s. Toledo has been Muslim, Jewish and very Christian, all at the same time. In fact, the fruitful cohabitation of the three great religions in Toledo in the last 300 years of the first millennium AD is often considered unique in the Western world. It was a centre for the *Mozárabes*, Christians who lived under Muslim rule with a semi-Arabic liturgy, and later *Mudéjares*, Muslims who did the reverse after the Christian conquest.

Which is why it is a shame that most visitors spend only half a day snapping photos, flashing past the El Grecos and haggling over local handicrafts before hopping back on the bus for Madrid. Toledo and its labyrinth of steep, cobbled streets and alleys are magical at dawn or dusk, when the summer's heat lessens and shadows evoke the ghosts of the past. Or under the light Castilian autumn and winter rain. Or when the fragrances of spring suddenly, unexpectedly invade the city one fine April day after four months of winter. At night, when the tourists

Blending in with the brown earth, the mudéjar *walls of* **Toledo***.*

have gone back to Madrid and the metal grates have come down over shop windows, Toledo's streets brim with strolling Toledanos enjoying their jewel of a city.

Beyond its human side, Toledo is an architectural delight, and there is too much to be seen in a day. If you can't spend a night or two here, this one-day itinerary – one of many possibilities – will give a taste of its treasures.

The starting point of any visit must be the eleventh-century **Puerta de Bisagra**, the only Moorish gate remaining in the city walls (and near the arrival point for buses from Madrid). Before entering, however, visit the museum of the **Fundación Duque de Lerma** on the street behind you as you face the city, just past the Tourist office. It is housed in the Hospital de Tavera, built in 1541. Inside are a chapel containing Cardinal Tavera's tomb, Renaissance courtyards and an interesting collection of works by Tintoretto, Zurbarán and, of course, El Greco, just the first you will see in his adopted home.

Enter the city through the Puerta de la Bisagra (really two gates, the Moorish one and one from 1550). Walk uphill through the Puerta del Sol, past a ninth-century mosque now called **Cristo de la Luz** (normally locked). This leads to the heart of the city, the **Plaza de Zocodover**, a triangular square lined with pleasant cafés and shady trees, and sundry things for sale. Off to the right rises the **Alcázar**, the enormous fortress that towers over the city (the museum inside mainly deals with the 1936 siege of the building by the Republicans, and the Francoist defence). Nearby is the magnificent Renaissance **Hospital de Santa Cruz**, now a museum, with works by El Greco and Ribera and superb tapestries. It also has a very fine interior courtyard and staircase.

Next, walk down the **Calle de Comercio**, the main street leading off Plaza de Zocodover, to the **Cathedral**. Completed one year after Columbus discovered America, work on it had actually begun 250 years earlier, and a Christian church is said to have been founded here in the first century AD by Saint Eugene, first Bishop of Toledo. Outside, a 91m- (298ft-) high tower, flying buttresses and enormous doors catch the eye. Inside, the dark, cavernous space is divided into five naves supported by 88 columns, with 750 stained-glass windows. There are fine paintings in the sacristy (*Sacristia*), remarkable tombs in the Treasury (*Tesoro*) and the sanctuary contains a spectacular carved altarpiece from 1504. Perhaps most extraordinary of all is the choir, carved with scenes of the fall of Granada and Biblical stories. Also unforgettable is the *Transparente*, a remarkable baroque *trompe-l'oeil* side chapel painted by Narciso Tomé in 1732, with an opening in the roof through which sunlight streams over cherubs and billowing clouds.

After lunching on regional specialities such as venison, partridge *a la Toledana* or pickled quail, there are more sights to take in downhill from the cathedral. The first is the medieval church of **Santo Tomé**, with a beautiful *mudéjar* tower. Inside the church is a room housing El Greco's oversize masterpiece *The Burial of Count Orgaz*, in the place for which it was originally commissioned. On another side of the same square is the **Casa de El Greco**. It has never actually been confirmed that the artist lived here, but it's an attractive reconstruction of a Toledan home of that era, with several works by him and period furnishings.

This area was once the *Judería*, the Jewish area of medieval Toledo, and contains some of the finest works of Jewish-*mudéjar* architecture. The Jewish presence in Toledo has been much easier to appreciate since extensive restoration work was carried out for 1992, as a symbolic act of atonement on the 500th anniversary of the expulsion of Jews from Spain. Near the Casa de El Greco on Calle Samuel Levi is the **Sinagoga del Tránsito**, built in the 1360s for Samuel Ha-Levi, Treasurer of King Pedro the Cruel of Castile, and one of the most powerful figures in Toledo's Jewish community. A remarkable architectural mix of ornate Moorish columns, Gothic touches and Hebrew inscriptions, it now houses a fascinating museum of Sephardic Jewish culture, tracing Sephardic customs in Spain and in the diaspora since 1492 (closed Mon). On Calle de los Reyes Católicos (ironically) is the **Sinagoga de Santísima María la Blanca**, begun as a mosque in the twelfth century, then a synagogue, and then a Christian church for centuries, until its recent restoration. The simple interior is extremely beautiful. On the same street is the convent of **San Juan de los Reyes**, built, ironically, for Ferdinand and Isabella, with an awesome Gothic cloister.

Information

Getting there: *by bus* Galeano Continental from Estación Sur, departures every ½ hour from 6.30am, last return at 10pm, Mon-Sat; first at 8.30am, last return at 11.30pm, Sun, holidays. There are direct (on the hour) and local stopping services (on the ½ hour). Journey time direct is 50 min; *by car* N401; *by train* from Atocha, 9 trains each day, roughly every 2 hours Mon-Fri 7am-8.25pm; 8 trains Sat, 7 trains Sun, 8.25am-8.25pm. Last return 9pm daily. Note that from Toledo's dainty 1920s neo-*mudéjar* station it's an uphill walk to the town, so the bus, while a less attractive ride, is both more frequent and more direct than the train. Or grab a taxi.
Tourist office: *Puerta de Bisagra (925 22 08 43)*. **Open** *Oct-June* 9am-6pm Mon-Fri; 9am-7pm Sat; 9am-3pm Sun; *July-Sept* 9am-7pm Mon-Sat; 9am-3pm Sun.
Where to eat: **Asador Adolfo** *C/Granada 6 (925 22 73 21)*, and **Venta de Aires** *C/Circo Romano 35 (925 22 05 45)* both serve fine traditional Toledano food.
Where to stay: **Parador Conde de Orgaz** *Paseo de los Cigarrales (925 22 18 50)*. On a hill across the river from the town, with superb views, and lavishly appointed. **Carlos V** *Plaza Horno de los Bizcochos 1 (925 22 21 00)*. A simpler but pleasant alternative.

The Sierras

When it's sweltering down in the city, a different view on the world and a complete change of air can be found only an hour away in Madrid's magnificent ring of mountains.

From Las Vistillas, just south of the Palacio Real, and many other places in central Madrid it's very easy to see the giant peaks of the Guadarrama, the massive mountain screen that runs across the northern and western horizon. It's an often repeated fact that, with an altitude of 650m (2,135ft), Madrid is the highest capital in Europe, but it's less appreciated that this is also one of the European cities closest to high mountain ranges, with peaks over 2,000m (6,600ft) less than 50km (31 miles) from the centre. In less than an hour's journey from the city it's possible to be amid superb, wild mountain scenery, with any number of walks to choose from ranging from gentle country strolls to routes for serious mountaineers. Many outdoor sports are also available (*see pages 240-1*).

The standard commonsense rules for mountain walking apply in the Sierras. It's essential to have local maps and know how to use them, and also advisable to carry a compass. Many routes can be done in summer in trainers, but light walking boots with good ankle support are a better option. Summer temperatures are high and the sunlight intense, so high-factor sun-cream, sunglasses and a hat are indispensable. In winter, temperatures drop below freezing and there can be dangerous patches of ice and snow. Only experienced, fully equipped walkers should try the higher walks in winter. Also, the weather in the mountains is notoriously changeable: check forecasts before you go.

Buy food and water in Madrid or on the way before your walk. Water is often scarce in the mountains, and you'll need an adequate supply.

Organised walks

Arawak Viajes

C/Peñuelas 12 (91 474 25 24). Metro Embajadores, Acacias/bus all routes to Embajadores. **Open** 10am-2pm, 5-9pm, Mon-Sat.
A small agency with young staff that offers a wide choice of weekend one- and two-day group walking tours in the Sierras around Madrid, and also longer trips in Spain and abroad, course in climbing, map-reading, orienteering and so on and one-day caving trips. Prices are very reasonable (from 1,700ptas for one-day trips, from about 10,000ptas for two days, hotel included), and some routes are specially designed for families with children. It also functions as a general travel agency, with budget flights to many destinations. **Branch**: C/Floridablanca 2, San Lorenzo de El Escorial (91 890 27 69).

Azimut

C/Jardines 3, 4º 7ª (91 521 42 84). Metro Gran Vía, Sol/bus all routes to Puerta del Sol. **Open** 5-9pm Mon-Fri. **Map E7**
A group that organises one- and two-day walking tours many weekends of the year. One-day trips are mostly to the Guadarrama and other mountains within a 60km radius of Madrid. Prices include a guide, route information, transport, board, accommodation and insurance. Gatherings are held on Thursday evenings to welcome new walkers to the group.

Haciendo Huella

C/José Abascal 32 (91 593 04 41). Metro Gregorio Marañón/bus 3, 12, 37, 149. **Open** 9am-2.30pm, 4.30-7.30pm, Mon-Fri.
The most professional agency of its kind in Madrid, which organises one-, two-day and longer group walking tours almost every weekend of the year. Again, one-day tours are mostly to the Guadarrama; Gredos normally features in longer trips. Prices include guide, transport, board and lodging (half-pension) and insurance. Routes are well planned and suitable for anyone in reasonable health. Meetings are held every Tuesday to welcome new walkers to the group.

Maps & information

Perseo

C/Fernández de los Ríos 95 (91 549 31 07). Metro Moncloa/bus all routes to Moncloa. **Open** 9.30am-2pm, 4.30-8.30pm, Mon-Fri; 10am-2pm Sat. **Credit** MC, V. **Map C1**
For maps and travel guides to Spain.

La Tienda Verde

C/Maudes 23 & 38 (91 534 32 57). Metro Cuatro Caminos/bus all routes to Cuatro Caminos. **Open** 9.30am-2pm, 4.30-8.30pm, Mon-Fri; 9.30am-2pm, 5-8pm, Sat. **Credit** AmEx, DC, V.
The best general travel book and map shops in Madrid.

Sierra de Guadarrama

The Guadarrama, sometimes just called the Sierra de Madrid, runs from El Escorial in the south-west to Somosierra in the north-east, and separates the two Castilian *mesetas*. It has been appreciated for centuries for its clear air, abundance of natural springs and forests and wealth of game and other wildlife. Many Madrileños have second homes in the villages of the Sierra, and many others regularly travel the 50km (31 miles) there to enjoy walking, climbing, skiing and a host of other activities away from the big city. The following is only a selection of the many walks possible in the area.

El Escorial

The best place from which to get an overview of the monastery of El Escorial (*see p225*), is **La Silla de Felipe II** (Philip II's Chair), a rocky promontory from which the King watched the progress of his great edifice. This vantage point also provides a splendid view of leafy oak forests and *dehesas*, the pastureland with scattered trees characteristic of Castile. With your back to the main façade of the monastery, turn left to leave the monastery esplanade by the Puerto de la Cruz Verde and take the track heading left that traverses the oak woods at Las Herrerías. Cross the M-505, and you will come to the asphalted track that climbs to La Silla. Once you get to the Ermita de la Virgen de Gracia, follow the red-and-white striped markings of the GR10 long-distance footpath. This is intended to run from Valencia to Lisbon, but its condition varies greatly. The walk to La Silla and back takes about 2½ hours, on easy, shaded paths.

If you have six or seven hours to spare, you can follow the classic *Cumbres Escurialenses* route. It is typically walked on 10 August, the day of the patron saint of El Escorial, Saint Laurence. From La Silla, continue north to the Collado de Entrecabezas (1,180m/3,870ft), the only place to pick up drinking water along the way; then follow the run of the spur north and east to the peak of Abantos (1,754m/5,756ft), before dropping down back to El Escorial from the Puerto de Malagón. The path is clear, but the walk takes you over five peaks, and so involves a bit of effort. For transport and other details on El Escorial, *see p226*.

Puerto de Guadarrama

Also known as the Alto de los Leones, the Guadarrama pass was a battlefront during the Civil War, and is the location of some of the most important action in Hemingway's *For Whom the Bell Tolls*. The nearest public transport is the train station at Tablada, 3km (2 miles) below the Puerto on the Madrid side. Once you've walked or otherwise made your way up to the pass, it's possible to walk, cycle or (if you have an off-road vehicle) drive along a dirt road south-west all the 30km (19 miles) to the village of Peguerinos, from where there are buses and a fully paved road to El Escorial. The signposted track veers off to the left as you come up the hill from the village of Guadarrama, among a jumble of radio towers and satellite dishes. The first part of the route is littered with bunkers from the war. Before setting off, check out the timewarp café Casa Hilario, with excellent views westward over the valley of San Rafael, and great-value rolls for an impromptu picnic. Set back from the road, on the right on the brow of the hill, Casa Hilario's original premises (there is a restaurant opposite) date back several decades to a time when getting this far out of Madrid on the way to Segovia merited a stopover for lunch. The track also gives access to a line of several campsites, including Camping La Nava, 4km (2½ miles) from the Puerto, and Valle de Enmedio, 11km (6½ miles) towards Peguerinos. Both are open April to October only.

There is another good walk to the north of the Puerto de Guadarrama. From Tablada train station, walk up 2km (not all the way to the pass) to km 56 and take the well-marked forestry track to the Peña del Arcipreste de Hita (1,527m/5,010ft), a rocky crag declared a 'natural monument' in honour of Juan Ruiz, Archpriest of Hita and author of the *Libro del Buen Amor*, a bawdy fourteenth-century classic. The route takes about three hours to walk, passing pines bent into fantastic shapes by the wind. It also allows you to orient yourself with respect to some of the most important villages and towns of the Sierra, away in the valley to the south, such as Guadarrama, Los Molinos and Cercedilla. The track drops steadily to reach the station at Los Molinos (1,045m/3,430ft).

One to share with the wild boar: the **Guadarrama** *contains hundreds of miles of peaceful pine woods.*

Information

Getting there: *by car* N-VI to Puerto de Guadarrama (55km/34 miles); *by train* from Atocha or Chamartín to Tablada, on Segovia line. **Getting back: from Peguerinos** *by bus* Herranz **665** to San Lorenzo de El Escorial; *by car* via El Escorial, 23km (14 miles). **From Los Molinos** *by bus* Larrea **683** from Los Molinos to Moncloa, last bus 6.45pm daily; *by car* M-995 from Los Molinos to N-VI; *by train Cercanías* C-8b from Los Molinos, trains hourly until 10.40pm.
Where to stay: **Camping La Nava** *(908 11 20 38)* or **Valle de Enmedio** *(no phone)* campsites, both on the Peguerinos road *(April-Oct only)*.
Where to eat: **Casa Hilario** *(no phone)*; **Casa Longinos** *Puerto de Guadarrama (91 852 05 57)*. A restaurant right on the pass.

Cercedilla & Valle de la Fuenfría

Cercedilla, the next town east after Los Molinos, stands at the foot of a valley that leads up to the pass that forms the oldest-known route across the Sierra, the Puerto de la Fuenfría (1,796m/5,895ft). Along the valley there is a *Calzada Romana* or Roman road dating back to the first century AD, with two fine Roman bridges at El Descalzo and Enmedio. The pass itself is also an important junction of paths.

From the main station in Cercedilla, a half-hour walk along the M-966 will bring you to a stretch of open woodland known as Las Dehesas, past the Casa Cirilo restaurant. This area offers natural spring swimming pools in summer, and all year round a range of walks to suit all abilities. They are conveniently signposted and mapped out on a noticeboard beside the *Calzada Romana*. The Roman road, well and poorly conserved by turns, climbs several steep slopes to reach the Puerto itself, three hours' walk away. Walk back down the Carretera de La República, the alternative track heading south, to return to Cercedilla station in another two hours.

Cercedilla also offers a narrow-gauge rail journey (*Cercanías* line C-9) up to the Cotos ski station, a charming, albeit lazy way to get up to and beyond the Puerto de Navacerrada (*see below*), especially when it's snowing.

Experienced walkers can try La Mujer Muerta (the Dead Woman), the Sierra's most famous silhouette. It overlooks La Acebeda, clothed in pine forests; the whole walk is a substantial hike of nine hours or so, complicated by having to follow narrow paths and cross spectacular scree slopes. From the top of the Roman road at Puerto de la Fuenfría, head north-west towards the Collado del Montón de Trigo, ascending to the west up to La Pinareja (2,193m/7,197ft), the 'head', to finish at the Puerto de Pasapán (1,843m/6,049ft), the 'feet'. On the north side, drop down to the San Rafael-Segovia road (N603) and at km 81, turn off to Navas de Riofrío-La Losa station.

Information

Getting there: *by bus* Larrea **684** hourly from Moncloa to Cercedilla; *by car* N-VI to Guadarrama, M-622 to Cercedilla, M-966 to Puerto de la Fuenfría (56km/35 miles); *by train Cercanías* C-8b to Cercedilla, trains hourly. **Getting back**: The same way (last return train from Cercedilla 10.37pm), or from La Losa; *by car* from km 81 on N603 to San Rafael, then N-VI; *by train* from La Losa (Segovia line) to Chamartín.

Puerto de Navacerrada.

The pass of Navacerrada (1,860m/6,104ft) is the main skiing centre of the Sierra. Outside the winter season, the ski station offers other activities (*see p240*), and there are great mountain walks nearby. Los Siete Picos (2,187m/7,178ft) is a magnificent walk along one of the Sierra's main ridges, through the seven granite peaks west from the Puerto de Navacerrada. There are superb views over the pine forests of Valsaín, home to much of the area's most characteristic wildlife. From Navacerrada, walk up under the *Telégrafo* skilift and skirt the peaks, which consist of huge rocky boulders, following the path until the saddle between the fifth and sixth peaks; once there, dip down and south towards Camorritos. This walk is easy and takes about four hours.

La Cuerda Larga (the Long Cord) is a much longer walk in the opposite direction, eastwards from Puerto de Navacerrada to the Puerto de la Morcuera (1,800m/5,908ft), for the most part above 2,000m/6,560ft. There are panoramic views to the south of La Pedriza and its ever-present colony of watchful griffon vultures, and over the pine forests in the Valle de Lozoya to the north. From Puerto de Navacerrada, walk east past the TV masts on Bola del Mundo, all the way to La Morcuera. Descend to Miraflores de la Sierra by following the M-611 for 2km (1¼ miles). The whole walk takes seven hours, and the path is clear enough, but hardgoing in stretches. Drinking water is very scarce in summer.

Information

Getting there: *by bus* Larrea **691** from Moncloa, every 2 hours; *by car* N-VI to Collado Villalba, then M-601 to Puerto de Navacerrada (57km/36 miles); *by train Cercanías* C-8b to Cercedilla, then C-9 to Puerto de Navacerrada; 4 trains daily Mon-Fri, hourly Sat, Sun. **Getting back**: *from Camorritos, by car* M-966 to Cercedilla, M-600 to Guadarrama, then N-VI; *by train Cercanías* C-9 to Cercedilla, then C-8b (last train approx 7.30pm). **From Miraflores de la Sierra**, *by bus* Colmenarejo **725** to Plaza Castilla, last bus 8.10pm Mon-Fri, 9.55pm Sat, 9pm Sun; *by train* Burgos line to Chamartín.
Where to eat: **Casa Gómez** *(no phone)*. A pleasant restaurant right in front of the station at Puerto de Navacerrada.

Puerto de los Cotos, Rascafría & El Paular

The Valle de Lozoya is a magnificent broad mountain valley that runs north-east, parallel to the main ridge of the Sierra, from the pass of Puerto de los Cotos (1,830m/6,006ft), north-east of Navacerrada. It can be reached by car from Navacerrada by continuing over the Puerto de los Cotos on the M-604, or directly from Madrid via Colmenar Viejo and Miraflores de la Sierra. The village of Rascafría at the western end of the valley and **Monasterio de El Paular** are both well worth a visit. The Benedictine monastery, 1km south of the village, dates back to the fourteenth century and is still partly occupied by monks, even though most of it has now become a hotel. The monastery entrance can be visited.

There is an ancient path across the Sierra between El Paular and the palace of **La Granja** *(see p229)*, which runs through Rascafría. Walk west out of the village of Rascafría, past the new schools, and cross the dense oak woods, looking out for wild boar. Climb up to the Puerto del Reventón (2,034m/6,675ft), cross it, and continue downhill on the Segovia side of the Sierra until you reach Scots pines again and the gardens of La Granja. The paths are poorly marked, but the walk is easy. The whole hike takes about five hours.

Another path, El Palero, links El Paular with the Puerto de los Cotos. This is one of the historic paths of the Sierra, and its construction predates that of all the existing roads. It is now part of the GR10 *(see above* **El Escorial***)* and so is marked in red and white. From the monastery, head south along the M-604 road for about 800m/875yds and then turn off to the right (south-west) alongside La Umbría stream. After about two-three hours this will bring you to a popular café, Casa Marcelino, about 500m/550yds below the pass at Cotos. On the way you cross leafy pine forests at the head of the Lozoya valley, refuge of the last roe deer in the Sierra, and any number of streams and springs.

For serious walkers there's also the trek up the highest peak in the Guadarrama, Peñalara (2,430m/7,970ft), reachable from Puerto de los Cotos. It's not hard to get to the top in about three hours, although the climb is quite steep. The complete walk round the cirque takes about six hours; the path is tricky only because it is so rocky. From Cotos station, walk up under the Zabala chairlift (or take the lift, if you prefer), pass the Dos Hermanas and continue to the summit, from where you can see right to the southernmost point of the Sierra and north to Lozoya. Walk down by heading in an arc north past the Risco Claveles, Laguna de Los Pájaros and the Laguna Grande until you regain the Puerto de los Cotos.

Information

Getting there: **to Puerto de los Cotos**, *by car* N-VI to Collado-Villalba, M-601 to Puerto de Navacerrada, then M-604 (64km/40 miles); *by train Cercanías* C-8b to Cercedilla, then line C-9 to Cotos; 4 trains daily Mon-Fri, hourly Sat, Sun. **To Rascafría**, *by bus* La Castellana **194** from Plaza Castilla, 2 buses at 2.30pm, 6pm, Mon-Fri, 8am, 6pm, Sat, 1 bus at 8am Sun; *by car* via Cotos *(see above)* or M-607 to Colmenar Viejo, M-609 to Soto del Real, M-611 to Rascafría (80km/50 miles). **Getting back**: the same routes; last **194** buses from Rascafría to Plaza Castilla 5pm Mon-Fri, 10.30am Sat, 6pm Sun.
Where to stay and eat: **Briscas** *Plaza España 13 (91 869 12 26)*. An excellent-value restaurant in Rascafría's main square, with a lively terrace in summer.
Santa María de El Paular *(91 869 10 11)*. With impressive views of the mountains, this grand hotel has 57 rooms amid the (admittedly austere) splendour of the monastery. It also has two restaurants, and rooms for about 13,000ptas. In addition, male readers (only) seeking a place of contemplation amid the peace of the valley can stay alongside at the **Monastery** itself *(91 869 14 25)* for 2,000ptas a night – for a minimum three nights' stay, and a maximum of ten.

Manzanares el Real & La Pedriza

La Pedriza is a wild region, almost exclusively of scattered and stacked granitic rock, located just south of the main Sierra. It surrounds the upper stretches of the Manzanares, which is suitable for swimming at this level, and overlooks the Santillana reservoir. Its inaccessible crags are home to the Sierra's biggest colony of griffon vultures, protected in the Parque Regional de la Cuenca Alta del Manzanares.

The area's outstanding landmark is El Yelmo (1,716m/5,630ft), a dome-shaped rock, visible from the **castle** of Manzanares el Real. To get to its peak, from the Plaza Mayor in Manzanares el Real, head for the river, without crossing it. Take the road signed to El Tranco just before the bridge, and get on to the path behind the small bars. Follow this path for three hours to the foot of El Yelmo. It's a 10m (33ft) scramble up a wide, easy chimney to the very top. The return walk to Manzanares takes about 1½ hours, along a well-marked but boulder-strewn path.

Information

Getting there: *by bus* Colmenarejo **724** from Plaza Castilla, buses approx hourly 7.20am-9.40pm Mon-Fri, 8.45am-9.30pm Sat, 8am-8pm Sun. Last return 9.45pm Mon-Fri, 7.55pm Sat, 9pm Sun; *by car* M-607 to Colmenar Viejo, M-609 towards Soto del Real, M-862 and M-608 to Manzanares el Real (53km/33 miles)
Where to stay: **La Fresneda** campsite at Manzanares el Real *(see chapter* **Accommodation***)*.

The Sierra Pobre

East of the N-I, the Carretera de Burgos, and beginning about 60km (37 miles) north of Madrid is the so-called *Sierra Pobre*, the Poor Sierra, running north-east toward Guadalajara. It is only *pobre* in comparison to the Guadarrama to the west, and inasmuch as its relative isolation has restricted the local economy, so that some villages have been all but abandoned. However, with far fewer visitors, it is less discovered and perhaps more 'authentic' than the main Sierra, and its rolling, at times forbidding, hills and peaks host some of the region's finest deciduous forests. Even at the height of summer the area is never crowded, and in spring or autumn its woods are a delight.

Buitrago de Lozoya is the main town of the Sierra Pobre. Its old centre dates back to the Middle Ages, and a walk around the walls – the inner part of which survives from Arab times – is essential. More surprising is that Buitrago has a **Picasso Museum** in its town hall, consisting of some 60 works, mostly from his later years, that the great (and bald) man donated to his hairdresser and friend Eugenio Arias, a native of the town.

Buitrago is also the best starting point for exploring the area. Reasonable roads now run round the main villages of the Sierra, but there are still several places with no direct bus from Madrid; however, from Buitrago a variety of microbuses run into the hills. Another option is to hire a bike in Madrid, take it on the bus and tour the Sierra from Buitrago. **Buitrabike** (91 868 07 19) is a cycle club in Buitrago that organises guided trips.

Among the first places of interest after Buitrago is **Montejo de la Sierra**, 16km (10 miles) to the north-east, and a good central point for excursions on foot. The jewel in Montejo's crown is a magnificent beech forest, the most westerly in Europe. Unless you phone previously for permission (91 869 70 58), access is limited to guided tours. Information on walking and cycling routes nearby can be obtained from the *Centro de Recurso de Montaña* (91 896 70 58), 8km (5 miles) east of the village towards the remote pass and mountain village of **La Hiruela** (1,477m/4,847ft).

South of here, at the bottom of a magnificent valley at the very heart of the Sierra Pobre, lies **Puebla de la Sierra**. With a population of just 77, this mountain hamlet represents a trip back into the past of rural Spain, only 100km from the capital. Much of the village has been restored, and it makes an ideal base for walks to the surrounding reservoirs. Information is available at the Parador de la Puebla – not an official state *Parador* – in the centre of the village.

About 25km (16 miles) south-west of Puebla (as the crow flies, not as the road winds) is **El Berrueco**, the village closest to the huge El Atazar reservoir. It boasts a splendid thirteenth-century church, and a range of water sports is on offer at the reservoir. **Patones**, on the southernmost edge of the Sierra and south of El Atazar, is reached via the Torrelaguna road, which turns off the N-I 51km (32 miles) north of Madrid. Once on the verge of being abandoned, the two villages of Patones (**de Arriba** and **de Abajo**) have been

extensively restored, and many of the ancient slate houses of Patones de Arriba have been turned into holiday homes and restaurants. The place, though, retains its character. A road north-east from Patones towards El Atazar leads on 12km (7½ miles) to the **Cueva del Reguerillo**, which contains prehistoric cave paintings.

Information

Getting there and back: *by bus* Continental **191** to Buitrago, **196** to Buitrago and Acebeda via El Berrueco, **199** to Montejo de la Sierra via El Berrueco (very infrequent), all from Plaza Castilla. 191 leaves every 2 hours from 8am; last return from Buitrago 6pm Mon-Sat, 8pm Sun. Many local microbus services run from Buitrago; *by car* from Madrid, N-I north direct to Buitrago de Lozoya (75km/47 miles), or turn right in Venturada (51km/32 miles; signposted to Torrelaguna) for Patones, or just north of La Cabrera (62km/39 miles) for El Berrueco. From Navacerrada and Rascafría on the M-604, continue to the N-I, and turn left for Buitrago.
Tourist office: **Centro de Turismo de la Sierra Norte** *La Cabrera* (91 868 86 98). The tourist office for the whole area. It is in La Cabrera, about 15km (9 miles) south of Buitrago, on the main street. The town hall at **Buitrago** also has a lot of information on activities in the Sierra, on the floor above the Picasso Museum.
Museo Picasso *Plaza Picasso, Buitrago de Lozoya* (91 868 00 56). **Open** 11am-2pm, 4-6pm, Tue-Fri; 10am-2.30pm, 3.30-6.30pm, Sat; 10am-2.30pm Sun, holidays. Closed Mon. **Admission** free.
Where to stay and eat:
Buitrago: **Hostal Madrid-París** *Avda de Madrid 23* (91 868 11 26). A typical old stone house with 25 bargain rooms and an excellent-value restaurant.
Asador Jubel *C/Real 33* (91 868 03 09) is an old-fashioned eating-house with old-fashioned, meaty food.
Montejo de la Sierra: **Hotel Montejo** *Vereda del Zarzal* (91 869 71 25). Wonderful views and immaculately kept rooms for around 5,000ptas. **Casa Benito** *C/Real* (91 869 70 63). Home cooking in a family atmosphere. **Mesón del Hayedo** *C/del Turco* (91 869 70 23) is much livelier, smaller and more crowded.
Patones: **El Tiempo Perdido** *Travesía del Ayuntamiento 7* (91 843 21 52). At 23,000ptas a pop, this restored five-room house is a hillbilly heaven. Still, it's a privilege to stay here. A good deal cheaper are the renovated school buildings in C/Escuelas (91 843 20 26). **El Rey de Patones** *C/Asas* (91 843 20 37). An old world, cottagey restaurant with typical local food.
Puebla de la Sierra: **El Parador de la Puebla** *Plaza de Carlos Ruiz 2* (91 869 72 56). This hotel has only five rooms (6,500ptas), so it's best to book. However, there are other houses in the village that let rooms: ask around.

Sierra de Gredos

The craggy peaks and lush valleys of the Sierra de Gredos – the part of Spain's central *cordillera* straddling southern Avila – were little known until two decades ago. When roads brought them within an easy drive from Madrid, though, the Gredos became a playground, and walkers, climbers, campers, mountain bikers, hang-gliders, fishermen, hunters, swimmers, skiers and city-dwellers simply in search of peace now flock in year round.

Where and how you go will depend on the time of year: in summer, the reservoirs are packed with Madrileños swimming or windsurfing, while

Mountain adventures

A choice of ways to get to grips with the countryside around Madrid.

For facilities in the city, *see chapter* **Sport & Fitness.**

Climbing & mountaineering

Escuela Madrileña de Alta Montaña
C/Apodaca 16, 1° (91 593 80 74). Metro Tribunal/bus 3, 37, 40, 149. **Open** *Sept-June* 10.30am-2pm, 6-8pm, Mon-Thur; 10.30am-2pm Fri; *July-Aug* 10.30am-2pm Mon-Fri.* **Map G4**
Provides practical and theoretical mountaineering and climbing classes throughout the year. Basic membership of the *Federación Madrileña de Montañismo*, based here, costs around 7,500ptas a year and includes accident insurance, access to the library, discounts for courses, use of mountain refuges and equipment in several sports shops, and other benefits. They can also suggest climbing and walking clubs to join in Madrid, according to your level of experience.

Estacion del Puerto de Navacerrada
Edificio Deporte y Montaña, Puerto de Navacerrada (91 852 33 02). Bus Larrea 691 from Moncloa/by car N-VI to Collado Villalba, then M-601 to Puerto de Navacerrada (57km/36 miles)/by train Cercanias line C-8b to Cercedilla, then C-9 to Puerto de Navacerrada.
Outside the skiing season, the Navacerrada ski station stays open and offers a range of organised activities including mountain biking, rock climbing, mountain walks and tours. They're also a good source of information on other sporting facilities such as golf, tennis, football, swimming, archery, horse riding and canoeing in the Sierras.
Madrid office: *C/Sagasta 13, 5° (91 594 30 34). Metro Alonso Martinez/bus 3, 7, 21, 37, 40.* **Open** 9am-6pm Mon-Thur; 9am-3pm Fri. **Map G3**

Fishing permits

Licencias de Caza y Pesca, Dirección General del Medio Ambiente
C/Princesa 3 (91 580 16 53). Metro Plaza de España, Ventura Rodriguez/bus all routes to Plaza de España. **Open** 9am-2pm Mon-Fri. **Map D4**
Fishing licences are issued on the spot. You must pay the licence fee (about 1,200ptas) into the authority's bank account, details of which are provided, and show the bank payment slip as proof you have paid, together with your passport. The same office also issues **shooting permits**: for these you will need a passport-size photograph, firearms licence from your home country and insurance (which is also bought here, about 2,000-2,500ptas).

Horse riding

Las Palomas
Club Hípico, Carretera de Colmenar Viejo km 28.9 (908 728 795/91 803 31 76). By bus 721, 724, 725, 726 from Plaza de Castilla/by car Carretera de Colmenar Viejo. **Open** 10am-2pm, 6-8pm, Tue-Sun.
Offers riding courses for all levels, and accompanied one-day one-to-one-week trekking excursions in the Guadarrama.

La Pasá
Urbanización La Cabezuela, Cercedilla (91 852 21 21/ 989 437 638). By bus Larrea 684 from Moncloa; by car N-VI to Guadarrama, M-622 to Cercedilla, M-966 to Puerto de La Fuenfria; by train Cercanias C-8b. **Open** by appointment.
Horse- and pony-treks in the Guadarrama from Cercedilla up to Navacerrada or Rascafria, across to Segovia or whichever route suits you, for around 6,000ptas a day. No experience is necessary. They're very busy on summer weekends, less so at other times; call a few days ahead to make an arrangement and discuss possible routes.

Mountain biking

For more on bike hire in Madrid, *see page 252.*

Bicibus
Puerta del Sol 14 (91 522 45 01). Metro Sol/ bus all routes to Puerta del Sol. **Open** 9.30am-1.30pm, 4.30-8pm, Mon-Fri; 10am-1.30pm Sat. **Credit** AmEx, MC, V. **Map E7**
Two-day and longer excursions for small groups into the Guadarrama or further afield. Prices for two-day trips start at 8,000ptas and include tour leader, insurance, transport, back-up vehicle and accommodation and breakfast. Also bike hire in Madrid, from around 1,200ptas per day.

Bicimanía
C/Palencia 20 (91 533 11 89). Metro Alvarado/bus 3, 43, 64, 66, 124, 127. **Open** 10am-2pm, 5-8.30pm, Mon-Fri. **Credit** AmEx, MC, V.
Organised group excursions through the year. Prices start at about 1,000ptas, and include tour leader and a light snack on the trip.

Sport Karacol
C/Tortosa 8 (91 539 96 33). Metro Atocha/bus all routes to Atocha. **Open** 10.30am-8pm Mon-Wed, Fri; 10.30am-10pm Thur; 10.30am-2pm Sat; *Aug only* closed Sat. **Credit** MC, V.
A big cycle hire shop that runs group excursions throughout the year. Prices start at around 7,000ptas and include bike hire, tour leader, insurance, transport and back-up vehicle, plus half-board and lodging on longer trips. *See also chapter* **Directory.**
Branch: *C/Montera 32 (91 532 90 73).*

Skiing

ATUDEM Phoneline
(91 350 20 20).
Recorded information (in Spanish only) on snow conditions at ski resorts.

Ski resorts
Of the four resorts near Madrid, **Valcotos** has the prettiest setting, and **Valdesquí** usually has the best snow. **La Pinilla** is directly north of Madrid near Riaza; the others are in the central Guadarrama. There is hotel accommodation only at Puerto de Navacerrada. The lifts get very

crowded on Friday afternoons and weekends. These ski stations offer limited skiing only and are of little interest to intermediate and advanced skiers, but are great for day trips out of Madrid, and the pleasure of swinging up the mountainside on a chairlift with the city away to the south is undeniable. Weekend packages at these stations and other ski resorts in Spain can be booked at virtually any Madrid travel agent.

La Pinilla *(921 55 03 04)*: 1 telecabin, 3 chairlifts, 8 button lifts; runs: 2 green, 5 blue, 8 red, 1 black; 15km of runs; snow cannons (7½km); lift passes from 2,000ptas.

Puerto de Navacerrada *(91 852 33 02)*: 5 chairlifts, 3 button lifts; runs: 3 green, 8 blue, 2 red, 2 black; 9km of runs; snow cannons (1½km); lift passes from 1,500ptas.

Valcotos *(91 563 60 31)*: 2 chairlifts, 5 button lifts; runs: 2 green, 2 blue, 3 red; 5km of runs; lift passes from 1,300ptas.

Valdesquí *(91 570 96 98)*: 3 chairlifts, 7 button lifts; runs: 10 green, 11 blue, 2 red; 18km of runs; lift passes from 1,400ptas.

Getting there: **La Pinilla** *by car* N-I to km104, N110 to Cerezo de Arriba, N112 to La Pinilla. **Puerto de Navacerrada, Valcotos** and **Valdesquí** *by bus* Larrea **691** from Paseo de la Florida 11, terminates at Valdesquí; *by car* N-VI to Collado-Villalba, M-601 to Puerto de Navacerrada, then M-604 to Puerto de los Cotos. (64km/40 miles); *by train* Cercanías C-8b to Cercedilla, then line C-9 to Navacerrada and Cotos.

Water sports

The reservoirs that ring Madrid offer a welcome break from soaring summer temperatures. The largest is **San**

Juan, depository for the Alberche river, in the Sierra de Gredos some 50km (31 miles) west of Madrid (*see p242*). As well as its own 'beach', San Juan has many places to eat. Several water sports clubs are based there, but there is nowhere for casual visitors to hire equipment. The **Valmayor** reservoir between Galapagar and El Escorial has a range of windsurfing and water sports facilities; **Club Deportivo Canal** (91 535 12 29) has boats for hire and runs sailing courses.

Escuela de Agua Bravas 'Los Gancheros'

C/Cuesta Negra 44 (91 306 72 78/989 429 728).
Metro Las Musas/bus 38, 140.
Open *information* 10am-11pm Mon-Fri.

A pioneer in the field, Iñaki San José runs one-day kayak and canoe trips through white water sections of an 80km (50 mile) stretch of the upper Tagus. The countryside is spectacular, and offers a unique opportunity to get to know one of Europe's most dramatic and least-known canoe descents. The starting point is the village of Cifuentes, some 130km (81 miles) north-east of Madrid. English is spoken.

Sport Natura

Avda Donostiarra 4 (91 403 61 61). Metro Ventas, El Carmen/bus 21, 48, 146. **Open** 9am-2pm, 4-7pm, Mon-Fri. **No credit cards.**

Windsurfing, sailing, paragliding, caving and rafting classes and group trips are organised throughout the year, mostly in Gredos. Basic prices include teaching, equipment hire and insurance, but not transport and board and lodging.

above them walkers stride the slopes and camp or sleep in mountain refuges; in winter, roads into the mountains may be blocked by snow. All year round, too, there is a difference in temperatures between the cooler northern and the southern slopes. Locals consider May-June the ideal months.

From Madrid, there are fast approaches from the north (N-VI/A6) and N110) or the south (N-V), or you can cut in through more attractive country roads from El Escorial or Brunete. Plan to spend at least two days in the Sierra to make a visit worthwhile, given that the journey from Madrid (133km/83 miles to Arenas de San Pedro) can easily take three hours.

The Gredos runs, roughly speaking, from the River Alberche in the east to the Aravalle valley in the west. Within this, it divides naturally into three sections. In the eastern triangle between **San Martín de Valdeiglesias**, **Cebreros** and the pass at the **Puerto del Pico** (the area most accessible by bus from Madrid), the land climbs from the mild, leafy Valle del Tiétar through bare hills to the first real peaks at the Puerto. Here, a dramatically steep stretch of Roman road drops into the delicious valley of **Mombeltrán**, with a medieval castle, sixteenth-century church and surrounding villages. Another major sight in this area are the mysterious stone **Guisando** bulls near **El Tiemblo** (north of San Martín) – massive sculptures of pre-Roman, Celtiberian origin. The woods around El Tiemblo, full of wild flowers, are unmissable. Other stopoffs could be the reservoirs of **San Juan** (often very crowded) or, further up the valley, **Burguillo**, prettier and marginally less hectic. **Cebreros** is a small wine-making town.

The heart of the Sierra is the massif centred on the **Pico Almanzor**, protected since 1905 as a royal hunting ground (the *Coto Real*) – a forerunner of today's nature reserve. Serious climbing is concentrated around the **Galayar**, a series of spectacular rock needles. For walkers, several paths lead into the mountains, from north and south. Here you may find ibex gambling around on the peaks, while eagles, vultures and kites cruise the thermals overhead.

The main bases here are, to the south, **Arenas de San Pedro**, which bulges with tourists at peak times, and 18km (11 miles) further west, **Candeleda**, less picturesque but less crowded. Both offer lots of walking possibilities. At **Ramacastañas**, near Arenas, there are the caves of **Cuevas del Aguila**, with spectacular rock formations, and near to Candeleda at **El Raso** there's a walled Celtic fortress. The northern access points are the quieter, cooler villages along the River Tormes, such as **Hoyocasero** and **Hoyos del Espino**, from where a road cuts into the mountains. This valley, with its cattle pastures and beautiful pine forests along the stony river bed, is the prime area for horseback treks and fishing.

The western flank of the Gredos is dominated by the **Tormantos** mountains and, in particular, the **Covacha** peak. To the south runs the valley of **La Vera**, with a string of half-timbered villages known in Spain for their tobacco and paprika. In the autumn, strings of dried peppers hang off the rickety wooden balconies. Attractive spots are Jarandilla, Pasarón, Losar and Cuacos de Yuste, above which stands the monastery of **Yuste**, where Charles V retired from the world to die. It's a humble monument, but as rewarding as the grander model his son Philip II built at El Escorial.

On the north side of these westerly mountains is **El Barco de Avila**, with its fourteenth-century church, the castle of **Valdecorneja** (open weekends only) and a Monday morning cattle and food market. However, since Barco is most famous for the quality of its dried beans (*judías* and larger *judiones*), many come here to tuck in at the town's restaurants. There are plenty of other possibilities. A short drive west is **Hervas**, a marvellously preserved hill village with a Jewish quarter, and further on is the medieval city of **Plasencia**, on the River Jerte, which has a superb double cathedral.

Whatever your interests, to make the most of a visit to Gredos you need a good map and a detailed walking guide, since local roads are confusing and information for visitors is scant. To date all such guides are in Spanish only. Very useful is *Anaya's Ecoguía*, by Rafael Serra, with detailed walks and itineraries. One warning: while there are still plenty of remote spots, the most popular places in the Sierra can be very crowded at peak weekends and holidays; it's much better to go midweek.

Information

Getting there: *by bus* Alvarez **551** from Estación Sur to San Martín de Valdeiglesias, El Tiemblo/Burguillo and Cebreros, about every 2 hours, last return 6.30pm, 8.30pm Sun; more services run from Avila; *by car* (main route) N-V to Alcorcón, then C501.

Where to stay and eat (heading west from Madrid):
Mombeltrán: Hostal Albuquerque *Parque de la Soledad (920 38 60 32).* An atmospheric family hostal in the centre of the town, with rooms for 4,000ptas, and an excellent base for the valley. Good basic cooking.
Navarredonda: Parador de Gredos *(920 34 80 48).* The first-ever *Parador*, a grey stone hunting lodge in a pine forest, opened in 1928 by Alfonso XIII. Very good food but formal atmosphere. Rooms about 10,000ptas.
Navacepeda de Tormes: Hostal Capra Hispánica *Carretera de Avila 40 (920 34 91 77).* An informal small hostal with bar and restaurant, and rooms for 5,000ptas.
El Barco de Avila: Hotel Manila *(920 34 08 44).* Best base for the west. Also organises riding, walking, mountain biking and so on, and has a campsite. **Casa Gamo** *Plaza Campillo 12 (920 34 00 85).* Of the town's clutch of restaurants offering traditional home cooking and local beans as a speciality, this is reliable.
Losar de la Vera: Carlos V *Avda de Extremadura 45 (927 57 06 36).* Great Castilian food and mountain views.
Jarandilla de la Vera: Parador Carlos V *(927 56 01 17).* Rooms overlook the beautiful Renaissance courtyard of this former castle of the counts of Oropesa. Doubles cost around 14,000-15,000ptas.

Further Afield

**Four very different destinations for weekends in the
Spain beyond Madrid.**

A packed day trip may be enough to get a flavour
of the famous towns near Madrid, but beyond
them there are naturally thousands more places to
explore that can only be appreciated with a
stopover. Spain's enormous diversity is reflected
in towns and cities that offer a complete contrast
in atmospheres. Here are just four possibilities.

Avila

The highest and coldest corner of Old Castile, capital of a threadbare province consisting of seven
parts mountain to one part tufted rock. If it weren't
for its medieval walls, who would come to Avila?
The saintly among us, presumably, for the city is
also famous for the dour piety of its inhabitants.

Had Avila ever known real prosperity and
change we probably would have lost the walls. It
hasn't, and there they are, a perfectly preserved
mile and a half of them, with 22 watchtowers and
nine gates, still encircling most of the town. If you
approach from the small modern part of Avila,
walk straight through the centre of the town and
out at the northern end to catch the superb view
from the Salamanca road. The walls can be
climbed in one spot only, from the gardens of the
Parador (*see below*).

The medieval city is stately and elegant, not
least the stark, fortified **Cathedral** embedded in
the walls. There's no mistaking its twelfth-century
origins, although the main portal is full-blown
Gothic. Another stylistic hybrid, the **Basilica de
San Vicente**, rivals the Cathedral in size and
grandeur. In contrast, outside the walls is the pure
Romanesque church of **San Andrés** and the palatial sixteenth-century **Santo Tomás** monastery,
wherein lie the bones of the son Ferdinand and
Isabella had hoped would succeed them.

Avila was settled by the knights who had a
hand in chucking out the Moors in 1089, one year
before work began on the walls, so noble palaces
are plentiful. The city is most famous, however, as
the home of Saint Teresa, greatest of Spanish mys-
tics, and a reformer, administrator, brilliant writer
and self-assured woman of the Renaissance.
Kitschy souvenirs apart, she is remembered with
a little exhibit in an annexe to the **San Juan
Bautista** church, with manuscripts and relics,
including a couple of knuckle bones – but not the
mummified arm which Franco kept at his bedside.

As any Spaniard can tell you, this is because it
made such a wonderful backscratcher.

Information

Getting there: *by bus* Larrea from Paseo de la Florida
11 or Estación Sur; 3 buses daily. Journey time 1¾ hours;
by car N-VI/A6 to Villacastín, then N110 (113km/70
miles); *by train* 16 trains daily from Chamartín or Atocha
6.40am-8.32pm. Last return at 10.16pm. Journey time
(*Regional Exprés* services) 1½ hours.
Tourist office: *Plaza de la Catedral 4*
(920 21 13 87). **Open** 9am-2pm, 5-7pm, Mon-Fri; 10am-
2pm, 5-8pm, Sat, Sun.
Where to eat: **Mesón del Rastro** *Plaza del Rastro 1*
(920 21 12 18). The usual Castilian fare plus beef and
veal from the Amberes valley, stewed kid and stewed
beans. Reliable. **El Molino de la Losa** *Bajada de la
Losa 12 (920 21 11 02)*. A simulacrum of a seventeenth-
century grain mill, on the banks of the Adaja river. Great
if the weather lets you sit outside, especially at night
when the walls are lit up. They also grill a superior slab
of steak, and the house wine is a bargain.
Where to stay: **Palacio de Valderrábanos** *Plaza de
la Catedral 9 (920 21 10 23)*; **Parador Raimundo de
Borgoña** *C/Marqués de Canales de Chozas 2 (920 21 13
40)*; **Hostería de Bracamonte** *C/Bracamonte 6 (920
25 12 80)*. Three converted Renaissance palaces, each
one lavishly endowed with atmosphere and antique
furnishings. The smallest, Bracamonte, has the best
interior, while the official *Parador* has a restaurant that
deserves a visit in its own right.

Salamanca

Being home to the third-oldest university in
Europe (after Bologna and Paris) has paid off for
Salamanca to a degree that other monumentally
lush but comparatively lifeless cities could envy.
Coffee shops or cathedrals (yes, there are two), art
galleries or architecture, blues from the basement
or baroque in the basilica, make it obvious that all
that burnished bronze stonework is pulsing with
vitality as well as pervaded by history.

The porticoes of the spacious, stunning **Plaza
Mayor** admit a plethora of people coming and
going, or stopping to natter: even the prostitutes
congregate under the same archway they did
almost as soon as this high baroque showpiece
was finished in 1753. Nearby, the old **University**
building draws crowds risking terminal eyestrain
trying to spot the one incongruous detail on the
incredibly elaborate façade bearing the medal-
lioned effigies of Ferdinand and Isabella. The trick
is to pick out the frog squatting on a skull amid all
the detail of griffons, flowers and popes. You have

to pay for a glimpse of the carved wooden stair-case, showing men and women making love and playing ball. The treasures of the library are housed in baroque bookcases by the architect Churriguera. Opposite, the patios of the **Escuelas Menores** house offices and an exhibition gallery.

The original **Cathedral**, an eminent example of late Romanesque reduced to the ranks as a mere parish church, is attached to, and dwarfed by, its flamboyantly Gothic successor, most of which was completed by 1577. The older one has a fifteenth-century altarpiece with beautiful narrative imagery recapping the life of Christ, while the new cathedral boasts finely carved ornamentation around the portals.

Salamanca's surfeit of outstanding religious buildings covers the gamut from Romanesque through Gothic, Renaissance and various baroque subcategories. But they're never overwhelming. One is dedicated to Saint Thomas à Becket, consecrated within a few years of his canonisation.

The shell-studded exterior of the **Casa de las Conchas** attests to its original owner's prominence in the Order of Santiago (the shell was the symbol of the Order), but in some ways is more interesting on the inside, where the original six-teenth-century layout is preserved. Getting into the city takes you across the Tormes river by way of the still solid **Roman bridge**. At least 15 of its arches date from the reign of Vespasian.

Information

As you might expect, Salamanca is loaded with tapas bars and student drinking hangouts. Try **La Covachuela**, at Portales de San Antonio 24 (north-west of the Plaza Mayor), said to be the tiniest bar in Spain. Salamanca province is also renowned as one of Spain's great ham and chorizo heavens, but cured specialities from acorn-fed, free-ranging Ibérico piggies do not come cheap.

Getting there: *by bus* Auto-Res from Conde de Casal, 18 buses daily Mon-Sat; 15 buses Sun, holidays, from 8am-9.30pm. Buses take a variety of routes; journey time for the most direct is 2½ hours; *by car* N-VI/A6 to Avila turn (N110), then N501 (215km/134 miles); *by train* from Chamartín: 3 trains 9.30am-7.15pm, Mon-Thur; 4 trains, Fri, Sun, 3 trains 9.30am-4.10pm Sat. Last return at 9.50pm. Journey time 3½ hours. All Salamanca-bound trains pass through Avila, so the two can be combined in one longish overnighter.

The flying **Museo Guggenheim Bilbao**.

Where to eat: El Mesón *Plaza del Poeta Iglesias 10 (923 21 72 22)*. The most reliable of three restaurants on different angles of the same plaza, all specialising in classic Castilian cooking. **Restaurante Félix** *C/Pozo Amarillo 10 (923 21 72 81)*. A little distant from the student scene, but a reliable budget favourite.

Where to stay: Gran Hotel *Plaza del Poeta Iglesias 3 (923 21 35 00)*. Looks like a piano warehouse from the outside, but after a deluxe overhaul this is now quite posh and comfy – and expensive. So close to the Plaza Mayor you'll be eternally grateful for the double glazing. **Hotel Don Juan** *C/Quintana 6 (923 26 14 73)*. Behind the emblazoned stone façade the rooms are all tiny, but immaculate and quiet; they cost about 9,500ptas.

Bilbao

How much difference can one museum make? As the millennium approaches, cities around the world (and above all in Spain) are eager to acquire a prestige cultural project in the hope that it will transform their international profile. Nowhere seems to have cracked it, though, quite like Bilbao. Since the opening of the dramatic Guggenheim Bilbao museum at the end of 1997, Spain's one-time capital of dirty smokestack industry has suddenly become an international must-see.

Unless you fly, it's hard to get from Madrid to Bilbao in much under five hours, so if you're going to the city it's worth taking enough time to look around the area and maybe visit other parts of the Basque Country as well. It can also be a good stopover on the way to France, or the twice-weekly ferry to Portsmouth.

Bilbao had already begun to do a lot to bright-en its image before it landed the Guggenheim plum. The wide streets of nineteenth-century Bilbao have an elegant bustle, centred on the smartly flower-bedded **Plaza Moyúa**. Many buildings have been renovated. Getting around is speeded up by a recently-opened Norman Foster-designed Metro running the length of the Nervión river valley, along which Bilbao and its suburbs are laid out in line. The **Casco Viejo**, the old city of Bilbao on the east bank of the river, used to be covered in a thick layer of black soot, but after serious sand-blasting has now emerged as a rather gracious eighteenth-century ensemble in yellowish stone, almost the same colour as Bath.

The heart of the Casco Viejo is the **Plaza Nueva**, a grand neo-classical arcaded square lined with pavement cafés. This square and the narrow streets a few turns to the south, the *Siete Calles* or 'Seven Streets', are among the best places to begin sampling the very distinctive atmosphere of the Basque Country and, especially, its food. Basques are a special and paradoxical people. They cultivate an un-Mediterranean down-the-line brusqueness that can seem positively rude (even when they're being friendly), but with some things, such as food, show a sense of refinement that by force of contrast can almost appear prissy. Instead of the simple guts-and-*patatas bravas* tapas of so many bars in Madrid, Basque bars are laden with trays of sophisticated canapés, subtle, wonderfully varied combinations of seafood, sauces or peppers. In each bar all the different tapas are the same price, and the tradition is to take as many as you want and tell the barman the total when you leave. Another tradition is to have a couple of tapas and a drink in one bar and then go on to the next, for the bar-crawl is a Basque institution. To help this along, areas like the *Siete Calles* – and Calle Licenciado Pozas, another drink-and-food zone in the new town – have the highest concentration of bars anywhere in Europe, even greater than that in Madrid.

The city's great new attraction, the **Museo Guggenheim Bilbao**, is on the western side of the new town, two Metro stops from the Casco Viejo and then a brief walk from Plaza Moyúa up Alameda Recalde. Frank Gehry's spectacular interplay of flowing shapes in titanium, stone and glass is an extraordinarily daring reworking of the urban landscape, which has immediately taken over Bilbao's river frontage and become an instant monument. Not the least of its qualities is that – in spite of its absolute modernity – no one seems not to be impressed by it. In its first year of opening it already attracted over a million visitors. Amid all the attention lavished on the building the resident collection has remained less of a known quantity, but it consists of a wide sample of works by major international artists: specially commissioned for Bilbao were pieces by Jenny Holzer, Eduardo Chillida, Richard Serra and Sol LeWitt, among others (although 'permanent collection' is a bit of a misnomer here, as nearly all the works will at some point be rotated around the other Guggenheim museums in New York, Berlin and Venice). One that is permanent is Jeff Koons' giant dog, entirely covered in wallflowers, that adds colour to the esplanade in front of the museum. The museum also hosts an impressive programme of temporary exhibitions, many drawn from the huge Guggenheim holdings: 1999 will begin with a major retrospective of Robert Rauschenberg.

Information

Getting there: *by air* Iberia, approx 10 flights daily; lowest return fare is 16,100ptas for a four-day trip, 20,100ptas for a weekend return; single fare is more than a four-day return. Flight time about 50 min, plus check-in; *by bus* Continental Auto from C/Alenza 20 (Metro Cuatro Caminos), buses approx every hour 7am-1.30am daily; fare 3,245ptas single, 5,850ptas return. Journey time 4½-5 hours; *by car* N-I via Burgos, 500km (310 miles). *by train* from Chamartín, 2 trains daily, a fast Talgo at 3.45pm (arrives 9.25pm) and a sleeper at 10.45pm (arrives 7.55am). Normal fare 4,110ptas single, 7,900ptas return. **By ferry from the UK** P&O from Portsmouth, sailings Tue, Sat at 8pm; journey time 35hrs; from Bilbao 12.30pm Mon, Thur, journey time usually shorter (29hrs). Minimum fare £59 (foot passengers).
Tourist office: *Plaza Arriaga 1 (94 416 00 22)*. **Open** 9am-2pm, 4-7.30pm, Mon-Fri; 9am-2pm Sat; 10am-2pm Sun.
Museo Guggenheim Bilbao: *Avda Abandoibarra 2 (information 94 435 90 80/reservations 94 435 90 90)*. **Open** 11am-8pm Tue-Sun. Closed Mon. **Admission** 700ptas; 350ptas students, over-65s; free accompanied under-12s; group discounts.
Admission is for a whole day, so with the one ticket you can leave and return as many times as you wish the same day.
Where to eat: **Victor Montes** *Plaza Nueva 8 (94 415 70 67)*. A classic Casco Viejo tapas bar that also serves full meals. **Zortziko** *Alameda Mazarredo 17 (94 423 97 43)*. Smart new-town restaurant serving widely admired modern Basque cuisine.
Where to stay: **Hostal Mardones** *C/Jardines 4, 3° (94 415 31 05)*. Near the *Siete Calles*, a pleasant, friendly traditional *hostal*. Doubles 5,000ptas with bath, 3,500ptas without. **Iturrienea Ostatua** *C/Santa Maria 14 (94 416 15 00)*. In the same area, an old hostal that's been given an imaginative, smart and very comfortable makeover. Doubles from 7,490ptas; very popular, so book.

The AVE to Córdoba & Seville

The AVE, Spain's high speed train, was one of the most controversial (and expensive) projects undertaken prior to Seville's Expo '92. Whether it was all worth it will forever remain an open question, but, thanks to this high-tech French-German-Spanish creation, with speeds of over 300kph (186mph), the wonders of Córdoba and Seville are just one hour 40 minutes and 2½ hours respectively from Madrid. Moreover, RENFE (Spanish Railways) offers many special fare deals, so that return tickets to Seville can cost around 13,000ptas off-peak. Trains leave hourly (7am-10pm) from **Atocha** station every day (RENFE information 91 328 90 20). Lunching at an Andalusian café and sipping on a few *finos* before heading back north to Madrid is thus no longer a pipe dream.

Córdoba

After passing through the rugged olive- and oak-strewn Sierra Morena, the AVE descends into the Guadalquivir valley and pulls into Córdoba station. The largest city in the world around the year 1000, and capital of Muslim Spain, Córdoba is now a rather provincial place of some 200,000 inhabitants. Still, its *Andalús* character makes a nice change from the hustle and bustle of Madrid.

Córdoba is not without relics of its former splendour, including a **Roman bridge** and some spectacular Arab mills. Greatest by far, though, is the eighth-century **Mosque**, one of the supreme works of Islamic architecture, which dominates the centre of the city. For an idea of its enormous size, consider that inside, in addition to 850 onyx, marble and granite columns reflecting light below its delicately carved cedar ceiling, is a grotesque Christian cathedral, crudely implanted in 1523.

The first half of May is the best time to visit Córdoba. As well as the fine weather, Cordobeses celebrate their *Festival de los Patios*, potting even more geraniums than usual and opening up their courtyards for visitors, and neighbours, to admire.

Information

Tourist offices: *C/Torrijos 10 (957 47 12 35); Plaza Judah Levi (957 20 05 22)*. **Open** 9.30am-8pm Mon-Sat; 10am-2pm Sun.
Where to eat: Almudaina *Campo de los Santos Mártires 1 (957 47 43 42)*. **El Caballo Rojo** *C/Cardenal Herrero 28 (957 47 53 75)*. One of Andalusia's finest.
Where to stay: Albucasis *C/Buen Pastor 11 (957 47 86 25)*. **Hostal-Residencia Séneca** *C/Conde y Luque 7 (957 47 32 34)*.

Seville

As the on-board movie comes to an end, the AVE arrives in Seville, capital of Andalusia. With its orange-blossom and jasmine-scented air, and bougainvillea climbing up and around pitch-black painted grillwork over the windows of whitewashed houses, this is one of the most beautiful cities in the world. A walk around the famous **Barrio de Santa Cruz**, the heart of old Seville, is a heady experience at any time of the year.

The **Cathedral** is the world's largest Gothic structure, and third-largest church in Europe after Saint Peter's in Rome and Saint Paul's in London. It is best known, though, for its emblematic tower the **Giralda**, only surviving part of the twelfth-century mosque that once stood on the site and a twin of the Koutoubia tower built by the same Almohad dynasty in Marrakesh. Not far away on the banks of the Guadalquivir sits the **Torre de Oro** (the Gold Tower), also built by Seville's last Muslim rulers. It is so named not for its colour but because gold and silver from the Americas was stored there. The **Reales Alcázares**, a fourteenth-century *mudéjar* palace with luxurious tiled courtyards and flower-scented gardens, is perhaps the most beautiful example of the architecture developed by the Muslim craftsmen who stayed on to work under Christian overlords.

Seville has been greatly marked by exhibitions. The **Plaza de España** in Parque Maria Luisa was built for the Spanish-American Exhibition of 1929. More recently, Expo '92 left Seville with motorways, modernistic bridges and a landscaped island that no one has known what to do with, and **Cartuja**. Most of the Expo pavillions have been

*In the Barrio de Santa Cruz, **Seville**.*

demolished and the area is being slowly recycled as a culture-and-leisure park, but it rarely draws a crowd. Much more lively is the traditional *barrio* of **Triana** – across the river from the Torre de Oro – one of the great homes of flamenco.

The most popular times to visit the city are during its world-renowned *Semana Santa* (Holy Week) and *Feria de Abril* (April Fair) celebrations. Hotel rooms must be booked far in advance, even though the city normally has a bit of a hotel glut due to building for the Expo. The religious fervour exhibited – in many very idiosyncratic ways – during the Easter Processions is unrivalled in Western Europe. The *Feria*, a couple of weeks later, draws thousands of Sevillanos with their horses and carriages, not to mention visitors, to tents and wooden *casetas* mounted along the river bank for a non-stop week of sherry-sipping, dancing, bullfights and general merrymaking.
Tourist offices: *Avda de la Constitución 21 (95 422 14 04)*. **Open** 9am-7pm Mon-Fri; 10am-2pm, 3-7pm, Sat; 10am-2pm Sun. **Branches** at train station, airport and Plaza de las Delicias.
Where to eat: El Corral del Agua *Callejón del Agua 6 (95 422 48 41)*. In a beautiful old patio near the Reales Alcázares. **San Marco** *C/Cuna 6 (95 421 24 40)*.
Where to stay: Hotel Internacional *C/Aguilas 17 (95 421 32 07)*. An attractive small hotel with charming patios; double rooms about 9,000ptas. **La Rábida** *C/Castelar 24 (95 422 09 60)*. Occupying an old palace with great patios, but with doubles for under 10,000ptas.

Directory

Directory

Getting Around

The best way to get around Madrid is on foot. Most of the main attractions, restaurants and nightlife are within comfortable walking distance of the main axes of Puerta del Sol, Plaza Mayor, Gran Vía and the Paseo del Prado. The Puerta del Sol is the undisputed centre of the city, and the main hub of the bus and Metro systems. Street numbers in Madrid all run outwards from Sol. Paseo del Prado continues into Paseo de Recoletos and the great avenue of the Castellana, most direct route to the modern business areas in the north of Madrid. Drivers become very familiar with the M-30, the

motorway that skirts the city in a loop south and along the River Manzanares, and also the M-40, an outer ring road that forms a full circle around the city.

Madrid has a cheap, very comprehensive and efficient public transport system. A car is rarely an asset within the city; a bike or scooter is more handy for those brave enough to face the traffic. Transport services in Madrid region are co-ordinated by the **Consorcio Regional de Transportes** (information 91 580 19 80). For transport to places outside Madrid, *see page 224* **Getting Started**.

Note: all transport and taxi fares are subject to revision each January.

Arriving & leaving

By air

Madrid's **Barajas Airport** is 16km (10 miles) to the east on the Barcelona motorway (A2). In the International Arrivals building there are 24-hour exchange facilities, a tourist office (*see page 261*), hotel booking desks (*see chapter* **Accommodation**) and a rail reservations desk. At present there are two ways to get from there into town: bus or taxi.

Before arriving

Visas & immigration

Visas are not needed by European Union nationals, or by US, Canadian and New Zealand citizens for stays of up to three months. British and all non-EU citizens must have full passports. Citizens of Australia, South Africa and some other countries need a visa to enter Spain. They can be obtained from Spanish consulates in other European countries as well as in your home country. Spain is also a signatory of the EU Schengen agreement, so visas issued in another Schengen state should also be accepted here.

EU citizens hoping to work, study or live permanently in Spain should register with the police within 15 days of arrival to obtain a Residence Card (*tarjeta de residencia*). Non-EU nationals who wish to work or study in Spain for more than three months should, officially, have the relevant visa before entering the country. For more on living in Spain and dealing with bureaucracy, *see pp262-3*.

Customs

EU residents do not have to declare goods imported into Spain from other EU countries for their personal use if tax has been paid in the country of origin. However, Customs officers can question whether large amounts of any item really are for your own use, and random checks are made for drugs. Quantities accepted as being for personal use include:
• up to 800 cigarettes, 400 small cigars, 200 cigars and 1kg of loose tobacco
• 10 litres of spirits (over 22% alcohol), 90 litres of wine (under 22% alcohol) and 110 litres of beer

Limits for non-EU residents and goods brought from outside the EU:
• 200 cigarettes **or** 100 small cigars or 50 cigars **or** 250 grams (8.82 ounces) of tobacco
• 1 litre of spirits (over 22% alcohol) or 2 litres of fortified wine (under 22% alcohol)
• 50 grams (1.76 ounces) of perfume

There are no restrictions on cameras, watches or electrical goods, within reasonable limits, and visitors can also carry up to 1 million pesetas in cash. Non-EU residents can also reclaim Value Added Tax (IVA) paid on some large purchases when they leave Spain. For details, *see chapter* **Shopping**.

Insurance

EU nationals are entitled to use the Spanish state health service, provided they have an E111 form, which in Britain is available from post offices, health centres and Social Security offices. This will cover you for emergencies, but using an E111 will necessarily involve dealing with some of the complexities of Spanish health bureaucracy, and for short-term visitors it's generally simpler to take out private travel insurance before departure, particularly as this will cover you for stolen or lost cash or valuables as well as medical costs.

Some non-EU countries have reciprocal health-care agreements with Spain, but, again, for most travellers it will be more convenient to have private travel insurance for all eventualities before arriving in the country. For more information on health services, *see p256*.

However, this is due to change in late 1999 with the opening of a **Metro** station at Barajas (line 8) providing a much faster route into town, via a change at Mar de Cristal (line 4). An exact opening date for the Barajas Metro will only be confirmed shortly before it happens.

This Metro link is part of a major facelift and extension programme at Barajas. A third runway, which is being built to the north, which should also be in use by the beginning of 2000, and a Norman Foster-designed new terminal building is due to open in summer 1999. It is not yet clear how flights will be distributed around the new 'Gran Barajas'. In the meantime, travellers can expect a certain amount of delay and disruption as this work affects the day-to-day running of the airport.

For **airport information**, call 91 305 83 43 or 91 305 83 46.

Airport bus
City Terminal Plaza de Colón (91 431 61 92). Metro Colón/bus all routes to Plaza de Colón. **Map I4**
The special airport bus runs between all the Barajas terminals and the Plaza de Colón, on the Paseo de la Castellana in the centre of the city. There are officially six stops en route, although the bus usually only stops at Canillejas, Avenida de América and Colón. At Colón the bus terminal is underground, beneath the main plaza. The nearest Metro station is Colón, on the other side of the Castellana, which can be reached by taking the underpass at the corner of Calle Goya. Buses run between Barajas and Colón and vice versa every ten minutes, 6am-10pm, and about every 20 minutes throughout the night. The trip should take 45 min-1hour, depending on traffic, but can take much less. A single ticket costs 380ptas. Buses are not accessible to wheelchairs. At Colón there is an office of the **Brújula** accommodation agency (*see chapter* **Accommodation**).

Taxis from the airport
A taxi to central Madrid from Barajas should cost about 2,300ptas, including a 350ptas special airport supplement. There are further supplements at night, on Sundays and for each item of luggage placed in the car boot (*see below* Taxis). Taxis are abundant at Barajas – in fact too much so. Some drivers specialise in hanging round the airport, and may try a variety of scams, such as taking you to your destination

by the longest possible route. To avoid them, use only taxis from the official ranks signposted outside each terminal, and ignore drivers who approach you inside the building. Check the meter is at the minimum fare when you begin the journey. It's also a good idea, to avoid unwanted 'tours', to check a map first, and have in mind a landmark in the area to which you should be going.

Airlines
Aer Lingus *Edificio España, Gran Via 88, 10ª (91 541 41 16). Metro Plaza de España/bus all routes to Plaza de España.* **Open** 9am-5pm Mon-Fri. **Credit** AmEx, MC, DC, V. **Map D4**
American Airlines *C/Pedro Teixeira 8, 5° (91 597 20 68/900 10 05 56). Metro Santiago Bernabéu/bus 5, 27, 40, 43, 147, 150.* **Open** 9am-6.30pm Mon-Fri; 9am-2pm Sat. **Credit** AmEx, DC, MC, TC, V. *Airport office* (91 305 83 48). **Open** 8am-noon daily.
British Airways *C/Pinar 7 (902 11 13 33). Metro Gregorio Marañón/bus 7, 12, 16, 40, 147.* **Open** *office* 9am-5pm Mon-Fri; *central number* 9am-7pm Mon-Fri; 9am-2pm Sat. **Credit** AmEx, DC, JCB, MC, V.
Iberia *C/Velázquez 130 (91 587 75 92/reservations 902 400 500/ information line 917 229 600). Metro Avda de América/bus 9, 12, 19, 51.* **Open** *office* 9.30am-2pm, 4-7pm, Mon-Fri; *information line* 24 hours. **Credit** AmEx, DC, EC, MC, TC, V.
TWA *Plaza de Colón 2, 2ª (91 310 30 94). Metro Colón/bus all routes to Plaza de Colón.* **Open** 9am-5.30pm Mon-Fri. **Credit** AmEx, DC, MC, \$TC, V. **Map I4**. *Airport office* (91 305 82 90). **Open** 8am-3.30pm daily.

By bus
Virtually all international and long-distance coach services to Madrid terminate at the new **Estación Sur de Autobuses**, C/Méndez Alvaro (information 91 468 42 00; bus companies have their own lines), to the south of central Madrid. It is next to Metro and *Cercanías* stations, both called Méndez Álvaro. Taxi fares from the bus station carry a 150ptas supplement.

By train
Trains from France, Catalonia and northern Spain, and most of those from Portugal, arrive in Madrid at **Chamartín** station, on the north side of the city some distance from the centre. High-speed **AVE** trains from Seville, express services from Lisbon

and trains from southern and eastern Spain arrive at the renovated **Atocha** station, on the south side of the city centre close to Paseo del Prado. There are exchange facilities at both stations, and a tourist office at Chamartín (*see page 261*). Atocha is also the main hub of the local (*Cercanías*) lines of Spanish national railways (RENFE) for the Madrid area, some of which also run from Chamartín and Príncipe Pío (*see below* **Cercanías/Local trains**).

Both Chamartín and Atocha are on the Metro. From Chamartín line 10 runs direct to the city centre. Atocha Renfe (the train station; not the same Metro as Atocha) is four Metro stops from Sol on line 1.

A taxi fare from Chamartín to the centre should be about 1,500ptas, including a 150ptas station supplement. There are further supplements at night, on Sundays and for luggage. The same need for caution regarding cabs at the airport (*see above*) applies – drivers who tout for fares at the main rail stations are best avoided.

RENFE Information
general information for all stations
91 328 90 20. Open *information & reservations 24 hours daily.*
Atocha *Glorieta del Emperador Carlos V. Metro Atocha Renfe/bus all routes to Atocha.* **Map H10**
Chamartín *C/Agustín de Foxá. Metro Chamartín/bus 5, 80.*

Left luggage
At the Estación Sur bus station, luggage can be left in a staffed office 6.30am to midnight, Monday to Saturday (sometimes on Sundays), for 175ptas per day.

Luggage lockers
The airport and stations have automatic, coin-operated lockers.
Barajas Airport *International Arrivals terminal.* **Open** 24 hours. **Rates** 425ptas first 24 hours; 530, 740ptas per day thereafter, according to size of locker.
Train stations. Open *Chamartín* 7.30am-10.30pm, daily, *Atocha* 6.30am-10.30pm, daily. **Rates** 300ptas first 24 hours; 400-600ptas per day thereafter, according to size of locker.

Maps

Metro and central-area street maps are included at the back of this Guide. Metro maps are also available at all Metro stations: ask for '*un plano del Metro*'. The best free maps available are those of the Consorcio de Transportes, particularly the *Plano de los Transportes del Centro de Madrid*, from which the maps in this Guide are taken. It should be available at tourist offices, Metro stations and the bus information booths at Sol, Callao and Cibeles, but they often run out. If you wish to buy a map, the most detailed are those published by **Almax**, available from most bookshops (*see chapter* **Shopping**).

Public transport

Metro

The Metro is the quickest and simplest means of travelling to most parts of the city. Each of its 11 lines is identified by a number and a specific colour on maps and at stations. Metro stations are, too, more than just access points into the system: they make essential reference points, and 'Metro Sevilla', 'Metro Goya' and so on will often be given to you as tags with addresses. As a visitor it's useful to become familiar with the Metro map, and to use the nearest Metro stations (also indicated with entries in this Guide) as an aid to getting oneself oriented.

The Metro is open from 6am to 1.30am daily. Tickets are available at all stations from coin-operated machines and staffed ticket booths (*see page 251* **Just the ticket**). Trains run on each line every three to five minutes during weekdays, and about every ten minutes after 11pm and on Sundays. The Metro can get very crowded in rush hours (7.30-9.30am, 1-2.30pm, 7.30-9pm), but is rarely packed at other times.

Metro information

C/Cavanilles 58 (91 552 59 09). Metro Conde de Casal/bus 10, 14, 26, 32, 56, C. **Open** 8am-2.30pm Mon-Fri.

New developments

The Madrid Metro is in the midst of an ambitious expansion plan due to continue into the new millennium. Early in 1998 the link was completed between two older lines to create a new north-south through line (line 10, dark blue) connecting Chamartín station directly to the centre.

At the midway point on this link, Gregorio Marañón, it meets line 7 (orange) from Avenida de América, which in late 1998 was extended west to Guzmán el Bueno. This line will eventually reach the north-western suburbs to connect with the *Cercanías* network at Pitis. Of interest to visitors to the **Feria de Madrid** trade fair is the also-new line 8 (pink) to Campo de las Naciones. This line is due to reach **Barajas Airport** by late 1999. Another project will extend line 9 (purple) far into the south-east suburbs (well beyond the city limits) to Arganda.

Buses

Operated by the *Empresa Municipal de Transportes* (EMT).

EMT Information

C/Alcántara 24 (91 406 88 10). Metro Lista/bus 1, 21, 26, 53, 146. **Open** 8am-1.30pm Mon-Fri. **Map L3** EMT Kiosks *Plaza de Callao, Puerta del Sol.* **Open** 8am-8.15pm Mon-Fri, excluding public holidays.

Taking the bus

Route timings vary, but most run about 6am to 11.30pm daily, with buses every 10-15 minutes on each route, although more popular routes are more frequent. At other times night buses operate. Due to the many one-way systems buses do not always follow the same route in both directions, so a bus map is handy. You board buses at the front, and get off at the middle or rear of the bus. The fare is the same for each journey, however far you travel (*see p251* **Just the ticket**). Officially, there is a limit to the amount of luggage passengers can take on city buses: to some extent this depends on the individual driver, but travellers with suitcases can find they are not allowed to board.

Useful routes

2 From Avda Reina Victoria, near Moncloa, to Plaza de España, then along Gran Vía to Cibeles and past the Retiro to Plaza Manuel Becerra.
3 From Puerta de Toledo up Gran Vía de San Francisco and C/Mayor to Sol, then up C/Hortaleza and C/Santa Engracia to Cuatro Caminos and Plaza San Amaro, near the Estadio Bernabéu.

5 From the Puerta del Sol via the Plaza de Cibeles, Plaza de Colón and the Castellana to Chamartín station.
14 From Avda del Mediterráneo along Paseo Reina Cristina to Atocha , then along Paseo del Prado, Recoletos and the Castellana to Chamartín.
27 From Embajadores, a frequent service through Atocha and then all the way up the Castellana to Plaza Castilla.
C The 'Circular' route runs in a wide circuit around the city, via Atocha, Embajadores, Plaza de España, Moncloa, Cuatro Caminos, Plaza Manuel Becerra and the Retiro.

Night buses

Between midnight and 6am there are 20 night routes in operation, N1 to N20, called *Búho* ('owl') buses. All begin from Plaza de Cibeles and run out to the suburbs, and are numbered in a clockwise sequence; thus, N1 runs north to Manoteras, N2 a little further east to Hortaleza, and so on. The N18 runs along the Gran Vía to Moncloa and Tetuán; the N20 along the length of the Castellana to Fuencarral. On Friday and Saturday night buses run every 25 minutes on all routes till 6am; on other nights, they run every half-hour from midnight to 3am, and every hour after that. Tickets and fares are the same as for daytime services.

Cercanías/local trains

The *Cercanías* or local network of Spanish Railways (RENFE) for the Madrid area consists of 11 lines – not numbered 1-11, since some divide into branches – centred on Atocha. Several stations connect with Metro lines. They are most useful for trips to the suburbs, or to the Guadarrama and towns near Madrid such as Aranjuez or Alcalá de Henares. Also, though, lines C-7a and C-7b combine (with one change at Príncipe Pío) to form a circle line within Madrid that is quicker than the Metro for some journeys, and the RENFE link between Chamartín and Atocha (on C-1, C-7, C-8 and C-10) is the quickest connection between the two main stations. *Cercanías* lines run from 5-6am to midnight-1am daily, with trains on most lines about every 15-30 minutes. Fares vary by distance, but the lines are included in the monthly season ticket (*see above*). A map of the *Cercanías* network is included on *page 287* of this Guide.

Just the ticket

Single tickets both for the Metro, which are available from all stations, and city buses, bought only from the driver on board, cost 130ptas. Unless you really are just passing through, though, buying tickets this way wastes time and money. It's much better to use the multi-journey *metrobús* ticket, which since 1998 can be used on both systems. Valid for ten journeys, they can be shared between two or more people.

Current price of the *metrobús* is 670ptas. They are available from automatic machines and ticket booths at Metro stations, and tobacco shops (*estancos*) and the EMT information kiosks (*see page 250*). On the Metro, you insert the ticket into the machine at the gate through to the platform, which automatically cancels one unit for each trip, and will reject expired tickets. There is no checking or collection of tickets at station exits. On buses, the *metrobús*

should be inserted arrow-downwards into the blue and yellow machine just behind the driver. The tickets cannot be bought on the bus itself.

Abonos/season tickets

Anyone spending a few weeks in Madrid might be interested in acquiring a monthly season ticket (*abono transportes*). Unlike the *metrobús*, they are valid not only for the Metro and city buses but for *Cercanías* trains too, giving unlimited travel within a specified area. A one-month ticket for zone A (virtually the whole of Madrid-city), currently costs 4,365ptas, and there are substantial reductions for people under 21 or over 65. Your first *abono* must be obtained with an identity card, available only from *estancos*, for which you will need two passport-size photos and have to fill in a brief form. The *abono* is issued on the spot. In succeeding months you can buy tickets (*cupones*) to revalidate the card from Metro stations and EMT kiosks as well as *estancos*. Note, though, that an *abono* is valid for an actual calendar month, not 30 days from date of purchase, so that if your stay runs across two months it may not be particularly economical, unless you qualify for one of the discounts.

Receipts & complaints

Taxi drivers provide receipts on request – ask for '*un recibo, por favor*'. If you think you've been overcharged or have any other complaint, insist the receipt is made out in full, with details of the journey and the driver's signature. Make a note of the taxi number, displayed on a plaque on the dashboard. Take or send the receipt, keeping a copy, with a complaints form to the City taxi office at the address below. The form is included in the Taxi Information leaflet available from tourist offices.
Taxi complaints *Sección de Autotaxi y Vehículos de Alquiler, Ayuntamiento de Madrid, C/Vallehermoso 1, 28015 Madrid (91 588 96 31/32).*

Phone cabs

You can call for a cab from the following companies. Operators will not usually speak much English, but as a direction to the driver try giving the name of the street and a restaurant or bar where you wish to wait, or position yourself near a street corner and say, for example, '*Sagasta, esquina Larra*' ('Sagasta, corner [of] Larra'). You will also be asked your name. Cabs start the meter from the point when the call is answered. Radio-Taxi and Tele-Taxi have some cabs that take credit cards.
Radio Taxi Asociación Gremial *(91 447 51 80)*; **Radio Taxi Independiente** *(91 405 12 13)*; **Radio Teléfono Taxi** *(91 547 85 00)*; **TeleTaxi** *(91 371 21 31/ 91 371 37 11).*

Taxis

Madrid taxis are white, with a diagonal red stripe on the front doors. The city has over 15,000 taxis, so they are rarely hard to find, except maybe late at night when it's raining heavily. They are also relatively cheap. When a taxi is free there is a *Libre* ('Free') sign behind the windscreen, and a green light on the roof. If there is also a sign with the name of a district in red, this means the driver is on his way home, and not obliged to take you anywhere that isn't near that route.

There are taxi ranks, marked by a blue sign with a white T, at many places in the central area. However, drivers who spend all their time at ranks in the city

have a bad reputation for scams, and those in the know prefer to flag cabs down in the street (*see above* **Arriving & leaving**).

Fares

Official fare rates and supplements are shown inside each cab, on the right hand sunvisor and/or the rear windows. Currently the minimum fare is 175ptas, and that is what the meter should show when you first set off. The fare will then increase at a rate of 85ptas per kilometre, or on a time rate if you are travelling at under 20kph. These basic rates on the meter are the same at all times, but supplements are added between 11pm and 6am and on Sundays and public holidays (150ptas), for trips starting from the bus and train stations (150ptas), to and from the trade fair complex (150ptas), to and from the airport (350ptas), and for each item of luggage (50ptas). Also, the basic fare will increase for journeys outside the city limits, except to the airport.

Driving & cycling

Driving in Madrid may be a little wilder than you are used to. Jams and snarl-ups are frequent, as are horn-punching and a range of aggressive maneuvres to get ahead. Serious accidents, though, are less common than slow-speed bumps. In Madrid itself, driving is rarely the most convenient way of getting anywhere. A car is a great asset, though, for trips outside the city (*see page 224*). If you do drive here, points to bear in mind are listed below.
• You can drive in Spain with a valid licence from most other countries, but it is useful also to have an international driving licence, available in Britain from the AA and RAC.
• Keep your driving licence, vehicle documents and insurance Green Card with you at all times.
• It is obligatory to wear seat belts at all times in cities as well as on main highways, and to carry a warning triangle in your car.
• Children under 14 may not travel in the front of a car.

• Speeding fines imposed on motorways (*autopistas*) and main highways, policed by the Guardia Civil, are payable on the spot.
• Do not leave anything of value, including a car radio, in your car, and do not leave bags or coats in view on the seats. Take all luggage into your hotel when you park.
• In general drivers go as fast as they can irrespective of the speed limit. At traffic lights at least two cars will follow through on the amber light as it changes between green and red. Do not, therefore, stop sharply when you see a light begin to change, as the car behind will not be expecting this and could easily run into your back.
• When oncoming drivers flash lights at you this means they will **not** slow down (contrary to British practice). On main highways, the flashing of lights is usually a helpful warning that there's a speed trap ahead.

Car & motorbike hire

To hire a car you must be over 21 and have had a driving licence for over a year. You will also need a credit card, or have to leave a large cash deposit. Check whether insurance, IVA (VAT) at 16 per cent and unlimited mileage are included; it is always advisable to take out full rather than basic insurance cover. Price structures vary a lot, and there are often good weekend deals.

Alcar SL

Paseo de la Castellana 121 (91 555 10 10). Metro Cuzco/bus 5, 27, 40, 147, 150. **Open** *Oct-May* 9am-8pm, *June-Sept* 9am-1.30pm, 4-7pm, Mon-Fri; 9am-1pm Sat. **Credit** V.
A small, cheap local company. A Fiat Uno can be 2,600ptas per day, plus 1,490ptas insurance and IVA; about 33,000ptas for a week.

Eurodollar-Atesa

Paseo de la Castellana 130 (91 561 48 00/reservations 902 100 101). Metro Santiago Bernabeu/bus 27, 40, 147, 150. **Open** *Sept-June* 7.30am-2.30pm, 3.30-6pm, Mon-Thur; 7.30am-2.30pm Fri; *July-Aug* 7.30am-3.30pm Mon-Fri. **Credit** AmEx, DC, MC, V.
Spain's biggest car hire company. A Citroen Saxo costs 40,600ptas (incl insurance, tax, unlimited mileage) for a week, 15,712ptas for a weekend. **Branch**: Barajas Airport (91 305 86 60). **Open** 7am-midnight daily.

Europcar

Avda del Partenón 16-18 (91 722 62 26/901 102 020). Metro Campo de las Naciones/bus 122. **Open** 8.30am-6pm Mon-Fri. **Credit** AmEx, DC, MC, V.

An Opel Corsa costs 50,912ptas for a full week. 'Weekend' deals (five full days, which can be Wed-Mon or Thur-Tue) are 28,037ptas for the same model.
Branches: Barajas Airport (91 393 72 35); Atocha station (91 530 01 94); Chamartin station (91 323 17 21); C/San Leonardo 8 (91 541 88 92); C/Orense 29 (91 555 99 30).

Motoalquiler

C/Conde Duque 13 (91 542 06 57). Metro Noviciado/bus 2, 21, 44, 133, C. **Open** 8am-2pm, 5-8pm, Mon-Fri; 9am-1.30pm Sat. Closed Sat July & Aug. **Credit** AmEx, MC, V. **Map D4**
Motorcycle specialists: a Vespa costs 7,000ptas a day, 23,000ptas a week; a Yamaha 250cc 12,000ptas, 40,000ptas; big road bikes around 17,000ptas a day, 55,000ptas a week. VAT is extra.

Cycle hire

Cycle hire shops often demand that you leave proof of identity (take a photocopy to avoid having to leave your actual passport) plus a cash deposit. For more shops, and biking tours outside Madrid, *see page 240*.

Sport Karacol

C/Tortosa 8 (91 539 96 33). Metro Atocha/bus all routes to Atocha. **Open** 10.30am-8pm Mon-Wed, Fri; 10.30am-10pm Thur; 10.30am-2pm Sat; *Aug only* closed Sat. **Credit** MC, V.
Mountain bikes for 2,000ptas a day, with 5,000ptas deposit and ID. A weekend deal (Fri-Mon) costs less – 4,000ptas – with the same deposit. The shop also runs tours (*see p240*).
Branch: C/Montera 32 (91 532 90 73).

Breakdown services

If you take a car to Spain it is advisable to join a motoring organisation such as the AA or RAC in Britain, or the AAA in the US. They have reciprocal arrangements with the local equivalent, RACE, the most convenient source of assistance for drivers in distress. If you need more than emergency repairs, or spare parts, main dealers for most makes of European car will be found in the local Yellow Pages under *Automóviles*.

RACE (Real Automóvil Club de España)

C/José Abascal 10 (freephone 900 11 22 22/information 91 593 33 33/office 91 447 92 00). Metro Ríos Rosas/bus 3, 5, 12, 16, 37. **Open** *phoneline* 24 hours; *office* 8.30am-5.30pm Mon-Fri.

The RACE has English-speaking staff and will send immediate breakdown assistance. If you are outside Madrid, you should still call the emergency freephone number, but you will be referred on to a local number. Repairs are carried out on the spot when possible; if not, your vehicle will be towed to the nearest suitable garage. Members of foreign affiliated organisations are not charged for call-outs, but non-members pay around 7,000ptas for basic breakdown service. The RACE also provides a range of other services for foreign drivers and members of affiliated organisations.

Parking

For car-owning Madrileños parking is a daily trauma. The Municipal Police give out tickets readily, although locals commonly never pay them. Be careful, though, not to park in front of doorways with the sign '*Vado Permanente*', indicating an entry with 24-hour right of access. Parking is banned in most main streets in the centre, but in most sidestreets the **ORA** pay-and-display parking system applies.

ORA

The ORA (*Operación Regulación Aparcamiento*) is a slightly complicated system, but its main features are: within the central ORA zone (roughly between Moncloa, C/José Abascal, C/Doctor Esquerdo and Atocha), residents park for free if they have an annual sticker. From 9am to 8pm (9am to 3pm in August), non-residents can also park here with a special card, labelled *ZER*, valid for a maximum of two hours. The cards can be bought from *estancos* or newsstands, cost 40-160ptas (for a half hour and multiples thereof) and should be displayed behind the windscreen. All streets within this zone that do not have additional restrictions signposted are ORA parking areas. In other zones time allowances are slightly more generous (a plan is also under consideration to introduce parking meters into central Madrid). All fines are cheaper if paid within 15 days; cars parked in the ORA zone without a card can also be towed away (*see below*).

Car parks

Central car parks Plaza de las Cortes, Plaza Santa Ana, C/Sevilla, Plaza Jacinto Benavente, Plaza Mayor, C/Descalzas Reales, C/Tudescos, Plaza de España. **Open** 24 hours daily. **Rates** 130ptas for first 30 min; 110ptas each subsequent half-hour; 2,220ptas 24 hours.

The 28 municipal underground *parkings* around the city are indicated by a white P on a blue sign, with an illuminated sign by the entrance to show whether spaces are available: *Lleno* means full, *Libre* means there are spaces. You are especially recommended to use a car park if you have a car with foreign plates.

Towing away & car pounds

(*91 345 00 50*). **Open** 24 hours daily. **Main pounds**: *Plaza del Carmen. Metro Sol/bus all routes to Puerta del Sol.* **Map E7**
Avda de Alfonso XIII 135. Metro Colombia/bus 7, 40, 52.

If your car seems to have been towed away by the Municipal Police, call the central number and quote your car number plate to be told which of the car pounds your vehicle has gone to. Staff do not normally speak English. It will cost 16,000ptas to recover your vehicle, plus 240ptas for the first hour and 220ptas per hour after that, timed from the moment it was towed away.

Petrol

Most petrol stations (*gasolineras*) have unleaded fuel (*sin plomo*) as well as regular (*súper*). Diesel fuel is *gas-oil*.

24-hour petrol stations

Atocha: Repsol junction of Paseo de Infanta Isabel and Avda Ciudad de Barcelona, next to Atocha station. **Credit** AmEx, MC, V. **Map I1**
Campsa: Paseo de Santa Maria de la Cabeza 18, on southward exit from Glorieta del Emperador Carlos V. **Credit** AmEx, MC, V. **Map H10**
Both have 24-hour shops on site.
Avda de América: Repsol C/Maria de Molina 21. **Credit** AmEx, MC, V.
Salamanca: Repsol C/Goya 24, junction with C/Núñez de Balboa. **Credit** AmEx, DC, MC, V. **Map J4**
Cuatro Caminos: Carba C/Rios Rosas 1, junction of C/Bravo Murillo. **Credit** AmEx, MC, V.

Directory A-Z

Communications

Mail

The main centre for all postal services is the **Palacio de Comunicaciones**. If you just need normal-rate stamps it's easier to buy them in any *estanco* (tobacco shop; *see page 254*).

Palacio de Comunicaciones

Plaza de Cibeles (91 521 65 00/91 537 64 94/information 902 197 197). Metro Banco de España/bus all routes to Cibeles. **Open** 8.30am-9.30pm Mon-Fri; 9.30am-9.30pm Sat; 8.30am-2pm Sun. **Map H7**
In the magnificent central post office, all manner of postal services are available at separate windows around the main hall: parcel post, telegrams, telex and so on. Faxes can be sent and received at all post offices, but their rates are very expensive, so it's better to use a private fax bureau. There is an information desk near the main entrance. Note that within the general opening times not all services are available at all times. Letters sent Poste Restante (General Delivery) should be addressed to *Lista de Correos, 28000 Madrid, Spain*. To collect them, go to windows 17-20 with your passport. For express post, say you want to send a letter *urgente*. For more on the building itself, *see p45 and chapter* **Architecture**.
Other city centre post offices
(open 9am-2pm Mon-Fri):
El Corte Inglés, C/Preciados. Metro Sol/bus all routes to Puerta del Sol. C/Hermosilla 103.
Metro Goya/bus 21, 26, 53, 61, C. C/Mejia Lequerica 7. Metro Tribunal/bus 3, 37, 40, 48, 149. Gran Via de San Francisco 13. Metro Puerta de Toledo/bus all routes to Puerta de Toledo.

Postal rates & postboxes

Letters and postcards weighing up to 20g cost 35ptas within Spain, 60ptas to EU countries, 70ptas to the rest of Europe and North Africa, 115ptas to the Americas and most of Africa and Asia and 155ptas to South-east Asia and Australasia. Cards and letters to other European countries generally arrive in 3-4 days, to North America in about a week. Aerogrammes (*Aerogramas*) cost 80ptas to all destinations. Normal postboxes are yellow, with two horizontal red stripes. There are also a few special red postboxes for urgent mail, with hourly collections.

Postal Exprés

Available at all post offices, this is an efficient express post system with next-day delivery anywhere within Spain of packages up to 1kg, for 715ptas. A similar package abroad costs 1,495ptas.

Telephones

The Spanish national phone company (*Telefónica*) has recently been privatised and now has a competitor, *Retevisión*. With time this may have an effect on charges. *Telefónica* charges are high, especially for international calls. It is cheaper to call after 10pm and before 8am, Monday to Saturday, and all day on Sundays.

Phone numbers

Since April 1998 it has been necessary to dial provincial area codes with all phone numbers in Spain, even within the same area. Hence, all numbers in the Madrid area are preceded by *91*, whether you're calling within Madrid, from elsewhere in Spain or from abroad. Many signs, hotel ads and so

on still do not show the *91*, which can cause confusion. Numbers beginning *900* are freephone lines. Calls made to mobile phones are not preceded by *91*, and cost more.

Public phones

The most common model of phone now in use accepts coins, phonecards and credit cards, and has a digital display with instructions in four languages including English. The minimum charge for a local call is currently 20ptas. If you use larger coins, this type of phone will also give you credit to make further calls without having to reinsert your money. If you're likely to make more than one or two calls it's better to get a phonecard, available for 500, 1,000, 2,000 or 5,000ptas and bought in post offices or *estancos*. There are also still some older-model phones around, with which you insert the coins into a slot or aperture at the top of the phone before dialling; the coins will begin to drop when the call is answered. For a local call you will need to insert four *duros* (5pta coins) and will not get change if you put in a 25 or 50ptas coin. In addition, most bars and cafés have a telephone for public use. They usually accept 5 and 25ptas coins, but in some bars they are set to take only 25ptas, an illegal but not-uncommon practice.

International & long-distance calls

To make an international call from any phone, dial 00, wait for a loud continuous tone and then dial the country code: **Australia** 61; **Canada** 1; **Irish Republic** 353; **New Zealand** 64; **United Kingdom** 44; **USA** 1, followed by the area code (omitting the first zero in UK codes) and individual number. To call Madrid from abroad, dial the international code (00 in the UK), then 34 for Spain (and the 91 for Madrid).

Essential vocabulary

Like other Latin languages, Spanish has different familiar and polite forms of the second person (you). Many young people now use the familiar *tú* form most of the time; for foreigners, though, it's always advisable to use the more polite *usted* with people you do not know, and certainly with anyone over 50. In the phrases listed here all verbs are given in the *usted* form. For help in making your way through menus, *see also chapters* **Restaurants** *and* **Tapas**.

Pronunciation basics

c, before an **i** or an **e**, and **z** are like **th** in **th**in
c in all other cases is as in **c**at
g, before an **i** or an **e**, and **j** are pronounced with a guttural **h**-sound that does not exist in English – like **ch** in Scottish lo**ch**, but much harder
g in all other cases is pronounced as in **g**et
h at the beginning of a word is normally silent
ll is pronounced almost like a **y**
ñ is like **ny** in can**y**on
A single **r** at the beginning of a word and **rr** elsewhere are heavily rolled

Basics

hello *hola;* hello (when answering the phone) *hola, diga*
good morning, good day *buenos días;* good afternoon, good evening *buenas tardes;* good evening (after dark), good night *buenas noches*
goodbye/see you later *adiós/hasta luego*
please *por favor;* thank you (very much) *(muchas) gracias*
you're welcome *de nada*
do you speak English? *¿habla inglés?;* I don't speak Spanish *no hablo español*
I don't understand *no entiendo*
what's your name? *¿cómo se llama?*
speak more slowly, please *hable más despacio, por favor*
wait a moment *espere un momento*
Sir/Mr *señor (sr);* Madam/Mrs *señora (sra);* Miss *señorita (srta)*
excuse me/sorry *perdón*
excuse me, please *oiga* (the standard way to attract someone's attention, politely; literally 'hear me')
OK/fine/(or to a waiter) that's enough *vale*

where is... *¿dónde está...?*
why? *¿porqué?;* when? *¿cuándo?;*
who? *¿quién?;* what? *¿qué?;*
where? *¿dónde?;* how? *¿cómo?*
who is it? *¿quién es?*
is/are there any... *¿hay...?*
very *muy;* and *y;* or *o*
with *con;* without *sin*
open *abierto;* closed *cerrado*
what time does it open/close? *¿a qué hora abre/cierra?*
pull (on signs) *tirar;* push *empujar*
I would like... *quiero...* (literally, 'I want...'); how many would you like? *¿cuántos quiere?*
I like *me gusta*
I don't like *no me gusta*
good *bueno/a;* bad *malo/a;*
well/badly *bien/mal;* small *pequeño/a;* big *gran, grande;*
expensive *caro/a;* cheap *barato/a;* hot (food, drink) *caliente;* cold *frío/a*
something *algo;* nothing *nada*
more/less *más/menos*
more or less *más o menos*
the bill/check, please *la cuenta, por favor*
how much is it? *¿cuánto es?*
do you have any change? *¿tiene cambio?*
price *precio;* free *gratis;*
discount *descuento*
bank *banco;* alquilar *to rent;* (en) alquiler (for) *rent, rental;*
post office *correos;* stamp *sello;*
postcard *postal;*
toilet *los servicios*

Getting around

airport *aeropuerto;* railway station *estación de ferrocarril/estación de RENFE* (Spanish Railways); **Metro** station *estación de Metro*
entrance *entrada;* exit *salida*
car *coche;* bus *autobús;* train *tren*
a ticket *un billete;* return *de ida y vuelta;* bus stop *parada de autobús;* the next stop *la próxima parada*
excuse me, do you know the way to...? *¿oiga, señor/señora/etc, sabe como llegar a...?*
left *izquierda;* right *derecha*
here *aquí;* there *allí*
straight on *recto;* to the end of the street *al final de la calle;* as far as *hasta;* towards *hacia*
near *cerca;* far *lejos*

Accommodation

do you have a double/single room for tonight/one week? *¿tiene una habitación doble/para una persona para esta noche/una semana?*

where is the car park? *¿dónde está el parking?*
we have a reservation *tenemos reserva*
an inside/outside room *una habitación interior/exterior*
with/without bathroom *con/sin baño;* shower *ducha;* double bed *cama de matrimonio;*
with twin beds *con dos camas*
breakfast included *desayuno incluido*
air-conditioning *aire acondicionado;* lift *ascensor;*
swimming pool *piscina*

Time

morning *la mañana;* midday *mediodía;* afternoon/evening *la tarde;* night *la noche;* late night (roughly 1-6am) *la madrugada*
now *ahora;* later *más tarde*
yesterday *ayer;* today *hoy;*
tomorrow *mañana;*
tomorrow morning *mañana por la mañana.*
at what time...? *¿a qué hora...?*
in an hour *en una hora*
the bus will take 2 hours (to get there) *el autobús tardará dos horas (en llegar)*
at 2 *a las dos;* at 8pm *a las ocho de la tarde;* at 1.30 *a la una y media;* at 5.15 *a las cinco y cuarto;*
at 22.30 *a veintidós treinta*

Numbers

0 *cero;* 1 *un, uno, una;* 2 *dos;* 3 *tres;* 4 *cuatro;* 5 *cinco;* 6 *seis;* 7 *siete;* 8 *ocho;* 9 *nueve;* 10 *diez;* 11 *once;* 12 *doce;* 13 *trece;* 14 *catorce;* 15 *quince;* 16 *dieciséis;* 17 *diecisiete;* 18 *dieciocho;* 19 *diecinueve;* 20 *veinte;* 21 *veintiuno;* 22 *veintidós;* 30 *treinta;* 40 *cuarenta;* 50 *cincuenta;* 60 *sesenta;* 70 *setenta;* 80 *ochenta;* 90 *noventa;* 100 *cien;* 1,000 *mil;* 1,000,000 *un millón*

Days, months & seasons

Monday *lunes;* Tuesday *martes;* Wednesday *miércoles;* Thursday *jueves;* Friday *viernes;* Saturday *sábado;* Sunday *domingo*
January *enero;* February *febrero;* March *marzo;* April *abril;* May *mayo;* June *junio;* July *julio;* August *agosto;* September *septiembre;* October *octubre;* November *noviembre;* December *diciembre*
Spring *primavera;* summer *verano;* autumn/fall *otoño;* winter *invierno*

Phone centres

At phone centres (*locutorios*) you are allotted a booth and pay at the counter when you have finished all your calls, thus avoiding the need for pocketloads of change.

Telefónica phone centre
Gran Via 30. Metro Gran Via/bus all routes to Gran Via. **Open** 9am-midnight Mon-Sat; noon-midnight Sun, public holidays. **Credit** AmEx, MC, V. **Map E6**

There are also private *locutorios* such as **Sol Telecom**, which provides phone and fax services, Internet access, e-mail, money changing and facilities for sending and receiving money. Cheap rates start from 6pm. Branch opening hours vary.

Sol Telecom branches: *Puerta del Sol 6 (91 531 03 82). Metro Sol/bus all routes to Puerta del Sol.* **Map E7** *Plaza del Callao 1 (91 532 79 77). Metro Callao/bus all routes to Plaza del Callao.* **Map D6** *Gran Via 84 (91 559 79 77). Metro Plaza de España/bus all routes to Plaza de España.* **Map D5**

Operator services

Normally in Spanish only.
National directory enquiries 1003
International directory enquiries 025
International operator *Europe & North Africa* 1008; *Rest of World* 1005
Telephone breakdowns 1002
Time 093
Weather information *Madrid* 906 36 53 28; *national* 906 36 53 65.
Alarm calls 096
Once the message has finished (when it starts repeating itself), key in the number you are calling from followed by the time at which you wish to be woken, in four figures, ie 0830 if you want to be called at 8.30am.
General information 098
A local information service provided by Telefónica, with information on duty pharmacies in Madrid. Otherwise, it is less reliable than the 010 line (*see p261*).

Computers/IT

Quick access to cyberspace is available at the **Net Café** and **Café Comercial** (*see chapter* **Cafés & Bars**).

Bitmailer

C/Juan Bravo 51 (91 402 15 51). Metro Diego de León/bus 26, 29, 52, C. **Open** 9am-2pm, 4-7pm, Mon-Fri. **Map K2**
An Internet service provider with a helpful and efficient back-up service. Unlimited Net access costs 3,500ptas per month (24,000ptas annually) plus tax, and there's a range of other price offers. Also software for sale.
Website: www.bitmailer.com

Data Rent

C/Montearagón 3 (91 759 62 42). Metro Arturo Soria/bus 9, 70, 72, 87. **Open** *Sept-June* 9am-2pm, 4-7pm, *July-Aug* 8am-3pm, Mon-Fri. **Credit** MC, V.
PCs, printers and OHP projectors for rent by the day, the week or the month.

WORKcenter

C/Alberto Aguilera 1 (91 448 78 77/902 11 50 11). Metro San Bernardo/bus 21, 147. **Open** 24 hours daily. **Credit** AmEx, EC, MC, V. **Map E3**
WORKcenter is conceived as an office that anyone can visit whatever their needs. You can send or receive faxes and e-mails, access the Net, work on a computer, print from a disk, make photocopies or passport photos. It also runs courses and sells stationery.
Branches Guzmán el Bueno 98 (91 533 50 50); Reina Mercedes 9 (91 533 35 95).
Website: www.workcenter.es

Courier services

Cheapest way of sending small packages within Spain is via **Postal Exprés**, available at all post offices (*see page 253*).

DHL

Phoneline for collection and delivery 902 12 24 24. **Open** *phoneline* 24 hours daily. **Credit** AmEx, MC, V.
One of the most expensive of the international courier companies, but also one of the most reliable. All business is done by phone. Orders can be placed at any time, but pick-ups and deliveries are made 9am-8pm Mon-Sat.

MFR Distribución Urgente

Avda del Manzanares 202 (91 476 71 61/fax 91 500 39 84). Bus 23, 79, 123. **Open** 8am-8pm Mon-Fri. **No credit cards.**
Rates for deliveries within Madrid begin at 998ptas for 50kg, but service is very fast. Call by 6pm for same-day delivery; outside office hours there is a 50% surcharge. They will also collect luggage from hotels to take to the airport and rail stations, and have long-distance and international services.

RUM

C/Galileo 91 (91 535 38 16). Metro Quevedo/bus 2, 12, 16, 61. **Open** *Oct-June* 9am-8pm, *July-Sept* 9am-7pm, Mon-Fri. **No credit cards.**
An efficient local courier company. Pick-ups and deliveries can be made by bike or van. A 1kg package for delivery by bike within Madrid costs 450ptas for non-account customers.

Trébol

C/Esperanza 3 (91 530 32 32). Metro Lavapiés/bus 6, 26, 32. **Open** *Sept-July* 9am-7pm, *Aug* 9am-3pm, Mon-Fri. **No credit cards. Map F9**

Madrid's first all-cycle courier company provides fast service at low prices. Parcels under 2kg for delivery within the M-30 cost 395ptas (with occasional discounts), and there is a competitive long-distance courier service. Services to the rest of Spain start at 995ptas (to Barcelona); abroad prices begin at 3,995ptas to European capitals. Services can also be provided outside office hours, at a premium rate.

Disabled travellers

Madrid is not yet a city where disabled people, especially wheelchair users, can get around freely, although little by (very) little the situation is improving. Access to public transport is patchy; buses and taxis are the most accessible forms of transport (*see below*).

There is no general guide to accessibility in the city. Access with lifts or ramps for wheelchair users is already provided at the major museums. Recent legislation requires all public buildings to be made fully accessible by 2003, but in practice the law is more demanding with new than existing buildings. Thanks to the ONCE (Spain's powerful lottery-funded organisation for the blind) more has been done on behalf of blind and partially sighted people. Most street crossings in the centre have identifiable, knobbled paving and low kerbs.

Coordinadora de Minusválidos Físicos de Madrid (COMFM)
C/Ríos Rosas 54 (91 535 06 19). Metro Ríos Rosas/bus 3, 12, 37, 45, 147. **Open** 8am-3pm Mon-Fri. An umbrella organisation for disability groups in the city collects information on changes in access and facilities.

Buses

There are seats reserved for people with mobility problems, slightly lower than others, behind the driver on most buses. The majority of buses on most routes are now of the *Piso Bajo* (Low Floor) type with low entry and exit doors and space for wheelchairs. Users complain, however, of limited access owing to parked cars at bus stops.

Metro & rail stations

Madrid's Metro system is not suited to disabled travellers. Metro stations have a lot of steps, and there are only a handful of lifts for wheelchair users. The ambitious but

Emergencies

Madrid has a **general emergency number** for calling for the police, ambulance or other emergency services, **112**. Some staff speak English, French and/or German. You can also call the relevant services direct.

Ambulance/*Ambulancia* 061/092/91 335 45 45/91 522 22 22
Fire Service/*Bomberos* 080
Municipal Police/*Policía Municipal* 092
National Police/*Policía Nacional* 091
Guardia Civil 062/91 533 1100/900 123 505

Emergency repairs

The electricity company you need to call will be indicated on the electricity meter.
Electricity Unión Fenosa *(91 406 80 00)*; Iberdrola *(91 364 88 88)*
Butane Gas *Repsol Butano* *(901 100 100/901 121 212)*
Gas *Gas Natural* *(91 589 65 55/91 589 61 16)*
Water *Canal de Isabel II* *(901 516 516/901 512 512)*

---

slow Metro expansion programme in principle includes the provision of access at new stations, and this has already been implemented at Gregorio Marañón, the new stations on line 4, and Mar de Cristal and Campo de las Naciones on line 8. Changing lines once on the Metro is another question. Of the main-line railway stations, Atocha has good access facilities, but Chamartín has stairs to the Metro and is only accessible to wheelchairs with assistance, which must be requested from the station authorities. *Cercanías* trains also have very limited access, but some new stations such as Méndez Álvaro (by the Estación Sur coach station) have lifts connecting Metro, train and bus stations.

Taxis

Special taxis adapted for wheelchairs can be called through **Euro-Taxi** on 91 547 82 00/85 00/86 00. This is also a general phone cab service, so when calling you must make clear you want an adapted model. There are currently around 30 such taxis functioning in Madrid, and the waiting time can be up to half an hour. Fares are the same as for standard cabs, but since they are so scarce and may have to come from far away the cost can be quite high, as the meter is started as soon as the request is received.

Embassies

For a full list look in the local phone book under *Embajadas*. Outside office hours all the embassies have answerphones that will give you an emergency number. For more on what to do if you lose a passport, *see page 260*.

Embassies/consulates

American Embassy
C/Serrano 75 (91 587 22 00). Metro Rubén Darío/bus 9, 19, 51, 61.
Open *phoneline* 24 hours; *office* 9am-1pm Mon-Fri. **Map I2**
Australian Embassy
Plaza del Descubridor Diego de Ordás 3 (91 441 93 00). Metro Ríos Rosas/bus 3, 12, 37, 45, 149.
Open 10am-1pm Mon-Fri.
British Embassy *C/Fernando el Santo 16 (91 308 06 18). Metro Alonso Martínez/bus 7, 21, 147.*
Open 8am-8pm Mon-Fri. **Map H3**
British Consulate *C/Marqués de la Ensenada 16 (91 308 52 01). Metro Colón/bus all routes to Plaza de Colón.*
Open 8am-2pm Mon-Fri. **Map H4**
Canadian Embassy *C/Núñez de Balboa 35 (91 431 43 00). Metro Velázquez/bus 1, 9, 19, 51, 74.* **Open** *embassy* 9am-12.30pm, *phoneline* 8.30am-1pm, 2-5pm, Mon-Fri. **Map J4**
Irish Embassy *Paseo de la Castellana 46 (91 576 35 00). Metro Rubén Darío/bus 5, 27, 45, 150.*
Open 10am-2pm Mon-Fri. **Map I2**
New Zealand Embassy *Plaza de la Lealtad 2 (91 523 02 26). Metro Banco de España/bus 9, 10, 14, 27, 34, 37, 45.* **Open** 9am-1.30pm, 2.30-5.30pm, Mon-Fri. **Map H7**

Health

All visitors can obtain emergency health care through the Spanish national health service, the *Seguridad Social*. EU citizens are entitled to basic medical attention for free if they have an E111 form (if you can get an E111 sent or faxed within four days, you are still exempt from charges). Many medicines

---

will be charged for. In non-emergency situations, short-term visitors will usually find it more convenient to use private travel insurance rather than the state system. Similarly, non-EU nationals with private medical insurance can make use of state health services on a paying basis, but other than in emergencies it will be simpler to use a private clinic.

If you become a resident and contribute to the *Seguridad Social*, you will be allocated a health clinic within the state system (*see page 262-3*).

Emergencies

In a medical emergency the best thing to do is to go to the casualty (*Urgencias*) department of any of the major hospitals. All are open 24 hours daily. In the central area, go to the Clínico or the Gregorio Marañón.

Hospitals

Ciudad Sanitaria La Paz *Paseo de la Castellana 261 (91 358 28 31). Metro Begoña/bus 66, 67, 132, 135.*
The largest city hospital, in north Madrid near Plaza Castilla.
Hospital Clínico San Carlos *Plaza de Cristo Rey (91 330 37 48). Metro Moncloa/bus 1, 12, 44, C.*
Enter from Calle Isaac Peral, just off the Plaza de Cristo Rey.
Hospital General Gregorio Marañón *C/Dr Esquerdo 46 (91 586 80 00). Metro Ibiza, O'Donnell/bus 2, 28, 143, C.* **Map L6/7**
The *Urgencias* entrance is in C/Ibiza.
Hospital Ramón y Cajal *Carretera de Colmenar Viejo, km 8 (91 336 83 13). Bus 124, 135/train Cercanías C-7, C-8 to Ramón y Cajal.*
In the north of the city. The *Cercanías* station is inside the hospital complex.

Emergency first-aid centres (*Casas de Socorro*)

If you have no E111, no insurance and are not within the Spanish health system, you will still be attended at the Gregorio Marañón (*see above*). Alternatively, go to a *Casa de Socorro*, where you will receive first aid and if necessary be sent to a hospital. Most are open 24 hours daily.
Central area *C/Navas de Tolosa 10 (91 521 00 25). Metro Callao/bus all routes to Plaza de Callao.* **Map D7**
Goya area *C/Montesa 22 (91 588 51 01). Metro Manuel Becerra/bus 1, 43, 53, 74, C.*

Retiro/Atocha area
C/Gobernador 39 (91 420 03 56).
Metro Antón Martín, Atocha/bus all
routes to Atocha. **Map G9**
Tetuán area C/Aguileñas 1 (91 588
66 89/69). Metro Plaza de Castilla,
Valdeaceras/bus 49, 66, 124.

Ambulances

Phone the general emergency line
(112), the *Seguridad Social* (061), the
Red Cross (*Cruz Roja*, 91 522 22 22), or
the city SAMUR service (via the
Municipal Police, on 092).

Private health care

Unidad Médica
Anglo-Americana

C/Conde de Aranda 1 (91 435 18 23).
Metro Retiro/bus all routes to Plaza de
la Independencia.
Open office 9am-8pm Mon-Fri; 10am-
1pm Sat; Aug 10am-4pm Mon-Fri.
Closed public holidays. **Map I6**
A British-American clinic whose staff
will make house and hotel calls. It has a
complete range of services, including
gynaecology and dentistry.

AIDS/HIV

Centro Dermatológico
de la Comunidad

C/Sandoval 7 (91 445 23 28). Metro
San Bernardo/bus 21, 147. **Open**
9am-noon Mon-Fri. **Map E3**
An official clinic that carries out free
confidential HIV tests. Queues are long.

Fundacíon Anti-SIDA

C/Juan Montalvo 6 (freephone 900
11 10 00/91 536 15 00). Metro
Guzmán el Bueno/bus 2, 12, 44, 45,
128, C. **Open** 10am-8pm Mon-Fri.
The best organisation to go to for sup-
port and advice about HIV and AIDS.
The volunteers don't generally speak
English, but efforts are made to do so.

Alternative medicine

Instituto de
Medicina Natural

Plaza de la Independencia 4 (91 576
26 49). Metro Banco de España,
Retiro/bus all routes to Plaza de la
Independencia. **Open** 8.30am-2pm, 5-
8pm Mon-Fri; 9am-2pm Sat. **Map H6**
A central clinic offering acupuncture,
homeopathy, chiropractics and other
forms of complementary medicine, with
some English-speaking practitioners.

Contraception &
women's health

Condoms (*profilácticos* or
condones) are available in
pharmacies, vending machines

and even supermarkets. A few
pharmacies still refuse to sell
condoms on religious grounds.
Abortion is available only up
to 12 weeks, and only in
limited circumstances.

Clínica Duratón

C/Colegiata 4 (91 429 77 69). Metro
Tirso de Molina/bus 6, 17, 23, 26,
50, 65. **Open** Sept-June 9.30am-
1.30pm, 4.30-8.30pm, July, Aug 4.30-
8.30pm, Mon-Fri. **Map D8**
Family planning centre run exclusively by its women doctors and staff.

Dator Médica

C/Hermanos Gárate 4 (91 571 27
00). Metro Tetuán/bus 3, 126, 127.
Open 9am-9pm Mon-Fri; 9am-
6.30pm Sat, Sun.
A specialised gynaecological clinic
with English-speaking staff, and
authorised to carry out terminations.

Espacio de Salud Entre
Nosotras

Avda de Alfonso XIII 114 (91 519
56 78). Metro Colombia/bus 7, 11,
40. **Open** 10am-1pm Mon-Thur.
A feminist medical association run
by doctors and health workers. They
offer free advice, counselling and
group-therapy treatment for women
on a wide range of problems.

Dentists

See also **Private health care.**

Clínica Dental Cisne

C/Magallanes 18 (91 446 32 21).
Metro Quevedo/bus 16, 37, 61, 149.
Open 10am-1.30pm, 3-8pm, Mon,
Thur; 2-8pm Tue, Wed, Fri.
No credit cards. Map E2
British dentist Dr Ian Daniel is based at
this clinic. Consultations cost 3,000ptas;
after that, fillings cost from 7,000ptas
and cleaning from 6,000ptas. Hours can
vary in summer, and the clinic may be
closed in August. Note that dentistry is
not covered by the E111 form, so you
must pay all charges yourself.

Pharmacies

Pharmacies (*farmacias*) are
signalled by large green, usually
flashing, crosses, and are
plentiful in central Madrid.
Pharmacies within the official
system of the College of
Pharmacies are normally open
9.30am to 2pm, 5 to 8pm,
Monday to Saturday. At other
times a duty rota operates. Every
pharmacy has a list of the
College's *farmacias de guardia*

(duty pharmacies) for that day
posted outside the door, with the
nearest ones highlighted. Many
have now substituted the paper
list for a computerised panel,
operated at the touch of a button.
Duty pharmacies for the whole
city are also listed in local
newspapers, and information is
available on the 010 and 098
phonelines (recorded message, in
Spanish only, between 9.30pm
and 8.30am). At night duty
pharmacies may appear to be
closed, and you have to knock on
the shutters to be served.

Currently there are two **24-
hour pharmacies,** open every
day of the year:

Farmacia Central

Paseo de Santa María de la Cabeza
64 (91 473 06 72). Metro Palos de la
Frontera/bus 6, 55, 59, 78, 85, 148.
No credit cards.
In Arganzuela, just far south of the
Glorieta de Embajadores.

Farmacia Lastra

C/Conde de Peñalver 27 (91 402 43
63). Metro Goya/bus, 26, 61. **Credit**
AmEx, DC, MC, V. **Map L3**
A handy standby, a good general
pharmacy in Salamanca that's open
permanently throughout the year.

Alcoholics Anonymous

C/Juan Bravo 40 (91 341 82 82/91
309 19 47). Metro Núñez de Balboa/
bus 26, 29, 52, 61. **Open** phoneline
10am-10pm daily. **Map J2**
The English-speaking AA group in
Madrid meets regularly.

Red Cross Centres
(Centros de la Cruz Roja)

C/Fúcar 8 (91 429 19 60). Metro
Antón Martín/bus 6, 26, 32, 57.
Open 8am-3pm Mon-Fri. **Map G9**
C/Marroquina 22 (91 470 60 77).
Metro Vinateros/bus 30, 32, 71.
Open 9am-5pm Mon-Fri.
These two centres offer counselling
and help on a variety of problems,
including drug-related ones. English-
speakers are sometimes available.

Teléfono de la Esperanza

C/Francos Rodríguez 51 (91 459 00
50). Metro Estrecho/bus 44, 64, 66,
127. **Open** phoneline 24 hours daily.
A privately funded local helpline that
caters for a wide range of needs, from
psychiatric to legal and financial. Some
of the staff speak English, but they
may not be available at all times.

Directory

Holidays

On public holidays (*fiestas*), virtually all shops, banks and offices, and many bars and restaurants, are closed. There is, though, a near-normal public transport service, except on Christmas Day and New Year's Day, and many museums are also open, for shorter-than-usual hours. Madrileños now take slightly fewer days off than in the past, but when a holiday falls on a Tuesday or Thursday many people still take the intervening day before or after the weekend off as well, in a long weekend called a *puente* (bridge). Many offices and businesses are also closed for the whole of Easter Week. For a calendar of the city's festivals, *see chapter* **Madrid by Season**. The city's usual official holidays, with some variations each year, include:

New Year's Day (Año Nuevo) 1 January; **Three Kings (Reyes Magos)** 6 January; **Good Friday (Viernes Santo)**; **May (Labour) Day (Fiesta del Trabajo)** 1 May; **Madrid Day (Día de la Comunidad de Madrid)** 2 May; **San Isidro** 15 May; **Virgen de la Paloma** 15 August; **Discovery of America (Día de la Hispanidad)** 12 October; **All Saints' Day (Todos los Santos)** 1 November; **Virgen de la Almudena** 9 November; **Constitution Day (Día de la Constitución)** 6 December; **Immaculate Conception (La Inmaculada)** 8 December; **Christmas (Navidad)** 25 December.

Libraries

For a complete list of libraries in Madrid, check the local Yellow Pages under *Bibliotecas*. Most will only ask you to show your passport to be admitted. University libraries can only be used by registered students.

Ateneo Científico y Literario de Madrid
*C/del Prado 21 (91 429 17 50).
Metro Antón Martín/bus 6, 9, 26, 32.*
Open 9am-1am Mon-Sat; 9am-10pm Sun. **Map F8**
A literary, scientific and philosophical club founded in 1820, Madrid's Ateneo has often been a focal point in the cultural life of the city, as a meeting place for artists, writers and politicians.

It also has the second-largest and most valuable library in the country, with the added advantage of being open when others are closed. If you are planning to stay in Madrid long enough, it could be of interest to take out membership (15,000ptas per year). Members have access to cultural events, seminars, talks and many other activities. To join, you will need the signature of two members of the Ateneo. *See also p56.*

Biblioteca Nacional
Paseo de Recoletos 20 (91 580 78 00). Metro Colón/bus all routes to Plaza de Colón. **Open** 9am-9pm Mon-Fri; 9am-2pm Sat. **Map I5**
Spain's national library has many manuscripts and early editions on display, in the **Museo del Libro** (*see chapter* **Museums**). The library is also home to the **Hemeroteca Nacional**, the national newspaper library, which also has many foreign publications. To use the library regularly and take out books on loan you will need some accreditation from a university or similar institution, but a one-day pass can usually be obtained on presentation of a passport or residency document.

Biblioteca Pedro Salinas
Plaza de la Puerta de Toledo 1 (91 366 54 07). Metro Puerta de Toledo/bus all routes to Puerta de Toledo. **Open** 8.30am-8.45pm Mon-Fri; 9am-2pm Sat, except July-Sept. **Map C10**
The most attractive and convenient of Madrid's public libraries. Books can be taken out on loan.

Hemeroteca Municipal
C/Conde Duque 9, 11 (91 588 57 71). Metro Noviciado, Plaza de España/bus all routes to Plaza de España. **Open** Oct-June 9am-9pm, July, Sept 9am-8pm, Aug 9am-1pm, Mon-Fri. **Map D4**
The city newspaper library, founded in 1918, is one of several institutions housed in the **Centro Conde Duque**. To be admitted you need a researchers' card, for which you need to provide a photocopy of your passport and two passport-size photos.

Washington Irving Library
Paseo de la Castellana 52 (91 564 55 15). Metro Rubén Darío/bus 5, 14, 27, 150. **Open** 2-6pm Mon-Fri. Closed July-Aug. **Map 3/G3**
A small English-language library run by the US Embassy. Books can be taken out on loan; membership is free.

Lost property

Airport & rail stations
If you lose something land-side of check-in at Barajas Airport, report the loss immediately to the *Aviación Civil* office in the relevant terminal. You can also call 91 393 60 00. If you think you have mislaid anything on the RENFE

rail network, look for the *Atención al Viajero* desk or *Jefe de Estación* office at the main station nearest to where your property has gone astray. For information by phone on lost property at main rail stations call the main RENFE information number. In all cases, ask for *'Objetos Perdidos'*.

Buses
EMT *C/Alcántara 24 (91 406 88 10). Metro Lista/bus 1, 21, 26, 53, 146.* **Map L3**
For items losts on city buses.

Metro/Taxis/Municipal Lost Property Office
Negociado de Objetos Perdidos, Plaza de Legazpi 7 (91 588 43 46/44). Metro Legazpi/bus all routes to Legazpi. **Open** Oct-June 9am-2pm, July-Sept 9am-1.30pm, Mon-Fri.
This office primarily receives articles found on the Metro or in taxis, but if you're lucky, something lost in the street may also be handed in and turn up here.

Money

The Spanish currency is the *peseta*, the usual abbreviation of which is *ptas*. There are coins for 1, 5, 10, 25 (with a hole in the centre), 50, 100, 200 and 500ptas. A 5pta coin is called a *duro*, 25ptas is *cinco duros* and so on. Notes are green 1,000ptas, 2,000 (red), 5,000 (brown) and 10,000ptas (blue).

Euro-philia
Spain will be in the first wave of countries to join the euro zone. A public awareness campaign is in full swing, and supermarkets, bills and cashpoint receipts increasingly give prices and accounts in pesetas and euros, allowing easy comparison. One euro is currently worth 168ptas, but the rate will fluctuate until 1 January 1999, when its value will become fixed against the member currencies. This is the day it will become usable for transactions between banks, but for the public the euro-era does not really take over until 2002. For six months up to 30 June 2002 both currencies will be in circulation; the peseta will be withdrawn as of 1 July. For queries regarding the euro in Spain, ring 902 11 20 02.

Banks & foreign exchange

Banks and savings banks (*cajas de ahorros*) readily accept cash and travellers' cheques (you must show your passport), but are less keen to take personal cheques with the Eurocheque guarantee card. Commission rates vary considerably between banks, and it's worth shopping around before changing money; also, given the rates charged by Spanish banks, the cheapest way to obtain money is often through a cash machine by credit card rather than with travellers' cheques, despite the fees that are charged for cash withdrawals. It is quicker and more trouble-free to change money at major bank offices than at local branches.

There are also many small bureau de change (*cambio*) offices, particularly on the Gran Via. They do not charge commission, but exchange rates are usually worse than bank rates. If you need to have money sent to you, the most convenient methods are via **American Express** or **Western Union**.

Bank hours

Banks and savings banks are normally open 9am-2pm, Monday to Friday. Between 1 October and 31 May many branches also open from 9am to 1pm on Saturdays. Hours vary a little between different banks, and some open slightly earlier or later, while some have branches that stay open until around 5pm one day a week, usually Thursday. All banks are closed on public holidays.

Out-of-hours services

Outside normal hours you can change money at the **airport** (24 hours), at the main train stations (Atocha, 9am-9pm, **Chamartín**, 8am-10pm, daily), in **El Corte Inglés** (*see chapter* **Shopping**), in large hotels, at private *cambios* and at the places below. With a major credit card you can also obtain money from bank ATMs (*see below*). At the airport, Chamartin and outside some banks in Gran Via and Puerta del Sol there are automatic cash exchange machines that accept notes in major currencies, in good condition (but avoid the ones at Gran Via and Puerta del Sol late-night).

American Express

Plaza de las Cortes 2 (91 572 03 03). Metro Banco de España/bus 9, 14, 27, 37, 45. **Open** 9am-5.30pm Mon-Fri; 9am-noon Sat. **Map G8**
All AmEx services such as bureau de change, poste restante, travellers' cheque refund service and cash machine. Money can be transferred from AmEx offices worldwide in 24 hours. Charges are paid by the sender.
Branch: C/Francisco Gervás 10 (91 572 03 03). **Open** 8.30am-4.30pm Mon-Fri.

Chequepoint

Puerta del Sol 8 (91 521 67 02). Metro Sol/bus all routes to Puerta del Sol. **Open** 9am-11.30pm daily.
Map E7
An international money-exchange company with several branches in central Madrid. Opening hours vary between the branches.
Branches: C/Preciados 7 (91 531 02 60); Gran Via 56 (91 559 03 06); Plaza de Callao 3 (91 532 15 90); Plaza del Callao 3 (91 532 29 22).

Western Union Money Transfer

Carrera de San Jerónimo 11 (freephone for all branches 900 633 633). Metro Sol/bus all routes to Puerta del Sol. **Open** 9am-10.30pm daily. **Map E7**
The Change Express *cambio* is the local agent for Western Union. This is the quickest, if not the cheapest, way to have money sent from abroad, which should be available at the Madrid office within an hour. Commission is paid by the sender on a sliding scale.
Branches: Gran Via 16, 25, 44, 46, 51, 53; Plaza Cánovas del Castillo 4.

Credit cards

Major credit and charge cards are very widely accepted in hotels, shops, restaurants and for many other services. Most bank branches also have ATM machines through which you can withdraw cash with major cards, and which provide instructions in different languages at the push of a button.

Exchange rates and charges often work out to be more favourable for card withdrawals than they do with cash or travellers' cheque transactions. Banks also advance cash against credit cards over the counter, but prefer you to withdraw the money directly from a cashpoint.

Card Emergencies

All lines have English-speaking staff and are open 24 hours daily:
American Express
(card emergencies 91 572 03 20/ travellers' cheques freephone 900 99 44 26).
Diners' Club *(91 547 40 00).*
MasterCard/Eurocard *(freephone 900 971 231/91 519 21 00).*
Visa *(freephone 900 974 445/900 991 216).*

Today not many Madrileños take a nap for their afternoon *siesta*, but they do operate to a distinctive schedule. Foreigners who fail to adapt to (or even recognise) this often complain the place is dead when they try to go for a walk at 4pm, without realising that the same streets might be bustling 3-4 hours later, or even after 1am. You get far more out of Madrid if you take this into account.

Shop hours are flexible, but most individual shops open from 9.30-10am to 2pm, and 5-5.30 to 8-8.30pm, Monday to Saturday, although many stay closed on Saturday afternoons. Food markets open earlier in the day, at 9am. In summer many shops and businesses open and close slightly later in the afternoons, or, in the case of most offices, not at all. The times when summer schedules apply vary, but most commonly run through July and August. Major stores and shopping malls are open from 10am to 9pm without a break, Monday to Saturday. For more on shops that open on Sundays, *see chapter* **Shopping**.

Madrileños eat, drink and go out later than their neighbours in virtually every other European country. Most restaurants are open 1 to 4pm, and 9pm to midnight, and you will find it hard to get a full evening meal before 9pm. Many restaurants, especially in the centre, close on Sundays, and many restaurants and shops also close for the whole of August.

Police & crime

Street crime is no more a problem in Madrid than in other major cities, but naturally there are parts of the city where you should be extra careful. The area around the junction of Gran Via and Calle Montera is a centre of street prostitution, and can be heavy at night. You should of course avoid empty, unlit streets at night, particularly in the old city. On the other hand, on weekend nights in nightlife areas such as Huertas or Calle Fernando VI the number of people in the street creates a sense of security that's often hard to find late-night in Northern European cities.

Pickpocketing or bag-snatching are more likely than mugging here. Places to be on your guard are the Puerta del Sol, the Plaza Mayor, the Plaza Santa Ana and its bars, and, above all, the Rastro. Watch out for pickpockets, also, on the Metro. Street thieves, however, often prey very deliberately on the unwary, and their chances can be limited greatly by the following simple precautions.
• When sitting in a café, especially at an outside table, **never** leave a bag or coat on the floor, on the back of a chair, or on a chair where you cannot see it clearly. If in doubt, keep it on your lap.
• Wear shoulder bags pulled to the front, not at your back. Keep the bag closed and keep a hand on top of it.
• Avoid pulling out large-denomination notes to pay for things, especially in the street at night; try not to get stuck with large notes when changing money.
• Be aware that street thieves often work in pairs or groups; if someone hassles you for money or to buy something in the street, or pulls out a map and asks you for directions, keep walking, as this can be a ruse to distract you so that the 'partner' can get at your bag. The attempt to get your attention is often done pretty crudely, and so not hard to recognise.

Police forces

Spain has several police forces. In Madrid the most important are the local *Policía Municipal*, in navy and pale blue, and the *Policía Nacional*, in black and white uniforms. Each force has its own set of responsibilities, and at times they overlap. The *Municipales* are principally concerned with traffic and parking problems and various local regulations. The force with primary responsibility for dealing with crime are the *Nacionales*. The *Guardia Civil*, in military green, are responsible for policing inter-city highways, Customs posts, and guarding many government buildings. A recent move by the city council has introduced *Policías Locales* in some neighbourhoods.

Reporting a crime

If you are robbed or attacked, you should report the incident as soon as possible at the nearest *Policía Nacional* station (*comisaría*).

Jefatura Superior de Policía

C/Fomento 24 (91 541 71 60). Metro Santo Domingo, Plaza de España/bus all routes to Gran Via. **Map D6**
The *Policía Nacional* headquarters for Madrid, near the Plaza de España. If you report a crime you will be asked to make an official statement (*denuncia*), which will be typed out for you. It is unlikely that anything you have lost will be recovered, but you will need the *denuncia* to make an insurance claim. A very few officers speak some English. Some other police stations in the city centre are listed below; all are open 24 hours daily.
Centro *C/de la Luna 29 (91 521 12 36). Metro Callao/bus all routes to Plaza de Callao.* **Map E5**
Santa Ana *C/Huertas 76 (91 249 09 94). Metro Antón Martín/bus 14, 27, 34, 37.* **Map G8**
The most convenient station for any incidents that occur around Huertas and the main art museums.
Chamberí *C/Rafael Calvo 33 (91 322 32 78). Metro Iglesia/bus 3, 16, 40, 61, 147.* **Map H2**
Sol *inside Sol Metro, by C/Carretas exit (91 521 09 11).* **Map E7**

Lost passports

The loss or theft of a passport must be reported to the nearest *comisaría* and to your consulate (*see p256*). If you lose a passport over a weekend and have to travel immediately consulates will charge for opening the office specially to issue an emergency passport. Spanish authorities and most airlines are often prepared to let you out of the country even without this document if you do not look suspicious and have other documents with you, including the police *denuncia* confirming the loss of your passport, but in such cases it's advisable to be at the airport in plenty of time, and be suitably prepared. You will also have to explain your lack of documents when you arrive at the other end.

Public toilets

Public toilets are not common in Madrid. There are some with an attendant in the Retiro, at the north end of the lake, and good facilities at Atocha and Chamartín stations and in the central boulevard of the Paseo del Prado. At several locations there are also pay-on-entry cubicles that cost 25ptas. Apart from that, you are best advised to pop into a bar or café. Major stores and fast-food restaurants are as usual useful standbys.

Anglican & Protestant

British Embassy Church (Saint George's) *C/Núñez de Balboa 43 (91 576 51 09). Metro Velázquez/bus 1, 9, 19, 21, 51, 74.* **Services** *Sept-June* 8.30am, 10am, 11.15am Sun; *July-Aug* 8.30am, 11.15am Sun. **Map J3**
Saint George's attracts a multi-cultural congregation.
Community Church *C/de la Viña 3 (91 730 03 49). Metro Metropolitano/bus 132, C.* **Services** 11am Sun.
International congregation, and a children's Sunday School.

Catholic Mass in English

Capilla de Nuestra Señora de la Merced *Avda de Alfonso XIII 165 (91 533 59 35/91 554 28 60). Metro Colombia/bus 7, 11, 40.* **English mass** 11am Sun.
Sunday Schools for children and adults. Also a party for Saint Patrick's Day.

Jewish

Sinagoga de Madrid *C/Balmes 3 (91 445 98 43). Metro Iglesia/bus 3, 5, 16, 37, 61, 149.* **Prayers** 8am, 8pm Mon-Fri; 9.15am Sat. **Map G1**
A Sephardic congregation. No evening services July to September.

Muslim

Centro Cultural Islámico de Madrid *C/Salvador de Madariaga 4 (91 326 26 10). Metro Barrio de la Concepción/bus 53.* **Open** *cultural centre* 10am-8pm Sat-Thur; 4-8pm Fri.
Known as the 'Mosque of the M-30' because of its dramatic appearance, looming beside the Madrid ring road, this Saudi-financed complex is one of the largest Islamic centres in Europe. In addition to the mosque, it houses a bookshop, restaurant, school, gym, exhibition space and social centre.

De Haan

Polígono Industrial Los Fraires, Nave 46, Daganzo de Arriba (91 884 13 89/fax 91 884 13 00). **Open** 8.30am-6pm Mon-Fri. **No credit cards.**
A Dutch-based international removals company with many years experience in Spain. Provides moving and storage services and help with pets, art collections, shipping cars and so on.

World Pack

C/Preciados 29 (91 522 24 71/fax 91 521 43 71/mobile 909 15 58 77). Metro Sol/bus all routes to Puerta del Sol. **Open** 9am-2pm, 4-7pm, Mon-Fri. **Credit** AmEx, DC, MC, V.
Local, national and international home and office moves, with personal service. World Pack also transports antiques and fine art. English spoken.

Seasons

Madrid's dry, mountain climate has been melodramatically described as 'six months of winter (*invierno*) and three months of hell (*infierno*)'. This is a gross exaggeration, but the city's weather does tend to extremes.

Spring *Average temperatures 6.5-18.5°C (43.7-65.3°F)*. One of the most pleasant times of year, with moderate sunshine and clear skies, although there are occasional bursts of rain. Pavement cafés fill the streets from Eastertime, and late spring and early summer is one of the liveliest times in Madrid. May is dominated by the city's biggest fiesta, **San Isidro**.

Summer *Average temperatures 15.5-30.5°C (59.9-86.9°F)*. June and early July are another time when Madrid is at its best. Temperatures only regularly approach 40°C (104°F) from mid-July to mid-August, although in recent years the weather has been less predictable. In the midsummer heat activity steadily winds down, and many people become semi-nocturnal, so that whole streets can be silent at 4pm but bustling after midnight. Traditionally, anyone who can leaves the city for the whole of August. This means it's less crowded, but many places are closed and it's hard to do much in such heat. One solution is to get up early (or see the night through), as the early morning air is so fresh you could drink it. In the last few years more staggered holidays have become fashionable; the August exodus has been smaller and more places have stayed open. After mid-August the peak of the heat passes, and the atmosphere is more pleasant.

Autumn *Average temperatures 7.5°-20.5°C (45.5-68.9°F)*. The weather is lovely, particularly in September. The return from holidays is greeted by new arts programmes, and the new football season. When summer finally departs in October there is often heavy rain. Most cafés take in pavement tables by late October.

Winter *Average temperatures 0.5-10.5°C (32.9-50.9°F)*. January is the coldest month: temperatures can drop to freezing point and snow is not unknown, although the air is usually more crisp than wet. A busy time culturally, and Madrileños still go out, if less than at other times of year.

Tipping

Tipping is now less generalised than it once was in Spain. There are no fixed rules, nor any expectation of a set ten per cent or more, and many Spaniards tip very little. It is still customary to leave around five to ten per cent for a waiter in a restaurant, up to and rarely ever over 500ptas, and many people also leave some coins in a bar, maybe part or all of the small change, according to the level of service. It's also usual to tip hotel porters and toilet attendants. In taxis a usual tip is around five per cent; more is given for longer journeys, or if a driver has helped with luggage.

Tourist information

City and regional authority (*Comunidad de Madrid*) tourist offices all provide similar basic information on attractions and events in Madrid and its region, plus free maps (*see also page 250*). The city also runs a phone information line for local citizens, 010, that can be equally useful to visitors. Tourist offices do not make hotel bookings, but can advise on vacancies; for booking agencies, *see pages 92-3*.

Useful publications in Spanish and English free at tourist offices are *En Madrid*, an events guide, and the monthly *Vive Madrid*. Full information on what's on at any time is in local papers and listings magazines. The English-language magazines *The Broadsheet* and *In Madrid* are also handy (*see chapter* **Media**).

Oficina Municipal de Turismo

Plaza Mayor 3 (91 588 16 36). Metro Sol/bus 3, 18, 23, 31, 50. **Open** 10am-8pm Mon-Fri; 10am-2pm Sat. **Map D8**

Oficinas de Información Turística de la Comunidad de Madrid

Duque de Medinaceli 2 (91 429 49 51). Metro Banco de España/bus 9, 14, 27, 34, 45. **Open** 9am-7pm Mon-Sat; 9am-2pm Sat. **Map G8**
Branch offices:
Barajas Airport International Arrivals *(91 305 86 56)*. **Open** 8am-8pm Mon-Sat; 8am-3pm Sun.
Chamartín Station *near platform 14, (91 315 99 76). Metro Chamartín/bus 5, 66, 80.* **Open** 8am-8pm Mon-Sat; 8am-2pm Sun.
Mercado Puerta de Toledo *(91 364 18 76). Metro Puerta de Toledo/bus 3, 17, 23, 35, 60, C.* **Open** 9am-7pm Mon-Fri; 9.30am-1.30pm Sat. **Map D10**

Summer Information Officers

During July and August pairs of young information officers, easily identifiable by their yellow and blue uniforms, are sent out by the city *Patronato de Turismo* to roam the central area ready to answer enquiries in a courageous variety of languages. They also staff information stands at various locations, including Puerta del Sol, Plaza Mayor and by the Prado. **Hours of service**: *July-Aug* 10am-3pm, 4-9pm, daily.

010 phoneline

Open 8am-9pm Mon-Fri.
A city-run information line that will answer enquiries of any and every kind on Madrid, and particularly on events promoted by the city council. Calls are accepted in French and English, but you may have to wait for an English-speaking operator. To call from outside Madrid, ring 91 366 66 04/05.

Useful points

Addresses

Individual flats in apartment blocks have traditionally been identified by the abbreviations *izq* (*izquierda*, left) or *dcha* (*derecha*, right) after the floor number (C/del Prado 221, 5ª dcha); in newer buildings they may be indicated more simply (C/del Prado 223, 4B). Many budget hotels occupy single apartments rather than whole buildings. When a building has no street number (usually because it's too big, like a station or hospital) this is written *s/n* (*sin número*).

Electricity

The standard current in Spain is now 220v, but a few old buildings still have 125v circuits, so check before using electrical equipment in hotels, especially in older, cheaper places. Plugs are all of the two-round-pin type. The 220v current works fine with British 240v products, with a plug adaptor, available at **El Corte Inglés** (*see chapter* **Shopping**). With US 110v appliances you will need a current transformer.

Estancos (tobacco shops)

Although no longer as ubiquitous as a few years ago, the tobacco shop or *estanco* (identified by a brown and yellow sign with the word *tabacos*) is still an important Spanish institution. Their main role is, as the sign suggests, to supply a nation of smokers with all tobacco-related products, but they are also the places to buy postage stamps, *metrobus* and monthly *abono* tickets for buses and the Metro, and phonecards. *Estancos* are also the only places where you can obtain the official money vouchers (*papel de estado*) that you may need if you have many dealings with Spanish bureaucracy. Some *estancos* also have photocopiers.

Living & working in Madrid

Although foreigners (especially EU citizens) now work in a variety of fields in Madrid – medicine, dentistry, business – unemployment is high and jobs can be hard to find. For newcomers the best chances of finding work are still in English teaching and/or translation. It is advisable to have a relevant teaching qualification, preferably the full RSA Diploma. If you get work in a school, initially it will usually be on only a nine-month contract. There is always private work available; the going rate for classes is between 1,500 and 3,000ptas an hour. To get your first students, try putting up ads at the **British Institute**, C/Miguel Angel 1 (91 337 35 01/03), and the **International Bookshop** (*see chapter* **Shopping**).

If you stay and work here there are various bureaucratic hurdles to negotiate; you can maybe ignore them for a while, but in the long run this will be counter-productive. If you come to work contracted from your country of origin, paperwork should be dealt with by your employer. When the Spanish State's love of form-filling has you terminally baffled, the quickest way to cut through it is to resort to one of the agencies called *gestorías*. A combination of lawyer, notary and accountant, a decent *gestor* may not be cheap but will help with all kinds of procedures and contracts, and show a path through the bureaucratic jungle. For English-speaking *gestorías, see page 264*.

Residency/paperwork

The Interior Ministry has a freephone information line for immigration enquiries, *900 15 00 00*, but it's frequently engaged.

EU citizens working for a company/*Cuenta ajena*

In recent years, paperwork has become a little easier for EU citizens working in Spain. Work permits as such no longer exist, but you must become a resident to work legally, and will also require an NIE/NIF (*see below* **EU citizens working freelance**). To become a resident, you will need a contract or firm offer of work (which can be for only three hours a week and with no stipulated duration) and an application form, which is obtained

from the police stations that deal with foreigners' affairs, the **Comisarías de Extranjería** (*see below*). When your application has been considered you will get a letter asking you to go the *comisaría* to collect your resident's card, taking with you a copy of the application, passport and proof that you have paid 990ptas into the Ministry of the Interior's account in a branch of the Argentaria bank. Keep photocopies yourself of all documents submitted. You may also be asked, arbitrarily, for a medical certificate and/or proof of sufficient funds. You will normally be given a Type A residency permit, valid for 12 months and not automatically renewable. This ties you to the company, region and business sector for which you have registered and, technically, you must leave the country on its expiry. Should you reapply successfully at that time, you will be issued a Type C permit, which lasts for five years and is renewable.

EU citizens working freelance/ *Cuenta própia*

To be able to work legally as a freelance, as a *trabajador autónomo/a* or *trabajador por cuenta própia*, an essential first step is to obtain a *Número de Identificación Fiscal* or *NIF* (tax code), which as you are a foreigner will be the same as your *Número de Identificación de Extranjero* (NIE). It will be very difficult to do any consistent business without one. Most people also find it near-indispensable to contract the services of a *gestor* to advise on legal procedures and tax, as without their help you can waste both time and money. An NIF/NIE can be obtained from the **Comisaría de Extranjería** (*see below*), your local Tax Office (*Delegación de Hacienda*), the address of which will be in the phone book, or through your *gestor*, which is the least stressful way of doing it. Once you have this *NIF* number you can open a bank account, request a telephone line, be paid by other businesses (perhaps the most important reason for having one) and so on.

The next stop is also in the Tax Office: at the *Actividades Económicas* desk fill in form 845, specifying which sector (*Enseñanza*, for teaching) you wish to work in, and form 036, the *Declaración Censal*, and keep copies of both. This done, you then visit your local Social Security office (*Delegación de Seguridad Social*) and say you want the *'alta como autónomo'*: this is one point where the advice of a *gestor* is particularly important, as the contribution band in which you are theoretically obliged to pay can be very high, and he/she can suggest alternatives. As an *autónomo* you will have a Social Security number, and in future will be obliged to make three-monthly or annual tax declarations, according to your earnings. Once you have your initial documentation you can apply for a *Cuenta Própia* residency permit from the *Comisaría de Extranjería*, with the same information (passport, proof of earnings, etc) as for the employee *Cuenta Ajena* permit (*see above*).

Queuing

Although it may not be immediately visible, Spaniards have a very highly developed queuing culture. Lining up resignedly if irritatedly at official counters has been a constant of local life since Madrileño bureaucracy was first invented. In small shops and at market stalls people may not be stand-

ing in line, but they generally have a very clear idea of when it is their turn. One common practice is to ask when you first arrive, to no one in particular, *'¿Quién da la vez?'* or *'¿Quién es el último/la ultima?'* ('Who's last?'); see who nods back at you, and follow on after them. Say *'yo'* ('me') to the next person who asks the same question.

Smoking

Despite belated health campaigns, most adult Spaniards still smoke – a lot. Tobacco prices remain low, and it's quite common for people to ask strangers for a cigarette as well as a light on the street. It is very unusual to find designated non-smoking areas in restaurants or bars, although

Non-EU citizens

The relative ease with which EU nationals can now legally establish themselves in Spain is not reflected in the situation for people from the rest of the world, for whom immigration laws have been tightened and who are subject to police checks. US and Australasian passport holders usually suffer less at the hands of the police than Africans and Asians, but all non-EU citizens should try to keep their papers in order to avoid trouble.

First-time applicants officially need a special visa, for which you must apply at the nearest Spanish consulate in your home country, although you can start the ball rolling in Spain if you don't mind making at least one trip back home. The basic documents needed are a contract or firm offer of work from a registered Spanish company, a medical certificate and a certificate of good conduct from your local police force. You must present these with some passport-size photos and translated copies of relevant qualifications to the consulate, who pass them on to the Labour Ministry in Madrid. If they approve them, the consulate will then issue your special visa (this can take six months). If you apply to work freelance or start your own business the procedures are slightly different and you will also be asked for proof of income. Once back in Spain, the procedures for applying for a residency permit are similar to those for European citizens (*see above*).

The Labour Ministry also publishes a guide to working in Spain, available in English at Spanish consulates.

Comisarías de Extranjería

For EU citizens Applications from EU citizens are now handled at the *comisaría* in **Tetuán**, *Pasaje de Maestros Ladrilleros 2 (91 571 92 00) Metro Valdeacederas/bus 42, 49, 124, 125.* **Open** 9am-2pm Mon-Fri.
Once the permit has been granted you will receive a letter of notification and can pick up the residency card.
For non-EU citizens
Non-EU citizens (referred to as *régimen general*) must apply at Calle Moratin 43 (91 429 0994, ext 1053; Metro Antón Martin). Once the permit has been issued it can be collected from the *comisaría* that formerly handled all foreigners' business, at *Calle de los Madrazo 9 (91 521 93 50/91 521 82 96) Metro Banco de España.* **Open** 9am-2pm, 4-7pm, Mon-Fri.

Legal help

Advice on employment law, contracts and so on can be obtained through the English-speakers' department of the trade union **Comisiones Obreras (CCOO)** at Calle Lope de Vega 38 (91 536 51 00). If you are working and have reason to believe your employer has not been paying your Social Security contributions (*cotizaciones*), go to your nearest Social Security office, show your SS number and ask for a *vida laboral* (contributions record). If no contributions have been paid, you can report your company.

Students

Students who stay in Spain for over three months, including EU citizens, also officially require a residence permit, and students enrolled on full-time courses may find it creates difficulties if they do not obtain one. To do so, you will need to show the **Comisaría de Extranjería** a confirmation of enrolment on a recognised course; proof of income for the duration of the course, currently estimated at a minimum of 800,000ptas for a 12-month period; and proof of health insurance status, private or public.

Renting a flat

Despite a drop in prices since the early '90s, Madrid is still not a cheap place to rent a flat. However, due to the anomalies of Spanish rental law, it is possible to find a one-bedroom flat with roof terrace in a good location for around 60,000ptas (£250/$410) a month, and if you share large properties are available for 190,000ptas (£810/$1,300) a month. It's also worth haggling for a reduction of the rent from the initial offer.

The best place to look for flat ads is the ads magazine *Segundamano*. Another option is to choose an area and look for '*Se alquila*' ('To let') signs in windows and doorways.

Legislation on rents is now quite simple: whether it suits you or the landlord to stick strictly to it is another issue. *Contratos de alquiler* (rental agreements) generally cover a five-year period, within which the landlord cannot ask you to leave, and can only raise the rent each year in line with inflation, set in the official price index (*Índice de Precios al Consumo*, IPC). Landlords can ask for the equivalent of one month's rent as a *fianza* (deposit) and a month's rent in advance before allowing you into the flat. In theory, if you move out before a year is up you lose the deposit (most people give a month's notice, and then don't pay that month's rent). Don't sign a *contrato* unless you are fully confident of your Spanish and/or a lawyer or *gestor* has looked over it. Main points are usually agreed verbally before being put in writing; responsibility for repairs is one thing that needs to be made very clear. For residents rent is tax deductible, so long as you keep the relevant receipts.

smoking bans in cinemas, theatres and on main-line trains are generally respected. Smoking is officially banned in every part of the Metro system, but many people take this to mean on the trains only, and not the station platforms. For more on buying cigarettes and tobacco, *see chapters* **Cafés & Bars** *and* **Shopping**.

Time

Spanish time is usually one hour ahead of British time, and so six hours ahead of US EST. At the beginning and end of summer clocks have traditionally been changed earlier than in the UK, so that for a while the two coincided. In future, though, the change-over to daylight saving may happen on the same day.

Water

Madrid's water no longer comes from the fast-flowing streams that earned the city its name, but local tap water is good and safe to drink, with none of the chlorine taste of some Spanish cities. There are occasional water shortages in summer, and signs are posted in hotels urging guests to avoid wasting water.

Business

As seat of government, Madrid is Spain's most important business centre. Despite the ending of the country's long '80s boom, business carries on apace here, in part due to the integration of Spain into the EU and the drive towards privatisation.

Anybody wanting to conduct business here must familiarise themselves with the intricacies of EU legislation and its often *sui generis* application within the Spanish legal-bureaucratic maze. They should also be ready for a more laid-back approach by clients regarding delivery and payment, and more paperwork and overheads than they may be used to. Chambers of commerce, consulates and a good *gestoria* can help you in getting started.

Institutions & info

Government

Ayuntamiento de Madrid *Plaza de la Villa 5 (91 588 10 00). Metro Sol, Opera/bus all routes to Puerta del Sol.* **Open** *Sept-June* 9am-2pm, Mon-Fri. The city council is important in many aspects of doing business; responsibility for issuing licences to open a business falls on the local council of the district where you plan to set up. *Distrito Centro*, for example, is at Plaza Mayor 3 (91 588 23 04/02). The city department to whom you will have to pay local taxes is at Calle Sacramento 5 (91 588 16 78).
Delegación de Hacienda Your business will need a tax number, *Código de Identificación Fiscal* (CIF), issued by the local tax office. It is best to obtain this through a *gestoria*.
EU office: Oficina de la Comisión Europea *Paseo de la Castellana 46 (91 432 33 71). Metro Rubén Dario/bus 5, 27, 45, 150.* **Open** 9.30am-1pm Mon-Fri. **Map I2** Information on EU directives in Spain, grants and so on.
Instituto Español de Comercio Exterior (Spanish Institute for Foreign Trade) *Paseo de la Castellana 14 (91 349 61 00/fax 91 577 07 50). Metro Colón/bus all routes to Plaza de Colón.* **Open** *mid-Sept-mid-June* 9am-2pm, 3-5pm, Mon-Thur; 9am-2pm Fri; *mid-June-mid-Sept* 8.30am-2.30pm Mon-Fri. **Map I4** The state trade organisation has a useful service to aid small to medium-sized businesses exporting from Spain. Ask for *Servicio de Información*.

Other institutions

The American Club *Edificio España, Gran Via 88, 9ª (91 547 78 02). Metro Plaza de España/bus all routes to Plaza de España.* **Map D4** A meeting point for US businessmen, diplomats and guests. Membership is open to all nationalities. The club has a magazine, *Guidepost*. Call the answerphone and they will get back to you.
Bolsa de Comercio de Madrid (Stock Exchange) *Plaza de la Lealtad 1 (91 589 26 00/investor assistance 91 589 16 59/fax 915 891 417). Metro Banco de España/bus 10, 14, 27, 34.* **Open** 10am-5pm Mon-Fri. **Map H7**
Cámara de Comercio e Industria de Madrid *Plaza de la Independencia 1 (91 538 83 00). Metro Banco de España, Retiro/bus all routes to Puerta de Alcalá.* **Open** 9am-2pm Mon-Fri. **Map B6** The Chamber's services are oriented toward local business, but it has information services for foreign investors, especially if they export from Spain.
Consejo Superior de las Cámaras de Comercio de España *C/Velázquez 157 (91 590 69 00). Metro República Argentina/bus 9, 16, 19, 51.* **Open** 9am-1pm Mon-Fri. Joint body of all the Spanish chambers.

Business services

Conference services

IFEMA/Feria de Madrid

Recinto Ferial Juan Carlos I (91 722 80 00/51 80/fax 91 722 57 99). Metro Campo de las Naciones/bus 73, 122. **Open** *office* 9.30am-6.30pm Mon-Fri. Madrid's lavish state-of-the-art trade fair centre, on the north-east side of the city near the airport, opened in 1991. It has eight main pavilions, a 600-seater auditorium and many smaller facilities, plus 20 catering outlets and 14,000 parking spaces. By the entrance is the **Palacio Municipal de Congresos**, a 2,000-capacity conference hall. The site hosts many events of different sizes through the year. Among the most important are the **ARCO** art fair (*see chapter* **Art Galleries**) and the Madrid Fashion Week (*see chapter* **Madrid by Season**), both in February, and the *Semana Internacional del Habitat* interior design fair, in April.

Oficina de Congresos de Madrid (Madrid Convention Bureau)

C/Mayor 69 (91 588 29 00/fax 91 588 29 30). Metro Sol, Opera/bus 3, 148. **Open** *Oct-May* 8am-3pm, *June-Sept* 8.30am-2.30pm, Mon-Fri. **Map D7**

An office of the city council to assist organisations or individuals wishing to hold a conference or similar event in Madrid, and facilitate contacts with local venues and service companies.

Palacio de Exposiciones y Congresos

Paseo de la Castellana 99 (91 337 81 00). Metro Santiago Bernabéu/bus 27, 43, 147, 149, 150. **Open** 9am-2.30pm, 4.30-7pm, Mon-Fri. Longer-established than the Feria, with a dramatic Miró frieze across the façade, and used for several major international conferences. It has conference rooms, auditoria and galleries of all sizes; ancillary facilities are excellent.

Recintos Feriales de la Casa de Campo

Avda de Portugal (91 463 63 34/fax 91 470 21 80). Metro Lago/bus 31, 33, 36, 39. **Open** *Sept-June* 8am-3pm, *July-Aug* 8am-2pm, Mon-Fri. A compact exhibition site with three main halls and open-air space in the Casa de Campo. Mainly hosts shows of food, fashion and consumer services.

Gestorías — administrative services

The *gestoria* is a very Spanish institution, which combines the function of lawyer, bookkeeper, business adviser and general aid with bureaucracy. They can be very helpful in taking you through paperwork and pointing out short-cuts that foreigners are often unaware of. Most local residents employ a *gestor* at some point. English is spoken at the *gestorias* listed below.

Gestoría Calvo Canga

Plaza Tirso de Molina 12 (91 369 35 03). Metro Tirso de Molina/bus 6, 26, 32. **Open** 9am-2pm, 5-8pm, Mon-Fri. **Map E8** Traditional *gestoria* dealing with labour law, tax, accountancy and residency.

Gestoría Cavanna

C/Hermosilla 4 (91 431 86 67). Metro Serrano/bus all routes to Plaza Colón. **Open** *Sept-June* 9am-2pm, *July-Aug* 9am-2pm, Mon-Fri. **Map I4** Specialists in tax and employment law.

Work Manager

C/Bravo Murillo 3 (91 593 96 22/fax 91 593 20 28). Metro Quevedo/bus 16, 37, 61, 149. **Open** *Sept-July* 9am-8pm, *Aug* 9am-2.30pm, Mon-Fri. **Map E2**

A friendly, efficient, women-run *gestoria* that provides comprehensible advice and assistance in dealing with all kinds of legal and bureaucratic problems, and at amenable rates.

Legal services

José M. Armero, Abogados
C/Velázquez 21 (91 431 31 00). Metro Velázquez/bus 1, 9, 19, 51, 74. **Open** 9am-2pm, 4-7.30pm Mon-Fri. **Map J4**
Commercial legal advice and representation in Spanish and English.

Office services

Office space
American Service Organization
Gran Via 88, Edificio España (91 548 30 46). Metro Plaza de España/bus all routes to Plaza de España. **Open** 10am-6pm Mon-Fri. **Map D4**
Assists the international business community with housing and rentals (private and business).

Regus *Paseo de la Castellana 93 (91 555 87 72/fax 91 555 99 57). Metro Santiago Bernabéu/bus 27, 40, 43, 149, 150.* **Open** 9am-7pm Mon-Fri. **Credit** AmEx, DC, MC, V.
Fully equipped business centre with offices from 90,000-290,000ptas a month. Secretarial services on request.

Temp agencies
Manpower *C/Génova 5, bajos (91 319 74 04/fax 91 319 25 66/ information line 902 20 20 26). Metro Alonso Martínez/bus 3, 7, 21.* **Open** 9am-7pm Mon-Fri. **Map H4**
Sélect Recursos Humanos ETT *Gran Vía 1 (91 531 27 01). Metro Gran Vía/bus all routes to Gran Vía.* **Open** *Sept-June* 9am-2pm, 3-7pm, *Aug* only to 6pm, Mon-Fri. **Map F7**
English-speaking secretarial staff.

Translation agencies
Many Madrid translation agencies also provide conference and seminar services.
ALTIF SL *C/General Arrando 5 dcha (91 593 85 56/fax 91 445 04 57).*

Metro Rubén Darío/bus 3, 7, 40, 147. **Open** *Sept-June* 9am-2pm, 5-7pm; *July-Aug* 9am-3pm Mon-Fri. **Map H2**
CL Servicios Lingüísticos *Torre Europa, Paseo de la Castellana 95 (91 456 71 00). Metro Nuevos Ministerios/bus 5, 27, 40, 149, 150.* **Open** 8.30am-8.30pm Mon-Fri.

Traductores Jurados (Official translators)
In Spain, official and some other bodies often demand that foreign documents be translated by legally certified translators. Rates are higher than for other translators. Many consulates also provide these services; *see p256.*
Concepción Pardo de Vera *C/Costa Brava 20, 1° (91 734 23 31).* **Open** by appointment.
Polidioma *C/Espronceda 33 (91 554 47 00/fax 91 534 47 59/ e-mail polidioma@bitmailer.net). Metro Ríos Rosas, Gregorio Marañón/bus 5, 12, 45.* **Open** *Sept-July* 10.30am-2.30pm, 4-7pm, *Aug* 10.30am-2.30pm, Mon-Fri.

Students

Most Spanish university courses last four years. Fees are low, but overcrowding is a consistent source of discontent, although conditions are often better on courses for foreign students. The Spanish state universities are adopting a pan-European system of credits and semesters. This should simplify the process of convalidation of foreign degrees, at least for students from the EU.

Foreign students who stay over three months, including EU citizens, require a residency permit. Non-EU students will also need a visa (*see page 263*).

Consejería de Educación y Cultura
C/Alcalá 32 (91 380 42 60). Metro Banco de España/bus all routes to Plaza de Cibeles. **Open** 9am-2pm, 5-8pm, Mon-Fri. **Map G7**
Regional government (CAM) office with details of courses and grants. Young artists can present work for inclusion in the CAM network of exhibition spaces, and resident foreigners under 26 can obtain the *Tarjeta Joven*, a youth card giving the holder a range of discounts.

Instituto de la Juventud
C/José Ortega y Gasset 71 (91 347 77 00). Metro Lista/bus 1, 74. **Open** *Sept-June* 9am-2pm, 4-6pm, Mon-Fri; 9am-2pm Sat; *July-Aug* 9am-2pm, 4-6pm, Mon-Fri. **Map L3**

This official youth information centre provides advice and free information on courses, educational exchanges and a range of student and youth activities.

TIVE
C/Fernando el Católico 88 (91 543 02 08). Metro Moncloa/bus 1, 16, 44, 61, 133, C. **Open** 9am-2pm Mon-Fri; *information only* 9am-noon Sat. **Credit** V. **Map C2**
The official local government (CAM) student and youth travel agency issues student and youth hostel cards, and has discounts available on air, rail and coach tickets to anyone under 26, or to students up to the age of 30.

Universities

EU programmes: Erasmus, Socrates & Lingua
The **Erasmus** student-exchange schemes and **Lingua** project (specifically for language learning) are the most important parts of the EU's **Socrates** programme to help students move freely between member states. Madrid's universities have exchanges set up with many British and Irish colleges, covering a range of subjects. To be eligible you must be studying at an exchange institution; they are open to students from their second year onwards, and prospective applicants should approach their college's Erasmus co-ordinator. General information is available in Britain from the *UK Socrates and Erasmus Council, R & D Building, The University, Canterbury, Kent CT2 7PD (01227 762 712).*

Universidad de Alcalá de Henares
Plaza de San Diego, Alcalá de Henares, 28071 Madrid (91 885 40 03). Train Cercanías lines C-1, C-2, C-7a. **Open** *office* 9am-2pm Mon-Fri.
Seat of Madrid's oldest university, founded in 1498 and moved to Madrid in 1836; the university reopened in 1977. *Website: www.alcala.es*

Universidad Autónoma de Madrid
Ciudad Universitaria de Cantoblanco Carretera de Colmenar Viejo (91 397 51 00). Train Cercanías C-1, C-7b. **Open** *office* 9am-2pm, 4-6pm, Mon-Fri.
On the northern fringes, the Autónoma is accessible by train from Atocha or Chamartín. Founded in 1968, it now has 32,000 students and competes in prestige with the Complutense. *Website: www.uam.es*

Universidad Carlos III
C/Madrid 126, Getafe (91 624 95 00). Train Cercanías C-4. **Open** *office* 9am-2pm, 4-6pm, Mon-Fri.
Madrid's newest public university, founded in 1989, Carlos III has two campuses, in Getafe and Leganés, and about 10,000 students (with a growing number of Erasmus students). *Website: www.uc3m.es*

Universidad Complutense de Madrid
Avda de Séneca 2 (91 394 10 00/1). Metro Ciudad Universitaria, Metropolitano/bus 82, 132, F, Y, G. **Open** *office* 9am-2pm, 4-6pm, Mon-Fri.

Madrid's main university derives its name from the Roman name for Alcalá de Henares, its original home. The current site, the *Ciudad Universitaria Complutense*, was opened by King Alfonso XIII in 1928, and became a Civil War battlefield before it was completed. It was rebuilt under the Franco regime to become the sprawling, monotonous compound of today. Home to 130,000 students, 3,000 from abroad. *Website: www.ucm.es/ INFOCOM/infocom.htm*

Private universities

Instituto de Empresa de Madrid *C/Maria de Molina 11-13 (91 562 25 60/91 411 65 11). Metro Avenida de América/bus 9, 12, 16, 89, C.* **Open** *office* 10am-2pm, 4-8pm Mon-Fri. One of Madrid's most prestigious private schools for post-grad studies in business, law and economics, including the International MBA.

Schiller International University *C/San Bernardo 97-99 (91 448 20 61/fax 91 593 44 46). Metro San Bernardo/bus 2, 16, 21, 61.* **Open** *office* 9.30am-6pm Mon-Fri. **Map E2** The only foreign university with full international accreditation in Madrid, with a four-year degree in business, economics and international relations, or a two-year International MBA.

Universidad Pontificia Comillas *C/Alberto Aguilera 23 (91 542 28 00/fax 91 559 65 69). Metro Argüelles/bus 2, 21.* **Open** *office* 9am-2pm, 4-6pm, Mon-Fri. **Map D3** One of the most prestigious Catholic colleges in Spain: theology is a speciality, but its other degrees are highly regarded. Of its 10,000 students, around 300 are usually foreigners. It also offers summer courses in international relations, law and business.

Language learning

If you wish to obtain a Spanish-language qualification, the most useful are the examinations of Spain's official language institute, *Instituto Cervantes*.

Universities

Universidad Autónoma de Madrid *Information: Servicio de Idiomas, Univ. Autónoma de Madrid, Ciudad Universitaria de Cantoblanco, 28049 Madrid (91 397 46 33).* Programmes similar to those at the Complutense, with all-year and summer courses, but fees are slightly lower.

Universidad Complutense *Secretaria de Cursos para Extranjeros, Facultad de Filosofía y Letras, Edificio A, Ciudad Universitaria, 28040 Madrid (91 394 53 25).* **Open** (office) *Sept-June* 10am-1pm, 3-6pm, *July-Aug* 10am-1pm, Mon-Fri.
Courses for foreign students during the academic year and in summer. Higher-level students can study grammar, linguistics, literature and culture; for those with a lower level in Spanish there are intensive language courses. Most run two to three weeks, and cost 45,000-80,000ptas. Accommodation is not provided. Spanish for foreigners is also offered in the college year (not summer), at the Universidad de Alcalá de Henares.

Language schools

Aliseda *C/Goya 115 (91 309 11 76). Metro Goya/bus 15, 21, 53, 61, C.* **Open** 8am-10pm Mon-Fri; *Sept-June only* 8am-2.30pm Sat.
A private school with courses for the *Instituto Cervantes* exams (*see above*).
Escuela Oficial de Idiomas *C/Jesús Maestro s/n (91 533 58 05). Metro Guzmán el Bueno/bus 2, 12, 44.* **Open** *Sept-June* 10am-1pm, 4-7pm, Mon-Fri.

This government-run school offers courses in several languages, including Spanish for foreigners, during the academic year (but no summer courses). Admission is problematic, as fees are lower than at private schools, and demand is very high. Registration takes place in the first two weeks of September; to have the best chance of being admitted, it can be worth camping out by the school the previous night, and putting up with the incredible queues. *Website: www.chester.es*
Idiomas XXI *C/Bárbara de Braganza 12 (tel/fax 91 319 41 73). Metro Colón/bus 3, 37, 40, 149.* **Open** 9am-8pm Mon-Fri. **Map H5** A small school specialising solely in Spanish courses for foreigners using dynamic, modern methods. Timetables are flexible, groups are small and courses (longer-term or intensive) cover all levels.
International House *C/Zurbano 8 (91 310 13 14). Metro Alonso Martínez/bus 3, 7, 21.* **Open** 9am-8.30pm Mon-Fri. **Map H3** IH offers a wide range of possibilities for Spanish-learners, at all levels and throughout the year. As well as regular full-time programmes there are cheap shorter courses.
Tandem *C/Marqués de Cubas 8 (91 532 27 15). Metro Banco de España/ all buses to Cibeles.* **Open** 9am-2pm, 5-8pm, Mon-Fri. **Map G7** Imaginative courses in English, German and Spanish, including intensive and combined (classes plus one-to-one sessions) courses. Courses last two weeks to four months, and there are also cultural programmes and preparation for official exams. Tandem can also arrange accommodation.

Women

Perhaps the single most noticeable change in Spanish society in the last 20 years has been in the position of women. More women than ever before hold positions of responsibility in professional and public life, and young women form a (dynamic) majority of university students.

The birth rate is now the lowest in the world, and single-parent families are common. The extended family, though, is still important: indeed, it is often family support that allows women to have a career and a child.

Women-only spaces, apart from lesbian clubs (*see page 196*), are scarce, but there are popular

women-run venues such as **La Madriguera** (*see chapter* **Cafés & Bars**). Also, in most cafés a woman can drink alone without anybody making a deal of it.

Publications

Dirección General de la Mujer has a quarterly magazine, *8 de Marzo*, and *El Boletín*, on women's themes in the Mediterranean area, in French and Spanish with some articles in Arabic. Also useful issues is *Trabajadoras*, published by the CCOO trade union.

Organisations

See also p264 **Work Manager**.
Centro de la Mujer *C/Barquillo 44 (91 319 36 89). Metro Chueca/bus 3, 37, 40.* **Open** 4-8pm Mon-Fri. **Map H5** A women's centre used by a variety of independent organisations.

Dirección General de la Mujer de la Comunidad de Madrid *Plaza de Carlos Trias Beltrán 7 (91 580 38 00). Metro Santiago Bernabéu/bus 27, 43, 149.* **Open** 9am-2pm Mon-Fri. Counselling, legal advice and other services for women, plus information on training and job opportunities.
Instituto de la Mujer *C/Condesa de Venadito 34 (91 347 80 00). Metro Barrio de la Concepción/bus 11, 53.* **Open** 9am-8pm Mon-Fri. A government organisation that acts as an umbrella for many smaller bodies. The Institute has a documentation centre (91 347 80 46; open 9am-2pm Mon-Fri), with reports, videos, guides and other publications related to women. Some are in languages other than Spanish. At C/Génova 11 (91 391 58 80; Metro Alonso Martínez), the institute has a legal advice office for women.

Further Reading

Art & architecture

Brown, Jonathan *Velázquez: Painter and Courtier*
The most comprehensive study in English.
Elliott, JH, and Brown, Jonathan *A Palace for a King: The Buen Retiro and the Court of Philip IV*
A vivid reconstruction by historians of art and politics of the life, culture and spectacle of the Habsburg Court, and the grandest of Madrid's palaces.
Gassier, Pierre *Goya, A Witness of His Times*
A thorough biography and study.
Goya, Francisco de *Disasters of War; Disparates, or the Proverbs; Los Caprichos*
Dover Books publish good-value, high-quality reproductions of Goya's three most remarkable series of etchings.
Jacobs, Michael *Madrid Observed*
A lively survey by one of the best current foreign writers on Spain. An excellent travelling companion
Mitchell, Angus
Spain: Interiors, Gardens, Architecture, Landscape
Lavishly illustrated.

Food & drink

Boyle, Christine, and Nawrat, Chris
Spain and Portugal
One of the Traveller's Food and Wine Guide series, a very useful, pocket-sized handbook and glossary.
Casas, Penelope *Food and Wines of Spain*
An informative general guide.

History, politics, culture

Braudel, Fernand *The Mediterranean and the Mediterranean World in the Age of Philip II* (two vols)
A huge, multi-faceted study of society, economics and culture during Spain's Golden Age, with Madrid's godfather as its central figure. There is a one-volume edition, *The Mediterranean*.
Elliott, JH *Imperial Spain, 1469-1716*
The standard history.
Fletcher, RA *Moorish Spain*
Varied account of a little-known period in European history.
Fraser, Ronald *Blood of Spain*
An oral history of the Spanish Civil War and the tensions that preceded it, the most vivid and human account of Spain's great crisis.
Lalaguna, Juan *A Traveller's History of Spain*
A handy introduction.

Gibson, Ian *Fire in the Blood*
Idiosyncratic vision of modern Spain by Lorca's biographer.
Gilmour, David *Cities of Spain*
With an informative, impressionistic chapter on Madrid.
Hooper, John *The New Spaniards*
By far the best survey of post-1975 Spain, updated to cover the country at the end of the González era.
Jacobs, Michael
Between Hopes and Memories: A Spanish Journey
A quirky account of a voyage through modern Spain in its year of glory, 1992.
Preston, Paul *Franco*
A massive and exhaustive biography.
Preston, Paul *The Spanish Civil War*
A good concise account.
Shubert, Adrian *A Social History of Modern Spain*
A little heavy, but comprehensive.
Thomas, Hugh, ed *Madrid, A Traveller's Companion*
A great anthology of writings on Madrid from the Middle Ages to the 1930s, by authors as varied as Casanova, Pérez Galdós and the Duke of Wellington.

Literature

Almodóvar, Pedro
Patty Diphusa Stories and Other Writings
Frothy, disposable, but full of the sparky, sexy atmosphere of *Movida* Madrid.
Cela, Camilo José *The Hive*
Nobel-prizewinner Cela's sardonic masterpiece on Madrid in the aftermath of the Civil War, with hundreds of characters centred on a group of do-nothing writers sheltering literally and metaphorically around a café table.
Cela, Camilo José *Journey to the Alcarria*
A vivid account of rural Guadalajara between traditional isolation and modernisation.
Cervantes, Miguel de *Don Quixote*
The classic portrait of Golden-Century Spain, although the Don only actually visits Madrid very briefly.
Cervantes, Miguel de *Exemplary Stories*
A collection of Cervantes' shorter pieces.
Múñoz Molina, Antonio *Prince of Shadows*
A psychological thriller based on the legacy of the recent past in modern Madrid.
Pérez de Ayala, Ramón *Honeymoon, Bittermoon*
Two short novels from 1923 by one of the most prolific of pre-Civil War Madrileño writers.
Pérez Galdós, Benito *Fortunata and Jacinta*
The masterwork of Spain's greatest 19th-century novelist, a story of love and class of great depth set amid the poltical conflicts of 1860s Madrid.
Pérez Reverte, Arturo *The Flanders Road* and *The Club Dumas* (also published as *The Dumas Club*)
Two complex thrillers by one of the most lauded of current Spanish writers: *Flanders* deals with intrigues in the Madrid art world; *Dumas* with Satanistic goings on among antiquarian booksellers.
Quevedo, Francisco de, and anon (Penguin edition) *Two Spanish Picaresque Novels*
The anonymous *Lazarillo de Tormes* and Quevedo's 1626 *El Buscón* (translated as 'The Swindler'), an earthy, cynical masterpiece, the second-greatest work of classical Spanish prose and an essential text on the atmosphere of the 'Golden Century'. Also a lot shorter than *Quijote*.

Index

language **254**
menu **108, 129**
language schools 266
Larra, Mariano José de 22
La Latina, Rastro, Lavapiés **59-61**
  art galleries 90
  cafés & bars 136-137
  nightlife 151-2
  restaurants 117-119
  tapas bars 129-130
laundrettes 174
Lavapiés *see* La Latina, Rastro,
  Lavapiés
Lázaro Galdiano, José 71
leather goods repairs 175
leather goods shops 165
legal help 263
legal services 265
leisure parks 180
libraries 258
  Museo Nacional Centro de Arte
    Reina Sofía 77
  newspapers in 197
Lichtenstein, Roy 74, *81*
light aircraft tours 180
lingerie & underwear shops 163
Los Molinos 237
lost property 258
lotteries **64**
Lotti, Cosimo 15
Lucía, Paco de 209

Machado, Antonio 25
Madrid en Danza (dance
  festival) 5, 7-8, 186
magazines 198-199
Mahou brewery 67
mail *see* post
Malasaña & Chueca **61-64**
  art galleries 89-90
  cafés & bars 137-138
  gay & lesbian Chueca 190
  nightlife 143, 152-4
  restaurants 119-123
  tapas bars 130-131
Malasaña, Manuela 61, 81
Manzanares river 49
maps 250
markets **170**
  Mercado de Maravillas 67
  Mercado de San Miguel 46
  the Rastro flea market 60-61, **167**
  stamp & coin market 42, 173
Martínez Feduchi, Luis 55
media **197-9**
Mendian, Loreak 161
metro 250
  disabled travellers 255
Ministerio de Agricultura, Atocha
  33, 65
Ministerio de Aire 34, 66
Monasterio de El Paular 238
monastery museums **79**
Moncloa *see* Conde Duque,
  Moncloa, Argüelles
Moneo, Rafael 34, 42, 44
money **258-259**
Montejo de la Sierra 239
Morral, Mateo 24
mosques
  Córdoba 246

Cristo de la Luz 234
motorbike hire 252
motorsports 214
mountain biking 240
mountaineering 240
Movida 29
Mulot, J-B 60
Muralla Árabe (Arab Wall) 31, **46**
Museo Africano **79**
Museo del Aire **84**
Museo de América 69, **79-80**
Museo Ángel Nieto **84**
Museo de Antropología/Etnología **80**
Museo Arqueológico Nacional 44, **80**
Museo de Carruajes 69
Museo Casa de la Moneda **84**
Museo de Cera 69
Museo Cerralbo 69, **70-71**
Museo de Ciencias Naturales 69, **84**
Museo de la Ciudad **81**
Museo del Ejército 15, 69, 73, **81**
Museo de Escultura al Aire Libre 45
Museo Ferroviario 69
Museo Geominero **84**
Museo Guggenheim, Bilbao 76,
  244, 245
Museo Lázaro Galdiano 69, **71, 78**
Museo del Libro **81-83**
Museo Municipal 19, 33, 69, **83**
Museo Nacional de Artes
  Decoratives **78**
Museo Nacional Centro de Arte
  Reina Sofía 34, 42, **76-77**, 87, 203
Museo Nacional Ferroviario (Antigua
  Estación de Delicias) **84**
Museo Naval 69, **83-84**
Museo Postal y de
  Telecomunicaciones **84**
Museo del Prado 15, 19, 33, 42, 69,
  72-73 , 226
Museo de la Real Academia de Bellas
  Artes de San Fernando 69, *71*,
  78, 201
Museo Romántico **78**
Museo Sorolla **78**
Museo Taurino 69, **80**
Museo Thyssen-Bornemisza 34, 42, 69,
  74-75, *81*
Museo Tiflológico 87
museums **69-84**
  archaeology & anthropology 79-80
  art 42, 226, 234, 239, 245
  bullfighting 69, 80
  cafés in 70
  carriages 69
  for children 178
  fine & decorative arts 69-78
  hunting 69
  Jewish culture 234
  literary & historical 80-84
  military 81, 83-84
  monastery museums 79
  natural history 84
  Paseo del Arte ticket 42, 69
  Picasso 239
  science 69, 178
  stamps & coins 84
  tickets 69
  times 69
  transport 84
  wax 69, 178
music
  classical & opera **200-3**
  flamenco 209-12
  rock, roots & jazz **204-8**
musical instrument shops 171
music magazines 198

National Museum of Decorative Arts
  see Museo Nacional de Artes
  Decorativas
Navidad (Christmas) **10**
newspaper libraries 197
newspapers 197
Nieto, Ángel 84
Nightlife **143-55**
  gay & lesbian 190-6
Noche Vieja (New Year's Eve) **10**
Nuevos Ministerios 34, **45**

Observatorio Astronómico 33, 57
office services 265
Oficina Municipal de Turismo 261
Oficinas de Información
  Turística *see* tourist information
Olivares, Count-Duke of 15, 18
opening times 259
opticians 176
ORA (Operación Regulación
  Aparcamiento) 252
orchestras 201
Orquestra Nacional de España 201
Ortega, Gómez 45
Otamendi, Joaquín 34, 45, 55
Otamendi, José María 34, 55
Oyarbide, Jesús María 114

Palacio, Alberto del 44
Palacio Buenavista 41
Palacio del Buen Retiro 72, 73
Palacio de Cristal 87
Palacio de Comunicaciones
  (Correos) 24, 34, 41, **45**
Palacio de El Pardo 227
Palacio de Justicia 64
Palacio de Linares 41
Palacio de Liria 66
Palacio Longoria 64
Palacio Real (Palacio
  de Oriente) **46, 50**
Palacio Real de La Granja
  de San Ildefonso 19, **229**, 238
Palacio de Riofrío 229
Palacio de Santa Cruz
  (Foreign Ministry) 32, 43
Palacio del Senado 52
Palacio de Velázquez 87
Palacios, Antonio 34, 45, 53, 55
La Paloma fiestas 8, 9
parking **252-253**
parks
  Capricho de la Alameda de Osuna **60**
  Casa de Campo **58-59**, 195
  Parque de Atenas 195
  Parque Juan Carlos I **60, 179**
  Parque del Oeste 26, **60**, 179
  Parque del Retiro **57**, 179, 195
  Parque Tierno Galván 179
  Plaza Picasso 45
Partido Popular (PP) 30, 35, 76, 185,
  197, 198, 200, 204
Paseo del Prado **45**, 145, 178
passports 248, 260
Pastori, Niña 211
Pastrana 230
Pedraza 228

Advertisers' Index

Maps

1664 de KronENbourg

SeGún Pep Carrió

Nunca cuAtro cifRAS DiJeroN tANto

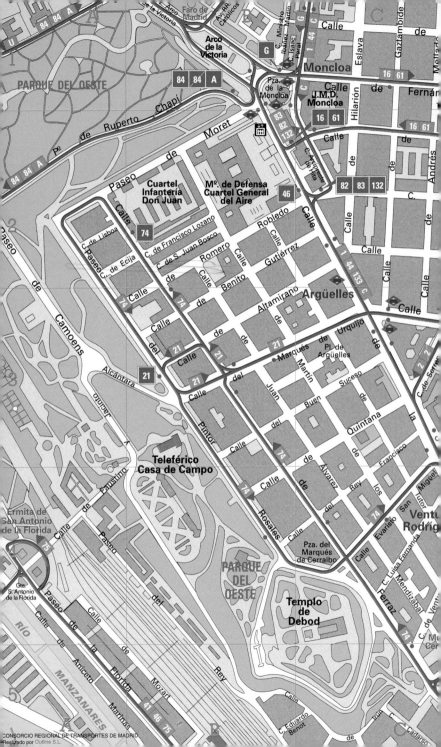

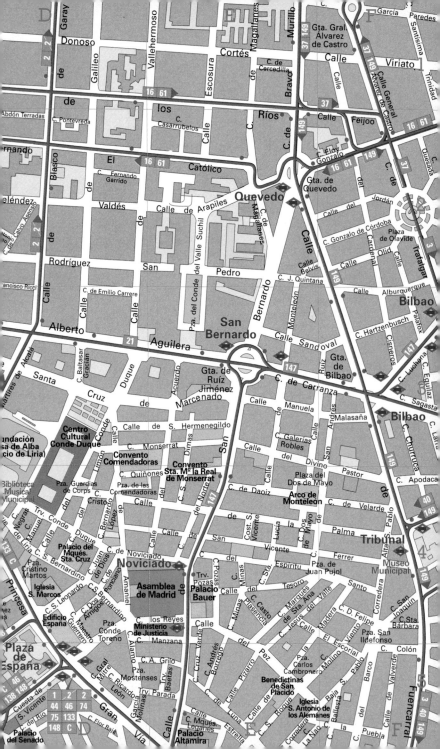

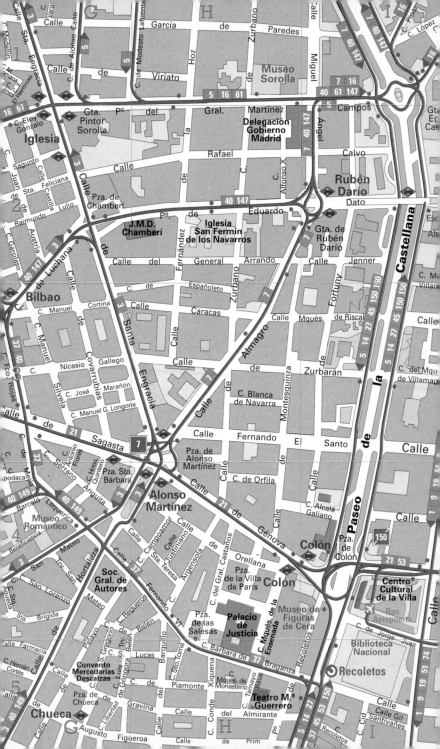

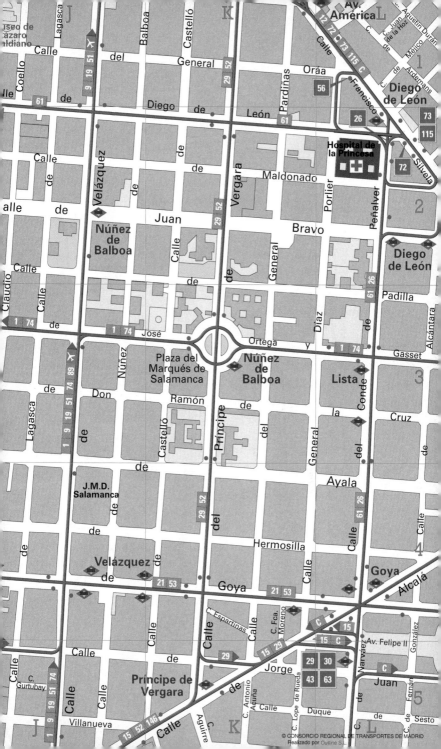

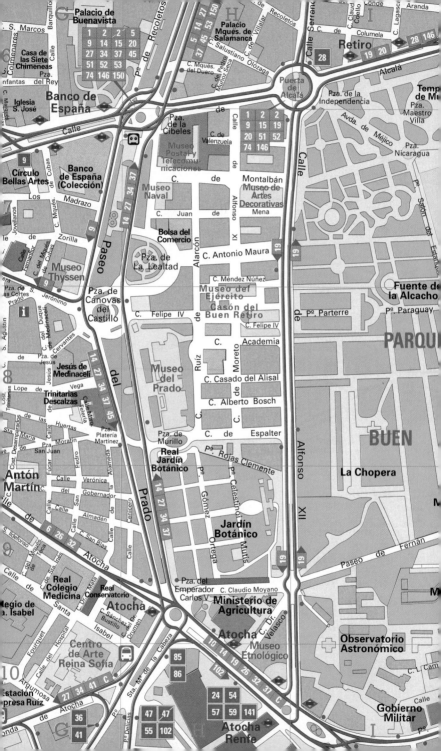

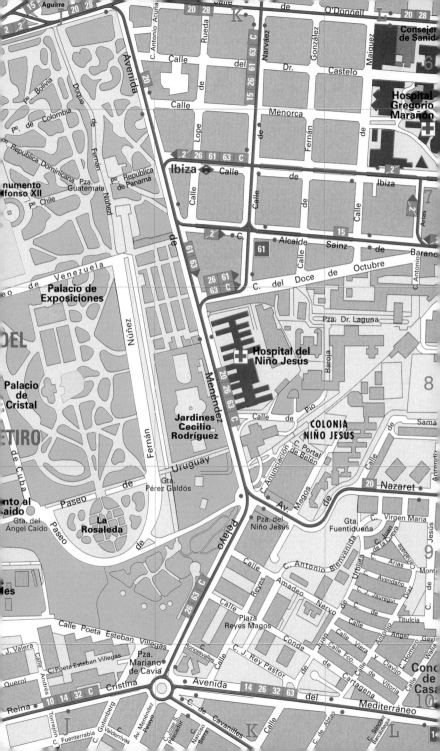

Street Index

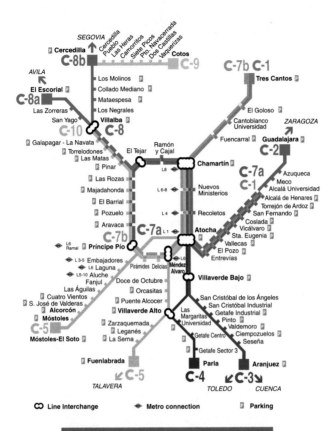

CO Line Interchange   ◆ Metro connection   🅿 Parking

CERCANÍAS LINES

- **C-1** Alcalá de Henares / Tres Cantos
- **C-2** Guadalajara / Atocha / Chamartín
- **C-3** Atocha / Aranjuez
- **C-4** Atocha / Parla
- **C-5** Móstoles -El Soto / Atocha / Fuenlabrada
- **C-7a** Alcalá de H. / Chamartín / Príncipe Pío
- **C-7b** Príncipe Pío / Atocha / Tres Cantos
- **C-8** Atocha / Chamartín / Villalba
- **C-8a** Atocha / Chamartín / El Escorial
- **C-8b** Atocha / Chamartín / Cercedilla
- **C-9** Cercedilla / Cotos
- **C-10** Villalba / Príncipe Pío / Atocha / Chamartín

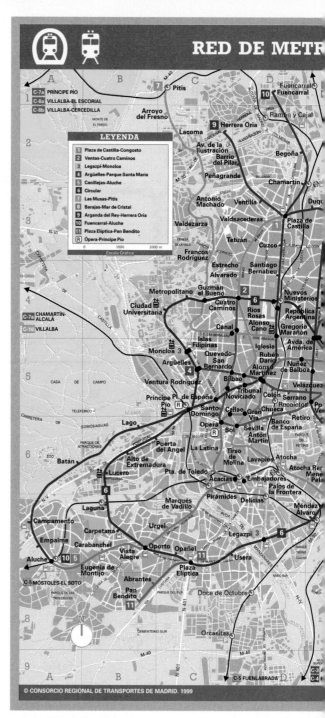

RED DE METR

C-7a PRÍNCIPE PÍO
C-8a VILLALBA-EL ESCORIAL
C-8b VILLALBA-CERCEDILLA

C-7a CHAMARTÍN-ALCALÁ
C-10 VILLALBA

C-5 MÓSTOLES-EL SOTO

C-5 FUENLABRADA

CERCANÍAS

Metro

SIMBOLOGÍA

- Transbordo entre estaciones de Metro
- Transbordo largo entre estaciones de Metro
- Estación de Metro con ascensor
- Estación de Cercanías Madrid
- Trazado de líneas de Cercanías
- Estación largo recorrido Renfe
- Terminal de autobús interurbano
- Autobús aeropuerto Barajas
- Aparcamiento en estación
- Terminales Aeropuerto

Servicio de Información de Transporte 91 580 19 80

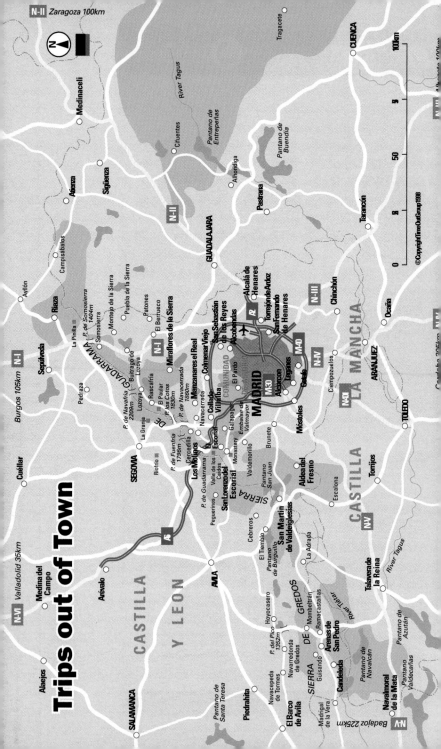